The Art of
Interpretative Speech

Charles Henry Woolbert
and

Severina E. Nelson
University of Illinois

The Art of
Interpretative Speech

PRINCIPLES & PRACTICES

FIFTH EDITION

New York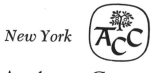

Appleton · Century · Crofts
Division of Meredith Corporation

PREFACE

The philosophy of this book continues to be that of former editions: namely, the student approaches artistry in interpretative speech by means of certain techniques. First, he builds a deliberate impression of the writer's meaning through an understanding of literary craft; second, he attempts, as an integrated and highly motivated individual, to express his impression through controlled use of vocal and bodily skills.

Some users of previous editions have recommended a slightly increased emphasis on literary craftsmanship; consequently, in this fifth edition certain portions have been expanded and documented by writers and critics of stature. Material for the student's literary appreciation of *how* literature is created has been broadened and deepened; chapters on structure, meaning and point of view in literature are now included. The critical observations given of any literary work, however, make no claim to being either comprehensive or definitive. Their purpose is rather to help the student begin to inform himself and to motivate him to further investigation of his own.

The majority of those who sent us their views have urged that no radical changes be made in the emphasis on voice and bodily activity. Others have asked for a fuller anthology of literature. Both requests have been heeded. In order to add literature acceptable for purposes of practice, the chapter on vocal pitch has been shortened to permit a final chapter, *Total Expression of the Impression*, which consists of poems, narratives and dramatic excerpts. These works should prove stimulating in strengthening vocal and bodily skills as well as in reviewing literary techniques.

Interpretative theories are considered carefully from the point of view of both the instructor and the student. Suggestions offered for effectiveness in interpretation are inserted only as incentives for further student motivation and adaptation, not as ultimata on the *how* of a writer's work and its oral expression. The student, guided by the artistry of the "interpreter-teacher," should thus find progressive appreciation for the *sound* of literature. In this way, meaning in a work and vitality in its oral re-creation can be united and memorable experiences provided for all —student, audience and instructor.

S. E. N.

CONTENTS

III—THE TECHNIQUE OF EXPRESSION

I

THE SOURCES OF
INTERPRETATIVE SPEECH

1

An Inventory of Sources

Historically, the active sharing of literary experiences—whether in festivals of drama on the hillsides of ancient Greece or in balladry throughout the courts and streets of medieval Europe—has left a heritage that still speaks of man's communicative enjoyment. Literature of the past, and of the present, may speak even more meaningfully when one understands the principles and practices best used to re-create them for others. The spirit of the arts today is admittedly less active and communal, more passive and individual. For, as life has quickened in pace and expanded in scope, it has often left the observer with less spontaneous participation. An effective performer, however, whether his appearance is immediate or is assisted by film and electronic devices, can still cause audiences to respond profoundly.

THE "COMMUNICATIVE" SOURCE

Man's intricate and revealing vocal pattern has its source in the physical activity of vocal grunts and attacks practiced by his earliest antecedents. Vocal expression, made possible by skillful use of the vegetative system—chewing, sucking, swallowing, breathing—is essential in the successful act of communication. Everyone now enjoys the result of this sharing of thoughts that has increased into live communication over the centuries. Today, as yesterday—since no one likes to be lonely—this verbalizing seeks an audience that is motivated to listen, enjoy and respond. This outgoing urge to communicate, governed by stimuli that are physical, visual and vocal, promotes the output of speech.

The foundation word in the title of this book is *speech*. Its basis lies in the communicative possibilities that speech exerts as a powerful and pleasurable mode for sharing meaning, feeling and attitude through various experiences. Involved in the procedure of a successful speaking act is the coordinated activity of the body and voice, integrated by the direction of an efficiently timed central nervous system. In like manner, the communicating part of the vocal mechanism cannot function effectively without the integrated coordination of the respiratory system and the hearing mechanism governed also by the central control. You speak as well as you do because you hear, and more importantly, because your nervous system is intact. Speech authorities repeatedly cite the fact that speech is a learned process, but a child will imitate or learn speech only so far as that system of nerve impulses and signals will permit—no matter how cultured the speech he may hear. In summary then, the motivation for the speech act is communication by means of vocal and bodily skills, all directed by an efficient and intact nervous system.

COMMUNICATION & INTERPRETATIVE SPEECH

The title includes, as you have noticed, a limiting word, namely, *interpretative*. "Interpretation" mirrors and projects the words of a text in a special way to arouse many mixed emotions. It is not expository speech, not discursive speech, not argumentative speech, but *interpretative* speech! These two words together imply speech that re-creates the impression of a meaning, emotion, attitude, as expressed by a literary master, with the hope that others may enjoy the writer's particular pattern of meaning. The emphasis in this text is thus not on *how* to give a speech persuasively or *how* to build your ideas into a good exposition of personal ideas but on *how* to find the meaning of the printed page and *how* to use your assets to create a controlled impression for listeners. Of course, you may have to defend the meaning you think the author intended or argue with another person concerning how he has misrepresented the tone or central meaning. Good critical discussion should help to point up *how* the writer's pattern of meaning will temper its interpretation through skills of body and voice.

MEANING & THE TECHNIQUE OF IMPRESSION

Interpretative communication involves two major skills: (1) the technique of impression, or the craft that will assist you in finding the pattern of meaning or sequence of images embodied in the works; and (2) the technique of expression, the craft that will help you to re-create or express an impression, that is, your emotional and intellectual understanding of a work through the controlled management of your voice and body.

You are concerned here briefly with the understanding of the technique of impression which will be discussed fully in part II. Your first step in interpretative speech will depend on how impressions are received by you from the black marks on the page and on the extent of your literary experiences as they relate to the writer's meaning. In other words, how does the author or poet make the black marks meaningful, and how do you utilize your literary talents in constructing an impression of the meaning?

To extend this last statement further remember that no meaning exists on the page independent of your own experience and that of others. Words live neither on a printed page nor in the air between one person and another while spoken. Only sound waves travel through the air. Words as counters of meaning remain solely and everlastingly and inevitably *within* a human being.

These characters on the printed page, however, are not just ordinary black marks. They are symbols that can possess a sort of magic if they relate to you. They do things to you: they can make you smile or weep or groan or laugh—or talk! On closer analysis, they really make you *talk to yourself.* Reading to yourself is nothing more than talking to yourself, or more technically, exercising *inner speech*—speech you learned to utilize in your very early attempts to speak.

When, as a child, you had some slight ability to make noises, grunts and groans, as well as syllables, you did most of your thinking openly. After a time, you learned to chatter endlessly. You soon discovered through continual checks from your parents that you were wise not to think aloud for others to hear. Accordingly, by some hard lessons, you managed to go through these same motions of talking without letting anyone hear you. So you cultivated the habit of inner speech, the source for all those complex ideas later designated as thought. You were really employing the same sound-making mechanism but with less energy than when you talk to a listener. Thus, the marks on the page make you talk to yourself as you read silently.

Words come into existence only when the symbols stir in you a *meaning,* and this meaning is called a *word.* Symbols that mean nothing in your experience do not startle you into doing anything meaningful; symbols that represent an unknown tongue or nonsense language mean nothing to you because they do not start you talking to yourself. Try the following marks, *oiaio.* Now these marks form a symbol that might be called a word, but not to a speaker of the English language. The sounds they represent constitute the Hawaiian word for "truth." This difficulty exists not only in foreign languages but in your native tongue. If you enjoy reading Frost's poetry, perhaps the symbol "heal-all" in his sonnet "Design" (page 182) fits easily into the meaning of the poetic lines. This may have happened if your experience with this particular flower makes you more knowledgeable than others who have never seen the "heal-all"—not even a picture of one. On the other hand, the printed marks of Frost's which tell that "The woods are lovely, dark and deep" are rich in meaning to all because of the basic level of the meaning: rich in the extent of familiar things they recall. For each reader that recall will be different, even as likes and dislikes, habits of living, enjoyment of nature are different. To some, however, the meaning will go beyond this basic pattern and extend into a symbolic pattern—the "woods" relating perhaps to the darkness or peace of death or to man's desire for a life of quiet contentment.

You read with delight and wonder only those lines for which your experience provides a key. Meaning is conditioned by a blend of your experiences—social, psychological, educational, physical. Many persons cannot enjoy Shakespeare because they find the characteristic words and sentence structures of Elizabethan English difficult to understand. Consequently, the black marks appear as a foreign language and do nothing to stir the imagination. Some symbols on the printed page are for those who enjoy only the simple pattern of meaning; others are for those who seek the deeper and unknown patterns.

It is clear, then, that the experiences of the writer will not have the same meaning for every reader, interpreter or listener, or even for other writers of fiction and poetry. The meaning that comes to you is yours, directed by the writer as far as he can go with the literary devices employed. Even *he* has little control over what the symbols will mean to others. Roethke, on hearing a student interpret one of his poems with a greenhouse environment, was delighted that the lines had been extended to an experience in her own life, one he had never intended. As long as you are reading to yourself, you may be happy with the impression giving you the greatest pleasure. When you take on the role of an interpretative communicator, you are assuming the status of the interpreter of the writer's meaning.

The words, to repeat again, will carry no *absolute* meaning, because the black marks do not always reveal the overtones of the author's feeling or attitude. In seeking the meaning, you will profit by recalling Frost's remark that "everything that is written is as good as it is dramatic." Frost would have the "speaking tone of voice" in some way "entangled in the words and fastened to the page for the ear of imagination." He believes vocal tones must be heard in order that "poetry can be 'saved' from itself." Frost is one poet who practices what he preaches, for you can hear his voice "entangled" in his poetry.[1]

To understand the patterns of meaning Frost relates to the *speaking tone* of the voice, try reading this sample sentence of four words, "Yes, I like her," and note some of the interpretations that may be given, according to the context in which the sentence is placed. There are others besides these:

1. Yes, I like her. (She is probably all right, but I am not eager for her friendship; or, I'd better say I like her, but don't believe it.)
2. *Yes*, I like her. (I'm sure of it.)

[1] Robert Frost, "Introduction," *A Way Out* (New York: The Harbor Press, 1929).

3. Yes, *I* like her. (Whatever others think, she suits me; or, I like her, though my friend does not.)
4. Yes, I *like* her. (I like her, but not more than that.)
5. Yes, I like *her*. (I like her but not the other girl, her family, etc.)
6. *Yes*, I *like* her. (Who said I did not?)
7. *Yes*, I *like her*. (I think she is a fine girl.)
8. *Yes, I like her*. (She's wonderful!)

The only reasonable conclusion you can make about the author's meaning is that within you a feeling exists that says, "Oh, yes, I have it now; I see what it means!" But do you? May not another individual find something quite different? For example, the following short scene can evoke several interpretations. Since you probably have never been near a murderer as he backs away from his monstrous deed, you may not appreciate the tension enveloping Lady Macbeth and her husband. With *bloody* hands, Macbeth comes out of the chamber after murdering the sleeping Duncan.

> LADY M.: Alack, I am afraid they have awak'd,
>   And 'tis not done. The attempt and not the deed
>   Confounds us. Hark! I laid their daggers ready;
>   He could not miss 'em. Had he not resembled
>   My father as he slept, I had done 't.
>
> *Enter* MACBETH
>
> MACBETH: I have done the deed. Didst thou not hear a noise?
> LADY M.: I heard the owl scream and the crickets cry.
>   Did you not speak?
> MACBETH: When?
> LADY M.:   Now.
> MACBETH: As I descended?
> LADY M.: Ay.
> MACBETH: Hark!
>   Who lies i' the second chamber?
> LADY M.:   Donalbain.
> MACBETH: This is a sorry sight.
>
> Shakespeare, *Macbeth*
> Act II, Scene 2

Shakespeare, the great dramatist, indicated the hurried and tense rhythm of the scene by his spacing of the lines, until he reached the line, "This is a sorry sight." In reacting to the horror felt by Macbeth, you may find several interpretations for the last line. You may envision a Macbeth so tortured yet so fascinated by his hands that he whispers, "This is a *sorry* sight"; or one who thrusts his hands out of sight and blurts out rapidly, *"This is a sorry sight"*; or one whose eyes are fixed on his hands and

whose speech is broken, tense and low, "This—is—a—sorry—sight"; or one
who has lost all control and is on the verge of hysterics, "This is a *sorry*
SIGHT!" Why not? You hear these various interpretations on the stage
from professional actors.

A more detailed discussion of literary sources involved in finding the
meaning will be offered in the section on *The Technique of Impression:*
the discovery and reconstruction of the writer's pattern of meaning.

MEANING & TECHNIQUE OF EXPRESSION

The second step in securing effective "interpretative speech" is directly concerned with the interpreter's communication to others through
the coordinated activity of voice and body, a speaking procedure intended
to hold the attention of listeners. This is the *technique of expression,* involving a skill that employs the spoken re-creation of the author's meaning. You become the objective and indirect voice of the writer, not the
writer himself. You become one who says, "I have an impression of these
lines, and I would like to express that impression for you." This interpretation implies effectiveness in manner and speech production and is not to
be confused with mechanical reading of words.

MEANING OF INTERPRETATION

In this text the term *interpretation* is used instead of *reading* to indicate and connote effective re-creation of the black marks on the page.
These two designations are often used interchangeably and quite acceptably by some who consider them synonymous in their denotative meaning,
and perhaps they are. They do not, however, have the same connotation.
Even the words *oral reading* do not imply the standard of effectiveness of
interpretation. Unfortunately, oral reading can be dull and monotonous
and yet seem satisfactory if the pronunciation of words is distinct and
accurate so everyone can hear easily. In an interpretative performance,
you should not be satisfied in calling off words as words, nor should you
attempt to read passively or casually. You are underselling an author if you
do not try to re-create tone, atmosphere and mood. Moreover, you should
seek thoughts and attitudes that represent the complex meaning of the
writer—who is another interpreter of ideas.

The sister arts, *impersonation* and *acting,* are not involved in this
study. The critical differences among these three types of speech artistry
consist in the directness of communication and the performer's involvement in the character of another individual, whether in a narrative, play
or poem. Certainly, the interpreter does not seek the direct audience contact of the public speaker; yet he does recognize the audience in a more
direct manner than either the impersonator or actor. A fine balance exists

in interpretation between the direct approach and restraint, depending on the form of literature.

One never speaks of impersonation in connection with a poem, except perhaps in the presentation of a dramatic monologue, in which a character is usually caught in a tense moment of decision or action. Even then the characterization requires more restraint than is usually experienced in an impersonation. Those who have heard Hal Holbrook[2] give his Mark Twain program have witnessed an impersonator in action—with typical attire, postures, walk, small gestures as well as facial and vocal expression. Holbrook impersonates Mark Twain in a most successful manner, as far as anyone today can know, through studied Mark Twain mannerisms, personality and vocal eccentricities. In his recording you will be impressed with his interpretative excellence.

Acting is the least direct of these three arts. Seldom does the actor of today try to establish direct, personal contact with the audience, except when the dramatist elects to have one of his characters serve as a narrator, as in Wilder's *Our Town* (see page 120). An *actor* assumes *complete* identification with the character he is portraying; the whole individual is involved and integrated with the movements of the other actors on stage. In addition, the art of acting employs memorization of lines; appropriate make-up and a harmony of costume and color with the action and the period of the play. It also involves lighting to focus attention on certain events or people or to create atmosphere; stage settings to give realistic or psychological or dream backgrounds; properties to give reality to the scene and to aid in action; and finally, adaptation of all actors on stage to reproduce a unified and forward-moving rather than a static scene. The actor will create only one part (unless he has to "sub" for someone), with the assistance of many others. In contrast, the *interpreter* stands alone, probably suggesting several parts, perhaps trying only to create the meaning of a poem. His goal is to move the listeners not only to understand but to capture and to appreciate the intensified meaning.

Therefore, in order to avoid confusion about the kind of *reading* expected, the words *interpretative speech* will be used, in the hope that each student can become aware of his ability to stir up meaning for an audience through *vital* expression. This *standard* of presentation is eminently sensible. Manifestly, the ideas a writer intended to put in black on white meant something to him; he felt the urge to express himself in written form; he thought those ideas significant enough for the struggle of composition. The performer must thus find the way to integrate his voice and body movement in order to show his auditors *how* the ideas mean.

Accomplishment of this end does not demand great histrionic display, vocal gymnastics or rare impersonative technique, but you should at least give the impression that you are interested in what you are interpret-

[2] *Mark Twain Tonight!* Recorded by Hal Holbrook. Columbia, OL 5440.

ing and believe it worthy of the attention of your hearers. In trying for this standard, you must not use the hit-or-miss method or just an emotional surge of words. You must know how to start, how to take stock of the subtleties of meaning, how to evaluate your own assets and how to use those abilities. Furthermore, you should attempt to build your own individual manner of interpretation, always keeping in mind the meaningful impression of literature as a unified *organic* structure which moves, lives and breathes with the temperament of the writer. You should also anticipate your final test before an audience, whether composed of few or many listeners, whether reached electronically through television sets or faced live in a general auditorium. Consideration of the audience—its tastes, age, number and sex—and in turn, a development of your own literary taste, will offer you many opportunities to find and interpret memorable literature, the motivating source of your interpretative attempts.

INTERPRETATIVE SPEECH AS AN ART

The high standard of effectiveness anticipated in this study is characterized by the word *art* in the title of this book. Perhaps few students will be able to reach a level of near-artistic accomplishment. A good principle to follow is to aim as high as you can if you are to attain the greatest possible satisfaction in enjoying literary communication.

TECHNIQUE AS A BASIC APPROACH TO ART

Any artistic endeavor has its beginning in technique with its basic patterns, formulae and devices: all sources for securing effects and utilizing materials and skills. Craftsmanship is merely a way of doing something well, a way of accomplishing in an effective way some desired end. A plan of workmanship, which will give the illusion of reality, must be perfected and controlled if an interpretation is to be a work of *art*. In other words, any accomplishment placed in the category of art does not stop with the technique but moves beyond this beginning range to the creation of true individuality and style. Every production, whether in painting, music, singing, acting, writing or any lasting monument, has its source in the knowledge of *how* to operate in a particular endeavor, *how* to use skills, and finally, *how* to select from the basic patterns to produce the illusion of reality.

For a moment, consider how knowledge of a craft or technique will help you to a better performance. The word *technique* was used earlier in explaining the initial procedure of securing an impression of the meaning, and the final oral expression of that meaning. At the beginning of your efforts, your performance may appear stilted, without too much warmth or vital understanding—perhaps even mechanical. Much of this kind of interpretation will be improved through "out-loud" practice of your expressive skills. You may even be astonished at your successes!

When this book was first published years ago, many comments were made about the use of the word *technique,* a word of ill-repute for those experts who were following the "natural" and "think the thought" methods. Some believed a mechanical procedure was being urged and that suggestions for the most feasible way of controlling voice and body, and assistance in securing meaning through knowledge of literary patterns, would tend to make the interpretative performance superficial. Naturally, if you stop with only an understanding of rudimentary principles, a mechanical superficiality may result. Artists in many professions, especially in writing, recognize today, however, the necessity of an orderly process in acquiring techniques of knowing *how.* No longer are the symbols *technique* and its companion synonym *craft* outlawed in any skill procedure that is touched in its later stages by individuality. Now libraries are stacked with books on the craft of many artistic productions—fiction, poetry, musical composition, painting, sculpture and ceramics: books that explain to the uninformed but motivated person how one works to attain a memorable creation through controlled execution.

A series of interviews originally published in *The Paris Review*[3] include perceptive "off-the-cuff" remarks about how technique has functioned for the artist interviewed. The writers talk candidly about the craft of their profession. They discuss the skills of craftsmanship and how they learned and practiced them only to blend and submerge them so that an individual form, style and approach might later be built; others note they have learned how to *select* among techniques used by well-known writers but not always with a successful result.

Most of the persons interviewed believe that after techniques are mastered, the writer approaches his own individuality and style. Robert Penn Warren reports that his experience as a teacher has made him think "a lot about the craft of other people." He believes those "deeply interested in art" are interested in the *how* of production, citing that superb example of craft found in the first scene of *Hamlet.*

Capote, in his inimitable manner, reports that the only device for improving technique is work and that certain principles of light and shade are present in writing as in painting and music. He realizes that one may intuitively know literary rules; if not, however, one must learn them, and later the techniques can be rearranged to fit in with one's stylistic pattern. He pays homage to Joyce, who, even though he is considered an outstand-

[3] The interviews quoted and paraphrased in the following pages are from WRITERS AT WORK: PARIS INTERVIEW SERIES, ed. Malcolm Cowley. Copyright © 1963 by the Paris Review, Inc. Reprinted by permission of The Viking Press, Inc.

ing "disregarder," is also a fine craftsman. Furthermore, he believes Joyce could "write *Ulysses because* he could write *Dubliners.*"

Capote's statement that he has to deplete an emotion before he is in a clinical position to get the perspective for analysis and writing reminds one of Burgess Meredith's comment on his projected acting practice to round out a characterization. Meredith overdoes the emotional activity of the character and then begins to control the part by taking away gradually all excess, thus presenting finesse and polish in his final performance. Eliot's interview also reveals much of his dramatic aspirations. In speaking of technique, he says he wanted to know theatrical procedures so well that he could forget them. He believes one should not break rules until one has acquired the proper respect for them. Porter recalls she spent at least fifteen years just learning to write, practicing every possible literary manner she could find. Finally she began to write in her own individual style. She compares the struggle of any artist to that of a pianist who works for ten years to obtain fingering automatically, for, as she says, "He can't be thinking of his fingering or his hands; he has to be thinking of his interpretation of the music he's playing. He's thinking of what he is trying to communicate. And if he hasn't got his technique perfected by then, he needn't give the concert at all."

Critics agree that if a craftsman is ineffective in his mastery of technique, then his meaning will lack spontaneity, unity, spirit. When the weaving of various skills into the warp and woof of meaning produces a haphazard pattern, not of a whole impression but of nonintegrated parts, or when the pattern repeats itself over and over without any highlights to relieve the monotony, then one may say that the technique has not been sufficiently mastered.

Inasmuch as you practice techniques every day to make yourself more attractive, intelligent, useful or perhaps eccentric, you should not consider the process unusual. You make continual adjustments in order to live more happily and successfully; you master techniques to gain assurance, control and a general *savoir faire;* you learn quickly how to adjust your student techniques to the eccentricities of an instructor; you learn "small talk" to give ease to a situation; you have a way of greeting people to make them more responsive; you watch your diet so your figure will conform; you know the achievement of tasteful color combinations will remain a wasted procedure if the "how-to-wear-it" element is absent. The correct blend of make-up with the color of the blouse, hat or hair and the contrasting accessories in both men's and women's clothes are more than a matter of good taste: these are attention-getting devices to make yourself more attractive, and hence, to make a good impression. As soon as your technique becomes too obvious, however, due to lack of taste and judgment—such as using a heavy make-up or repeating a color to the extent of monotony—then the desired illusion of beauty is not attained.

So it is with interpretation: if the pattern of expression repeats itself over and over, never deviating in form or emphasis, then the presentation becomes monotonous and the audience loses interest. Or if the interpreter appears to have a studied awareness of *his* performance, of *his* skills, then again the audience will think about the performer and his technique instead of the meaning of the author. Some of these difficulties occur because the student has been advised wrongly in his study. Unfortunately, some instructors will insist that you find one particular meaning in a piece of literature; otherwise, you do not understand it. Since in some cases, this may be true, each meaning should be examined with care and consideration for all details related to your experience. Occasionally you may be told how to present the material by pausing here and emphasizing there and using a certain inflection on the last word. Suggestions such as these are sometimes helpful; if you rely upon them entirely, however, your performance may lack spontaneity and individuality.

Watch your instructor employ different techniques to stir you into vocal activity. This procedure is legitimate and will assist in establishing an *esprit de corps* among those working for control. He may seek to promote your vocal skill by having you listen to a recording of your own voice. In this way you will receive a valuable auditory stimulus as well as help in getting acquainted with the sound of your voice. He may urge you to listen to recordings of professional interpreters, as Dylan Thomas's production of *Under Milk Wood,* in which you will hear an amazing range of vocal impressions. He may wish to interpret for the class members to show them how he secures a certain meaning or how he approaches an audience. He may wish to stimulate by creating discussion and offering positive criticism of each student's interpretation. He might contrast the interpretative work of students by having three or four interpret the same poem or story or scene. As your instructor becomes better acquainted with his students, he will temper their ways of expressing meaning to emphasize their personal and physical assets. A student of muscle and brawn, clutching an imaginary flower as he tries to express the beauty of Tennyson's lines, "Flower in the Crannied Wall," needs to learn how to channel his vigor and strength temporarily in another direction in order to do justice to the philosophy of those famous six lines. The instructor will realize the student should be encouraged for having selected that particular poem and help him eventually to acquire the tone and touch and awareness needed. So your instructor is a technician first; he approaches the *art* of teaching when he considers individually your assets and liabilities; and finally, he attempts to inspire you to reach a performance worthy of your individuality. The heavy part of this load—at least 75 percent—lies in your willingness to develop your skills.

To repeat, the beginning of an artistic presentation occurs through the understanding of sources that will heighten your interpretative skills.

You will attempt to secure the right reactions in the listeners, to become sensitive to the sound values of words and images as your voice utters them and to know how to secure mastery of your body and voice so no distractions occur to block the meaning. Much of your impression can be improved by practice before a mirror, a friend or any audience that is willing to listen or by a recording. One coed, after experiencing severe shock on the platform, solved her problem by practicing on top of a dining-room table before a very critical peer audience. Students learn to bring their ordinary skills in communication to the fore by various means. Some day, you will have made the great effort in some unexpected way to smooth over your interpretative difficulties, to find that you, too, have re-created an impression which meets with great approval. You may be surprised, however, if you sense only failure in your next attempt. Continued success is always broken by *seeming* failures, by which you can learn what not to do. Trying to find the pattern of artistry appears at times to be an almost intangible procedure.

THE ARTIST AT WORK

Every artist functions in a different way to get his imaginative and impressive results. He builds a philosophy, as he goes along, of how his work should appear. You will notice in every creative performance or production, the artist shows the temper and sensitivity of his work by touching it here and there with imaginative skill and pervading it with his own creative impulse. In this way you recognize play directors of great repute, you know novelists and short story writers who are characteristically individual in their writing, you know instructors who teach in such a way that you will never forget them or the subject matter.

Take a specific example of two contrasting architects, rather than writers or teachers. Probably any unnamed architect can draw plans for the typical straight-edged, box-like buildings that sometimes loom up in a narrow spot never meant to hold a twelve-apartment complex. From the street, it presents a solid brick prison-like wall, with no windows and with back entrances jutting out to the front walk. Convenience has been the major design consideration here—certainly not beauty or regard for the shaded, attractive homes along either side of the street. Yet this architect has conformed as far as building rules are concerned, for there are no flaws. He understands the procedures involved in plumbing, roofing, plastering, flooring and heating; unfortunately, he has stopped short in planning this building as an artistic part of a living environment.

In contrast to this architect is Frank Lloyd Wright, who knew how to go beyond brick walls and straightness of design and monotony of appearance and still build solidly. Wright's philosophy centers in organic architecture, an organicity that involves a growing, a developing, and a fusing so "the whole is to the parts as the parts are to the whole." His differentiation between conventional and organic buildings is a structural one. The organic is "locked together as fingers are locked," a merging to get "continuity," to give the "element of strength," also to give "tenuity rather than rigidity which could be broken." The site chosen, as well as the make-up of the family matrix, determines the features of the home. If the site is in the valley, then one builds close to the soil and makes something beautiful of the surroundings. "Never build," insists Wright, "on top of the hill because then there is no hill; rather reach toward it so that you will not lose it." Wright favors the innovation of the corner window which permits light to come in where it was never seen before; consequently, the corner window opens a whole new "vista" and "the box is gone." Clearly, Wright had the philosophy of an artist, and he functioned as an artist. The unnamed architect, of whom there are many, never saw the light stream in through any corner window. These comments point up the difference between a person who knows techniques but has no idea how to use them effectively and another person who possesses the imaginative perspective of the whole vista, and so functions as an artist.

ART & ILLUSION

How does art mean? What has happened to you when you breathlessly use the cliché, "This is a work of art"? The definition of what constitutes art is as difficult as the description of a poem, about which hundreds and hundreds of lines have been written. Probably for your purpose, the simplest, most direct answer is that art is the creation of any experience, production, object or "thing" so unusually impressive that you as observer, interpreter and listener participate in the illusion of reality created and store the experience away as a memorable one.

This created illusion is the keynote of your admiration. Not that you say so; not that you realize it immediately since you are immersed in the artistic experience of wonder and awe. Nor do you even murmur, "He is very artful," or "His use of artifice is excellent." You are not interested at this time in how this feeling has happened to you. Certainly if you were, the experience of witnessing and being caught by the illusion might be deflated. You leave that kind of analysis to the critic, who is often taken to task for detaching the parts from the whole to show how the illusion has been realized by selectivity.

SELECTIVITY IN ART

People tend to avoid these words: *artful,* meaning full of artistic devices, and *artifice,* meaning a skillful contrivance, because of the connotation indicating some action that is undesirable, and not real or honest. You have had the experience, however, of peering up to the top of a church spire, which seems to reach unknown heights—seemingly to the heavens—but you know it only *seems* that way because the constructing artist cleverly used the artifices of line and form. You buy a car that has the sleekest, smoothest "stream-lines," lines suggestive of speed and swiftness; yet you know these body lines are artifices because the basis for speed rests mainly in the precision motor controlled by the pressure of the human foot. Certainly the building of a cathedral is not accomplished solely by inspiration and an unpremeditated outpouring of the soul. It cannot be done. Nor can you create an inspiringly spontaneous improvisation on a piano, for into that performance goes much of your past training. Consider the improvisations of a novice: the result may be perfectly natural—and quite terrible.

So art in a measure is *artificial*, because everything is planned and consciously selected to produce the right effect. The way of art is not a natural process: it will *seem* to be natural, however, if the illusion of reality has been effected. By definition, the word artificial is opposed to the natural, the genuine, the honest-to-goodness reality. According to the dictionary, it pertains to "something made by human skill and labor." Consider the production of drama: the stage setting, if it has been made an intrinsic part of the play, has been accomplished by selected artifices arranged to establish a mood, a movement, a theme through the artificial, but seemingly artistic, use of lighting, color, costuming and arrangement of properties as well as the grouping of the actors. You watch an actor, knowing but never admitting that he is using every artifice of vocal play and bodily attitude to build an impression of a character. He may be making the attempt to have the audience capture the spirit of Hamlet's lines; yet you know that a Hamlet never happened in real life and that no one ever spoke Hamlet's lines naturally. Hamlet was created by a master technician. He must be acted by another artist-technician who understands the meaning of the lines, is able to interpret the beauty of the poetry and simulates the enveloping torture of Hamlet's soul. This performance will be artistic in so far as the actor has integrated technical cues and Shakespearean language with his own expression of the lines in order to give the impression of *being* Hamlet.

Poems, short stories, novels, drama, which deal with sentiments and themes selected from everyday experiences, are couched in language that is chosen carefully by the author to build the desired illusion. This matter of selection becomes a very important source since whatever does not support or is extraneous to the idea or theme must be discarded. The writer consciously selects his man-made relationships—the artifices—that make emotion, characterization and action as real and impressive as possible; he leaves unsaid many things that may have happened in the real experience. He knows what effects and meaning he wants to produce and plans accordingly. "Catching the very note and trick, the strange irregular rhythm of life," James insists, "is the attempt of the writer of fiction." This artifice, of course, furthers the author's purpose and is not art which means "rose-colored window panes," nor does the selection mean "picking a bouquet for Mrs. Grundy."[4] It *is* art that calls for direction of the writer's energy and restraint in making an effective selection. Hemingway's style has always been accounted unusual in its compression and restraint. Some writers have tried to copy his style without success. In his interview concerning the way in which he writes, Hemingway says:

> *The Old Man and the Sea* could have been over a thousand pages long and had every character in the village in it and all the processes of how they made their living, were born, educated, bore children, etc. That is done excellently and well by other writers. In writing you are limited by what has already been done satisfactorily. So I have tried to learn to do something else. First I have tried to eliminate everything unnecessary to conveying experience to the reader so that after she or he has read something it will become a part of his or her experience and seem actually to have happened. This is very hard to do and I've worked at it very hard.
>
> Anyway, to skip how it is done. I had unbelievable luck this time and could convey the experience completely and have it be one that no one had ever conveyed. The luck was that I had a good man and a good boy and lately writers have forgotten there still are such things. Then the ocean is worth writing about just as man is. So I was lucky there. I've seen the marlin mate and know about that. So I leave that out. I've seen a school (or pod) of more than fifty sperm whales in that same stretch of water and once harpooned one nearly sixty feet in length and lost him. So I left that out. . . . But the knowledge is what makes the under-water part of the iceberg.[5]

Faulkner relates how he wrote *The Sound and the Fury* five times in trying to tell its story and thus rid himself of the dream that continued to "anguish" him. He did not complete it to his satisfaction until fifteen years later, at which time he wrote an appendix[6] to another book. This selectivity is practiced also by Frost. Many believe the poet is merely employing speech typical of New England speech. The insight and culmination of meaning, however, should not be attributed to the particular speech of that area, or anywhere else. Frost is so skillful in the art of selecting colloquial rhythms and particular phrasing of words and incidents that flash into the experiences of many that his poetry reaches the dramatic level. As he has written, a poem "begins in delight"—an idea, a character, an incident no doubt comes to the fore; then "inclines to impulse"—that is, thoughts begin to gather around a central point and fuse into a meaning. The finished poem is a "performance," an extremely artful one.[7]

[4] Henry James, *The Art of Fiction and Other Essays* (New York: Oxford University Press, 1948), pp. 16-17.

[5] *Paris Interview Series,* p. 236. On page 37, an explanation of the knowledge learned from the iceberg is given.

[6] William Faulkner, *The Portable Faulkner* (New York: The Viking Press, 1949).

[7] Robert Frost, "The Figure A Poem Makes," *Complete Poems of Robert Frost* (New York, Holt, Rinehart and Winston, Inc., 1964), p. vi.

SELECTIVITY IN THE ART OF INTERPRETATIVE SPEECH

Now you are ready to turn to the artistic problems of the interpreter. To approach the standard of artistry, the interpretation must *seem* "natural." Remember, however, the core of this art is creation of an *illusion* through appropriate selection of vocal skills and bodily attitudes; and consequently, to make meaningful your impression of the black marks. The author has led the way; you must follow in his steps by making his artistry audible and visible in a manner the printed page cannot reveal. If you will pardon a cliché, you must breathe life into the words. Enrich the meaning as much as you can from your own experience, but at the same time, treat fairly your impressions extracted from the author's literary work. Harmony and coordination of the principles involved in techniques must be considered, just as the writer has sought to do.

The endeavors of any artist always seem so effortless that they create empathy—the feeling of participating in a situation—in those who watch or listen. Here, too, "art conceals art." A skillful ski expert can send an observer gliding down the snowy slopes with amazing grace and then get him ready for the big jump into the air. In no endeavor is this apparent ease so necessary as in the art of interpretative speech, for you must make the thoughts, feelings and spirit of the writer live for others. Care must be taken, however, that your own feelings do not override those of the author. To reach the point where the literature speaks for itself instead of through an interpreter is the highest peak of artistry, the finest illusion of reality.

Before going forward with this most human of all arts, you must dispel the mistaken notion that good interpretation is possible only for those who are naturally gifted. In this area, as in all others, gifts make a difference; even when you decide to capitalize on gifts, you must still spend energy and work on the project. Schiller writes, "All art is dedicated to joy"—that is, joy in native talents, joy in the opportunity to re-create successfully. Schiller, who worked so intensely, is a good example of a doctrine paraphrased from his own dictum: "All art is dedicated to hard work." Although the skill of interpretation will come more readily to some than to others, any performance in the realm of art never comes by chance or luck. It is always pondered, blocked out, planned, sketched, blueprinted, tried and retried. For a total interpretative effect, the creation of the illusion of reality requires study, training and patience in order to understand source materials and the procedures of selectivity and to master the necessary skills for their expression.

2

Control: The Basic Source

SKILLFUL CONTROL OF THE "WHOLE OF YOU"

You must discard the notion, if you have it, that any artistic production comes by nature or is natural—if and when it comes. Some will question, "Why not be natural in interpreting instead of working for a controlled technique?"; "why worry about how the voice sounds or how the larynx, lips, tongue, teeth and palates function or what your body is doing as long as you can stand before an audience and interpret?" Certainly, a few have this so-called innate ability to perform artistically. In most individuals this adeptness is probably due not to nature but to the outgoing environment in which they have lived, the experiences they have had with artistic endeavors and people.

If interpretation is an art, and it is agreed it is, then it demands planning and foresight by a person who understands it. The interpreter must thus consider these sources for control of that art: assessment of personal attitude toward and appreciation of literature; ability to make a successful decision as to the central meaning of the literary selection through a command of sensibilities and good sense; skill in expressing emotional content meaningfully by coordinated vocal and bodily activity. An artistic interpretation will require these talents controlled by the "whole of you."

You should be warned, however, that the final effectiveness of a performance before an audience, whether a class group or a large number of listeners, can never be anticipated. It will vary according to the kind of literature selected, the personality and skills of the interpreter and the situation in which the literature is presented. Even with an apparently workable control system, no set of didactic rules will ever cover every situation, audience and personality.

CONTROL OF MEANING

As an interpreter you will build—as the creative writer does—an imaginative skill that reflects *your* individuality only on the foundation of your knowledge of known techniques. Your personal adjustment to literature and its techniques, your spirit of enthusiasm and willingness to share

19

experiences gained from the expert writer are important in carrying the meaning effectively. The marks on the page will stir in you some definite and vital reactions: emotional involvement through word associations, interest in the way words sound and mean, desire to repeat lines aloud to hear the sound and feel the rhythm, appreciation of the structural arrangement of meaning. Moreover, if you wish to become an outstanding student in the understanding and expression of literature, you should bring to the task a variety of experiences from different sources to give sensitivity to the meaning: versatile daily living, conversations, newspapers, books, concerts, operas, plays, painting and travel. Your emotional experiences should range from the light and the humorous to the serious, breath-taking emotions. In short, you need at least some of the same sensibilities as the author in order to understand and appreciate his work.

CONTROL OF EMOTIONS

Those who cannot re-create meaning for others may have difficulty revealing or demonstrating *how* they feel in *any* situation. Many are reticent about expressing their feelings by means of overt action, simply because their way of living has always been quiet and restrained. Although they may sense inwardly the emotional values of meaning, they cannot show any outward sign of sparkle, enjoyment or drama through the release of deeper emotions. The difficulty can be partly alleviated through the practice of "letting go." The French have found the right word for this procedure in the concept of *abandon* which means "cutting one's cables," "burning one's bridges," "being free from natural restraints." After you sense some of this emotional release, then you should learn how to "tone down" to secure the illusion of reality. This kind of control, which is not easy, can be gained by exaggerating initially and then by gradually polishing the rough spots so that the glow seems real.

The instructional problem varies with the student's emotional difficulty. Should he be urged to "live the part," to "submerge his identity," to "lose himself," so that he is oblivious to all about him? Each of these exhortations may be valuable for the young and inexperienced interpreter, if he will be helped to "let go," but must be taken with some allowance for endurance. They are helpful only if you know what they mean. Complete absorption in a performance is beneficial only when you are a skilled technician in control of the artistic reins. For instance, it is nonsense to believe that in order to interpret Macbeth with sincerity, you must be overpowered with ambition to the point of committing murder; or to characterize Katherine, the shrew, you should *be* an uncontrolled, spoiled and selfish young woman.

Further explanation is needed on this matter for it is the key to the control of the emotions in re-creating the author's meaning. To be successful as an interpreter, you must be sensitive to the meaning of the lines and be moved by them as the author intended. If you lack this sensitivity, your interpretation will be ineffectual. If, however, you are capable of experiencing anger, remorse, love or serenity, or any other mood that the author created, you will have a chance at re-creating the meaning with some success. Because all art requires headwork and planning, however, you should not become so absorbed in an emotion that you weaken your judgment and sense of values. No matter how moved you may be, you must have sufficient control at all times to know exactly what you are doing, to know whether or not you have gone too far or not far enough in portraying the emotional depth of the feeling.

The psychology of the situation reaffirms this control. You cannot go through the motions and tensions of being angry or passionate or frightened without feeling something of anger, passion and fear. After all, emotion itself is an organic pattern of tensing and relaxing, because of the rhythmic integration of the neuromuscular system. In some instances, you may experience deep emotion as you read the lines to yourself and absorb the impact of the literature. Then as you practice aloud, you may be disappointed at your failure to reach the emotional depth of the meaning. Whatever reaction you have, you know that control is the next step: to find the happy mean, study and criticize what you are doing, decide how realistic you sound and gauge the effect on your listeners. Tape-recorders can always provide an objective approach to your control of vocal sound.

In brief, then, you must feel the emotion deeply and sincerely enough to interpret, but not so much that you are lost in your emotional reactions and thus have little control of yourself. Sincerity is not a saving grace in itself: the only interpreter whose sincerity helps him to success is the one who knows what he is doing, vocally and bodily, and with regard to meaning. In the last analysis, art rests on selectivity and skill. In actual achievement, these two abilities come first in importance; then absorption, sincerity and spirit follow.

CONTROL OF BODILY MOVEMENT

The first problem, most noticeable on the platform, is control of bodily movement—inner as well as outward control of muscular tension. The sea of faces before you may present a sudden input from stimuli that could cause rigidity, followed by trembling of muscles before you speak your first words. The nerve fibers, contained within your body structure, receive the signals of outside stimulation and are quickly activated without warning to you. Immediately the tiny cerebral body in the center of the brain, known as the hypothalamus, strives for equilibrium of the body mechanism. In this process of readjustment in which an output in the form of release is necessary, you may freeze on the platform for a moment or two with a dry mouth, a tongue like leather, hands that are damp and cold, and eyes that see nothing: a body out of control!

This condition can be alleviated by practice and by conditioning your body to meet the concentrated attention of expectant listeners. Coordination and centralization of movements and tensions can be acquired, just as you learn control in any physical activity: dancing, skating, fencing, racing, ski-jumping, golfing, swimming. The most adept person in any of these competitive sports is the one who knows how to make his body do the necessary work skillfully, with ease and economy. If the state of the body plays a part in your success or failure, and if it is so easy to dislocate the equilibrium of the muscular mechanism, then what do you do in an emergency? The answer is found in the emotional quality every artist has to have: the art of "letting go" at the right time of his habitual natural instincts.

To be natural, really natural—not the illusion of naturalness, but naively natural—is to show a certain amount of restraint. By nature man is full of caution and has a certain amount of craving for quiet and safety. On the other hand, the artist is full of the desire to get out "in front" where he knows he may encounter greater risks than during the quiet of everyday life. He has to be a great "taker-of-chances," a volunteer for hazardous commissions; he must be willing to cut loose from his moorings. The diver on the springboard demonstrates this idea: if he is to make an expert dive, he abandons all hope of hanging on to the board or of keeping anything solid underneath his feet. He must literally cut himself off from his foundations through the control of his whole body. He works for form—not disintegration—of movement in "cutting himself loose." So, too, does the ski-jumper. So, too, does every artist! The history of the world represents the great writers, painters, sculptors, actors and leaders as people who took the plunge and never openly flinched at the possible consequences.

Failure to project yourself into the limelight, to offer yourself as a target for others, will be one of your first obstacles in interpretative speech. The advice "Be yourself" was never intended for those interested in creative activity before a group of listeners. You can understand why the rule of practice should be: *Begin with overdoing.* Be sure to go far enough at first. Halfway practice and work will leave you unwilling to spring from the diving board to make your plunge. With each dive, your form will improve until you finally operate with economy of control. Some few may well fear and should avoid the evils of exaggeration and bombast, but the majority of American students will be effectively outgoing and will cherish the virtue of going two miles initially when only one seems necessary.

CONTROL OF VOICE

Your most powerful instrument on the platform, on the street, in the classroom, in your home, is your *voice;* for it conveys your thoughts and arouses emotional responses in others, so that perhaps they too begin to think, feel, believe as you do! Do not forget you have a communicative heritage and you live in a world by and for communication. Inasmuch as your voice gives you so much personal enjoyment, you should never forget that vocal power is produced by the intricate innervation of very delicate muscles. According to the manner in which the voice is treated much of the time, the vocal mechanism would appear to be made of iron and steel. You seldom think in terms of the control of voice, even in your everyday activities. You accept this great gift of speech in a matter-of-fact manner, use your speech mechanism to the limit of its endurance and subject it to all kinds of hazards. At a football game, you whoop yourself into a state of hoarseness and "sore throat"; you tense the delicate vocal muscles beyond their normal functioning power. Only when the voice becomes a whisper or seems to have disappeared and the tissues of the larynx are inflamed and nodules appear, do you begin to evaluate the voice as a possession—one that may mean dollars and cents to you later in your chosen profession.

The first step involved in vocal control is to learn how to listen to voices, to become conscious of the sound of other voices, as well as your own. Listen to recordings of speaking voices. Notice how the personality of the speaker is often reflected in the voice. Compare the vigorous voices of famous leaders, such as Franklin D. Roosevelt, Winston Churchill and John F. Kennedy, with the dramatic voices of Dylan Thomas, Tyrone Power and Charles Laughton and with the lyrical voices of Siobhan McKenna, Edna St. Vincent Millay and Helen Hayes. Then listen to the voices of students and teachers. After your study of how the vocal mechanism operates, you will be able to *hear* with greater discrimination the pleasant voice, the well-modulated tones. Train your ear to detect a voice that is nasal, monotonous, inarticulate, too high. Then listen to tape after tape of your own voice. Try every vocal effect you can think of in order to evaluate the range and effectiveness of your vocal potential. These listening moments are extremely important because they also tell much of how people think, act and control themselves through vocal activity.

The next step in your study is to know something of the operation of the vocal mechanism. You do not need the scientific information of a speech pathologist, but you should know how to utilize the body mechanism involved in the production of sound. Furthermore, you will be aided through this control in the re-creation of meaning. The artful use of the voice as it may reflect meaning is discussed fully in part III.

CONTROL THROUGH PERSONALITY

In no artistic production is the personality of the creator more pertinent and crucial than in the art in which man uses himself as the instrument to express meaning. The interpreter finds no chisels and marble, no oils and canvas, no bricks, stones or steel—just black marks to guide his way and a controlled body and voice for expression. Like the actor, the interpreter needs mastery of *how* the lines mean, ability to ease into the spirit of the poem, story or character through control of the complete person. If this desire to communicate as an alive and interesting person is not added to other techniques, then the presentation will be ineffective. You as an interpreter should feel motivated to "give" through your personality and character. Your "brains" count, your appearance and your manners—indeed the total impression you give as a person.

One of the vague terms used in the description of self is *personality*. What can be its make-up? It is character, of course; it is physical structure and operation; it is a matter of manners and habits; it includes training, skill, accomplishment, the result of your labors and struggles; it is the positive and outward acknowledgment of your experience. All these it is surely. One more important item should be added to the make-up of personality: effective communication through speech. Personality is often gauged by the person's speech coordinated with bodily activity: effective quality of speaking, bodily control, emotional balance through choice of words and language; control of vocal timbre or quality, vocal intensity, vocal tempo, the modulations and nuances of vocal pitch. Listen to people discussing personalities, and note how much stress is placed on the main speech characteristics, such as vivacity of thought, speech mannerisms and style, quick verbal adjustments.

Some people use the word *magnetic* in describing an impressive personality. They probably are thinking of how the bodily structure and coordination, aided by training, study and experience, make this person attractive or exert a "drawing-power" to others. Coeds have been heard to say of a male performer, "Um-m-m—what chemistry!": a phrase with expressive organic or physical associations similar to those connected with *magnetism*—a word belonging to the language of the 1890's. This "chemistry," this "come hither," is something intangible which you sense about the organicity of a person: his bodily structure and speech adjustments, his manner of moving, his assurance, his alive and easy remarks seemingly directed to you personally. He is very different from one who appears impatient, disturbed, tense, irritable and jittery. The voice will often betray the inner man by being harsh, high and hard-hitting; just as the body may show indecisive actions, hurried movements, lack of composure. The speech and body, operating as a unit, tend to become a barometer of how this personality thinks, lives, works and socializes. This exterior manner is grounded in the chemistry of the intricately winding bloodstream on its circulatory way to feed the neuromuscular system. Indirectly, outward manifestations are the result of the operation of the "chemical or electrical" synapses responding to situations. Could this be the main motivating force of a "personality"? Perhaps.

This willingness to reach out to others must exist within the make-up of an interpreter so that he can breathe life, understanding and emotion for overtones of meaning, thereby enhancing the moment as a memorable experience for the listener. This "something" may be called *personality*—a factor to be merged effectively with other techniques of control.

II

THE TECHNIQUE OF
IMPRESSION

3

Patterns of Literary Form

THE *HOW* OF LITERARY FORMS

ANALYSIS OF LITERATURE

In earlier editions of this text, it was thought that the majority of students interested in interpretative speech would have an informative background of literary forms. Yet, in the course of years, explanations had to be given many times concerning various forms of literature before the author's point of view could be treated. Most students seemed to know the drama form, probably because of their experiences on- or off-stage, watching or taking part in performances. For this edition, short summaries of literary forms have been included, in addition to discussions of the writer's point of view. Even though explanations have been curtailed, it has been difficult not to get too involved in the intricacies of form and literary devices which authors employ to convey meaning vividly. These following discussions are intended only as a possible springboard for further reading, inasmuch as these summaries are not conclusive. You must reach out for the unknown in the excellent critical books found on the library shelves and in the bookstores.

Unfortunately, knowledge of the forms of literature will not guarantee you the ability to interpret effectively. If this were true, then all well-informed instructors of literature would be competent to convey orally the tone, mood, atmosphere, rhythm and overtones of meaning. You will find someone who can; and when you have had that experience, you will never forget the consummate skill of the teaching. An understanding of the craftsmanship and artistry involved in the creation of memorable literature will strengthen your appreciation of the writer's struggle to create impressions. You will also gain a hint or two of how the same kind of effort should be reflected in the final goal of the interpreter to re-create impressions.

Although the analysis of a literary selection is very intriguing, this is not the goal of interpretative speech. Rather it is the means to the end. Your aim is to try to make others *hear* what you find on the printed page; the more perceptive you are about the meaning, the greater is your chance

in establishing a sincere approach to your performance on the podium.
Students of literature, who attempt this kind of study, add incentive to
group procedures because of their literary appreciation; they also have to
learn how to tackle the problem of using their assets, vocally and bodily,
to re-create meaning for others. To know you are studying a ballad or a
villanelle may show some elementary erudition, but the important principle is to know how to express the overall impression the poet has given you
in his particular form. To know a sonnet is composed of fourteen lines,
sometimes divided into an octave and a sestet and sometimes ending with
a succinct couplet, will assist you as an interpreter *only* if you know how
to help the audience *hear* the shift in mood, tone or philosophy between
the first lines and the last six lines, or if you know how to make impressive
the emphasis of the ending couplet. The study of form for your own understanding is excellent. Even top authorities on structure, meter, form, imagery—and distinguished writers who interpret their own works—often do
not know how to re-create meaning audibly. Literary intricacies are a
fascinating subject for study in their own right, but they will not reach
an audience unless you know how to express them.

FORM & STRUCTURE

At this time, a clarification of the terms *form* and *structure* as used in
the following discussions might be helpful, inasmuch as they are often
employed as of equal technical prominence and sometimes are treated
synonymously. Because an attempt is being made here to simplify rather
than to argue, *form* characterizes not only the outward or external identifiable design but also is dependent on the internal structure of the literature. In other words, form will be considered an all-inclusive term that will
include the outward design supported by external organizational and developmental patterns and by the internal structural composition. Every
item in the literary masterpiece will then be unified into an organic central
meaning, thus giving the desired tone, texture and feeling.

The following list of items characterizes the *form* of various types of
literature discussed in this particular study of interpretative speech:

1. The outward design of form—by stanzas or paragraphs—may be observed easily as belonging either to prose or poetry.
2. Form is identified within the twofold classification of prose and poetry.
   a. In prose the forms are known as essay, short story, novel and drama
      —sometimes called by various other names, such as narratives, ex-
      positions, fantasies, allegories, commentaries and characterizations.
   b. In poetry the forms are known under the broad classification of
      narrative, lyrical and dramatic poems, and are subdivided for com-
      positional purposes as ballads, songs, sonnets, epics, odes, elegies and
      dramatic lyrics and monologues.

3. Form is characterized by developmental patterns of narration, exposition, description, persuasion and dramatization.
4. Form is tempered by the point of view of the writer.
5. Form can be observed easily by the metrical and stanzaic pattern in poetry characterized by distinctive rhythmical cadences of lines; and by the paragraph progression of ideas in prose characterized by distinctive stylistic arrangement.
6. Form is given perspective by the internal compositional and structural pattern that integrates the inherent poetical and prose qualities for intensification of meaning; by the development and arrangement of images, metaphors, symbols; by the associative word combinations and stylistic patterns to support characterizations, events, tone, mood and atmosphere; and by the development through balance and contrast of ideas, characters and incidents moving toward a culminating thought or climax.

Although isolation of form, structure and meaning is almost impossible, to a certain extent this procedure is necessary for clarifying purposes. The theory that a literary form has an organic unity of developing parts is still inherent in discussions of this book, even though certain items may seem at times to be pulled apart from the meaning. Perceptive meaning will never be expressed by isolating parts but rather by observing how the developing elements are synthesized to support the meaning.

You must decide for yourself whether paraphrase and explication of meaning will assist you in finding the meaning. You may believe that the most creative part of the meaning has been left unsaid. Hopefully, you will enjoy finding the unknown rather than having it handed to you in the arbitrary form known as the explication. If you study earnestly the *how* and *why* of lines, and if you are in control of your vocal and bodily mechanisms, then you should be able to express the significant thought.

Since the study of literary elements necessary to make literature memorable to listeners, or even solitary readers, may be found mainly in the poem, the short story, the novel, the play and the essay, the text could develop into a literary evaluation of the philosophy and techniques of many authors as indicated by their writing of prose and poetry: how the idea originates; how it develops; how form and structure are utilized for meaning and theme; how the writer employs literary devices to make lines and meaning impressive; and how, finally, the literary piece arrives at its full development with the author directly involved in its audible construct or indirectly looking on from the sidelines.

Whirlpools of argument would arise with detailed discussions, no doubt, as are evidenced in any volume by anthologists, dimensionists, poets, prose writers, explicators and critics. One of the first items noticeable in any volume is the classification and selection of literature. A generally accepted practice is to establish differences between prose and poetry, although some would prefer to think these variations are minimal, or at least, merely a matter of degree. Some authors even report that one form—such as the short story—may serve as a disciplinary function for the creation of a differently concentrated structure—such as the poem. Professional interpreters of literature believe the differences among forms call for a distinctive way to interpret prose as opposed to poetry; or at least, they believe, and rightly so, the procedure is more orderly if distinctions of form, point of view and development are pointed out to the naïve interpreter.

PROSE & POETRY: FORMAL DIFFERENCES

Many think of the differentiating line of prose and poetry as a straight, decisive form line: that is, prose is literature which shows sentence structure conforming to normal speech syntax and rhythm, and paragraphs indicating a change in the direction of thought development. The language may be characterized by everyday colloquialisms, imitative of American or dialectal speech as well as by a style of high literary level. Generally the thought moves along easily because of well-ordered sentences. Poetry, on the other hand, is recognized by lines that are broken, that conform with a certain brevity, and that are usually irregular in syntax and structured in a stanzaic pattern. These are visual differences of which everyone is aware; this is the form the eye sees!

You perhaps have an elementary background of the writer's craft as it is employed in building interrelationships of form, structure, meaning, points of view or approach and various literary patterns to create the illusion of reality. To help you recall some of these factors important as background in the interpretation of literature, it may be helpful to review briefly the differentiating characteristics of writers in finding the idea, forming it, finding the right point of view and developing it. These factors contribute essentially to *how* the pattern of meaning will be structured into a particular form.

TONE IN LITERARY FORMS

The impact of literature can come from various sources, as these discussions will reveal. The initial emotional impact will probably recall some memorable experience you have had or perhaps an extension of one of your beliefs. Generally, however, the literary master, not knowing who his audience will be, relies on certain resources to create the direct impression through a given form. Later this topic will be examined in greater detail.

For the present discussion of form, you should remember three elements, important in creating a totality of impression: *tone, atmosphere* and *mood. Tone* is characterized by the voice of the author, sometimes submerged but still recognized or sensed through his individual style, whether by overstatement or understatement, by arrangement of phrases and sentences or by rhythmical fluency. Remember that tone establishes the writer's attitude. *Atmosphere* encompasses movement and meaning in some form as suspense, mystery, inevitability, fantasy, horror, irony, humor. *Mood* is expressed through the intermingled attitudes, feelings and speech of the characters toward themselves, others and events or through images expressing the predominant emotion of the writer.

Although the appreciation of atmosphere and mood is an important source of motivation for the interpreter's presentation, the most urgent factor to be considered is the author's underlying tonal attitude to his central theme or "center of vision," as Lubbock calls it in *The Craft of Fiction.*

The word *tone* is taken from its vocal and physical environment. Your tone of voice—its intonations, inflections, emphasis, rhythm—can give a meaning orally, which might not be evident if you, the amateur, tried to put that meaning on the printed page. You should have little difficulty, however, interpreting reactions with variations of vocal tones, bodily manner, and especially facial expression. On the campus, a coed can be heard between classes greeting her friends; listen to the different tones that show her particular happiness in seeing various persons. You may hear, "Hi!" (abrupt and quick manner; no time for talk; eyes shift); "Hi!" (surprise attitude; haven't seen you for a long time; touch on the arm); "Hi." (light and indifferent; what *you* again; brief nod); and then suddenly you hear the soft melodious singing voice, expressing warmth and satisfaction—

$$\text{``H}^{e}{}_{l}{}^{l}{}_{o}{}^{o}{}^{o}{}_{o}{}_{o}{}_{o}\,o!\text{''}$$

—(as she snuggles up to her boyfriend).

Tone, however, expresses the writer's attitude by means of his intonational stylistic quality toward his subject and relationship with the reader. The closeness of this attitude is made possible by the right choice and arrangement of words giving overtones and activating experiences for the listener instead of lulling him to sleep with an impersonal attitude, reminiscent of the rhetorical approach. The writer will vary the tone in poems and stories, depending on the way in which he wishes his meaning to be understood through the form he has decided to use.

POETRY

In poetry you are conscious of concentration within a few lines. No doubt you have experienced many moments of struggle with printed symbols, hoping to understand the involved meaning caused by quick shifts in phrasing and imagery and by gaps you cannot span because of the eccentricity of the author's style and thought. You probably have realized the images are packaged in a small bundle of relationships; the phrases and lines are carried by a sustained tone; the meaning is heightened emotionally; but alas, you are many times conscious only of obscurity. Fortunately, you may have been repaid after several readings with a sudden impact of the meaning through the understanding of interrelated symbols. Poetry is expected to have this concentrated meaning pressured into a series of images contained in an intonational pattern. When Eliot's poems were first published, students found difficulty in translating his way with words into their way. If you still find his meaning not sufficiently clear for your literary understanding, just remember that the poet has admitted when writing *Waste Land,* "I wasn't even bothering whether I understood what I was saying." Thomas's unusual images too are being explicated, and perhaps exploited, today in many critical volumes: his phrases are being analyzed, his images are being explained, his personal life is being torn apart to make his images clear. Sometimes a poet like Frost can give enjoyment to all people who read his poetry, because of his different levels of cadenced meaning. Although much has been written about his use of the implied metaphor, Frost has never offered his own solution of the thought inherent in his poetry.

Poets and critics today stress this concentration on an image that grows into a more complex, and usually a more obscure, meaning when the poet attaches other related or contrasting images to the first one. Pound's compressed use of images in the lines of "In a Station of the Metro" (*metro* is a Paris subway), has intrigued many anthologists and critics because of the impact of the images (the second line has been spaced as it appears in most books):

> The apparition of these faces in the crowd
> Petals   on a   wet   black   bough.[1]

You may wonder how these two lines happened. Pound tells of the development of his experience:

> Three years ago in Paris (1911) I got out of a "metro" train at La Concorde, and saw suddenly a beautiful face, and then another and another and another beautiful woman . . . and I tried all that day for words for what that had meant for me. . . . And that evening . . . I found suddenly, the expression . . . not in speech but in sudden splotches of colour. It was just that—a "pattern" or hardly a pattern if by pattern you mean something with a "repeat" in it. But it was a word, the beginning for me of a new language in colour. . . .[2]

[1] From PERSONAE by Ezra Pound. Copyright 1926, 1954, by Ezra Pound. Reprinted by permission of the publishers, New Directions.
[2] From THE FORTNIGHTLY REVIEW, "Vorticism," September 1, 1914, p. 465. For and on behalf of THE CONTEMPORARY REVIEW CO. LTD.

He relates how he wrote a thirty-line poem and then destroyed it because it was work of the "second intensity"; six months later he tried again with fifteen lines. Still not satisfied, he finally wrote the finished lines a year later, in the manner of the Japanese imagist poetry called *Haiku*, consisting of seventeen syllables in three lines of five, seven and five syllables. Pound called the above one-image "metro" poem a form of "super-position," indicating that one idea was set on top of another to secure the completed image.

For the interpreter, this concentrated poetic form with its tonal quality calls for rich and varied experiences in order to call up associations stimulated by the images ,which, more than any other item, give meaning to the poem. If the meaning is obscure to you, the interpreter, you can be sure that it will not be revealed to listeners merely by uttering words. No literature, especially poetry, should be considered for presentation before an audience unless the images create meaning to the interpreter.

THE ESSAY

The essay is a brief discursive composition on some phase of a subject, large or small, important or trivial, so written to reveal deliberately the author's tone and indirectly his personality. An essayist never tries to exhaust a subject; he merely finds a new glance at an idea. In so doing, he will use a developmental pattern to fit his mood or his idea—description, exposition, narration, persuasion—even the dramatic pattern.

The essay had its christening when the amiable, rambling voice of Michel de Montaigne, a Frenchman of the sixteenth century, named his three collections of "experiments," *Essais.* He writes concerning his attempts:

It is a natural, simple and unaffected speech that I love, so written as it is spoken, and such upon the paper as it is in the mouth, a pithy, sinewy, full, strong, compendious, and material speech, not so delicate and affected as vehement and piercing. . . . I decided to walk with my pen as I go with my feet, and let my mind move with its own natural step, not the steps of the dancing school or as those who leap on horseback because they are not strong enough in their legs to march on foot.

Of course, Plato, Cicero, Seneca, Confucius, Plutarch and others had preceded him by many centuries, even as the scribes of The Book of Proverbs, Judges, and Ecclesiastes of the Bible; as well as the numerous "sayings," epigrams, maxims, epistles and superstitions, many of which were handed down by word of mouth. Inasmuch as no one had ever named the particular literary form, Montaigne used the word *essai,* with the connotation of experiment, attempt, endeavor. His was an attempt to delight, entertain—and he succeeded!

Every student knows, of course, Irving's *Sketch Book,* typically American but modeled in some ways after the well-known *Tatler* and *Spectator* of Addison and Steele. He knows, too, Theodore Roosevelt, Robert Louis Stevenson and most important of all, Mark Twain: each writer having his own preference for subjects and each with his own particular tone. The essayist is like the short story writer in giving you a glimpse of the wheels going round, but the wheels belong to him personally and not to the characters who are projected on the story screen.

The essay, sometimes considered the literary form having the least impact, in truth wields a greater daily influence than any other form. You are bombarded with essayists at every turn of events and many times during the day. This form provides a means of keeping abreast in many fields —politics, art, finance, government, medicine, safety and hygiene. When you hear commentators on news broadcasts with their scintillating and succinct—sometimes cryptic—remarks on a chosen subject of the moment, you are listening to essays or attempts to give a personal way of thinking about a subject, either serious or light in tone. The news columnist is an essayist; the editor is an essayist; so is the critic of any feature story or play; so is the travel narrator of adventure; and so are those who like to write character portrayals or the philosophers who would set the world in its right course. Your listening world, as well as your reading world, is tempered every day by the tone of the essayist, who tells you what he thinks.

THE SHORT STORY

As the poet labors for compression of images to obtain tone and unity of meaning, so does the author of the twentieth-century short story utilize a condensed form of prose to get compact unity. Poe, because of his criticism of Hawthorne's *Twice-told Tales,*[3] is credited for giving impetus to the prevalent short story in America: the narrative must be short enough to be read at one sitting and long enough to give a unified impression and so produce a deep emotional response. Moreover, to Poe the atmosphere is the most important element in the short story and gives the narrative its concentrated unity. Characters are subordinate to the creation of the atmosphere. Indeed, the first sentence of the story should establish the particular tone of the author, as Poe demonstrates in his story, "The Fall of the House of Usher":

During the whole of a dull, dark and soundless day in the autumn of the year, when the clouds hung oppressively low in the heavens, I had been passing alone, on horseback, through a singularly dreary tract of country; and at length found myself, as the shades of the evening drew on, within view of the melancholy House of Usher.

[3] Edgar Allan Poe, "Literary Criticism," *The Works of Edgar Allan Poe* (New York: Charles Scribner's Sons, 1914), V. vii, pp. 38-42.

And Poe proceeds to pile horror upon horror throughout the pages of his story.

Critics agree, however, that Poe's influence has given the short story a tight and rigid form, yet variable according to the structure of the meaning. Typically the short story contains little or no analysis and no excessive discussion or description—sometimes none; but the narrative moves forward according to the author's stylistic arrangement and approach. The reader is permitted to draw his own conclusions about the theme and the significance of characters and situations in the evolvement of meaning. The impression—the "after-image" of the short story—is like a flash upon the screen held long enough to show the total picture and then released quickly.

James, in writing "The Middle Years," a story in the form of a "concise anecdote," relates his effort "to squeeze his subject" for tone and meaning into five or six thousand words, and his "struggle to keep compression rich" or rather to "keep accretions compressed"—a struggle similar to the "anxious effort of some warden of the insane engaged at a critical moment in making fast a victim's straight jacket." Having planned his formula of "working from the outside in," he found "after boilings and reboilings of the contents of the small cauldron, after pounds of salutary sugar, as numerous as those prescribed in the choicest recipe for the thickest jam," and "after innumerable repeated chemical reductions and condensations," the experience was one of the "costliest, even, if, like the hard, shining sonnet, one of the most indestructible forms of composition in general use."[4]

In her *Letters*, Katherine Mansfield tells how she wrote *Miss Brill* (page 503). She read the story aloud many times to get the "sound and fall," the tone, of the sentences so they would seem to fit Miss Brill "on that day and at that very moment." Although this story is not considered one of Mansfield's best, the narrative does show tremendous impact because of the detail work. In contrast, Hemingway explains the technique of compression in a different manner. He emphasizes the need of keeping in reserve observation of things known and seen, and then choosing carefully at the time of composing:

> I always try to write on the principle of the iceberg. There is seven-eighths of it underwater for every part that shows. Anything you know you can eliminate and it only strengthens your iceberg. It is the part that doesn't show. If a writer omits something because he does not know it then there is a hole in the story. I have tried to eliminate everything unnecessary to conveying experience to the reader so that . . . it will become a part of his or her experience and seem actually to have happened . . . But knowledge is what makes the underwater part of the iceberg.[5]

[4] Henry James, "Preface," *The Author of Beltraffio, The Middle Years, Greville Fane and Other Tales* (New York: Charles Scribner's Sons, 1909), pp. v-vi, xvi.

[5] *Paris Interview Series*, pp. 235-236.

This condensation of the short story decrees that only a few characters, sometimes only one, will be captured in a particular environment at a certain dramatic moment. Since brevity and unity of total effect and theme are the concern of the writer, continuous development of a character is not possible as in the novel. Instead, the major character and his subordinates are portrayed, directly or indirectly, in some phase of living in which their traits, under the stress of allotted time, are revealed; usually they are caught at some turning point of positive or deteriorating activity, either shown implicitly or explicitly. Consequently, the author's framework on which he builds his theme supports active characterization with little or no description or exposition. In Mansfield's story, "Miss Brill," the action *is* Miss Brill, who is etched against the background of a "cupboard" of a room and the park, the latter offering her an escape and freedom from loneliness. Other characters merely form a background on which Miss Brill's thoughts are projected.

In Hemingway's "The Snows of Kilimanjaro," you become immersed in the struggle of Harry—writer, hunter, degenerate—a man who knows death is near. The main struggle, however, concerns not life and death but his own failure to make use of his writing talent because of his general deterioration. This part of his personality is accomplished by means of memory flashbacks to earlier episodes of his life. Then, momentarily, you are brought back to the isolated location in Africa, where you hear his insolence and indifference to his wife and become acutely aware of borrowed time for him as he moves in and out of consciousness. In these twenty-four hours before Harry's death, Hemingway has blended the reality of the day of suffering with the tonal fantasy of recalled experiences to intensify indirectly the heartbreaking destruction of Harry's talent, "by drinking so much that he blunted the edge of his perceptions, by laziness, by sloth, and by snobbery, by pride and by prejudice."

The memory flashbacks are written in rhythmical prose quite different in tone from the heartless, abrupt talk with his wife, the final controlling reason he had traded his talents for security. The memories recall to him certain unforgettable experiences in faraway places, about which he one day intended to write: trout streams in the Black Forest; Constantinople; snow-bound winters in Schrunzthe with bright Christmas days; surroundings enhanced by "solid bamboo slopes," "a pink sifting cloud," "forests sculptured into peaks and hollows," a log house "chinked with white mortar" on top of a hill with a lake below and beyond, a timber forest; and Paris:

No, he has never written about Paris. Not the Paris that he cared about. But what about the rest that he had never written?

What about the ranch and the silvered gray of the sage brush, the quick, clear water in the irrigation ditches, and the heavy green of the alfalfa. The trail went up into the hills and the cattle in the summer were shy as deer. The bawling and the steady noise and slow moving mass raising a dust as you brought them down in the fall. And behind the mountains, the clear sharpness of the peak in the evening light and, riding down along the trail in the moonlight, bright across the valley. Now he remembered coming down through the timber in the dark holding the horse's tail when you could not see and all the stories that he meant to write. . . .[6]

ERNEST HEMINGWAY, *The Snows of Kilimanjaro*

In contrast to this story, Hemingway's "The Killers" is a narrative with the drama of the theater in it, the action being directed by means of short dialogue scenes as the characters move in and out from the wings of the stage set. During the short period of one day, momentum is built toward the presence of Andreson, the man who is being hunted by three gangsters. The consequent denouement is concerned directly with the theme of the story: the sudden knowledge of the consequences of evil for the youngest character, Nick.

A different tone is found in Frank O'Connor's "First Confession" (page 526), a story combining the deft humor and penerating understanding of the priest with the belligerence of a small boy "with death in his heart," being dragged by his "vixen" sister to his first confession. The basic human qualities of the three characters, revealed through ironic intensity of tone and amazing economy of words, are caught at fleeting but impressionable moments of activity—moments sometimes delightfully and shrewdly funny. These four stories, so different in tone, form and approach, affirm the critics' repeated statements: (1) every short story has its own individual form and style; and (2) the author's frame of reference will never contain a human life in its totality, as is possible in the novel.

The interpreter must *see* from all sides the "moment" of the story and observe how intensity of tone is created. He should try to re-create in his own thoughts preceding events that may have precipitated the action or conflict, as in "The Killers," "The Snows of Kilimanjaro," "First Confession" and "Miss Brill." He will then, as an interpreter, be partially prepared through his own background to release the impact to listeners. This procedure is the "spadework," the preparation for the foundation of tone and meaning.

THE NOVEL

In contrast to the short story with its few characters imaged in a "momentary slice-of-life" incident, the novel contains a series of episodes usually extending over a longer period of time, characters who develop

[6] Excerpt from the work of Ernest Hemingway is used by permission of Charles Scribner's Sons: "The Snows of Kilimanjaro." (Copyright 1936 Ernest Hemingway; renewal copyright © 1964 Mary Hemingway.)

and move within that period of time and generally in many different environments. James characterizes the novel as an "ado" about something; the "larger the form it takes, the greater, of course, the ado."[7] The author of the novel creates a continuous and contrasting combination of occurrences, dialogues and characterizations to show the participating characters in activity. This arrangement finally culminates in a climax and sometimes includes a denouement, a settlement of the conflict. The perspective, as limited by the element of time in which the characters move, becomes important in the building toward the climax in these two forms of fiction. O'Connor, in the *Paris Interview Series,* distinguishes between time as shown in the novel and in the short story:

Creating in the novel a sense of continuing life is the thing. We don't have that problem in the short story, where you merely suggest continuing life. In the novel, you have to create it. . . . To me, a novel is something built around the character of time, the nature of time, and the effects that time has on events and characters.[8]

So the novelist makes use of the time factor to establish the conflict of his main character in relation to his environment and his consequent development, as well as to make plausible the climax of the narrative, through his selection of certain well-timed episodes.

The form of the novel is not too often considered challenging to the average reader. Inasmuch as the words and syntax are ordinarily those of everyday communication, heightened by the novelist's tone or style of writing, the reader moves casually and sometimes superficially over the pages to find the outcome. Too seldom does he reread or pause to wonder about the design of the author or how the scenes are put together. In other words, technique is accepted rather indifferently because of the narrative interest. No doubt most readers of fiction are more concerned with *what* is going to happen than *why* certain events occur, or *why* this character responds as he does, or *how* this sequence or arrangement furthers the author's meaning. Although the *where* and *when* provide the setting as in the short story, environments can change in a kaleidoscopic manner, bringing about unusual coincidences and events. Whereas the *why* probably will not be commented on in the short narrative, it always gives clues to the central meaning and is often explained in the novel. Moreover, the *why* is supported by the *who,* the assemblage of characters who may be many in number in the novel and only a few in the short story. Thus, the novel form includes many elements, all of which are interrelated to give intensification of tone to the central meaning.

Inasmuch as James's *The Portrait of a Lady* has been read by most

---

[7] Henry James, "Preface" to *The Portrait of a Lady, The Novels of Henry James* (New York: Charles Scribner's Sons, 1908), p. xiii.

[8] *Paris Interview Series,* p. 165.

students, many will remember his main character, Isabel Archer. Some may not be familiar with the story behind her creation. First of all, James thought about this "vivid" character, Isabel, "affronting her destiny" for a long time; he had observed her "in motion" and "in transit" and felt he must create an "ado" about this "complex" young woman of his imagination. So he planned a structured balance to obtain the necessary psychological conflict by means of contrast of characterizations in such a way that Isabel would be the center around which her satellites would converge, as the title implies. He would be interested in the actions of the others only in so far as they would demonstrate the conflict *within* Isabel's own consciousness. This would be the key to the meaning. He tells how he reached his decision about the balance of conflict:

"Place the center of the subject in the young woman's own consciousness," I said to myself, "and you get as interesting and as beautiful a difficulty as you wish. Stick to *that*—for the center; put the heaviest weight in *that* scale, which will be so largely the scale of her relation to herself. . . . Place meanwhile in the other scale the lighter weight; . . . press less hard . . . on the consciousness of your heroine's satellites, especially the male; make it an interest contributive only to the greater one."⁹

Having made this decision, James awoke one morning to find all his characters assembled, much as a group of people who had arrived to be present at a party. He was then ready to start. His next problem was "What should she do?" He initiates the "ado" by sending the American-born Isabel with her aunt to England. She makes her first appearance among three gentlemen who will form a group of her satellites: Mr. Touchett, an invalid American financier who has lived in England for thirty years and is the husband of the aunt who brought Isabel to England; his son, Ralph, a semi-invalid; and their friend, the handsome Lord Warburton. The scene opens with the three men enjoying a leisurely afternoon tea on the spacious lawn of Mr. Touchett's country home. In this beautiful and dramatic setting, Isabel makes her first appearance. As the men finish their tea, Ralph is aware of the indistinct form of a young lady in the "ample doorway" some distance from the group; then a voice is heard greeting Bunchie, the "bristling, bustling terrier"; hands are seen to reach out to hold him face to face as he continues his "quick chatter." As Bunchie's new friend comes closer, Ralph sees a "tall girl in a black dress, who at first sight looks pretty." No further description is given for several pages; then the author builds Isabel into the setting: "She was looking at everything, with an eye that denoted clear perception—at her companion (Ralph), at the two dogs (a collie leaves Mr. Touchett to greet her by 'slowly setting his tail in motion'), at the two gentlemen under the trees, at the beautiful scene before her. 'I've never seen anything

⁹ From *The Novels of Henry James, op. cit.,* p. xv.

so lovely as this place.' " After a few words to Ralph about her arrival with her aunt, Isabel as a person is centered in relation to Ralph. "She remained standing where they had met making no offer to advance or to speak to Mr. Touchett, and while she lingered so near the threshold, slim and charming, her interlocutor (Ralph) wondered if she expected the old man to come and pay her his respects. American girls were used to a great deal of deference, and it had been intimated that this one had a high spirit. Indeed Ralph could see that in her face." Then after the introductions to the other two gentlemen, James focuses the attention of the reader more pointedly on the reactions of his "vivid" character to the environment in which he has placed her:

She had been looking all round her again—at the lawn, the great trees, the reedy, silvery Thames, the beautiful old house; and while engaged in this survey she had made room in it for her companions; a comprehensiveness of observation easily conceivable on the part of a young woman who was evidently both intelligent and excited. She had seated herself and had put away the little dog; her white hands, in her lap, were folded upon her black dress; her head was erect, her eye lighted, her flexible figure turned itself easily this way and that, in sympathy with the alertness with which she evidently caught impressions. Her impressions were numerous, and they were all reflected in a clear, still smile. 'I've never seen anything so beautiful as this.'[10]

In addition to the above character clues, James leaves the reader with two key sentences (see italicized below), further characterizing Isabel as a person of spirit and independence. In answer to her explanation of how Ralph's mother found her in America and had brought her to England, Ralph replies:

"I see. She adopted you."
"Adopted me?" the girl stared, and her blush came back to her, together with a momentary look of pain, which gave her interlocutor some alarm. He had underestimated the effect of his words. . . .
"Oh no; she has not adopted me. *I'm not a candidate for adoption.*"
"I beg a thousand pardons," Ralph murmured. "I meant—I meant—" He hardly knew what he meant.
"You meant she has taken me up. Yes; she likes to take people up. She has been very kind to me; but," she added with a certain visible eagerness of desire to be explicit, "*I'm very fond of my liberty.*"[11]

The last words of this chapter are given to Lord Warburton, as happened also in the preceding chapter before Isabel's entrance. The contrast is interesting because the reader's interest is extended by the beginning of the first big "ado." In the preceding chapter when the three men were alone on the terrace, they discussed the anticipated visit of the

[10] *Ibid.*, pp. 20-21.
[11] *Ibid.*, p. 23-24.

American girl and her marriageable status. Mr. Touchett, remarking that Lord Warburton would probably not make a remarkable husband, added, "Try as much as you please (to be a good husband) but don't try on my niece." Lord Warburton replied, "Ah, well" . . . perhaps, after all, she's not worth trying on!" Then after Isabel's exit in the following scene, Lord Warburton, left standing with Ralph, said after a moment, "You wished a while ago to see my idea of an interesting woman. There it is!" The "ado" has started, with the involvement of all three men, in the leisurely manner of the novel rather than the abrupt plunging approach of the short story.

The above cursory discussion indicates how James combines dramatic, narrative, descriptive and dialogue elements to set the stage for the development of his character, Isabel, in an English environment. With a few deft strokes, the novelist awakens interest in a young American woman among her English friends, prepares the reader for Isabel's relationship to others and to her environment and indicates how she will probably sustain her own convictions. This beginning suggests a characterization to be continually developed until the climax in Isabel's life is reached. These few words here are intended to point up James's theory that he cannot imagine a "passage of description that does not have for its intention narrative," nor a "dialogue that is not in its intention descriptive," nor an "incident" that is not "illustrative." This belief is echoed in much of the critical writing of the twentieth century, as well as in James's contention that a novel is a "living thing, all one and continuous, like any other organism;" and because it is "living," it will have "each of its parts revealed in each of the other parts." He believes, for instance, a woman standing with her hand resting on a table and looking at another person in a certain way is an incident, and also an "expression of character." Consequently, the artist who sees this episode as character, undertakes to record it as such for the reader.[12]

Although the developmental pattern of the novel may not appear to be as concentrated as the poem or the short story, the novelist rearranges, deletes and builds, and also employs the same care with imagery, symbols and concentration of scenes and dialogue to strengthen the climax. Even though you have no opportunity to go backstage and observe the novelist at work, you should be aware of the arrangement of scenes for mounting progression of interest, each incident impinging upon the one following to intensify and make more vivid the movement toward the central meaning. Lubbock's dramatic recording of Tolstoy's penetrating selectivity should increase your appreciation of the way the great novelist creates:

His hand is plunged into the scene, he lifts out of it great fragments, right and left, ragged masses of life torn from their setting; he selects. And upon

[12] Henry James, *The Art of Fiction and Other Essays* (New York: Oxford University Press, 1948), p. 13.

these trophies he sets to work with the full force of his imagination; he detects their significance, he disengages and throws aside whatever is accidental and meaningless; he re-makes them in conditions that are never known in life, conditions in which a thing is free to grow according to its own law, expressing itself unhindered; he liberates and completes. And then, upon all this new life, . . . that is now so much more intensely living than before, Tolstoy directs the skill of his art; he distributes it in a single, embracing design; he orders and disposes.[13]

This same kind of selectivity is credited to James by those who write of his ability to "undercut" for suspense and to intensify key incidents. Even James admits with a bit of satisfaction, that Isabel's all-night meditative vigil to arrive at a decision or a solution of her inner conflict "throws the action forward more than twenty incidents." This technique makes seemingly inert or implicit action anticipate movement in the narrative.

Katherine Anne Porter, when questioned about how the writing of her novel, *The Ship of Fools*, differed from the writing of shorter fiction, replied:

It's just a longer voyage, that's all. It was the question of keeping everything moving at once. There are about forty-five main characters, all taking part in each other's lives, and then there was a steerage of sugar workers, deportees. It was all a matter of deciding which should come first, in order to keep the harmonious moving forward. A novel is really like a symphony, you know, where instrument after instrument has to come in at its own time, and no other. I tried to write it as a short novel, you know, but it just wouldn't confine itself. I wrote notes and sketches. And finally I gave in. "Oh, no, this is simply going to have to be a novel," I thought. That was a real horror. But it needed a book to contain its full movement: of the sea, and the ship on the sea, and the people going round the deck, and into the ship, and up from it. That whole movement felt as one forward motion: I can feel it while I'm reading it. I didn't "intend" it, but it took hold of me.[14]

As Porter introduces many facets of characterization in her novel, broadening the incidents and uniting them into her theme, so other novelists often choose the world as their stage, create shifts in time and environment and build an intricate form to take care of a group of characters. They may select a particular environment as Faulkner does in his Yoknapatawpha saga; or they may limit the time to twenty-four hours as Joyce does in *Ulysses*. By reading extensively among the novels, past and present, you will be able to evaluate perceptively the writer's success in making each incident with its attendant characters grow out of the preceding events; in building effectively through movement, conflict and suspense; and also in creating tone, atmosphere and mood to intensify the central idea.

[13] From THE CRAFT OF FICTION by Percy Lubbock. Copyright © 1957 by The Viking Press, Inc. Reprinted by permission of The Viking Press, Inc., p. 18.
[14] *Paris Interview Series*, p. 162.

THE DRAMA

Unlike a novel, a play—whether comedy, tragedy, melodrama, farce or one of the less common types—is written usually for spectator approval. Expert actors, assisted by other artists of the stage, including the perceptive director and the inventive production staff, give vitality to the playwright's lines. This desire to see the play come to life does not imply that drama cannot be enjoyed by the literary reader nor prove stimulating on its own merit. The enjoyment of watching a play take on life usually gives the imaginative touch of reality, which the ordinary reader may not have sensed. Furthermore, as in the era of your forefathers, pleasure also stems from the need for community participation found in a communicating art. The play will always be remembered more vividly when brilliantly produced and received by an appreciative audience.

Many times, too, a director can save a play as well as the name of the author by his perceptive understanding of how people should react in a pictured stage setting to secure the playwright's meaning. Chekov, the great Russian playwright, was having little success with the production of *The Sea Gull* until that great directing artist Stanislavski produced it as an initial performance of the Moscow Art Theater in December, 1897. According to drama critics, he employed the subjective approach in his directing of the lines, thus projecting mellow temper and tone instead of the typical bombast and declamation prevalent in that era. The drama was proclaimed a success; and much in the manner of an "honor" epilogue, an emblem of the sea gull still decorates the façade of that theater. Eliot, in his experience as a playwright during rehearsals of *Murder in the Cathedral,* learned that lines must "act," and that it is "no use putting in nice lines that you think are good poetry if they don't get the action on at all." According to the *Paris Review,* he remembers the producer remarking to him, "There are very nice lines here, but they've nothing to do with what's going on on stage."

If the dramatic structure is a one-act play, the similarity of the technique employed with that of the short story is quite marked. The "one-act" playwright strives for a single striking effect, a quickening of attention, which he tries to sustain to the end. He may build toward an intense climax or a resolution of the conflicting forces—a "fade out," to use theater jargon. Characters are few; usually one main character dominates the scene, as in the short story; the action moves swiftly and with great economy to the conclusion, without the clutter of unnecessary words, movements or incidents. The author, in creating an emotional tone, gives impact to the moment of crisis by means of action and dramatic dialogue. A secondary action may serve as a frame of reference to establish a relationship to the central idea, but this minor activity serves only as support to the tonal impression.

The mechanical form of the three- and four-act play is clearly developed by acts and scenes and is usually limited to three hours or less, including intermissions. The latter are deemed necessary for physical reasons inasmuch as the human body needs a relaxation of muscular tension; furthermore, they are advisable for psychological reasons, giving the audience a chance to readjust to the play, think over and talk about the action with their neighboring observers and then come back with renewed interest and attention.

The play is objective in its presentation as far as the playwright is concerned. You may think you hear his voice expounding his theme; in reality, you hear the voice of the director, who has arranged the vocal effects. You will find no explanation, description or comment on why some character is responding as he is, except through dialogue and stage directions, interpreted by the director. The author is backstage, in the wings, a submerged onlooker. His play is in the hands of others, who must understand the nuances of the dialogue as it defines character and points up action, suspense and conflict.

The dramatic form is concentrated into the above mentioned patterns and maintains direct and seemingly spontaneous, immediate action by means of dialogue or soliloquy. In other words, the interplay of the speech of characters must show dynamic tone, plus strength and power, to pull the movement of the play in the desired direction. Like the novel, the long play may cover years instead of the moments or hours of the short story; even then, action always appears to be happening for the first time. Wilder, winner of three Pulitzer awards for his novel *The Bridge of San Luis Rey* and his plays *Our Town* and *The Skin of Our Teeth,* can speak with authority on the essential difference in the use of the time element in the play and novel. In the *Paris Interview Series* he comments that anything that happens on the stage "is always *now;* the personages are standing on that razor-edge, between the past and the future" and "the words are rising to their lips in immediate spontaneity." The novel, on the other hand, "is what *took* place." No matter how the author tries to efface himself, "we hear his voice recounting, recalling events that are past and over."

THE ART OF THE PLAYWRIGHT

The ingenuity of the playwright is shown in his art of impregnating his tonality into the speech and activity of his characters, all of whom have a reason for being present. Like artists of other literary forms, he too has selected and arranged his characters, action and scenes from the mass of episodes encountered in life situations. He puts them into a fluid acting form, rejecting those not pertinent to the total effect and indirectly focusing the attention of the listener or reader on the rhythmical sweep of events moving in the direction of the climax. He practices economy in his choice of words, searching always for symbols appropriate to the vocabulary and speech rhythm of his cast. Maugham, one of the greatest short story writers, believes his skill in story writing stemmed from his training as a dramatist:

> I did not take to writing stories seriously till I had had much experience as a dramatist, and this experience taught me to leave out everything that did not serve the dramatic value of my story. It taught me to make incident follow incident in such a manner as to lead up to the climax I had in mind. I am not unaware of the disadvantages of this method. It gives a tightness of effect that is sometimes disconcerting. You feel that life does not dovetail into its various parts with such neatness.[15]

This orderly process is a familiar one in writing or in any artistic form. As someone has said, "The pen is mighty but the blue pencil is mightier" in the art of writing. This tightness of effect means also the writer cannot have a static scene motivated only by brain waves or silent thought processes of a character thinking his way through a situation. Rather, the character must verbalize and show through his outward actions how he thinks and feels inwardly—this is his means of communication. Decidedly, the impact of the character's immediate reaction and the seeming spontaneity in drama are made possible by deft strokes of the playwright's pen; by dramatic effects of tone, emphasis and contrast; and by conflict, verbally and actively produced by the art of the director and his expert cast. Actors cannot assume the flat, one-dimensional person of the printed page; instead they lift impressions from the black marks to show personalities with temperament, color and animation through vocal and bodily control. Moreover, this technique is similar to that of the interpreter. The latter, of course, has no director or other characters, nor does he have the support of artifices used in producing a play. The interpreter stands alone and must depend on his own ability to re-create.

By this time you have become acquainted with the *how* of an art and the selectivity involved to give the desired illusion. In no writing craftsmanship is the *how* so inherently necessary as it is in the building of a play structure and its meaning. Drama, whether comedy or tragedy, involves the "how-process" of bringing people and their individualized actions and reactions into some kind of dramatic conflict, without exposition or description. The playwright says to the actors, "This is how I meant the play to mean." In some instances, he gives direct cues by supplying stage directions, which may mean one thing to him and another to the director of the play or to the actor. A stage direction might read: *Mrs. M. laughed lightly as she turned away.* All that the cue says is that

---

[15] From *The Saturday Review Treasury,* ed. John Haverstich *et al.* "How I Write Short Stories" by Somerset Maugham. Simon and Schuster, 1957 (July 28, 1934), p. 87.

she laughed lightly and turned away. What precisely does it mean? How can it be translated into tonal meaning by the director? Is a "light laugh" ironic, playful, scornful, happy, mocking, agreeable, indifferent? Furthermore, how will the "turning away" add to the meaning of the "light laugh?" Is it a matter of turning away from conflict or accepting a role Mrs. M. secretly is enjoying? Is it to be emphasized by facial expression, by a shrug of the shoulders, by hand movement, by hesitation or by movement of the whole body in a decisive "turn away?" Mrs. M. has to *show* a composite of voice and bodily expression to make the light laugh and the turning away mean what she thinks the author meant. Of course, the context of the dialogue and action will help in the understanding of the meaning, for the author must have had a reason for including the stage direction. So the director tries to show the actress how this cue fits into the scheme of the play: how it relates to the meaning and action of the scene: how it typifies Mrs. M.'s reaction under pressure; how it and Mrs. M's other movements anticipate the conflict; how it may influence the quickening action of other characters. Yes, he is showing the cast *how*, which the playwright assumes is explained in the stage directions. As a result of the director's skills, the listener no longer recognizes the one-dimensional character of the printed page; he finds instead an individual with depth, tone, light and shadow—and the organic whole is given life. Truly, the play is a "showing," inasmuch as it has been discussed, worked over, analyzed and now holds the breath of life to create the illusion of three-dimensional characters caught in a web of activity.

The possibility of re-creating vivid, immediate, emotional responses is greater in the art of drama than in any other literary form. By this time, you have discovered that the art of interpretation falls within the art of acting and is an important initial key to the emotional expression of the play.

THE ORIGIN & DEVELOPMENTAL PATTERN OF AN IDEA

HOW THE IDEA ORIGINATES

You have wondered at times how literary artists begin, how they find their idea. Recorded conversations and writings indicate that the *germ* of an idea strikes them first. The accounts of *how* that germ is caught and built into literature reveal that the motivation and inspiration to create arise from an incident, an impression, an almost forgotten memory suddenly flashing across the thought: a face, a phrase, a character seen only once in a "fleeting but impressionable moment," as noted in Pound's lines about the metro. With this remembrance as a starting place, the germ of an idea grows and develops into a form.

The poet, for instance, centers his thought mainly on images and so produces a more immediate and intense reaction than the prose writer. Poets emphasize continually this concentration on imagery, seeking a combination of several images to support and enhance the meaning. Marianne Moore has found laboratory studies in biology exhilarating and is sure that her poetry has been influenced by science courses. "Precision, economy of statement, logic employed to ends that are disinterested, drawing and identifying"—these she found "liberating" to the imagination. In reading her poetry, you can understand how her training has sharpened the penetrating observation that enables her to pack lines with images showing unique relationships. How does a poem start for her? "A felicitous phrase springs to mind—a word or two, say—simultaneous with some thought or object of equal attraction. Words cluster like chromosomes, determining the procedure."[16] Study the development of thought in "Nevertheless."

Nevertheless

you've seen a strawberry
    that's had a struggle; yet
    was, where the fragments met,

a hedgehog or a star-
    fish for the multitude
    of seeds, What better food

than apple-seeds—the fruit
    within the fruit—locked in
    like counter-curved twin

hazel-nuts? Frost that kills
    the little rubber-plant-
    leaves of *kok-saghyz*-stalks, can't

harm the roots; they still grow
    in frozen ground, Once where
    there was a prickly-pear-

leaf clinging to barbed wire,
    a root shot down to grow
    in earth two feet below;

as carrots form mandrakes
    or a ram's-horn root some-
    times. Victory won't come

[16] *Paris Interview Series*, p. 75.

to me unless I go
        to it; a grape-tendril
        ties a knot in knots till

knotted thirty times,—so
        the bound twig that's under-
        gone and over-gone, can't stir.

The weak overcomes its
        menace, the strong over-
        comes itself. What is there

like fortitude! What sap
        went through that little thread
        to make the cherry red![17]
                        MARIANNE MOORE

    Hopkins's *Journals* contains vivid observations of color and shape as seen in nature: "brindled clouds," "sky minted into golden sequins," "clouds touched here and there with spots of colours," "chestnuts as bright as coals or spots of vermilion," "the wind . . . gliding over the ground in white wisps that between trailing and flying shifted and wimpled like so many silvery worms to and from one another," "the sundown yellow, moist with light but ending at the top in a foam of delicate white pearling and spotted with big tufts of cloud in colours russet between brown and purple but edged with brassy light," "a brindled heaven, the moon just marked by a blue spot pushing its way through the darker cloud," "the sun itself dappled with . . . flowers-in-damask of cloud and joy," "moonlight hanging or dropping on tree-tops like blue cobweb."[18]

    Hopkins writes, "All the world is full of inscape and chances left free to act fall into an order as a purpose." By "inscape" he is referring to the individualism or characteristic action of all things in nature. No wonder then that he could write "Pied Beauty" with "its access of delight and joy," "the light rhythm and the heavy rhythm, the easy meaning and the deeper meaning," coalescing, "rocking back and forth," as Frankenberg writes.

Pied Beauty

Glory be to God for dappled things—
        For skies of couple-colour as a brinded cow;
        For rose-moles all in stipple upon trout that swim;

    [17] Reprinted with permission of The Macmillan Co. from COLLECTED POEMS by Marianne Moore. Copyright 1944 by Marianne Moore.

    [18] Gerard Manley Hopkins, *The Journals and Papers of Gerard Manley Hopkins* (New York: Oxford University Press, 1959), pp. 3-25. See also *A Hopkins Reader,* John Pick, ed. (Oxford University Press, 1953), Chapter 2, "Observation of Nature: Inscape"; and Chapter 3, "Poetic Theory."

Fresh-firecoal chestnut-falls; finches' wings;
Landscape plotted and pieced—fold, fallow and plough;
And all trades, their gear and tackle and trim.

All things counter, original, spare, strange;
Whatever is fickled, freckled (who knows how?)
With swift, slow; sweet, sour; adazzle, dim;
He fathers-forth whose beauty is past change:
Praise him.[19]

GERARD MANLEY HOPKINS

Frankenberg's above notation contains this final penetrating comment on the last line: "It's as if, saying 'Bless you!' to a sneeze, we were suddenly to experience, in the reflex phrase, its full pristine power of benediction."[20]

In David McCord's delightful collection of verses in *What Cheer*, Ernest G. Moll, the Australian poet, has generously contributed the origin of the idea of the famous ballad, "Waltzing Matilda." Although you may have joined groups in singing "Waltzing Matilda," do you know what the words mean and how the ballad started? Here is Mr. Moll's note on this Australian "unofficial national anthem":

The story of how *Waltzing Matilda* came to be written is recorded by an Englishman, Thomas Wood, who, during extensive travels in Australia, kept an eye out for anything in the nature of folk song. In Winton a local man told him: "Banjo Paterson used to come and stay with old Robert McPherson, out at Dagsworth Stations, years ago. They were driving into Winton one day, in the buggy, along with McPherson's sister and Jack Lawton, the drover. He's told me the tale many a time. On the way they passed a man carrying his swag. 'That's what we call *Waltzing Matilda* in these parts,' said McPherson; and Banjo Paterson was so struck with the phrase that he got a piece of paper and wrote the verses there and then. When they got to Winton, his sister, who was a bit of a musician, wrote the tune; and they all sang it that night."

Though there have been some changes in music and words, they are singing it still—Australia's unofficial national anthem. The swagman is a familiar figure in the Australian landscape. To call him hobo or tramp is to do him a grave injustice. Like the snail he carries his house with him, but unlike the snail he is a great wanderer. His house is the blanket roll (*swag*), which he carries on his back. In one hand he bears a tin can with a wire handle (*billy*), a can blackened on the outside by the smoke of many fires and stained brown on the inside by the boiling of much tea. Sometimes, especially in hot country, he carries a canvas bag full of water. Hooked to the straps of his swag he has a bag (*tucker-bag*) for the food which he buys or begs or for which he does odd jobs on the farms along his track. Though by reputation he is an honorable

[19] From *Poems of Gerard Manley Hopkins*, Third Edition, edited by W. H. Gardner. Copyright 1948 by Oxford University Press, Inc. Reprinted by permission.
[20] Lloyd Frankenberg, *Invitation to Poetry* (Garden City, N.Y.: Doubleday & Company, Inc., 1956), p. 294. Reprinted by permission.

man, sometimes the desire for a little fresh mutton takes hold of him and then he takes hold of the sheep (*jumbuck*) that belongs to another. This gets him into trouble with the large landowner (*squatter*) and with the police, as the poem tells us.

But the spirit of him? Like Lamb's borrower, he has risen above the humdrum ways of the world; he has rejected the idea that man shall live by the sweat of his brow; he finds no call to burden himself with wife and child and home. The road is his home—all the roads in all Australia. . . . He lights his campfire by the pools in dry creekbeds (*billabongs*); in the heat of the day he rests in the shade of the gum trees (*coolibahs*). He is free as a bird, and over a pipe in the evening he meditates on that freedom and knows that it is good. Perhaps that is why Australians celebrate him in song.[21]

ERNEST MOLL, *The Story of the Swagman*

In the ballad or Australian anthem of "Banjo Paterson," what folk ballad characteristics are obvious?

Waltzing Matilda

Once a jolly swagman camped by a billabong
Under the shade of a coolibah tree.
And he sang as he watched and waited till his billy boiled:
"You'll come a-waltzing, Matilda, with me!"

CHORUS

Waltzing, Matilda, waltzing, Matilda,
You'll come a-waltzing, Matilda, with me.
And he sang as he watched and waited till his billy boiled,
"You'll come a-waltzing, Matilda, with me!"

Down came a jumbuck to drink at the billabong,
Up jumped the swagman and grabbed him with glee.
And he sang as he stowed that jumbuck in his tucker bag:
"You'll come a-waltzing, Matilda, with me!"

CHORUS

Waltzing, Matilda, waltzing, Matilda,
You'll come a-waltzing, Matilda, with me.
And he sang as he stowed that jumbuck in his tucker bag:
"You'll come a-waltzing, Matilda, with me!"

Up rode the squatter mounted on his thoroughbred,
Down came the troopers, one, two, three,
And his "Where's that jolly jumbuck you've got in your tucker bag?"
"You'll come a-waltzing, Matilda, with me!"

[21] From *What Cheer*, by David McCord, "After All." New York, Coward-McCann, Inc., 1945. Part 2, p. 400. Reprinted with permission of the author.

CHORUS

Waltzing, Matilda, waltzing, Matilda,
You'll come a-waltzing, Matilda, with me.
And his "Where's that jolly jumbuck you've got in your tucker bag?"
"You'll come a-waltzing, Matilda, with me!"

Up jumped the swagman, sprang into the billabong,
"You'll never catch me alive," said he.
And his ghost may be heard as you pass by that billabong:
"You'll come a-waltzing, Matilda, with me!"

CHORUS

Waltzing, Matilda, waltzing, Matilda,
You'll come a-waltzing, Matilda, with me.
And his ghost may be heard as you pass by that billabong:
"You'll come a-waltzing, Matilda, with me!"

A. B. PATERSON

Novelists and story writers also find ideas developing inwardly and casually; then suddenly they recognize that their images are clustering around a central idea. Faulkner relates how his novel, *The Sound and the Fury,* started:

It began with a mental picture. I didn't realize at the time it was symbolical. The picture was of the muddy seat of a little girl's drawers in a pear tree, where she could see through a window where her grandmother's funeral was taking place and report what was happening to her brothers on the ground below. By the time I explained who were and what they were doing and how her pants got muddy, I realized it would be impossible to get all of it into a short story and that it would have to be a book. And then I realized the symbolism of the soiled pants, and that image was replaced by the one of the fatherless and motherless girl climbing down the rainpipe to escape from the only home she had, where she had never been offered love or affection or understanding.[22]

Porter, author of "The Flowering Judas" and *The Ship of Fools,* reports that she never wrote a story unless she was sure it had a firm foundation. It was

somebody else's experience quite often, but an experience that became my own by hearing the story, by witnessing the thing, by hearing just a word perhaps. It doesn't matter, it just takes a little, a tiny seed. Then it takes root, and it grows. It's an organic thing. That story (referring to "The Flowering Judas") had been on my mind for years, growing out of this one little thing that happened in Mexico.[23]

[22] *Paris Interview Series*, p. 130.
[23] *Paris Interview Series*, p. 153.

In answer to what little thing it was that happened in Mexico, Porter explains that as she was going through a courtyard and past the flowering judas tree one evening, she saw her friend Mary with fear in her face, sitting at a window with a great fat man beside her. This "little thing" was the motivation for her idea.

Her novel, *The Ship of Fools,* started with her first voyage of twenty-eight days to Europe in 1931 on a crowded German ship with a

great mixture of nationalities, religious, political beliefs—all that sort of thing. I don't think I spoke a half-dozen words to anybody. I just sat there and watched. . . . It's a parable . . . of the ship of this world on its voyage to eternity. . . . There seems to be a kind of order in the universe, in the movement of the stars and the turning of the earth and the changing of the seasons, and even in the cycle of human life. But human life itself is almost pure chaos. Everyone takes his stance, asserts his own rights and feelings, mistaking the motives of others and his own. . . . Don't forget I am a passenger on that ship; it's not the other people altogether who are the fools! . . . Misunderstanding and separation are natural conditions of man. We come together only at these pre-arranged meeting grounds; we were all passengers on that ship, yet at his destination, each one was alone.[24]

Maugham, traveling from Honolulu to Pago Pago, jotted down notes on his fellow passengers, three of whom served as inspiration for the characters in his well-known story, "Rain." He described Miss Thompson in her late twenties, dressed in white, noticeable for her rather "coarse" beauty. Supposedly she was escaping arrest, after having been seen in a raid just before the boat sailed. The missionary and his wife were an interesting couple. As Mr. W. moved his tall, thin, loosely-jointed figure here and there, the look of "suppressed fire" in his eyes and manner hinted of a goal to be reached. Mrs. W. had the alert movements of a bird, and a high-pitched, "metallic," monotonous voice, irritating the nerves much like the "ceaseless clamor of a pneumatic drill."[25] The elaborate hair fashion, gold-rimmed pince-nez and gold chain from which hung a cross completed the picture of her small figure. You will recognize these characters in his story.

Cary tells how he noticed a girl on a steamer, sitting by herself on the other side of the deck, a woman about thirty with a "nice" expression but with a wrinkled forehead—in fact, "a good many wrinkles." He and his friend talked about her, wondering if she were a schoolteacher, and finally decided she was probably sensitive and intelligent. The following day he began a story; later in polishing it, he was conscious of "wrinkles"

24 *Paris Interview Series,* pp. 161-162.
25 From *The Saturday Review Treasury,* ed. John Haverstich et al. "How I write Short Stories" by Somerset Maugham. New York, Simon and Shuster, 1957. (July 28, 1934), p. 87.

appearing three times within a short space in the script. He realized then his heroine was the girl he had seen on the Manhattan boat.[26]

Too seldom do playwrights explain how a play has emerged as lucidly as Miller does in his discussion of the development of ideas and images in *Death of a Salesman*. The following excerpt will impress you with the realization that the poet is not the only literary master who thinks in terms of images.

The play grew from simple images. From a little frame house on a street of little frame houses, which had once been loud with the noise of growing boys, and then was empty and silent and finally occupied by strangers. Strangers who could not know with what conquistadorial joy Willy and his boys had once re-shingled the roof. Now it was quiet in the house, and the wrong people in the beds.

It grew from images of futility—the cavernous Sunday afternoons polishing the car. Where is that car now? And the chamois cloths carefully washed and put up to dry, where are the chamois cloths?

And the endless convoluted discussions, wonderments, arguments, belittlements, encouragements, fiery resolutions, abdications, returns, partings, voyages out and voyages back, tremendous opportunities and small, squeaking denouements—and all in the kitchen now occupied by strangers who cannot hear what the walls are saying.

The image of aging and so many of your friends already gone and strangers in the seats of the mighty who do not know you or your triumphs or your incredible value.

The image of the son's hard, public eye upon you, no longer swept by your myth, no longer rousable from his separateness, no longer knowing you have lived for him and have wept for him.

The image of ferocity when love has turned to something else and yet is there, is somewhere in the room if one could only find it.

The image of people turning into strangers who only evaluate one another.

Above all, perhaps, the image of a need greater than hunger or sex or thirst, a need to leave a thumbprint somewhere on the world. A need for immortality, and by admitting it, the knowing that one has carefully inscribed one's name on a cake of ice on a hot July day.

I sought the relatedness of all things by isolating their unrelatedness, a man superbly alone with his sense of not having touched and finally knowing in his last extremity that the love which had always been in the room unlocated was now found.

The image of a suicide so mixed in motive as to be unfathomable and yet demanding statement. Revenge was in it and a power of love, a victory in that it would bequeath a fortune to the living and a flight from emptiness. With it an image of peace . . . leaving the issues above ground and viable yet.

And always, throughout, the image of private man in a world full of strangers, a world that is not home nor even an open battleground but only galaxies of high promise over a fear of failing.

[26] *Paris Interview Series,* p. 64.

And the image of a man making something with his hands being a rock to touch and return to. "He was always so wonderful with his hands," says his wife over his grave, and I laughed when the line came, laughed with the artist-devil's laugh, for it had all come together in this line, she having been made by him though he did not know it or believe in it or receive it into himself. Only rank, height of power, the sense of having won he believed was real —the galaxy thrust up into the sky by projectors on the rooftops of the city he believed were real stars.

It came from structural images. The play's eye was to revolve from within Willy's head, sweeping endlessly in all directions like a light on the sea, and nothing that formed in the distant mist was to be left uninvestigated. It was thought of as having the density of the novel form in its interchange of viewpoints, so that while all roads led to Willy the other characters were to feel it was their play, a story about them and not him.[27]

Another one of the great playwrights, Tennessee Williams, reports on "Why It Is Called The Glass Menagerie" in the brochure enclosed in the Caedmon |IRS-F-301) recording of his play, *The Glass Menagerie.* When the Williams family moved to St. Louis from the South, their new living quarters were a "shocking change" from the spaciousness of their former home surrounded by shade trees. They found themselves in an apartment with few outside windows, and some in the bedrooms looked out upon a narrow, sunless areaway with only one opening to the street— in other words, a cul-de-sac. His sister, whose bedroom window opened into this passageway, kept her shades down because of the unsightly remains in the morning after the cat-and-dog fights at night. So her room had a "perpetual twilight gloom," until they decided to paint the furniture white, put up white curtains and arranged on the shelves around the room a collection of little glass articles. Williams describes the room as then taking on a "light and delicate appearance."

He writes:

When I left home a number of years later, it was this room that I recalled most vividly and poignantly when looking back on our home in St. Louis. Particularly the little glass ornaments on the shelves. They were mostly little glass animals. By poetic associations they came to represent, in my memory, all the safest emotions that belong to recollection of things past. They stood for all the small and tender things that relieve the austere pattern of life and make it endurable to the sensitive. The areaway where the cats were torn to pieces was one thing—my sister's white curtains and tiny menagerie of glass were another. Somewhere between them was the world we lived in. . . .[28]

[27] From DEATH OF A SALESMAN by Arthur Miller. Copyright © 1949 by Arthur Miller. Reprinted by permission of The Viking Press, Inc., pp. 29-30.

[28] From WHY IT IS CALLED THE GLASS MENAGERIE by Tennessee Williams, as printed originally in the "New York Herald Tribune," 1945. Reprinted by permission of New Directions, publishers.

Before leaving the subject of "Whence Come Ideas," you may remember that some musical plays are not original in their ideas, their source originating from fiction and dramas of merit[29]: for example, *Carousel* was adapted by Hammerstein and Glazer from Molnar's *Liliom; My Fair Lady* by Lerner and Loewe from Shaw's *Pygmalion; South Pacific* by Rodgers, Hammerstein and Logan from Michener's *Tales of the South Pacific; Guys and Dolls* by Swerling and Burrows from Runyon's story with the same name; *Oklahoma* by Rodgers and Hammerstein from Rigg's *Green Grow the Lilacs; Hello Dolly* by Stewart and Hermann from Wilder's *The Matchmakers; Oliver!* by Bart from Dicken's *Oliver Twist*. Each adapter found a germ, an idea, and developed it to win popular acceptance with song and dance. Lerner reports that on first examination, he and Loewe decided that *Pygmalion* could not be arranged for a musical. On second perusal, however, they were surprised to find that the plot would not have to be enlarged. Instead they found they merely had to "add what Shaw had happening offstage," and *My Fair Lady* was on its way! Hammerstein tells how he was so deeply impressed with the stage directions at the opening of the play *Green Grow the Lilacs* by Riggs that he decided the words describing an impression of a "visible golden emanation," a morning made radiant with sparkling streams, young corn and cattle in the meadows should not be wasted on stage directions the audience would never hear. So Hammerstein, put them into song, opening the play "to an atmosphere of relaxation, peace and tenderness," along with the "cattle and corn and golden haze," and most importantly, at the character level of the cowboy, Curley.[30] The result—the lyrics and melody of "Oh, What a Beautiful Mornin'!"

HOW THE THEME EVOLVES

From the germ, the initial idea, a theme evolves—a centrifugal meaning around which the author's developing pattern in prose or poetry revolves. Stylistic reinforcement interrelates episodes, environment and character. Evidently, no writer is ever certain how much he will eventually change the elements of emphasis and contrast to secure the organic—the developing interrelationship—unity of meaning. Abram writes understandingly about organic unity: "Organic growth is an open-ended process, nurturing a sense of the incomplete, and the glory of the imperfect. . . . And only in a 'mechanical' unity are the parts sharply defined and fixed; in organic unity, what we find is a complex interrelation of living, indeterminate, and endlessly changing components." In a work of art, Abrams

---

[29] David Ewen, *Complete Book of American Musical Theatre* (New York: Holt-Rinehart & Winston, Inc., 1958), p. 199.
[30] Oscar Hammerstein II, "Where The Song Begins," *Saturday Review Treasury,* John Haverstich, ed. (New York: Simon and Shuster, 1957), p. 379.

believes the "gauge of greatness" is shown by the richness of the related and diverse parts as they are bound together into an organic whole. To make this theory more explicit, he comments on Shakespeare's greatness due to the variant power of his themes and techniques: "the reconciliation into unity of tragedy and farce, laughter and tears, the trivial and sublime, kings and clowns, the high style and low, pathos and puns; and the delineation in high tragedy of man at once the glory, jest and riddle of the world."[31]

Sometimes the novelist talks of the way in which characters take over and assume a sort of independence. Porter's remarks in answer to a question about the possibility of a character taking a different turn suddenly is startling, yet typical of an author's way with his characters:

Well, in the vision of death at the end of "Flowering Judas," I knew the real ending—that she was not going to be able to face her life, what she'd done. And I knew that the vengeful spirit was going to come in a dream to tow her away to death, but I didn't know until I had written it that she was going to wake up saying "No!" and be afraid to go to sleep again.[32]

James reports in his "Preface" to *The Portrait of a Lady* that his characters fell into place with ease. Porter senses this same cooperation at times, for she tells how the "dark cloud" moving around in her head finally dissolves itself into a train of thoughts, then into words and finally, into images; and by the time she is ready to write her people are "alive and walking around, and taking things into their own hands."

Cary remarks concerning his characters:

I rewrite a great deal. I work over the whole book and cut anything that does not belong to the emotional development, the texture of feeling. . . . You've got to find out what people *believe,* what is pushing them on . . . a matter of the simple emotional drives—like ambition and love. These are the real stuff of the novel and you can't have any sort of real form unless you've got an ordered attitude towards them.

You can now appreciate Cary's theory that "your form is your meaning, and your meaning dictates your form." If, however, "you make your scheme too explicit, the framework shows and the book dies. If you hide it too thoroughly, the book has no meaning and therefore no form."[33] You may remember Cary's procedure later when you study the technique of expression in interpretation.

Many times, too, words create more intensity of meaning than was intended—even in poems. As a result, critics and other writers find symbolic directions through imagery that the author may not have intended.

---

[31] From *The Mirror and the Lamp* by M. H. Abrams. Copyright 1953 by Oxford University Press, Inc., p. 221. Reprinted by permission.

[32] *Paris Interview Series,* p. 152.

[33] *Paris Interview Series,* pp. 55 and 59.

Porter relates she did not name her story "Flowering Judas" until it was completed; then she recognized the symbolic pattern of which she had been unaware at the time of writing. The imaginative impetus to stimulate miraculous play of meaning in black on white is experienced in various ways and not always easily. Sometimes the climax or ending of a novel or play or poem is created before the beginning is well on its way. Cary writes his big scenes first, "the ones that carry the meaning of the book"— the emotional experience; then he plans a plot into which they fit. Lowell wrote the last two stanzas of his poem "Skunk Hour" first because they contained the essential meaning. Eventually the last four stanzas were completed; finally, the first stanzas were created to give the poem an "earth to stand on and space to breathe."[34]

In an amusing way, writers tell how they get ready for the creative session by getting into a physical "set." Wilder takes long walks; Hemingway would "get set" for the day's writing by sharpening twenty pencils. Capote sees everything in a flash and writes it down in longhand. He describes his manner of writing: "I am a completely horizontal author. I can't think unless I'm lying down, either in bed or stretched on a couch with a cigarette and coffee handy. I've got to be puffing and sipping. As the afternoon wears on, I shift from coffee to mint tea to sherry to martinis." On the other hand, Thurber surely existed in a continual "writing" stage, for in his unique way, he tells his interviewer, "I never know when I'm not writing. Sometimes my wife comes to me at a party and says, 'Dammit, Thurber, stop writing.' She usually catches me in the middle of a paragraph. Or our daughter will look up from the dinner table and say, 'Is he sick?' 'No,' my wife says, 'He's writing something.'" Thurber, however, explains that he writes in this way because of his failing vision, and instead of using black crayon to write twenty words on one sheet of yellow paper.[35]

You have now taken the initial steps in understanding how the germ of an idea intrigues and motivates skillful and imaginative writers to develop a theme into a unique literary pattern. As you proceed, your interest will increase with the introduction of how various techniques are employed in the artistic creation of a literary work.

[34] Robert Lowell, "On Robert Lowell's 'Skunk Hour,'" *The Contemporary Poet as Artist and Critic,* Anthony Ostroff, ed. (New York: Little, Brown and Co., 1964), pp. 109-112.

[35] *Paris Interview Series,* pp. 96, 294.

4

Writer's Point of View in Literature

THE POET

Earlier in this discussion, the importance of the author's tone for meaning was emphasized. Now the poet's point of view or approach adopted in certain kinds of poems should be examined. Inasmuch as the developmental pattern of his thought has much to do with the intensification of the theme, poetry has been classified into three main groups: narrative, lyrical and dramatic poems. In certain types of poetry, as in the dramatic monologue, the poet takes an objective point of view of the characterization he has planned; whereas in a song he may personalize the meaning through his own immediate voice. Naturally you may expect overlapping in this classification as in any other type of category, but generally speaking, this pattern is followed.

Next to the essayist, the poet has the greatest opportunity to express himself personally. In poetry, the point of view varies according to the immediacy of the poet's voice through arrangement of words and phrases, in his rhythm and relationship to his subject. The approach varies also in the way his tone conforms to his chosen mode of framing the thought,— that is, whether he decides to use narrative, lyrical or dramatic forms, or a combination of all these developmental methods.

Since everyone is acquainted with Frost, observe his way with a poem. No doubt his poetry has given memorable experiences to many people for it deals with everyday, and seemingly insignificant, episodes within the reach of the American public. They respond to the tone and surface pattern of meaning, as Frost's images carry recollections intensely and poetically expressed. Thus, the participators enjoy the moment or two of emotional release, even though they may not realize much of their pleasure has come from the immediate association with certain episodes in their lives. The unbelievable rebellion of some readers of *Saturday Review* to John Ciardi's discussion of Frost's composition and symbolic meaning in the poem " Stopping by Woods on a Snowy Evening" is evidence of their great need for meaning growing out of their own experiences. Obviously from their comments they consider Ciardi's kind of analysis heresy. They wish none of his "dissection," his explanation of Frost's "duplicity and symbolism," his "spectimetric analysis," his "probing, poking, and picking," his "blown-up explication," his "mechanic's hammer." The shock was so great that one person called Ciardi a "humorless pathologist slicing away with his microtome at a biopsy." In other words, Frost's popular readers heard the personal, immediate voice of Frost and wanted the impact of the first sensation left intact. Perhaps one should not steal that enjoyment from them, for almost everyone approaches a poem to get "something" from the first reading. If he is stopped by some obstruction in thought, he may turn away; or fortunately, he may reread to find new images and a deeper meaning. By repeated reading, this scope of understanding may be enlarged to include other meanings. The average person who reads for enjoyment only, however, is not always too interested in delving for riches underground. Take another look at Frost's poem. Can you burrow below the first emotional impact you received? If not, read Ciardi's discussion in *Dialogue With an Audience*[1] for assistance.

Stopping by Woods on a Snowy Evening

Whose woods these are I think I know.
His house is in the village though;
He will not see me stopping here
To watch his woods fill up with snow.

My little horse must think it queer
To stop without a farmhouse near
Between the woods and frozen lake
The darkest evening of the year.

He gives his harness bells a shake
To ask if there is some mistake.
The only other sound's the sweep
Of easy wind and downy flake.

The woods are lovely, dark and deep.
But I have promises to keep,
And miles to go before I sleep,
And miles to go before I sleep.[2]

ROBERT FROST

[1] From DIALOGUE WITH AN AUDIENCE by John Ciardi. Copyright © 1958 by John Ciardi. Published by J. B. Lippincott Company, pp. 157-168.
[2] From COMPLETE POEMS OF ROBERT FROST. Copyright 1916, 1921, 1923, 1928, 1930, 1939 by Holt, Rinehart and Winston, Inc. Copyright 1936, 1942, 1944, 1951, © 1956, 1958, by Robert Frost. Copyright © 1964 by Lesley Frost Ballantine. Reprinted by permission of Holt, Rinehart and Winston, Inc.

THE POET—"A PERFORMER": FROST

These criticisms of Ciardi's analysis mean Frost has created his illusion of reality so convincingly that inexperienced critics cannot believe as Ciardi writes—and as the authors of this book wrote in the first edition—that "art is artifice": it involves selection, arrangement and integration of elements to create the illusion. Obviously this statement implies duplicity to many people. Certainly Frost would agree with Ciardi that a "writer must learn beyond any flicker of doubt within himself that art is not life itself but a representation of life. The writer's subject is reality but his medium is illusion. Only by illusory means can the sense of reality be transmitted in an art form."[3] Frost confirms this principle when he admits he looks upon a poem as a "performance," something experienced and heard, spoken lines similar to those of an actor playing his part on the stage. "I look on the poet as a man of prowess, just like an athlete. He's a performer. And the things you can do in a poem are very various. You speak of figures, tones of voice varying all the time. I'm always interested, you know, when I have three or four stanzas, in the way I *lay* the sentences in them. I'd hate to have the sentences all lie the same in the stanzas. Every poem is like that: some sort of achievement in performance."[4] And Frost does set his stage: the setting gives background, the characters are present, as heard in the voice of the speaker, with the point of view of "the first-person narrator," talking to his imagined auditor. For instance, read the following poem, "Mending Wall." The setting includes two expansive country landscapes, one all apple trees offering shade (*note the familiar image*), the other a woods of pine trees extending beyond the hill (*note the contrasting scenes*). These two scenes are separated by a wall of boulders, irregular in shape, some like "loaves," some nearly like "balls" (*note familiar images*). The scene is a quiet one except for dogs yelping after occasional rabbits who have been holed up in the wall during the winter and now leave through the gaps in the wall (*note familiar incident*). No cows disturb the pines, and the apples cannot "eat" the cones (*note whimsical humor*) lying under the pine trees. So the setting is made ready for Frost's performance and for those "dramatic tones of voice," necessary to reveal the meaning of the poem. The characters are the owner of the apple tree orchard and his neighbor over the hill, the owner of the pine trees. You can visualize the staunch and rigid owner of the pines listening to the thoughtful and kindly voice of the apple orchard owner and answering stolidly, " Good fences make good neighbors." (*Note familiar saying.*) How could a more personal, and still a dramatic, tone be uttered than "He is all pine and I am apple orchard";

[3] Ciardi, *op. cit.*, pp. 259-260.
[4] *Paris Interview Series*, p. 30.

or how could the vocal intonations be more explicit than in the arrangement of these words,

> Before I built a wall I'd ask to know
> What I was walling in or walling out,
> And to whom I was like to give offense.
> Something there is that doesn't love a wall,
> That wants it down.

How could you miss the body turn of the apple orchard owner, who, with a twinkle in his eyes and a chuckle in his voice, remarks slyly to his listener, "I could say 'Elves' to him" (tongue in cheek); but of course, he realizes his neighbor knows nothing of the fantasy of elves, especially among pine trees, though he does believe in boundaries. Here is the poem:

Mending Wall

> Something there is that doesn't love a wall,
> That sends the frozen-ground-swell under it,
> And spills the upper boulders in the sun;
> And makes gaps even two can pass abreast.
> The work of hunters is another thing:
> I have come after them and made repair
> Where they have left not one stone on a stone,
> But they would have the rabbit out of hiding,
> To please the yelping dogs. The gaps I mean,
> No one has seen them made or heard them made,
> But at spring mending-time we find them there.
> I let my neighbor know beyond the hill;
> And on a day we meet to walk the line
> And set the wall between us once again.
> We keep the wall between us as we go.
> To each the boulders that have fallen to each.
> And some are loaves and some so nearly balls
> We have to use a spell to make them balance:
> "Stay where you are until our backs are turned!"
> We wear our fingers rough with handling them.
> Oh, just another kind of outdoor game,
> One on a side. It comes to little more:
> There where it is we do not need the wall:
> He is all pine and I am apple orchard.
> My apple trees will never get across
> And eat the cones under his pines, I tell him.
> He only says, "Good fences make good neighbors."
> Spring is the mischief in me, and I wonder
> If I could put a notion in his head:
> "*Why* do they make good neighbors? Isn't it
> Where there are cows? But here there are no cows.

Before I built a wall I'd ask to know
What I was walling in or walling out,
And to whom I was like to give offense.
Something there is that doesn't love a wall,
That wants it down." I could say "Elves" to him,
But it's not elves exactly, and I'd rather
He said it for himself. I see him there
Bringing a stone grasped firmly by the top
In each hand, like an old-stone savage armed.
He moves in darkness as it seems to me,
Not of woods only and the shade of trees.
He will not go behind his father's saying,
And he likes having thought of it so well
He says again, "Good fences make good neighbors."[5]

ROBERT FROST

As you read this poem several times, would you, as many do, find the only meaning to be that of neighborly interest in walls? Does the wall extend in meaning beyond the wall structured of irregular boulders that cannot be held fast? Does the line "He is all pine and I am apple orchard" concern only two owners? Would you be surprised if someone suggested a contradiction in the poem indicating Frost accepts this way of living as typical of all men striving in the world of men? Why did Frost repeat these two opposing statements twice: "Something there is that doesn't love a wall" and "Good fences make good neighbors"? Untermeyer believes this contradiction is the heart of the lines and that its answer is found in the "paradox of people, in neighbors, in competitors, in the contradictory nature of man."[6]

THE POET—"HEARD" VOICE: HOPKINS

These remarks are intended as an opening wedge to the appreciation of the *heard* voice of the poet. More time could be spent speaking of other poets who believe their poetry has for its completion the voice that must be heard. Hopkins, in explaining his theory of "inscape of speech"—that is, particularized penetration through the sound of speech—believes "poetry is . . . speech framed to be heard for its own sake and interest, even over and above its interest of meaning."[7] He expects his poetry to be heard, not just read but "declaimed," "recited," so the sounds related to the meaning and the rhythm of his verse can be experienced just as one feels the

---

[5] Frost, *op. cit.*, p. 47.

[6] Robert Frost, *Come In*, with commentary by Louis Untermeyer (New York: Jonathon Cape, 1943), p. 73.

[7] Gerard Manley Hopkins, *Journals and Papers of Gerard Manley Hopkins* (New York: Oxford University Press, 1959), p. 289.

melody of music and the design in painting. In a letter to Robert Bridges, August, 1877, he writes, "Poetry must have down to its least separable part, an individual touch. . . . Poetry is designed to be read aloud." He remarks of his own poetry, "it is altogether for recital, not for perusal," and it must be "declaimed," so the "strange constructions will be dramatic and effective." His verse, "as living art should be," is made for "performance"—performance that is not "reading with the eye but loud, leisurely, poetical (not rhetorical) recitation, with long rests, long dwells on the rhyme and other marked syllables." He exhorts those who read his poetry aloud to "take a breath and read it with the ears," as he always wishes to be read: then the auditor can enjoy the "inscape of spoken sound." Some poets, like Eliot, believe certain poems are written mainly for the poet's own pleasure and some, for no audience. He agrees the poetic voice, dramatic in the sense that the poet is speaking in the role of a narrator, is recorded for others to hear. Inasmuch as the interpreter will find these roles to be varied—as the lover, satirist, naturalist, religious prophet, philosopher—he should listen for cues that give the tone its particular melody and overtones; he should appreciate a certain concentration of word-groups giving a particular sound-pattern, and a design giving a tonal quality important to the meaning. Brooks and Warren are writing about this when they explain "poetry is a specialization of speech";[8] Hopkins is talking about this when he creates the phrase "inscape of speech"; and Frost means this when he writes "a poem is a reproduction of the tones of actual speech," and most important, when he says "poetry is made of words that have become deeds."[9]

POINT OF VIEW IN NARRATIVE POETRY

THE FOLK BALLAD

The earliest narrative poem took the form of the folk ballad.[10] This poem has an objective approach because of its communal universality. You never hear the poet's voice, for as Lloyd Frankenburg writes, "It's the collaboration of centuries." Originally some person must have designed the poem that has become the property of many peoples. Most authorities agree it made a distinctive contribution to mass communication during the Middle Ages. The derivation of the word *ballad* is from the French word *baller*, meaning to dance. So it is easy to understand how, as every-

[8] Cleanth Brooks and Robert Penn Warren, *Understanding Poetry* (New York: Holt, Rinehart and Winston, Inc., 1960), p. 7.
[9] Robert Frost, "Introduction," *A Way Out* (New York: The Harbor Press, 1929).
[10] Note: An excellent selection of ballads, as well as a perceptive introduction, can be found in *Traditional British Ballads* by Bartlett Jere Whiting, published by Appleton-Century-Crofts, Crofts Classics Edition, 1955.

one danced, everyone sang and beat out rhythms to the repetitions and refrains. With adaptations from the wandering minstrels as the years rolled by, the lyrics grew, and authorships with their variations increased. Even if originally the ballad might have been claimed by one individual, the variations, which have occurred through the centuries, have made his identity impossible to discover. The tone you hear now in the ballad does not characterize one poet's point of view but the culmination of many voices in many countries, especially in England, Scotland and Norway.

This ballad is formed in four-line stanzas, with the second and fourth lines rhyming and ending many times in a refrain. The language is simple and repetition of phrases is evident, always part of the joy in singing—from childhood through adulthood. The story is told in the form of short dramatic episodes, usually tragic and bloody, and recorded by means of brief dialogues. The latter are characteristically abrupt, leaving gaps in the story for the reader's inventive imagination. Minor episodes have been eliminated through the years, leaving only the high points of the action. The result is a directness and swiftness of movement by means of "dialogue" action of episodes. The magical surprise of the folk ballad originates from various sources: the dramatic *tour de force* of both speech and song; the refrain that sometimes adds an ironical touch to the action; the rapid, direct movement to the implied climax; the tragic culmination with death, estrangement of lovers, shipwrecks, suicides and partings. In other words, the action is centered in tales of heroic deeds and of adventure ending in disaster. Occasionally you will find a ballad with a humorous touch, as shown in "Get Up and Bar the Door " (page 400).

The lines of the traditional ballad, as Hopkins says about his own poetry, must be heard "with the ears" to capture the sound and dramatic emphasis of the voices, and to sense the rhythmical cadences. The simplicity, forward movement, intensity and climax will then be fully appreciated. Not only should every student be acquainted with the speech pattern of the ballad, but he should also attempt singing one, for the melody of the song will bring out the plaintive cadences not always heard as distinctly in speech.

The folk ballads listed below are among the best known of the earliest narrative poems. The ballad devices are evident: short dramatic dialogues of repetition and of refrain; absence of minor explanatory episodes; simplicity of language; rhythm; climax; and usually a story of death and tragedy.

"Sir Patrick Spens," a famous Scottish ballad, tells the story of the anticipated death of Sir Patrick Spens and his men at sea, and of their ladies with gold combs in their hair waiting for their lords' return. Meanwhile, you learn the good Sir Patrick Spens lies fifty fathoms deep half way to Aberdour, with the Scotch lords at his feet. Although longer forms of this story exist, in this version all nonessentials have been obliterated or forgotten in the oral transmission of the story: only the high peaks of the action are given, the emphasis being placed on the tragedy of no return rather than on the courage of the men. Observe how a few words characterize the persons involved in the action; also how quickly the story gets underway, yet gives a background setting. Read aloud the last three lyrical stanzas, catching their plaintive singing melody.

"Sir Patrick Spens" commemorates a twelfth century shipwreck; and according to Frankenberg, the ballad has "curious anticipations of moving picture technique." He observes cleverly that the scene, the pace, even the tense, keep changing:

It opens with a long shot: "The king sits in Dumferling toune," drinking technicolor wine. Truck to the elderly knight, who "up and spak." Quick dissolve to king, finishing a letter: "The king has written a braid letter." Does he use wide stationery? broad, rather than courtly, speech? Is he issuing extensive commands? "braid" or deceitful orders, sending his lords and his best sailor to their certain doom? The overtones of all the possible ways it may have been heard coalesce; an audible palimsest.

Flash to Sir Patrick Spens, "Was walking on the sand" (sometimes "strand"). Close-up of tear blinding his eye. And later the future comes into the picture: "For they'll see thame na mair."

This constant change of focus creates the illusion of a great deal happening. Yet for all its momentum, doesn't it have the quality of arrested motion, like an old woodcut of a wave? All its action is about to take place or has already gone by. The shipwreck is hats bobbling on the water.[11]

LLOYD FRANKENBERG, *Invitation to Poetry*

Sir Patrick Spens

The king sits in Dumferling toune,
    Drinking the blude-reid wine:
"O whar will I get guid sailor,
    To sail this schip of mine?"

Up and spak an eldern knicht,
    Sat at the kings richt kne:
"Sir Patrick Spens is the best sailor,
    That sails upon the se."

The king has written a braid letter,
    And signd it wi his hand,
And sent it to Sir Patrick Spens,
    Was walking on the sand.

---

[11] Lloyd Frankenberg, *Invitation to Poetry* (Garden City, N. Y.: Doubleday and Company, 1956), p. 112. Reprinted by permission.

The first line that Sir Patrick red,
  A loud lauch lauched he;
The next line that Sir Patrick red,
  The teir blinded his ee.

"O wha is this has don this deid,
  This ill deid don to me,
To send me out this time o' the yeir,
  To sail upon the se!

"Mak haste, mak haste, my mirry men all,
  Our guid schip sails the morne,"
"O say na sae, my master deir,
  For I feir a deadlie storme.

"Late, late yestreen I saw the new moone,
  Wi the auld moone in hir arme,
And I feir, I feir, my deir master,
  That we will cum to harme."

O our Scots nobles wer richt laith
  To weet their cork-heild schoone;
Bot lang owre a' the play wer playd,
  Thair hats they swam aboone.

O lang, lang may their ladies sit,
  Wi thair fans into their hand,
Or eir they se Sir Patrick Spens
  Cum sailing to the land.

O lang, lang may the ladies stand,
  Wi thair gold kems in their hair,
Waiting for thair ain deir lords,
  For they'll se thame na mair.

Half owre, haf owre to Aberdour,
  It's fiftie fadom deip,
And thair lies guid Sir Patrick Spens,
  Wi the Scots lords at his feit.[12]

In these five stanzas of "Lord Randal," the dramatic action is suggested by means of five questions and answers, with repeated phrases and refrains dominating the form. On the first reading, the action may seem muted and characterized mainly by repetitions. When the stanzas are

[12] Notes on word-meanings: *Aberdour,* a port on the Firth of Forth; *Dumferling,* inland from Aberdour; *braid,* broad; *lauch,* laugh; *yestreen,* yesterday evening; *laith,* loth; *cork-heiled schoone,* cork-heeled shoes; *aboone,* above; *kems,* combs; *half owre,* halfway over.

read aloud, however, the movement becomes more intense and dramatic with each succeeding question and answer. Suddenly you realize why Lord Randal would "fain lie down," for the action is climaxed with the change in the repetitive phrase, "For I'm sick at the heart." This story is more condensed than any among these quoted. No motive is given for Lord Randal's death as the story unfolds typically through the dialogue. The reader may only surmise the implied motivation for the poisoning.

Lord Randal

"O where hae ye been, Lord Randal, my son?
O where hae ye been, my handsome young man?"
"I hae been to the wild wood; mother, make my bed soon,
For I'm weary wi hunting, and fain wad lie down."

"Where gat ye your dinner, Lord Randal, my son?
Where gat ye your dinner, my handsome young man?"
"I dined wi my true-love; mother, make my bed soon,
For I'm weary wi hunting, and fain wad lie down."

"What gat ye to your dinner, Lord Randal, my son?
What gat ye to your dinner, my handsome young man?"
"I gat eels boiled in broo; mother, make my bed soon,
For I'm weary wi hunting, and fain wad lie down."

"What became of your bloodhounds, Lord Randal, my son?
What became of your bloodhounds, my handsome young man?"
"O they swelled and they died; mother, make my bed soon,
For I'm weary wi hunting, and fain wad lie down."

"O I fear ye are poisoned, Lord Randal, my son!
O I fear ye are poisoned, my handsome young man!"
"O yes! I am poisoned; mother, make my bed soon,
For I'm sick at the heart, and I fain wad lie down."

"The Wife of Usher's Well" differs slightly from "Lord Randal" in its format. The setting of a farm home, with a bright glowing fire and a red, red cock and a bonny lass to tend the fire, serves as a dramatic contrast to the present resting place of the three sons. The characters are described briefly: a wealthy wife with three stout and stalwart sons who were sent to sea and whom she would never again see. The wife is a bustling house-wife who now believes her sons will visit her again. She has the fire made, the water brought in from the well, a feast prepared and a large, wide bed made ready. The typical breaks in the story of a ballad occur: the sons are neither greeted nor seen, but the devoted mother draws her mantle about her as she sits by the side of the bed. Another break occurs; then the red,

red cock awakens the eldest son who decides that the brothers must away. It is the youngest son, however, who presses their departure so that their "mother dear" will not suffer too much pain; and it is he who gives the lyrical farewell to his "mother dear," his home and the bonny lass. All these images intensify the haunting memory of three stalwart sons who have left a warm comfortable home and love—and a bonny lass—for a grave at the bottom of the sea, although this contrast is never mentioned overtly in the poem.

The Wife of Usher's Well

There lived a wife at Usher's well,
　And a wealthy wife was she;
She had three stout and stalwart sons,
　And sent them o'er the sea.

They hadna been a week from her,
　A week but barely ane,
When word came to the carline wife
　That her three sons were gane.

They hadna been a week from her,
　A week but barely three,
When word came to the carline wife
　That her sons she'd never see.

"I wish the winds may never cease,
　Nor fashes in the flood,
Till my three sons come home to me,
　In earthly flesh and blood!"

It fell about the Martinmas,
　When nights are lang and mirk,
The carline wife's three sons came hame,
　And their hats were o' the birk.

It neither grew in syke nor ditch,
　Nor yet in ony sheugh;
But at the gates o' Paradise
　That birk grew fair eneugh.

"Blow up the fire, my maidens!
　Bring water from the well!
For a' my house shall feast this night,
　Since my three sons are well."

And she has made to them a bed,
　She's made it large and wide;

And she's taen her mantle her about,
   Sat down at the bedside.

Up then crew the red, red cock,
   And up and crew the gray;
The eldest to the youngest said,
   " 'Tis time we were away."

The cock he hadna crow'd but once,
   And clapped his wings at a',
When the youngest to the eldest said,
   "Brother, we must awa'."

"The cock doth craw, the day doth daw,
   The channerin' worm doth chide;
Gin we be missed out o' our place,
   A sair pain we maun bide."

"Lie still, lie still but a little wee while,
   Lie still but if we may;
Gin my mother should miss us when she wakes,
   She'll go mad ere it be day."

"Fare ye weel, my mother dear!
   Fareweel to barn and byre!
And fare ye weel, the bonny lass
   That kindles my mother's fire!"

THE LITERARY BALLAD

From these traditional ballad forms, many devices are carried over in the literary ballad. Keats's "La Belle Dame Sans Merci" (page 407), tells a story in four-line stanzas with the typical rhyme scheme, repetitions and simplicity of manner. The dialogue episodes, however, are cut down, giving prominence mainly to a single narrator, and mystical and symbolical elements are present. In "The Rime of the Ancient Mariner," Coleridge also follows the folk ballad approach in some respects. The Mariner establishes a personal point of view but tells his story to a "forced" listener. The language is simple and the imagery is extremely vivid in its sensory appeal; not only did "slimy things" crawl, but they crawled *with legs upon the slimy sea.* The unusual episodes, which follow in swift succession, hold the attention because they are grounded in supernatural events, involving folk superstitions. The symbolic meaning increases the intensity of the poem. The breaks between dialogues are not evident; instead a smooth progression of events gives unity to the final effect. Neither is the psychological complication, such as the moral atonement for the Mariner's evil deed, found in the folk ballad. Observe how the story is told:

The bright-eyed Mariner, as the narrator of the story, holds with his skinny hand and glittering eye one of three Wedding-Guests, one who becomes a "three-years' child" under the will of the Mariner as he begins his story abruptly, without explanation:

> "The ship was cheered, the harbor cleared,
> Merrily did we drop
> Below the kirk, below the hill,
> Below the light-house top."

Note the downward speed of the lines.

The Wedding-Guest remonstrates, beats his breast, for he is next of kin to the bride, who, red as a rose, now paces into the hall, but he is forced to listen. Throughout the story, the Wedding-Guest interposes with dramatic tones,

> "God save thee, ancient Mariner!
> From the fiends, that plague thee thus!"—

and with fear:

> "I fear thee, Ancient Mariner!
> I fear thy skinny hand!
> And thou art long, and lank, and brown,
> As is the ribbed sea-sand.
>
> I fear thee and thy glittering eye,
> And thy skinny hand, so brown;"

Nothing, however, stops the Mariner, and finally, having listened perforce to the end, the Wedding-Guest

> "—went like one that hath been stunned,
> And is of sense forlorn:
> A sadder and a wiser man,
> He rose the morrow morn."

The ballad was not isolated with the intention of suggesting this is the only poetical form that tells a dramatic story. You can find many poems based on a narrative or an episode; the folk ballad, however, is unique because of its unusual heritage from the populace whose literary effects were not consciously sought and attained, as in the literary ballad.

Most students are acquainted with "Danny Deever" from Kipling's *Barrack-Room Ballads.* A story is told through the concentrated direction of dialogue episodes, very much like the folk ballad; and the rhythm is closely bound up with the implied action. In fact, the dialogues constitute the dramatic action and must be heard to appreciate the movement, intensified by the mood and the singing quality found in the refrain.

Danny Deever

"What are the bugles blowin' for?" said Files-on-Parade.
"To turn you out, to turn you out," the Colour-Sergeant said.
"What makes you look so white, so white?" said Files-on-Parade.[13]
"I'm dreadin' what I've got to watch," the Colour-Sergeant said.
   For they're hangin' Danny Deever, you can 'ear the Dead March play,
   The regiment's in 'ollow square—they're hangin' him today;
   They've taken of his buttons off an' cut his stripes away,
   An' they're hangin' Danny Deever in the mornin'.

"What makes the rear-rank breathe so 'ard?" said Files-on-Parade.
"It's bitter cold, it's bitter cold," the Colour-Sergeant said.
"What makes that front-rank man fall down?" said Files-on-Parade.
"A touch o' sun, a touch o' sun," the Colour-Sergeant said.
   They are hangin' Danny Deever, they are marchin' of 'im round,
   They 'ave 'alted Danny Deever by 'is coffin on the ground;
   An' 'e'll swing in 'arf a minute for a sneakin' shootin' hound—
   O they're hangin' Danny Deever in the mornin'!

" 'Is cot was right-'and cot to mine," said Files-on-Parade.
"E's sleepin' out an' far to-night," the Colour-Sergeant said.
"I've drunk 'is beer a score o' times," said Files-on-Parade.
"E's drinkin' bitter beer alone," the Colour-Sergeant said.
   They are hangin' Danny Deever, you must mark 'im to 'is place,
   For 'e shot a comrade sleepin'—you must look 'im in the face;
   Nine 'undred of 'is county an' the regiment's disgrace,
   While they're hangin' Danny Deever in the mornin'.

"What's that so black agin the sun?" said Files-on-Parade.
"It's Danny fightin' 'ard for life," the Colour-Sergeant said.
"What's that that whimpers over'ead?" said Files-on-Parade.
"It's Danny's soul that's passin' now," the Colour-Sergeant said.
   For they're done with Danny Deever, you can 'ear the quickstep play,
   The regiment's in column, an' they're marchin' us away;
   Ho! the young recruits are shakin', an' they'll want their beer to-day,
   After hangin' Danny Deever in the mornin'.[14]

Rudyard Kipling

THE EPIC

The epic, in contrast to the narrative ballad with its short episodic dialogues, is a long, involved poem of adventure, celebrating heroic deeds

---

[13] Note: *Files-on-Parade,* a noncommissioned officer, in charge of military files; *Colour-Sergeant,* in charge of flags during the parade.

[14] "Danny Deever" by Rudyard Kipling, From RUDYARD KIPLING'S VERSE: Definitive Edition. Reprinted by permission of Mrs. George Bambridge, and Doubleday & Company, Inc.

involving a central figure of renown. The poet employs various developmental forms—narrative, descriptive, expository and dramatic. Usually the aid of some mythical force is invoked at the beginning of the poem; for instance, Milton in "Paradise Lost" invokes the assistance of the heavenly muse to "justify the ways of God to Man," the theme of the epic. Although the poem may begin with a personal approach, the dramatic presentation of bravery and conflict is usually more objective, as soon as the episodes begin to move forward. Even though diversions may occur as distinct from the main flow of the story—asides in which the author describes some character or laments some incident—the poet attempts to unify all into a theme that progresses, as it would in a novel. The central meaning, however, is expanded and directed to give a perspective of national or spiritual progress helpful to all mankind. Milton employs another device often found in fiction today: the action starts in the middle of the struggle; and later a flashback to past events leads to the opening disaster. You may recall that the introductory dramatic scene in "Paradise Lost" describes how Satan and his "fellow" angels, having been evicted from Heaven, are chained to the burning lake in Hell.

The classical epic is a poem of former centuries, tedious often in its descriptives asides, yet charged with great poetry presented with a tone that at times shows a distinctive subjective attitude superimposed on the basic objective approach. Today, *John Brown's Body* by Stephen Vincent Benét has been called an American epic. It dramatizes the action of the Civil War through the characters involved: the conflict that drew into its mesh "lives of millions of ordinary men and women who lived together through war and peace, strove, struggled, failed, built something together." The poem, writes Benét, is made up of "realities," "legends," "ways of living," "faces of men," who belonged to *our* country. It has for its background the "look of mountains and the flow of rivers, heat and cold, wind and rain, the stories in the old burying grounds and the casual ballads of the people." Those who participated were "living people," facing "our problems and making decisions that still affect us."

Probably the epic poem which has drawn the most favorable attention in this era is *The Odyssey, A Modern Sequel* (1938), by Nikos Kazantzakis, a Greek poet. Even though Kimon Friar, the eminent translator, and William B. Stanford, author of *The Ulysses Theme,* have named it the greatest heroic epic of modern times, the poet considers its genre immaterial. According to Friar, Kazantzakis calls it a "new epical-attempt of modern man to find deliverance by passing through all the stages of contemporary anxieties by pursuing the most daring hopes."

If you become acquainted with this amazing epic, you will recognize that although the poet uses the general framework of Homer's *Odyssey,* the pattern is strikingly different. You will be surprised at the romantic tone and overwhelmed by its "profusion of metaphors and similes, of allegorical and symbolic characters and episodes, of fables and legends." It is an unending array of fantastic and mythical events, written with modern verve and intensity. You will also be intrigued with Stanford's appraisal of the two great "elaborate portraits" as "symbols of contemporary aspirations and perplexities." One is Joyce's "epic" prose narrative, *Ulysses* (1922), which appeared 3,000 years after the first appearance of this mythical theme; the other is the Greek epic poem by Kazantzakis. Although the wanderer motif is present as in the Homeric tradition, Joyce tells a tightly woven story of the activities and thoughts of the two Dubliners, Dedalus and Bloom, who "re-enact experiences of Telemachus and Odysseus among modern equivalents of Odyssean places." Furthermore, Bloom's rewards and punishments are "personal and subjective" in the form of exalted as well as miserable thoughts in his own heart. "For him," writes Stanford, "hell, purgatory, paradise are in Dublin." In *The Odyssey,* as Stanford indicates, the design is more spacious, set in a greater environmental scope to permit the extrovert, Odysseus, to initiate "spectacular heroic deeds and decisions but not aspirations"—nor regrets.[15]

These remarks were introduced here so that you would think of these literary masterpieces—epics—as concerned with modern thought, with "modern man in search of a soul." Each one would require the skillful art of an experienced interpreter. A few lines from the invocation of Kazantzakis's poem, following the Homeric tradition, are reprinted so that you may sense the power and brilliance in the creation of his images. You can also appreciate the poetic symbolism that permeates the entire poem: note how he invokes the aid of the Sun, "great Oriental," the "golden cap" of his "proud mind," his "red-haired hound," his "quick coquetting eye," the power that transforms all "stones, water, fire and earth to spirit."

from *Prologue*

O Sun, my quick coquetting eye, my red-haired hound,
sniff out all quarries that I love, give them swift chase,
tell me all that you've seen on earth, all that you've heard,
and I shall pass them through my entrails' secret forge
till slowly, with profound caresses, play and laughter,
stones, water, fire, and earth shall be transformed to spirit,
and the mud-winged and heavy soul, freed of its flesh,
shall like a flame serene ascend and fade in sun.[16]

Nikos Kazantzakis, *The Odyssey, A Modern Sequel*

[15] W. B. Stanford, *The Ulysses Theme* (Oxford: Basil Blackwell & Mott, Ltd., 1954), p. 222.
[16] From *The Odyssey, A Modern Sequel* by Nikos Kazantzakis, trans. by Kimon Friar. Copyright © 1958 by Simon and Schuster, Inc. Reprinted by permission of the publishers.

In a totally different tone, Tolkien has written his prose "epic-fantasy," *The Hobbit*. The narrator establishes reality immediately with his chatty introduction of Bilbo Baggins, the hobbit, and by creating an atmosphere appropriate to the moods and personalities of the characters, who speak, think and react like Big People. Bilbo, the hero, is not an Odysseus but a mild home-loving hobbit who enjoys the comfort of his hobbit-hole. His father, Bungo Baggins, built the dwelling hole, so they say, partly with his wife's money. He arranged the rooms on a modern scale—"no going up-stairs"; all rooms—kitchens, bathrooms, bedrooms and pantries (of which there were many because hobbits like to eat) and wardrobes full of clothes —were planned for the ground floor with windows on the left side looking out to meadows and gardens. As a gentle descendant of the Baggins, Bilbo is fastidious about his dress, especially his pocket handkerchief; enjoys bacon and eggs—fried not poached—and the warmth of his fireside. Bilbo's mother, the famous Belladonna Took, was one of the wealthy Took-clan, several of whom, it was whispered, were thought to have married into the fairy-family, inasmuch as they sometimes discreetly disappeared in search of adventure. The "Took-side" of Bilbo's heritage takes over when courage and daring action are needed. When he first hears inadvertently from the dwarves that he looks more like a grocer than a burglar who could steal the treasure from the red dragon, "something Tookish wakes up inside" and he becomes "Tookishly determined" to hunt for the gold and gems.

If you attempt an interpretation of one of the scenes, you will realize that the narrator's stylistic prose pattern results in dramatic responses realized from the blending of fantasy and character reality. In this world unknown to Men, dwarves, elves, trolls, goblins and spiders are those who follow the typical human struggle for survival and fight for control through physical strength, revenge, cunning and domination against intruders. The tale, however, takes on the charm of fantasy with enchanting word combinations: "bewildered and bewithered," "confusticate and bebother," "witchments with fire and lights," "flummoxed," "staggerment," "disappeared in a jumble of smithereens," These are juxtaposed against colloquialisms as "tighten their belts," "lost their wits," "a good deal of traffic went in and out," "a nasty cold in the nose," "not on speaking terms," "a nice pickle they were in now."

The fairy-tale imagery pervades the narrative, giving color, delight and magic in the names of places, characters and descriptive passages of adventure, as well as the singing of ballads. Eventually the possession of the magic ring, which Bilbo, by the way, carries home in secret, gives courageous support to the hero's "Tookish determination." At the end of the story, however, a realistic episode occurs as Bilbo arrives home to find a great deal of commotion around his hobbit-hole: people coming and going with Bilbo's possessions, not even stopping to wipe their feet on the doormat, much to his annoyance. An auction of his household goods is in progress![17] Thus the author gives credence to the preceding events of fantasy by this final incident so characteristic of man's typical habits and eccentricities of living.

POINT OF VIEW IN LYRICAL POETRY

THE LYRIC

The lyrical poem usually includes the song, sonnet, ode and elegy. Often *song* is used interchangeably with *lyric,* probably because the lyric originally was accompanied by lyre instrumentation. The song has many variations in form, always showing, however, a distinctive melody and subjective emotional tone. The poem may be based on an emotional conflict; an episode of dramatic tension; the result of some incident, using the narrative element; some passing thought descriptive of the beauty of nature; a meditative expression of death; some betrayal as of love; a reflection of some great happiness—the range is endless. The poet writes of a personal, sometimes almost rhapsodic, feeling towards some subject: philosophical, emotional, analytical.

Shakespeare employed the song in his plays, not to further the story of the drama particularly but rather to give atmosphere and sometimes to serve as a musical interlude for his audience. Here are several of the memorable songs you have heard sung in his productions.

Who Is Sylvia?

Who is Sylvia? what is she,
    That all our swains commend her?
Holy, fair and wise is she;
    The heaven such grace did lend her,
That she might admiréd be.

Is she kind as she is fair?
    For beauty lives with kindness.
Love doth to her eyes repair
    To help him of his blindness,
And being helped, inhabits there.

Then to Sylvia let us sing,
    That Sylvia is excelling;
She excels each mortal thing
    Upon the dull earth dwelling:
To her let us garlands bring.

SHAKESPEARE,
The Two Gentlemen of Verona
Act IV, Scene 2

[17] J. R. R. Tolkien, *The Hobbit* (New York: Houghton Mifflin Company, 1965).

Under The Greenwood Tree

Under the greenwood tree,
Who loves to lie with me,
And tune his merry note
Unto the sweet bird's throat—
Come hither, come hither, come hither!
Here shall he see
No enemy,
But winter and rough weather.

Who doth ambition shun,
And loves to lie in the sun,
Seeking the food he eats,
And pleased with what he gets—
Come hither, come hither, come hither!
Here shall he see
No enemy,
But winter and rough weather.

SHAKESPEARE, *As You Like It*
Act II, Scene 5

Where The Bee Sucks

Where the bee sucks, there suck I;
In a cowslip's bell I lie;
There I couch when owls do cry.
On the bat's back I do fly
After summer merrily.
Merrily, merrily, shall I live now,
Under the blossom that hangs on the bough.

SHAKESPEARE, *The Tempest*
Act V, Scene 1

The beau-brummel sophistication of Sir John Suckling, a Cavalier poet of the seventeenth century, finds its paradoxical expression in the gay, nonchalant lyrical attitude:

The Constant Lover

Out upon it, I have loved
    Three whole days together!
And am like to love three more,
    If it prove fair weather.

Time shall moult away his wings,
    Ere he shall discover

In the whole wide world again
  Such a constant lover.

But the spite on 't is, no praise
  Is due at all to me:
Love with me had made no stays,
  Had it any been but she.

Had it any been but she,
  And that very face,
There had been at least ere this
  A dozen dozen in her place.

SIR JOHN SUCKLING

Why So Pale and Wan?

Why so pale and wan, fond lover?
  Prithee, why so pale?
Will, when looking well can't move her,
  Looking ill prevail?
  Prithee, why so pale?

Why so dull and mute, young sinner?
  Prithee, why so mute?
Will, when speaking well can't win her,
  Saying nothing do 't?
  Prithee, why so mute?

Quit, quit for shame! This will not move;
  This cannot take her.
If of her self she will not love,
  Nothing can make her.
  The devil take her!

SIR JOHN SUCKLING

Jonson will always be remembered for his song "To Celia," but perhaps not so well known is the following lyric. Note how the well-turned phrase gives compactness, especially to the epigram.

It Is Not Growing Like a Tree

It is not growing like a tree
In bulk, doth make man better be;
Or standing long an oak, three hundred year,
To fall a log at last, dry, bald, and sear;
    A lily of a day
    Is fairer far in May,

Although it fall and die that night,
It was the plant and flower of light.
In small proportions we just beauties see;
And in short measures, life may perfect be.

BEN JONSON

Herrick's approach is personal even though the appeal is universal.

To The Virgins, to Make Much of Time

Gather ye rosebuds while ye may,
Old Time is still a-flying;
And this same flower that smiles today
Tomorrow will be dying.

The glorious lamp of heaven, the Sun,
The higher he's a-getting,
The sooner will his race be run,
And nearer he's to setting.

That age is best which is the first,
When youth and blood are warmer;
But being spent, the worse and worst
Times still succeed the former.

Then be not coy, but use your time;
And while ye may, go marry;
For having lost but once your prime,
You may forever tarry.

ROBERT HERRICK

Frankenberg remarks in his inimitable way that in "A Red, Red Rose" he would "expect *my* to be lightly stressed, with a proud lilt, in 'O, my luve's like a red, red rose.'" This stress would give a shift in the trite meaning usually heard, and consequently, in the attitude.[18]

A Red, Red Rose

O, my luve's like a red, red rose,
That's newly sprung in June:
O, my luve's like the melodie
That's sweetly played in tune.

As fair art thou, my bonie lass,
So deep in luve am I:

[18] Lloyd Frankenberg, *Invitation to Poetry* (Garden City, N.Y.: Doubleday and Company, 1956), p. 171. Reprinted by permission.

And I will luve thee still, my dear,
   Till a' the seas gang dry.

Till a' the seas gang dry, my dear,
   And the rocks melt wi' the sun:
I will luve thee still, my dear,
   While the sands o' life shall run.

And fare thee weel, my only luve,
   And fare thee weel awhile!
And I will come again, my luve,
   Tho' it were ten thousand mile.

ROBERT BURNS

This poem is typical of Dickinson's exacting restraint:

I Died for Beauty

I died for beauty, but was scarce
Adjusted in the tomb,
When one who died for truth was lain
In an adjoining room.

He questioned softly why I failed?
"For beauty," I replied.
"And I for truth,—the two are one;
We brethren are," he said.

And so, as kinsmen met a night,
We talked between the rooms,
Until the moss had reached our lips,
And covered up our names.[19]

EMILY DICKINSON

You will discover many lyrics showing the personal approach in this volume as well as in many anthologies. Interpret several of the poems clustered around one theme before your group.

THE SONNET

In the song, you may have noticed the form of the stanzas varies greatly, demonstrating freedom in the expression of the poet's lyrical tone by means of fusion of rhythm, tuneful phrasing, word sounds, repetition; and by subjects of universal appeal, like love, spring, youth, memories and

---

[19] Emily Dickinson, *The Complete Poems of Emily Dickinson* (Boston: Little, Brown and Company, 1960).

the happy way of living. These elements add to the emotional experience, making the poem memorable.

The sonnet form requires a rigorous condensation of thought, usually expanded through simile and metaphor, to fit a traditional fourteen-line structure of iambic pentameter and a particular rhyme scheme. Consequently, that rigidity, quite different from the freedom of the song lyrics, never allows the emotional appeal to get out of hand. Because of the need for this masterful restraint, sonnets belong to the craft of great artists. You are acquainted with the two main forms of the sonnet: the Italian (Petrarchan) and the Elizabethan (Shakespearean). In the twelfth century, Petrarch originated the Italian sonnet, in which the thought is accentuated by the division of lines into an octave, the first eight lines and the sestet, the last six lines—the lines rhyming *abba abba cde cde* (or *cd cd cd* in the sestet). The Shakespearean sonnet is formed by using three balanced quatrains, in which the thought may be initiated by simile or metaphor, and concluded with a final couplet—the lines rhyming *abab cdcd efef gg*. The rhyme units in this sonnet also mark the development of thought. The final couplet shows a counter-motion of the preceding thought, or as Ciardi[20] calls it, a point of balance or "fulcrum" between two differing thoughts, indicated by a pause. This counter-motion is noticeable when a shift in tone or attitude, as expressed in the quatrains, occurs in the rhymed couplet. Shakespeare's sonnet "That Time of Year," which follows shortly, shows this thought development in the quatrains and the counter-motion in the couplet.

The questions as to whether form controls meaning or meaning regulates form, or whether form and meaning are one, are argued pro and con by literary specialists. In the sonnet, as in many other poems, the form offers signposts directed to the development of meaning. The total effect as produced by a combination of all elements is more important to the interpreter than a critical announcement of certain stress patterns or rhyming structures. Certainly the manipulation of words and phraseology in the sonnet requires masterful handling not only to support form but also to give fluency of rounded thought. The early dinning of the formalized sonnet elements into your literary background may be responsible for a mechanical approach to this poem in interpretation. You should be constantly aware of the challenge of structural meaning, recognizing the component parts as they are united into a whole pattern, but be sure to show sensitive rather than studied, automatic interpretation. You must so arrange your manner of re-creating the impression that the auditor will wonder at the thought so beautifully and compactly expressed rather than to squirm at its rigid and contrived effect.

[20] John Ciardi, *How Does a Poem Mean* (New York: Houghton Mifflin Company, 1959), pp. 994-995.

A dignified yet personal approach gives a persuasive tone to this Shakespearean sonnet, indicating a limited rather than a universal audience.

That Time of Year

That time of year thou may'st in me behold
When yellow leaves, or none, or few, do hang
Upon those boughs which shake against the cold,
Bare ruined choirs where late the sweet birds sang.
In me thou see'st the twilight of such day
As after sunset fadeth in the west,
Which by-and-by black night doth take away,
Death's second self, that seals up all in rest.
In me thou see'st the glowing of such fire
That on the ashes of his youth doth lie,
As the deathbed whereon it must expire,
Consumed with that which it was nourished by.
  This thou perceiv'st which makes thy love more strong,
  To love that well which thou must leave ere long.

SHAKESPEARE

In the next sonnet, the tone begins with the intimacy of light conversation—concerning the physical beauty of the listener—between two loved ones; then after the consideration that deterioration occurs "sometime" (to give reality to the thought), the conviction becomes increasingly earnest in the third quatrain with the assurance "thy eternal summer shall not fade . . . when in eternal lines to time thou grow'st." The following famous couplet shows a counter-motion (fulcrum) to the preceding thought. Read it aloud for melody, for sureness but lightness of tone and for the distinctive falling cadences suggesting certainty. In rereading this couplet, one always thinks of how Shakespeare's plays and sonnets have given *him* an immortality lasting thus far some four hundred years—

As long as man can breathe or eyes can see,
So long lives this, and this gives life to thee.

Shall I Compare Thee

Shall I compare thee to a summer's day?
Thou art more lovely and more temperate:
Rough winds do shake the darling buds of May,
And summer's lease hath all too short a date;
Sometimes too hot the eye of heaven shines,
And often is his gold complexion dimm'd;
And every fair from fair sometimes declines,

By chance or nature's changing course untrimm'd:
But thy eternal summer shall not fade
Nor lose possession of that fair thou ow'st;
Nor shall Death brag thou wander'st in his shade,
When in eternal lines to time thou grow'st;
So long as men can breathe or eyes can see,
So long lives this, and this gives life to thee.

SHAKESPEARE

In Shelley's "Ozymandias," you will find a different tone from the preceding sonnets: the elements of narration and characterization are presented in a dramatic tone, with three voices speaking.

Ozymandias

I met a traveller from an antique land
Who said: "Two vast and trunkless legs of stone
Stand in the desert. Near them, on the sand,
Half sunk, a shattered visage lies, whose frown,
And wrinkled lip, and sneer of cold command,
Tell that its sculptor well those passions read
Which yet survive, stamped on these lifeless things,
The hand that mocked them, and the heart that fed:
And on the pedestal these words appear:
'My name is Ozymandias, king of kings:
Look on my works, ye Mighty, and despair!'
Nothing beside remains. Round the decay
Of that colossal wreck, boundless and bare
The lone and level sands stretch far away."

PERCY BYSSHE SHELLEY

In Milton's sonnet "When I Consider How My Light Is Spent," some find a tone of "self-abasement," an unusual "exhaustion of vitality," revealing the tragic consequences of great suffering. Others think the lines contain an eloquent statement of courage. You will remember Thurber's statement concerning how he wrote all day long as he moved about, even at meals and parties. Yet Thurber, who was also visually handicapped, is one of the greatest humorists. The difference in the personality of the two writers is the difference between an extrovert and an introvert. Thurber never imposed his difficulty on others; he wrote because he thought people needed humor. Read his sketch on "University Days" (page 498) and laugh with him at his partial loss of sight when as a student at Ohio State University he tried to see plant cells through a microscope but saw only a "phenomenon of maladjustment." Yes, it is true these two men lived in different ages! They must also have had distinct personalities!

When I Consider How My Light Is Spent

When I consider how my light is spent,
 Ere half my days, in this dark world and wide,
 And that one talent which is death to hide
 Lodged with me useless, though my soul more bent
To serve therewith my Maker, and present
 My true account, lest He returning chide,
 "Doth God exact day-labor, light denied?"
 I fondly ask. But Patience, to prevent
That murmur, soon replies, "God doth not need
 Either man's work or his own gifts; who best
 Bear His mild yoke, they serve Him best. His State
Is Kingly. Thousands at His bidding speed
 And post o'er land and ocean without rest;
 They also serve who only stand and wait."

MILTON

A postscript can be added to this last sonnet: some believe that Milton was not blind at the time the poem was written. If the date of writing is accepted as 1652, and the Biblical three-score and ten years are accepted as the span of life, then Milton would have been about thirty-five years old and not blind. Then "light" would have the meaning of "inspiration." Would that interpretation change the tone?

These sonnets are classical examples known to you through your literary study. For comparison, read the following sonnet of your generation—Frost's "Meeting and Passing." The lines as usual are typical of Frost's voice: the reminiscent narrative, the personal tone, the unusual way of placing simple words in phrases to make meaning perceptively imaginative and finely etched and the caesuras in the couplet to be sure that your voice will do justice to the thought. Most important is the manner in which the idea is held in quiet and guarded restraint through understatement and is subtly and intimately revealed in the final couplet.

Meeting and Passing

As I went down the hill along the wall
There was a gate I had leaned at for the view
And had just turned from when I first saw you
As you came up the hill. We met. But all
We did that day was mingle great and small
Footprints in summer dust as if we drew
The figure of our being less than two
But more than one as yet. Your parasol
Pointed the decimal off with one deep thrust.
And all the time we talked you seemed to see

Something down there to smile at in the dust
(Oh, it was without prejudice to me!)
Afterward I went past what you had passed
Before we met and you what I had passed.[21]

ROBERT FROST

If you are a sonnet analyst, your attention should be brought to the poet's Italian rhyme scheme in the octave and the Shakeaspearean pattern in the sestet. Does this arrangement in any way change your interpretation? Do you think the repetition of words in the couplet is more effective than the usual rhyming words?

THE ODE

The ode, in comparison with the song and even most sonnets, usually has a more sustained, exalted tone, a formality to its utterance, a dignity of rhythmical movement and a variable stanzaic arrangement. It often begins with a simple lyrical form increasing in emotional tone to a steady incantation of lines. For the present interpretative purposes, the formalized Pindaric form of strophe, antistrophe and epode—a design imitated from the chorus movement and chant of the Greek drama—will not be discussed.

The romantic poets of the nineteenth century excel in the ode, notably Shelley, Wordsworth and Keats. Their themes are in praise of some person, object or natural phenomenon, with symbolic implications in the development of the thought. The tone of the ode is meditative, but it may soar to poetic heights as the poet reaches the culmination of his thought. In this lyric type, the voice of the poet does not reach out intimately to an auditor rather it is heard as the ecstatic voice of the poet releasing his emotional meaning.

Although many students find the ode uninteresting, some memorable lines should be part of the "growing-up" with literature. Shelley's "Ode to the West Wind" is a personal expression of his own ideals and ambitions fused with the forces of nature. Wordsworth's "Ode on Intimations of Immortality," perhaps not always appreciated in one's younger days due to the intricacy of thought, contains many unforgettable lines. Keats, best known for his "Ode On a Grecian Urn," has also demonstrated his versatile poetic charm in "Ode To A Nightingale." The last two lines of the latter ode have been quoted by some as the touchstone of romantic poetry: "Charmed magic casements, opening on the foam/ Of perilous seas, in faery lands forlorn."

In another ode framework, Herrick meditates with warmth and long-

[21] From COMPLETE POEMS OF ROBERT FROST. Copyright 1916 by Holt, Rinehart and Winston, Inc. Copyright 1944 by Robert Frost. Reprinted by permission of Holt, Rinehart and Winston, Inc.

ing on his good friend Ben Jonson. The rhythm is not the measured, stately one of most odes. The tone, instead of a culminating ecstasy, reflects rather the delightful, conversational remembrance of happy, frolicking friendship. The rhyme adherence and the line structure suggest interesting interpretative possibilities:

An Ode for Ben Jonson

Ah Ben!
Say how, or when
Shall we thy guests
Meet at those lyric feasts
Made at the Sun,
The Dog, the Triple Tun,
Where we such clusters had
As made us nobly wild, not mad;
And yet each verse of thine
Outdid the meat, outdid the frolic wine.

My Ben!
Or come again,
Or send to us
Thy wit's great overplus;
But teach us yet
Wisely to husband it,
Lest we that talent spend,
And having once brought to an end
That precious stock, the store
Of such a wit the world should have no more.

ROBERT HERRICK

Tate's "Ode to the Confederate Dead" takes the lead among present-day odes. The comparison of his poem with some of the preceding quoted lines in subject, tone and point of view will intrigue you. It is not reprinted here because the lines are difficult for the "learning" interpreter; if, however, it stirs wonder and admiration in you, try to interpret the meaning. The poet's discussion of the ode can be found in his volume *Collected Essays*.[22] The poem and discussion are reprinted in Engle's *Reading Modern Poetry*.[23]

THE ELEGY

The elegy is a poetic lamentation and praise for one who has been lost to the poet through death; or it may be a reminiscent lyric describing

[22] Allen Tate, *Collected Essays* (Denver: Alan Swallow, 1959), pp. 248-262.
[23] Paul Engle and Warren Carrier, *Reading Modern Poetry* (Chicago: Scott, Foresman and Company, 1955), pp. 204-219.

past pleasureable experiences and friendships never to be replaced. The classical tradition of the sixteenth and seventeenth centuries of presenting characters in the guise of shepherds in an idyllic setting has disappeared in contemporary literature, as you would expect in these days of urban living. These lyrics might be called "special occasion" poems, usually quite immediate in tone inasmuch as the poet is personally involved in the loss of a friend or in the remembrance of past events. Milton's "Lycidas" in honor of Edward King, Shelley's "Adonais" in memory of John Keats, Tennyson's "In Memoriam" in remembrance of Arthur Henry Hallam, Whitman's "When Lilacs Last in the Dooryard Bloom'd" as a dedication to a monumental and beloved President are elegiac landmarks. Gray's "Elegy in a Country Churchyard" has a generalized attitude, a quiet meditative appeal and is not as deeply intensive, inasmuch as a lost friend is not being eulogized.

Elegies are interesting in their own environmental setting and era and in their memorable lyrical expression of one who is dead. An interpreter has difficulty, however, making them "talk" to a contemporary audience, even though they are masterpieces of poetry. On the other hand, this kind of poem must not be dismissed as something beyond the reach of interpretative skill, not only because of Whitman's commemoration of Lincoln's death but for present-day elegies, such as Auden's "In Memory of W. B. Yeats" and Thomas's famous threnody, "Fern Hill," called one of the major poems of this century (page 385).

Whitman starts his impressive elegy in a quiet, familiar tone, describing the farm-house setting, lilacs growing at the dooryard, the great star drooping in the western sky, the solitary thrush warbling his song. He then develops the images of the lilac, star and thrush as symbols in his commemoration of Lincoln: lilacs suggesting love for the slain President; the star, the President; and the bird, the poet singing of the dead. They culminate in the thought of the last lines: "Lilac and star and bird twined with the chant of my soul,/ There in the fragrant pines and cedars dusk and dim." At times you may become so involved in the trend of the symbolic meaning, you may not notice other means by which the poet has caught your attention, as through the immediacy of his voice and the rhythmical cadences. Later the poet's tone becomes exalted as he serenades "lovely and soothing death" in the memorable lines, "Carol with Joy to Thee O Death."

These beginning lines introduce you to the symbols of his poem:

from *When Lilacs Last in the Dooryard Bloom'd*

When lilacs last in the dooryard bloom'd,
And the great star early droop'd in the western sky in the night,
I mourn'd, and yet shall mourn with ever-returning spring.

Ever-returning spring, trinity sure to me you bring,
Lilac blooming perennial and drooping star in the west,
And thought of him I love.

O powerful western fallen star!
O shades of night—O moody, tearful night!
O great star disappear'd—O the black murk that hides the star!
O cruel hands that hold me powerless—O helpless soul of me!
O harsh surrounding cloud that will not free my soul.

In the dooryard fronting an old farm-house near the white-wash'd
 palings,
Stands the lilac-bush tall-growing with heart-shaped leaves of rich green,
With many a pointed blossom rising delicate, with the perfume strong
 I love,
With every leaf a miracle—and from this bush in the dooryard,
With delicate-color'd blossoms and heart-shaped leaves of rich green,
A sprig with its flower I break.

WALT WHITMAN

Carol with Joy to Thee O Death

Come lovely and soothing death,
Undulate round the world, serenly arriving, arriving,
In the day, in the night, to all, to each.
Sooner or later delicate death.

Prais'd be the fathomless universe,
For life and joy, and for objects and knowledge curious,
And for love, sweet love—but praise! praise! praise!
For the sure-enwinding arms of cool-enfolding death.

Dark mother always gliding near with soft feet,
Have none chanted for thee a chant of fullest welcome?
Then I chant it for thee, I glorify thee above all,
I bring thee a song that when thou must indeed come, come unfalteringly.

Approach strong deliveress,
When it is so, when thou hast taken them, I joyously sing the dead,
Lost in the loving floating ocean of thee,
Laved in the flood of thy bliss O death.

From me to thee glad serenades,
Dances for thee I propose saluting thee, adornments and feastings for thee,
And the sights of the open landscape and the high-spread sky are fitting,
And life and the fields, and the huge and thoughtful night.

The night in silence under many a star,
The ocean shore and the husky whispering wave whose voice I know,
And the soul turning to thee O vast and well-veil'd death,
And the body gratefully nestling close to thee.

Over the tree-tops I float thee a song.
Over the rising and sinking waves, over the myriad fields and the prairies wide,
Over the dense pack'd cities all and the teeming wharves and ways,
I float this carol with joy, with joy to thee O death.

WALT WHITMAN, When Lilacs Last in the Dooryard Bloom'd

THE PASTORAL LYRIC

The pastoral setting as shown in the early elegy is reflected in other lyrics of the sixteenth century. Two of these poems should interest you: Marlowe's "The Passionate Shepherd to His Love" and Raleigh's "The Nymph's Reply to the Shepherd." In Marlowe's lyric, the youthful lover speaks of the many delightful pastoral pleasures he can offer his loved one; in Raleigh's reply, the nymph answers stanza by stanza, or image by image. Here, the stanzas in italics are those of Raleigh's poem and are so inserted to demonstrate the different tonal quality of the voices. These companion lyrics "talk" when two interpreters integrate their vocal efforts in this pastoral experience.

The Passionate Shepherd to His Love
and
The Nymph's Reply to the Shepherd

Come live with me and be my love,
And we will all the pleasures prove,
That valleys, groves, hills and field,
Woods or steepy mountain yield.

If all the world and love were young,
And truth in every shepherd's tongue,
These pretty pleasures might me move
To live with thee and be thy love.

Where we will sit upon the rocks,
Seeing the shepherds feed their flocks
By shallow rivers, to whose falls
Melodious birds sing madrigals.

Time drives the flocks from field to fold
When rivers rage and rocks grow cold,

Then Philomel becometh dumb;
The rest complains of cares to come.

And I will make thee beds of roses,
And a thousand fragrant posies,
A cap of flowers and a kirtle
Embroidered all with leaves of myrtle;

The flowers do fade, and wanton fields
To wayward winter reckoning yields;
A honey tongue, a heart of gall,
Is fancy's spring, but sorrow's fall.

A gown made of the finest wool,
Which from our pretty lambs we pull;
Fair-lined slippers for the cold,
With buckles of the purest gold;

Thy gowns, thy shoes, thy beds of roses,
Thy cap, thy kirtle, and thy posies
Soon break, soon wither, soon forgotten,—
In folly ripe, in reason rotten.

A belt of straw and ivy-buds,
With coral clasps and amber studs;
And if these pleasures may thee move,
Come live with me and be my love.

Thy belt of straw and ivy-buds,
Thy coral clasps and amber studs,
All these in me no means can move
To come to thee and be thy love. . . .

The shepherd swains shall dance and sing
For thy delight each May morning;
If these delights thy mind may move,
Then live with me and be my love.

But could youth last and love still breed,
Had joys no date nor age no need,
Then these delights my mind might move,
To live with thee and be thy love.

CHRISTOPHER MARLOWE
AND SIR WALTER RALEIGH

You may be interested to learn that two students of interpretation presented this arrangement.

POINT OF VIEW IN DRAMATIC POETRY

THE DRAMATIC POEM

In a way, every good poem has a dramatic tone, some more intense than others, some more subjective, depending on the manner in which the words and phrases fall into place under the poet's creative hand, and the way in which his voice "talks" to get attention. If he is successful in creating an experience in which you can participate, he certainly is dramatic in tone and approach. Frost, who believes, as you recall, "everything written is as good as it is dramatic," created his poetry with the "feel" of the dramatist but with such discriminating understatement that at first glance the intensity of meaning may not be felt. Students sometimes feel no initial emotional impact on first reading "The Death of the Hired Man." On the other hand, they are quite sensitive to the emotional tones of the voices recorded at high tension in "Home Burial" (page 394).

You can recall many dramatic lines: remember

> Some say the world will end in fire,
> Some say in ice.
> > Frost

> For God's sake, hold your tongue, and let me love;
> > Donne

> Fear death?—to feel the fog in my throat,
> The mist in my face,
> > Browning

> Tiger! Tiger! burning bright
> In the forests of the night,
> > Blake

> Since there's no help, come let us kiss and part.
> Nay I have done, you get no more of me;
> > Drayton

> But at my back I always hear
> Time's wingèd chariot hurrying near,
> > Marvell

> "Ah, are you digging on my grave
>   My beloved one?—planting rue?"
> > Hardy

O, I can hear you, God, above the cry
  Of the tossing trees—
SARETT

It beats in the head, it beats in the head,
It ties the heart with a scarlet thread,
This is the last,
This is the last,
Hurry, hurry, this is the last.
BENÉT

"Is there anybody there?" said the Traveller,
  Knocking on the moonlit door;
DE LA MARE

And what rough beast, its hour come round at last
Slouches to Bethlehem to be born?
YEATS

Midnight shakes the memory
As a madman shakes a dead geranium.
ELIOT

Every one's voice was suddenly lifted,
And beauty came like the setting sun;
SASSOON

The force that through the green fuse drives the flower
Drives my green age;
THOMAS

We lash with the best or worst
Word last! How a lush-kept plus-capped sloe
Will, mouthed to flesh-burst
Gush!
HOPKINS

Since many have read the forty-three stanzas of Keats's "The Eve of St. Agnes," you may not need to be reminded that this poetry has the elements discussed here: you may call it a narrative, and it is; you may decide it is a lyric, and it is; or you may be more impressed by the dramatic tones and incidents, and you should be. Without the fusion of the story, dialogue, lyricism and imagery, how dramatic would the poem be? For you, one creative element may offer greater participation in the interpretative experience than another will. If you consider carefully the blending of all elements, Keats's romantic theme built into lyrical and dramatic episodes will probably make the greatest impression on you; in other words, the poem unites all factors important for feeling and dramatization.

You will remember that St. Agnes' Eve, January 20, is, according to myth, always bitterly cold.

from *The Eve of St. Agnes*

I

St. Agnes' Eve—Ah, bitter chill it was!
The owl, for all his feathers, was a-cold;
The hare limped trembling through the frozen grass,
And silent was the flock in woolly fold:
Numb were the Beadsman's fingers while he told
His rosary, and while his frosted breath,
Like pious incense from a censer old,
Seemed taking flight for heaven, without a death,
Past the sweet Virgin's picture, while his prayer he saith.

The chambers were glowing to receive a thousand guests and among them, one Lady Madeline, was hopeful, on this anniversary of the martyrdom of the Roman virgin, Agnes, that she might, as legend promised, dream and feast with her future husband.

IV

That ancient Beadsman heard the prelude soft;
And so it chanced, for many a door was wide,
From hurry to and fro. Soon, up aloft,
The silver, snarling trumpets 'gan to chide:
The level chambers, ready with their pride,
Were glowing to receive a thousand guests.
The carved angels, ever eager-eyed,
Stared, where upon their heads the cornice rests,
With hair blown back, and wings puts crosswise on their breasts.

V

At length burst in the argent revelry,
With plume, tiara, and all rich array,
Numerous as shadows haunting faerily
The brain new-stuffed, in youth, with triumphs gay
Of old romance. These let us wish away,
And turn, sole-thoughted, to one Lady there,
Whose heart had brooded, all that wintry day,
On love, and wingèd St. Agnes' saintly care.
As she had heard old dames full many times declare.

VI

They told her how, upon St. Agnes' Eve,
Young virgins might have visions of delight,
And soft adorings from their loves receive

Upon the honeyed middle of the night,
If ceremonies due they did aright:
As, supperless to bed they must retire,
And couch supine their beauties, lily white;
Nor look behind, nor sideways, but require
Of Heaven with upward eyes for all that they desire.

VII

Full of this whim was thoughtful Madeline:
The music, yearning like a God in pain,
She scarcely heard: her maiden eyes divine,
Fixed on the floor, saw many a sweeping train
Pass by—she heeded not at all: in vain
Came many a tiptoe, amorous cavalier,
And back retired; not cooled by high disdain,
But she saw not: her heart was otherwhere:
She sighed for Agnes' dreams, the sweetest of the year.

VIII

She danced along with vague, regardless eyes,
Anxious her lips, her breathing quick and short:
The hallowed hour was near at hand: she sighs
Amid the timbrels, and the thronged resort
Of whispers in anger, or in sport;
'Mid looks of love, defiance, hate, and scorn,
Hoodwinked with faery fancy; all amort,
Save to St. Agnes and her lambs unshorn,
And all the bliss to be before to-morrow morn.

IX

So, purposing each moment to retire,
She lingered still. Meantime, across the moors,
Had come young Porphyro, with heart on fire
For Madeline. Beside the portal doors,
Buttressed from moonlight, stands he, and implores
All saints to give him sight of Madeline,
But for one moment in the tedious hours,
That he might gaze and worship all unseen;
Perchance speak, kneel, touch, kiss—in sooth such things have been.

And now comes the hero to win his fair lady with the help of the "aged creature." The plot is slim perhaps, but the episodes are enhanced by the secrecy of the dialogue and the imagery of the lines:

X

He ventures in: let no buzzed whisper tell,
All eyes be muffled, or a hundred swords

Will storm his heart, Love's feverous citadel:
For him, those chambers held barbarian hordes,
Hyena foemen, and hot-blooded lords,
Whose very dogs would execrations howl
Against his lineage; not one breast affords
Him any mercy in that mansion foul,
Save one old beldame, weak in body and in soul.

XI

Ah, happy chance! the aged creature came,
Shuffling along with ivory-headed wand,
To where he stood, hid from the torch's flame,
Behind a broad hall-pillar, far beyond
The sound of merriment and chorus bland:
He startled her; but soon she knew his face,
And grasp'd his fingers in her palsied hand,
Saying, "Mercy, Porphyro! hie thee from this place:
They are all here to-night, the whole blood-thirsty race!"

XII

"Get hence! get hence! there's dwarfish Hildebrand;
He had a fever late, and in the fit
He cursed thee and thine, both house and land:
Then there's that old Lord Maurice, not a whit
More tame for his gray hairs—Alas me! flit!
Flit like a ghost away."—"Ah, Gossip dear,
We're safe enough; here in this arm-chair sit,
And tell me how"—"Good Saints; not here, not here;
Follow me, child, or else these stones will be thy bier."

XIII

He follow'd through a lowly archèd way,
Brushing the cobwebs with his lofty plume,
And as she mutter'd "Well-a—well-a-day!"
He found him in a little moonlight room,
Pale, lattic'd, chill, and silent as a tomb.
"Now tell me where is Madeline," said he,
"O tell me, Angela, by the holy loom
Which none but secret sisterhood may see,
When they St. Agnes' wool are weaving piously."

XIV

"St. Agnes! Ah! it is St. Agnes' Eve—
Yet men will murder upon holy days:
Thou must hold water in a witch's sieve,
And be liege-lord of all the Elves and Fays,

To venture so: it fills me with amaze
To see thee, Porphyro!—St. Agnes' Eve!
God's help! my lady fair the conjuror plays
This very night: good angels her deceive!
But let me laugh awhile, I've mickle time to grieve."

XV

Feebly she laugheth in the languid moon
While Porphyro upon her face doth look,
Like puzzled urchin on an aged crone
Who keepeth closed a wond'rous riddle-book,
As spectacled she sits in chimney nook.
But soon his eyes grew brilliant, when she told
His lady's purpose; and he scarce could brook
Tears, at the thought of those enchantments cold,
And Madeline asleep in lap of legends old.

XVI

Sudden a thought came like a full-blown rose,
Flushing his brow, and in his painèd heart
Made purple riot: then doth he propose
A stratagem, that makes the beldame start:
"A cruel man and impious thou art:
Sweet lady, let her pray, and sleep, and dream
Alone with her good angels, far apart
From wicked men like thee. Go, go!—I deem
Thou canst not surely be the same that thou didst seem."

XVII

"I will not harm her, by all saints I swear!"
Quoth Porphyro: "O may I ne'er find grace
When my weak voice shall whisper its last prayer,
If one of her soft ringlets I displace,
Or look with ruffian passion in her face.
Good Angela, believe me, by these tears;
Or I will, even in a moment's space,
Awake, with horrid shout, my foemen's ears,
And beard them, though they be more fanged than wolves and bears."

So the plot was made. The rest you must read in a volume of Keats's poetry, except for the description of Madeline's room, so typical of Keats's lush imagery:

XXIV

A casement high and triple-arched there was,
All garlanded with carven imag'ries

Of fruits, and flowers, and bunches of knot-grass,
And diamonded with panes of quaint device,
Innumerable of stains and splendid dyes,
As are the tiger-moth's deep-damasked wings;
And in the midst, 'mong thousand heraldries,
And twilight saints, and dim emblazonings,
A shielded scutcheon blushed with blood of queens and kings.

XXV

Full on this casement shone the wintry moon,
And threw warm gules on Madeline's fair breast,
As down she knelt for heaven's grace and boon;
Rose-bloom fell on her hands, together prest,
And on her silver cross soft amethyst,
And on her hair a glory, like a saint:
She seemed a splendid angel, newly drest,
Save wings, for heaven:—Porphyro grew faint:
She knelt, so pure a thing, so free from mortal taint.

"All's well that ends well" as at the end,—

XLI

They glide, like phantoms, into the wide hall;
Like phantoms, to the iron porch they glide;
Where lay the Porter, in uneasy sprawl,
With a huge empty flagon by his side:
The wakeful bloodhound rose, and shook his hide,
But his sagacious eye an inmate owns:
By one, and one, the bolts full easy slide:—
The chains lie silent on the footworn stones;—
The key turns, and the door upon its hinges groans.

. . .

And they are gone: aye, ages long ago
These lovers fled away into the storm.

JOHN KEATS

You have just read parts of a truly dramatic poem, a romantic story, with atmospheric setting, sensuous imagery, poetic language and vivid characterizations sustained through dialogue and action—united by literary artistry. "The Eve of St. Agnes" is one of the greatest romantic poems written in the early part of the nineteenth century by a young and creative poet who lived only until his twenty-fifth year.

THE DRAMATIC MONOLOGUE

Among the dramatic poems, a genre called the dramatic monologue is so written and staged that the author is completely detached from the scene, very much as the playwright is from his play. The character revelation can be as dramatic as one seen on the stage; it can be similar to one found in the short story or novel. In fact, the dramatic monologue resembles the short story in that moment of intensity in an individual's life when an episode is dramatized to reveal the person's way of living and thinking, overtly as well as covertly. Browning's "My Last Duchess" has been called a condensed novel since it presents the accumulated life history of the Duke. The goal of the poet in this form is to reveal through speech and actions the temperament, personality and philosophy of the narrator. Your emotional reaction to this kind of character analysis is not unlike the impact you receive as you study the details of a portrait, such as the *Mona Lisa,* trying to discern the underlying traits by means of observing the outward integrating details.

Because the poet's approach is objective in the dramatic monologue, he arranges an opportune situation in which the character may create the dramatic tone. Then he stands offstage to observe the unveiling of his portrait. The tone is created through the speech of the narrator as he talks to himself, or to another person or group of persons who do not audibly participate. Sometimes the speaker is alone, grappling with inner tensions, such as you find in the famous soliloquies of Shakespeare's plays: Juliet's "I have a faint cold fear thrills through my veins," Macbeth's "If it were done, when 'tis done," Othello's "Put out the light, and then put out the light." These interior monologues are objective portrayals of a character caught in a tense moment of indecision, fear or self-deprecation: a moment of revelation, of inner turmoil, culminated eventually in decisive action. No matter whether you call this moment a monologue, a soliloquy, an interior monologue or lyrical poetry, the scene exists in its intense entirety as a dramatic episode. The sharp division used in classification of types is not as important as the realization of the tonal impression the poet wants to create.

Browning has always been considered the forerunner of the dramatic monologue, being motivated by the artistry of the Renaissance painters in their revelation of character. His montage of voices consists of an enviable collection, among them the Bishop who orders a tomb, the Duke who selects a new Duchess, the unnamed monk who hurls his hatred at Friar Lawrence. Tennyson's "Ulysses," although considered one of the poet's best poems, never quite reaches the penetrating dramatic peak found in Browning's poems. This may be due to the legendary figure whose heroic actions seem foreign today, although the inability of Ulysses to meet old age adequately is also typical in contemporary society. Arnold's "Dover Beach" is lyrically beautiful but lacks the dramatic intensity of Browning, the tonal impression being one of philosophical reflection in a twilight mood.

Arnold is looking out over Dover Beach along the coast of England at the time of evening when he can no longer see the light from the French Coast beyond the Straits of Dover. How does this favorite poem—sometimes called a love lyric—compare in tone, character and vividness with the two preceding poems? How does the moonlight affect the tone? What details do you observe in the portrait? Which one of these dramatic monologues would you prefer to interpret?

Dover Beach

The sea is calm tonight.
The tide is full, the moon lies fair
Upon the straits;—on the French coast the light
Gleams and is gone; the cliffs of England stand,
Glimmering and vast, out in the tranquil bay.
Come to the window, sweet is the night-air!
Only, from the long line of spray
Where the sea meets the moon-blanched land,
Listen! you hear the grating roar
Of pebbles which the waves draw back, and fling,
At their return, up the high strand,
Begin, and cease, and then again begin,
With tremulous cadence slow, and bring
The eternal note of sadness in.

Sophocles long ago
Heard it on the Ægean, and it brought
Into his mind the turbid ebb and flow
Of human misery; we
Find also in the sound a thought,
Hearing it by this distant northern sea.

The Sea of Faith
Was once, too, at the full, and round earth's shore
Lay like the folds of a bright girdle furled.
But now I only hear
Its melancholy, long, withdrawing roar,
Retreating, to the breath
Of the night-wind, down the vast edges drear
And naked shingles of the world.

Ah, love, let us be true
To one another! for the world, which seems

To lie before us like a land of dreams,
So various, so beautiful, so new,
Hath really neither joy, nor love, nor light,
Nor certitude, nor peace, nor help for pain;
And we are here as on a darkling plain
Swept with confused alarms of struggle and flight,
Where ignorant armies clash by night.

MATTHEW ARNOLD

Eliot is credited with renewal of interest in this type of poetry. "The Waste Land" has been discussed as a collection of dramatic monologues. "Journey of the Magi" (page 300), "The Love Song of J. Alfred Prufrock" (page 480), "The Hollow Men" (with a chorus of voices speaking as one) (page 387), as well as those poems of Yeats and Frost and others found in this text, will give you excellent opportunities to burrow into the meaning and present a selection with dramatic tones.

Two examples, Tennyson's "Ulysses" and Browning's "Soliloquy of the Spanish Cloister" (page 298) illustrate differences in characterizations through immediacy of tone, intonational phrases and speech rhythm: one showing dignity of speech and the other following a colloquial pattern.

Ulysses

It little profits that an idle king,
By this still hearth, among these barren crags,
Matched with an agèd wife, I mete and dole
Unequal laws unto a savage race,
That hoard, and sleep, and feed, and know not me.
I cannot rest from travel; I will drink
Life to the lees. All times I have enjoyed
Greatly, have suffered greatly, both with those
That loved me, and alone; on shore, and when
Through scudding drifts the rainy Hyades
Vext the dim sea. I am become a name;
For always roaming with a hungry heart
Much have I seen and known,—cities of men
And manners, climates, councils, governments,
Myself not least, but honored of them all;
And drunk delight of battle with my peers,
Far on the ringing plains of windy Troy.
I am a part of all that I have met;
Yet all experience is an arch wherethro'
Gleams that untraveled world, whose margin fades
For ever and for ever when I move.
How dull it is to pause, to make an end,
To rust unburnish'd, not to shine in use!
As tho' to breathe were life! Life piled on life

Were all too little, and of one to me
Little remains: but every hour is saved
From that eternal silence, something more,
A bringer of new things; and vile it were
For some three suns to store and hoard myself,
And this gray spirit yearning in desire
To follow knowledge like a sinking star,
Beyond the utmost bound of human thought.
　　This is my son, mine own Telemachus,
To whom I leave the sceptre and the isle—
Well-loved of me, discerning to fulfil
This labor, by slow prudence to make mild
A rugged people, and thro' soft degrees
Subdue them to the useful and the good.
Most blameless is he, centred in the sphere
Of common duties, decent not to fail
In offices of tenderness, and pay
Meet adoration to my household gods,
When I am gone. He works his work, I mine.
　　There lies the port; the vessel puffs her sail:
There gloom the dark, broad seas. My mariners,
Souls that have toil'd, and wrought, and thought with me,—
That ever with a frolic welcome took
The thunder and the sunshine, and opposed
Free hearts, free foreheads—you and I are old;
Old age hath yet his honor and his toil;
Death closes all: but something ere the end,
Some work of noble note, may yet be done,
Not unbecoming men that strove with Gods.
The lights begin to twinkle from the rocks:
The long day wanes: the slow moon climbs: the deep
Moans round with many voices. Come, my friends,
'Tis not too late to seek a newer world.
Push off, and sitting well in order smite
The sounding furrows; for my purpose holds
To sail beyond the sunset, and the baths
Of all the western stars, until I die.
It may be that the gulfs will wash us down:
It may be we shall touch the Happy Isles,
And see the great Achilles, whom we knew.
Tho' much is taken, much abides; and tho'
We are not now that strength which in old days
Moved earth and heaven, that which we are, we are;
One equal temper of heroic hearts,
Made weak by time and fate, but strong in will
To strive, to seek, to find, and not to yield.

ALFRED TENNYSON

Tennyson portrays a heroic figure, Ulysses, an aged Trojan warrior who, after having roamed about the Mediterranean area for twenty years at the end of the war, comes home to his wife, Penelope, and his son, Telemachus. He is pleased with his honored name, his heroic dimensions, but restless and unhappy with the trials of an old man who would like to conquer new fields. (Whether or not this is the typical masculine trait of wanting to get away from home is your decision.) Are there listeners or is he talking to himself? Some believe Tennyson has portrayed a senior citizen, so to speak, in a mood of reverie, one who dreams he may pry himself free to conquer again. Which tone predominates: masculine impatience, heroic vanity, restlessness, or is the poem a dream of symbolized endeavor?

In Browning's "Soliloquy of the Spanish Cloister" (page 298), the central figure has none of the characteristics of a great hero. The contemporary psychologist could make a good case study of the monk with his deviating phrases that show how deeply his hatred has touched the inner man; he might also wish to investigate Friar Lawrence as the "motivation" for the monk's hatred; he could also analyze Ulysses in an interesting way. These are characters whose speech shows their inner torments, their psychological complexities.

Any one of Shakespeare's interior monologues presents the same vivid characterization; for instance, read the following soliloquy from *Hamlet*. Here a tormented young man reveals his inner thoughts concerning the faithlessness of his mother to his dead father, as he tries to find a solution to his perplexed and anxious thoughts. His speech tones are broken as he shifts from one agonizing picture to another, rising and falling with varied intensity until finally his voice breaks on the last line.

> HAMLET: O that this too too solid flesh would melt,
> Thaw, and resolve itself into a dew!
> Or that the Everlasting had not fix'd
> His canon 'gainst self-slaughter! O God! O God!
> How weary, stale, flat, and unprofitable
> Seem to me all the uses of this world!
> Fie on't! O fie, fie! 'Tis an unweeded garden,
> That grows to seed; things rank and gross in nature
> Possess it merely. That it should come to this!
> But two months dead. Nay, not so much, not two.
> So excellent a king; that was, to this,
> Hyperion to a satyr; so loving to my mother
> That he might not beteem the winds of heaven
> Visit her face too roughly. Heaven and earth!
> Must I remember? Why, she would hang on him,
> As if increase of appetite had grown
> By what it fed on; and yet, within a month,—
> Let me not thing on't!—Frailty, thy name is woman!—

A little month, or ere those shoes were old
With which she follow'd my poor father's body,
Like Niobe, all tears,—why she, even she—
O God! a beast, that wants discourse of reason,
Would have mourn'd longer—married with mine uncle,
My father's brother, but no more like my father
Than I to Hercules; within a month,
Ere yet the salt of most unrighteous tears
Had left the flushing in her gallèd eyes,
She married. . . .
It is not nor it cannot come to good.—
But break, my heart, for I must hold my tongue.

SHAKESPEARE, *Hamlet*
Act I, Scene 2

From this discussion you should realize the difficulty involved in classifying poems according to subjective and objective points of view and to narrative, lyrical and dramatic tones. This classification, which has been offered in good faith, must be understood only as a frame of reference. Probably every poem has a narrative motivation; probably every lyric has a dramatic setting and immediacy of voice; certainly every dramatic poem is lyrical if it is considered great poetry. Although a merging of all literary elements is expected, poetry is placed usually in the category showing the dominant form and tone.

POINT OF VIEW IN THE ESSAY

THE ESSAYIST AS PERSONALIZED AUTHOR

The essay is author-oriented in a special way. The essayist differs from other literary writers in his acknowledged attitude and direct approach. He offers no camouflage about the source and direction of his thoughts. He is "speaking his piece" as an identifiable person, not as an unknown writer who lurks behind the story or verse or play. He is voicing his opinion on some subject, which may be important or trivial as far as critical, moral and public opinions are concerned. Depending on the character of the voice heard—whether formal or informal, instructive or entertaining, impersonal or personal—a distinctive style showing the tone and temper of the essayist will be noticeable.

VOICE OF THE INFORMAL ESSAYIST

The voice you hear may be conversational in an intimate way—chatty, alive, animated, genial or humorous in its tone and colored by the mood of the writer. This essay will then have a personal tone or attitude, intriguing because of its sparkle, quick turn of the phrase, unusual combination of words and associations, reminiscent mellowness or cleverly concealed satiric edge, which the naïve might not easily experience. The author exposes himself as a certain kind of person with particular convictions, prejudices, whims and fancies, but he does it in an informal, conversational manner more engaging in style than everyday humdrum conversation. He draws you into his confidence also by allowing personal involvement. You enjoy being included in his thoughts and likes and dislikes, which may be quite similar to yours. This is the informal essay of Montaigne's so-called "experiments." In the early years of the essay in this country, the essayist might have been a gently tempered but whimsical Charles Lamb writing "A Dissertation Upon Roast Pig":

He must be roasted. I am not ignorant that our ancestors ate them seethed, or boiled—but what a sacrifice of the exterior tegument!

There is no flavour comparable, I will contend, to that of the crisp, tawny, well-watched, not over-roasted, *crackling*, as it is well called—the very teeth are invited to their share of pleasure at this banquet in overcoming coy, brittle resistance—[24]

Charles Lamb

In those days you might have enjoyed the essays of Henry David Thoreau, who hoped to live deeply but sturdily as he meditated on "Where I Lived, and What I Lived For" and concluded with his well-known metaphor: "Time is but the stream I go a-fishing in. I drink at it; but while I drink I see the sandy bottom and detect how shallow it is. Its thin current slides away but eternity remains."

Perhaps you could not have resisted the brilliantly verbose Carlyle, who wrote "Silence is golden" but failed to be impressed personally with his own dictum—the essayist who was never able to curb his biting tongue or his wayward hand as it moved over the page yet could always stimulate with his energetic and perceptive tone. Where could a more paradoxical and penetrating portrait be found than in the word picture he painted of DeQuincey, another essayist. Be sure to appreciate his imagery: "wire-drawn ingenuities," "bankrupt enthusiasms," "bankrupt pride," "elaborate gently-winding courtesies," "shaped like a pair of tongs;" and the surprise ending:

He was a pretty little creature, full of wire-drawn ingenuities; bankrupt enthusiasms, bankrupt pride; with the finest silver-toned low voice, and most elaborate gently-winding courtesies and ingenuities in conversation. One of the smallest man-figures I ever saw; shaped like a pair of tongs; and hardly about five feet in all; when he sat, you would have taken him, by candlelight, for the

---

[24] Charles Lamb, "A Dissertation Upon Roast Pig," *Select Essays* (New Rochelle, N.Y.: The Peter Pauper Press, 1934), pp. 76-77.

beautifullest little child; blue-eyed, sparkling face—had there not been a something, too, which said, *"Eccovi, the Child has been in Hell!"*

Setting the pace for those today who haunt their childhood experiences for happy recollections was Kenneth Grahame who wrote with a
dramatic touch of "The Magic Ring"—the circus ring.

A thud of unseen hoofs first set us a-quiver; then a crash of cymbals, a jangle
of bells, a hoarse applauding roar, and Coralie was in the midst of us, whirling
past 'twixt earth and sky, now erect, flushed, radiant, now crouched to the flowing mane; swung and tossed and molded by the maddening dance-music of the
band. The mighty whip of the count in the frock-coat marked time with pistol-
shots; her war-cry, whooping clear above the music, fired the blood with a
passion for splendid deeds, as Coralie, laughing, exultant, crashed through the
paper hoops. We gripped the red cloth in front of us, and our souls sped round
and round with Coralie, leaping with her, prone with her, swung by mane or
tail with her. It was not only the ravishment of her delirious feats, nor her
cream-colored horse of fairy breed, long-tailed, roe-footed, an enchanted prince
surely, if ever there was one! It was her more than mortal beauty . . . that
held us spellbound. What princess had arms so dazzlingly white, or went delicately clothed in such pink and spangles? Hitherto we had known the outward
woman as but a drab thing, hour-glass shaped, nearly legless, bunched here,
constricted there, slow of movement, and given to deprecating lusty action of
limb. Here was a revelation! . . . I saw myself and Coralie, close enfolded,
pacing the world together, o'er hill and plain, through storied cities, past rows
of applauding relations,—I in my Sunday knickerbockers, she in her pink and
spangles.[25]

KENNETH GRAHAME, *The Magic Ring*

This list of excerpts could go on and on because every essayist is different in tone and style; just as every short story writer reveals something
of the tonal impact of his individuality—but behind the scenes.

VOICE OF THE FORMAL ESSAYIST

The essay voice may have another purpose than to delight and entertain as in the informal essay. For those who have learned how to plan a
speech, nothing new will be observed in the use of speech devices by the
formal essayist: he gives facts, comparisons, examples; and employs re-
statement and amplification. The form will show a direct, impersonal approach; the ideas will be logically arranged and move toward a definite
goal. The voice will be reminiscent of the instructor or speaker who is
formal, serious, sometimes aloof, sometimes satirical, and who is talking to a
large group rather than to a few individuals. The subject matter often

[25] Kenneth Grahame, "The Magic Ring," *Dream Days* (New York: John Lane
Co., 1904), pp. 105-107.

becomes more important than the manner or style of the writer. The outgoing character or eccentricity of the writer is subordinated. This is the formal essay, employed by Sir Francis Bacon, whose manner was known to be not too smoothly tempered. As Alexander Smith wrote in his meditative and whimsical essay "On the Writing of Essays," Bacon seemed to "write with his ermine on." Critical essays on literature, culture, morality, religion, science and art are part of this great essay heritage led by Hazlitt, Coleridge, Arnold, Poe, Macaulay and Huxley. The warm feeling of being talked to personally is missing, but you will recognize a distinguished style, if not a personal one. Richard Le Gallienne has suggested the formal essayist does not always make magic of his recollections and associations. Nor does he fit into Carl Van Doren's belief that the ideas must take root inside the writer and must show some of the soil clinging to them and be shaped by the composition of the soil.

PRESENT DEVELOPMENT OF THE ESSAY

A flood of essay writing can be found today in critical books, editorials, book reviews and political comments, but the delight of hearing the voice of a writer as the center of interest is often negligible. The formal objective essay, which seems to be taking the lead in critical articles, is not adaptable usually for interpretative purposes.

At times formal and informal points of view are merged. For instance, a curious exchange of an essay title from Jarrell's *Poetry and the Age*[26] was made in reprinting the essay in Fiedler's *The Art of the Essay:*[27] "Some Lines From Walt Whitman" was changed to "Walt Whitman: He Had His Nerve." This shift from formal to informal tone certainly is more appropriate to the content which has the imprint of Jarrell's personal and ingenious manner and tone. His point of view, as usual, presents his outspoken and direct analysis, suggesting "You can take my ideas or leave them, but this is the way Whitman will be judged in the years ahead."

Perhaps Fiedler, whose excellent collection of essays should be read by every student, has the perspective of what is happening today when he writes that those writers who are sensitive observers are turning back to the place they know best in their past, as shown in Thomas's "A Visit to Grandpa's," Cowley's "Big Town High School," Powers's "St. Paul: Home of the Saints," Kazin's "The Open Street" and even as shown in Joyce's *Dubliners* and in the return of Faulkner to Oxford, Mississippi. Nor in this respect can you forget that Mark Twain's Mississippi River serves as a recognized symbol in his writing and that even the pseudonym he adopted

[26] Randall Jarrell, "Some Lines from Walt Whitman," *Poetry and the Age* (New York: Alfred A. Knopf, Inc., 1953), pp. 587-597.
[27] Leslie Fiedler, *The Art of the Essay* (New York: Thomas Y. Crowell Company, 1958), pp. 112-133.

is a "river" expression meaning "two fathoms deep." To Fiedler the typical motion of the informal essayist is back through time, from recent events to recaptured moments of the past and the "search for discovery and identity of self which leads outward as well as inward."

POINT OF VIEW IN FICTION

AUTHORITY OF THE NARRATOR'S VOICE

The point of view, the "center of vision," becomes more complex in the telling of a story than in other literary types because the form of fiction requires a wider scope of episodes and characterizations to reach the central meaning. Furthermore, consistency on the part of the writer in sustaining his point of view is necessary to secure organic unity. The narrative authority, delegated by the author, must give his story the tone of reality in vivid relating and must be one with whom the author wishes to be identified, even though objectively. Once the story starts, the narrator has control of the characters and movement of the theme to be built into a dynamic pattern. The records of authors' experiences in choosing the most meaningful point of view indicate they often change from one character to another in an attempt to find one who will realistically present the story. An example is Faulkner's struggle to find the right individual to narrate *The Sound and the Fury*. He first tried Benjy as the "eyes" of the tale, inasmuch as the child could see what happened but would not know *why* certain actions took place because of his level of intelligence. Then the author decided to make the second brother the narrator, and again he was unsuccessful. He tried the third brother and still was unsatisfied; neither was he content with himself as the story-teller. Finally, as he tells his interviewer, he added an appendix to the end of another novel to satisfy his desire for the right approach to his theme [28] (page 17).

The relationship of the narrator to the story will depend on the knowledge of what is happening, the manner in which events unfold, the extent of details that can be told and the focus of views—either panoramic, long-distance views or close-ups involving the immediate scene. The procedure is similar to the operation of the screen and television photographer who secures relationships of far and near action.

The first observation of the interpreter in preparing a piece of fiction is to determine who is telling the story, who is the authority in control of events. Decide what voice is reaching you and how the particular focus presents reality. Any critical book on fiction will explain points of view in telling a story, but perhaps a brief outline will be helpful now.

Three main types of approach are used extensively in the short story

[28] *Paris Interview Series*, pp. 130-131.

and novel: (1) first-person narrator, who may be the author, the main character or a minor character; (2) omniscient or third-person narrator, sometimes called the roving narrator (often called the approach of "central intelligence"); (3) effaced narrator who assumes a distinctly objective attitude by not revealing himself at any time. Another point of view, difficult to manage and characteristic of recent authors, involves the technique of "stream of consciousness," in which the action is carried forward through the revelation of inner thoughts, usually of the main character.

FIRST-PERSON NARRATOR

The first-person narrator is an eye-witness who presents a close-up view of events; consequently, his tone and observations are immediate. He tells you only what he sees and hears, so his authority as narrator may be limited. He may appear at times biased in his reporting, due to the boundaries of his knowledge and intrusion of his personal attitude. He may decide either to withdraw from some action or may report on the significance of some episode.

Variations in the placement of the first-person narrator are possible, depending, of course, upon how the author wants his theme developed. He can be the author, but the immediate recounting will be more realistic if the narrator is a major character, an actor in the action. If he is a direct participant, the tone of the story will be heightened. In other words, the narrative becomes more credible because "he was there." What he sees, you see; what he hears, you hear; what he senses, you sense. Since his experiences are limited in giving the total action, you cannot expect him to explain what he does not observe. Poe, in "The Fall of the House of Usher," has a first-person narrator who reports the environment and situations as they occur with increasing intensity.

You recall that the "ancient Mariner," as first-person narrator, *makes* the "Wedding-Guest" listen to his story. In *A Farewell to Arms*, Hemingway places the hero, Lt. Henry, in the part of the story-teller. Thus, the emotional tone is immediately noticeable at the beginning of the story, a tone that deepens as the two lovers are caught in the vagaries of war-time action and that penetrates more and more into the movement of the story until finally the climax is reached by the separation of the lovers through death. The first paragraph is often quoted, for Hemingway's artful and lyrical cadences establish the mood of the tale and tone of the narrator, which suggest impending desolation of the soldier traveling along the "road bare and white except for the leaves," the leaves being reminiscent of the past spring-time of one's life. Ford Madox Ford, in the "Introduction," gives his total impression of the story, "It [the story] may close with tears but it is like a spring morning." The narrator starts the story:[29]

[29] Notice the repetition of images of "dust," "dry," "white," "falling leaves."

In the late summer of that year we lived in a house in a village that looked across the river and the plain to the mountains. In the bed of the river there were pebbles and boulders, dry and white in the sun, and the water was clear and swiftly moving and blue in the channels. Troops went by the house and down the road and the dust they raised powdered the leaves of the trees. The trunks of the trees too were dusty and the leaves fell early that year and we saw the troops marching along the road and the dust rising and leaves, stirred by the breeze, falling and the soldiers marching and afterward the road bare and white except for the leaves. . . .[30]

In a widely read novelette, *The Heart of Darkness,* Conrad puts Marlow in the specific role of storyteller. Five men bound together by the love of the sea are on the cruising yawl "Nellie," looking out over the vast waterway of the Thames. The air to the West is heavy with "brooding gloom," and a "mist on the Essex marshes" gives the impression of "transparent gauze draping the shores." The day is ending and the men are sitting in a meditative mood. In this atmosphere, one character, Marlow, with sunken cheeks, yellow complexion and straight back, sitting cross-legged and leaning against the mizzen-mast, starts his story of a trip to the South Seas. This preliminary descriptive part sets the mood and atmosphere for his narrative as well as explains how he was commissioned for the trip. Moreover, it adds to the credibility of his search for Kurtz, an Englishman who had lost his identity as a civilized person among the jungle tribes to become engulfed in the deteriorating savagery of the jungle inhabitants. In the following reprinted portion, the entry into the jungle by means of a "two-penny-half-penny river-steamboat with a penny whistle attached" exemplifies the outward reality of the whole experience. Conrad emphasizes that reality by the use of the personal "you," "I tell you," and by Marlowe's avowal of how incredible the story of the jungle seemed to him: "the reality—the reality, I tell you—fades. The inner truth is hidden— luckily, luckily." These last two words are prime agents of suspense and premonition.

Going up that river was like traveling back to the earliest beginnings of the world, when vegetation rioted on the earth, and the big trees were kings. An empty stream, a great silence, an impenetrable forest. The air was warm, thick, heavy, sluggish. There was no joy in the brilliance of sunshine. The long stretches of the waterway ran on, deserted, into the gloom of overshadowed distances. On silvery sandbanks hippos and alligators sunned themselves side by side. The broadening waters flowed through a mob of wooded islands; you lost your way on that river as you would in a desert, and butted all day long against shoals, trying to find the channel, till you thought yourself bewitched and cut off for ever from everything you had known once—somewhere—far away—in another existence perhaps. There were moments when one's past came back to one, as it will sometimes when you have not a moment to spare to your-

[30] Excerpt from the following work of Ernest Hemingway is used by permission of Charles Scribner's Sons: A FAREWELL TO ARMS (Copyright 1929 Charles Scribner's Sons; renewal copyright © 1957 Ernest Hemingway).

self; but it came in the shape of an unrestful and noisy dream, remembered with wonder amongst the overwhelming realities of this strange world of plants, and water, and silence. And this stillness of life did not in the least resemble a peace. It was the stillness of an implacable force brooding over an inscrutable intention. It looked at you with a vengeful aspect. I got used to it afterwards; I did not see it any more; I had no time. I had to keep guessing at the channel; I had to discern, mostly by inspiration, the signs of hidden banks; I watched for sunken stones; I was learning to clap my teeth smartly before my heart flew out, when I shaved by a fluke some infernal sly old snag that would have ripped the life out of the tinpot steamboat and drowned all the pilgrims; I had to keep a look-out for the signs of dead wood we could cut up in the night for next day's steaming. When you have to attend to things of that sort, to the mere incidents of the surface, the reality—the reality, I tell you—fades. The inner truth is hidden—luckily, luckily."[31]

Sometimes, as in Ring Lardner's "Haircut," the narrator is a subordinate character who observes part of the action and is not personally involved in the complete action. In this story, Whitey, a barber of limited character and intellectual dimensions, sees the action at his meagre level of understanding; consequently, the reader acquires with some satisfaction, insight and appreciation for the author's total meaning. Whitey tells the story as he knows it, but what he does not observe or sense are the ironic overtones of the tragedy. He merely misses the wisecracking chap who was in the habit of playing crude jokes on people and dominating the talk of the barber shop with his stories. Due to the barber's lack of perception, Lardner is able to build to an ironic and dramatic climax. This he accomplishes so subtly the reader may find himself going back to reread portions to see if he has missed the key to the ending.

OMNISCIENT OR ROVING NARRATOR

The discussions of the omniscient point of view are sometimes confusing because critics use various names for this technique of narration. Very simply, the narrator is one who stands on the hilltop and surveys *all* the action. He utilizes the panoramic technique, for at times he is interested in the far view; at other times he looks through his binoculars to get the details of a close-up scene. He is the "know-all" teller of tales, going from one group of characters to another and then perhaps to an individual, commenting, if he wishes, on some significant activity. You can understand why some call him the omniscient, or roving, narrator. James calls this viewpoint the "post of observation" which is similar to that of "central intelligence." He explains how a "single superior mind" should be placed in the center of the main dramatic situations in order to give the "immediacy of the eye-witness" account without "the narrow and biased view of

---

[31] From HEART OF DARKNESS by Joseph Conrad. Copyright 1893, 1903. Reprinted by permission of J. M. Dent & Sons Ltd.: Publishers, and the Trustees of the Joseph Conrad Estate.

the first-person narrator." Certainly James's method is not as limited as the first-person point of view, but, according to critics, it tends to increase the difficulty of sustaining a well-knit episodic pattern in a story.

When Crane published "The Open Boat" in 1898, he provided fiction writers with a technique of securing vivid suggestive effects through sensory reactions of a character in the midst of the action—an omniscient character, one who witnessed and was moved by events in which he was immersed. Critics believe that Crane was the first to give the illusion of reality by means of a character's insight into selected details of association rather than a telling *about* events and characters. Everything in "The Open Boat" that is seen, heard, feared, touched, felt, sensed, is experienced by you through the correspondent's mood, reactions and observations. In the words of an interpreter of literature, you feel empathically the activities and emotions of those in the boat so small that "many a man ought to have a bath-tub larger." You experience a "feeling *into*," not *with*, the fearful hazards awaiting those in the boat, perched one moment on the top of the waves and then swept suddenly down a long incline. You are *there*, cramped up with four men, sharing their panoramic views: your eyes are "fastened upon the waves" rushing toward you; you see the ominous slate-colored waves with foaming white tops; you watch with a sickening feeling the horizon narrow and widen, dip and rise. From a close-up perspective you watch breathlessly the cook squatting in the bottom of the boat, looking "at the six inches of gunwale which separated him from the broken ocean," at the same time bailing out water with the exclamation "Gawd! That was a narrow clip"; you unconsciously labor with the oiler trying to maneuver the boat with one thin oar; you feel the concern of the correspondent pulling on the other oar and "wondering why he was there." And then you look down at the injured captain, lying in the bow, dejected and indifferent about consequences.

This vivid tale is based on a real experience of the author in contrast to his famous novel, *The Red Badge of Courage*, which was written without any war experience. As a war correspondent during the Cuban insurrection against Spain in 1896, Crane was on his way to Cuba aboard the "Commodore," when the ship went down. Crane and his three companions climbed into the last open boat. Their experience is revealed in "The Open Boat," further labeled by Crane as "A Tale Intended to be after the Fact: Being the Experience of Four Men from the Sunk Steamer, 'Commodore.'"

from *The Open Boat*

None of them knew the color of the sky.[32] Their eyes glanced level, and were fastened upon the waves that swept toward them. These waves were of the hue

[32] Notice the quick plunge into the story with the short dramatic opening sentence of direction.

of slate, save for the tops, which were of foaming white, and all of the men knew the colors of the sea. The horizon narrowed and widened, and dipped and rose, and at all times its edge was jagged with waves that seemed thrust up in points like rocks. Many a man ought to have a bath-tub larger than the boat which here rode upon the sea. These waves were most wrongfully and barbarously abrupt and tall, and each froth-top was a problem in small-boat navigation.

The cook[33] squatted in the bottom and looked with both eyes at the six inches of gunwale which separated him from the ocean. His sleeves were rolled over his fat forearms, and the two flaps of his unbuttoned vest dangled as he bent to bail out the boat. Often he said: Gawd! That was a narrow clip." As he remarked it he invariably gazed eastward over the broken sea.

The oiler, steering with one of the two oars in the boat, sometimes raised himself suddenly to keep clear of water that swirled in over the stern. It was a thin little oar and it seemed often ready to snap.

The correspondent, pulling at the other oar, watched the waves and wondered why he was there.

The injured captain, lying in the bow, was at this time buried in that profound dejection and indifference which comes, temporarily at least, to even the bravest and most enduring when, willy nilly, the firm fails, the army loses, the ship goes down. The mind of the master of a vessel is rooted deep in the timbers of her, though he commanded for a day or a decade, and this captain had on him the stern impression of a scene in the grays of dawn of seven turned faces, and later a stump of a topmast with a white ball on it that slashed to and fro at the waves, went low and lower, and down. Thereafter there was something strange in his voice. Although steady, it was deep with mourning, and of a quality beyond oration or tears.

"Keep 'er a little more south, Billie," said he.

" 'A little more south,' sir," said the oiler in the stern.

A seat in this boat[34] was not unlike a seat upon a bucking broncho, and by the same token, a broncho is not much smaller. The craft pranced and reared, and plunged like an animal. As each wave came, and she rose for it, she seemed like a horse making at a fence outrageously high. The manner of her scramble over these walls of water is a mystic thing, and, moreover, at the top of them were ordinarily these problems in white water, the foam racing down from the summit of each wave, requiring a new leap, and a leap from the air. Then, after scornfully bumping a crest, she would slide, and race, and splash down a long incline, and arrive bobbing and nodding in front of the next menace.[35]

Stephen Crane

You have observed that the omniscient narrator, in the role of "interpreter," has an analytic approach, revealing inner thoughts not only

---

[33] Notice how the characters are introduced, each in his particular environment of the boat.

[34] Now you are introduced to the action of the boat.

[35] Stephen Crane, *The Open Boat and Other Tales of Adventure* (Garden City, N.Y., Doubleday, Page & Co., 1898).

through the speech and action of the characters but through reactions of the main characters. In some stories, the third-person narrator takes part in the action and indicates what he sees and hears but does not analyze motives. His point of view is therefore limited, inasmuch as he, unlike the correspondent in "The Open Boat," does not sense the innermost feelings of the characters. The third-person narrator relates in terms of what he observes the central character and others do and say. In James's "The Beast in the Jungle," which is too long for complete reprinting here but which should be read, you will find a story told by the third-person narrator. The title of the story is most apt, because the main character, John Marcher, through his lack of insight and his unbelievably selfish and egocentric responses to May Bartram, is oblivious to anything but his own jungle of thoughts. The clues occurring throughout are not emphasized, nor are they discussed. A portion of the first dialogue, beginning with the second meeting of John Marcher and May Bartram after a lapse of some ten years, will help you to understand the tone of the story. In this passage John Marcher is trying to recall their last conversation but realizes from her opening remark that May Bartram remembers more about it than he does. Finally, she supplies the link he had "frivolously managed to lose."

from *The Beast in the Jungle*

"You know you told me something I've never forgotten and that again and again has made me think of you since; it was that tremendously hot day when we went to Sorrento, across the bay, for the breeze. What I allude to was what you said to me, on the way back, as we sat under the awning of the boat enjoying the cool. Have you forgotten?"

He had forgotten and was even more surprised than ashamed. But the great thing was that he saw in this no vulgar reminder of any "sweet" speech. The vanity of women had long memories, but she was making no claim on him of a compliment or a mistake. With another woman, a totally different one, he might have feared the recall possibly even some imbecile "offer." So, in having to say that he had indeed forgotten, he was conscious rather of a loss than of a gain; he already saw an interest in the matter of her mention. "I try to think—but I give it up. Yet I remember the Sorrento day."

"I'm not very sure you do," May Bartram after a moment said; "and I'm not very sure I ought to want you to. It's dreadful to bring a person back at any time to what he was ten years before. If you've lived away from it," she smiled, "so much the better."

She waited as if it might come to him; but as, only meeting her eyes in wonder, he gave no sign, she burnt her ships. "Has it ever happened?"

Then it was that, while he continued to stare, a light broke for him and the blood slowly came to his face, which began to burn with recognition. "Do you mean I told you—?" But he faltered, lest what came to him shouldn't be right, lest he should only give himself away.

"It was something about yourself that it was natural one shouldn't forget— that is if one remembered you at all. That's why I ask you," she smiled, "if the thing you then spoke of has ever come to pass?"

Oh then he saw, but he was lost in wonder and found himself embarrassed. This, he also saw, made her sorry for him, as if her allusion had been a mistake. It took him but a moment, however, to feel it hadn't been, much as it had been a surprise. After the first little shock of it her knowledge on the contrary began, even if rather strangely, to taste sweet to him. She was the only other person in the world who would have it, and she had had it all these years, while the fact of his having so breathed his secret had unaccountably faded from him. No wonder they couldn't have met as if nothing had happened. "I judge," he finally said, "that I know what you mean. Only I had strangely enough lost any sense of having taken you so far into my confidence."

"Is it because you've taken so many others as well?"

"I've taken nobody. Not a creature since then."

"So that I'm the only person who knows?"

"The only person in the world."

"Well," she quickly replied, "I myself have never spoken. I've never, never repeated of you what you told me." She looked at him so that he perfectly believed her. Their eyes met over it in such a way that he was without a doubt. "And I never will."[36]

HENRY JAMES

EFFACED NARRATOR

The effaced narrator is appropriately named. He obliterates himself completely, and the resulting objectivity comes very close to the dramatic action found in a play. The story is not narrated; instead you watch the characters and hear their voices as they take their places center stage. You find little explanation of why something is happening, why a character speaks as he does or why he is part of the action. Description is limited to a few sentences, which, of course, must be powerfully and significantly expressive. No reflection is offered on the motivation of characters; supposedly the characters reveal motives as they go through their paces. The immediacy of action, characterization and episode presents a dramatic tone, as you will find in Hemingway's superb story of "The Killers." Without too much effort or change, this story could be produced easily as a play: it has a dramatic form consisting of several scenes made up mainly of dialogue. The few descriptive sentences characterize, colloquial speech rhythms characterize and mannerisms add their particular cultural meaning.

[36] Henry James, "The Beast in the Jungle," *The Novels and Tales of Henry James* (New York: Charles Scribner's Sons, 1961), v. 17, pp. 68-70.

Caroline Gordon, in *How to Read a Novel*,[37] reprints a well-known, dramatic scene from Flaubert's *Madame Bovary*, an excellent example of how the effaced narrator operates. This scene is reprinted here, translated, however, by Steegmuller. Emma, or Madame Bovary, has just received a note from her secret lover which says that he is renouncing her love and is on his way to a distant location. As Gordon writes, Flaubert does not tell you how Emma feels, but he does show her emotions as she stands at the window in the hot attic. You will get a tremendous empathic response merely by reading the passage to yourself. You will have the same hypnotic feeling that Emma has, as dazed by the intense, stifling heat and by the dazzling light streaming in from the attic windows, she looks at the paving stones below and feels drawn to the lathe, stridently humming its monotonous recurrent rhythm.

Here is the effaced narrator giving you the immediacy of the scene, revealing Emma's emotions and inner thoughts as she stands on the edge of the vast space, yet interposing none of his reactions or comments:

. . . she hurried on up the second flight of stairs, breathless, distracted, reeling, clutching the horrible piece of paper that rattled in her hand like a sheet of tin. At the third-floor landing she stopped outside the closed attic door.

She tried to calm herself: only then did she think of the letter. She must finish it—she didn't dare. Besides, where could she read it? How? She'd be seen.

"I'll be all right in here," she thought; and she pushed open the door and went in.

There the roof slates were throwing down a heat that was all but unbearable; it pressed on her so that she could scarcely breathe. She dragged herself over to the dormer, whose shutters were closed; she pulled back the bolt, and the dazzling sunlight poured in.

Out beyond the roof-tops, the open countryside stretched as far as the eye could see. Below her the village square was empty; the stone sidewalk glittered; weathervanes on the houses stood motionless. From the lower floor of a house at the corner came a whirring noise with strident changes of tone: Binet was at his lathe.

Leaning against the window frame she read the letter through, now and then giving an angry sneer. But the more she tried to concentrate, the more confused her thoughts became. She saw Rodolphe, heard his voice, clasped him in her arms; and a series of irregular palpitations, thudding in her breast like great blows from a battering ram, came faster and faster. She cast her eyes about her, longing for the earth to open up. Why not end it all? What was holding her back? She was free to act. And she moved forward. "Do it! Do it!" she ordered herself, peering down at the pavement.

The rays of bright light reflected directly up to her from below were pulling the weight of her body toward the abyss. The surface of the village square seemed to be sliding dizzily up the wall of her house; the floor she was standing on seemed to be tipped up on end, like a pitching ship. Now she was at the very edge, almost hanging out, a great emptiness all around her. The blue

[37] Caroline Gordon, *How to Read a Novel* (New York: The Viking Press, 1957), p. 108.

of the sky was flooding her; her head felt hollow and filled with the rushing of the wind: all she had to do now was to surrender, yield to the onrush. And the lathe kept whirring, like an angry voice calling her.[38]

GUSTAVE FLAUBERT, *Madame Bovary*

STREAM OF CONSCIOUSNESS

The stream-of-consciousness method is demonstrated brilliantly in the fiction of Joyce, Woolf, Proust and others. This technique probes deeply into the inner rationalization of thoughts, motives and actions. The stream flows between the outer manifestations of one's feeling and the dreamlike semiconscious state, revealing the deep recesses of thought and emotion that one tries to keep from the public eye. In other words, the story involves the inner revelation of one's own private way of handling decisions, actions and motives. Eliot's interesting character "Prufrock" (page 480) dares to reveal, but only to his ego, his troubled inner rationalization about the "big question." Joyce's masterpiece, *Ulysses*, is written skillfully with this technique. For an example of Woolf's use of it in her fictional works, consider the inner rationalization of Mabel in her heartbreak story, "The New Dress."

Mabel, forty and a mother of two children, receives an invitation to Mrs. Dalloway's party. Since she cannot be groomed fashionably as the other women, she decides to look charming in a pale yellow, old-fashioned dress—renovated. The scene at the party is a kaleidoscopic flow of Mabel's introspections concerning those who offer no comment about her charm or dress, even when she projects her doubts aloud by saying, "I feel like some dowdy, decrepid, dingy old fly." She rationalizes inwardly about her "creeping, crawling life"—just like that of a fly. Miserably she reads her own feeling of nonacceptance into the silence about her dress and the indifferent actions of the guests. She feels as she leaves, wrapping herself, "round and round and round, in the Chinese cloak she had worn these twenty years," just like the flies trying to "crawl over the edge of the saucer."

In this paragraph from the party scene, she identifies herself with the flies trying to crawl over the edge of the saucer: words that show how deeply a woman may crave acceptance.

"We are all like flies trying to crawl over the edge of the saucer," Mabel thought, and repeated the phrase as if she were crossing herself, as if she were trying to find some spell to annul this pain, to make this agony endurable. Tags of Shakespeare, lines from books she had read ages ago, suddenly came to her when she was in agony, and she repeated them over and over again. "Flies

[38] From MADAME BOVARY by Gustave Flaubert, translated by Francis Steegmuller. © Copyright 1957 by Francis Steegmuller. Reprinted by permission of Random House, Inc.

trying to crawl," she repeated. If she could say that over often enough and make herself see the flies, she would become numb, chill, frozen, dumb. Now she could see flies crawling slowly out of a saucer of milk with their wings stuck together; and she strained and strained (standing in front of the looking-glass, listening to Rose Shaw) to make herself see Rose Shaw and all the other people there as flies, trying to hoist themselves out of something, or into something, meagre, insignificant, toiling flies. But she could not see them like that, not other people. She saw herself like that—she was a fly, but the others were dragonflies, butterflies, beautiful insects, dancing, fluttering, skimming, while she alone dragged herself up out of the saucer.[39]

Virginia Woolf, The New Dress

POINT OF VIEW IN DRAMA

OBJECTIVE ATTITUDE

From the dramatic poem, discussed earlier, it is only a few steps to the objective and impersonal tone employed by the playwright as he places his characters in acting relation to one another. The dramatist writes his play, impregnating it with his philosophy by means of the thoughts and activity of his characters and hopefully leaving the interpretation, as conveyed by the actors, to his audience.[40] Interpretations will vary, depending on the temperament of the players, producers and listeners; for instance, Gielgud's vocal intonations and handling of his body in a Shakespearian play are quite different from those of Olivier or Burton. Consequently, the author may find that audience response differs from the reaction he anticipated.

After watching several productions of his play *Death of a Salesman,* Miller expressed surprise to observe some members of the audience moved to tears at the suicide of Willy, the struggling yet pitifully hopeful salesman. This reaction might mean that Miller, since he thinks of dramatic form as "organic," had "collapsed and drawn together" events into a tight sequence of frustrating incidents, heightened by dramatic and colloquial speech that could not be born except through emotional release. Instead of experiencing the death of Willy on an exalted level, the listeners had empathized into the emotions of this confused, bruised and tormented Willy. In other words, the ineffectual struggle was very close to the everyday experiences of futility in trying to reach a standard of success, of "saving face" before the great American public, of leaving, as Miller writes, "a thumbprint somewhere on the world." The empathy felt by the audi-

---

[39] Virginia Woolf, "The New Dress," *A Haunted House and Other Short Stories* (New York: Harcourt, Brace & World, Inc., 1944), pp. 48-49. Reprinted by permission.

[40] Note: In the chapter on Vocal Tempo, several recordings, interpreted by means of the "inner thought" technique, are listed.

ence of being pulled down into an abyss of failure while still groping for the ledge which might save them could not be restrained. The impact of a "small" man struggling against odds, instead of a "giant" of a man deteriorating, was so strong and so immediate that Willy's failure could well become an intensification of their failures. In witnessing the production, the audience probably did not immediately sense that Willy had a distorted hope of the kindness and helpfulness of people, nor that he was pushed beyond the world of stark reality into that dream-like misty world of his for relief, contentment—and escape.

In discussing the images that motivated this play, you will remember Miller relates how his structural images took form (page 55): "The play's eye was to revolve from within Willy's head, sweeping endlessly in all directions like a light on the sea, and nothing that formed in the distant mist was to be left uninvestigated. It was thought of as having the density of the novel form in its interchange of viewpoints, so that while all roads led to Willy the other characters were to feel it was their play, a story about them and not him."[41] These statements reveal the objectivity of a playwright. No direct clarification of an event is to be expected, except as the explanation comes from a character or as an incident shows the influence of some character's reaction. Supposedly speech and action should work toward the revelation of the playwright's meaning to show deterioration or growth of character; to capture certain characters in a vise through coincidence of events; to deplore social customs or to portray the humor of eccentric people. The dramatist plans stage directions for the producer and actors, not for the audience. He also manages his word grouping for nuances of speech, tone and movement. Then he steps out of the picture and the play must speak for itself.

CHOICE OF DRAMATIC TONE

Occasionally, a play is written in which the point of view is more direct than in the typical drama, as in Albee's *The Ballad of the Sad Cafe* or Williams's *The Glass Menagerie* or Wilder's *Our Town*. In the latter play, the Stage Manager assumes the personal tone of the first-person narrator, telling the story of a small American village, Grover's Corners. In his kindly, easeful way, the Manager ties together the crucial events of daily living as it revolves in its old patterns and changes with deaths, new life, new ventures and new habits. As the narrator, he sets the tone of poignancy throughout the play. In the scene reprinted below, he creates the mood of contentment, peace and serenity of the cemetery with his colloquial philosophizing about eternity, basic to the meaning of the play. When Emily's unsuccessful attempt to return to life occurs, the audience

[41] From DEATH OF A SALESMAN by Arthur Miller. Copyright © 1949 by Arthur Miller. Reprinted by permission of the Viking Press, Inc., pp. 29-30.

begins to sense—with her cry, "Oh, earth, you're too wonderful for anybody to realize you"—the wonder of real living is not appreciated. Wilder
has remarked that deeper than his idea is one that surprised him because he
had been unconscious of the importance he had attached to it: the concept
of "hundreds," "thousands," "millions" is repeated over and over throughout the play, giving the impression that the audience is observing that
town as through a telescope, showing a past of unbelievable perspective
and distance.[42]

You recall during Acts I and II, the audience is introduced to Grover's
Corners, New Hampshire, on a typical day, centering around activities of
the inhabitants of the town, but with attention mainly directed to the
Gibbs and Webb families. In Act II, Emily Webb and George Gibbs form
the center of interest because of their marriage. Act III, the beginning of
which is reprinted here, takes place in the cemetery at the top of the hill
overlooking Grover's Corners. Graves can be seen; and in the background
are several rows of chairs, to which those who have died within the last
nine years approach quietly and seat themselves, facing out mostly to the
audience. During this scene, they sit without stiffness and wait patiently.
This episode prefaces Emily's funeral as well as the poignant scene in
which she expresses her wish to return to the living. The Stage Manager,
usually smoking a pipe and wearing a hat, stands downstage near the
proscenium pillar.

from *Our Town*

STAGE MANAGER

This time nine years have gone by, friends—summer 1913.
Gradual changes in Grover's Corners. Horses are getting rarer. Farmers com-
ing into town in Fords.
Chief difference is in the young people, as far as I can see.
They want to go to the moving pictures all the time.
They want to wear clothes like they see there . . . want to be citified.
Everybody locks their house doors now at night. Ain't been any burglars in
town yet, but everybody's heard about 'em.
But you'd be surprised though—on the whole, things don't change at
Grover's Corners.
Guess you want to know what all these chairs are here fur. Smarter ones
have guessed it already. I don't know how you feel about such things; but this
certainly is a beautiful place. It's on a hilltop—a windy hilltop—lots of sky, lots
of clouds—often lots of sun and moon and stars. You come up here on a fine
afternoon and you can see range on range of hills—awful blue they are—up
there by Lake Sunapee and Lake Winnapassaukee . . . and way up, if you've
got a glass, you can see the White Mountains and Mt. Washington—where

42 *Paris Interview Series,* see p. 113.

North Conway and Conway is. And, of course, our favorite mountain, Mt. Monadnock's, right here—and all around it lie these towns—Jaffrey, 'n East Jaffrey, 'n Peterborough, 'n Dublin and there, quite a ways down is Grover's Corners.

Yes, beautiful spot up here. Mountain laurel and li-lacks. I often wonder why people like to be buried in Woodlawn and Brooklyn when they might pass the same time up here in New Hampshire.

Over in that corner are the old stones—1670, 1680. Strong-minded people that come a long way to be independent. Summer people walk around there laughing at the funny words on the tombstones . . . it don't do any harm. And genealogists come up from Boston—get paid by city people for looking up their ancestors. They want to make sure they're Daughters of the American Revolution and of the *Mayflower*. . . . Well, I guess that don't do any harm, either. Wherever you come near the human race, there's layers and layers of nonsense. . . . Over there are some Civil War veterans too. Iron flags on their graves. . . . New Hampshire boys . . . had a notion that the Union ought to be kept together, though they'd never seen more than fifty miles of it themselves. All they knew was the name, friends—the United States of America. The United States of America. And they went and died about it.

This here is the new part of the cemetery. Here's your friend Mrs. Gibbs. 'N let me see—Here's Mr. Stimson, organist at the Congregational Church. And over there's Mrs. Soames who enjoyed the wedding so—you remember? Oh, and a lot of others. And Editor Webb's boy, Wallace, whose appendix burst while he was on a Boy Scout trip to Crawford Notch.

Yes, an awful lot of sorrow has sort of quieted down up here. People just wild with grief have brought their relatives up to this hill. We all know how it is . . . and then time . . . and sunny days . . . and rainy days . . . 'n snow . . . tz-tz-tz. We're glad they're in a beautiful place and we're coming up here ourselves when our fit's over.

This certainly is an important part of Grover's Corners. A lot of thoughts come up here, night and day, but there's no post office. Now I'm going to tell you some things you know already. You know'm as well as I do, but you don't take'm out and look at'm very often. I don't care what they say with their mouths—everybody knows that *something* is eternal, and that something has to do with human beings. All the greatest people ever lived have been telling us that for five thousand years and yet you'd be surprised how people are always losing hold of it. There's something way down deep that's eternal about every human being.[43]

THORNTON WILDER

Later, in your study of vocal tempo, you may like to interpret this scene, but read the whole play first. If you do try it, watch the reminiscent quality of your voice; foremost should be attention to timing, pauses and sustained silences combined with facial and bodily expression appropriate for the character of the Stage Manager, and to the mood and atmosphere of the scene.

[43] From *Our Town* by Thornton Wilder. Copyright 1938 by Coward-McCann, Inc. Reprinted by permission of the publisher.

Tennessee Williams did not wait long in *The Glass Menagerie* to establish the tone of the drama, identified by him as a "memory" play. The stage directions describe a setting that suggests the atmosphere of "events passed," of unreality from which escape is impossible. Williams offers descriptions of his characters to prepare for the emotional impact at the beginning of the drama. If you have read the entire script, you will remember this is a play of voices, dealing hauntingly with innermost hurts and desolation because of desires never realized: the unsuccessful rebellion of Tom to achieve the free life of a poet; the inability of Laura, his crippled sister, to cope with her own futile life; and the failure of Amanda —a "little woman of great and confused vitality clinging frantically to another time and place"—to help her children, because of her selfish and thoughtless domination. Another character, a young man, appears in the latter part of the play to raise the hopes of Amanda for Laura and to give Laura a fleeting glimpse into a world she does not know. As Tom reports, this youth is symbolic of the world of reality for which they all long—the symbol of the "long delayed but always expected something that we live for." The dialogue in the play reveals the patterns of inner desires and motivations of the three main characters; even the picture of the long-lost father is realistically expressive of his smiling escape.

In having Tom serve as the narrator, Williams places himself in an objective position; in reality, of course, he is talking through the narrating Tom, a wishful poet with a job in a warehouse. Tom rebels against the web enmeshing him: his mother's delusions and memories of her younger days that have taken on unrealistic proportions; and the fragility of Laura's life as it is echoed in the sheltered care of her tiny glass pieces—symbolic of her cloistered living, easily broken (hurt), deformed, even shattered when handled carelessly by the young man who comes to call from the outside world.

The stage directions set the tone, and Tom, the narrator, opens the play, creating the atmosphere. Recall how Williams was motivated in writing this play (page 56). Listed below is an excellent recording of the play by Caedmon.[44]

from *The Glass Menagerie*

ACT I, SCENE 1

The Wingfield apartment is in the rear of the building, one of those vast hive-
like conglomerations of cellular living-units that flower as warty growths in
overcrowded urban centers of lower middle-class population and are symp-
tomatic of the impulse of this largest and fundamentally enslaved section

[44] *The Glass Menagerie* recorded by M. Clift, J. Harris, J. Tandy, D. Wayne. Caedmon TRS 301.

of American society to avoid fluidity and differentiation and to exist and function as one interfused mass of automatism.

The apartment faces an alley and is entered by a fire-escape, a structure whose name is a touch of accidental poetic truth, for all of these huge buildings are always burning with the slow and implacable fires of human desperation. The fire-escape is included in the set—that is, the landing of it and steps descending from it.

The scene is memory and is therefore nonrealistic. Memory takes a lot of poetic license. It omits some details; others are exaggerated, according to the emotional value of the articles it touches, for memory is seated predominantly in the heart. The interior is therefore rather dim and poetic.

At the rise of the curtain, the audience is faced with the dark, grim rear wall of the Wingfield tenement. This building, which runs parallel to the footlights, is flanked on both sides by dark, narrow alleys which run into murky canyons of tangled clotheslines, garbage cans and the sinister lattice-work of neighboring fire-escapes. It is up and down these side alleys that exterior entrances and exits are made during the play. At the end of TOM's *opening commentary, the dark tenement wall slowly reveals (by means of a transparency) the interior of the ground floor Wingfield apartment.*

Downstage is the living room, which also serves as a sleeping room for Laura, the sofa unfolding to make her bed. Upstage, center, and divided by a wide arch or second proscenium with transparent faded portieres is the dining room. In an old-fashioned what-not in the living room are seen scores of transparent glass animals. A blown-up photograph of the father hangs on the wall of the living-room, facing the audience, to the left of the archway. It is the face of a very handsome young man in a doughboy's First World War cap. He is gallantly smiling, ineluctably smiling, as if to say, "I will be smiling forever." . . .

The narrator is an undisguised convention of the play. He takes whatever license with dramatic convention as is convenient to his purpose.

TOM *enters dressed as a merchant sailor from the alley, stage left, and strolls across the front of the stage to the fire-escape. There he stops and lights a cigarette. He addresses the audience.*

TOM: Yes, I have tricks in my pocket, I have things up my sleeve. But I am the opposite of a stage magician. He gives you illusion that has the appearance of truth. I give you truth in the pleasant disguise of illusion.

To begin with, I turn back time. I reverse it to that quaint period, the thirties, when the huge middle class of America was matriculating in a school for the blind. Their eyes had failed them, or they had failed their eyes, and so they were having their fingers pressed forcibly down on the fiery Braille alphabet of a dissolving economy.

In Spain there was revolution. Here there was only shouting and confusion.

In Spain there was Guernica. Here there were disturbances of labor, sometimes pretty violent, in otherwise peaceful cities such as Chicago, Cleveland, St. Louis. . . .

This is the social background of the play.

Music.

The play is memory.

Being a memory play, it is dimly lighted, it is sentimental, it is not realistic.

In memory everything seems to happen to music. That explains the fiddle in the wings.

I am the narrator of the play, and also a character in it.

The other characters are my mother, Amanda, my sister, Laura, and a gentleman caller who appears in the final scenes.

He is the most realistic character in the play, being an emissary from a world of reality that we were somehow set apart from.

But since I have a poet's weakness for symbols, I am using this character also as a symbol; he is the long delayed but always expected something that we live for.

There is a fifth character in the play who doesn't appear except in this larger-than-life-size photograph over the mantel.

This is our father who left us a long time ago.

He was a telephone man who fell in love with long distances; he gave up his job with the telephone company and skipped the light fantastic out of town. . . .

The last we heard from him was a picture post-card from Mazarlan, on the Pacific coast of Mexico, containing a message of two words—"Hello—Good-bye!" and no address.

I think the rest of the play will explain itself. . . .

He divides the portieres and enters the upstage area. The interior has lit up softly and through the scrim we see Amanda and Laura seated at the table in the upstage area.

Tom, who finally escapes his unbearable life, comes back at the end of the play, haunted by the memory of Laura. Here is the poet speaking; listen to his rhythmical prose as he speaks again of the futility of living for Laura, who has no escape from her cloistered life with her glass menagerie and makes no effort to seek another life:

TOM: I didn't go to the moon, I went much further—for time is the longest distance between two places—

Not long after that I was fired for writing a poem on the lid of a shoe-box.

I left Saint Louis. I descended the steps of this fire-escape for a last time and followed, from then on, in my father's footsteps, attempting to find in motion what was lost in space—

I traveled around a great deal. The cities swept about me like dead leaves, leaves that were brightly colored but torn away from the branches.

I would have stopped, but I was pursued by something. It always came upon me unawares, taking me altogether by surprise. Perhaps it was a familiar bit of music. Perhaps it was only a piece of transparent glass—

Perhaps I am walking along a street at night, in some strange city, before I have found companions. I pass the lighted window of a shop where perfume is sold. The window is filled with pieces of colored glass, tiny transparent bottles in delicate colors, like bits of a shattered rainbow.

Then all at once my sister touches my shoulder. I turn around and look into her eyes. . . .

Oh, Laura, Laura, I tried to leave you behind me, but I am more faithful than I intended to be!

I reach for a cigarette, I cross the street, I run into the movies or a bar, I buy a drink, I speak to the nearest stranger—anything that can blow your candles out *(Laura bends over the candles.)*—for nowadays the world is lit by lightning! Blow out your candles, Laura—and so good-bye. . . *She blows the candles out.*

The scene dissolves.[45]

TENNESSEE WILLIAMS

A student who had interpreted this latter part of the play, paused a moment at the ending, then said: "And there my memory ends and your imagination begins." This was an impressive and conclusive remark for an interpretative presentation.

[45] From THE GLASS MENAGERIE by Tennessee Williams. Copyright 1945 by Tennessee Williams and Edwina D. Williams. Reprinted by permission of Random House, Inc.

5

Toward Patterns of Meaning

THE AUTHOR'S PATTERN

You are now in the midst of the most controversial phase of understanding literature—to paraphrase or not to paraphrase! Is it possible, ask some critics, to tear apart a selection and then put it back together again to regain the first impression? Many believe you should be satisfied with the enjoyment received from the sound of words and melody in poetry and from the suspense and characterization in prose. If a piece of literature, however, can stand the wear and tear of numerous critics over many years, it should not lessen the student's appreciation to try to understand the ways and means in which the writer creates impressions. If, however, you think of a selection only through paraphrasing and forget the total emotional impression, then you are squeezing the lines and forgetting the personality behind them.

"MENTION THE NAME: AND A MAN APPEARS"

No literature should be examined as anonymously created. Someone "lives" in the lines you enjoy. He is the poem, the story, the play, the essay; he fashioned the experience for you. What kind of person appears to you when you read the author's name? Is he a myth—some old "fellow" who lived a long time ago? If so, do you wonder how he lived and was known in his environment? Was he once young and spirited? Did he live in a world of "make-believe" or was he a person of active individuality? If he lives today, is he approachable, agreeable; does he have interesting ideas? Do you feel the life stream of the person who is giving you pleasure, or are you satisfied to accept the gift from an anonymous donor?

The person directing the pen over the page must be a unique individual to know: a Byron perhaps, with piercing gray eyes, arrogant, handsome; known as a tireless swimmer in rough water even though slightly lame, as an excellent horseman and as one perfectly groomed even to the point of initiating men's styles, but alas, one with a "gloom that was almost Satanic." Perhaps he is an Eliot, distinguished in mien, stooped in posture, certainly not the romantic Byronic type, but a poet and dramatist with a fine dramatic sense, even in his dissembling characterizations of "Practical Cats";[1] a Yeats, a mystic with the magic of fantasy; a Millay, who at nineteen years astounded the literary world with *Renascence;* a Crane, writer for newspapers and magazines after finishing two years of college and at twenty-four years, the author of the famous *The Red Badge of Courage* and of ten other volumes before his death at the age of twenty-nine.

You must wonder why events have directed and challenged these authors. What kind of person would Faulkner have been if he had lived in Manhattan? Why did Lindsay follow the heritage of minstrelsy to sing his ballads on his journeys? Would Masters's characters have found the same niche in Chicago or New York as in "Spoon River"? Why is Frost so unique? Marguerite Wilkinson in 1927 wrote that a post-Victorian imitator of the great Victorians would never have composed a line like "Something there is that doesn't like a wall." Rather he would have written, "A wall, I think, is quite superfluous!"[2] Why did Woolf and Hemingway find the hard, courageous way to die? Would Mansfield ever have become a critic for journals or have written the stories in *The Garden Party*, if she had not left the sheltered Beauchamp home of colonial pioneering stock in London and New Zealand to become the rebellious, lonely, restless, wandering soul, often destitute and always crippled with arthritic pain, happy and unhappy in her love for John Middleton Murry and always nervously motivated to write? On her tombstone is her answer in the words of *Hotspur:* "But I tell you, my lord fool, out of this nettle, danger, we pluck this flower, safety."[3] Porter,[4] on the other hand, did not start writing at nineteen years' of age as Mansfield did, yet she ran away from her home in New Orleans at sixteen years and married. At twenty-one, she reports, "I bolted again," and sang old Scottish ballads in Texas and Louisiana. Then she found work as a reporter in Chicago while "hashing" in a restaurant; ninety percent of her time was spent in "keeping her head above water" and ten percent in writing. She also tells of her trip to a movie studio to get a news story: how she got in the wrong line and soon found herself acting in a courtroom scene with Francis X. Bushman. She kept the acting job for a week at five dollars a day, then went back to the newspaper office, only to get fired. She now possesses one of the Pulitzer awards of 1966 for *The Collected Stories of Katherine Anne Porter.*

Who is this man Carl Sandburg, with a shock of white hair over one eye, who writes of rugged America and of Lincoln; was once a porter, scene-shifter, truck-handler and soldier; and who still likes to sing ballads?

---

[1] T. S. Eliot, *Old Possum's Book of Practical Cats* (New York: Harcourt, Brace & World, Inc., 1930).

[2] Marguerite Wilkinson, *New Voices* (New York: The Macmillan Company, 1927), p. 63.

[3] William Shakespeare, *King Henry IV, Part I*, Act II, Scene 3.

[4] *Paris Interview Series*, pp. 145-146.

Certainly one can admire the romantic Robert Browning, who found Elizabeth Barrett, an invalid, through her poetry and carried her off to Italy as his bride in spite of the furor caused by the elder Mr. Barrett. Read the dramatic scene, from *The Barretts of Wimpole Street*, of the first meeting between Browning and his future wife (page 536). If it is possible, listen to the beautiful voice of Katherine Cornell, who played the part of Elizabeth on the legitimate stage, in the recording of that scene.[5] For an outsider's point of view, read Woolf's *Flush*, a delightful story portraying Browning's courtship of Elizabeth Barrett as seen through the jealous eyes and sensitive feelings of her cocker spaniel, "Flush." On Browning's first visit to the Barrett home, Flush looked over this strange visitor: "Twisting his yellow gloves in his hands, blinking his eyes, well-groomed, masterly, abrupt, Mr. Browning strode across the room. He seized Miss Barrett's hand, and sank into the chair at her side. Instantly they began to talk." To Flush, a dog who had lived in the warmth, seclusion and stillness of Miss Barrett's room for four or five years, this "dark, taut, abrupt, vigorous man, with his black hair, his red cheeks, and his yellow gloves," was an enemy to be attacked. "The very sight of him, so well tailored, so tight, so muscular, screwing his yellow gloves in his hand, set his teeth on edge. Oh! to let them meet sharply, completely in the stuff of his trousers!" So thought Flush as he lay watching his arch enemy, the "hooded" man who had suddenly turned his world with Miss Barrett into turmoil, and more than that, had deprived him of Miss Barrett's undivided attention.[6]

Open the books on the library shelves and look further for some kinship with the writer. Let him come to life! Have you an animated picture, for instance, of Frost in action? Every description of him includes his whimsical manner, his droll expression, his amused detachment as if he were looking you over for a final impression. Watch him as he talks and John Holmes listens:

The man's talking presence is unforgettable. With one or two present for an evening, he starts all but flat on his back, deep in a big chair, in his house in Cambridge, or at the cabin near Bread Loaf. He looks tired; perhaps he is. But you learn never to underestimate the powerful physique, the durability, the tough-bodied liveliness of this old Roman. He begins, casting here and there with a question or two. Then as he warms up to his favorite occupation, he sits up a little, then more, until he is in full swing, carrying the evening away. He rumples his hair with a hand now and then. He likes to be easy when the occasion requires—and he will chuckle at the next thing he is going to say. The

[5] Caedmon, TC 1071. "Sonnets from the Portuguese" by Elizabeth Barrett Browning; and *The Barretts of Wimpole Street* by Rudolf Besier. Recorded by Katherine Cornell and Anthony Quayle.

[6] From FLUSH by Virginia Woolf, copyright, 1933 by Harcourt, Brace & World, Inc.; copyright, 1961, by Leonard Woolf. Reprinted by permission of the publishers.

deep-set eyes glint; the full lower lip pushes out; and some wise or wicked or very funny remark comes forth. He loves nothing better than to work away at his talking until he surprises himself into saying a new thing. He keeps this state of readiness of mind always.[7]

JOHN HOLMES, *Robert Frost*

You can imagine Frost enjoying himself in that state of readiness, when he once said to Untermeyer—"There are two types of realist. There is one who offers a good deal of dirt with his potato. And there is one who is satisfied with the potato brushed clean. I am inclined to be the second kind. To me, the thing that art does for life is to clean it, to strip it to form."[8]

The author is a personality worth knowing! Inasmuch as the person is usually shown in some aspects through his writing, you would be careless to ignore the individual behind the scenes. You may not always be helped in your interpretation, but your audience will doubtless be charmed to know something about the person who wrote for you and them. You will have added to your background of literary forms and points of view and to your general communicative spirit. When you mention a name, let a live person appear and not a shadow.

Although literary devices are important to an author, images, word connotations, sentence structure and metaphorical language cannot be combined mechanically if a literary creation is to grow in meaning or live a long life. Only the final merging and interweaving of one into another will result in an organic whole—and literature long remembered. Some writers, of course, build only around sound, others emphasize tone and rhythm, and some use imagery to establish a characteristic style. All these devices support the dominant idea and give distinct movement to the central meaning.

A poem, play or story was never intended to become a static unit; rather the writer hopes for a developing relationship of ideas, images and rhythm through a kind of metamorphosis. This organic growth changes with the times and experiences of people. The lines may have the same printed appearance, but they are revitalized as the centuries go by. So the author's idea that starts with the germ enlarges and, at times, assumes a growth even the writer had not expected—if he lives to appreciate the development. This organicity will continue to develop in relation to various living conditions of the era and to man's ever-changing environment. For instance, Donne's poetry has reached a high peak of interest in the present cultural climate, and Keats has boomed to a popularity among

---

[7] John Holmes, "Robert Frost," *The New York Times Book Review* (March 26, 1950), p. 220.

[8] Louis Untermeyer, *The Road Not Taken* (New York: Holt, Rinehart and Winston, 1951), p. 18.

university students which would have delighted the young poet. Eliot's poetry, when first published, was disparaged as unintelligible by many who were not ready for his range of thought, whereas now his work is greatly appreciated by those who enjoy the challenge it provides.

Since the medium through which you secure meaning consists of the action of words—their arrangement for rhythmical movement of ideas and their combination into phrases, images, metaphors and symbols that will connote meaning through your experiences—a brief summary of what the writer, especially the poet, can do with his medium to create meaning is next on the agenda. If you can learn something about the integration of literary devices for meaning in poetry, you will be able to identify their arrangement and impact in prose.

PATTERNS OF MOVEMENT IN POETRY

METRICAL PATTERN

The study of the mechanics of meter is not one of the main purposes of this volume. Unfortunately, the versification underlying rhythm is an intricate problem, due to present variations now imposed upon the structure of lines. Then, too, since disagreement concerning the proper scansion has always been a problem even among experts, too much time would have to be given to decisions unimportant to this study.

Any poet, even in writing free verse, establishes some kind of framework in order to discipline his writing within certain boundaries. He, like the architect, may have a blueprint of speech figures and a design showing the "footage" along with the number of words requiring special accent; the sketch, however, may not reveal how the whole will be personalized by the artistic treatment of the designer through the pattern of color and tone. Remember that in a poem, syllabic accents, contained within a certain number of metrical feet, give a dimensional base—one that is subordinated necessarily to the stress of sound, speech rhythm and meaning in the finished literary selection.

The poet has the privilege of reporting he has a five-foot line with two syllables in every foot, the accent on the second syllable of each foot —thus building the lines on "the basic English pattern" known as iambic pentameter. He will acknowledge, however, the irregularities within his metrical scheme in order to give the sound and sense stress he wishes to convey. The necessity, however, of placing the accent stress in a certain manner does not involve interpretation of meaning. Examine the customary marks of the second line of Gray's "Elegy" to be found in almost any book on prosody:

The lŏw|ĭng hérd | wĭnd slŏw|lў o'ér |thĕ léa

The general pattern here is typical: the word *wind* is unaccented and the unimportant word *o'er* is given the accent. If you read the line aloud, you will not be conforming to the sense stress of speech rhythm or to the flow of sound and meaning.

In contrast, Hopkins's marking of the sprung rhythm in "The Wind-hover" presents interesting sense accents: for instance, the sense of the phrase *dapple-dawn-drawn* is established through the accents:

> Ĭ caught│this mŏrn│ĭng, mŏrn│ĭng's mĭn│ĭŏn. kĭng-│
> dŏm ŏf dáy│light's daúph│ĭñ, dáp│plĕ- daw̆n- dráwn│Fál cŏn│
> ĭñ hĭs ríd│ĭñg.

The next line also shows understandable metrical accents with a sprinkling of unaccented syllables, typical of Hopkins's rhythm:

> Hígh theře│hów hĕ│rúñg ŭp│oñ thĕ reín│ŏf ă wímp│lĭñg wíng.

The following lines from a skilled maker of free verse could be slashed to pieces if the accent stress rather than the sense stress were followed. Whitman's lines,

> When lilacs last in the doorway bloom'd
> And the great star early dropp'd in the western sky at night,

would lose the rhythmical lilt and cadence if each syllable were isolated into a mechanical pattern. Furthermore, any study of phonetics emphasizes the elision and assimilation of sounds in American speech rhythm, not the isolation of each word. Even though highly poetic, Shakespeare's lines always follow the stress of speech rhythm blended into the poetic rhythm. For instance, read this short excerpt aloud, sensing the flow of sound and meaning:

> All the world's a stage,
> And all the men and women merely players,
> That have their exits and their entrances;
> And one man in his time plays many parts.

You may think this metrical point is being overstressed, but too many times the marks of scanning can be heard in interpretations, noticeably in the rigid sonnet form, with disastrous results for meaning.

If you enjoy beating out accents of a metrical design, then you should pursue your interest in a study of prosody. This procedure cannot be used as a substitute for interpretation. Eventually you will agree with Eliot, who remarks that, in the study of meter, he cannot tell why one line is good and the other bad; furthermore, he doubts the study of anatomy will "teach you how to make a hen lay eggs." He believes also the melody or rhythm of verse is not a "line by line matter"; rather it should pertain to the whole poem.[9]

[9] From T. S. Eliot, *On Poetry and Poets* (New York: Farrar, Strauss & Giroux, 1957), pp. 27 and 36.

According to reputable critics, the classical idea of consistent metrical patterns is on the wane. No longer is the once popular iambic pentameter of Chaucer's verse employed with regularity; nor is any other combination of *accent* stresses used consistently throughout one poem. The pulse and flow of *sense* stresses appear to be gaining prominence since greater diversity is noticeable in the syllabic accents forming the base of a poem. Somewhere, however, you have enjoyed learning the game of scanning: the iambic as in *Mărié;* the trochaic as in *Marÿ;* the anapestic as in *Mári-anne;* the dactyllic as in *Marilyn;* the spondee as in *Márée.* No stress for sense is needed in a repetitive, monotonous and mechanical directive. Listen to an instructor's voice in a women's gym class: *slǐde-kǐck, slǐde-kǐck, tuřn-kǐck, tuřn-kǐck, slǐde-kǐck, slǐde-kǐck* . . . and *ad infinitum* to *dismissed.*

In summary, the quantitative terms of this "dead pattern" appear no longer applicable to modern poetical forms. Ciardi gives the proper lift to the rhythmical spirit when he remarks that the traditional meters are "simply rules of thumb, any one of which may be violated by a master."[10] Pound is reported to have stated characteristically that the "first heave is to break the pentameter."

RHYTHMICAL PATTERN: SOUND

The cadences of rhythm will depend partially on sound heard through the many variations of rhyme: end-rhyme (rhyme at the end of the line); internal rhyme (rhyme within the line); initial rhyme or alliteration (repetition mainly on initial consonants, sometimes medial and final); identical rhyme (same word repeated); slant rhyme or near rhyme as in consonance (initial or final consonants are similar); assonance (repetition of identical or related vowels). All of these rhyme schemes can be found in Hopkins's "The Windhover" or in a number of poems in this book. Find them, read them aloud and note how the auditory pattern supports rhythm and intensifies meaning—and also gives pleasure.

RHYTHM: WORD QUANTITIES & PAUSES

Sound related to word quantities is extremely important to the enhancement of rhythm as well as to tone and mood: if the movement is to be quick, abrupt, bright or light, the poet will choose words with vowels short in quantity and consonants (plosives) that can be given a definite stroke, as *t, d, k, g, p, b.* This method of selection is called *cacophony.* If the movement is to be more slowly paced, the words will be chosen usually for their sonority of vowels, for measured heaviness of sound or for blending and smoothness. This method is called *euphony.*

[10] From DIALOGUE WITH AN AUDIENCE by John Ciardi. Copyright © 1958 by John Ciardi. Published by J. B. Lippincott Company, p. 253.

Gilbert, the great master of cacophony, makes fascinating use of the hard plosive sounds in the following:

> To sit in solemn silence in a dull dark dock,
> In a pestilential prison, with a life-long lock,
> Awaiting the sensation of a short, sharp shock,
> From a cheap and chippy chopper on a big black block!
> A big, black block, a short, sharp shock,
> From a cheap and chippy chopper on a big black block!
>
> W. S. GILBERT, *The Mikado*

This movement is quite different from that of Coleridge's lines, in which he makes use of sustained vowels:

> Alone, alone, all, all alone,
> Alone on a wide wide sea!
>
> SAMUEL TAYLOR COLERIDGE, *The Ancient Mariner*

In addition to the sound value through rhyme and word quantities, listen for the pause, the sound of silence. The poet often employs the caesura, the break, the pause within the line. Even though it may be almost imperceptible, the pause can change the lilt and melody of cadences; it can also give a clue to the rhythm. Shakespeare's lines establish through cacophony and pauses a light, gay rhythm:

> It was a lover and his lass,
>   With a hey, and a ho, and a hey nonino,
> That o'er the green corn-field did pass
>   In the spring time, the only pretty ring time,
> When birds do sing, hey ding a ding, ding;
> Sweet lovers love the spring.

Now contrast a stanza, characterized by euphony, from Sarett's *Wéeng:*

> If Wéeng-oosh comes at the end of this day,
> And finds you asleep he will hurry away . . .
> Do you hear him cry on the winds that blow?—
> And walk on the earth as soft as a doe?—
> To-and-fro . . . . to-and-fro . . .
> Hi-yah! he has crept away from my lap!
> For he found my little boy taking a nap."
> Oh, weep no more and whisper low,
> I hear the feet of Sleepy-eye go—
> Tip-toe . . . . tip-toe.[11]

[11] From *Covenant With Earth,* by Lew Sarett. Gainesville: University of Florida Press, 1956. Reprinted by permission of Mrs. Lew Sarett.

Instead of the smooth rhythm of the two preceding examples, you find in Dickinson's flash of remembrance, as expressed in these lines, a rhythm broken by pauses as she gropes for the recollection. Since the pauses, however, are not abrupt, the rhythm is sustained:

A Thought

A Thought went up my mind today—
That I have had before—
But did not finish—some way back—
I could not fix the Year—

Nor where it went—nor why it came
The second time to me—
Nor definitely, what it was—
Have I the Art to say—

But somewhere—in my Soul—I know—
I've met the Thing before—
It just reminded me—'twas all—
And came my way no more—[12]

EMILY DICKINSON

Closely allied to rhyme is *onomatopoeia,* or the use of word-symbols that echo their meaning in sound, such as *hiss, crackle, buzz, crunch, boom, snap, murmur.* Images are made memorable through the sensory reactions triggered by this type of associative words. They make vivid tone, mood and atmosphere, as well as rhythm. Added to these sound elements, of course, is the vocal manner in which you lift the words from the page to give them color, vividness, vitality and life, and thus move the poem into action.

The sound of your voice is equally important in creating intensity, vigor or lightness suggested by these aural values of words. So also must your own speech rhythm capture the elision of word combinations as they reflect the poet's rhythmical sensitivity. Since the poet must have felt the power of the words from their sound as well as their meaning, you must be able to re-create these audible values in order to draw the meaning into motion.

From these remarks, perhaps you can now understand that, unlike metrical pattern, rhythm cannot be considered in isolation; nor can images serve vividly in associative reactions unless you hear their rhythmical and sound values.

---

[12] Emily Dickinson, *The Complete Poems of Emily Dickinson* (Boston: Little, Brown and Company, 1960).

PATTERNS OF WORDS & MEANINGS

"WORDS, WORDS, WORDS!"

You may remember the famous short scene in *Hamlet* in which Polonius, ever-inquisitive and prying in his concern for Hamlet's sanity, makes a second approach to Hamlet, who apparently is lost in the contents of a book. He asks, "What do you read, my lord?" Hamlet, with a faraway, quizzical look on his face, lifts his eyebrows and, with revealing inflections and pauses, replies, "Words, words, words." Polonius, rebuffed once again, is amazed, to the delight of the audience. Seldom would you think these *three words,* so evidently flat and inconspicuous as printed, could evoke laughter—but Hamlet, the actor, does it with relish.

Perhaps many times in reading literature you will think "words, words and more words, and what do they mean?" Assuredly you are not alone in this predicament. This book could tell you the meaning of the words. Your search for the understanding of the author's thought, however, will be more profitable if you try to solve your difficulty; then seek critical explanation to make your final judgment more complete. In the following chapter, you will encounter analyses by literary critics, in which the desire is frequently expressed to know more about the writer's experiences as reflected in his images. These critics support the idea that meanings are often evoked according to the author's literary interests and philosophy. For instance, true appreciation of Hopkins's "Pied Beauty" is gained only after you have thumbed through his *Journals.* Then you will know how sensitively the poet watched every small change in color, shape, movement and form in natural life and how expertly he framed his philosophy of "inscape" in eleven lines.

From everyday comunications with friends you know that word relationships and grouping can shift emphasis in meaning, and stress on certain words can bring contrast of ideas and highlight characterizations. You will be exposed in these pages to analyses of poems, with the hope that if you have realized the importance of such details in the concentrated form of poetry, you will know how to look for them in broader, enlarged literary forms, such as the story, novel and drama. Even fiction writers and dramatists sometimes find the meaning they were hoping to express is not the one that finally evolves. For instance, remember Wilder's realization that instead of giving the impression of sensing life to the full as you live it in *Our Town,* he found he had emphasized unconsciously the enormous span of thousands and millions of years—of eternity—as the background. He also tells of receiving letters from interested people: some reported the play had been a great comfort to them, and others commented that the last act was almost too difficult to bear because of man's inability to "realize" life.[13]

When his novel *The Bridge of San Luis Rey* was published, he again received letters from organized groups with different philosophies, reading into the story their own beliefs and experiences.[14] A group of atheists, for instance, wrote the novel had provided an "artful exposure of shallow optimism." In reality, the author wanted to express his belief that the meaning of love over the centuries had acquired many new dimensions, extending beyond the love of man and woman into philanthropy and man's relationships with the order of the universe, and so had become a motivating force to help man better himself in his world of activity and beliefs.

To repeat, words mean according to your experiences. The ballad "Jabberwocky" is intriguing for its combination of nonsense syllables. They do not have to make sense (although they do) if you enjoy them, as one coed remarked, "for their tickling and associative combinations." In some intangible way you become a part of the details of the narrative executed with lavish strokes of sound and action.

Jabberwocky

'Twas brillig, and the slithy toves
    Did gyre and gimble in the wabe;
All mimsy were the borogoves,
    And the mome raths outgrabe.

"Beware the Jabberwock, my son!
    The jaws that bite, the claws that catch!
Beware the Jubjub bird, and shun
    The frumious Bandersnatch!"

He took his vorpal sword in hand:
    Long time the manxome foe he sought—
So rested he by the Tumtum tree,
    And stood awhile in thought.

And as in uffish thought he stood,
    The Jabberwock, with eyes of flame,
Came whiffling through the tulgey wood,
    And burbled as it came!

One, two! One, two! And through and through
    The vorpal blade went snicker-snack!
He left it dead, and with its head
    He went galumphing back.

[13] *Paris Interview Series,* p. 111.

[14] See also Arthur Miller's reaction to audience response in *Death of a Salesman,* p. 561.

> "And hast thou slain the Jabberwock?
> Come to my arms, my beamish boy!
> O frabjous day! Callooh! Callay!"
> He chortled in his joy.

> 'Twas brillig, and the slithy toves
> Did gyre and gimble in the wabe;
> All mimsy were the borogoves,
> And the mome raths outgrabe.

LEWIS CARROLL

As in any ballad—a form many think Carroll was satirizing—conflict is shown through the typical dialogue action: in this case a battle of some sort between the youth and the Jabberwock. Just what the battle is concerned with has never been decided exactly. Essays and books have been written indicating the poem means many things to many groups of people. Mathematicians, scientists, literary critics and philosophers have found allusions to their own professional deficiencies, as well as to their strengths, in this amiable satire. Children still enjoy it as a poem of fantasy with imaginative tonal effects, as do adults with a zany sense of humor. No matter what Carroll was satirizing, regardless of the meaning, you need a "frabjous," "Callooh! Callay!" spirit in interpreting the poem.

The narrative is not difficult to follow: it is about four o'clock in the afternoon—"brillig" or broiling time—when suddenly the "son" appears with vorpal sword in hand looking for the Jabberwock. After hunting a long time for the enemy, he finally rests in "uffish thought" under the "tum-tum tree," awaiting the creature with "jaws that bite" and "claws that catch." Eventually, the Jabberwock comes "whiffling" and "burbling" through the "tulgey wood." The youth's sword goes "snicker-snack" and the "beamish boy" goes "galumphing" back with head in hand. What fantastic words! What combinations suggesting action not only through their sound but through their connotative associations! In the sixth stanza you too "chortle" over the victorious outcome with "O frabjous day! Callooh! Callay!" The last stanza brings you back to the quiet scene with the toves, borogroves and raths going about their business of burrowing holes and building their nests. McCord comments in his humorous book *What Cheer* that the poem illustrates the fact that "the *sound* of Basic English translations of verse is older than Basic English," and then he proceeds to set the stage for Carroll's "Basic preview" of the poem. "It was evening, and the smooth active badgers were scratching and boring holes in the hillside; all unhappy were the parrots, and the green turtles squeaked out."[15]

Carroll explains how he packed two meanings into one word in this "frabjous" piece of satiric art:

[15] David McCord, *What Cheer* (New York: Coward-McCann, Inc., 1945), pp. 432-433.

Take the two words "fuming" and "furious." Make up your mind that you will
say both words but leave it unsettled which you will say first. Now open your
mouth and speak. If your thoughts incline ever so little towards "fuming," you
will say "fuming-furious"; if they turn, by even a hair's breadth towards "furious," you will say "furious-fuming;" but if you have that rarest of gifts, a perfectly balanced mind, you will say "frumious."

Today the word *brunch,* a combination of *breakfast* and *lunch,* is
quite acceptable in American speech; so are the words, *motel* or *motor*
plus *hotel,* and *smog* or *smoke* plus *fog.* The word *chortle* has also become
a part of our vocabulary.

Carroll elaborates more definitely in the scene between Alice and
Humpty Dumpty in *Through The Looking Glass:*

from *Humpty Dumpty*

"You seem very clever at explaining words, Sir," said Alice. "Would you
kindly tell me the meaning of the poem called 'Jabberwocky'?"

"Let's hear it," said Humpty Dumpty. "I can explain all the poems that ever
were invented—and a good many that haven't been invented just yet."

This sounded very hopeful, so Alice repeated the first verse:

> *'Twas brillig, and the slithy toves*
> *Did gyre and gimble in the wabe:*
> *All mimsy were the borogoves,*
> *And the mome raths outgrabe.*

"That's enough to begin with," Humpty Dumpty interrupted: "there are
plenty of hard words there. *'Brillig'* means four o'clock in the afternoon—the
time when you begin *broiling* things for dinner."

"That'll do very well," said Alice: "and *'slithy'?*"

"Well, *'slithy'* means 'lithe and slimy.' 'Lithe' is the same as 'active.' You see
it's like a portmanteau—there are two meanings packed up into one word."

"I see it now," Alice remarked thoughtfully: "and what are *'toves'?*"

"Well, *'toves'* are something like badgers—they're something like lizards—
and they're something like corkscrews."

"They must be very curious-looking creatures."

"They are that," said Humpty Dumpty: "also they make their nests under
sun-dials—also they live on cheese."

"And what's to *'gyre'* and to *'gimble'?*"

"To *'gyre'* is to go round and round like a gyroscope. To *'gimble'* is to make
holes like a gimblet."

"And *'the wabe'* is the grass-plot round a sun-dial, I suppose?" said Alice,
surprised at her own ingenuity.

"Of course it is. It's called *'wabe,'* you know, because it goes a long way
before it, and a long way behind it—"

"And a long way beyond it on each side," Alice added.

"Exactly so. Well then, *'mimsy'* is 'flimsy and miserable' (there's another portmanteau for you). And a *'borogove'* is a thin shabby-looking bird with its feathers sticking out all round—something like a live mop."

"And then *'mome raths'?*" said Alice. "I'm afraid I'm giving you a great deal of trouble."

"Well, a *'rath'* is a sort of green pig: but *'mome'* I'm not certain about. I think it's short for 'from home'—meaning that they'd lost their way, you know."

"And what does *'outgrabe'* mean?"

"Well, *'outgribing'* is something between bellowing and whistling, with a kind of sneeze in the middle: however, you'll hear it done, maybe—down in the wood yonder—and when you've once heard it you'll be *quite* content. Who's been repeating all that hard stuff to you?"

"I read it in a book," said Alice. "But I had some poetry repeated to me, much easier than that, by—Tweedledee, I think it was."

"As to poetry, you know," said Humpty Dumpty, stretching out one of his great hands, "*I* can repeat poetry as well as other folk, if it comes to that—"

"Oh, it needn't come to that!" Alice hastily said, hoping to keep him from beginning.

LEWIS CARROLL, *Through the Looking Glass*

With ingenuity, you may find other combinations:[16] *whiffle* could be a blend of *whistle* and *puffily; galumphing—galloping* and *triumphantly; frabjous—fragrant* and *joyous* or *fabulous* and *joyous; chortle—chuckle* and *snort.* What the *Jabberwock* is or means has never been explained. You immediately think of one who talks too much and without sense; it may refer to *jabs* and *whacker* (meaning *whopper* in colloquial British or something enormous). Perhaps you have some other ideas. Carroll may have been satirizing the use of pompous poetical language; he may have wished to present a mock-heroic ballad. Who is to know at what customs, what hypocrisies in philosophy and social culture his motley but intriguing array of connotative word sounds were pointed. He is a great satirist because he does not depend on the keen edge to get his point across to the reader.[17] Remember Alice saying in astonishment to the Duchess, "You're nothing but a pack of cards." One is reminded of Lorenzini's story of "Pinocchio," a delight for children but also the "best book ever written on child psychology," according to a well-known psychologist.

[16] Gardner in *The Annotated Alice* reports that many dictionaries now define the "portmanteau word" as a word that is packed, like a suitcase, with more than one meaning. To him, the great master of the portmanteau word is James Joyce, who uses them "by the tens of thousands" in *Finnegan's Wake* "(like the Alice books, a dream)." Among the "ten hundred-letter thunderclaps" that symbolize the fall of Tim Finnegan, is Humpty Dumpty, packed up in the seventh thunderclap: "Bothallchoracterschumminaroundgansumuminarumdrumstrumtruminahumptadumpwaulttopoofoolooderamaunsturnup!" From *The Annotated Alice* by Lewis Carroll; ed. by Martin Gardner (New York: Clarkson N. Potter, Inc., 1960), p. 271.

[17] *Ibid.,* p. 88, for discussion of one of the most quoted passages in the *Alice* books. Throughout this work note how extensively Carroll's ingenuity applies to the philosophies of many professions.

MEANING: DENOTATIVE & CONNOTATIVE

Words can be expressed very simply to carry an impression of reality, but they can also be so alive with feeling that they create a memorable experience for you. They must "talk," they must act on you so you can empathize with the emotion they offer. Then, too, words, like all literature, can have more than one meaning: the denotative definitions, found in the dictionary, identifies a word syntactically and in its different concepts; the connotative meaning is the emotional meaning, the meaning associated with your experiences and found in your memory, your imagination and your heart. *Susan* is just a name attached to any girl until you meet *the* Susan; then the name becomes everything your Susan *is* or seems to be to *you*.

Knowing the denotation of words is the first step necessary to the basic meaning of literature, to the explicit obvious impression. Superimposed on this stated factual information is the suggestive association, giving tone, mood and atmosphere—that is, the emotional tinge. Word connotations offer implied comparisons and feelings, because they are stimulated by previous experiences not indicated in the printed symbol. The sentence, "He is a nice man," may be a statement of fact; but who, except the person who writes it, can know exactly what thought is involved. *Nice* has various denotative meanings—pleasant, precise, subtle, accurate, refined in manners, proper—and certainly can stir up various connotative meanings according to the emphasis and inflection you choose to employ. This unexpressed meaning causes differences in impressions in interpretative speech.

Very often the dictionary goes beyond the denotative meaning, as in the word *dog:* (1) a domesticated carnivore, bred in a great many varieties; (2) any animal belonging to the same family; (3) any of the various animals suggesting the dog, as the prairie dog; (4) *a gay dog;* (5) any of the various mechanical devices, as for gripping or holding something; (6) *go to the dogs: colloq.,* to go to ruin; (7) *put on the dog: colloq.,* to behave pretentiously; put on airs. The slang expressions, called *colloquial,* have more than a mere denotative meaning, for they have attached to their denotation, through emotional associations and reactions, a way of living, of experiencing, hence they become connotative in meaning. To you a *dog* is more likely to be a playmate of the woods, fields or streams—something for you to love and cuddle. An *automobile* is a kind of locomotive machine, and also your cherished companion on many adventures. A *plane,* especially in wartime, is not merely a mechanical automaton to the pilot and his crew but is a symbol of "life" and "luck," and becomes charged with emotion as it is identified and personalized with their experiences. *Home* is a place of residence but is not easily separated from a particular spot loaded with memories and feelings.

In the following excerpts, the differences in connotation suggested by the word *home* are marked. Does any one of them connote your feeling of *home?*

YANK: It must be great to stay on dry land all your life and have a farm with a house of your own with cows and pigs and chickens, 'way in the middle of the land where yuh'd never smell the sea or see a ship. It must be great to have a wife and kids to play with at night after supper when your work is done. It must be great to have a home of your own, Drisc.[18]

EUGENE O'NEILL, *Bound East for Cardiff*

Willie John had been home for a month and he had made no move toward returning—not that it was ever out of his mind for an instant, but it pleased him to stay there and savor the ripe mellowness of everything as he might savor a fruit. Summer was fairly in and the yellow blossoms had fallen from the gorse, but roses were blooming in every garden, great creamy ones and others with the vivid red of an autumn sunset.

The horse-chestnuts were heavy with balloons of white flowers, and every evening the bees returned drowsy from the heather of the purple mountains. There was something in it all that he had missed for years and that he was greedy for.[19]

BRIAN DONN-BYRNE, *The Barnacle Goose*

MRS. KEENEY: My memory is leaving me—up here in the ice. It was so long ago. . . . It's June now. The lilacs will be all in bloom in the front yard at home—and the climbing roses on the trellis to the side of the house—they're budding.[20]

EUGENE O'NEILL, *Ile*

"Home is the place where, when you have to go there,
They have to take you in."
"I should have called it
Something you somehow haven't to deserve."[21]

ROBERT FROST, *The Death of the Hired Man*

LYDIA (*half in reverie, is speaking of her feelings during Mass at St. Eustache*):
If I cried just now in church it wasn't for the reason that you thought. . . . I felt so lonely. All those people, they have a country; and in that country, homes; to-morrow they'll spend Christmas Day together, father and mother and children; some of them, like you, went only to hear the

[18] Eugene O'Neill, "Bound East for Cardiff," *Plays of Eugene O'Neill* (New York, Liveright Publishing Corp., 1926), p. 236.
[19] Brian Donn-Byrne, "The Barnacle Goose," *The Changeling and Other Stories* (New York: Meredith Press, 1923), p. 65.
[20] Eugene O'Neill, "Ile," *Plays of Eugene O'Neill* (New York: Liveright Publishing Corp., 1926), p. 308.
[21] Robert Frost, "The Death of the Hired Man," *Collected Poems* (New York: Holt, Rinehart and Winston, Inc., 1964), p. 49.

music, and some have no faith, but just then, all of them, they were joined together by a common feeling. . . . it is part of the recollections of their childhood, the gardens they played in, the countryside, the streets of the towns. It binds them together, it makes them one, and some deep instinct tells them that they belong to one another. But I am a stranger. I have no country, I have no home, I have no language. I belong nowhere. I am an outcast.[22]

W. Somerset Maugham, *Christmas Holiday*

In the passage below, Duffus challenges you to give the meaning of some words. Try out the list of words among members of your interpretative group for meanings.

What, if you pardon my asking, does the word "Bolshevik" mean to you? Or "Nordic"? Or "Jew"? Or "Catholic"? Or "German"? Or "Mexican"? Or "tariff"? Or "pacifist"? Or "militarist"? Or "Prohibition"? . . . Or "motion picture"? Or "chewing-gum"? Or any one of a thousand other words?

One answer you may safely make. They do not mean the same to you that they do to me, or to your uncle, your wife, your next-door neighbor, . . . or the milk man. We assume that there is such a thing as the English language—and perhaps there is. But each of us speaks a different dialect. All we say is like an imperfectly heard conversation over the telephone. The connection is always poor. We are always getting the wrong number. This is because every important word has to carry around, in addition to its dictionary definition, the meaning that each one of us has attached to it as the result of his life's experiences. "Automobile" signifies one thing to a man who is in the hospital recovering from an argument with one, and quite another to a man who has just made a successful speculation in General Motors.[23]

Robert Duffus, *Where Do We Get Our Prejudices*

ALLUSIONS

Authors add meaning to their literary work by the use of allusions. A word or phrase that, either directly or by implication, refers to a past event or is quoted from some familiar literary or historical source adds interest and significance to a passage. Speakers of this generation still like to arouse their audience emotionally by recalling a fighting Churchill and his famous phrase "blood, sweat and tears"; or they enjoy using the phrase "at long last," first heard when King Edward VIII of England abdicated the throne. Lincoln's "government of the people, by the people and for the people" frequently brings applause. Often today you will use clichés that

[22] From "Christmas Holiday" copyright 1939 by W. Somerset Maugham. From THE MAUGHAM READER. Reprinted by permission of Doubleday & Company, Inc., p. 1014.
[23] Robert Duffus, "Where Do We Get Our Prejudices," *Harper's Magazine* (September, 1926), p. 503.

recall the plays of the great sixteenth-century dramatist Shakespeare: "milk of human kindness"; "who steals my purse steals trash"; "what fools these mortals be"; "all the world's a stage"; "midsummer madness"; "keep a good tongue in your head"; "every inch a king"; "there's a small choice in rotten apples"; "that which we call a rose by any other name would smell as sweet"; "it was Greek to me"; "some are born great, some achieve greatness, and some have greatness thrust upon them."

The interpreter should be sufficiently alert to recognize words and phrases that in currently accepted usage have come to carry allusions to some habit or action among people or to some phase of man's customs or social adjustment. In his enlightening book on language, Mario Pei[24] cites idioms and words that shows such an evolution: *don't give a rap* refers to an Irish counterfeit halfpenny of an early century, known as *rap; don't give a continental* is a reference to one of our early monetary units; *spud* was formed from the initials of the title of an organization of Englishmen who did not like potatoes and so called themselves the Society for the Prevention of Unwholesome Diet"; *salary* alludes to salt money, having its origin in the Roman custom of paying part of the soldier's wages in salt, much needed to preserve perishable foods in ancient and medieval times; *square meal,* a typical American idiom, alludes to the New England custom of preparing food in square tins in the eighteenth century; *Mardi Gras* is French for *fat Tuesday,* referring to the last day on which fat food (that is, meat) may be eaten before Lent; *propaganda,* today used almost exclusively in the political sense, comes from the Catholic organization known as *Congregatio de Propaganda Fide,* meaning "Congregation for the Propagation of the Faith," or, more literally, "the faith to be propagated."

Idioms that allude directly to certain American activities are prevalent today: "according to Hoyle," "behind the eight-ball," "to pinch hit for another," "hit-and-run drivers," "to jump the gun." Nor is it unusual to hear phrases indicating manner or disposition: "he was Janus-faced," "he had a Rotarian manner," "he had a Midas touch," "he was no Pegasus," "he had an Achilles heel." The *dark horse,* glibly used today in campaigns and races, may have had its origin from Disraeli, who in 1831 wrote: "A dark horse, which had never been thought of, and which the careless St. James has never observed in the list, rushed past the grand stand in sweeping triumph." The *kiss of death,* often used in connection with a present-day newspaper syndicate, originated with Alfred Smith, who used the expression in alluding to the support of W. R. Hearst for Ogden Mills, who campaigned unsuccessfully for the governorship of New York State in 1926. The term *iron curtain* is sometimes credited to Winston Churchill, who, in an address at Westminster College in 1946, said: "An iron curtain has

[24] Mario Pei, *The Story of Language* (Philadelphia: J. B. Lippincott Company, 1949), pp. 201-233.

descended across the Continent." In reality, however, the expression was first used by Hitler's ministers, Goebbels and von Krosigk. History will probably record this period in which you are living as the "Space Age," an allusion vastly different from that evoked by the phrase "The Gay Nineties."

You are acquainted with many of the following statements that have become clichés, but do you know who said them?

1. Tell that to the marines—the sailors won't believe it.—SIR WALTER SCOTT
2. What a sight for sore eyes that would be!—WILLIAM HAZLITT
3. Fat, fair and forty.—SIR WALTER SCOTT
4. I git thar fustest with the mostest men.—NATHAN B. FORREST
5. The reports of my death are greatly exaggerated.—MARK TWAIN
6. She's no chicken; she's on the wrong side of thirty, if she be a day.—JONATHAN SWIFT
7. All the world is queer save thee and me, and even thou art a little queer.—ROBERT OWEN
8. Neat, not gaudy.—CHARLES LAMB
9. He was not merely a chip of the old block, but the old block itself.—EDMUND BURKE
10. We must all hang together, or assuredly, we shall all hang separately.—BENJAMIN FRANKLIN
11. She looks as if butter wouldn't melt in her mouth.—JONATHAN SWIFT
12. Let sleeping dogs lie.—CHARLES DICKENS
13. In this world nothing is certain but death and taxes.—BENJAMIN FRANKLIN
14. Keep cool: it will be all one a hundred years hence.—RALPH WALDO EMERSON
15. She has more goodness in her little finger than he has in his whole body.—JONATHAN SWIFT

EPIGRAPHS

One form of allusion is the epigraph, or quoted material usually found at the beginning of a literary work, which suggests the ensuing theme and symbolic relationships. Eliot often supports his meaning by this device. In "The Hollow Men" (see page 387) he underscores his title with two epigraphs: (1) *Mistah Kurtz—he dead,* a reference you will not appreciate until you have read Conrad's *The Heart of Darkness* and can then understand the despair of Kurtz, the man who succumbed to the savagery of the jungle and whose death was announced by one of the steamer helpers; (2) *A penny for the Old Guy,* referring to Guy Fawkes Day in England, at which time straw effigies of Guy Fawkes, the man who initiated the Gunpowder Plot to blow up the House of Commons, are sold for a penny. This same literary device will intrigue you in "The Love Song of J. Alfred Prufrock" (see page 480) in which six lines from Dante's *Inferno* give overtones of meaning. An understanding of the significance of Benét's epic, *John Brown's Body* (see page 365), entails knowledge of the history of Brown's raid at Harper's Ferry and of his trial in which he was declared guilty and executed, even though he pleaded innocence. Hemingway also uses the epigraph indirectly by titling one of his novels *For Whom the Bell Tolls.* This phrase originates in Donne's "Devotion XVII" in a well-known excerpt that expresses the author's philosophy:

No man is an island, entire of itself; every man is a piece of the Continent, a part of the Main; if a Clod be washed away by the Sea, Europe is the less, as well as if a Promontory were, as well as if a Manor of thy friends or of thine own were; any man's death diminishes me, because I am involved in Mankind; and therefore never send to know for whom the bell tolls; it tolls for thee.

JOHN DONNE, Devotion XVII

Familiarity with the paragraph above sharpens and deepens the meaning of Hemingway's novel.

IRONY & PARADOX

To discuss thoroughly the literary devices that intensify literature is impossible in this book; however, the terms *irony* and *paradox,* based on contrasts, should be a part of your vocabulary. Briefly, irony involves a duality of possible meanings, insofar as words mean one thing as printed or said, and another thing to the person reading or listening. It can take the form of understatement, which has the impact of a shock at times, or it can be managed through overstatement of an idea. Irony should not be mistaken for sarcasm, which involves ridicule. As an interpreter, you will realize much depends on vocal inflections and pauses to convey the double meaning basic to irony of statement.

The playwright also likes to achieve a startling effect through irony of situation—as do fiction writers. This ironic situation occurs when the opposite happens from what is expected on the basis of preceding incidents. Robinson, in his poem "Richard Cory," uses irony of situation; Hardy employs the device in "Ah, Are You Digging On My Grave?" Check also Shelley's "Ozymandias." Suckling's "The Constant Lover" shows a light touch of irony with "tongue-in-cheek": note the title and then the twist of the lines.

The author also employs contrast of ideas, characters and events by means of paradox—a contradictory statement that seems to be true. In other words, some idea may be expressed that appears to contradict another idea and yet may state a truth. Paradox can be based on irony, which, if accomplished with finesse, will leave the reader stunned, incredulous until the whole idea is grasped. Lovelace's famous lyric will demonstrate the clever use of paradox better than a longer literary selection at this point. In a later chapter Brooks's discussion of paradox in Keats's "Ode on a Grecian Urn" will interest you.

To Lucasta, Going to the Wars

Tell me not, Sweet, I am unkind,
    That from the nunnery
Of thy chaste breast and quiet mind
    To war and arms I fly.

True, a new mistress now I chase,
    The first foe in the field;
And with a stronger faith embrace
    A sword, a horse, a shield.

Yet this inconstancy is such
    As you too shall adore;
I could not love thee, Dear, so much,
    Loved I not Honor more.

RICHARD LOVELACE

PATTERNS OF METAPHORICAL LANGUAGE IN POETRY

IMAGERY

Most people like words that *do* things to them—muscularly or empathically; they like words that make them *feel*, rather than words used merely for identification. A textbook can be dull if every page is full of definitions, scientifically designed to clarify content rather than associate a new idea with an old. You enjoy the feeling of elation, the compulsion to react, precipitated by figurative language interestingly chosen to stir up earlier associations. Knowing this psychological power of recall, the poet and prose writer stimulate through the memory of impressive images.

What is an image? For a moment, imagine you are looking at a sunset glowing behind a high mountaintop. You stand enthralled, moved by the ever-changing harmony of light and color: red and orange melting into green and mauve, deep purple blending gradually into the dusky blue of the evening sky. You are experiencing impressions of sight, warmth, color; these are your sensations. You have also recognized the object of your attention as the sunset; this is your perception, the act of taking in, of perceiving, an object or shape. The scene shifts. Now sitting alone in your room, you close your eyes and think of that sunset. You will find you are able to reproduce it, not in its fullest details but in your recollection of its myriad of colors. This reproduction is called an image and serves as a substitute for the direct sensation and perception. You store these images in your memory; eventually in reading literature or in hearing someone speak in an unusual manner you will recall a certain association connected with an image, adding to your insight of the moment.

The greatest difficulty in securing meaning from images arises from the diversity of sensory appeal aroused in you, according to your experiences. The recall will exist for you only insofar as it revitalizes some association. For each interpreter, the image planned by the writer may be different; the image stimulated in you may not be the one intended by the author or the one experienced by another interpreter. Your aim should be to reproduce as fully as possible the author's intention, to recapture his hoped-for impression. Care must be taken not to misinterpret his meaning without good reason. An image of a cat may stir unpleasant emotions in some—claws, an arched back and a body that seems not to hang together inside; to others, the soft purr and cuddling nature of a cat are most pleasant. As someone has said, the "red, red rose" may not call up the same image to you that it did for Burns; furthermore, you may prefer the orchid image, depending on the girl who is so loved.

Images, then, have emotional value because of what they do to you sensorily and are usually grouped in the following categories: *visual*—images of color, shape, hue; *kinesthetic*—images of movement, action; *auditory*—images of sound; *tactile*—images of pressure, touch, contact (sharp, hard, soft, wet, moist, blunt); *thermic*—images of temperature (hot, cold, warm); *olfactory*—images of smell; *gustatory*—images of taste (sweet, sour, bitter). Images of pain, hunger, thirst and equilibrium, sometimes placed in another category, may also be classified under *kinesthetic* and *tactile* images, whereas images of hunger and thirst fall under *gustatory* images.

Be alive to your interpretation of sensory impressions: the warmth of a slowly burning log fire, the cold tang of a wintry blast, the hazy, mysterious autumn nights; the blue-white of a brilliant moon; the shell-like pink of the Peace rose. How do you react to these images: "the rough male kiss of blankets"; the "scythelike interference" of the "swivel-hipped" football captain; they were struggling in "abysmal goo"; the "ground-devouring" quarterback "churned through the middle" for six points; "clogging weeds enwreathed and held him back with evil embrace"; "he argued, he cajoled, he threatened, he thundered, he exploded, he blazed, he fairly dazzled"; "the blue bitter smoke of wood"; "butter-ball legs under a butter-ball body"; "twenty-four years remind the tears of my eyes"; "now as I was young and easy under the boughs"; "silver filaments, golden flakes settling downward"; "The barge she sat in, like a burnish'd throne,/ Burned on the water: the poop was beaten gold"; "cancer cells/Sinister shapes with menacing attitudes"; "the hectic dance of the passionate cancer cells"? These images evoke sensory associations, arouse emotional reactions; capture, if you can, the awareness of the kinesthetic, tactile, visual —especially color—and sound experiences. Not only will you feel the desire to reread when you discover what the images *do* to you but your audience will also delight in the sensory reaction.

Images create the tone, atmosphere and mood of a poem, story or play and support the rhythmical cadences. They can also indicate action without a description of it. Turn back to Keats's "The Eve of St. Agnes" with its lush imagery. Read some lines aloud to note how vivid the sensory input is.

In contrast, one of the finest examples of how imagery can be inherent in the dramatic action of a poem is demonstrated by Browning in two companion lyrics. Instead of the luxuriant images of Keats's poem, this swift and emotional action is contained in sixteen lines.

Meeting at Night

The gray sea and the long black land;
And the yellow half-moon large and low;
And the startled little waves that leap
In fiery ringlets from their sleep,
As I gain the cove with pushing prow,
And quench its speed i' the slushy sand.

Then a mile of warm sea-scented beach;
Three fields to cross till a farm appears;
A tap at the pane, the quick sharp scratch
And blue spurt of a lighted match,
And a voice less loud, through its joys and fears,
Than the two hearts beating each to each!

ROBERT BROWNING

Parting at Morning

Round the cape of a sudden came the sea,
And the sun looked over the mountain's rim:
And straight was a path of gold for him,
And the need of a world of men for me.

ROBERT BROWNING

These images suggest vividly the story, never stated directly in narrative form. You know what the lover is doing, seeing and feeling through dramatic phrases conveyed by the imagery. You follow him sensorily: "gray sea," "long black land," "yellow half-moon," "startled little waves that leap in fiery ringlets"—images that reveal the time of night, mode of travel and environment, and also create atmosphere. The next stanza gives you the feeling of eagerness, urgency and suspense, ending with "tap at the pane," "quick sharp scratch," sudden illumination of a "blue spurt of a lighted match"—and the meeting of the lovers. The action moves continually and dramatically through images only Browning could create.

The tone of "Parting At Morning" has changed, as well as the movement of the four lines. The poet does not elaborate as Keats does in "The Eve of St. Agnes"; nevertheless an impression of a dramatic event, seldom equalled in restraint except in Frost, is sensed. When asked at one time what the relationship of love is in the two poems, Browning remarked the second poem is man's admission of how fleeting is the belief that such raptures are as enduring and sufficient as they appear at the moment.

Now consider again the images that motivated Arthur Miller to write *Death of a Salesman;* consider, too, Tennessee Williams's recollection of his sister's room in *The Glass Menagerie;* remember the images in *The Open Boat*. In fact, most of the literary selections in this text are built on vivid imagery, which makes for the best interpretative material.

If writers were satisfied with simple, sensory imagery, your difficulties in understanding would not be too great. Authors enjoy, however, interrelating images so that the meaning is expressed implicitly by means of a simile, metaphor or symbol, with personification usually merged into these three distinctive types. Literature today is sometimes troublesome to understand because of the intricacies involved in the extension of meaning through the use of metaphorical language. If the meaning is obscure, be sure you know the denotative meanings, in order to solve the literary puzzle through the black and white meaning and arrangement of words, phrases, images. You will then begin to add color to the black and white by building connotative values through your experiences. As you come to an image that seems to be out of place, see if it fits into the pattern of the preceding image in some unusual way you had not realized. Sometimes you need the one extra idea to make the puzzle complete; and it may be you never will understand completely the meaning, especially in poetry. In fiction, this difficulty is not so great because explanations of why some action happens or why some character speaks as he does usually are woven into the story by the narrator and by the way events happen and the climax is reached.

SIMILE

Since you may have forgotten the distinguishing characteristics of the simile, metaphor and symbol, a short time given to definitions may be profitable. A simile is not difficult to identify, inasmuch as it involves the explicit likening of one thing, characteristic or person to a natural object, usually by employing the words *like* or *as* to indicate the similarity. Hopkins and Housman can provide you with two interesting language similes:

Language rich as clotted cream—GERARD MANLEY HOPKINS

English language as clear and pure as water—A. E. HOUSMAN

Which of the following are most vivid in their connotative power?

Over your cheeks old Wéeng will go,
With feet as soft as the falling snow—
LEW SARETT

Kindness as large and plain as the prairie's wind
STEPHEN VINCENT BENÉT

I could a tale unfold whose lightest word
Would harrow up thy soul, freeze thy young blood,
Make thy two eyes, like stars, start from their spheres,
Thy knotty and combined locks to part
And each particular hair to stand on end,
Like quills upon the fretful porpentine.
SHAKESPEARE

I saw Eternity the other night.
Like a great ring of pure and endless light,
    All calm, as it was bright;
And round beneath it, Time, in hours, days, years,
    Driven by the spheres
Like a vast shadow moved;

.   .   .   .

The darksome statesman, hung with weights and woe,
Like a thick midnight fog moved there so slow,
    He did not stay nor go.
HENRY VAUGHAN

Thou, from whose unseen presence the leaves dead
Are driven, like ghosts from an enchanter fleeing,
Yellow, and black, and pale, and hectic red,
Pestilence-stricken multitudes.
PERCY BYSSHE SHELLEY

My heart is like a singing bird
CHRISTINA ROSETTI

For thoughts like waves that glide by night
Are stillest when they shine.
OWEN MEREDITH

Thine arms are as young saplings under the bark
Thy face as a river of lights.

EZRA POUND

When the evening is spread out against the sky
Like a patient etherized upon a table;

T. S. ELIOT

Pocahontas's body, lovely as a poplar, sweet as a red haw in
November or a pawpaw in May, did she wonder?

CARL SANDBURG

He clasps the crag with crooked hands;
Close to the sun in lonely lands,
Ringed with the azure world, he stands.

The wrinkled sea beneath him crawls;
He watches from his mountain walls,
And like a thunderbolt he falls.

ALFRED TENNYSON

METAPHOR

The metaphor is an implied likeness or similarity, such as "You have a heart of gold" and "She's a modest violet." Writers of this era are inclined to suggest indirectly through metaphorical language rather than through direct statement. Often a metaphor is extended throughout a selection to become the dominant metaphor, called a symbol. The less perceptive reader may not always realize the meaning is centered in an extended metaphor and may therefore miss certain overtones and implications. Thomas tells how the center of his poems exists in a "host of images": the poem begins with one image, is intensified by a contradictory image, which results in a third image absorbing the first two images. For this reason you will need to study his lines intensely to decode the meaning. Many critics praise this kind of literary writing, likening it to motifs that are built into the theme of a musical composition. So in the writing of literature, authors repeat, reinforce, supplement and blend images to support the incidents, characters and action in order to sharpen the central meaning. Sensitivity to key phrases and imagery must be acquired as well as attentiveness to the direction in which the words move.

This language problem should not be too difficult, inasmuch as you belong to a metaphor-loving people who enjoy unusual word groupings. Hayakawa makes some interesting comments about metaphoric assimilation in everyday speech:

When we talk about the "head" of a cane, the "face" of a cliff, the "bowels" of a volcano, the "arm" of the sea, the "hands" of a watch, the "branches" of a river or an insurance company, we are using metaphor. A salesman "covers" an area; an engine "knocks"; a theory is "built up" and then "knocked down"; a government "drains" the taxpayers, and corporations "milk" the consumers. Even in so unpoetical a source as the financial page of a newspaper, metaphors are to be found: stock is "watered," shares are "liquidated," prices are "slashed" or "stepped up," markets are "flooded," the market is "bullish"; in spite of government efforts to "hamstring" business and "strangle" enterprise, there are sometimes "melons" to be "sliced"; although this is—but here we leave the financial page—"pure gravy" for some, others are left, "holding the bag."[25]

S. I. HAYAKAWA, *Language in Action*

Slang draws heavily on metaphors for its effectiveness. You may not be a more effective interpreter after reading this paragraph, but your attention will be directed to the close relationship between connotative meaning and metaphor. You say of someone: he's "all thumbs," "chicken-hearted," "dyed-in-the-wool"; he's a "big cheese," "meal ticket," "pill," "crumb," "big noise," "snake-in-the-grass," "wet blanket," "gold-mine," "smoothie," "butterfingers"; or you might say let's "talk turkey," "chew the rag," "make the fur fly," "egg them on," "eat humble pie," "put up a squawk," "shoot the bull," "make no bones about it," "foot the bill." You understand what is meant; a foreigner, however, might have some difficulty in understanding these metaphorical allusions. Sometimes even you are puzzled by the lingo of the waiter in the restaurant who calls out, "Adam and Eve on a raft, wreck 'em!"—but any American should know that scrambled eggs on toast are "coming up," even as you know "Two on a slice of squeal" will bring your order of bacon and eggs.

Evaluate the metaphors found in these lines as far as their effectiveness is concerned.

1. New York, the nation's thyroid gland.—CHRISTOPHER MORLEY

2. Diplomats: babies in silk hats playing with dynamite.—ALEXANDER WOOLL-COTT

3. Our lives are merely strange dark interludes in the electrical display of God the Father!—EUGENE O'NEILL

4. April prepares her green traffic light and the world says Go.—JOHN MISTLE-TOE

5. Cauliflower is nothing but cabbage with a college education.—MARK TWAIN

6. Atom bomb: A mushroom of boiling dust up to 20,000 feet.—PAUL TIBBETT, JR.

7. Life's but a walking shadow, a poor player

25 From S. I. Hayakawa, *Language in Action* (New York: Harcourt, Brace & World, Inc., 1914), p. 196.

That struts and frets his hour upon the stage,
And then is heard no more.
> SHAKESPEARE, *Macbeth,*
> Act V, Scene 5

8. Night's candles are burnt out, and jocund day
Stands tiptoe on the misty mountains.
> SHAKESPEARE, *Romeo and Juliet,*
> Act III, Scene 5

Many times personification is merged with the metaphor inasmuch as objects and elements of nature are given animate characteristics or described as if they had life and were capable of human activity. Herbert Hoover, for instance, created a vivid association with the decimal point, with which every one has struggled, when he said, "When I comb over these accounts of the New Deal, my sympathy arises for the humble decimal point. His is a pathetic and hectic life, wandering around among regimented ciphers, trying to find some old places he used to know." Winston Churchill too gave his metaphoric reaction to a Gallup Poll: "Nothing is more dangerous in wartime than to live in the temperamental atmosphere of a Gallup Poll, always feeling one's pulse and taking one's temperature."

Ulysses, in speaking to Achilles in *Troilus and Cressida,* uses images, similes, metaphors and also personification. Can you identify them?

> Time hath, my lord, a wallet at his back,
> Wherein he puts alms for oblivion,
> A great-siz'd monster of ingratitudes.
> Those scraps are good deeds past, which are devour'd
> As fast as they are made, forgot as soon
> As done. Perseverance, dear my lord,
> Keeps honour bright. To have done is to hang
> Quite out of fashion, like a rusty nail
> In monumental mock'ry. Take the instant way;
> For honour travels in a strait so narrow
> Where one but goes abreast. Keep then the path,
> For emulation hath a thousand sons
> That one by one pursue. If you give way,
> Or hedge aside from the direct forthright,
> Like to an ent'red tide they all rush by
> And leave you hindmost;
> Or, like a gallant horse fall'n in first rank,
> Lie there for pavement to the abject rear,
> O'errun and trampled on. Then what they do in present,
> Though less than yours in past, must o'ertop yours;
> For Time is like a fashionable host,
> That slightly shakes his parting guest by th' hand,
> And with his arms outstretch'd as he would fly

Grasps in the comer. The welcome ever smiles,
And farewell goes out sighing. Let not virtue seek
Remuneration for the thing it was!

SHAKESPEARE, *Troilus and Cressida,*
Act III, Scene 3

In one long sentence, Frost has interwoven metaphoric meaning in his sonnet "The Silken Tent." The poet creates skillfully the "silken" femininity, with perfection arising from virtuous stability and awareness of duty. At the end of the poem, he suggests with metaphoric artistry, the fleeting desire for a summer's capricious whim.

The Silken Tent

She is as in a field a silken tent
At midday when a sunny summer breeze
Has dried the dew and all its ropes relent,
So that in guys it gently sways at ease,
And its supporting central cedar pole,
That is its pinnacle to heavenward
And signifies the sureness of the soul,
Seems to owe naught to any single cord,
But strictly held by none, is loosely bound
By countless silken ties of love and thought
To everything on earth the compass round,
And only by one's going slightly taut
In the capriciousness of summer air
Is of the slightest bondage made aware.[26]

ROBERT FROST

Pound, writing in the manner of the Haiku technique of restraint and delicate images, presents another form of his super-position poems "Liu Ch'E." Compare his lines with those of Frost's "The Silken Tent," especially the metaphoric language. Which poem gives the greater intensity? Which the more impressive images? Which the greater empathy? Which the greater tonal impression?

Liu Ch'E

The rustling of the silk is discontinued,
Dust drifts over the courtyard,

---

[26] From COMPLETE POEMS OF ROBERT FROST. Copyright 1916, 1921, 1923, 1928, 1930, 1939 by Holt, Rinehart and Winston, Inc. Copyright 1936, 1942, 1944, 1951, © 1956, 1958 by Robert Frost. Copyright © 1964 by Lesley Frost Ballantine. Reprinted by permission of Holt, Rinehart and Winston, Inc.

There is no sound of foot-fall, and the leaves
Scurry into heaps and lie still,
And she the rejoicer of the heart is beneath them:

A wet leaf that clings to the threshold.[27]

EZRA POUND

Another poem involving the feminine personality is Herrick's "Delight in Disorder." Is the empathy felt by the poet or narrator really brought about through his delight in disorder of dress, or is an implicit meaning skillfully suggested through a cluster of images that appear to be a delight in something other than dress. What of the metaphorical significance of words like *kindles, wantonness, distraction, erring, enthralls, confusedly, winning, tempestuous, careless, wild, bewitch?*

Delight in Disorder

A sweet disorder in the dress
Kindles in clothes a wantonness:
A lawn about the shoulders thrown
Into a fine distraction,
An erring lace, which here and there
Enthralls the crimson stomacher,
A cuff neglectful, and thereby
Ribbands to flow confusedly,
A winning wave (deserving note)
In the tempestuous petticoat,
A careless shoe-string, in whose tie
I see a wild civility,
Do more bewitch me, than when art
Is too precise in every part.

ROBERT HERRICK

In summary then, the metaphor has to be discovered inasmuch as it is implied rather than stated; the simile, however, is acknowledged through the introductory words *as* and *like*. Writers believe the illusiveness of the implied meaning gives their literary work greater depth and more effectively points up contrasts.

Examine now a poem from the point of view of masculine loneliness. "Mr. Flood's Party," like many of Robinson's poems, is intensified through metaphorical language.

[27] From PERSONAE by Ezra Pound. Copyright 1926, 1954 by Ezra Pound. Reprinted by permission of the publishers, New Directions.

Mr. Flood's Party

Old Eben Flood, climbing alone one night
Over the hill between the town below
And the forsaken upland hermitage
That held as much as he should ever know
On earth again of home, paused warily.
The road was his with not a native near;
And Eben, having leisure, said aloud,
For no man else in Tilbury Town to hear:

"Well, Mr. Flood, we have the harvest moon
Again, and we may not have many more;
The bird is on the wing, the poet says,
And you and I have said it here before.
Drink to the bird." He raised up to the light
The jug that he had gone so far to fill,
And answered huskily: "Well, Mr. Flood,
Since you propose it, I believe I will."

Alone, as if enduring to the end
A valiant armor of scarred hopes outworn,
He stood there in the middle of the road
Like Roland's ghost winding a silent horn.
Below him, in the town among the trees,
Where friends of other days had honored him,
A phantom salutation of the dead
Rang thinly till old Eben's eyes were dim.

Then, as a mother lays her sleeping child
Down tenderly, fearing it may awake,
He set the jug down slowly at his feet
With trembling care, knowing that most things break.
And only when assured that on firm earth
It stood, as the uncertain lives of men
Assuredly did not, he paced away,
And with his hand extended paused again:

"Well, Mr. Flood, we have not met like this
In a long time; and many a change has come
To both of us, I fear, since last it was
We had a drop together. Welcome home!"
Convivially returning with himself,
Again he raised the jug up to the light;
And with an acquiescent quaver said:
"Well, Mr. Flood, if you insist, I might.

"Only a very little, Mr. Flood—
For auld lang syne. No more, sir; that will do."
So, for the time, apparently it did,
And Eben evidently thought so too;
For soon amid the silver loneliness
Of night he lifted up his voice and sang,
Secure, with only two moons listening,
Until the whole harmonious landscape rang—

"For auld lang syne." The weary throat gave out,
The last word wavered; and the song being done,
He raised again the jug regretfully
And shook his head, and was again alone.
There was not much that was ahead of him,
And there was nothing in the town below—
Where strangers would have shut the many doors
That many friends had opened long ago.[28]

EDWIN ARLINGTON ROBINSON

Robinson is known for his restrained and subtly ironic—sometimes harsh—approach to his character delineations, generally etched in black and white. You will find yourself filling in the background because of what is left unsaid. In this poem, a clue is given to the suspected metaphor immediately in the name "Eben Flood"; but certainly the lines would lose much of their flavor if you pointed the emphasis in that direction. You will observe the title is "Mr. Flood's Party," rather than the more obvious "Eben Flood's Party." Furthermore, the name of the poem brings to the fore the gracious, convivial host entertaining "Mr. Flood" under the harvest moon. A subtle irony is suggested through the situation by the poet. On first reading, you may be carried away by the pathos of the old soul, lonely, companionless, except for his friend, "Mr. Flood," and the jug that he handles "with trembling care, knowing that most things break." Later you might become aware of the quiet amusement offered by the situation: the effort toward dignified conversation with "Mr. Flood"; the acquiescent quaver of "Well, Mr. Flood, if you insist, I might," reminiscent of familiar experiences; the singing of "Auld Lang Syne" in the "silver loneliness of night," "with two moons listening." The situation never reaches the comic because of the undercurrent tone of irony blended with tenderness and pathos. Even the one-sided chat reveals his longing for friends and brings your thoughts back to the moonlit hill overlooking the panoramic view of Tilbury Town, where friends of long ago had opened their doors to him.

[28] From *The Children of the Night* by Edwin Arlington Robinson. Copyright Scribner's and Sons, 1897. *Collected Poems* by Edwin Arlington Robinson, copyright The Macmillan Company, 1921.

You will note that your sympathy as well as your enjoyment are reached through the point of view of Eben Flood, not the poet. Look through the poem for images that suggest character delineation; then look for those that bring the smile due to the situation. How are they merged into a unit? Decide, if you can, whether the predominant tone is one of loneliness and pathos, as shown through characterization, or whether the humor of the situation involving a decorous little drinking party with "Mr. Flood" and the jug wins in giving you enjoyment. Do you like the allusion to Roland, nephew of Charlemagne? Does Eben Flood bear a likeness—even though it is ghostly—to the courageous Roland, who in his last battle with the Moors finally blew his horn for help, but in vain? How about the sound of *Tilbury Town?* The poet has made it attractive rhythmically if you can give it the British pronunciation; it may have other connotations if you pronounce it with the midwestern "burr."

Finally, do you find a metaphoric meaning; if so, does it extend into a symbolic meaning (see next paragraph), involving the ebb and flow of life? the tides of men? the old order and the new? life's instability and insecurity? Examine these phrases: "scarred hopes outworn"; "a phantom salutation of the dead"; "And only when assured that on firm earth it stood, as the uncertain lives of men/ Assuredly did not"; "he lifted his voice and sang,/ Secure, . . . / Until the whole harmonious landscape rang." You make your decision about the meaning as it involves the use of metaphorical language.

SYMBOL

The symbol is less specific and consequently more illusive than the metaphor. Although at times the metaphor will be extended into a symbol, no explicit explanation is ever presented indicating that the symbol is, so to speak, in operation, or completing an implicit design of the author's thought. As in the metaphor, you are expected to arrange extended experiences—if you find them—into new patterns of association and of comparison, which can be reached through new overtones of meaning. The more you study poetry or prose, the more conscious will you become of meaning which is more than the surface idea.

You may be helped in this kind of "meaning" exercise, if you realize that the symbol connected with a word-to-word connotation is used often in your everyday communication. Your nation's flag implies unity; the three marines who planted your flag on a knoll in Iwo Jima constitute a symbol of that unity. The coin implies wealth: Sarett's poem "Requiem for a Modern Croesus" (page 334) employs the symbol of coins, not only in the name of "Croesus," an ancient king of great wealth, but in the silver dollar, the golden coin, the dimes and finally, the pennies on his eyes. The tree, which suggests great strength and "uprightness," is used to symbolize Lincoln's enduring stature and vitality, as in a "gaunt, scraggly pine," and a "kingly cedar green with boughs." You will remember that Whitman integrates in his great "elegy" the symbol of the bird for the poet singing; the lilac for love of Lincoln; the star for the slain President; and the black cloud for the assassination. Because the top hat is considered a symbol of authority and superiority, Eisenhower (so the story goes) refused to wear the formal hat at his inauguration ceremony. You may remember other symbols: the evergreen—eternal life; the albatross—the bird of ill-omen, creating a symbolic meaning which permeates Coleridge's "The Rime of the Ancient Mariner"; white—purity and innocence; red—passion and love. With these two latter symbols, O'Reilly's lyric "A White Rose," evokes symbolic and realistic meaning:

A White Rose

The red rose whispers of passion,
    And the white rose breathes of love;
Oh, the red rose is a falcon,
    And the white rose is a dove.

But I send you a cream-white rosebud,
    With a flush on its petal tips;
For the love that is purest and sweetest
    Has a kiss of desire on the lips.

JOHN BOYLE O'REILLY, *In Bohemia*

Nor should you have too much trouble with Browning's "My Star," to be enjoyed as a delightfully rhythmical lyric with the ecstatic tone so often found in Browning. Notice the pauses Browning has suggested and the fulcrum at the end. Eventually, you will realize that "the star," a known symbol of inspiration, is not a planet in the heavens. The poet could be referring to his beloved wife, Elizabeth Barrett Browning; he could be thinking of his own imaginative star in the creation of poetry. Think of other symbolic meanings for the "star" in Browning's life. You are offered an opportunity to make the poem mean what you prefer.

My Star

All that I know
    Of a certain star
Is, it can throw
    (Like an angled spar)
Now a dart of red,
    Now a dart of blue;

Till my friends have said
    They would fain see, too,
My star that dartles the red and the blue!
Then it stops like a bird; like a flower, hangs furled:
    They must solace themselves with the Saturn above it.
What matter to me if their star is a world?
    Mine has opened its soul to me; therefore I love it.

ROBERT BROWNING

In contrast to these less complicated symbols in Browning's and O'Reilly's poems is the classical symbolic enigma of Blake's "The Tiger."

The Tiger

Tiger! Tiger! burning bright
In the forests of the night,
What immortal hand or eye
Could frame thy fearful symmetry?

In what distant deeps or skies
Burnt the fire of thine eyes?
On what wings dare he aspire?
What the hand dare seize the fire?

And what shoulder, and what art,
Could twist the sinews of thy heart?
And when thy heart began to beat,
What dread hand? And what dread feet?

What the hammer? what the chain?
In what furnace was thy brain?
What the anvil? what dread grasp
Dare its deadly terrors clasp?

When the stars threw down their spears,
And watered heaven with their tears,
Did he smile his work to see?
Did he who made the Lamb make thee?

Tiger! Tiger! burning bright
In the forests of the night,
What immortal hand or eye
Dare frame thy fearful symmetry?[29]

WILLIAM BLAKE

[29] Listen to Dame Edith Evans interpreting "The Tiger" in the record album *The Voice of Poetry* (Columbia, MM-375), sponsored by The National Council of the Teachers of English.

Little agreement can be found concerning the author's symbolic meaning as projected from the tense, fiery, fierce and primarily kinesthetic imagery, cast in short, abrupt and awesome rhetorical questions. The images flash out so suddenly and with such intensity that you feel compelled to associate them with an inner meaning. Because of the contrast shown in Blake's companion poem, "The Lamb," concerning the creature that symbolizes the Christian spirit, the eternally good and righteous, many think of the tiger as a symbol of God's anger or wrath, designed to make mortals feel the force of destructive power in the face of evil. Others believe it may imply the evil of souls who live in the darkness of their destructive thoughts and then inflict their fierceness on those who live in the "light." Furthermore, the tiger with its burning brightness and sinewy strength could symbolize the early emergence of evil from the darkness of the womb, suggested by the first heartbeat. An interpretation on the positive side might emphasize that the mood, instead of one of fear and dread, is one of brute beauty and fiery strength to contrast with the mildness of the lamb. You would think, however, the tone would then have to be offset by a stronger line than "Did he smile his work to see?" Today the image of destructive war could possibly be found in the tiger whose eyes burn with fire, whose fearful symmetry is awesome, whose sinews of the heart have been twisted, whose terror brings dread so that even the stars in fearful amazement throw down their spears and weep at the disaster. The terse doubts are brought together in a final repetition of the first stanza with the fearful question concerning the tiger's creation still unanswered, "What immortal hand or eye/ Dare frame thy fearful symmetry?" It is left without an answer, but upon that answer depends the symbolization.

No matter what your decision will be, you must examine closely the means by which the poet gives strength and power to his lines. He starts with a strong, dominant call, "Tiger! Tiger!" with heavy stress on the two words. The short phrases with their insistent monosyllabic words give a sharp hard rhythm. Note the repetitions throughout the poem of intense color; of images that hurt and burn kinesthetically and produce fear; of questions starting with *What* and made abrupt by short phrases separated by the caesura; of sounds that must be hit hard rather than lightly; of contrasts, especially of black and burning and fiery brightness; of the viselike reinforcement shown in the first and last stanzas.

No discussion about symbols, however meagre, can be ended without a look at the rough, slouching beast of Yeats's "Second Coming" that leaves you shivering with dread. This poem should be studied with "Sailing to Byzantium" and "Byzantium," for these three dramatic poems form the essence, along with "The Vision," of Yeats's theories on culture and the transient moral energy of an era "Sailing to Byzantium" (page 484) will be examined later.

The Second Coming

Turning and turning in the widening gyre
The falcon cannot hear the falconer;
Things fall apart; the centre cannot hold;
Mere anarchy is loosed upon the world,
The blood-dimmed tide is loosed, and everywhere
The ceremony of innocence is drowned;
The best lack all conviction, while the worst
Are full of passionate intensity.

Surely some revelation is at hand;
Surely the Second Coming is at hand.
The Second Coming! Hardly are those words out
When a vast image out of *Spiritus Mundi*
Troubles my sight: somewhere in sands of the desert
A shape with lion body and the head of a man,
A gaze blank and pitiless as the sun,
Is moving its slow thighs, while all about it
Reel shadows of the indignant desert birds.
The darkness drops again; but now I know
That twenty centuries of stony sleep
Were vexed to nightmare by a rocking cradle,
And what rough beast, its hour come round at last,
Slouches towards Bethlehem to be born?[30]

WILLIAM BUTLER YEATS

Yeats's theory of the cyclical movement of the world is unique: the study of history, he believes, reveals a cycle of the beginning, development and death for one civilization after another. Each cycle, containing 2000 years to coincide with his symbolization of the moon cycles, presents an opposite trend from the preceding era. Although this poem was written in 1921 just before the fascist movement developed, he believed that the moral life of his era, which had shown strength at times, was in the process of deteriorating in conduct as well as in beliefs and that the era would die because of the domination of mechanical force. Then a new age would be born.

The opening lines of "The Second Coming" convey the idea that Yeats's age had reached its peak and was on its way to destruction through loss of perceptive values: "Turning and turning in the widening gyre/ The falcon cannot hear the falconer" would indicate the power of intellectual supremacy had been weakened and so "things fall apart." The widening gyre (one of Yeats's favorite phrases) suggests potentially de-structive forces swirling about in an ever-enlarging circle with centrifugal energy, eventually pulling apart the center of culture and morals.

The second stanza must be examined for its symbolic meaning. *Spiritus Mundi*,[31] the world spirit, symbolizes the source of man's imagina-tion, memory and intellect. The Sphinx is symbolized as timeless Nature by some—the creative force from which this civilization is trying to seek freedom. In its place will come a shape, a monster of huge dimensions, with the body of a lion, the head of a man and a blank, pitiless gaze as it moves its slow thighs—a symbol that might imply mechanical and ruth-less rather than creative and perceptive activity.

How do all these symbols merge into a central symbol emphasized by the rough slouching beast? The symbol could suggest the death or end of spiritual ideals; it could stand for anything or everything that destroys rather than builds and creates. Strangely enough, the poem today appears to many as a striking prophecy; and so, too, as you come closer to the end of the era of 2000 years—"twenty centuries of stony silence"—you may wonder how Yeats's question will be answered!

Donne, like all metaphysical poets, requires the reader to delve into his inner thoughts for the complete meaning; sometimes, the depth of his ideas is difficult to fathom. You should accept the challenge of "A Valedic-tion: Forbidding Mourning," called one of the greatest masterpieces of imagery because of the unusual metaphorical language employed. The poet wrote the poem in 1612, a farewell gift to his wife before he em-barked on a journey to the Continent.

A Valediction: Forbidding Mourning

As virtuous men pass mildly away,
   And whisper to their souls to go,
Whilst some of their sad friends do say,
   The breath goes now, and some say, no:

So let us melt, and make no noise,
   No tear-floods, nor sigh-tempests move,
'Twere profanation of our joys
   To tell the laity our love.

Moving of the earth brings harms and fears,
   Men reckon what it did and meant,
But trepidation of the spheres,
   Though greater far, is innocent.

[31] *Spiritus Mundi* is also thought by some to be the habitat of the souls of the dead, located somewhere in "outer space."

Dull sublunary lovers' love
    (Whose soul is sense) cannot admit
Absence, because it doth remove
    Those things which elemented it.

But we by a love, so much refined
    That our selves know not what it is,
Inter-assurèd of the mind,
    Care less, eyes, lips, and hands to miss.

Our two souls, therefore, which are one,
    Though I must go, endure not yet
A breach, but an expansion,
    Like gold to airy thinness beat.

If they be two, they are two so
    As stiff twin compasses are two,
Thy soul, the fixed foot, makes no show
    To move, but doth if the other do.

And though it in the center sit,
    Yet when the other far doth roam,
It leans and hearkens after it,
    And grows erect as that comes home.

Such wilt thou be to me, who must,
    Like the other foot, obliquely run;
Thy firmness makes my circle just,
    And makes me end where I begun.

JOHN DONNE

You will observe the tone, in keeping with the title, is restrained and unemotional in its approach. After several readings, you recognize a series of images presented from a rational, physical, scientific and spiritual point of view, involving man's adjustment to death, life and the world. Perhaps you wonder how these images support and extend the central theme of the poem: the strength of their deep, spiritual love calls for no tears, tempest, noise or unusual action or movement when they part. Let us remember, writes the poet, the death of virtuous men who "pass mildly away" rather than through resistance, tempest and tears. Thus "let us melt and make no noise," suggests through the unique word "melt" quietness and ease of manner in their separation. Let us not profane our love by telling the laity—those less refined in spiritual conduct and perhaps more outspoken and talkative—of our love and separation. Let us compare the movement of the earth—the sublunary habitat of dull lovers whose interest is in material things and physical love—to the larger vibratory movements of its nine encircling spheres. These spheres, being in closer spiritual relationship to God, cause each other less trepidation, agitation, alarm than the movements they exert on the smaller central force of the earth. Let us believe the refinement of our love can be likened not to "material" gold but to gold beaten to airy thinness, making it more precious and less "material" and thus causing an expansion rather than a breach.

Donne then builds a final metaphor around the structure and action of "stiff twin compasses," probably one of the most discussed figures of speech in poetry. If you think of the movements of a compass, as operated by a person, you know that in completed action, the two prongs draw a circle, the symbol of unity. The poet's wife is likened to the fixed and constant part of the compass to which the poet must always return. This nicely rounded closing completes his circle of thought: "Thy firmness makes my circle just,/ And makes me end where I begun."

This surface analysis of symbolic meaning needs deeper penetration. You should think about the wording of the imagery in its exactness and depth and realize Donne has incorporated much of his own theory of the Ptolemaic universe, mentioned briefly in the preceding remarks concerning the movements of the spheres and earth. You should consider also the metaphor of the "compasses," remembering the instrument is not self-activating but needs outside pressure to complete the circle. Would this thought interfere with Donne's metaphoric language?

As a final observation in checking the interrelationship of literary devices of rhythm and sound, and of meaning to be evaluated through denotative, connotative and metaphorical sources, study Hopkins's "The Windhover," often named the foremost sonnet of the era. First contrast Pope's celebrated lines about the pheasant with those of Hopkins about the falcon, observing that each poem describes the flight of a bird by means of different figurative language: Pope's vivid imagery of the whirring pheasant's death after his short triumphant flight; and Hopkins's weaving of symbolic meaning of the physical endurance and ecstatic flight of the windhover as compared to the spiritual activity of one dedicated to Christ.

The Whirring Pheasant

See! from the brake the whirring pheasant springs,
And mounts exulting on triumphant wings:
Short is his joy; he feels the fiery wound,
Flutters in blood, and panting beats the ground.
Ah! what avail his glossy, varying dyes,
His purple crest, and scarlet-circled eyes,

The vivid green his shining plumes unfold,
His painted wings, and breast that flames with gold?

ALEXANDER POPE, Windsor Forest

The Windhover
to Christ our Lord

I caught this morning, morning's minion, king-
      dom of daylight's dauphin, dapple-dawn-drawn Falcon, in
        his riding
Of the rolling level underneath him steady air, and striding
High there, how he rung upon the rein of a wimpling wing
In his ecstasy! then off, off forth on swing,
      As a skate's heel sweeps smooth on a bow-bend: the hurl
        and gliding
Rebuffed the big wind. My heart in hiding
Stirred for a bird,—the achieve of, the mastery of the thing!

Brute beauty and valor and act, oh, air, pride, plume, here
      Buckle! AND the fire that breaks from thee then, a billion
Times told lovelier, more dangerous, O my chevalier!
      No wonder of it: shéer plód makes plough down sillion
Shine, and blue-bleak embers, ah my dear,
      Fall, gall themselves, and gash gold-vermillion.[32]

GERARD MANLEY HOPKINS

In the vivid images of Pope's lines, you will find enjoyment and also sorrow, realizing the beauty and life of the bird is struck down by the "fiery wound." The images of "whirring" and "panting" are kinesthetic in their recall; perhaps more effective are the contrasting images of color. The poet is not interested in comparing the flight of the bird and its sudden death with any other thought, person or thing. The lines exist in a moving way for their beautiful and intact images.

When you read Hopkins's famous sonnet, you are faced with a challenge of word and phrase meanings. You should appreciate the poet's technique in building images that extend into a sustained metaphor which becomes a Christ symbol. As an interpreter, the arrangement and sound of words and phrases, as well as the meaning gained from the images, will prove interesting. Hopkins would approve of your vocal presentation for he liked his poems to be "declaimed" for the sound values. Some clues may help you to reach your decision about the meaning. Critics,

---

[32] From *Poems of Gerard Manley Hopkins*, Third Edition, edited by W. H. Gardner. Copyright 1948 by Oxford University Press, Inc. Reprinted by permission.

among them Gardner[33] and Richards,[34] have worked together to secure the intangible meanings and to clarify the fascinating direction of Hopkins's thinking.

The title, "The Windhover," has a subtitle, "To Christ our Lord," which should give you pause. In a quick glance over the poem, you observe words seemingly jumbled together and lines that seem to roll into one another. Before you decide you cannot understand anything except "it's about a falcon," take another look at the puzzle. Start with denotative meanings first, with the dictionary in hand. What does *windhover* mean? Note the pronunciation first; then you find it is a European *kestrel*. Continue your search on *kestrel* and discover it is a small *falcon*. If you read further, you find the kestrel is notable for hovering in the air with its head toward the wind: so the name *windhover*. Continue with *minion:* a favorite or patron (here the favorite or the prince of the kingdom of daylight). Consider the meanings of *wimpling*—rippling or undulating; *buckle* (see below); *sheer*—very thin, unmixed with anything else, extending up and downward very steeply, abrupt, perpendicular or the British meaning of bright or shining; *sillion,*—furrow; *gall,*—to make sore by rubbing, chafe severely, irritating.

Now try to decipher the meaning of certain phrases with a *double entendre.* Your main difficulty will lie with the lack of connectives to show relationships of words within phrases; or from a cluster of images that on first glance seem to be thrown together heedlessly, certainly not for comfortable reading and understanding; or from startling unfamiliar words placed in unusual combinations. To read the implicit meaning that Hopkins intended is perhaps impossible, as evidenced in the numerous explications of it on the literary-critical market: especially noticeable is the juggling over the word *buckle* and over the point of whether the poet is addressing the windhover or Christ (to be noted later).

One of the baffling phrases on first reading is *dapple-dawn-drawn Falcon.* If you remember "Pied Beauty" with its dappled images, and if you remember how the poet's theory of "inscape" is formed from the unique formation, color and movement of all natural objects, then you will realize this is a typical Hopkins image. Every descriptive word was carefully selected from his scintillating observations of nature. Now reread the phrase *dapple-dawn-drawn Falcon.* What does it mean? *Drawn* is the verb that suggests a double meaning. The falcon could be drawn *toward* the *dapple-dawn* and he could also be drawn in silhouette *against* the *dapple dawn.* Perhaps you can find another meaning. Thus far the images in the octave create the beauty and controlled freedom of physical activ-

---

[33] W. H. Gardner, "Themes and Imagery," *Gerard Manley Hopkins* (New Haven, Conn.: Yale University Press, 1949) V. 1, pp. 180-184.

[34] I. A. Richards, *Principles of Literary Criticism* (New York: Harcourt, Brace & World, Inc., 1957).

ity: the windhover's superb mastery in his ecstatic flight as he rebuffs the *big wind.* Your attention is now directed to Hopkins's first hint of the conflict between the physical and spiritual, occurring in the lines *My heart in hiding/Stirred for a bird.* Although he, as a Jesuit priest, has dedicated his heart to the praise of Christ, he is still moved by the physical and natural beauty of the windhover's flight.

The sestet shifts from the mortal beauty of outward physical action to the spiritual or eternal course of man's activity. Overtones of symbolic meaning are suggested through word connotations. Critics are concerned with the first three lines: *Brute beauty and valor, act, oh air, pride, plume, here/Buckle! AND the fire that breaks from thee then, a billion/Times told lovelier, more dangerous, O my chevalier!* The meaning centers around the word *buckle.* Gardner, the eminent authority on Hopkins, senses the underlying religious cry of the priest in the imperative use of *buckle.* He translates the poet's thought of self-discipline in this way: "As the bird coordinates all its faculties in graceful flight and dangerous swoop so the poet asks Christ's help in buckling or enclosing within the belt of the Jesuit rule all his own rich faculties." To some explicators, *buckle* suggests *disintegrate, break-down, pull apart.* Gardner believes that "the example of Christ's life linked together three relevant and complementary meanings of *buckle:* buckle within (discipline), buckle to (labour), buckle under (sacrifice)." The two lines following are intensified in meaning by the capitalized AND, which creates a pause for reinforcement and emphasis for the next thought: the discipline of controlled spiritual activity, the inner flame that comes from buckling, as opposed to the action of physical endeavor is "a billion times told lovelier, more dangerous, O my chevalier!"

At this point the meaning is directed in one of two ways, depending on the interpretation of *chevalier.* Gardner, who knows Hopkins as a Jesuit priest as well as a poet, believes that *chevalier* is addressed to Christ because of the necessary stress on *my.* Furthermore, this interpretation emphasizes the spiritual activity and eternal beauty as revealed in the life of Christ. On the other hand, if the windhover is being addressed, then the sonnet's meaning is reduced to the vivid description of the falcon's flight.

These lines lead directly into another confusing combination of predominantly monosyllabic words: *shéer plód makes plóugh down sillion/Shine.* If you examine the words for denotative meanings, you may find an idea similar to one of these: plodding very deeply or under difficulty makes the plough as it goes down the furrow shine; or as the plough makes progress toward its goal, it gives brilliance to the furrow; or a shining glory exists in any task—however menial—if accomplished under difficulty. How do you translate this symbol into the meaning of the previous lines?

The last cluster of images in the final tercet, expressed also in abrupt monosyllabic words—*blue-bleak . . . fall, gall . . . gash, gold*—give decision, vigor and intensity to the concluding thought; namely that reward is forthcoming after suffering and toiling. These images may seem difficult to grasp but they are familiar ones. Have you ever watched the dying embers of a wood-fire—blue-bleak embers, ashy in appearance, finally fall to the hearth and break open; and through the galling—the breaking of one part against another—have you seen flames flash out gold and vermillion from the inner fire that still glows? These images suggest not only the "blue-bleak embers" of the suffering and martyrdom of Christ but the reward of the "golden crown"; and to the Jesuit priest his reward in the dedication of his life to Christ. The final impression of the poem, according to Gardner[35] and Richards,[36] should be one of catharsis, "that sense of relief, of repose in the midst of stress, of balance and composure, given by Tragedy."

You should now be ready to put the pieces of the puzzle together, adding your own imaginative ideas. You are at least conscious of a sustaining symbol in the lines: the mastery and beauty of the windhover as he surmounts his physical difficulty and thus withstands the onslaught of the buffeting wind even as the glory of Christ in his suffering and dying for mankind gained spiritual mastery a billion times told lovelier and more dangerous. Whether or not you accept this meaning, or part of it, is unimportant. You cannot discard the poem as unimportant merely because you are unable in your initial attempt to integrate the images. Resolve your acceptance of the poem through your understanding of the meaning.

Hopkins's technique in utilizing sound values to support meaning, tone and rhythm is unique for its "heard" values. The octave shows a sustained smoothness characteristic of the flight of the bird by means of the repetitive sounds *m,n,ng*. "Read with your ears," repeating these words aloud: *morning, minion, kingdom, dauphin, dawn-drawn, falcon, rein, riding, rolling, wing, him, striding, rung, upon, wimpling, swing, bend, gliding, wind, hiding, thing.* You recognize the repetition of the vowel sound in *dauphin dapple-dawn-drawn Falcon* as assonance; you know the repetition of the consonant *d* in the second line is alliteration. Phrases like *"rolling level," "rung upon the rein of a wimpling wing," "as a skate's heel sweeps smooth on a bow-bend"* have interesting sound values to support rhythmical cadences.

In the sestet, do not overlook the plosive sounds made by damming up the breath stream: *b, p, d, g* and the blends *pl, bl*; the intermittent use of sibilants, *sh, s, ch*, as in *chevalier, sheer, sillion, shine;* and in the last

[35] W. H. Gardner, "The Religious Problem in G. M. Hopkins," *Critiques and Essays,* Robert Wooster Stallman, ed. (New York: The Ronald Press, 1949), pp. 349-352.

[36] See above, p. 167.

line, the near similarity of vowels and the repetition of *g*, in *fall, gall, gash, gold*. As you note the rhyme of *billion, sillion, vermillion,* you may wonder what imaginative effort could discover these three totally different words as far as meaning is concerned.

Finally, observe how Hopkins has employed the "sprung rhythm," providing him, he says, with more freedom. He arranges one to four syllables to the foot, always stressing the first syllable and thus giving at times peculiar stress and meaning. In his "Preface" to *Collected Poems,* he explains that if the first line "has one or more syllables at its end, the other must have so many the less at the beginning." Furthermore, the "scanning runs on without break from the beginning, say, of a stanza to the end, and all the stanza is one long strain, though written in lines asunder." He creates his particular rhythm in an effort to get away from the too rigid iambic, trochaic and anapestic patterns.

PATTERNS OF METAPHORICAL LANGUAGE IN PROSE

IMAGERY, SIMILE, METAPHOR

The writer of prose employs metaphorical language on a more extended basis than the poet; consequently, the intensity and compactness is not felt as in the tightly packed poetic lines. The images are interwoven with the direction of meaning and may not be noticed because of interest in the plot of the story or play. They are there, however, to telescope the author's final perspective. Caroline Gordon[37] gives a striking example of James's dramatic use of imagery to suggest the character of Madame de Vionnet in *The Ambassadors.*[38] Lambert Strether, who had come to Paris on a mission which involved Madame de Vionnet, met her for the first time: "She was dressed in black that struck him as light and transparent; she was exceedingly fair, and though she was as markedly slim, her face had a roundness with eyes far apart and a little strange. Her smile was natural and dim; her hat not extravagant; he had only perhaps a sense of the clink, beneath her fine black sleeves, of more bracelets and bangles he had ever seen a lady wear." Gordon remarks that James, to be sure that the reader gets the implication that the woman is unconventional in her living, has underlined the clink of the bracelets and bangles underneath her fine black sleeves.

Remember the boat in Crane's story "The Open Boat"—the small boat which one had a right to expect should be larger than a bath tub. "A seat

[37] Caroline Gordon, *How to Read a Novel* (New York: The Viking Press, 1957), p. 135.

[38] Henry James, *The Ambassadors* (New York: Charles Scribner's Sons, 1961), V. 21, p. 210.

in this boat was like a seat upon a bucking broncho"; she was like an animal prancing, rearing and plunging, trying to make a fence "outrageously high." Here are immediate impressions through images and similes!

The same technique employing vivid imagery, similes and metaphors can be discovered in essays, as shown in the following excerpts.

The most beautiful thing I have seen at sea, all the more so that I had never heard of it, is the trail of a shoal of fish through the phosphorescent water. It is like a flight of silver rockets, or the streaming of northern lights through that silent nether heaven. I thought nothing could go beyond that rustling star foam which was churned up by our ship's bows, or those eddies and disks of dreamy flame that rose and wandered out of sight behind us.[39]

James Russell Lowell, *At Sea*

Poor old Britain! Her infirmities are mortal, not because cure is impossible, but because, blithely, stupidly, fatuously, her governing élite will never recognize her malady, let alone accept the remedy. She has "class" the way some people have arthritis; her joints are inflamed and so crooked that opportunities slip from her swollen fingers as she limps towards a future of growing immobility and decay.

J. H. Plumb, Comment in *Saturday Review*, March 7, 1964

Women have served all these centuries as looking glasses, possessing the magic and delicious power of reflecting the figure of man at twice its natural size.[40]

Virginia Woolf, *A Room of One's Own*

SYMBOLISM

In poetry, images may come to the fore and sometimes take over completely to build or merge into symbolic meaning, as in Thomas's and Hopkins's poetry. In fiction images are usually interwoven through symbols to give a lighting effect to a character or to illuminate the central meaning. In Joyce's story "The Dead," the image of snow is brought in very unobtrusively at the beginning—merely evident on the husband's boots. Gradually the snow begins to grow and to merge into atmosphere and mood; it falls more heavily; and at the end of the story, the whole landscape is white. The author has also put a strong connotative value on the title of his narrative, extending it not only to the dead lover of the wife but also to the husband who has not been too perceptive about his wife.

[39] James Russell Lowell, "At Sea," *Fireside Travels* (Boston: Houghton, Mifflin and Company, 1864), p. 160.
[40] Virginia Woolf, *A Room of One's Own* (New York: Harcourt Brace & World, Inc., 1929), p. 60.

A clue to symbolic meaning is often found in the title. Smith, in the foreword of her novel *A Tree Grows in Brooklyn,* points to the symbolic meaning when she writes:

There's a tree that grows in Brooklyn. Some people call it the Tree of Heaven. No matter where the seed falls, it makes a tree which struggles to reach the sky. It grows in boarded-up lots and out of neglected rubbish heaps. It grows up out of cellar gratings. It is the only tree that grows out of cement. It grows lushly . . . survives without sun, water, and seemingly without earth. It would be considered beautiful except that there are too many of it.[41]

Steinbeck's delightful sketch entitled "How to Tell Good Guys from Bad Guys" reveals the simple and naïve approach of the "young fry" in differentiating among status symbols of the "good guys" and the "bad guys" as portrayed in the Westerns on television. Steinbeck learned inadvertently from his son Catbird, who was disgusted with his father's ignorance, that the Good Guy always wore the White Hat in contrast to the Bad Guy who donned a Black Hat. So the father watched to learn more: the Good Guy with his White Hat showed little emotion under pressure, being "brave and pure"—and he was always clean and shaved. The Bad Guy with his Black Hat and dark clothing was not too clean, had a "stubble of beard," a face that "leered" and "sneered" and a voice that shouted and laughed a "nasty laugh." The decision was as simple as that to Catbird, and finally, to his father, Steinbeck.[42]

One must always look carefully at the title of a short story, play or poem, for it may indicate the intent of the inner meaning, as in "The Beast in the Jungle," "The Flowering Judas," "Cat in the Rain," "The Dill Pickle," "The Glass Menagerie," "Death of a Salesman."

ALLEGORY

Another kind of story that related to the symbolic tale is the allegory, a narrative with a concrete meaning noticeable as you first read the pages. Then, without the suggestive clues given by metaphors or symbols, an abstract meaning is sensed, an underlying meaning that relates to the physical counterpart. According to the dictionary, an allegory is a "presentation of an abstract or spiritual meaning under concrete or material forms." The author establishes an intangible relationship between the abstract idea and the "assumed" pattern of the concrete meaning.

At first you may be baffled at the direction of the narrative, but you will soon realize that the writer is trying to turn a concrete experience

[41] From A TREE GROWS IN BROOKLYN by Betty Smith. Copyright 1943, 1947 by Betty Smith. Reprinted with the permission of Harper & Row, Publishers.
[42] From John Steinbeck, "How to Tell Good Guys from Bad Guys," *The Reporter* (March 10, 1955).

into a concurrent impression of an abstract idea. It is interesting to note how he keeps the connection between the two ideas. Coleridge's "The Rime of the Ancient Mariner" is called a ballad, and is also considered an allegory of Coleridge's life, a spiritual adventure of the terrors he experienced on his "mental voyages," his "inner life adventures." This idea is also discounted vigorously by some literary critics. Forster's "The Other Side of the Hedge" is reprinted later so that you can understand how subtly the author follows his pattern of fantasy.

THEMATIC PATTERNS

These literary devices and many more are available to the great writer who wants his literature to endure through the centuries. He molds and supports his theme, his controlling idea, by skillful and ingenious integration of these various techniques. He chooses his subject matter (what the work is about) and then develops his theme, his attitude toward his subject matter, his representation of actions, characters and episodes.

Many subjects intrigue writers—death, love, desolation, deterioration, religion. In this book, for some reason many selections involve the universal subject of escape—escape from oneself, others, situations, environment, destiny. As an exercise, state the theme of the narrator of three or four of the following, noting also the point of view and how the theme is developed: "The Heart of Darkness" by Conrad; "Impulse" by Aiken; *Escape* by Galsworthy; "The Daughters of the Late Colonel" and "Miss Brill" by Mansfield; "The Secret Life of Walter Mitty" by Thurber; "The Open Boat" by Crane; "The Other Side of the Hedge" by Forster; "Courage" by Fitzgerald; *The Glass Menagerie* by Williams; *Death of a Salesman* by Miller; *Adam* by Lewisohn; *Hello Out There* by Saroyan; "The Woman at the Washington Zoo" by Jarrell; "Rhapsody on a Windy Night," "The Hollow Men," "The Love Song of J. Alfred Prufrock" by Eliot; "Design," "Out, Out—," "Home Burial," "Fire and Ice" and "After Apple-Picking" by Frost; "The End of the World" by MacLeish; "Father and Son" by Kunitz; "Snake" by Lawrence; "Do Not Go Gentle Into That Good Night" by Thomas; "Escape" from *John Brown's Body* by Benét. If only an excerpt is reprinted, you should read the complete selection.

6

Nine Poems:
Poets & Critics in Dialogue

This chapter is devoted to selected dialogues between poets and their critical readers; it even includes cases in which the readers are themselves the poets commenting on their earlier poems. By listening to several such dialogues, you may improve your skill in discoursing with any writer, whether poet, novelist or dramatist. Your own dialogue with a given work is simply a process of refining your impressions of that work before beginning the complementary process of expressing them before an audience.

JOHN CIARDI & THE CITIZEN: THE CONTEXT FOR CRITICAL DISCUSSION

John Ciardi, a poet in his own right and Poetry Editor of *Saturday Review*, sets the context for critical discussion between every poet who desires to be read with understanding and his audience whose desire is to understand what it reads. Wallace Stevens's "Anecdote of the Jar" is the poem that initiates the dialogue between the Poet (perhaps you) and the Citizen (more likely you). Although the Citizen considers himself to be literate, he wonders why he cannot understand modern poetry. The Poet replies that this difficulty happens to everyone, even he has never fully comprehended Blake's "The Tiger." The Citizen then claims that, although he understands every word and sentence in "Anecdote," he still is not sure about Stevens's meaning. He reads the poem aloud, and their dialogue ensues.

Anecdote of the Jar

I placed a jar in Tennessee,
And round it was, upon a hill.
It made the slovenly wilderness
Surround that hill.

The wilderness rose up to it,
And sprawled around, no longer wild.
The jar was round upon the ground
And tall and of a port in air.

It took dominion everywhere.
The jar was gray and bare.
It did not give of bird or bush,
Like nothing else in Tennessee.[1]

WALLACE STEVENS

The Citizen finishes reading and looks up. "I was bothered at first by 'port,'" he says, "but I checked the word in the dictionary and I think I see what he's doing with it. But how am I supposed to understand 'It made the slovenly wilderness surround that hill'? How can a jar make a jar make a wilderness surround a hill? The wilderness was already surrounding the hill, and long before Stevens and his jar came along."

"In a sense, yes," says the Poet, "but only in the most usual prose-sense. Poetry constantly makes over that usual sense of things. The jar is a made-form; as such it stands for all artifice. The wilderness is nature as-it-happens, the opposite of made-form. But to 'surround' is 'to take position around a center.' And what is formless has no center. It is human artifice, the assertion of human artifice, that puts a center to the wilderness. Because the wilderness is formless it still 'sprawls' but now it sprawls 'up to' the jar. It approaches form, that is, and therefore it 'is no longer wild.'"

"Wait a minute," says the Citizen, "aren't you the one who is doing the paraphrasing now?"

"Yes, surely. I have no quarrel with paraphrase: only with paraphrase as a substitute for the poem. I am not trying to say, 'This is what the poem comes to.' Far from it. I am trying to point out the symbolic areas in which the poem moves. The two poles of Stevens's thought seem clearly enough to be 'artifice' and 'formless nature.' Why shouldn't those poles be identified? But the poles are not the poem. The poem is much better seen as those poles plus the force-field they create."

"That does it!" says the Citizen and slams the book shut, "symbolic areas, force-fields, artifice versus formless-nature—what is all this jargon? Didn't you write once that a poem is an emotion or nothing?"

"I certainly did."

"Then tell me how on earth I am supposed to get an emotion from this sort of haywire theorizing?"

The Poet smiles sadly. "I'm about ready to grant you that all criticism is in fact haywire, but would you grant me that criticism is not the poem? At that, one can still rig a weathervane out of haywire, and that vane can point to the weather. The poem is not the vane, nor is it the haywire from which the vane is improvised: the poem is the weather that is pointed to.

"Stevens, as it happens, had very strong feelings about form versus the formless. Those feelings crowd all his poems. They are fundamental to his very sense of reality. His emotions, to be sure, are intellectual things. If you refuse to think a sense of aesthetic-reality, as opposed to some other more common ideas of reality, is worth an emotion, you are breaking no law, but Stevens is obviously not for you. And that, I find myself thinking, is your loss rather than his."

"Maybe so," says the Citizen, but now he is sitting up as if squared for battle. "I'll even say he is obviously not for me. Who *is* he for? I'm the one who brought up Stevens, and I'll grant he may be a special case. But Stevens is not the only one who is obviously not for me. Who *are* you modern poets for? Is there no such thing as an audience?"

This charge, too, is a familiar one to the Poet. "You've fired a lot of questions," he says, "and a full answer would call for a long sermon. Let me try the short form.

"What is the idea of 'the audience'? Is it enough to argue, 'I have bought this book of poems and therefore I have certain audience-rights'? I think, first, one must distinguish between two ideas of 'the audience.'

"One idea may be called the horizontal audience and the other the vertical audience. The horizontal audience consists of everybody who is alive at this moment. The vertical audience consists of everyone, vertically through time, who will ever read a given poem.

"Isn't it immediately obvious that Stevens can only 'be for' a tiny percentage of the horizontal audience? Even Frost, who is the most seemingly clear and the most widely loved of our good poets, certainly does not reach more than a small percentage of the total population, or even of that part of the population that thinks of itself as literate—as at least literate enough to buy a best seller. The fact is that no horizontal audience since the age of folk poetry has been much interested in good poetry. And you may be sure that a few spokesmen sounding off in the name of that horizontal audience are not going to persuade the poets.

"All good poets write for the vertical audience. The vertical audience for Dante, for example, is now six centuries old. And it is growing. If the human race has any luck at all, part of Dante's audience is still thousands of years short of being born.

"Now try a flight of fancy. Imagine that you held an election tomorrow and asked the horizontal audience to vote for Dante as opposed to Eddie Guest. Guest would certainly swamp Dante in such an election. More people in the horizontal audience have read Guest and even, God save the mark, been moved by him—if only to their own inanition. But moved, nevertheless. And we're a democracy, aren't we? The majority rules: bless the majority?

"Not in art. Not horizontally at least. The verdict in art is vertical. Take the idea of majority vote a step further. Imagine that you held the same election on Judgment Day, calling for a total vote of the human race down through time. Can you fail to believe that Dante would then swamp Eddie Guest plus all the horizontalists from Robert Service to Carl Sandburg?

"The point is that the horizontal audience always outnumbers the vertical at any one moment, but that the vertical audience for good poetry always outnumbers the horizontal in time-enough. And not only for the greatest poets. Andrew Marvell is certainly a minor poet, but given time enough, more people certainly will have read 'To His Coy Mistress' than will ever have subscribed to

Time, Life, and *Fortune.* Compared to what a good poem can do, Luce is a piker at getting circulation."

"Impressive, if true," says the Citizen, "but how does any given poet get his divine sense of this vertical audience?"

"By his own ideal projection of his own best sense of himself. It's as simple as that," says the Poet. "He may be wrong, but he has nothing else to go by. And there is one thing more—all good poets are difficult when their work is new. And their work always becomes less difficult as their total shape becomes more and more visible. As that shape impresses itself upon time, one begins to know how to relate the parts to their total. Even Keats and Shelley confounded their contemporary critics as 'too difficult' and 'not for me.' "

The Citizen throws his hands up. "All right, all right: I've been out-talked. But who *does* write for me?"

The Poet spreads his hands palms out. "Keats and Shelley—now that they have lost their first difficulty."

"And are dead enough?" says the Citizen. "Well, maybe. But why is it so impossible for you to think about writing for me? I'm willing to give it a try."

The Poet shrugs. "The sort of try you gave Stevens? But no matter. The point is, why *should* I write for you?—you're going to be dead the next time anyone looks. We all are, for that matter. But not the poem. Not if it's made right. If I make it for you I have to take the chance that it will die with you. I'm not sure you're that good an investment. Besides which, I have to invest in myself. If we happen to share some of the same sense of poetry, it may work out that I do happen to write for you. But that would be a happy bonus at best. I still cannot think of you as a main investment—not till you show a better 'vertical-sense.' "

"We who are about to die," says the Citizen, "salute the poems we cannot grasp. Is that it?"

"Like nothing else in Tennessee," says the Poet, bowing.[2]

JOHN CIARDI, *Dialogue With an Audience*

Ciardi's implication is not simply that live citizens are condemned to understand only dead poets and that live poets exist in limbo awaiting just evaluation of their work by generations of citizens yet unborn. He emphasizes also that a poet, in his poem at least, outlives, if he is good, the citizen as well as himself. By the same token, a citizen, because he can compare his own reading with that of others in both vertical and horizontal audiences, is more likely to grasp all levels of meaning in a poem from the past than from those of the present.

The nine poems that follow are approached by readers—whether citizens, critics, poets or all three—who offer, in dialogue, some of their thoughts on the creativity of poets living and dead.

[2] From DIALOGUE WITH AN AUDIENCE by John Ciardi. Copyright © 1958 by John Ciardi. Published by J. B. Lippincott Company, pp. 33-37.

DIALOGUE 1: MARK VAN DOREN /
WALT WHITMAN'S "THE NOISELESS SPIDER"

The first poem is by the great poet of democracy, the free verse poet who loved humanity and the streets of Manhattan—Walt Whitman. He sang lustily, vigorously, expansively of his beloved America. "I sound my barbaric yawp over the roofs of the world," he wrote. His poetry usually swings along in broad movements, with many repetitive phrases and with a rhythm that surges with life and enthusiasm. He was an American, living in America, hobnobbing with Americans of all classes.

In reality the most important thing he was doing in all these years was what people called his loafing. Young Walt Whitman never seemed in a hurry. Something of a Broadway dandy, carrying a cane, wearing a bud in his buttonhole, he stopped on his way to the office to see workmen tinning a roof, or to talk with a policeman. He saw the crowd pour from the ferryboat. He rode on the Broadway omnibuses for hours. He sat there beside Broadway Jack, the driver, or Pop Rice or Old Elephant. Jack and Pop would spin a yarn, or Walt would recite *Julius Caesar*.[3]

JOSEPH AUSLANDER & FRANK E. HILL, *The Winged Horse*

He will live in the memories of Americans for his devoted allegiance to Lincoln and for his elegy (to that great man)—"When Lilacs Last in the Dooryard Bloom'd." Sandburg has called the poem the "most majestic threnody to death in the English language." He will be remembered also for *Leaves of Grass*, in which his philosophy, motivation and temperament have been expressed by this succinct expression, "Who touches this touches man." When the volume was first published in 1865, praise and condemnation greeted the printing. To Sandburg, however, *Leaves of Grass* was the "most wildly keyed oath that America means something and is going somewhere that has ever been written; it is America's most classic advertisement of itself as having purpose, destiny, banners, and beacon fires."[4]

Your attention is now directed to a Whitman poem, which you might otherwise skip over without realizing the strength of the meaning supported by form, restraint of manner, tone, unusual choice and placement of words in stress positions to further the rhythmical movement.

[3] Joseph Auslander and Frank E. Hill, *The Winged Horse* (New York: Double-day and Company, Inc., 1927), p. 350.
[4] From "Introduction" by Carl Sandburg in *Poems* by Walt Whitman (New York: Liveright Publishing Corp., 1921).

A *Noiseless Patient* Spider

A noiseless patient spider,
I mark'd where, on a little promontory, it stood, isolated;
Mark'd how, to explore the vacant, vast surrounding,
It launch'd forth filament, filament, filament out of itself;
Ever unreeling them—ever tirelessly speeding them.

And you, O my Soul, where you stand,
Surrounded, surrounded, in measureless oceans of space,
Ceaselessly musing, venturing, throwing—seeking the spheres, to
  connect them;
Till the bridge you will need, be form'd—till the ductile anchor
  hold;
Till the gossamer thread you fling, catch somewhere, O my Soul.

WALT WHITMAN

Mark Van Doren analyzes the solitude of the poem for you:

Here is solitude with a vengeance, in vacancy so vast that any soul seen at
its center, trying to comprehend and inhabit it, looks terribly minute. Whitman's spider on its little promontory—a twig, a stalk, a leaf of grass—is no more
helpless than the soul of a man must be, laboring to launch itself in the universe
and connect the spheres; or even to catch anywhere, at one fact, one friend, one
lover, and thus no longer be alone. Emily Dickinson's soul had the society of
one person, and was content with that one. Here there are no persons yet—only
the soul newborn in space, hoping to conquer its measureless environment.

The verse of the poem is free, yet not altogether so. It is bound to the task
of saying for the poet how strenuous the effort is he has set himself to describe.
It arranges itself in two sections—hardly stanzas, though they are almost that
—and keeps a certain symmetry in those sections, a symmetry consistent with
the parallel Whitman wants to maintain between the spider and the soul. After
a relatively short line, each section throws out four longer ones. These have five,
six, or seven stresses as the case may be; but they are roughly uniform in the
time they take and in the nature of their movement. Their movement is the
movement of throwing, of putting out, of launching forth filaments of themselves, of sending loops and spirals into space. "Ever unreeling them—ever tirelessly speeding them." This expresses the poem as well as the spider. Short as it
is, it never seems to be done, except in so far as the last line promises some sort
of success, somewhere, sometime. The soul, as if it were itself a spider, has put
forth gossamer threads. One of them—the suggestion is clear—may catch.

The two adjectives in the first line are more cunning than we may suspect.
Their order is eloquent of the creature referred to—not a patient, noiseless
spider, but one whose silence strikes us first, and then its industry. In another
poem, Whitman has spoken, not of the few large stars that glorify the night, but

of "the large few stars." The difference is wonderful, as it is here. And the spider has the whole of the beginning line to itself, as if there were no observers. But there is one. "I mark'd." There, on its little promontory, says Whitman, "it stood isolated." And then he marked how it had work to do, how it strove to overcome its isolation, its immense isolation in the space between the twig it clung to and any other object whatever. Not only did it feel out with its arching, delicate feet; from its very self it sent out filament, filament, filament —more and more of them all the time, as if it contained infinities of thread—in search of something with which contact could be made and a web begun. "Filament," used three times in precisely this place, becomes a more forceful word than we could have supposed it would be. It is a light word, like the thing it names; but the three *f*'s fill it with an energy which does not leave us surprised when we learn in the next line that the spider never became tired. The filaments went forth fast, too—faster and faster, and farther and farther away. Nothing could be compared with this. Nothing, except the soul.

My own soul, says Whitman, stands in the same fashion, surrounded by the same sea of vacancy. Or seas—or oceans, a better word—of empty air. The sentence he addresses to this essence of himself is never completed. The sentence about the spider was in the past tense and described an action; the action was not completed, but the observation of it was, and so the sentence could be. But the second half of the poem hangs unfinished, unconnected, in syntax, time, and space. *This* is the situation *now*. The soul keeps on, ceaselessly, throwing out filaments of itself—thoughts, theories, desires—and will do so forever until the day when contact is made with that reality which is as far away as the stars in their spheres. Such a day will undoubtedly come, but it has not come yet. There is not merely the hope that it will come, there is the purpose and the certainty; and somehow we are assured of this by the sound of the last five words in line 9. "Till the ductile anchor hold"—and the moment is forecast with an authority we cannot question, since the thing itself is happening in our eyes and ears. Particularly our ears. The hard *c*'s in "ductile" and "anchor" verify the competence of the one filament that is successful at last; it is flexible, but it is strong; and it will *hold;* the merest gossamer, it will nevertheless catch (another hard *c*) and stay caught. The near-rhyme of "Soul" with "hold" already commences the operation of sewing and tying the anchor tight.

The effort, meanwhile, has been immense. It is an ancient idea, this of man's mind or soul that in its little sphere of flesh can achieve a correspondence with the great sphere of creation around it. And there have been times when this correspondence was spoken of as easy to bring about—indeed, it almost happened by itself. Not so with Whitman, whose modern soul was haunted by the difficulties of the task. Whitman studied loneliness like a scholar, and made his various music out of solitude, his great subject. Here his music is urgent and anxious. The spider and the soul may fail. And yet they may not—indeed they must not, as the rolling energy of the verse by its own might declares. And as the adjectives, so intelligently and powerfully placed, assure us if we listen well. Not only "noiseless" and "patient," but "vacant" and "vast," and "ductile," and "gossamer," which stitch the sections together, giving us to understand that as the spider is assisted by the very genius for survival that can be assumed in its species, so the soul must be similarly assisted, though Whitman does not know how. Yet "somewhere, O my Soul."[5]

MARK VAN DOREN, *Introduction to Poetry*

Plan a dialogue contrasting the poem "The Noiseless Patient Spider" with these lines from *Leaves of Grass:*

> Give me faces and streets—give me these phantoms incessant and
>   endless along the trottoirs!
> Give me interminable eyes—give me women—give me comrades
>   and lovers by the thousand!
> Let me see new ones every day—let me hold new ones by the
>   hand every day!
> Give me such shows—give me the streets of Manhattan!
>
> . . .
>
> Give me the shores and wharves heavy-fringed with black ships!
> Oh, such for me! Oh, an intense life, full to repletion and varied!
> The life of the theatre, barroom, huge hotel, for me!
> The saloon of the steamer! the crowded excursion for me! the
>   torchlight procession!
> The dense brigade bound for the war, with high-piled military
>   wagons following;
> People, endless, streaming, with strong voices, passions, pageants,
> Manhattan streets with their powerful throbs, with beating
>   drums as now,
> The endless and noisy chorus, the rustle and clank of muskets,
> Manhattan crowds, with their turbulent musical chorus!
> Manhattan faces and eyes forever for me.
>
> . . .

WALT WHITMAN, *Leaves of Grass*

DIALOGUE 2: RANDALL JARRELL & REUBEN A. BROWER / ROBERT FROST'S "DESIGN"

You can now compare the point of view, tone, mood and meaning of Whitman's lyric about the "noiseless, patient spider" with Frost's sonnet about the spider and the moth in "Design." Frost has caused interesting speculation concerning this sonnet.

Jarrell dramatically introduces the poem as the "most awful of Frost's smaller poems." Be sure you understand the word "awful" as used by this essayist. Brower offers an equally scintillating dialogue but with a different approach. You will be amazed at Frost's imaginative ability to include

[5] From *Introduction to Poetry*, by Mark Van Doren, copyright © 1951. Reprinted by permission of Holt, Rinehart and Winston, Inc., pp. 43-45.

so many perceptive associations within fourteen lines; and to integrate them into deep philosophical thought centered on this "albino catastrophe."

Design

I found a dimpled spider, fat and white,
On a white heal-all, holding up a moth
Like a white piece of rigid satin cloth—
Assorted characters of death and blight
Mixed ready to begin the morning right,
Like the ingredients of a witch's broth—
A snow-drop spider, a flower like froth,
And dead wings carried like a paper kite.

What had that flower to do with being white,
The wayside blue and innocent heal-all?
What brought the kindred spider to that height,
Then steered the white moth thither in the night?
What but design of darkness to appall?—
If design govern in a thing so small.[6]

ROBERT FROST

Jarrell is commenting:

. . . And this little albino catastrophe is too whitely catastrophic to be accidental, too impossibly unlikely ever to be a coincidence: accident, chance, statistics, natural selection are helpless to account for such designed terror and heartbreak, such an awful symbolic perversion of the innocent being of the world. Frost's details are so diabolically good that it seems criminal to leave some unremarked; but notice how *dimpled, fat,* and *white* . . . come from our regular description of any baby; notice how the *heal-all,* because of its name, is the one flower in all the world picked to be the altar for this Devil's Mass; notice how *holding up* the moth brings something ritual and hieratic, a ghostly, ghastly formality, to this priest and its sacrificial victim; notice how terrible to the fingers, how full of the stilling rigor of death, that *white piece of rigid satin cloth* is. And *assorted characters of death and blight* is, like so many things in this poem, sharply ambiguous: a *mixed bunch of actors or diverse representative signs.* The tone of the phrase *assorted characters of death and blight* is beautifully developed in the ironic Breakfast-Club-calisthenics, Radio-Kitchen heartiness of *mixed ready to begin the morning right* . . . , and concludes in the *ingredients* of the witch's broth, giving the soup a sort of cuddly shimmer that the cauldron in *Macbeth* never had; the *broth*, even, is brought to life—we realize that witch's broth is broth, to be supped with a long spoon. For sweet-sour, smiling awfulness *snow-drop spider* looks unsurpassable, until we come to the almost obscenely horrible (even the mouth gestures are utilized) *a flower like froth; . . .*

And then, in the victim's own little line, how contradictory and awful everything is: *dead wings carried like a paper kite!* The *dead* and the *wings* work back and forth on each other heartbreakingly, and the contradictory pathos of the *carried* wings is exceeded by that of the matter-of-fact conversion into what has never lived, into a shouldered toy, of the ended life. *What had that flower to do with being white,/ The wayside blue and innocent heal-all?* expresses as well as anything ever has the arbitrariness of our guilt, the fact that Original Sin is only Original Accident, so far as the creatures of this world are concerned. And *the wayside blue and innocent heal-all* is, down to the least sound, the last helpless, yearning, trailing-away sigh of too-precarious inno-cence, of a potentiality cancelled out almost before it began to exist. The *way-side* makes it universal, commonplace, and somehow dearer to us; the *blue* brings in all the associations of the normal negated color . . . ; and the *inno-cent* is given a peculiar force and life by this context, just as the name *heal-all* here comes to sad, ironic, literal life: it healed all, itself it could not heal. The *kindred* is very moving in its half-forgiving ambiguity; and the Biblical *thither in the night* and the conclusive *steered . . .* are very moving and very serious in their condemnation, their awful mystery. The partly ambiguous, summing-up *What but design of darkness to appall* comes as something taken for granted, a relief almost, in its mere statement and generalization, after the almost unbear-able actuality and particularity of what has come before. And then this whole appalling categorical machinery of reasoning-out, of conviction, of condemna-tion—it reminds one of the machine in *The Penal Colony*—is suddenly made merely hypothetical, a possible contradicted shadow, by one off-hand last-minute qualification: one that dismisses it, but that dismisses it only for a pos-sibility still more terrifying, a whole new random, statistical astronomical abyss underlying the diabolical machinery of the poem. "In large things, macroscopic phenomena of some real importance," the poem says, "the classical mechanics of design probably *does* operate—though in reverse, so far as the old Argument from Design is concerned; but these little things, things of no real importance, microscopic phenomena like a flower or moth or man or planet or solar system . . . are governed by the purely statistical laws of quantum mechanics, of ran-dom distribution, are they not?". . .[7]

RANDALL JARRELL, To the Laodiceans

Brower talks over Frost's intent in "Design":

This is a poem of finding evil in innocence, a song of experience, though the voice is hardly that of Blake's child-like singer. At first we hear the cheer-fully observant walker on back-country roads: "I found a dimpled . . ." The iambic lilt adds a tone of pleasant surprise: "I found a dimpled darling"—"Little Miss Muffet sat on a tuffet!" But in "spider" the voice betrays itself, and in "fat" and "white" the dimpled creature appears less charming. On a small scale the first line, like the whole poem, builds up a joke in tone, rhythm, and image that grows into a "joke" of another sort.

In the octet the joking discovery develops gradually through a series of contradictory pictures. "A white heal-all" suggests purity and safety, though the color echoes the white of the swollen spider. A satin-white moth has its charm, too, a party-going creature poised like Wordsworth's butterfly on its flower; but "rigid" is too frozen, too easily reminiscent of *rigor mortis* or the stiff shining satin of a coffin. In the aside of the next three lines, the speaker gives away his joke, but he does it *jokingly*, again partly by tricks of rhythm. First there is the very correct iambic of line 4,

> Assorted characters of death and blight . . .

in exactly ten syllables, every other one of which must be stressed, a little as in doggerel. The plain truth of the statement takes on a cheerful sing-song quality, an effect increased in the next line by reversing the stress and omitting the short in "Mixed ready." The tone now becomes quite jaunty, but "right" hovers on a pun for "rite," as the poet mixes a brew worthy of the Weird Sisters, Shakespeare's most evil images of evil. The adding of unstressed syllables speeds up and lightens the next line to soften the ugliness of what is being said:

> Like the ingredients of a witches' broth . . .

And with

> A snow-drop spider, a flower like froth,

more oblique joking is resumed in images of springtime freshness ("snow drop," "flower" "like," we hear). But the spider is there, and the fragility of "froth" hardly conceals the link with venom. A surface of elegant gaiety is kept up, however, through symmetry of sound, as o's and i's, alliterated syllables, and apparent compounds are balanced in each half of the verse. Again we are brought up short with "*dead* wings," and if kites are fun, a "kite" is also a bird of prey, and "a *paper* kite" is another image of death-like rigidity.

The sextet brings the expected change in tone, now no longer easily observing and half-singing though in mockery, but self-questioning and increasingly serious. The first question ("What had the flower to do . . .") sounds like ordinary annoyance at the fact that doesn't fit in, though "white" out of place begins to seem like "black." The next question ("What brought the kindred spider . . ."), in a voice of lost innocence, brings a new note and a harsher irony with "*kindred*" (as if the sweet flower and the spider had conspired to arrive at exactly that height and place). "Steered" is more sinister, and with the last question ironic puzzlement turns into vision:

> What but design of darkness to appall?—

Alliteration picks out salient impressions to give older theological and Emersonian arguments a reverse twist—"Design, yes—but for evil." But the natural theologian pauses—he is only asking, not asserting—and takes a backward step:

If design govern in a thing so small.

It may after all be absurd to see so much in a flower, a moth, and a spider. But the "if" stands out oddly because of the reversal of stress and because of the pause for the loss of a syllable,

I'f desigń || góvern . . .

There is a glimmer of a further joke: "If design *góvern* in anything at all . . ." —the subjunctive and a second reversal of stress alert us to the doubt. The soothingly humorous hesitation points to something many readers may find less agreeable than design of darkness, to no order whatever.[8]

REUBEN A. BROWER, *The Poetry of Robert Frost*

Evaluate each of the preceding dialogues according to the meaning you discover in the sonnet. Did the images and form take on new meaning after reading Jarrell and Brower? What do you consider interesting about these two essayists, particularly their ability to express their thoughts through images? A good starting point occurs with the expression "albino catastrophe."

From the comments of these two critics, a provocative dialogue could be created by you to emphasize their difference in attitudes and reactions to Frost's metaphoric language and meaning.

DIALOGUE 3: EARL DANIELS / WALTER DE LA MARE'S "THE MOCKING FAIRY"

Walter de la Mare is known as a poet of enchantment, fantasy and mysticism. His volume *Peacock Pie,* a delightful collection of "rhymes" for children, contains "The Mocking Fairy," under the section called "Witches and Fairies." Consequently, you may be surprised at Daniels's first convincing statement that this is not a child's poem.

The Mocking Fairy

"Won't you look out of your window, Mrs. Gill?"
  Quoth the Fairy, nidding, nodding in the garden;
"*Can't* you look out of your window, Mrs. Gill?"
  Quoth the Fairy, laughing softly in the garden;
But the air was still, the cherry boughs were still,
And the ivy-tod 'neath the empty sill,

---

[8] From *The Poetry of Robert Frost: Constellations of Intention,* by Reuben A. Brower. Copyright © 1963 by Reuben A. Brower. Reprinted by permission of Oxford University Press, Inc., pp. 105-107.

And never from her window looked out Mrs. Gill
    On the Fairy shrilly mocking in the garden.

"What have they done with you, you poor Mrs. Gill?"
    Quoth the Fairy, brightly glancing in the garden;
"Where have they hidden you, you poor old Mrs. Gill?"
    Quoth the Fairy dancing lightly in the garden;
But night's faint veil now wrapped the hill,
Stark 'neath the stars stood the dead-still Mill,
And out of her cold cottage never answered Mrs. Gill
    The Fairy mimbling mambling in the garden."[9]

WALTER DE LA MARE

Daniels speaks with a definite tone:

If this sounds, at first, like one more pretty, unpretentious fairy story, designed only for small children, read it again; if necessary, again and again, until you begin almost to be ghostly haunted by it and know that more is here than meets the casual eye. Mrs. Gill, from her name, seems like a harmless, home-loving old lady; but the fairy is, as the title tells us, not a good fairy; he is a *mocking* fairy, he has come by night, and his *mimbling mambling* hints that his haunting the garden is to no good purpose. Amused, at first, he laughs softly at Mrs. Gill with his invitation, "Won't you look out of your window?" which is pleasant enough. But his second question, "*Can't* you look out of your window, Mrs. Gill?" with the italics of emphasis for *can't* is a first hint that something is wrong. Mrs. Gill couldn't come out, even if she heard the fairy and wanted to. Then everything is so still: air, cherry boughs, and ivy bush (*tod*); the mill is *dead*-still; only the fairy is in motion. The cottage is *cold*. Now, the meaning should strike home. Mrs. Gill is dead. That is why she never answers, why she *can't* come out. De la Mare does not tell us what the fairy wanted of Mrs. Gill, nor whether he was anything more sinister than a *mocking* fairy. But if we know the ways of fairies with mortals, if we have read at all in the lore of witchcraft, we may well be disturbed about Mrs. Gill's fate. No, this isn't a child's poem. No slight part of its magic is in what is unsaid, in De la Mare's refusal to resolve all problems, answer all questions. Suggestion as a stimulus to imagination is more powerful than direct statement.

Another part of the magic is in the simplicity and surface naturalness which make the supernatural more supernatural. The scene is a domestic cottage garden—the kind of garden the speaker in Frost's poem might conceivably have had at home—on a quiet night with stars. There is a hill, and somewhere, not definitely located—the indefiniteness is part of the poet's intention—a mill, closed after the day's work. We are not very much disposed to quarrel with the fairy when he makes his appearance, for his *nidding, nodding* seems to tell of friendliness. But the details, held up for analysis, transform domesticity into gooseflesh, goblin terror as we watch. In addition to those already pointed out,

[9] *Collected Poems*, 1901-1918, by Walter de la Mare, Volume 1, 1920. Reprinted by permission of The Literary Trustees of Walter de la Mare and the Society of Authors as their representative.

observe how the fairy's voice becomes *shrill* at the end of the first stanza; how the night's *veil* is *faint*, barely wrapping the hill, so that the mill stands out *stark*. Stillness becomes stiller by the emphasis of repetition. Consider too the added force, once the meaning of the poem begins to strike home, of the contrasting, pleasant words like *laughing softly, brightly glancing, dancing lightly*. With all its ghostliness the poem maintains an easy, almost conversational tone. The poet does not raise his voice, does not become rhetorical. The real and the unreal are combined with telling effectiveness.[10]

EARL DANIELS, *The Art of Reading Poetry*

Now incorporate some of your thoughts about de la Mare's poem, "The Listeners," in a dialogue:

The Listeners

"Is there anybody there?" said the Traveller,
    Knocking on the moonlit door;
And his horse in the silence champed the grasses
    Of the forest's ferny floor:
And a bird flew up out of the turret,
    Above the Travellers' head:
And he smote upon the door again a second time;
    "Is there anybody there?" he said.
But no one descended to the Traveller;
    No head from the leaf-fringed sill
Leaned over and looked into his grey eyes,
    Where he stood perplexed and still.
But only a host of phantom listeners
    That dwelt in the lone house then
Stood listening in the quiet of the moonlight
    To that voice from the world of men:
Stood thronging the faint moonbeams on the dark stair,
    That goes down to the empty hall,
Hearkening in an air stirred and shaken
    By the lonely Traveller's call.
And he felt in his heart their strangeness,
    Their stillness answering his cry,
While his horse moved, cropping the dark turf,
    'Neath the starred and leafy sky;
For he suddenly smote on the door, even
    Louder, and lifted his head:—
"Tell them I came, and no one answered,
    That I kept my word," he said.

Never the least stir made the listeners,
  Though every word he spake
Fell echoing through the shadowiness of the still house
  From the one man left awake:
Ay, they heard his foot upon the stirrup,
  And the sound of iron on stone,
And how the silence surged softly backward,
  When the plunging hoofs were gone.[11]

WALTER DE LA MARE

Suggestions and clues are presented to give you a critical beginning. You will first notice the abrupt dramatic beginning, a situation not explained through a preceding event or lead. You are plunged into a scene of questioning that is attention-getting: you must read further to satisfy your curiosity.

Various interpretations have been elicited of the creative motive of the poem: one story reports the poet once said it was motivated by a class reunion which he attended and to which very few came. The poet felt so alone in the empty corridors and classrooms that he caught the impression embodied in this poem. Whether or not this is merely a facetious tale is not known. Other ideas are found in critical essays: the Traveller keeps his word even though the darkness of life's experiences surround him; he is knocking on the House of Death; he is an emissary from God sent to warn those on earth of evil deeds; he is a ghost returning to his former home. Some find no symbolic transference since the tone gives only silence instead of reassurance.

Do not push yourself to find symbolism if you enjoy the lyric as a mystical experience typical of de la Mare's poems. If, however, you find clues to direct you to an extended symbol, then your enjoyment may be increased. You may find your impression by studying the tone and action of the characters, seen and unseen. Make a list of images describing the action of the Traveller and his horse and those of the phantom listeners. Then check the contrasting imagery that creates sensory reactions. The auditory contrasts are excellent in accentuating the stillness of the shadowy house and its unseen listeners. The loud voice of the Traveller echoes through the eery, silent atmosphere as does the sound of iron on stone made by the horse's hooves.

The melodic cadences in "Stood thronging the faint moonbeams on the dark stair" are repeated effectively in "Fell echoing through the shadowiness of the still house." The lilt of the rhythm shows interesting contrasts also, shifting from general smoothness, as above, to "cropping the dark turf," and to the short hard beats of "they heard his foot upon the stirrup,/ And the sound of iron on stone"—images bringing you back mo-

11 *Ibid.*, see p. 186.

mentarily to reality. The movement and alliteration of the next line, however, "And how the silence surged softly backward," pull you backward into the silence, adroitly accomplished by the empathic phrase, "silence surged softly," and finally, "backward" dies away into the stillness surrounding the hidden listeners. Certainly the poem will live for its mysticism, tone, atmosphere and its rhythmical cadences supported by vivid imagery.

DIALOGUE 4: EARL DANIELS / T. S. ELIOT'S "RHAPSODY ON A WINDY NIGHT"

Daniels starts his evaluation of Eliot's "Rhapsody on a Windy Night" by explaining the denotative meaning of the word "rhapsody" as "an ecstatic highly emotional composition," epic in character. The poem has also been called a dramatic monologue. Aside from the kind of poem it portends to be, what ironic connotation does "rhapsody" suggest to you? What sensory images are predominant? Why would it be called a dramatic monologue?

Rhapsody on a Windy Night

Twelve o'clock.
Along the reaches of the street
Held in a lunar synthesis,
Whispering lunar incantations
Dissolve the floors of memory
And all its clear relations,
Its divisions and precisions,
Every street lamp that I pass
Beats like a fatalistic drum,
And through the spaces of the dark
Midnight shakes the memory
As a madman shakes a dead geranium.

Half-past one,
The street-lamp sputtered,
The street-lamp muttered,
The street-lamp said, "Regard that woman
Who hesitates toward you in the light of the door
Which opens on her like a grin.
You see the border of her dress
Is torn and stained with sand,
And you see the corner of her eye
Twists like a crooked pin."

The memory throws up high and dry
A crowd of twisted things;
A twisted branch upon the beach
Eaten smooth, and polished
As if the world gave up
The secret of its skeleton,
Stiff and white.
A broken spring in a factory yard,
Rust that clings to the form that the strength has left
Hard and curled and ready to snap.

Half-past two,
The street-lamp said,
"Remark the cat which flattens itself in the gutter,
Slips out its tongue
And devours a morsel of rancid butter."
So the hand of the child, automatic,
Slipped out and pocketed a toy that was running along the quay.
I could see nothing behind that child's eye.
I have seen eyes in the street
Trying to peer through lighted shutters,
And a crab one afternoon in a pool,
An old crab with barnacles on his back,
Gripped the end of a stick which I held him.

Half-past three,
The lamp sputtered,
The lamp muttered in the dark.
The lamp hummed:
"Regard the moon,
La lune ne garde aucune rancune,
She winks a feeble eye,
She smiles into corners.
She smooths the hair of the grass.
The moon has lost her memory.
A washed-out smallpox cracks her face,
Her hand twists a paper rose,
That smells of dust and eau de Cologne,
She is alone
With all the nocturnal smells
That cross and cross across her brain."
The reminiscence comes
Of sunless dry geraniums
And dust in crevices,
Smells of chestnuts in the streets,
And female smells in shuttered rooms,
And cigarettes in corridors
And cocktail smells in bars.

The lamp said,
"Four o'clock,
Here is the number on the door.
Memory!
You have the key,
The little lamp spreads a ring on the stair.
Mount.
The bed is open; the tooth-brush hangs on the wall,
Put your shoes at the door, sleep, prepare for life."

The last twist of the knife.[12]

T. S. ELIOT

Daniels discusses the poem.

First, the title requires attention. A rhapsody is either an ecstatic, highly emotional composition; or, more strictly, it is a portion of an epic, used for public recitation. This second meaning is more suggestive here, for it contains the germ of the poem's basic irony. The central character is an epic hero—a contemporary version of the epic hero—wandering like Odysseus, and like Odysseus finally arriving home. But his wanderings are confined to sordid streets in a modern city, during the early hours of the morning; they are punctuated by the sputterings of uncertain lamps. As there is little which is heroic in his journeyings, there is also little which is heroic about the man himself, a sensitive, morbid kind of individual, alert to beauty, finding only ugliness and meanness. When ancient epic is set against the contemporary scene in this fashion, modern life, at least in the present mood of the poet, appears empty and futile. The heroic has departed. The suggestion, at the end, of sleeping as preparation for living is to give to a stabbing knife one final, unendurable twist in the wound already made in the breast of the too-sensitive hero. . . .

Life has gone out of everything for the protagonist of the poem, just as it has gone out of the twisted branch, thrown up on the beach, out of the twisted, rusted spring in the factory yard. These objects are symbols and put the hero's mood concretely. They reach a kind of climax in the symbol of the crab—an old crab, who gripped the end of a stick poked at him through the water, acting automatically, without intelligence. (Is the hero of the poem very different from this crab?) Branch, spring, crab are, again, in harmony with the sordid human figures, like wraiths, haunting the scene, the woman in the ominous doorway, the empty-eyed child on the wharf. And there is that alley cat, furtively licking at a morsel of rancid butter! Even the moon brings neither brightness nor beauty: she is a worn-out woman, for whom are only paper roses, ugly, faded; she is a moon without enough character to guard a bitterness.

The poem is built around the clocks announcing the four separate hours, and around the speeches the hero imagines addressed to him by four different street lamps, in the course of his walk. Those speeches call up floods of impressions, for night, as we are told in the first section, has dissolved the floor of memory, so that all sorts of things seem to come slipping through. Actually, the order is precise, carefully directed to the goal the poet has set for himself, to the conveyance of bitterness and frustration. *It must be noted that this bitterness and frustration are the hero's; there is no warrant, in this poem, for assuming that they represent the poet's own and personal views on life.*[13]

EARL DANIELS, The Art of Reading Poetry

DIALOGUE 5: CLEANTH BROOKS, MIDDLETON MURRY, GILBERT HIGHET, ALVIN WHITELY & WALTER JACKSON BATE / JOHN KEATS'S "ODE ON A GRECIAN URN"

Keats was twenty-three years old when he wrote the "Ode on a Grecian Urn." His early death three years later deprived him of the joys of youth and his marriage to Fanny Brawne. He was never to know the mere acceptance of his poetry about which he often wondered. During the first realization of his love for Fanny Brawne, he wrote in twelve weeks—April, May, June, 1819—his greatest poems, "La Belle Dame Sans Merci" and all of the "Odes" except "Ode to Autumn." Biographers report that during this period Keats knew great happiness tempered by many misfortunes—his income was dwindling; his health, even his life, was doubtful; one brother died of tuberculosis and another went to America.

You have read and studied his famous "Ode"; now look at it with the perspective of an interpreter.

Ode on a Grecian Urn

> Thou still unravished bride of quietness,
>   Thou foster-child of silence and slow Time,
> Sylvan historian, who canst thus express
>   A flowery tale more sweetly than our rime:
> What leaf-fringed legend haunts about thy shape
>   Of deities or mortals, or of both,
>   In Tempe or the dales of Arcady?
>   What men or gods are these? What maidens loath?
> What mad pursuit? What struggle to escape?
>   What pipes and timbrels? What wild ecstasy?
>
> Heard melodies are sweet, but those unheard
>   Are sweeter; therefore, ye soft pipes, play on;

---

[13] Reprinted by permission from Earl Daniels: *The Art of Reading Poetry,* copyright 1941 by Earl Daniels. Holt, Rinehart and Winston, Inc., publishers, pp. 404, 405.

Not to the sensual ear, but, more endeared,
  Pipe to the spirit ditties of no tone:
Fair youth, beneath the trees, thou canst not leave
  Thy song, nor ever can those trees be bare;
    Bold Lover, never, never canst thou kiss,
Though winning near the goal—yet, do not grieve;
    She cannot fade, though thou has not thy bliss,
  For ever wilt thou love, and she be fair!

Ah, happy, happy boughs! that cannot shed
  Your leaves, nor ever bid the Spring adieu:
And, happy melodist, unweariéd,
  For ever piping songs for ever new;
More happy love! more happy, happy love!
  For ever warm and still to be enjoyed,
    For ever panting, and for ever young;
All breathing human passion far above,
  That leaves a heart high-sorrowful and cloyed,
    A burning forehead, and a parching tongue.

Who are these coming to the sacrifice?
  To what green altar, O mysterious priest,
Lead'st thou that heifer lowing at the skies,
  And all her silken flanks with garlands drest?
What little town by river or sea shore,
  Or mountain-built with peaceful citadel,
    Is emptied of this folk, this pious morn?
And, little town, thy streets for evermore
  Will silent be; and not a soul to tell
    Why thou art desolate, can e'er return.

O Attic shape! Fair Attitude! with brede
  Of marble men and maidens overwrought,
With forest branches and the trodden weed;
  Thou, silent form, dost tease us out of thought
As doth eternity: Cold Pastoral!
  When old age shall this generation waste,
    Thou shalt remain, in midst of other woe
Than ours, a friend to man, to whom thou sayst,
  Beauty is Truth,—Truth Beauty,—that is all
    Ye know on earth, and all ye need to know.

John Keats

Now listen to various points of view as to how the poem was motivated and also how literary devices assist in intensifying meaning.

The following excerpt from Brooks's penetrating commentary on
paradox in Keats's poem is helpful in understanding how a poet can

attain perspective for his meaning through this particular weaving and contrasting of thoughts that seem so opposed to one another. If you read Brooks's thoughts aloud, you can actually hear him conversing about the paradox of the "Cold Pastoral."

The recognition that the men and maidens are frozen, fixed, arrested, has run . . . through the second, third, and fourth stanzas as an ironic undercurrent. The central paradox of the poem, thus, comes to conclusion in the phrase, "Cold Pastoral." The word "pastoral" suggests warmth, spontaneity, the natural and the informal as well as the idyllic, the simple, and the informally charming. What the urn tells is a "flowery tale," a "leaf-fring'd legend," but the "sylvan historian" works in terms of marble. The urn itself is cold, and the life beyond life which it expresses is life which has been formed, arranged. The urn itself is a "silent form," and it speaks, not by means of statement, but by "teasing us out of thought." It is as enigmatic as eternity is, for, like eternity, its history is beyond time, outside time, and for this reason bewilders our time-ridden minds: it teases us. . . .

The marble men and women lie outside time. The urn which they adorn will remain. The "Sylvan historian" will recite its history to other generations.

What will it say to them? Presumably, what it says to the poet now: that "formed experience," imaginative insight, embodies the basic and fundamental perception of man and nature. The urn is beautiful . . . but it is also true. The sylvan historian presents us with beautiful histories, but they are true histories, and it is a good historian.

Moreover, the "truth" which the sylvan historian gives is the only kind of truth which we are likely to get on this earth, and furthermore, it is the only kind that we *have* to have. The names, dates, and special circumstances, the wealth of data—these the sylvan historian quietly ignores. . . . It takes a few details and so orders them that we have not only beauty but insight into essential truth. Its "history," in short, is a history without footnotes. It has the validity of myth—not myth as a pretty but irrelevant make-believe, an idle fancy, but myth as a valid perception into reality.

As to the objection often made that the final lines break the tone of the poem, Brooks summarizes:

. . . Throughout the poem the poet has stressed the paradox of the speaking urn. First, the urn itself can tell a story, can give a history. Then, the various figures depicted upon the urn play music or speak or sing. If we have been alive to these items, we shall not, perhaps, be too much surprised to have the urn speak once more, not in the sense in which it tells a story—a metaphor which is rather easy to accept—but, to have it speak on a higher level, to have it make a commentary on its own nature. If the urn has been properly dramatized, if we have followed the development of the metaphors, if we have been alive to the paradoxes which work throughout the poem, perhaps then, we shall be prepared for the enigmatic, final paradox which the "silent form" utters. But in that case, we shall not feel that the generalization, unqualified and to be taken literally, is meant to march out of its context to compete with the scientific and philosophical generalizations which dominate our world.

"Beauty is truth, truth beauty" . . . is a speech "in character" and supported by a dramatic context.[14]

CLEANTH BROOKS, *Keats's Sylvan Historian*

Brooks urges that the assertion of the poem be "taken as part of an organic context" and not be dealt with as isolated factors; rather the "dramatic wholeness" of the poem should be accepted instead of some "statement of theme abstracted by paraphrase."

As you can judge from the preceding remarks, the last couplet has always provoked controversial discussions among critics because it seems not to be interwoven with the meaning nor does it serve as a climax. Consequently, to many the couplet is not a part of the organic whole. Furthermore, the question of whether the poem was motivated by a certain urn Keats had observed or by an object of his own creation becomes involved. Perhaps the ideas of several well-known authors—Murry, Highet, Whitely and Bate—should be considered pertinent in rounding out Brooks's concepts.

Murry[15] emphasizes that Keats believed in a close relationship between Truth and Beauty. Several years before the creation of the "Ode," the poet wrote: "The excellence of every art is its intensity, capable of making all disagreeables evaporate from their being in close relationship with Beauty and Truth." The thought of the urn came to Keats as he was meditating on the artistic value of a painting: the urn was a means by which he could show the beauty of arrested action to indicate an immortality with continued happiness and with no deterioration. Murry believes the urn is a "symbol of a possibility of vision," or perception, for the urn will "whisper comfort" to those suffering misery and unhappiness. It has the impact of drama: some will "pass into the spellbound land of eternity" of which the "urn is a record of that enchantment." They will be lost to humanity for destiny will fall upon them, but the knowledge, the vision of knowing, the perceptive value of believing that "Beauty is Truth" is all they need to understand.

Highet[16] is more realistic than Murry in his speculation over what urn Keats might have seen. He recalls a beautiful Greek marble vase in the British Museum that throbs with life; the observer can feel the rhythm of the dancers and can almost hear the music. Highet believes, however, this is not Keats's urn since only the dancers in the wild are engraved and

[14] From THE WELL WROUGHT URN, copyright, 1947, by Cleanth Brooks. Reprinted by permission of Harcourt, Brace & World, Inc., pp. 149-151.

[15] John Middleton Murry, *Keats* (New York: The Noonday Press, 1962), pp. 218-222.

[16] Gilbert Highet, *The Powers of Poetry* (New York: Oxford University Press, 1960), pp. 237-243.

no contrasting procession is shown. Murry, on the other hand, disclaims the existence of any urn.

Highet puts his emphasis on the Grecian connotation for his understanding of the poem. Greek artists in the classical era would not have had two scenes so distinctly opposite in tone and character: the scene of the men, gods and maidens in "mad pursuit" and the "wild ecstasy" in their struggle to escape; and the calm, peaceful communal activity of the priest leading the "heifer lowing at the skies/ And all her silken flanks with garlands dressed" to the altar of sacrifice followed by a procession of worshippers who have come from some "little town by river or sea shore,/ Or mountain-built with peaceful citadel," leaving the streets empty, evermore to be silent. Consequently, Highet believes Keats must have seen two different urns depicting the conflict of the Greeks "between the life of reason and the dark forces of passions," or the struggle between power as personified by Dionysus, and reason and restraint as exemplified by Apollo. This tension produced Greek tragedy, Highet recalls, a tension reconciled through art showing sensuality as embodying beauty and restraint and purity as being "dignified and lovable." Thus in the souls of the Greeks, one could always be a "priest and a reveler, an outrageous satyr and a wise and tranquil god." To Keats, Highet concludes, beauty is expressed in both revel and reverence.

Whitely,[17] in "The Message of the Grecian Urn in Keats," reprints a "tracing or a drawing" by Keats of the Sosibios Vase taken from the *Musée Napoleon*. This vase, he conjectures, may have been the one Keats was "looking at," for he was not writing of a past experience "recollected in tranquility." For this reason, Keats was able to project himself "into the mood of the urn." Furthermore, the sacrificial scene was not on the urn but was merely a "thoughtful journey" by Keats into the Greek world. Whitely also mentions the harsh break into another mood and tone as the poet writes that paradoxical phrase, "Cold Pastoral," emphasizing the "warmth and coldness of a frozen beauty." The controversial couplet is explained as being the voice of the urn rather than a dual statement uttered by Keats *and* the urn. The critic's evidence is found in the British Museum in which four manuscripts are punctuated as if one voice were speaking:

> Beauty is Truth, Truth Beauty—that is all
> Ye know on earth, and all ye need to know.

More recently, Walter Jackson Bate, in his monumental study of Keats's life and art, agrees that the last couplet is meant as a message to men from the urn and is not a "subjective intrusion" by the poet. The message is that of a "shape," a "form," an "attitude" which will not be

---

[17] Alvin Whitely, "The Message of the Grecian Urn in Keats," *The Keats-Shelley Memorial* Bulletin, No. V, 1953.

understood until the work of art is able to "tease us out of thought." The urn thus maintains "decorum" and remains ready to "come alive" even as music comes alive "when the inked notes are scanned and interpreted by some later imagination." In another age, the urn's message may be translated into life and thus will continue to speak:

> More specifically, . . . the special and restricted character of the urn is stressed before its inscriptional message is permitted. Qualification is gradually built into the last two stanzas and particularly the closing sentence. Very much a part of the "truth" of human experience is the fact that every generation that views the urn is in the process of wasting, and living "in the midst of other woe/ Than ours." Aloof from the brevity and sharp claims of human life, the urn is not only freer but also more limited: freer to advance the message it does in a way that no human being could confidently do, and yet, as a work of art, limited to the realm in which the message applies. The message is like itself: "teasing," perpetually available for certain human experiences, and altogether oblivious of others. . . .[18]

This interplay of ideas on the superiority of art over nature is affirmed in another context by William Faulkner:

> The aim of every artist is to arrest motion, which is life, by artificial means and hold it fixed so that a hundred years later, when a stranger looks at it, it moves again since it is life. Since man is mortal, the only immortality possible for him is to leave something behind him that is immortal since it will always move. This is one artist's way of scribbling "Kilroy was here" on the wall of the final and irrevocable oblivion through which he must someday pass.[19]

WILLIAM FAULKNER

As an interpreter, check on the following: speaker-listener relationship; stanzaic form of the "Ode"; invocation in the first stanza; tone of exaltation and dignity; metaphoric language; slow, meditative cadence timed by iambic pentameter. You should come to your own conclusion as to whether or not the meaning of the lines leads to the last couplet, emphasized by a fulcrum, a shift in tone.

DIALOGUE 6: CLEANTH BROOKS, ROBERT PENN WARREN & REUBEN A. BROWER / ROBERT FROST'S "AFTER APPLE-PICKING"

Note the versatility of Frost as you compare the tone of "Design" with that of "After Apple-Picking," a dramatic lyric.

[18] Walter Jackson Bate, *John Keats* (Cambridge, Mass.: The Belknap Press of Harvard University Press, 1963), pp. 518-519.
[19] *Paris Interview Series*, p. 139.

After Apple-Picking

My long two-pointed ladder's sticking through a tree
Toward heaven still,
And there's a barrel that I didn't fill
Beside it, and there may be two or three
Apples I didn't pick upon some bough.
But I am done with apple-picking now.
Essence of winter sleep is on the night,
The scent of apples: I am drowsing off.
I cannot rub the strangeness from my sight
I got from looking through a pane of glass
I skimmed this morning from this drinking trough
And held against the world of hoary grass.
It melted, and I let it fall and break.
But I was well
Upon my way to sleep before it fell,
And I could tell
What form my dreaming was about to take.
Magnified apples appear and disappear,
Stem end and blossom end,
And every fleck of russet showing clear.
My instep arch not only keeps the ache,
It keeps the pressure of a ladder-round.
I feel the ladder sway as the boughs bend.
And I keep hearing from the cellar bin
The rumbling sound
Of load on load of apples coming in.
For I have had too much
Of apple-picking: I am overtired
Of the great harvest I myself desired.
There were ten thousand thousand fruit to touch,
Cherish in hand, lift down, and not let fall.
For all
That struck the earth,
No matter if not bruised or spiked with stubble,
Went surely to the cider-apple heap
As of no worth.
One can see what will trouble
This sleep of mine, whatever sleep it is.
Were he not gone,
The woodchuck could say whether it's like his
Long sleep, as I describe its coming on,
Or just some human sleep.[20]

ROBERT FROST

[20] *Frost,* see p. 182.

Many, intrigued by the symbolic extension in this poem, differ in their conclusions of the poet's meaning. Brooks and Warren evaluate this dramatic lyric as an interesting study in various contrasts: summer and winter; fact and fancy; labor and rest; effort and reward; wakefulness and sleep; everyday and confused visions. These critics, however, observe that the contrasts are blended into a unit of the real and the ideal: two experiences in life involving the completion of some achievement in the world of reality, followed by "reward, rest, dream." Should anyone question the dream as unpleasant, he should note the dream is not a nightmare but a fantasy evoked by images of swaying, scent and fragrance, of cherishing by touch and of the rumbling of apples, suggesting the satisfying completion of hard work. An application of this basic idea of an ideal stemming from the real world would appropriately fit Frost's way with poetry: the poem should develop from living experiences, reflecting the activities of ordinary living; "It should present apples magnified, but yet as apples." Brooks and Warren conclude that inasmuch as man is set off from nature, he *can* dream; on the other hand, he is also "of nature" since he seeks fulfillment in the world.[21]

Brower points out that the central metaphor is expressed in the phrase "the essence of winter sleep," a phrase permitting both the abstract meaning, "ultimate nature of sleep," and the natural one, "physical smell." Fragrance and sleep are blended in the same manner as sight and touch and are intensified by the line "I cannot rub the strangeness from my sight." The metaphor is further extended in the image of "magnified apples," fruit once seen clearly against the sky but now envisioned as "dream-like spheres."[22]

Everyone appreciates the effective description of remembered experience of similar fatigue not easily erased as he sinks into sleep. Your first impression is probably of an apple-picker, the narrator, who has pushed himself through days, perhaps weeks, of careful picking and sorting of the fruit—"ten thousand thousand fruit/ cherish in hand, and not let fall." He has experienced the same kind of after-effects from tedious work, the distortion of objects, the feel of the pressures and movements of his recent activity. For this worker the apples are magnified; "Stem end and blossom end" become more than minor details, as does the noticeable "fleck of russet." He sees the ladder reaching toward heaven—*still;* he feels the pressure of the ladder-round; he still sways with the ladder as the boughs bend; he still smells the fragrance—the scent of the apples; he still hears the rumbling sound of load on load of apples.

You can empathize with these sensory images—visual, tactile, kines-

---

[21] Cleanth Brooks and Robert Penn Warren, *Understanding Poetry,* 3rd ed. (New York: Holt, Rinehart and Winston, Inc., 1960), pp. 362-368.
[22] Reuben A. Brower, *The Poetry of Robert Frost* (New York: Oxford University Press, 1963), p. 26.

thetic, auditory, olfactory—because you too have been there! How easily, how casually, all these images are brought into the experience to make it real. You know the drowsiness, the inability to throw off the physical memory of repeated actions. This pattern of meaning with the dreamy mood, hovering between that illusive moment of consciousness and the dream, comes to you first. You enjoy it, you have a personal feeling about it, you are satisfied by the true and vivid description of the episode.

These impressions are first reactions; on reading further, images penetrate more deeply than the physical awareness of apple-picking. This is particularly true if you remember Frost's belief that a poem is a "metaphor saying one thing and meaning another." Gradually you are conscious of another meaning extending beyond the denotative one. You wonder if the apple-picker is having a typical dream of fatigue, if he is thinking of a near-experience of the great beyond or if he is reaching out beyond the apple-picking episode to another one of decision and effort in everyday life, an experience bringing eternal fulfillment. The pattern of thought appears to involve some kind of symbolic transference.

The meaning you find may not be that of another person. Before making a decision, be sure your connotative images fit Frost's pattern of a poem: after inclining to an impulse "it assumes direction with the first line laid down"; "it runs a course of lucky events";[23] "it ends in a clarification of life"; and "it has denouement." Inasmuch as the philosophy of this book is to suggest rather than to lay down an ultimatum about meaning in literature, you should follow your own decision about the direction toward a deeper impression. Question the connotative implication of these words and phrases: *two-pointed ladder*—life experiences or two desired activities pointing to the same goal or the ladder of success; *toward heaven*—hoped-for reward or end of life; *still*—task finished or to be continued; *essence of winter sleep*—distillate as perfume, fragrance or eternal permanence of "winter sleep"; *scent*—fragrance or reward as envisioned in the dream; *strangeness* of looking through a pane of glass held against a *world of hoary grass*—the beginning of "winter sleep" or death; *cherish, essence, scent, fleck of russet*—typical of the apple-picker's vocabulary; the *long sleep* of the woodchuck or *just some human sleep*— merely a dreamless sleep of the woodchuck who has no human worries of hard work in contrast to the confused sleep of men who cannot erase fatigue, numbness and weariness from their dreams or the sleep of death or hibernation; *this sleep of mine, whatever sleep it is*—deep "winter sleep" or only suggesting it?

You may apply your ingenuity in considering the images so implicitly interwoven as to almost defy a common understanding of the poet's central thought. If you are satisfied with the realistic description of the experience

23 Robert Frost, "The Figure a Poem Makes," *Complete Poems of Robert Frost* (New York: Holt, Rinehart & Winston, Inc., 1949), p. vi.

of apple-picking, no one will question your enjoyment. Others may wonder if the task is likened to a universal effort well-performed with a reward in the after-life. Some may find the images directed toward a premonition of death occurring after life episodes that have depleted the energy of the individual; some may find the dream a wish for immortality.

No doubt you have appreciated the images in this lyric containing the drama of man's inner thoughts and wish fulfillments. Have you also been aware of the tone of the narrator? Have you been conscious of the suggestive power of the words directed toward a central meaning? Have you caught Frost's whimsical touches? Have you noticed his device of understatement rather than the pressure of an idea extended too far in one direction? Do you have the impression that the poet is saying, "Here it is; it's yours for the finding"?

Have you thought about the devices that give the rhythmical movement of swaying, of drowsiness, of lulling to sleep? Notice the end-rhymes; the vowel repetitions, the sound echoes; word repetitions such as *sleep, stem end and blossom end, load on load, appear and disappear, ten thousand-thousand, essence and scent;* and the irregularity of lines not held rigidly to the same metrical pattern thus allowing sounds and words to support tone, mood and distinctive pattern. The empathic rhythm of many phrases, is evident, also, as in "I feel the ladder sway as the boughs bend," two balanced movements swaying back and forth, each one terminated firmly with the words *sway* and *bend.* These devices aid in the drowsy movement of the whole as the apple-picker sinks deeper and deeper into a sleep where he will no longer dream of *magnified apples,* feel the aches and swaying of the ladder, know the worries and disturbing after-effects of the apple-picking task.

Frost, however, has added "something" beyond these factors of imagery, repetitive sound, rhyme, rhythm. Perhaps one can say merely, "This is Frost's way with a poem." This illusive "something" has been called "texture" by the poet Ransom. Perhaps *you* can identify the intangibility inherent in the organic development. Certainly Frost's manner of discovering the proper niche for every word and phrase is vital for the universal appeal of his poems. In this lyric the narrator's voice could belong to any person because of the universality of that inner dreamlike, almost hypnotic trance that occurs with extreme fatigue and its release.

DIALOGUE 7: RANDALL JARRELL / RANDALL JARRELL'S "THE WOMAN AT THE WASHINGTON ZOO"

In his dramatic voice, Jarrell gives the student and the interpreter of literature an unusual insight into how he fused the images in his remarkable poem "The Woman at the Washington Zoo." Not too often does a poet or writer take the time to explain in detail the resolving of interwoven images in a literary masterpiece.

The poet's story of how images, accumulating daily from chance observations during his work in Washington, D. C. and during his visits to the zoo, merged into the final lines, illustrates the way in which flash impressions keep pushing the poet until the creative whole is found. Read the poem aloud several times before studying Jarrell's account of how the images became a part of the total meaning. Then check your impression with that of the poet.

The Woman at the Washington Zoo

The saris go by me from the embassies.

Cloth from the moon. Cloth from another planet.
They look back at the leopard like the leopard.

And I . . .
        This print of mine, that has kept its color
Alive through so many cleanings; this dull null
Navy I wear to work, and wear from work, and so
To my bed, so to my grave, with no
Complaints, no comment: neither from my chief,
The Deputy Chief Assistant, nor his chief—
Only I complain; this serviceable
Body that no sunlight dyes, no hand suffuses
But, dome-shadowed, withering among columns,
Wavy beneath fountains—small, far-off, shining
In the eyes of animals, these beings trapped
As I am trapped but not, themselves, the trap,
Aging, but without knowledge of their age,
Kept safe here, knowing not of death, for death
—Oh, bars of my own body, open, open!

The world goes by my cage and never sees me.
And there come not to me, as come to these,
The wild beasts, sparrows pecking the llamas' grain,
Pigeons settling on the bears' bread, buzzards
Tearing the meat the flies have clouded . . .

                    Vulture,
When you come for the white rat that the foxes left,
Take off the red helmet of your head, the black
Wings that have shadowed me, and step to me as man,
The wild brother at whose feet the white wolves fawn,

> To whose hand of power the great lioness
> Stalks, purring . . .
> > You know what I was,
> You see what I am: change me, change me![24]

RANDALL JARRELL

Jarrell recalls that his first impression of the hundreds of thousands of government clerks in Washington was the appearance in some women of the "aging-machine part." He wondered if one of them might not "feel all her dresses one dress, a faded navy blue print, and that dress her body." In his first attempt with composition, the woman speaks of the "dull null navy" she wears to and from work, with "no complaint, no comment" from her chief or any of his subordinates. The next creative work, according to the poet, introduces these images: *Body that no sunlight dyes, no hand suffuses* . . . then after a space there is *Dome-shadowed, withering among columns,/ Wavy upon the pools of fountains, small beside statues* . . . ." Jarrell explains:

No sun colors, no hand suffuses with its touch, this used, still-useful body. It is subdued to the element it works in: is shadowed by the domes, grows old and small and dry among the columns, of the buildings of the capital; becomes a reflection, its material identity lost, upon the pools of the fountains of the capital; is dwarfed beside the statues of the capital—as year by year it passes among the public places of this city of space and trees and light, city sinking beneath the weight of its marble, city of graded voteless workers.

The word *small*, as it joins the reflections in the pools, the trips to the public places, brings the poem to its real place and subject—to its title, even: next there is *small and shining*, then . . . , *small, far-off, shining in the eyes of animals;* the woman ends at the zoo, looking so intently into its cages that she sees her own reflection in *the eyes of animals, these wild ones trapped / As I am trapped but not, themselves, the trap.* . . . The lines have written above them, now, *The Woman at the Washington Zoo.* On the next page, the title and these twelve lines are recorded:

> *This print, that has kept the memory of color*
> *Alive through many cleanings; this dull null*
> *Navy I wear to work, and wear from work, and so*
> *To bed (with no complaints, no comment: neither from my chief,*
> *The Deputy Chief Assistant, nor her chief,*
> *Nor his, nor Congressmen, nor their constituents*
> > ~~wan~~
> *—Only I complain); this ~~plain~~ worn, serviceable*
> > *sunlight*
> *Body that no ~~sunset~~ dyes, no hand suffuses*

---

[24] From A SAD HEART AT THE SUPERMARKET by Randall Jarrell. Copyright © 1960 by Holt, Rinehart & Winston. Copyright © 1962 by Randall Jarrell. Reprinted by permission of Atheneum Publishers.

> *But, dome-shadowed, withering among columns,*
> *Wavy beneath fountains—small, far-off, shining*
> ~~wild~~
> *In the eyes of animals, these beings trapped*
> *As I am trapped, but not, themselves the trap* . . .

Written underneath this, in the rapid, ugly disorganized handwriting of most of the pages, is *bars of my body burst blood breath breathing—lives aging but without knowledge of age/Waiting in their safe prisons for death, knowing not of death;* immediately this is changed into two lines, *Aging, but without knowledge of their age,/Kept safe here, knowing not of death, for death*—and out at the side, scrawled heavily, is: *O bars of my own body, open, open!* She recognizes herself in the animals—and recognizes herself, also, in the cages.

Thus the poet finds that "the zoo was a whole group of pieces, a little Washington, into which the poem itself fitted."

The many visits of Jarrell and his wife to Rock Creek Park, "with its miles of heavily wooded hills and valleys, its rocky stream," permitting many animals unroofed cages in its ravines, suggest the setting of the poem. The poet recalls his experiences at the zoo with the lynx; the white timber wolves eager for meat; the lioness with her two cubs, purring and rubbing her head against the bars even as the lynx rubbed his head against the turkey-skin fed to him by the Jarrells; the foxes, curled up asleep in their unroofed cages, ignoring three rats, stiff and untouched on the concrete floor; the turkey buzzards that swooped down for the rats; the wolves that left big slabs of horsemeat, glazing, covered with flies; and finally, two black leopards, spotted "black on black, dingy somehow." He recalls that as a child, he had often seen "a turkey buzzard, with its black wings and naked red head, flap heavily up from the mashed body" of its prey.

These images are then assimilated in the composition of the poem. Jarrell continues:

A good deal of this writes itself on the next page, almost too rapidly for line-endings or punctuation: *to be and never know I am   when the vulture buzzard comes for the white rat that the foxes left   May he take off his black wings, the red flesh of his head, and step to me as man—a man at whose feet the white wolves fawn—to whose hand of power/The lioness stalks, leaving her cubs playing/and rubs her head along the bars as he strokes it.* Along the side of the page, between these lines, two or three words to a line, is written *the animals who are trapped but are not themselves the trap black leopard spots, light and darkened, hidden except to the close eyes of love, in their life-long darkness, so I in decent black, navy blue.*

As soon as the zoo came into the poem, everything else settled into it and was at home there; on this page it is plain even to the writer that all the things in the poem come out of, and are divided between, color and colorlessness. Colored women and colored animals and colored cloth—all that the woman sees as her own opposite—come into the poem to begin it. Beside the typed lines are many hurried phrases, most of them crossed out: *red and yellow as October maples   rosy, blood seen through flesh in summer   colors wild and easy natural   leaf-yellow cloud-rose leopard-yellow, cloth from another planet the leopards look back at their wearers, hue for hue   the women look back at the leopard.* And on the back of the vulture's page there is a flight of ideas, almost a daydream, coming out of these last phrases: *we have never mistaken you for the others   among the legations one of a different architecture women, saris of a different color envoy impassive   clear bullet-proof glass   lips through the clear glass of a rose sedan   color of blood   you too are represented on this earth. . . .*

In recalling these hues, Jarrell is reminded of the "women from the embassies of India and Pakistan, their sallow skin and black hair leopard-like, their yellow or rose or green saris exactly as one imagines the robes of Greek statues before the statues had lost their colors." Furthermore, as an "old reader of science fiction," the poet remembers how he was accustomed to "looking at the sun red over the hills, the moon white over the ocean, and saying to his wife in a sober voice: 'It's like another planet.'"—so the saris seemed "cloth from another planet" . . .

He then found he had the beginning of his poem:

It is almost as if, once all the materials of the poem were there, the middle and end of the poem made themselves, as the beginning seemed to make itself. After the imperative *open, open!* there is a space, and the middle of the poem begins evenly—since her despair is beyond expression—in a statement of accomplished fact: *The world goes by my cage and never sees me.* Inside the mechanical official cage of her life, her body, she lives invisibly; no one feeds this animal, reads out its name, pokes a stick through the bars at it—the cage is empty. She feels that she is even worse off than the other animals of the zoo: they are still wild animals—since they do not know how to change into domesticated animals, beings that are their own cages—and they are surrounded by a world that does not know how to surrender them, still thinks them part of itself. This natural world comes through or over the bars of the cages, on its continual visits to those within: to those who are not machine-parts, convicts behind the bars of their penitentiary, but wild animals—the free beasts come to their imprisoned brothers and never know that they are not also free. . . .

The poet interprets the last lines beginning with "Vulture" by explaining the woman has "become her own cage," living a "manless, childless, fleshless" existence. She becomes the stale bait finally seized by the turkey buzzard. The series of words *pecking, settling on, tearing* become a sexual metaphor. The overtones attached to these images demonstrate how deeply Jarrell probed:

. . . Her own life is so terrible to her that, to change, she is willing to accept even this, changing it as best she can. She says: *Vulture* (it is a euphemism that gives him distance and solemnity), *when you come for the white rat that the foxes left* (to her the rat is so plainly herself that she does not need to say so; the small, white, untouched thing is more accurately what she is than was the clouded meat—but, also, it is euphemistic, more nearly bearable), *take off the red helmet of your head* (the bestiality, the obscene sexuality of the flesh-eating death-bird is really—she hopes or pretends or desperately is sure—merely external), *clothes,* (an intentionally-frightening war-garment like a Greek or Roman helmet), *the black wings that have shadowed me* (she feels that their inhuman colorless darkness has always, like the domes of the inhuman city, shadowed her; . . . *and step* (as a human being, not fly as an animal) *to me as* (what you really are under the disguising clothing of red flesh and black feathers) *man*—not the machine-part, the domesticated animal that is its own cage, but man as he was first, still must be, is: the animals' natural lord,

> The wild brother at whose feet the white wolves fawn,
> To whose hand of power the great lioness
> Stalks, purring . . .

And she ends the poem when she says to him:

> You know what I was,
> You see what I am: change me, change me![25]

RANDALL JARRELL, *A Sad Heart at the Supermarket*

DIALOGUE 8: STANLEY KUNITZ / STANLEY KUNITZ'S "FATHER AND SON"

In the collected symposia of the volume, *The Contemporary Poet as Artist and Critic,* are found many uninhibited, critical discussions among various poets concerning eight poems. A fine orientation to poets' inventive ingenuity in conceiving the ideas, blocking out designs and building toward central meanings that have grown out of their own experiences is offered the literary student.

The poem "Father and Son," planned by Kunitz as a dramatic lyric but having many aspects of the dramatic monologue, provides provocative material for comments among the members of the symposium. Kunitz is revealed as a perceptive and undaunted personality in his reply to the questions raised. The poem is excellent for interpretative purposes, inasmuch as it has "talking" potential.

Father and Son

Now in the suburbs and the falling light
I followed him, and now down sandy road
Whiter than bone-dust, through the sweet

[25] Jarrell, *op. cit.,* pp. 161-173.

Curdle of fields, where the plums
Dropped with their load of ripeness, one by one.
Mile after mile I followed, with skimming feet,
After the secret master of my blood,
Him, steeped in the odor of ponds, whose indomitable love
Kept me in chains. Strode years; stretched into bird;
Raced through the sleeping country where I was young,
The silence unrolling before me as I came,
The night nailed like an orange to my brow.

How should I tell him my fable and the fears,
How bridge the chasm in a casual tone,
Saying, "The house, the stucco one you built,
We lost. Sister married and went from home,
And nothing comes back, it's strange, from where she goes.
I lived on a hill that had too many rooms:
Light we could make, but not enough of warmth,
And when the light failed, I climbed under the hill.
The papers are delivered every day;
I am alone and never shed a tear."

At the water's edge, where the smothering ferns lifted
Their arms, "Father!" I cried, "Return! You know
The way. I'll wipe the mudstains from your clothes;
No trace, I promise, will remain. Instruct
Your son, whirling between two wars,
In the Gemara of your gentleness,
For I would be a child to those who mourn
And brother to the foundlings of the field
And friend of innocence and all bright eyes.
O teach me how to work and keep me kind."

Among the turtles and the lilies he turned to me
The white ignorant hollow of his face.[26]

STANLEY KUNITZ

The first paragraph of the poet's answer to the questions raised most often by Josephine Miles, Robert Beloof and Robert Lowell concerns a poet's feeling after he has disengaged himself from his identity with the poem.

Once a poem has been distributed, it is no longer the property of the poet. By the time it is published he has become somebody else, and part of the change in him must be attributed to his knowledge that he is free from the necessity of making that poem again. Even if he could! He can try, of course, to remem-

[26] From SELECTED POEMS: 1928-1958, by Stanley Kunitz. Copyright, ©, 1958, by Stanley Kunitz. Reprinted by permission of Little, Brown and Co.—Atlantic Monthly Press.

ber who he was and how he felt during the event, but his memory is not wholly to be trusted, since it is stained with afterthought and prone to rationalize everything he has done, particularly when he has done something as unreasonable as writing poetry. The poet's professional identity is elusive even to himself: it is not a fixity to be recaptured, but rather an accumulation of quite special, often compulsive energies that disappear by flowing into the poem. After the event poet as well as reader is left with nothing but an arrangement of words on a page to testify that something more or less unusual or valuable has happened.[27]

Kunitz then explains that the poem was "born of a dream," written at the beginning of World War II—"whirling between two wars"—and that the details are true as dreams are true: there was a big house on the hill at the edge of the city; there was a sister who died; there was a bottomless pond "alive with snakes and pickerel and snapping turtles and pond lilies." These experiential details present an "overlay of episodes and images" which the poet worked into a myth or legend, not knowing now just where the myth begins. He settles the doubt concerning his father's death by drowning by telling his commentators that his father did not die in the pond, had never seen it and that he himself was the one who escaped drowning in the water.

The image of the orange nailed to his brow disturbed all critics, so he reports how the image became part of his experience:

Nobody, alas, seems to like my line, "The night nailed like an orange to my brow," but I have lived with it too long to think of changing a word. What is so outlandish about it? Throughout the poem the moon, though never named, is fiercely burning . . . shining in the bone-dust and the mist, reflected at the last in "the white ignorant hollow" of the father's face. Most of us must have known breathless nights, so heavy and close that the moon has walked with us. To suffer this night of the moon so intensely is to be impaled by it. To one who says flatly, "Oranges are not nailed," my flat answer is, "In this poem they are." The reader cannot be expected to know that when I was six years old, running barefoot, I stepped on a nail that protruded—God knows how—through a rotten peach and hobbled home with that impossible fruit hammered to my flesh.[28]

He adds that this particular image was not employed as an ornament but was felt by him as a reality, a truth:

Such moments in a poem, evident only by the pressure building behind them, can never fully explain themselves, but the poet must take the risk with them

[27] Reprinted from *The Contemporary Poet as Artist and Critic: Eight Symposia,* edited by Anthony Ostroff, by permission of Little, Brown and Company. Copyright © 1964, by Little, Brown and Company (Inc.). The commentary from which this selection is excerpted originally appeared in "The Poet and His Critics: A Symposium on Stanley Kunitz' 'Father and Son' " in *New World Writing,* 20, 1962, copyright © 1962 by J. B. Lippincott Company, pp. 211-215.
[28] *Ibid.*

as an article of faith. In the end, for whatever it may be worth, they constitute his signature.[29]

The poet emphasizes that the breaks in the grouping of lines do not indicate stanzas but rather blocks of narrative, each with its own distinctive rhythm. In the first block, you can observe how distance is "skimmingly" portrayed, the action being smooth and swift; in the second block, breaks and pauses of the broken rhythm of speech are obvious; in the third block, a dramatic crescendo, insistent in its movement and appealing in its tone, is built. The poet calls attention to the last two lines "which should be set off from the rest of the poem by a space." To Kunitz, this space or fulcrum is extremely important for the firmness of the structure.

In the paragraph below, note the way the poem develops for Kunitz, as well as his superb objectivity in the analysis of meaning:

The way that a poem develops is largely out of one's control, since the end is willed by the means, but I sense that my impulse toward a form generally tends to move along the lines of certain ineluctable archetypes, particularly those of death and rebirth, the quest, and the night-journey (or descent into the underworld). In all three patterns—which may be consubstantial—the progress is from a kind of darkness into a kind of light. If Miss Miles is correct in asserting that passivity and ignorance win out at the end of "Father and Son," I am most egregiously at fault. As I understand the main level of the action, the son in his quest is not looking for pity or pardon. It is to be noted that he makes no confession of sins. The losses that he reviews are those peculiar to the human condition and of special interest to the father, since they involve property and family. "Instruct me how to live" is the substance of his prayer, but in the irony of circumstance it is addressed to one who is dead and who, furthermore, has destroyed himself. Presumably the son who wants to be saved is unaware of the self-destructive elements in his nature that impel him toward the father; unaware till the very instant when his begetter enters the water and becomes one with it—both source and death-trap. The last two lines, constituting a simultaneous *peripeteia* and *anagnorisis*, reversal and discovery, announce for me the shock of recognition that moves beyond despair. Now that for the first time the father shows his terrible face, the son is delivered from his bondage, from his trance of love and yearning, from his seductive loyalties. His triumph is in what he *sees*. I read the ending on a note of tragic exaltation.[30]

DIALOGUE 9: ALLEN TATE / EMILY DICKINSON'S "THE CHARIOT"

One of the foremost critics, Allen Tate—also the poet who wrote the well-known "Ode to the Confederate Dead," ranks Dickinson's poem "The Chariot" as "one of the greatest in the English language," in his dialogue.

[29] *Ibid.*
[30] *Ibid.*

Tate talks about the "heart of this poem":

The Chariot

Because I could not stop for Death,
He kindly stopped for me;
The carriage held but just ourselves
And Immortality.

We slowly drove, he knew no haste,
And I had put away
My labor, and my leisure too,
For his civility.

We passed the school where children played
At wrestling in a ring;
We passed the fields of gazing grain,
We passed the setting sun.

We paused before a house that seemed
A swelling of the ground;
The roof was scarcely visible,
The cornice but a mound.

Since then 'tis centuries; but each
Feels shorter than the day
I first surmised the horses' heads
Were toward eternity.[31]

EMILY DICKINSON

If the word great means anything in poetry, this poem is one of the greatest in the English language. The rhythm charges with movement the pattern of suspended action back of the poem. Every image is precise and, moreover, not merely beautiful but fused with the central idea. Every image extends and intensifies every other. The third stanza especially shows Miss Dickinson's power to fuse, into a single order of perception, a heterogeneous series: the children, the grain, and the setting sun (time) have the same degree of credibility; the first subtly preparing for the last. The sharp *gazing* before *grain* instills into nature a cold vitality of which the qualitative richness has infinite depth. The content of death in the poem eludes explicit definition. He is a gentleman taking a lady out for a drive. But note the restraint that keeps the poet from carrying this so far that it becomes ludicrous and incredible; and note the subtly interfused erotic motive, which the idea of death has presented to most romantic poets, love being a symbol interchangeable with death. The terror of death is objectified through the figure of the genteel driver, who is

[31] Emily Dickinson, *The Complete Poems of Emily Dickinson* (Boston: Little, Brown and Company, 1960).

made ironically to serve the end of Immortality. This is the heart of the poem: she has presented a typical Christian theme in its final irresolution, without making any final statements about it. There is no solution to the problem; there can be only a presentation of it in the full context of intellect and feeling. A construction of the human will, elaborated with all the abstracting powers of the mind, is put to the concrete test of experience: the idea of immortality is confronted with the fact of physical disintegration. We are not told what to think; we are told to look at the situation.[32]

ALLEN TATE, *Emily Dickinson*

For the interpreter, this poem will need an easy, casual approach in vocal intensity and also careful timing. Pauses are important for reinforcement and suspense. Preparation for the shock treatment of the last stanza must be realized.

---

[32] Reprinted from *Collected Essays* by Allen Tate, by permission of the publisher, Alan Swallow. Copyright 1960 by Allen Tate, p. 206.

III

THE TECHNIQUE OF
EXPRESSION

7

Meaning Through Bodily Movement

HOW THE INTERPRETER EXPRESSES MEANING

Through the skills involved in the technique of impression, you have gained something of the author's impression from the black marks. You may not always be right about the meaning, but you will have made an attempt to understand how the author wants his words to carry the central idea.

You will now be concerned with the skills involved in the technique of expression: the ability to re-create this meaning for others. Your main concern is the control over total bodily and vocal response. Since the philosophy of this book centers on how you employ all parts of the body as a coordinated system, you must first consider how you perform *toute d'une piece*—all of one piece.

MEANING THROUGH BODILY TENSIONS & MOVEMENT

Inasmuch as you always see before you hear—that is, the eye is quicker than the ear—you recognize easily that bodily tension or activity is most important in stirring up meaning for an audience. Even as you face the listeners, before you say anything, you carry meaning as a person. The impression others get may be the wrong one or not one you hope for, but it is meaning. You may be unconsciously frowning, smiling, nervous or limp, without reason. You may be experiencing platform tensions that give a false impression of your skill as an interpreter. Watch a performer as he appears before you. What meaning do you as an observer receive? Do you get an impression of his ease or perhaps of his discomfort? If he is smiling, you smile back; if he is uncomfortable you fidget in your chair, unconsciously receiving the tension he shows. If this meaning can be carried without words, merely through facial expression and bodily tension—and it can be—think of the power of expression you may have if you employ the right distribution of bodily energy and play of muscles with the coordinated control of the voice!

MEANINGFUL RESPONSE THROUGH EMPATHY

How, then, can you best adapt yourself to an audience-interpreter situation, one that demands you arouse or stimulate in your listeners an emotional response similar to the one you received from the author's lines. The principle involved is one of empathy, the kinesthetic response you create in your listeners. Empathy, from the German word *einfühlung*, is a "feeling into," as contrasted with a "feeling with" or "sympathy for." The muscles of the observer tend to do what the object at which he is looking is doing or suggesting. Empathic reaction is a difficult response to study introspectively because it occurs spontaneously. It is not subject to your will; it is rather, a natural impulse. Listeners are not really aware that their facial expressions reflect those of the performer; that their bodies tense with anger when the interpreter shows anger; that their eyes open wide in a startled look when the performer has the same expression. They have been caught in an emotional "feeling into" that indicates the performer has been effective in his portrayal. So empathy is created most successfully when people are not conscious of what is happening to them or how they are responding physically or emotionally.

EMPATHIC EXPERIENCES

Empathy implies the response of "getting into the spirit of things." Analyze your own muscular reactions. How do you react to the different moods of your friends? What do you do when you observe some person walking with a prim, tense rhythm—stilted and rigid? Can you feel the pull in your muscles? Where do you feel the greatest urge for action when you observe bronzes of drooping maidens, of stern Indians watching the flight of an arrow, of a child wriggling his toe in glee, of a stealthy tiger ready to spring? Note the downward pull of your muscles when you observe a jet plane swooping earthward; or the upward pull as it swings back into space. Did you ever sit on the bleachers and watch the football hero tear down the field—stumbling, struggling, pulling, running, dodging, twisting—and finally, with a tremendous lunge, succeed in putting the ball over the line? If you thoroughly enjoyed what he was doing, if you were helping him along, exhorting, pushing your neighbor, whooping and yelling when the touchdown was made—then *you* made the touchdown, for your muscles were straining and pulling as his were and you probably felt the joyous relaxation that comes after strenuous exercise.

You watch dancers and, insofar as you can, you dance with them; you see the hero knock the villain down and find your fists doubled up and your arms taut trying to strike and hold still at the same time. You see the base runner "hit the dust" and you slide with him—on the bleachers. All this is empathy, a "feeling into."

You like or dislike a person very often because of the muscular tensions you observe in him. Sometimes these tensions are very noticeable; sometimes they are hidden from the casual observer. Many people, as they grow in experience, try to cover up any muscular movements that reveal how they feel. An individual of personality, for instance, is often one whose movements make others do things that are correct, proper and stimulating. In a large measure, men *are* what they are observing. You enter into the spirit of what is happening, you enjoy it and become lost in it because you *are taking part.* If you actually feel the beauty of the towering cathedral, it lifts you and carries you bodily to transcendent heights. When you appreciate a work of art, you are actually going through the bodily responses suggested by whatever you are enjoying. In this manner empathy is the essence of artistic appreciation.

The theater offers an excellent opportunity for the study of empathic responses. Everything about the mechanics of the stage picture, including furniture, properties, lights, color, make-up, line, movement, is arranged to create an illusion of reality, a necessity if the audience is to feel empathy. If the lights do not work, if an essential prop has been forgotten, if the gun does not go off when it should, if the telephone does not ring, then momentarily, the illusion has been lost and you are no longer in the spirit of the scene. Empathy—the kind of empathy the director has been trying to get from the audience—has been lost.

The greater number of tensions the actor stimulates in you, the better you like the play. If you do not experience any of the desired empathic responses, you are bored, cold, pained at the performance. You are not muscularly set to enjoy anything, for you will not permit yourself the emotion that the director and actors have tried to arouse in the audience. Usually, the more relaxed you are at the beginning of the performance, the greater your chance of empathic enjoyment. Empathy is the response that tingles, warms, exhilarates. When Cyrano de Bergerac, the great swordsman and soldier, draws his sword with a great flourish, every man feels the pull of that brandish; or if Juliet has conveyed the fear she feels as she drains the sleeping potion, then those watching feel the throat muscles tighten and the body go limp as she sinks down in the emotional climax. You have probably never liked the villain on the stage: if he is a convincing actor, he causes unpleasant tensions as you react empathically. Remember that when you get angry, you get angry all over—glands, muscles and nerves respond to the complete picture of anger. Your body experiences an increase of glandular secretions and of sugar in the blood stream; the beat of your heart will quicken, resulting in a corresponding tonicity of muscles—and you are angry!

You like comedies because they do pleasant things to your muscles—you laugh and are relaxed and refreshed. Real tragedy, if it accomplishes its purpose, should purify, cleanse and relax "body and soul." The tragedy so stark that it chokes you and leaves you rigid is the one you like to avoid. No matter what the writer's intention or purpose may be—to make his audience laugh or cry or both—he makes the body *do* things, and this *doing* may be called an empathic or emotional response, a reacting *into* the situation.

EMPATHY & COORDINATION

How do you communicate these tensions to the audience? How do you evoke empathic responses creating the desired emotion, exciting bodily activity to respond to your thought? The answer lies in a coordinated body showing a totality of response through economy of effort and a rhythmical follow-through of muscles, every part working *all of one piece.*

You cannot always get the wished-for response from everyone in the room because your listeners are people with individual differences, tastes and experiences. To make all of them like you is impossible, even for professionals. To stand before a group, however, with an expressionless face and with hands waving and whirling through the air as you utter the first line of de la Mare's "The Listeners," "Is there anybody there? said the Traveller," is not going to bring success because the body is out of control and therefore the mood established by the author has not been expressed. In this poem (page 187), you are not knocking on the door of your next-door neighbor's house to use the phone for an emergency call. The rhythmical cadences of Vachel Lindsay's "The Congo," as in these lines,

> Wild crap-shooters with a whoop and a call
> Danced the juba in their gambling hall
> And laughed fit to kill, and shook the town . . .

cannot be interpreted by standing inert from head to toe, if you wish to show the contrast of the primitive Negro with the redeemed Negro. This does not mean you have to stamp your feet, beat your hands and sway your body, but it does mean that you will never get the rhythm in your voice without feeling the pulse of the rhythm inherent in a coordinated bodily response. If you cannot suggest this to the audience, you cannot expect them to get the empathy inherent in Lindsay's word arrangements. Rhythm does not exist without coordination; hence, bodily coordination is not only advisable but necessary.

What is involved in this principle of coordination? Muscles and tonicity of muscles. A muscle can do only one thing—contract. Muscles are always in a state of contraction although the degree varies. When contraction is nil, the muscle is dead or flaccid. This relaxing state can be partially attained by an anesthetic but complete relaxation comes only when life is gone. The degree of muscle tone or contraction is proportional to the degree of attentiveness of the interpreter. If you are under great excitement, the tonus (partial contraction of the muscles) increases until the muscles become so tense they may ache, and you may experience great difficulty in relaxing. The more practice you give muscles in employing different degrees of relaxation, the more pliable they become and the greater the "muscle memory." A muscular sense or memory of muscle movement is requisite; you cannot fully experience a movement you have never made. This memory can be developed only by practice as in any activity requiring coordination. After many, many performances, the movement will tend to become reflexive. Without this muscle memory, you could not go about your daily tasks of eating, dressing, drinking with any economy. To make your bodily movements mean the maximum, you must practice; thus you build up muscle sense and memory, that, in turn, pave the way for coordination and economy of effort.

COORDINATION & TOTAL BODILY RESPONSE

In order to have a total bodily response, you must be emotionally or muscularly set, just as the track man "gets set" for his race, the punter poises himself for the punt, the golfer anticipates a "follow-through," the horseman gets the feel of his horse, the ski-jumper gets ready to sail through the air or the actor gets the mood of the character he is to portray. Each performer has his body coordinated for a situation that calls for complete muscular activity, not for some isolated movements that would destroy the goal he is seeking and would give the observer the wrong empathic response. Inasmuch as the audience assumes some kind of motor response toward the object it is watching, too many uncoordinated movements are likely to produce restlessness in the observers. An amateur acrobat whose muscles are not ready makes you uneasy, and a dancer whose gasping breath you can hear, makes you gasp. So the interpreter whose hands flabbily gesture from one side to another makes you flop too; and one who fails to grapple adequately with the thought makes you fumble. Everyone likes to do his observing as a whole: hence, the performer, in order to secure the desired empathic response, must learn to integrate all desired emotional processes. Command the attention of the audience upon yourself as a whole and not as an uncoordinated collection of parts. If an audience notices you are waving your hands through the air when you are talking about the "babbling brook" or the "blue clouds overhead," you may be sure something is wrong with your technique, and that something is usually a lack of coordination in addition to poor taste. Any unusual muscular set may reveal an attitude that may distort your meaning. Think of the many phrases descriptive of bodily responses identifying character and attitude as: "She gave me a cold shoulder";

"She was stiff-necked about it"; "He wears his heart on his sleeve"; "He did a complete turn-about"; "The teacher was a high brow"; "She wore a chip on her shoulder"; "He was two-faced"; "She opened her mouth and let her brains fall out."

These clichés represent gestures, movements inherent in bodily set, translated into metaphorical language. Too many times a gesture is considered a movement outside of the total bodily response or habit, an action taken on and off, to be used here and not there. Gesture rather should grow out of the total activity of the body and not be an isolated manifestation; it should come from within as a part of the whole.

You are endowed with physical parts that, if used skillfully, can carry the meanings you intend to your audience. If you feel a certain movement is necessary, try it out in front of your mirror. Work for a suggested activity that supports the thought. If your audience squirms every time you make any kind of movement, you are undoubtedly either overdoing or are uncoordinated. When you work *all of one piece*, your action will fit the thought and language; no one but an expert critic will be able to detect your body technique, and everyone will enjoy the added meaning such action contributes to your interpretation. Your objective should be to intensify meaning through coordinated movement.

Richard Blackmur[1] explains clearly the interweaving of language and gesture:

> Language is made of words, and gesture is made of motion. There is one half the puzzle. The other half is equally self-evident if only because it is an equally familiar part of the baggage of our thought. Words are made of motion, made of action or response, at whatever remove; and gesture is made of language—made of the language beneath or beyond or alongside of the language of words.

Blackmur then relates his experience watching a woman attempt to pay her fare and to get a seat on the bus, as it spurted forward at forty or fifty miles an hour. She was a woman with a "largish" French figure, with "noticeable waist and a more noticeable rear," "wearing heels too high for her balance," and a big floppy hat (worn askew) that had a way of interfering as she attempted to gain her composure with the upright post holding the coin box. In moving toward her seat, she "fair yawed to leeward every few yards," lurching in all directions as the bus increased its speed, and clutching each seat handle.

> During the whole business . . . she managed by sniffs and snorts, by smiles, by sticking her tongue out very sharp, by batting her very blue eyes about, and generally by cocking her head this way and that, to express fully, and without a single word either uttered or wanted, the whole mixed, flourishing sense of

[1] Richard Blackmur, *Language as Gesture* (New York: Harcourt, Brace and World, Inc., 1952), pp. 3-6.

her disconcertment, her discomfiture, her uncertainty, together with a sense of adventure and of gaiety, all of which she wanted to share with her companion behind me.

This activity, Blackmur remarks, is not only gesture that takes the place of language, but when occurring with it, "crowns" and "animates" language to its highest use.

COORDINATION & ECONOMY OF EFFORT

Coordination usually implies economy of effort. Your system of organicity is so arranged that with the stimulation of certain muscles, a relaxation of opposing muscles occurs. This rhythmic contraction and relaxation, if utilized, results in the expert performance that distinguishes the professional performer from the amateur.

Interpretation usually does not call for broad, expansive movements, excessive head and hand activity, such as Blackmur's character with the floppy hat indulged in; it does, however, call for suggestion of highly coordinated movements. Every muscle in the body of a skillful interpreter should perform its function of tension and relaxation to give ease of movement. Muscular selectivity will aid in carrying through your impression by intensifying your meaning, just as in an etching the fewest lines always carry the finest impression. The visual stimulation of your listeners will depend upon the effectiveness of your suggested, economical movement.

Economy of effort, however, does not mean an inert attitude, a slumped-over body, or a purposeless expression. The person who stands still is not particularly interesting; the person, however, who stands still with purpose, with meaning, commands attention. This same kind of difference can be found in the classroom between the student who listens without hearing and intention of purpose and the student who listens and hears thoughtfully.

Any audience will analyze your total bodily attitude in the same way. They like to feel you are confident, and are not embarrassed by the fact they are listening to you. The response of the audience to you personally begins as soon as you start to the platform. If you lope to the podium, sag at the waist, fumble with your book, clear your throat many times, shuffle your feet, fidget with a gadget, and finally, droop over the lectern, you can be certain the majority of the listeners will be wishing you could believe in your interpretation, or at least be aware that they are complimenting you by being present.

Purpose, intention and sincerity should be shown by your bodily set and movements. You expect this same kind of poise and assurance when you seek the services of a professional person, such as a doctor. If you are confronted by an evasive person who cannot look into your eyes, continually shifts his position, hems and haws, speaks indefinitely, what do you do? Believe in his decision? Allow him to operate with hands in continual motion? Usually you seek another person—one in whom you can place your confidence, one who knows how to make decisions. Why do you conclude he is competent? You recognize his directness, his decisiveness, his control!

COORDINATION & RHYTHM

To discuss rhythm as separate from coordination and economy of effort is to give a mistaken impression of how rhythm operates and influences movement of the body. Rhythm is inherent in these two factors, just as organic rhythm is inherent in breathing, walking, speaking and the beating of the heart. You may be one who has rhythm that adapts easily to learned activities such as skating, dancing, baseball, swimming. You have a rhythmical follow-through: bodily movements consisting of recurrent contraction and relaxation of certain muscles, timed to provide smooth, total muscular action. All jerky and angular movements, suggesting tension and rigidity, are excluded from your balanced timing and easeful effort.

Consider the smooth process of breathing. How do you breathe—deeply and fully or shallowly and quickly? Good rhythmical breathing habits are difficult for some persons, who, because of insufficient practice and control, go through life panting and puffing. An athlete develops certain breathing habits for greater speed and ease in physical effort; a singer learns to control the rhythm of breathing so no strain in the shoulder muscles will be obvious. Have you ever noticed you tend to follow the breathing pattern of the person with whom you are talking? Have you noted what happens to your breathing pattern when you are watching swift and unexpected movement on television or on the athletic field? You also tend to breathe in rhythm with the steps you are taking. Have you ever listened to your walking rhythm? Do your steps reveal a lagging foot or a mincing, quick step? Do you lift one foot higher than the other or swing one foot over to one side? Perhaps you use a free, swinging rhythm that pulses through the body with a pleasurable thrill of well-being. You empathize happily with a lithe, pleasing movement and you groan with heavy, plodding steps. Each person has a rhythm peculiar to himself: one may be a rhythm with economy of muscular movement and coordinated timing; the other a rhythm with many random and unnecessary movements and misdirected nervous energy that will soon tire the body. Ease of movement, whether in walking, dancing, running, acting or interpreting, brings joy to the onlooker because of the esthetic reaction received from the "form." To create the greatest pleasure empathically, you must educate your body, your neuromuscular mechanism, so it shows rhythmical control. Then perhaps you will be ready to convert your impressions of literature into bodily expression.

PLATFORM TENSION

Attending to an audience is brought about by muscle tensions of the body, called by some, attitude. Unfortunately, this attention can some-times be disrupted through audience stimulation, through sensory reactions of looking, listening and speaking.

You have seen the rabbit freeze when caught suddenly in the brilliant lights of an oncoming car. So too have you had the unforgettable experience of the same kind of rigidity before an audience: the body is "frozen," the voice quivers, the tongue is glued to the roof of the mouth, the hands are clammy and wet, the knees shake, you may feel faint or nauseated. Instead of the typical rhythm of contraction and relaxation of the muscles in these audience situations, you have contraction without relief from the opposing muscles. As a result, a trembling of muscles, held too long in a state of contraction, may occur. Any kind of movement that gives the muscles some biological relief is helpful.

This encounter with an audience is to be expected and not feared, since, after several attempts, you will realize you know more concerning the literary interpretation than the audience does and you become master of the situation. Sometimes you are wise to admit your fear in a practice session. Inasmuch as you have companions in similar distress, part of the awe-some audience confrontation should be lessened.

The following are some suggestions to help you control platform tension in order to secure favorable audience attention:

1. Breathe slowly and deeply before you walk to the platform.
2. Walk to the platform without too much haste; if you race to the po-dium, your breathing may be uncontrolled for you will tend to breathe in rhythm with your quick steps.
3. When you get to the podium, look directly at the audience. Take time to give them the "once-over." Remember this is your show and so you, for the time being, are master of the situation.
4. Let your audience settle down and look you over. Do not rush them—create some expectancy. Let them get an idea of your appearance, and hopefully, your enjoyment of the occasion. At the same time you can look them over in a gracious manner, noting the age range and interest shown in the faces and attitudes.
5. If your knees begin to shake or your voice begins to quiver, pause or move to another position without losing audience attention. Even shifting your weight from one foot to another will help, but do not sway.
6. Never be embarrassed by too much platform tension for everyone has experienced it. You may give a better performance if you feel a trifle

nervous and apprehensive. At any rate, you will be a better interpreter for having controlled your bodily tension.

7. Always watch your audience in your introductory remarks. If you look away from your listeners, tension will increase and you will find difficulty in turning back to them.

8. You will begin, probably, with an introduction explaining some pertinent item about your selection—why you are interpreting it, what its literary value is, what kind of person wrote it, how it relates to other similar pieces of literature. Do not make your introductory statement too long because attention can be fleeting.

9. If you are using a book or script, plan how to hold it or place it on the lectern, and when and how you will turn the pages. Remind yourself continually to let your eyes take only transitory glances at the page. You will know the selection well enough so that you will not have to hunt for the next phrase or line, and will not seem to be exerting great effort in following the page.

10. As you proceed with your presentation, notice the reaction of your audience: Are they hearing you? Are they listening? Are they restless? Are they looking out the window instead of at you? Are they reacting in a nervous, fidgety manner because you are ill at ease?

11. You wish for a sincere interpretation. If you feel inadequate, however, in the first few moments, *pretend* for your own happiness that you are a capable and confident interpreter. You have spent most of the day probably pretending to be intelligent or happy or interested; now try pretending you are confident.

12. When you finish, hold your body in the attitude appropriate to the meaning conveyed; do not break away from the moment too readily or immediately look down or away or fuss with your script. Hold your posture until your audience has caught up with the meaning and responded to an effective interpretation. After you have remained with them a moment or two, break away quietly; do not rush from the platform.

13. If tension has not eased after several platform attempts, read Edmund Jacobson's *You Must Relax*[2] or David Fink's *Release from Nervous Tension*.[3] Each author demonstrates practical methods in acquiring more ease. You will enjoy Fink's chapters on "Even Dogs Get Neurotic." "The Body Talks Back to You" and "Are You Allergic to Some People?"

To summarize: appropriate muscular tone and posture intensify meaning by creating empathic responses through coordinated bodily activity. In order to secure empathy in the listeners, the interpreter:

[2] Edmund Jacobson, *You Must Relax* (New York: McGraw-Hill Book Company, Inc., 1934).

[3] David Fink, *Release from Nervous Tension* (New York: Simon and Schuster, 1953).

1. Suggests rather than initiates extensive outward activity.
2. Avoids bodily mannerisms and random movements that detract rather than add to the total meaning.
3. Works for body form and poise emphasized through economy and ease of effort; and for rhythmical movement of bodily parts.

These bodily movements and tensions are coordinated with vocal control in producing the final impression. Even though the management of the voice has not been discussed, try this initial experiment in empathy. Each of the following selections in prose and poetry has a marked mood, that, if meaningfully expressed, will create empathy in your listeners. You may have a favorite literary selection to substitute for one of these. When you try this assignment, err on the side of doing too much rather than too little. Toning down is always easier than building up. At first, *abandon* is the word!

SELECTIONS

Masefield, always restless in his love of the sea and adventure, writes of his longing in "Sea Fever." Can you feel the cadences of the phrases that suggest pauses for rhythm and mood? Be careful not to let your voice drop at the end of all phrases.

Sea-Fever

I must down to the seas again, to the lonely sea and the sky,
And all I ask is a tall ship, and a star to steer her by,
And the wheel's kick and the wind's song and the white sail's shaking,
And a grey mist on the sea's face and a grey dawn breaking.

I must down to the seas again, for the call of the running tide
Is a wild call and a clear call that may not be denied;
And all I ask is a windy day with the white clouds flying,
And the flung spray and the blown spume, and the sea-gulls crying.

I must down to the seas again to the vagrant gypsy life,
To the gull's way and the whale's way where the wind's like a whetted knife;
And all I ask is a merry yarn from a laughing fellow-rover,
And quiet sleep and a sweet dream when the long trick's over.[4]

JOHN MASEFIELD

The mellow mood in this classic from Byron is not found too often in his poetry:

So We'll Go No More A Roving

So, we'll go no more a roving
  So late into the night,
Though the heart be still as loving,
  And the moon be still as bright.

For the sword outwears its sheath,
  And the soul wears out the breast,
And the heart must pause to breathe,
  And love itself have rest.

Though the night was made for loving,
  And the day returns too soon,
Yet we'll go no more a roving
  By the light of the moon.

GEORGE GORDON, LORD BYRON

Do not attempt to create sentimentality in Elizabeth Barrett Browning's famous sonnet. Experience the depth, quietness and sincerity of the mood, stressing shifts in thought through your eyes and facial expression, as well as with your voice. Listen to Katherine Cornell's recording.[5]

How Do I Love Thee?

How do I love thee? Let me count the ways.
I love thee to the depth and breadth and height
My soul can reach, when feeling out of sight
For the ends of Being and ideal Grace.
I love thee to the level of every day's
Most quiet need, by sun and candle-light.
I love thee freely, as men strive for Right;
I love thee purely, as they turn from Praise.
I love thee with the passion put to use
In my old griefs, and with my childhood's faith.
I love thee with a love I seemed to lose
With my lost saints,—I love thee with the breath,
Smiles, tears, of all my life!—and, if God choose,
I shall but love thee better after death.

ELIZABETH BARRETT BROWNING

[5] Caedmon TC 1071: "Sonnets from the Portuguese," *The Barretts of Wimpole Street*. Recorded by Katherine Cornell and Anthony Quayle.

The selection of connotative words and images creates a distinctive mood of solitude and deep rest in Lew Sarett's "Deep Wet Moss." The phrases "deep wet moss," "cool blue shadows," "purple solitude" should cue you for the mood.

Deep Wet Moss

Deep wet moss and cool blue shadows
  Beneath a bending fir,
And the purple solitude of mountains,
  When only the dark owls stir—
Oh, there will come a day, a twilight,
  When I shall sink to rest
In deep wet moss and cool blue shadows
  Upon a mountain's breast,
And yield a body torn with passions,
  And bruised with earthly scars,
To the cool oblivion of evening,
  Of solitude and stars.[6]

LEW SARETT

Note the casual irony in Hardy's poem:

The Man He Killed

Had he and I but met
  By some old ancient inn,
We should have sat us down to wet
  Right many a nipperkin!

But ranged as infantry,
  And staring face to face,
I shot at him as he at me,
  And killed him in his place.

I shot him dead because—
  Because he was my foe,
Just so: my foe of course he was;
  That's clear enough; although

He thought he'd 'list, perhaps,
  Off-hand like—just as I—

[6] From *Covenant with Earth* by Lew Sarett. Gainesville: University of Florida Press, 1956. Reprinted by permission of Mrs. Lew Sarett.

Was out of work—had sold his traps—
No other reason why.

Yes, quaint and curious war is!
You shoot a fellow down
You'd treat if met where any bar is,
Or help to half-a-crown.[7]

THOMAS HARDY

Notice the easy, forward movement in this lyric even though the pauses indicate shifts in direction:

I Like to See It Lap the Miles

I like to see it lap the Miles—
And lick the Valleys up—
And stop to feed itself at Tanks—
And then—prodigious step

Around a Pile of Mountains—
And supercilious peer
In Shanties—by the sides of Roads—
And then a Quarry pare

To fit it's sides
And crawl between
Complaining all the while
In horrid—hooting stanza—
Then chase itself down Hill—

And neigh like Boanerges—
Then—prompter than a Star
Stop—docile and omnipotent
At it's own stable door—[8]

EMILY DICKINSON

NARRATIVE & DESCRIPTION

In narrative selections, you may often find descriptions that are important to the mood and tone of the story. Avoid the tendency to hurry

[7] Reprinted with permission of The Macmillan Company from COLLECTED POEMS OF THOMAS HARDY. Copyright 1925 by The Macmillan Company.
[8] Emily Dickinson, *The Complete Poems of Emily Dickinson* (Boston: Little, Brown and Company, 1960).

over these passages to get on with the narrative. They may be quite necessary as mood background for the progression of events. The following descriptive accounts should create empathy because of the sensory appeal through vivid imagery. In the first selection, Tom Pinch rides the stage-coach to London for the first time.

from *The Life and Adventures of Martin Chuzzlewit*

When the coach came round at last, with "London" blazoned in letters of gold upon the boot, it gave Tom such a turn, that he was half disposed to run away. But he didn't do it; for he took his seat upon the box instead, and looking down upon the four greys, felt as if he were another grey himself, or, at all events, a part of the turn-out; and was quite confused by the novelty and splendor of his situation.

And really it might have confused a less modest man than Tom to find himself sitting next to that coachman; for of all the swells that ever flourished a whip, professionally, he might have been elected emperor. He didn't handle his gloves like another man, but put them on—even when he was standing on the pavement, quite detached from the coach—as if the four greys were, somehow or other, at the ends of the fingers. It was the same with his hat. He did things with his hat, which nothing but an unlimited knowledge of horses and the wildest freedom of the road could ever have made him perfect in. Valuable little parcels were brought to him with particular instructions, and he pitched them into his hat, and stuck it on again, as if the laws of gravity did not admit of such an event as its being knocked off or blown off, and nothing like an accident could befall it. The guard too! Seventy breezy miles[9] a day were written in his very whiskers. His manners were a canter; his conversation a round trot. He was a fast coach upon a downhill turnpike road; he was all pace. A wagon couldn't have moved slowly, with that guard and his key-bugle on the top of it.

These were all foreshadowings of London, Tom thought, as he sat upon the box, and looked about him. Such a coachman and such a guard never could have existed between Salisbury and any other place; the coach was none of your steady-going, yokel coaches, but a swaggering, rakish, dissipated, London coach; up all night, and lying by all day, and leading a terrible life. It cared no more for Salisbury than if it had been a hamlet. It rattled noisily through the best streets, defied the cathedral, took the worst corners sharpest, went cutting in everywhere, making everything get out of its way; and spun along the open country-road, blowing a lively defiance out of its key-bugle, as its last glad parting legacy.

It was a charming evening. Mild and bright. And even with the weight upon his mind which arose out of the immensity and uncertainty of London, Tom could not resist the captivating sense of rapid motion through the pleasant air. The four greys skimmed along, as if they liked it quite as well as Tom did; the bugler was in as high spirits as the greys; the coachman chimed in sometimes with his voice; the wheels hummed cheerfully in unison; the brass-

[9] Note the figurative language used here and in the following sentences.

work on the harness was an orchestra of little bells; and thus they went clinking, jingling, rattling smoothly on; the whole concern, from the buckles of the leaders' coupling-reins to the handle of the hind boot, was one great instrument of music.

Yoho! past hedges, gates, and trees; past cottages and barns, and people going home from work. . . . Yoho! by churches dropped down by themselves in quiet nooks, with rustic burial-grounds about them, where the graves are green, and daisies sleep—for it is evening—on the bosoms of the dead. Yoho! past streams, in which the cattle cool their feet, and where the rushes grow; past paddock-fences, farms, and rich-yards. . . . Yoho! down the pebbly dip, and through the merry water-splash, and up at a canter to the level road again. Yoho! Yoho! . . . Yoho! down countless turnings, and through countless many ways, until an old inn-yard is gained, and Tom Pinch, getting down, quite stunned and giddy, is in London.

Charles Dickens

Images create the intense mood in this description of a tropical sunset. What kind of feeling do you have after reading it?

from *A Midsummer Trip to the Tropics*

What a tropical sunset is this—within two days' steam-journey of the equator! Almost to the zenith the sky flames up from the sea—one tremendous orange incandescence, rapidly deepening to vermillion as the sun dips. The indescribable intensity of this mighty burning makes one totally unprepared for the spectacle of its sudden passing; a seeming drawing down behind the sea of the whole vast flare of light. . . . Instantly the world becomes indigo. The air grows humid, weighty with vapor; frogs commence to make a queer bubbling noise; and some unknown creature begins in the trees a singular music, not trilling, like the note of our cricket, but one continuous shrill tone, high, keen, as of a thin jet of steam leaking through a valve. Strong vegetal scents, aromatic and novel, rise up. Under the trees of our hotel I hear a continuous dripping sound; the drops fall heavily, like bodies of clumsy insects. But it is not dew, nor insects; it is a thick, transparent jelly—a fleshy liquor that falls in immense drops. . . . The night grows chill with dews, with vegetable breath; and we sleep with windows nearly closed.[10]

Lafcadio Hearn

NARRATIVE & CHARACTERIZATION

The emphasis in this short tale lies in the characterization of Della, whose strong points, as told by the great humorist Thurber, are her choice vocabulary and her thorough diagnosis of her master's mental condition.

[10] Lafcadio Hearn, *Two Years in the French West Indies* (Boston: Houghton Mifflin Company, 1923), V. 3, pp. 86-87.

What Do You Mean It Was *Brillig?*

I was sitting at my typewriter one afternoon several weeks ago, staring at a piece of blank white paper, when Della walked in. "They are here with the reeves," she said. It did not surprise me that they were. With a colored woman like Della in the house it would not surprise me if they showed up with the toves. In Della's afternoon it was always brillig; she could outgrabe a mome rath on any wabe in the world. Only Lewis Carroll would have understood Della completely. I try hard enough. "Let them wait a minute," I said. I got out the big Century Dictionary and put it on my lap and looked up "reeve." It is an interesting word, like all of Della's words; I found out there are four kinds of reeves. "Are they here with strings of onions?" I asked. Della said they were not. "Are they here with enclosures or pens for cattle, poultry, or pigs; sheep-folds?" Della said no sir. "Are they here with administrative officers?" From a little nearer the door Della said no again. "Then they've got to be here," I said, "with some females of the common European sandpiper." These scenes of ours take as much out of Della as they do out of me, but she is not a woman to be put down by a crazy man with a dictionary. "They are here with the reeves for the windas," said Della with brave stubbornness. Then, of course, I understood what they were there with: they were there with the Christmas wreaths for the windows. "Oh those reeves!" I said. We were both greatly relieved; we both laughed. Della and I never quite reach the breaking point; we just come close to it.

Della is a New England colored woman with nothing of the South in her accent; she doesn't say "d" for "th" and she pronounces her "r"s. Hearing her talk in the next room, you might not know at first that she was colored. You might not know till she said some such thing as "Do you want cretonnes for the soup tonight?" (She makes wonderful cretonnes for the soup.) I have not found out much about Della's words, but I have learned a great deal about her background. She told me one day that she has three brothers and that one of them works into a garage and another works into the incinerator where they burn the refuge. The one that works into the incinerator has been working into it since the Armitage. That's what Della does to you; she gives you incinerator perfectly and then she comes out with the Armitage. I spent most of an hour one afternoon trying to figure out what was wrong with the Armitage; I thought of Armistead and armature and Armentières, and when I finally hit on Armistice it sounded crazy. It still does. Della's third and youngest brother is my favorite; I think he'll be yours, too, and everybody's else's. His name is Arthur and it seems that he has just passed, with commendably high grades, his silver-service eliminations. Della is delighted about that, but she is not half so delighted about it as I am.

Della came to our house in Connecticut some months ago, trailing her glory of cloudiness. I can place the date for you approximately: it was while there were a great many fletchers about. "The lawn is full of fletchers," Della told me one morning, shortly after she arrived, when she brought up my orange juice. "You mean neighbors?" I said. "This early?" By the way she laughed I knew that the fletchers weren't people; at least not people of flesh and blood.

I got dressed and went downstairs and looked up the word in the indispensable Century. A fletcher, I found, is a man who makes arrows. I decided, but without a great deal of conviction, that there couldn't be any arrow-makers on my lawn at that hour in the morning and at this particular period in history. I walked cautiously out the back door and around to the front of the house— and there they were. I don't know many birds but I do know flickers. A flicker is a bird which, if it were really named fletcher, would be called flicker by all the colored cooks in the United States. Out of a mild curiosity I looked up "flicker" in the dictionary and I discovered that he is a bird of several aliases. When Della brought my toast and coffee into the dining room I told her about this. "Fletchers," I said, "are also golden-winged woodpeckers, yellow-hammers, and high-holders." For the first time Della gave me the look that I was to recognize later, during the scene about the reeves. I have become very familiar with that look and I believe I know the thoughts that lie behind it. Della was puzzled at first because I work at home instead of in an office, but I think she has it figured out now. This man, she thinks, used to work into an office like anybody else, but he had to be sent to an institution; he got well enough to come home from the institution, but he is still not well enough to go back to the office. I could have avoided all these suspicions, of course, if I had simply come out in the beginning and corrected Della when she got the words wrong. Coming at her obliquely with a dictionary only enriches the confusion; but I wouldn't have it any other way. I share with Della a form of escapism that is the most mystic and satisfying flight from actuality I have ever known. It may not always comfort me, but it never ceases to beguile me.

Every Thursday when I drive Della to Waterbury in the car for her day off, I explore the dark depths and strange recesses of her nomenclature. I found out that she had been married for ten years but was now divorced; that is, her husband went away one day and never came back. When I asked her what he did for a living, she said he worked into a dove-wedding. "Into a what?" I asked. "Into a dove-wedding," said Della. It is one of the words I haven't figured out yet, but I am still working on it. "Where are you from, Mr. Thurl?" she asked me one day. I told her Ohio, and she said, "Ooooh, to be sure!" as if I had given her a clue to my crazy definitions, my insensitivity to the ordinary household nouns, and my ignorance of the commoner migratory birds. "Semantics, Ohio," I said. "Why there's one of them in Massachusetts, too," said Della. "The one I mean," I told her, "is bigger and more confusing." "I'll bet it is," said Della.

Della told me the other day that she had had only one sister, a beautiful girl who died when she was twenty-one. "That's too bad," I said. "What was the matter?" Della had what was the matter at her tongue's tip. "She got tuberculosis from her teeth," she said, "and it went all through her symptom." I didn't know what to say to that except that my teeth were all right but that my symptom could probably be easily gone all through. "You work too much with your brain," said Della. I knew she was trying to draw me out about my brain and what had happened to it so that I could no longer work into an office, but I changed the subject.

There is no doubt that Della is considerably worried about my mental condition. One morning when I didn't get up till noon because I had been writing letters until three o'clock, Della told my wife at breakfast what was the matter with me. "His mind works so fast his body can't keep up with it," she said. This diagnosis has shaken me not a little. I have decided to sleep longer and work less. I know exactly what will happen to me if my mind gets so far ahead that my body can't catch up with it. They will come with a reeve and this time it won't be a red-and-green one for the window, it will be a black one for the door.[11]

JAMES THURBER

In this opening to the story "Impulse," you are introduced to the character and mood of Michael Lowes through his inner thoughts:

from *Impulse*

Michael Lowes hummed as he shaved, amused by the face he saw—the pallid, asymmetrical face, with the right eye so much higher than the left, and its eyebrow so peculiarly arched, like a "v" turned upside down. Perhaps this day wouldn't be as bad as the last. In fact he knew it wouldn't be, and that was why he hummed. This was the bi-weekly day of escape, when he could stay out for the evening, and play bridge with Hurwitz, Bryant, and Smith. Should he tell Dora at the breakfast table? No better not. Particularly in view of last night's row about unpaid bills. And there would be more of them, probably, beside his plate. The rent, the coal, the doctor who attended the children. What a life. Maybe it was time to do a new jump. And Dora was beginning to get restless again—.

But he hummed, thinking of the bridge game. Not that he liked Hurwitz or Bryant or Smith—cheap fellows, really—mere pick-up acquaintances. But what could you do about making friends, when you were always hopping about from one place to another, looking for a living, and fate always against you! They were all right enough. Good enough for a little escape, a little party— and Hurwitz always provided good alcohol. Dinner at the Greek's, and then to Smith's room—yes. He would wait till late in the afternoon, and then telephone to Dora as if it had all come up suddenly. Hello, Dora—is that you, old girl? Yes, this is Michael—Smith has asked me to drop in for a hand of bridge—you know—so I'll have a little snack in town. Home by the last car as usual. Yes. . . . Gooo - bye!

And it all went off perfectly, too. Dora was quiet, at breakfast, but not hostile. The pile of bills was there, to be sure, but nothing was said about them. And while Dora was busy getting the kids ready for school, he managed to slip out, pretending that he thought it was later than it really was. Pretty neat, that! He hummed again, as he waited for the train. Telooralooraloo. Let the bills wait, damn them! A man couldn't do everything at once, could he, when bad luck hounded him everywhere? And if he could just get a little night off, now and then, a rest and change, a little diversion, what was the harm in that?

[11] From THE THURBER CARNIVAL by James Thurber, published by Harper and Brothers. Copyright © 1939 by James Thurber. Orignally published in the *New Yorker*. Reprinted by permission of Mrs. James Thurber.

At half-post four, he rang up Dora and broke the news to her. He wouldn't be home till late.

"Are you sure you'll be home at all?" she said coolly.

That was Dora's idea of a joke. But if he could have foreseen—!¹²

CONRAD AIKEN

NARRATIVE & DRAMATIC ACTION

Most authors of fiction attempt to intensify meaning mainly by integration of either or both elements of description and characterization to support dramatic action leading to a climax. The skill by which they obtain this crescendo may vary from story to story, depending on which factor they consider most important for the final empathic response.

The following dramatic episode is one of many from the classic narrative, *The Red Badge of Courage*, written by Crane when he was twenty-three years old and without any war experience. Stuart Pratt Sherman, a perceptive essayist, has written that one cannot forget this story.

I see his vague shape (the hero's) creeping through the misty fringe of a forest, sniffing the whiffs of powder, hearing the bullets cut the leaves overhead, perceiving his gradual immersion in the battle, till the louder roar of cannon and drifting smoke and danger and charging men and flags and horses and wounds and thirst and death envelop him in a cloudy whirling confusion.¹³

Henry Fleming, the hero, is referred to in the story as "the youth," emphasizing his inexperience and age for the war as well as the universality of his reactions. After running away from a bloody battle, he falls in with a procession of disabled soldiers, who think he too is wounded. Their many questions make him feel desperately ashamed and he becomes enraged at them. "They were ever upraising the ghost of shame on the stick of their curiosity." Then seeing a quickly advancing troop ready for battle, he wondered

what those men had eaten that they could be in such haste to force their way to grim chances of death. As he watched, his envy grew until he thought that he wished to change lives with one of them. . . . He thought he was about to start for the front. . . . Then the difficulties of the thing began to drag on him. . . . He had no rifle. . . . it would be a miracle if he found his regiment. . . . his comrades would ask for an explanation. . . . he felt their scrutiny. . . . Furthermore . . . he had a scorching thirst. His face was so dry and grimy that he thought he could feel his skin crackle. Each bone of his body had an

¹² From THE COLLECTED SHORT STORIES OF CONRAD AIKEN. Copyright © 1922, 1923, 1924, 1925, 1927, 1928, 1929, 1930, 1931, 1932, 1933, 1934, 1935, 1941, 1950, 1952, 1953, 1955, 1956, 1957, 1958, 1959, 1960 by Conrad Aiken. Published by arrangement with The World Publishing Company, Cleveland and New York, pp. 159-160.

¹³ Stephen Crane, "Preface" by Max J. Herzberg, *The Red Badge of Courage* (New York: Meredith Press, 1942), p. xxxix.

ache in it, and seemingly threatened to break with each movement. His feet were like two sores. . . . There was a dull, weightlike feeling in his stomach, and when he tried to walk, his head swayed and he tottered. . . . Small patches of green mist floated before his vision. . . . He was a craven loon. Those pictures of glory were piteous things. He groaned from his heart and went staggering off.

In this physical state and in torture mentally, Fleming found himself engulfed in another battle scene.

from *The Red Badge of Courage*

The column that had butted stoutly at the obstacles in the roadway was barely out of the youth's sight before he saw dark waves of men come sweeping out of the woods and down through the fields. He knew at once that the steel fibers had been washed from their hearts. They were bursting from their coats and their equipments as from entanglements. They charged down upon him like terrified buffaloes.

Behind them blue smoke curled and clouded above the treetops, and through the thickets he could sometimes see a distant pink glare. The voices of the cannon were clamoring in interminable chorus.

The youth was horror-stricken. He stared in agony and amazement. He forgot that he was engaged in combating the universe. He threw aside his mental pamphlets on the philosophy of the retreated and rules for the guidance of the damned.

The fight was lost. The dragons were coming with invincible strides. The army, helpless in the matted thickets and blinded by the overhanging night, was going to be swallowed. War, the red animal war, the blood-swollen god, would have bloated fill.

Within him something bade to cry out. He had the impulse to make a rallying speech, to sing a battle hymn, but he could only get his tongue to call into the air: "Why—why—what—what's th' matter?"

Soon he was in the midst of them. They were leaping and scampering all about him. Their blanched faces shone in the dusk. They seemed, for the most part, to be very burly men. The youth turned from one to another of them as they galloped along. His incoherent questions were lost. They were heedless of his appeals. They did not seem to see him.

They sometimes gabbled insanely. One huge man was asking of the sky: "Say, where de plank road? Where de plank road!" It was as if he had lost a child. He wept in his pain and dismay.

Presently, men were running hither and thither in all ways. The artillery booming, forward, rearward, and on the flanks made jumble of ideas of direction. Landmarks had vanished into the gathered gloom. . . .

The youth, after rushing about and throwing interrogations at the heedless bands of retreating infantry, finally clutched a man by the arm. They swung around face to face.

"Why—why—" stammered the youth struggling with his balking tongue.

The man screamed: "Let go me! Let go me!" His face was livid and his eyes were rolling uncontrolled. He was heaving and panting. He still grasped his rifle, perhaps having forgotten to release his hold upon it. He tugged frantically, and the youth being compelled to lean forward was dragged several paces.

"Let go me! Let go me!"

"Why—why—" stuttered the youth.

"Well, then!" bawled the man in a lurid rage. He adroitly and fiercely swung his rifle. It crushed upon the youth's head. The man ran on.

The youth's fingers had turned to paste upon the other's arm. The energy was smitten from his muscles. He saw the flaming wings of lightning flash before his vision. There was a deafening rumble of thunder within his head.

Suddenly his legs seemed to die. He sank writhing to the ground. He tried to arise. In his efforts against the numbing pain he was like a man wrestling with a creature of the air.

There was a sinister struggle.

Sometimes he would achieve a position half erect, battle with the air for a moment, and then fall again, grabbing at the grass. His face was of a clammy pallor. Deep groans were wrenched from him.

At last, with a twisting movement, he got upon his hands and knees, and from thence, like a babe trying to walk, to his feet. Pressing his hands to his temples he went lurching over the grass.

He fought an intense battle with his body. His dulled senses wished him to swoon and he opposed them stubbornly, his mind portraying unknown dangers and mutilations if he should fall upon the field. He went tall soldier fashion. He imagined secluded spots where he could fall and be unmolested. To search for one he strove against the tide of his pain.

Once he put his hand to the top of his head and timidly touched the wound. The scratching pain of the contact made him draw a long breath through his clinched teeth. His fingers were dabbled with blood. He regarded them with a fixed stare.

Around him he could hear the grumble of jolted cannon as the scurrying horses were lashed toward the front. Once, a young officer on a besplashed charger nearly ran him down. He turned and watched the mass of guns, men, and horses sweeping in a wide curve toward a gap in a fence. The officer was making excited motions with a gauntleted hand. The guns followed the teams with an air of unwillingness, of being dragged by the heels. . . .

The blue haze of evening was upon the field. The lines of forest were long purple shadows. One cloud lay along the western sky partly smothering the red.

As the youth left the scene behind him, he heard the guns suddenly roar out. He imagined them shaking in black rage. They belched and howled like brass devils guarding a gate. The soft air was filled with the tremendous remonstrance. With it came the shattering peal of opposing infantry. Turning to look behind him, he could see sheets of orange light illumine the shadowy distance. There were subtle and sudden lightnings in the far air. At times he thought he could see heaving masses of men. . . .

He was overcome presently by a dragging weariness. His head hung forward and his shoulders were stooped as if he were bearing a great bundle. His feet shuffled along the ground.

He held continuous arguments as to whether he should lie down and sleep at some near spot, or force himself on until he reached a certain haven. He often tried to dismiss the question, but his body persisted in rebellion and his senses nagged at him like pampered babies.

At last he heard a cheery voice near his shoulder: "Yeh seem t' be in a pretty bad way, boy?"

The youth did not look up, but he assented with thick tongue. "Uh!"

The owner of the cheery voice took him firmly by the arm. "Well," he said, with a round laugh, "I'm goin' your way. Th' hull gang is goin' your way. An' I guess I kin give yeh a lift." They began to walk like a drunken man and his friend.

As they went along, the man questioned the youth and assisted him with the replies like one manipulating the mind of a child. Sometimes he interjected anecdotes. "What reg'ment do yeh b'long teh? Eh? What's that? Th' 304th N' York? Why, what corps is that in? Oh, it is? Why, I thought they wasn't engaged t'day—they're way over in th' center. Oh, they was, eh? Well, pretty nearly everybody got their share 'a fightin' t'day". . . .

Thunder, I wish we was sure 'a findin' our reg'ments t'night. It's goin' t' be long huntin'. But I guess we kin do it."

In the search which followed, the man of the cheery voice seemed to the youth to possess a wand of a magic kind. He threaded the mazes of the tangled forest with a strange fortune. In encounter with guards and patrols he displayed the keenness of a detective and the valor of a gamin. Obstacles fell before him and became of assistance. The youth, with his chin still on his breast, stood woodenly by while his companion beat ways and means out of sullen things.

The forest seemed a vast hive of men buzzing about in frantic circles, but the cheery man conducted the youth without mistakes, until at last he began to chuckle with glee and self-satisfaction. "Ah, there yeh are! See that fire?"

The youth nodded stupidly.

"Well, there's where your reg'ment is. An' now, good-by, ol' boy, good luck t' yeh."

A warm and strong hand clasped the youth's languid fingers for an instant, and then he heard a cheerful and audacious whistling as the man strode away. As he who had so befriended him was thus passing out of his life, it suddenly occurred to the youth that he had not once seen his face.[14]

STEPHEN CRANE

ESSAY

These two excerpts by Jacques Barzun and John Mason Brown should interest you. Barzun is an educator, Dean at Columbia University, a prolific essayist; Brown is a drama critic, a scintillating essayist who writes about actors, theater and speechmaking. Each writer indulges in humor, but the tone provides a different mood in each essay:

[14] A cutting from *The Red Badge of Courage*, recorded by Edmond O'Brien, is one of the best prose interpretations among the records. Note the versatility and range of his vocal powers. Caedmon TC 1040.

from *Let X Equal*

Then I have more than an impression—it amounts to a certainty—that algebra is made repellent by the unwillingness or inability of teachers to explain why we suddenly start using *a* and *b*, what components mean apart from their handling, and how the paradoxical behavior of + and − came into being. There is no sense of history behind the teaching, so the feeling is given that the whole system dropped down readymade from the skies, to be used only by born jugglers. This is what paralyzes—with few exceptions—the infant, the adolescent, or the adult who is not a juggler himself.

When you add to this the fact that many computers who teach are both impatient and inarticulate, you have reason enough for the child's hatred of ciphering. I well remember one college instructor, said to have been a brilliant discoverer, but whose students failed with alarming regularity. He used to write on the board difficult problems in integration, and after everyone had given up he would put the chalk to his lips, make a noise like a straining gear box, and write out the correct result. How he got to it he could never explain. "Don't you see?" he would plead. We never did see. But we had his exact opposite, a rather crude and coarse barrel of a man, whom I remember with gratitude for the phrase he never tired of using at every step, "What'll this *gim-me?*" That expressed the true spirit of calculation, and to symbolize this feeling we students made up the myth that he was a successful bootlegger on the side.[15]

JACQUES BARZUN

Brown evidently had allowed himself enough leisure in his busy day of writing and lecturing to read Mrs. Roosevelt's column, "My Day," recounting her varied activities.

from *Seeing the Sights*

But those indolent days are no more. Mrs. Roosevelt's example has brought them to an end. In almost every township in the land newspapers can be purchased which carry her Pepys's Diary. Devouring it fills one with shame. Shame and envy. For the First Lady's journal is more than America's Court Circular. It is an alphabet soup of vitamins which the slothful sip at their own peril. Its record of energies untiring and seconds unwasted curdles the conscience of those who have felt fatigue. Worse than that, just when we have surrendered to the need for doing nothing, or been tempted to indulge in a siesta, "My Day" has forced us to jump up guiltily and ask ourselves, "What *would* Mrs. Roosevelt be doing if only she were here?"

The question is sufficiently agitating to drive a bear out of hibernation. Certainly she would not be lolling in the noonday sun. Certainly she would not

---

[15] From TEACHER IN AMERICA by Jacques Barzun, by permission of Little, Brown and Co.—Atlantic Monthly Press, p. 82.

be napping. Nor would she be tired. The art museum would have taken twenty —at the most twenty-one—minutes of her time. The zoo she would have seen in ten minutes; the arrowheads in four. Her day would have been fuller than the fullest moon. From six in the morning until midnight she would have set us all a model of vitality without ever being victimized by that anemia which drives most of us to rest. For in one respect only does this good and gracious lady resemble Macbeth. She murders sleep, and makes us, who fancy ourselves strong men, feel like worms for ever having slept.

It is she who in her charming person has effected an industrial revolution in the lives of all of us who also lecture. No longer can any of us claim to have seen a town if we have encircled the Civil War monument. An interest in art is not now enough. If we would pattern our day on hers, we, too, must dash from Picasso to the picket lines. We, too, must vary Goya with the garment workers. We, too, must be concerned with the striking of more than chimes. We, too, must go down to the water front again and rejoice that the morning's at seven. We, too, must four-star in our Baedekers the settlement houses, the post-office murals, the clinics, the federal housing projects, and the local handicrafts.[16]

JOHN MASON BROWN

[16] From *Accustomed As I Am,* by John Mason Brown, W. W. Norton & Co., 142. Reprinted with permission of the author, pp. 138-139.

8

Speech Pattern

VOICE & MEANING

YOUR LISTENING WORLD

The world today is a listening world of radio, telstar, television, recordings, interviews and commentators. You have grown up with the everyday sounds of home life—the sounds of water running, bacon sizzling, dishes breaking, refrigerator and furnace noises, dogs scratching at the door; and also the outdoor sounds of trucks, hot-rods, motorcycles, cars, hail against the windows, destructive winds of hurricanes, devastating crash of cars. Through your sensitivity to noise, you have learned to connect meaning with sound: the whine of sirens and defense signals, the thundering boom of jets as they break the sound barrier, the crack of pistols and the noise of the action on television. You can even identify the voices of many actors, commentators and politicians without seeing them. The voice, instead of the pen, has taken over dramatically as the universal spokesman, motivating serious negotiations, commenting on news before it is printed, providing recorded entertainment by speech and song.

So, too, do you and your friends recognize one another over the phone or "on the air" because your vocal habits form a speech pattern with characteristic quality, emphasis, intonation and cadence. You have acquired your particular way of talking because of your experiences, environment, vocal mechanism and your bodily set and movement. Very seldom will two voices show an identical pattern, except for unconscious imitation of those with whom you live. Vocal expression is not so much a matter of whether your voice is slow or fast, high or low, resonant or muffled, forceful or weak. Rather it is a matter of how all these elements blend together to give a total pattern.

These identifying elements of sound found in the production of voice are (1) *quality* or *timbre,* or the resonant balance of voice, (2) *force* or *intensity,* or the vocal attack, (3) *tempo* or *timing* within and among phrases and sentences, (4) *pitch,* including *key, step* and *inflection,* or the up and down movement of vocal intonations. The infinite variety of combinations of these elements will be discussed in the following chapters.

Although for this study each element is considered separately, they merge to form your total speech pattern.

SPEECH RHYTHMS

SPEECH RHYTHM, ENVIRONMENT & PERSONALITY

Every speech pattern has its characteristic movement and rhythm, showing variable combinations of attack and release of sound, rise and fall of inflection, pause and flow of sound. Quality, the resonant tone of your voice, indirectly influences speech rhythm. If the voice is richly resonant, the movement probably will not be rapid except when the owner of the voice wishes to employ hurried or decisive speech. On the other hand, if the voice is high pitched and nasal, the vocal tempo is likely to quicken because the owner is not taking time to use his vocal mechanism effectively.

To a considerable degree your speech rhythm is typical of your general bodily rhythm. Precision of bodily movements will usually be accompanied by precision of vocal activity. A quickly moving person often will have a high, tense voice with a fast, staccato rhythm. The movements of an awkward, slow body will be reflected in a halting speech rhythm. The healthy outdoor person has a different speech rhythm from that of an invalid. Those who have mastered the muscular patterns involved in the "follow-through" of a golf club or a tennis racket, or those who have learned control of movements in swimming, running and hurdling, should have little difficulty in mastering rhythms of vocal expression. The hypotonic person (one with less than normal tonicity of muscles), because of a slowness of physical movement, will not have the speech pattern of the excitable, high-strung, hypertonic person (one with more than normal tonicity of muscles). The former will usually have a slower speech rhythm, with long pauses and little inflection; the latter a quick, broken rhythm, with abrupt pauses and breaks and probably a wide range of pitch.

Your speech pattern is likely to reflect your personality, to indicate how you think and feel. Others interpret your mood according to your vocal inflections, rapidity or slowness of your expression, forcefulness or ease of your speech pattern. You learn also to know how another will react because of his habitual approach through his bodily set and speech pattern. You, the interpreter, have a different environmental make-up than another interpreter. Each of you has lived through particular experiences; your reading interests may vary; your traveling may have been extensive or limited; your neighbors may have been friendly or aloof; your living abode may have changed every few years or it may have been established in one community. So your likes and dislikes are based on how you have lived, where you have lived and with whom you have lived. Some have creative ability; some know how to provide opportunities for socialization; some have the knack of self-direction and improvement; some are withdrawn. As a result, the voice often reveals reflections of these experiences. An individual's friendliness, his sense of "amongness," presents a personality with "give" that will be reflected in his speech pattern. Dividends will be realized by you, as soon as you build a reservoir of experiences.

Locale also plays its part in making speech rhythms distinctive. Different locales have their own provincial cadences. The interpreter soon learns that dialectal speech requires study of speech rhythms, of cadence, of the stressed and unstressed. The speech rhythm of the Bostonian is not that of the Kentuckian. The northwest side of Chicago produces cadences found in no other spot in that great city. Some southern Illinoisians show a nasality quite different from the tense, twangy nasality of many living in northern Illinois. So, in like manner, each nationality is recognized by its own peculiar speech pattern. The Italian has an irresistible lilt; the Russian, often with a guttural quality, hurries along with a staccato movement; the Frenchman indulges in an abundance of nasal resonance with an ecstatic upward swing; the Englishman uses clipped, precise speech, permitting little resonance and has a tendency to upward inflections.

SPEECH RHYTHM & ELISION

Inability to secure a varied rhythm often occurs if the student has been urged in earlier days to give every syllable equal value in the interest of distinct enunciation. No sensible or sensitive person, however, talks with all words and syllables evenly spaced, like a typewriter or metronome. If you do speak in this way, your speech is unnatural, indirect, laborious, stilted.

The standards of good speech are based upon conversational speech that will never sound like a metronome. Good rhythmical speech requires elision of syllables, subordination and superordination of words, a pattern of dots and dashes. Some syllables must be stressed, others must be unstressed. To emphasize everything is to emphasize nothing; and without emphasis, little sense is projected—just a string of monotonous, isolated syllables. Unless you are forced to do so, you will never say:

I—must—down—to—the—seas—a—gain,—to—the—lone—ly—seas—and—the—sky.

Rather, you will probably elide like this:

I mus'down toth'seasagain toth'lonely seas'n'th'sky.

One of the helpful hints in rhythmical speech is: make the long sounds long and the short ones short. When you have decided which sounds are to be held, prolong them as much as good communicative sense permits; and when you have decided which sounds can be shortened, cut them to the demands of distinctness. This problem of elision of the unimportant and insignificant is not in conflict with the needs of careful enunciation and communicative speech. Many spoken words are never pronounced as the dictionary would have them pronounced: such words as *the, and, in, of, to, be, from, that* (conjunction), *have, as, if, why* seldom have complete dictionary pronunciation unless the meaning calls for emphasis as in "I said that Bill *and* Mary went to the picnic."

SPEECH RHYTHM & MEANING

Variety in speech rhythm is necessary for meaning; if you cannot vary your timing, your meaning will not show important inflections that give pertinent emphasis; instead your speech will be monotonous and uninteresting. Neither do you wish for so much variety that you give the impression of an indecisive or superficial individual.

The realization, however, that good speech and effective interpretation need a thoroughly varied rhythm from the longest hold that may represent deep feeling or strong emphasis down to the merest click or grunt is most important. Yet this principle must be applied sensibly. It is applicable to a simple conversational situation, when you desire to create an air of directness and naturalness; it also applies to small audiences. Under the stress of deep emotion, before large audiences, and without a public address system, however, the need for careful enunciation of syllables must be considered. Absurdity arises when the "grand" manner is dragged into a situation calling for simplicity and ease.

OPERATIONAL PATTERN OF VOCAL MECHANISM

No other criticism of your voice will ever aid you as much as your own evaluation. Inasmuch as you never hear yourself as others hear you, you must learn to listen objectively to your speech pattern by the use of a tape recorder. Even the most experienced interpreter resorts to "listening" before a performance. You really will not understand *what* you hear until you have some knowledge of the operation of the vocal mechanism. You cannot read about the flexibility of vocal tones, the use of reinforcement in the resonant chambers and tonicity of vocal muscles controlling the vocal cords until you have elementary information on how you can capitalize on your vocal equipment. As an artist knows the techniques involved in using his strokes, brushes, canvas, paints, colors, highlights, shadows and balance, so you should know the apparatus you are attempting to control, not necessarily from a scientific or research point of view but as a functional mechanism man has adapted to speech.

Before you read an explanation of how the vocal mechanism functions to produce sound waves translated into communicative speech, you should be reminded that the speech mechanism cannot function alone, as an entity. Two important requisites to the production of intelligible speech are an intact central nervous system, especially in certain cerebral areas, and a hearing mechanism that functions satisfactorily in coordination with the central nervous system. If you hear normally, you learn perception of speech signals and voicing of the symbols by imitating others. You *may* hear but you may not understand *what* you hear due to some dysfunction of the central nervous system. You may not *hear* at all, but may with great difficulty *learn* to receive speech signals; and with greater difficulty, you may learn a *productive* output of adequate but not fluent speech responses.

The production of voice in its respiratory, phonatory, resonating and articulatory phases will be discussed as simply as possible: all controversial issues and innervations from the central nervous system will be omitted. With the following elementary information, your study of interpretation is not a haphazard venture but a study based on what you can do with what has been given you. This approach to the functioning of the speech mechanism will point out visible and known parts first, even though the procedure is reversed in producing sound.

ARTICULATORY STRUCTURE

The vocal mechanism is best explained with a model of the head and larynx, which can be borrowed from any speech laboratory. If a model is not available, take a mirror and observe first the articulatory structure. You see the lips, formed by a circular muscle. Upon opening the lips, you see two rows of teeth; the upper teeth are firmly entrenched in the *alveolar* or gum, *ridge* that is part of the bony structure called the *maxilla* or upper jaw; the lower teeth grow out of another bony structure called the *mandible* or lower jaw. Looking into the mouth, or *oral cavity*, beyond the teeth, you see a tongue—the only complex of muscular tissues in the body that has only one point of attachment. Consequently, the tongue muscles are capable of great flexibility. If you look upward, you see a dome or roof above the tongue; the forward body part of this roof is called the *hard palate*. In some people the palate is high and vaulted, in others it is a normally rounded vault; and in still others it is low and rather flat. If you allow your tongue to start at the alveolar ridge and move backward along the hard palate, it soon finds a portion of the palate that is no longer hard and bony but soft and flexible; this is the *soft palate* or *velum*. You will observe it seems to terminate in two archways called the *palatine arches*. The latter are separated in the center by pendulous tissue, the *uvula*, that is sometimes very short, sometimes very long, sometimes non-existent:

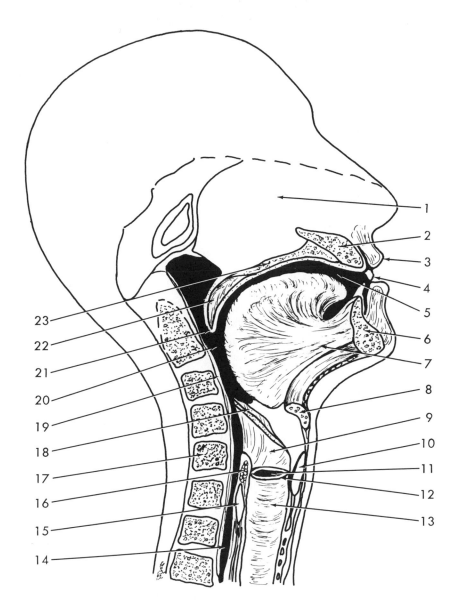

VOCAL MECHANISM

1. nasal cavity   2. maxilla   3. lip   4. teeth   5. oral cavity   6. mandible
7. tongue muscles   8. hyoid bone   9. opening into laryngeal cavity   10. thyroid
cartilage or "Adam's Apple"   11. glottis   12. vocal folds   13. trachea
14. esophagus (*posterior to trachea*)   15. cricoid cartilage   16. arytenoid
cartilages   17. vertebral canal   18. epiglottis   19. pharyngeal wall (*composed
of pharyngeal constrictor muscles*)   20. pharyngeal passageway (*extends from
entrance to nasal cavity down to entrance to larynx*)   21. uvula   22. soft palate
or velum   23. hard palate

normally it does not touch the tongue as it hangs relaxed. The side arches (like the proscenium arch of an auditorium or theatre) form the entrance to the pharynx, whose posterior wall can be seen beyond the archway. The pharynx is the irregular longitudinal cavity that extends from the posterior opening of the nasal cavity, down in back of the oral or mouth cavity to the esophagus and entrance to the larynx, just anterior to the esophagus. If you touch the soft palate with a tongue depressor, the uvula contracts, moving upward and backward with the soft palate to approximate the contracting muscles of the pharyngeal wall (the cyclorama of this setting). These contractions will partially close the passageway into the nasal cavity above and also the pharyngeal cavity below. When you drink from a fountain, for instance, the soft palate contracts, moving upward to meet the pharyngeal wall, which in turn moves forward to close off the nasal cavity so the water will go down the pharyngeal passageway instead of coming out the nose. When you gargle, the pharyngeal muscles contract, closing off the entrance to the passageway below.

These structures just mentioned—lips, teeth, tongue, palates, mandible and maxilla—are the articulators: their coordinated movements and articulation form the sounds of your language. The word *articulation,* as used here, means the adjustments and coordinated movements of parts involved in the formation of sounds.

Primarily, all these structures have a vegetative function for they support and aid your survival by functioning as chewing, sucking and swallowing parts. The lips, tongue and palates are used for sucking. The hard palate, separating the nasal cavity from the oral or mouth cavity, serves as a wall against which food may be pressed without allowing it to get into the nasal cavity; it is also vital for the pressure involved in sucking and swallowing processes. The soft palate by its contractibility keeps foreign objects out of the nasal cavity and assists in the swallowing function. The teeth, mandible and maxilla are mainly the chewing equipment. The teeth cut, grind and chew the food; the tongue swirls the bolus of food from one side to the other side of the mouth, in front and in back, and finally flips it through the archway and down the pharyngeal passageway to the esophagus, into the entrance of the stomach. The tongue thus aids in chewing, sucking and swallowing; and also has taste buds that make eating pleasurable. These vegetative activities—chewing, sucking and swallowing—are among the most primitive of your physiological functions necessary for survival.

Breathing or respiration also functions in the same way for it utilizes the nasal, oral, pharyngeal and laryngeal cavities for the inhaling of oxygen and the exhaling of carbon dioxide. Some call the coordination of all these parts for articulation of speech an "overlaid function," meaning that man has been able to initiate speech functions in addition to the vegetative activity of these structures. Finally, note that nature has safeguarded you with two entrances and two exits for the passage of air: the nasal and oral cavities.

In any discussion of speech activity, these moving parts are named articulators. The tongue, for instance, is the most versatile and mobile of all articulators, continually shifting and adjusting to other articulators to secure the coordinated movements necessary for the distinct articulation of sounds. It may impede or channel the outgoing air stream with the help of the teeth, lips and palates, in sounds like *t, d, k, g, f, v, th, s, sh, z, sh, dzh, tsh;* or it may assist in changing the size of the oral cavity for vowel formation and resonance by restricting its own activity; or it may provide pressure against the hard palate and teeth to aid in precision of articulation of certain sounds. Vowels require changes in the shape and size of the oral cavity that bring into action the versatile movements of the lower jaw and lips in shaping that cavity. All sounds but the nasal continuants—*m, n, ng*—require the approximation of the soft palate and the pharyngeal wall, in order to direct *most* of the air stream into the oral cavity for their proper resonation.

RESONATING STRUCTURE & VOCAL QUALITY

This direction of the air stream mentioned above is important not only for articulation of sounds but for the reinforcement or amplification of sounds, called vocal resonance. The various cavities pick up the tone frequencies adaptable to their particular frequencies and reinforce them. The cavities are variable in size, length and inner opening, as well as in their soft and hard surfaces: the *oral cavity* has the soft inner surfaces of the cheeks, a hard palate as well as a soft tissue palate, bony ridges that provide hard surfaces, and a tongue and jaws that can change its size momentarily; the *nasal cavity*, open at each end, is rather rigid in shape and size, contains cartilaginous turbinates and is divided by a medial bony septum and membrane; the *pharyngeal cavity* is a long tubelike structure, quite changeable in size because of the posterior constrictor muscles which move inward and then back to their relaxed position. The sound is started in the phonatory structure below these cavities and is reinforced to a certain amplification depending on (1) the tension of the soft surfaces, (2) the hard surfaces serving as sounding boards, (3) the articulators that provide the necessary openings to make resonance possible. Voices are not alike in resonance, principally because of the differences in the size, shape and nature of the cavities. Varying degrees of amplification of tones will be affected by: presence or absence of bones and cartilage, obstructions in the nasal cavity, high palates, low palates, free jaws, tense jaws, many teeth, few teeth, false teeth, flabby muscles, hard muscles. For instance, the wail of a newborn child has little resonance: the bony structures are soft, the teeth are absent, the cavities of the nose, mouth and pharynx are very small, and all surrounding tissue is soft. As the weeks pass, however, the wail develops into a lusty howl, aided by stronger breathing habits.

Your vocal cavities are peculiar to you; and depending on their structure and your control of the resonating mechanism will be your vocal quality. A voice that is pleasing to the ear has a balance of resonance. At times a noticeable imbalance is heard, such as too little or too much nasal resonance. The same principle applies to musical instruments; for instance, the violin is valuable because of its tonal quality, produced by certain kinds of woods. The vibrant tones that are heard, however, depend on the ability of the artist to produce a richness of tone through the knowledge and use of his instrument.

PHONATORY STRUCTURE

Turn now to the vocal chart to observe the phonatory structure. Following the posterior pharyngeal wall downward, you approach the opening of the esophagus, a collapsible tube through which food moves by the process of peristalsis to the stomach. Now following the *tongue* downward, you discover it is attached to a small horse-shoe-shaped bone, called the *hyoid bone,* or gullet bone, the only bone in the body not attached to the skeletal frame. From this bone is suspended, by means of muscular attachments, the larynx, in a position anterior to the esophagus. The larynx is the sound-production room where phonation originates for it houses the vibrating mechanism, the *vocal folds. Phonation* pertains to the production of sound waves by air as it is pressured against the approximated vocal folds. This system then sends out the sound waves that move upward along the pharyngeal pathway.

At the entrance to the laryngeal mechanism is a muscular tonguelike fold called the epiglottis. By contracting, it assists in making the laryngeal structure a valve for the purpose of building up air pressure for such biological acts as child-birth and defecation; for lifting objects, especially heavy ones; for keeping out foreign objects from the respiratory tract. The larynx thus serves its vegetative function as a valve: the epiglottis, along with the false folds (just below it) and the true vocal folds (below the false folds) in their contractile movements momentarily close off the trachea or windpipe—a continuing open passageway from the larynx to the lungs for the intake of oxygen and exhalation of carbon dioxide. When a bolus of food, nail, hairpin or some foreign object is aspirated, the quick contractions of these parts may keep the object from being drawn into the lungs—but often, the aspiration has such strong suction force that the object is too suddenly drawn in for the necessary contraction.

You are now looking down the throat and into the laryngeal opening through which you see the true vocal folds, extending across the larynx passageway in the form of an inverted V, as $\wedge$. The space between the true vocal folds is called the *glottis.* The apex of the inverted V folds is just behind the Adam's apple. If you put your fingers on this prominence, you can feel one of the most important cartilages of the larynx, the *thyroid cartilage,* shaped like a shield and serving as a shield to the vocal folds. The thyroid cartilage articulates on the *cricoid cartilage,* shaped like a signet ring—the signet portion forming the back of the larynx. Mounted on the top of the signet ring formation are two cartilages called *arytenoids.* Their main action of gliding in and out is important in causing tension and relaxation of the muscles controlling the action of the vocal folds: some laryngeal muscles have the function of opening the folds, some of closing them and some of maintaining the proper tension of the folds. Each vocal fold, however, has a point of attachment in one of the arytenoid cartilages; and the two folds join at the apex, just inside the thyroid prominence, or Adam's apple, to form an acute angle, as shown in the diagram (page 245). Extrinsic muscles of the larynx and throat area can also change the "up and down" position of the larynx, which, if pulled up too high into the lower region of the throat, can cause hypertension of the vocal folds. If you again put your fingers on the Adam's apple and repeat several sentences, you will feel the movement of the muscles supporting and surrounding the larynx. If your tones are harsh, nasal and tense, the thyroid cartilage, usually is pulled up almost to the area of the hyoid bone.

When you breathe, a gentle opening and closing of the *glottis* occurs but in a relaxed manner. Whenever speech is produced, however, the folds, because of the exerted air pressure, close or approximate or adduct; then the air forced up from the lungs causes vibration of the approximated edges, thus setting the air stream into vibration and producing sound waves that move upward to be amplified in the resonating chambers and articulated in the oral cavity.

RESPIRATORY PROCESS

The mechanism that provides the power for the vibrating action and vocal sound is the breathing structure, another vegetative mechanism with the function of inhaling oxygen and exhaling carbon dioxide. Since the outgoing pressured air stream produces vocal fold vibrations, lack of proper expulsion of air produces a greatly weakened voice. The vital relationship of respiration to speech is evident when you remember that you speak on exhalation, not inhalation. A person with a respiratory illness or one who cannot for some reason utilize the exhaled air stream efficiently has difficulty producing a normal, audible voice.

Understanding how the respiratory structure functions is necessary. In most books, breathing is explained first in the study of the production of the voice because it is the initiating process of speech production, the motor from which energy is supplied. Since you have proceeded from the visible to the invisible in this discussion, the power apparatus on the ground floor comes last.

Below the vocal folds, the trachea, held open by rings of cartilage to facilitate inhalation and exhalation, extends downward. This circular tube soon branches into two bronchi or air passageways, extending to the right and left. These bronchi, in turn, branch into many bronchioli that terminate in small air sacs called alveoli. The air sacs are lodged in the two large masses of spongy tissue called the lungs, which, with the heart, fill the thoracic cavity or chest. The left lung has only two lobes and is not quite as large as the right (which has three), thus making room for the heart. The lungs are passive and are acted upon by muscles for the exchange of oxygen and carbon dioxide. The thoracic cavity, containing the suspended lungs, is enclosed by the sternum or breastbone, the ribs and the spinal column or backbone.

Respiration is a process made possible by the creation of a vacuum in the thoracic cavity through the action of certain muscles. This action is caused by nerve impulses originating in the medulla, the respiratory center at the base of the brain. When there is too much carbon dioxide in the blood stream and a need for oxygen, nerve impulses are conducted to the muscles involved in breathing, causing the necessary contraction and relaxation. This process is carried on in a rhythmical pattern, so automatic in its occurrence that you seldom think about it until you participate in some activity calling for a quicker exchange of these two elements. Even speaking will change the respiratory rhythm.

One of the principal activating muscles in respiration is the *diaphragm*. It lies transversely of the torso, separating the lungs and heart in the thoracic cavity from the abdominal viscera; the stomach, liver and intestinal tract. The diaphragm—attached to the sternum, ribs and in back, to the spinal column—is not a heavy thick muscle, but is composed of a tendinous tissue extending into muscular fibers around its edge. When dissected and stretched out, it is not unlike the shape of an opened fan. In its relaxed position, the diaphragm is arched to a domelike structure in front, extending downward from the front to the back of the body where it is attached to the spinal column. Its innervating source comes from the phrenic nerve, which, if damaged or blocked in its innervation, will hinder or even stop the respiratory process.

In inhalation, this muscle contracts, thereby pushing downward and slightly compressing the viscera, causing the anterior wall of the abdomen to be distended briefly. The external intercostal muscles attached to the ribs also help to increase the size of the thoracic cavity by pulling the ribs upward and outward. Due to these actions, a potential vacuum is created in the thoracic cavity, causing an inrush of oxygen through the oral and/or nasal cavity, down the pharynx, past the relaxed (or raised) epiglottis, into the laryngeal cavity, through the glottis, down the trachea to the bronchi and then to the air sacs in the lungs. In exhalation, the action is reversed: the abdominal muscles push against the viscera, the diaphragm relaxes to its normal resting position, arching upward and the rib muscles relax. By these actions, air is expelled from the lungs, passes through the larynx and pharynx, and finally is emitted through the nasal or oral cavity—or both. Some air always remains in the lungs, called *residual air.* Poor speech habits can be acquired by trying to talk on residual air, especially at the end of phrases and sentences.

You will understand better what happens if you stand erect and place your fingers on the abdominal muscles just below the waistline. As you inhale deeply, keeping your shoulders quiet and relaxed, you feel a distention of the abdominal wall, indicating the expansion that occurs during inhalation. Note how your fingers are pushed outward. Now as you exhale, observe how the abdominal muscles recede to their original position. If you expel a vigorous "ho" on exhalation, you can feel the sudden inward direction of the muscles. Try laughing a "ha-ha-ha"—vigorously—to get the pressure of the muscles. Now put your hands on each side of the waistline and inhale. Feel the outward movement of the ribs. Extend your hands farther back and note again the enlarging of the thoracic cavity. Although speech authorities do not endorse this type of breathing as the only acceptable kind, certainly you can exercise more power and control without muscle strain, instead of the typical clavicular breathing that puts the biggest pressure on throat and shoulder muscles. In energetic or vigorous speech, the individual who resorts to clavicular breathing has a tendency to raise and lower the shoulders during the breathing cycle— just as the untrained singer does. In watching a professional singer, observe the ease with which tones are produced: shoulders do not hunch up nor do throat muscles show unusual strain nor are facial muscles distorted as if in pain. Use any muscles you wish to impound air but be certain the muscles of the shoulders and throat are not strained and rigid. The important factor in speech is not how much breath you can take in, but how *you control the outgoing air stream* for the purpose of sustaining tone for controlled speech. Ease, economy of effort and control are highly essential for this breathing motor mechanism to function satisfactorily. If you strain and tense in an effort to produce voice, your audience will also squirm in their effort to help you.

In involuntary breathing, the diaphragm and the assisting muscles maintain a balance between the oxygen and carbon dioxide supply due to nerve impulses from the respiratory center. The rhythm of this normal breathing process can be increased or decreased by age, physical vitality, a sudden stimulus or an emotional disturbance. When you are "out of breath" or when you yawn continually, your blood usually needs more oxygen. When you experience platform tension, you have difficulty sometimes in breathing due to muscular tension. You can control by enforced slow breathing. Remember that in speaking, you will change the normal rhythm of your breathing to a certain extent, just as the singer, swimmer, runner and skater do. Each has his own technique for control of the breath stream. The necessary controls for the interpreter may be summarized as follows:

1. Learn to use the outgoing air stream efficiently so you will not have to struggle to get to the end of the sentence.
2. Learn to control your breathing so the listener is never conscious of your lack of breath or of forced breath.
3. Learn to control your breathing muscles so that in projection of tones, your facial, throat or shoulder muscles will not show tension, strain or distortion.

SUMMARY: FUNCTIONING OF VOCAL MECHANISM

Having examined how structures operate in the production of speech, you now understand that speech depends for its audible success on the innervations received from the central nervous system that directs the energy for sound into the precisionlike functioning of the following mechanisms:

Respiration (motor mechanism): air stream expelled from the lungs by the action of the diaphragm, abdominal and thoracic muscles and pressured against the adducted (closed) vocal folds, furnishes the energy and power for speech production.

Phonation (vibrating or sound production mechanism): pressured air stream below the folds causes them to open slightly so that vibration occurs, causing sound waves of various compositions; thus phonation occurs, with tones differing in intensity, rate and pitch.

Resonation (resonating mechanism): vibrating sound waves are reinforced or amplified in the various cavities—oral, nasal, pharyngeal—by means of a frequency selectivity.

Articulation (sound formation mechanism): tones are then formed into various sounds by the actions of the articulators—lips, teeth, tongue and palates—as they channel, impede and direct the air stream between and within the cavities; and by the jaws, as they shape the size and opening of the oral cavity, especially for the vowels.

9

Vocal Quality

You know now that vocal quality refers to the predominant timbre of your tones, to the resonant or non-resonant voice by which your friends identify you. Although other factors such as pitch, tempo and intensity also characterize your voice, the essential quality of your fundamental tone and overtones—combining to produce the complex tone—are always heard and recognized as belonging to you.

THE COMPLEX TONE

Theories vary concerning the vibration of the vocal folds. The principle generally accepted is similar to that found in the vibrating tones of the piano, cello and violin, in which the vibrators move not only as a whole unit but also in segments: the vibrations of the parts blending (not always harmoniously) with the vibrations of the whole unit. The tone resulting from the vibrating whole is called the *fundamental*, the low frequency tone that is most prominent in the voice—the one most easily heard and recognized. The tones coming from the vibrations of the segments are known as *overtones*. The blending of the fundamental and the overtones produces the complex tone, heard in a vowel like *o*. If the overtones are amplified effectively by nicely balanced resonance and related harmoniously to the fundamental tone, vocal quality is said to have depth and fullness; in other words, the voice is pleasant to hear.

TONE REINFORCEMENT

Differences in the number and relative strength of the overtones account for the main variations in the quality of voices. This differential amplification through the selective action of the various resonating cavities gives character and timbre to the voice. To repeat, this tone reinforcement will depend on the management of the vibrating mechanism; and on the shape, size, flexibility and surfaces of these cavities. In the same way, certain musical instruments, like the trombone, cornet and horn produce different tonal qualities due to the sizes and shapes of the resonating chambers into which the musician can direct the vibrations set off by his lip and tongue movements. Vocal quality can be influenced also by securing an appropriate *balance* of oral, nasal and pharyngeal reinforcement. With some control, you should be able to vary your quality to interpret characterizations, mood, atmosphere and action for many different meanings.

ORAL RESONANCE

Most important in the reinforcement of the vowels is the shaping of the oral and pharyngeal cavities. The lips may be rounded, retracted, protruded, flattened or immobile. The tongue with its vertical, longitudinal and horizontal muscle fibers is equipped to do almost anything you wish with a little practice. The teeth can assist in making the oral cavity large or small with the help of the jaws and can serve also as sounding boards due to their hard surfaces. The bony structure of the hard palate assists further in reinforcement; and the soft palate, as a director of the air stream, closes off the nasal cavity to increase oral resonance, and relaxes to allow the air stream to enter the nasal cavity for nasal resonance.

If you would have better than average oral resonance, so important to the vowel formation, learn to keep these moving parts free from unnecessary tensions. Try to control the tight, tense lower jaw that seldom moves to give openness to the oral cavity; the lips that do not have the capacity to round, retract and be mobile; the tongue that humps up posteriorly on certain sounds when it should lie flat on the floor of the mouth; the tongue that is too large for the oral cavity or too rigid in its movements; the soft palate that cannot meet the pharyngeal wall to close off the nasal cavity. You should be reminded again that the shape of the resonator as well as the tonicity of the muscles and the surfaces involved must be considered in securing vowel resonance. For instance, observe how the lips function: try to sound the vowel *a* as in *father* with the corners of the mouth retracted: the vowel has changed from its characteristic quality produced when your lips and mandible are free to make the correct movement. Now try *e* as in *feet* with the articulators in their normal position; then try it with the lips pursed, observing how the resonance varies as the shape of the cavity changes. The more freedom you can give to the oral chamber, the greater your capability for oral resonance.

NASAL RESONANCE

Nasal resonance is often confused with nasality, a term implying an unpleasant vocal quality. Nasality may occur when a *lack* of nasal resonance is noticeable in the production of the nasal continuants, *m, n, ng.* Predominance of nasal resonance is likely to occur also on vowels when necessary oral and pharyngeal resonance are not sufficient. The lack of nasal resonance has various names: negative nasality, denasality, hyponasality; too much nasal resonance on vowels is called positive nasality or hypernasality. The nasal chamber, serving as the resonator for the nasal sounds—*m, n, ng*—must have an open port so the air stream can be directed into the cavity. If you hum a tune, you will soon be aware of the vibrating tones in the nasal cavity. If the entrance to this chamber is blocked either because of mucus, a deviated septum (the medial bone of the nose) or through poor speaking habits, you will have either suppressed nasal sounds or no nasals; instead you will substitute *b* for *m, d* for *n, g* for *ng*. The substituted sounds are formed in the oral cavity in much the same way as the nasals, except for the direction of the air stream. This substitution happens when you have a "cold in the nose" and are likely to say "sig be a sog" or "cub to see be sood."

You must understand also it is normal to use some nasal resonance on vowels when you are in animated conversation or in a large room where more amplification is needed for your voice to carry. An appropriate balance is acceptable for good vocal quality; a partial but not predominant emission of the vibrated air stream through the nostrils will be typical in vowel production.

Too much nasal reinforcement on the vowels will result in hypernasality. This kind of vocal quality can occur when you attempt to amplify sound in or around the vicinity of the nasal cavity. Unconsciously and perhaps through inertia or the habits of your environment, you utilize small pouches in the posterior area of the throat, instead of making use of the oral cavity. In large cities of the Midwest and in the East, you will hear an *assimilated* nasality: this occurs usually when a vowel precedes or follows a nasal consonant, as in *man, fine, grand*. Due to slovenly articulatory movements, you nasalize the vowel along with the proper nasalization of *m, n, ng*. Many variations occur in the amplification of your sounds if you misdirect or block the vibrating air stream. The common habit of those with nasal vocal quality is to keep the lower jaw rigid, the lips too immobile, the teeth too close together, the tongue humped up posteriorly, the throat muscles too tense.

In addition to these types of nasality, a quality often referred to as "nasal twang" can be heard. When it is present, it pervades the speech pattern. The cause of it appears to originate below the pharynx—in fact, near the larynx. If you try to imitate the "nasal twang," you feel a constriction of the muscles surrounding the larynx and suspect that the intrinsic muscles of the larynx have likewise been tensed. You hear this quality in certain parts of the South; in New England but with different intonations; and among people living under the tension and noise of a large city. Some radio and television artists cultivate it for portrayal of characters.

PHARYNGEAL RESONANCE

The pharyngeal cavity is considered the most important reinforcement chamber because of its potential flexibility in changing its size and shape. You will recall this tubelike cavity with sphincteric muscles lining its back wall (see diagram, page 245). These muscles make this cavity extremely flexible in size and adaptable as a resonator of the vibrations emerging from the larynx, as well as serving as a passageway for food to enter the esophagus. Improper tension, however, will affect the tonicity of these muscles, producing strained, harsh, nasal vocal quality. Business men who are in conference sessions most of the day may show this vocal tension; or high-powered insurance salesmen notice after continual talking that their voices become unpleasant; so do criminal lawyers, and also, school teachers.

This hypertension will influence the laryngeal muscles, in turn causing too much tension in the vocal folds. If the resulting harsh quality is not corrected, the vocal folds may become irritated, causing small growths to appear on the vibrating edges. The vocal quality may become breathy, hoarse, or husky; and medical attention may be needed.

VITALITY IN VOCAL QUALITY

Your physical and emotional vitality is often reflected in the character of your vocal quality, telling much of how you feel, how you live, how you think, what your attitudes are. This character factor revealed in vocal quality is utilized in radio, television and the theater. Think of your favorite actors. Each one uses a quality adapted to his particular "acting" personality—the one indicative of the principal bodily attitude of that character. The ability to change this vocal quality, along with vocal inflections, intensity and tempo, is part of your interpretative skill.

The flexibility and coordination of the muscles of the articulators are as important in producing good vocal quality as they are in the articulation of sounds. The strong amplification of overtones is not usually heard in the voice of a person too indifferent, weak or lazy to adjust his articulators properly or by a person whose vocal muscles are so rigid or weak that he cannot secure the flexibility necessary for the production of resonant tones. Good tones do not emerge between closed teeth, lips or rigid jaws; from too weak or too tense palatal and pharyngeal muscles; or with a tongue that does not conform in shape or mobility to its oral surroundings. Weakness in muscle tone will tend to give the voice a flat colorless quality; too much tension, on the other hand, may produce harsh, strident or metallic tones.

Furthermore, the vitality of a person is sometimes reflected in the

sustaining of an appropriate quality. If the breathing habits of the interpreter are such that he cannot sustain the power necessary to produce the
desired quality, then he tends to speak on residual air at the end of
phrases and sentences. His vocal quality diminishes in resonance and becomes a whisper. Proper phrasing and more attention to good breathing
habits will help to sustain tones; so will energetic production of sounds.

To the interpreter, vocal quality is the primary ingredient for intelligent and pleasant vocal expression. To the layman, the timbre of the voice
may not seem important or even noticeable. He is not too certain whether
the voice is harsh, breathy, hoarse, nasal or colorless, as long as he can
understand what is being said. Unfortunately, most people who have unpleasant tones are not certain how to make an asset of the voice. Every
interpreter should strive to use varied combinations and blends of the
fundamental tone and overtones. The one with trained and versatile vocal
quality can make literature overpoweringly beautiful; one who lacks harmonious balance of resonance can ruin the best literature.

The chief problem in building resonant vocal tones lies in the inability to hear yourself as others hear you. As you speak you hear the
reinforcement of your tones against the sounding board of the bones in
your head. If you put a finger lightly in each ear as you talk, you will to
some extent hear your voice as others do. The tape recorder will assist you
greatly in your task of listening to and improving vocal resonance. You
can also learn to appreciate pleasant, resonant voices of others. Your ear
must be educated to acknowledge reinforced tones. Radio and television
performances offer a chance to use both ears; so does a professional play;
so do your peers; so do recordings played over and over.

A word on *how* to listen may be of value. Train yourself to listen objectively. Listen first for the general impression and for vocal quality of
distinguished actors and poets; then play the recording again, listening
more intently to the meaning as revealed through vocal intonations; hear
how the voice manages images, rhythms, contrasts, crescendoes.

Before you start training your ear to hear, review the definitions of
tone, mood and atmosphere (page 72) so important in creating the immediate impression of the author. Then listen for changes of vocal quality
that intensify the episodes and action.

LISTEN TO AN ELEGY

The elegy is placed first on your listening program because the voice
of Dylan Thomas in his poem "Do Not Go Gentle Into That Good Night"
probably will never be equalled in a recording. Thomas has been ranked
by many as the finest dramatic interpreter in this country—"without peer"—
because of the dynamic power of his resonant vocal quality. No one can
mistake the warmth and sincerity of his emotional mood shown through

his vibrant quality and vocal intensity. His versatility in adapting his resonant quality to the tone of the literature is remarkable. The recording *A Child's Christmas in Wales and Five Poems*[1] demonstrates his ability to tell a story of his youthful Christmas experiences in Wales with simplicity and enjoyment—and with distinctive melody. On the same recording are five of his well-known poems, two of which are reprinted in this text: "Fern Hill" and "Do Not Go Gentle Into That Good Night."

This latter poem is a literary "must" for interpreters. First of all, remember Thomas was Welsh, and according to his biographers, had the "singing" temperament as well as the emotional intensity of his countrymen. Highet calls Thomas a "singing poet," because of "interlaced rhymes" and "intricacies of his rhythmical pattern." Certainly the latter is true but not always evident as you read silently from the page. When you hear Thomas interpreting his poetry, however, the rhythmical pattern supported by his vocal quality and rhyme schemes falls into a melody not often heard from a poet. Instead of the "regularity of the Saxon," Highet finds the "electrical excitement" typical of the Welsh: the intensity of suppressed feelings, "even their silences," shows the undertow of emotional pressure.[2] This characteristic of internal excitement appears to be part of Thomas's temperament as heard in his recording. Evidently, this sturdy, well-built, rather stocky poet could hold his audience spellbound with his voice. Unfortunately, his body—though apparently strong in build —could not withstand his particular way of living; so his life ended early at the age of thirty-nine years.

Here is the elegy, in the form of a villanelle, with five tercets, one concluding quatrain and only two end rhymes. Some critics find this structure, originally employed by the French for pastoral themes, not too appropriate for Thomas's vigorous, impelling tone.

Do Not Go Gentle Into That Good Night

Do not go gentle into that good night,
Old age should burn and rave at close of day;
Rage, rage against the dying of the light.

Though wise men at their end know dark is right,
Because their words had forked no lightning they
Do not go gentle into that good night.

Good men, the last wave by, crying how bright

---

[1] *"A Child's Christmas in Wales"* and *Five Poems*, recorded by Dylan Thomas, Caedmon, TC 1002.

[2] Gilbert Highet, *The Powers of Poetry* (New York: Oxford University Press, 1960), pp. 153-155.

Their frail deeds might have danced in a green bay,
Rage, rage against the dying of the light.

Wild men who caught and sang the sun in flight,
And learn, too late, they grieved it on its way,
Do not go gentle into that good night.

Grave men, near death, who see with blinding sight
Blind eyes could blaze like meteors and be gay,
Rage, rage against the dying of the light.

And you, my father, there on the sad height,
Curse, bless, me now with your fierce tears, I pray,
Do not go gentle into that good night.
Rage, rage against the dying of the light.[3]

DYLAN THOMAS

The tone of this lyric is quite personal: the poet is talking about a deep emotional experience, written at the time his father was dying. According to Brinnin,[4] the feeling between father and son was not too warm, at least not openly affectionate. The elder Mr. Thomas was known as academic, aloof, intelligent; one who put a "price on respectability" and had had an "early unrealized ambition" to be a poet. On the other hand, Dylan "remained at the bottom of all his classes but English." Dylan, however, became the poet even though he was not considered a scholar and the elder Thomas was never able to realize his poetic ambition even though he had been Senior English Master at Swansea Grammar School in Wales. The elegy was motivated no doubt because of the poet's early environment and relationship with his father.

As you listen to the recording, Thomas's voice will carry the full emotional meaning to you; moreover, you see his body moving and tensing in rhythm to the arrangement of the lines; and you hear words that are not "gentle" but cut into a pattern of intensity. You are likely to be so moved by the ringing surge of his vocal quality with its strong overtones that you may not even listen for the meaning. You are experiencing empathy initiated by full vocal power and resonant quality.

You hear Thomas's immediate voice as he plunges into the first line with a directive, "Do not go gentle into that good night." His vocal quality quickly attracts your attention and gives the clue to the tone of urgency and mood of persuasion; and blended together, the need and urgency to

[4] John M. Brinnin, *Dylan Thomas in America* (Boston: Little, Brown and Company, 1955), p. 112.

persuade. His distinctive pattern of meaning is directed first to a dramatic statement or plea that must be heard. "Do not go" is followed by "gentle" in an unusual arrangement for emphasis. The word is not "gently," nor is the line worded, "Do not go into that good night gently," syntax that would weaken the directive. Then two words "good night," generally run together in conversational speech, are here particularized with a different emphasis by the word "that." If properly interpreted, the line will offer a melody in its completeness of expression. The contrast in the phrases, as in the first line and "rage, rage, against the dying of the light" and the reinforcing line at the end of each stanza, must be emphasized.

The word choice and phrase combinations are typical of Thomas's poetic tone. Through his vocal propulsion of words and images, the impression of a dynamic emotion ready to break through all bounds is immediate. If you are not too immersed in listening to his voice, perhaps you will hear his rhyme schemes—end-rhyme and internal—and his alliterative use of sounds. Some of these pattern-making elements you will enjoy finding for yourself, but several arrangements are typical of Thomas: the use of action verbs to establish the tone as in *go, burn, rave, rage, forked, crying, danced, caught, sang, grieved, blaze, curse, bless;* the intensity of the powerful adjective-noun clusters and phrases to establish mood as in *close of day, dying of the light, dark is right, no lightning, frail deeds, green bay, sun in flight, blinding sight, blind eyes, like meteors, sad height, fierce tears;* the skillful use of alliterative sounds and of end-rhymes in the tercets that are repeated throughout the poem, as in *age, rage, rave, wave, blaze, grave, dying, wise, lightning, crying, might, wild, blinding, blind, eyes;* and the predominant use of plosive sounds, *g, d, k, dg* (*dg* as in *rage, age, gentle*) and the blends *gr* and *bl.* These sounds eliminate any softness in the lines and assist in making the impact of the meaning strike the listener dramatically.

The poet also persuades by citing how the wise men, the good men, the wild men, the grave men—all "do not go gentle into that good night." The quatrain intensifies the emotional undercurrent of Thomas's need for his father's love—at least, one can read that meaning into the lines. Clark Emery vividly accounts for the emotion felt:

The day of the death was a cold, dark day (one infers that it was the year's shortest day). But Dylan is not lamenting the day but the many sunless days that had preceded. This darkest day is an image of a life, as the father's blindness is an image of his failure to see the need in his son for outgoing love. 'Let him be fathered and found,' Thomas prays. His prayer arises from his own need.

Emery concludes wisely that Thomas does not accuse for he is too "proud to cry or to tell the truth." However,

Fancy can see the poem as the father's counterpart: the confining narrowness of the tercets; the cold, calculatedness of the wit and artifice; the burning of the emotion within the shell, epitomized in the eyes hot with unshed tears; the kindness of the sentiment. . . . Father and son meet in this poem as perhaps they never did in life. Arthur Symons's comment springs to mind: 'Pathos which can touch the intellect becomes so transfigured that its tears shine: you can see by their light!'[5]

LISTEN TO A LYRIC

You have listened to an elegy; now try several lyrics that usually create the personal tone of the poet. In contrast to the experience of listening to the unusual vibrancy of Thomas's vocal quality and Welsh temperament, your next "hearing" should be the voice of a woman, the Irish actress and interpreter, Siobhan McKenna. Her vocal quality should be the envy of every woman who is at all interested in a pleasant, resonant voice. As Thomas is all force, energy, propulsion in his masculine verbal activity, so is McKenna's voice all you could wish for in melody, quiet restraint and emotional depth. You imagine time waits breathlessly for her mellow tones and Celtic lilt, in contrast to Thomas who races with time trying to catch up with his own turbulent ideas. One voice soothes and starts you dreaming; the other stimulates and urges you to turbulent, emotional action. McKenna interprets the music of the poems of Yeats in a Spoken Arts recording. Listen to the lyrical magic of "The Brown Penny," "The Lake Isle of Innisfree," "After Long Silence," as well as those Gaelic verses, which you may not understand but can appreciate, because of the melodious quality of McKenna's voice.[6] You might like to compare the haunting melody of Helen Hayes's interpretation of "The Lake Isle of Innisfree" in the recording *Poet's Gold*[7] with the virile voice of Cyril Cusack recording *Poetry of Yeats,*[8] as well as with McKenna's lilting interpretation. Compare also, "The Song of the Wandering Aengus" (remembering *Aengus* is the Celtic god of love) as recorded by Michael MacLiammoir on Yeats's record, *The Poems of William Butler Yeats,* with the interpretation of Cyril Cusack in *Poetry of Yeats.*

You will recognize that the tone of these lyrics is reminiscent; consequently, the images reflect the tone, as well as the lyrical quality of the voice. Let them spring into life as you interpret them. Can you *hear* the melody of the lines? What is the metaphorical significance of the "brown penny"?

[5] From *The World of Dylan Thomas,* by Clark Emery, University of Miami Press, 1962, p. 55. Reprinted by permission of the publisher.

[6] *The Poems of William Butler Yeats.* Recorded by William Butler Yeats, Siobhan McKenna and Michael MacLiammoir. Spoken Arts Record, 753.

[7] *Poet's Gold.* Recorded by Helen Hayes, Raymond Massey and Thomas Mitchell. RCA Victor, IM 1813.

[8] *Poetry of Yeats.* Recorded by Cyril Cusack and Siobhan McKenna. Caedmon, TC 1081.

Brown Penny

I whispered, 'I am too young'
And then, 'I am old enough;'
Wherefore I threw a penny
To find out if I might love.
'Go and love, go and love, young man,
If the lady be young and fair.'
Ah, penny, brown penny, brown penny,
I am looped in the loops of her hair.
O love is the crooked thing,
There is nobody wise enough
To find out all that is in it
For he would be thinking of love
Till the stars had run away
And the shadows eaten the moon.
Ah, penny, brown penny, brown penny,
One cannot begin it too soon.[9]

WILLIAM BUTLER YEATS

The Lake Isle of Innisfree

I will arise and go now, and go to Innisfree,
And a small cabin build there, of clay and wattles made;
Nine bean rows will I have there, a hive for the honey bee,
        And live alone in the bee-loud glade.

And I shall have some peace there, for peace comes dropping slow,
Dropping from the veils of the morning to where the cricket sings;
There midnight's all a glimmer, and noon a purple glow,
        And evening full of the linnet's wings.

I will arise and go now, for always night and day
I hear lake water lapping with low sounds by the shore;
While I stand on the roadway, or on the pavements gray,
        I hear it in the deep heart's core.[10]

WILLIAM BUTLER YEATS

When You Are Old

When you are old and grey and full of sleep,
        And nodding by the fire, take down this book,

[9] William Butler Yeats, *Collected Poems* (New York: The Macmillan Company, 1951).
[10] *Ibid.*

And slowly read, and dream of the soft look
Your eyes had once, and of their shadows deep;

How many loved your moments of glad grace,
And loved your beauty with love false or true,
But one man loved the pilgrim soul in you,
And loved the sorrows of your changing face;

And bending down beside the glowing bars,
Murmur, a little sadly, how Love fled
And paced upon the mountains overhead
And hid his face amid a crowd of stars.[11]

WILLIAM BUTLER YEATS

The Song of the Wandering Aengus

I went out to the hazel wood,
Because a fire was in my head,
And cut and peeled a hazel wand,
And hooked a berry to a thread;
And when white moths were on the wing,
And moth-like stars were flickering out,
I dropped the berry in a stream
And caught a little silver trout.

When I had laid it on the floor
I went to blow the fire aflame,
But something rustled on the floor,
And some one called me by my name:
It had become a glimmering girl
With apple blossom in her hair
Who called me by my name and ran
And faded through the brightening air.

Though I am old with wandering
Through hollow lands and hilly lands,
I will find out where she has gone,
And kiss her lips and take her hands;
And pluck till time and times are done
The silver apples of the moon,
The golden apples of the sun.[12]

WILLIAM BUTLER YEATS

[11] *Ibid.*
[12] *Ibid.*

LISTEN TO A BALLAD

Although many records of folk songs can be found, the spontaneity of the communal spirit prevalent in the singing of the early ballads is not too often heard. It must have been similar, however, to contemporary participation in popular ballad experiences, especially the group singing of Christmas carols and folklore songs of this country. The three recordings listed here[13] offer varying tonal effects of balladry from different environmental backgrounds. *The Great Carl Sandburg* record will intrigue you, particularly if you have never heard the "guitar-singing" poet of Illinois. Learn to sing ballads—the best way to appreciate the folk song.

Several interpretations of Millay's literary ballad, "The Ballad of the Harp-Weaver," offer interesting comparisons. Listen to Millay record the poem in the *Edna St. Vincent Millay Album*[14] and then listen to Helen Hayes's interpretation in *Poet's Gold.*[15] Which recording presents the greater intensity? What would happen to the meaning if a dramatic vocal quality of heightened mystery had been employed?

This ballad offers a challenging study for the interpreter. Follow through as you did in Thomas's elegy, *Do Not Go Gentle Into That Good Night,* but here note ballad characteristics as far as stanza and word arrangements, dialogue and climax and melody of lines are concerned, as well as the mysticism and symbolism inherent in the meaning. Realize also the necessity for restraint in vocal quality and dramatic intensity in order to secure melody.

The Ballad of the Harp-Weaver

> "Son," said my mother,
>   When I was knee-high,
> "You've need of clothes to cover you,
>   And not a rag have I.
>
> "There's nothing in the house
>   To make a boy breeches,
> Nor shears to cut a cloth with,
>   Nor thread to take stitches.

[13] *Elizabethan Songs: Songs of Folk and Minstrelsy out of Elizabethan England.* Recorded by Alfred Deller and Desmon Dupré. Angel, 45016. *Irish Verse and Ballads.* Recorded by Siobhan McKenna. Spoken Arts, 707. *The Great Carl Sandburg.* Recorded by Carl Sandburg. Lyrichord, LL 66.

[14] *Edna St. Vincent Millay Album.* Recorded by Edna St. Vincent Millay. RCA Victor, M 836–1.

[15] *Poet's Gold,* see p. 261.

"There's nothing in the house
　　But a loaf-end of rye,
And a harp with a woman's head
　　Nobody will buy,"
　　And she began to cry.

That was in the early fall,
　　When came the late fall,
"Son," she said, "the sight of you
　　Makes your mother's blood crawl,—

"Little skinny shoulder-blades
　　Sticking through your clothes!
And where you'll get a jacket from
　　God above knows.

"It's lucky for me, lad,
　　Your daddy's in the ground,
And can't see the way I let
　　His son go around!"
　　And she made a queer sound.

That was in the late fall.
　　When the winter came,
I'd not a pair of breeches
　　Nor a shirt to my name.

I couldn't go to school,
　　Or out of doors to play.
And all the other little boys
　　Passed our way.

"Son," said my mother,
　　"Come, climb into my lap,
And I'll chafe your little bones
　　While you take a nap."

And, oh, but we were silly
　　For half an hour or more,
Me with my long legs
　　Dragging on the floor,

A-rock-rock-rocking
　　To a mother-goose rhyme!
Oh, but we were happy
　　For half an hour's time!

But there was I, a great boy,
  And what would folks say
To hear my mother singing me
  To sleep all day,
  In such a daft way?

Men say the winter
  Was bad that year;
Fuel was scarce,
  And food was dear.

A wind with a wolf's head
  Howled about our door,
And we burned up the chairs
  And sat upon the floor.

All that was left us
  Was a chair we couldn't break,
And the harp with a woman's head
  Nobody would take,
  For song or pity's sake.

The night before Christmas
  I cried with the cold,
I cried myself to sleep
  Like a two-year-old.

And in the deep night
  I felt my mother rise,
And stare down upon me
  With love in her eyes.

I saw my mother sitting
  On the one good chair,
A light falling on her
  From I couldn't tell where,

Looking nineteen,
  And not a day older,
And the harp with a woman's head
  Leaned against her shoulder.

Her thin fingers, moving
  In the thin, tall strings,
Were weav-weav-weaving
  Wonderful things.

Many bright threads,
    From where I couldn't see,
Were running through the harp-strings
    Rapidly,

And gold threads whistling
    Through my mother's hand.
I saw the web grow,
    And the pattern expand.

She wove a child's jacket,
    And when it was done
She laid it on the floor
    And wove another one.

She wove a red cloak
    So regal to see,
"She's made it for a king's son,"
    I said, "and not for me."
    But I knew it was for me.

She wove a pair of breeches
    Quicker than that!
She wove a pair of boots
    And a little cocked hat.

She wove a pair of mittens,
    She wove a little blouse,
She wove all night
    In the still, cold house.

She sang as she worked,
    And the harp-strings spoke;
Her voice never faltered,
    And the thread never broke.
    And when I awoke, —

There sat my mother
    With the harp against her shoulder,
Looking nineteen,
    And not a day older,

A smile about her lips,
    And a light about her head,
And her hands in the harp-strings
    Frozen dead.

And piled up beside her
And toppling to the skies,
Were the clothes of a king's son,
Just my size.[16]

EDNA ST. VINCENT MILLAY

LISTEN TO A DRAMATIC MONOLOGUE

The narrator of the dramatic monologue presents a sustained vocal quality characteristic of the temperament of the individual placed in a particular situation by the poet. The voice may vary in intonations and inflections for the subtleties of the personality, but basically, it should have a certain tonal quality expressive of the narrator. Raymond Massey, with his resonant and beautifully articulated voice interprets Browning's "My Last Duchess" in *Poet's Gold*.[17] As you listen, you may miss the undercurrent of the Duke's egocentricity; his interpretation is a bit too bland and sounds like a gentleman who has placed his cards on the table with an honest gesture. Certainly the Duke should not be treated as a broad villain with ominous traits; some intonations and pauses, however, should make you doubt his honest intentions. Or course, the facial expression, especially the eyes, convey much of the Duke's coldness and aloofness. The poem is printed in the next chapter.

LISTEN TO A PLAY

Variety in vocal quality is best heard in plays, where characters are revealed mainly through the voice. A familiar drama has been selected so that you can listen with greater ease to what the voice is doing, particularly in intensely dramatic scenes. In the recording *An Evening with Will Shakespeare*,[18] you will hear certain episodes from *Macbeth*, Shakespeare's "plotting tragedy," which demonstrate the quality range of those interpreting: Eva Le Gallienne, as Lady Macbeth, and Staats Cotsworth as Macbeth. The scenes are introduced by Margaret Webster, a well-known director of Shakespearean plays and one who presents the informative material in an excellent manner. Be sure to listen to the direct way in which she prepares for the environment and motivation for what is to happen. This technique can help you interpret narratives with expository information.

[16] From COLLECTED POEMS, Harper & Row. Copyright 1913, 1921, 1923, 1940, 1948, 1951 by Edna St. Vincent Millay and Norma Millay Ellis. Reprinted by permission of Norma Millay Ellis.

[17] *Poet's Gold, op. cit.*, p. 261.

[18] *An Evening with Will Shakespeare* (Theatre Masterworks, LP) features Eva Le Gallienne, Staats Cotsworth and Claude Rains under the direction of Margaret Webster; it includes scenes from *The Merchant of Venice, Henry V, The Tempest, Twelfth Night, Richard II* and *Macbeth*.

In order that the listening period will not be too long, start with Act 1, Scene 7 of *Macbeth*. You hear first one of the famous interior monologues—the vacillating and tormented Thane of Cawdor brooding over his anticipated murderous act. In this conspiracy scene, the mood is established by the hushed vocal quality of each character and toned to the tension and secrecy involved in conspiring for the King's death. Whenever Macbeth is pressed beyond his endurance, however, you will hear his voice take on a harshness and intensity:

from *Macbeth*

ACT I, SCENE 7

MACBETH *has left the banquet to ponder over the intended murder of* DUNCAN

> MACBETH: If it were done when 'tis done, then 'twere well
> It were done quickly. If the assassination
> Could trammel up the consequence, and catch
> With his surcease success; that but this blow
> Might be the be-all and the end-all here,
> But here, upon this bank and shoal of time,
> We'ld jump the life to come. But in these cases
> We still have judgement here, that we but teach
> Bloody instructions, which, being taught, return
> To plague the inventor. This even-handed justice
> Commends the ingredients of our poison'd chalice
> To our own lips. He's here in double trust:
> First, as I am his kinsman and his subject,
> Strong both against the deed; then, as his host,
> Who should against his murderer shut the door,
> Not bear the knife myself. Besides, this Duncan
> Hath borne his faculties so meek, hath been
> So clear in his great office, that his virtues
> Will plead like angels, trumpet-tongu'd, against
> The deep damnation of his taking-off;
> And pity, like a naked new-born babe
> Striding the blast, or heaven's cherubim, hors'd
> Upon the sightless couriers of the air,
> Shall blow the horrid deed in every eye,
> That tears shall drown the wind. I have no spur
> To prick the sides of my intent, but only
> Vaulting ambition, which o'erleaps itself,
> And falls on the other—

Enter LADY MACBETH

How now! what news?°

LADY M.: He has almost supp'd: why have you left the chamber?†
MACBETH: Hath he ask'd for me?
LADY M.:   Know you not he has?
MACBETH: We will proceed no further in this business: ‡
  He hath honour'd me of late; and I have bought
  Golden opinions from all sorts of people,
  Which would be worn now in their newest gloss,
  Not cast aside so soon.
LADY M.:   Was the hope drunk
  Wherein you dress'd yourself? Hath it slept since?§
  And wakes it now, to look so green and pale
  At what it did so freely? From this time
  Such I account thy love. Art thou afeard
  To be the same in thine own act and valour
  As thou art in desire? Wouldst thou have that
  Which thou esteem'st the ornament of life,
  And live a coward in thine own esteem,
  Letting "I dare not" wait upon "I would,"
  Like the poor cat i' the adage?
MACBETH: Prithee, peace!
  I dare do all that may become a man;
  Who dares do more is none.
LADY M.:   What beast was't, then,
  That made you break this enterprise to me?
  When you durst do it, then you were a man;
  And, to be more than what you were, you would
  Be so much more the man. Nor time nor place
  Did then adhere, and yet you would make both.
  They have made themselves, and that their fitness now
  Does unmake you. I have given such, you know
  How tender 'tis to love the babe that milks me;
  I would, while it was smiling in my face,
  Have pluck'd my nipple from his boneless gums,
  And dash'd the brains out, had I so sworn as you
  Have done to this.
MACBETH: If we should fail?
LADY M.:   We fail!
  But screw your courage to the sticking-place,
  And we'll not fail. When Duncan is asleep—‖
  Whereto the rather shall his day's hard journey

  ° Note the quick shift into the last line showing Macbeth's quick start and sudden
alertness as a release from his brooding torture.
  † Note Lady M's breathy quality in answer to Macbeth's startled question, indi-
cating that time is pressing and the moment is almost at hand.
  ‡ Note M's quiet, firm, resonant tones—he has made up his mind.
  § Note Lady M's fierce intensity as she jabs and probes her husband.
  ‖ Note Lady M now encourages, showing less intensity.

Soundly invite him—his two chamberlains
Will I with wine and wassail so convince
That memory, the warder of the brain,
Shall be a fume, and the receipt of reason
A limbeck only. When in swinish sleep
Their drenchèd natures lie as in a death,
What cannot you and I perform upon
The unguarded Duncan? what not put upon
His spongy officers, who shall bear the guilt
Of our great quell?

MACBETH: Bring forth men-children only;
For thy undaunted mettle should compose
Nothing but males. Will it not be receiv'd,
When we have mark'd with blood those sleepy two
Of his own chamber and us'd their very daggers,
That they have done 't?

LADY M.:   Who dares receive it other,
As we shall make our griefs and clamour roar
Upon his death?

MACBETH: I am settled and bend up
Each corporal agent to this terrible feat.
Away, and mock the time with fairest show;
False face must hide what the false heart doth know. *(Exeunt)*

The climax of the famous murder scene is intensified by voices that scarcely ever rise above terrified and guilty whispers, thus establishing mood and atmosphere. Full vocal resonance is not heard, except when the movement has been made dramatic by a quick change from a stealthy whisper to a sudden cry as in Macbeth's "Who's there? What, ho!" or when a high spot is reached as in Macbath's lines "Still it cried 'Sleep no more' to all the house." Listen also for the changing vocal quality of Lady Macbeth as she mutters, "Alack, I am afraid they have awak'd." This vocal variability is indicative of her underlying tension and fear. If you have not yet caught the movement of the scene, listen again for minor high points as in " 'Amen' stuck in my throat," or "Macbeth shall sleep no more," which finally builds to Macbeth's horrified voice, intensified by the knocking that grows louder and louder, as he cries out brokenly in a tremendous crescendo, "Wake Duncan with thy knocking! I would thou couldst!"

It is late at night. Macbeth is "about it"; Lady Macbeth "waits in an adjoining room."

ACT II, SCENE 2

LADY M.: That which hath made them drunk hath made me bold;
What hath quench'd them hath given me fire. Hark! Peace!
It was the owl that shriek'd, the fatal bellman,
Which gives the stern'st good-night. He is about it.

The doors are open; and the surfeited grooms
Do mock their charge with snores. I have drugg'd their possets,
That death and nature do contend about them,
Whether they live or die.

MACBETH (*within*): Who's there? What, ho!

LADY M.: Alack, I am afraid they have awak'd,
And 'tis not done. The attempt and not the deed
Confounds us. Hark! I laid their daggers ready;
He could not miss 'em. Had he not resembled
My father as he slept, I had done't.

Enter MACBETH

                              My husband!

MACBETH: I have done the deed. Didst thou not hear a noise?

LADY M.: I heard the owl scream and the crickets cry.
Did not you speak?

MACBETH: When?

LADY M.:   Now.

MACBETH: As I descended?

LADY M.: Ay.

MACBETH: Hark!
Who lies i' the second chamber?

LADY M.:   Donalbain.

MACBETH: This is a sorry sight. (*Looking at his hands*)

LADY M.: A foolish thought, to say a sorry sight.

MACBETH: There's one did laugh in's sleep, and one cried "Murder!"
That they did wake each other: I stood and heard them;
But they did say their prayers, and address'd them
Again to sleep.

LADY M.:   There are two lodg'd together.

MACBETH: One cried "God bless us!" and "Amen" the other;
As they had seen me with these hangman's hands,
List'ning their fear, I could not say "Amen,"
When they did say "God bless us!"

LADY M.:   Consider it not so deeply.

MACBETH: But wherefore could not I pronounce "Amen"?
I had most need of blessing, and "Amen"
Stuck in my throat.

LADY M.:   These deeds must not be thought
After these ways; so, it will make us mad.

MACBETH: Methought I heard a voice cry "Sleep no more!
Macbeth does murder sleep,"—the innocent sleep,
Sleep that knits up the ravell'd sleave of care,
The death of each day's life, sore labour's bath,
Balm of hurt minds, great nature's second course,
Chief nourisher in life's feast,—

LADY M.:   What do you mean?

MACBETH: Still it cried "Sleep no more!" to all the house;

"Glamis hath murder'd sleep, and therefore Cawdor
Shall sleep no more; Macbeth shall sleep no more."
LADY M.: Who was it that thus cried? Why, worthy thane,
You do unbend your noble strength, to think
So brainsickly of things. Go get some water,
And wash this filthy witness from your hand.
Why did you bring these daggers from the place?
They must lie there. Go carry them, and smear
The sleepy grooms with blood.
MACBETH: I'll go no more.
I am afraid to think what I have done;
Look on't again I dare not.
LADY M.:   Infirm of purpose!
Give me the daggers. The sleeping and the dead
Are but as pictures; 'tis the eye of childhood
That fears a painted devil. If he do bleed,
I'll gild the faces of the grooms withal;
For it must seem their guilt. (*Exit. Knocking within*)
MACBETH: Whence is that knocking?
How is't with me, when every noise appalls me?
What hands are here? Ha! they pluck out mine eyes.
Will all great Neptune's ocean wash this blood
Clean from my hand? No, this my hand will rather
The multitudinous seas incarnadine,
Making the green one red.
                Re-enter LADY MACBETH
LADY M.: My hands are of your conor; but I shame
To wear a heart so white. (*Knocking*) I hear a knocking
At the south entry: retire we to our chamber.
A little water clears us of this deed;
How easy is it, then! Your constancy
Hath left you unattended. (*Knocking*) Hark! more knocking.
Get on your nightgown, lest occasion call us,
And show us to be watchers. Be not lost
So poorly in your thoughts.
MACBETH: To know my deed, 'twere best not know myself.
                    (*Knocking*)
Wake Duncan with thy knocking! I would thou couldst!

The last scene is the sleep-walking scene in which two figures wait in the darkness to observe Lady Macbeth in one of her nocturnal wanderings. You hear whispering voices from the Doctor and the Gentlewoman; the fearful and intense horror of the previous scenes is now absent but the atmosphere is full of wondering suspense. These two voices serve as an effective undercurrent to emphasize Lady Macbeth's behavior; and also as a contrast to the wide range and rigid control in her voice, sometimes full and resonant; at other times, aspirate and then again harsh. Notice the vocal control in timing and intensity of the exit line, "To bed, to bed, to bed!"

ACT V, SCENE 1

The scene is an anteroom in the castle. Enter a DOCTOR OF PHYSIC *and a* WAITING-GENTLEWOMAN

DOCTOR: I have two nights watch'd with you, but can perceive no truth in your report. When was it she last walk'd?

GENTLEW.: Since His Majesty went into the field, I have seen her rise from her bed, throw her nightgown upon her, unlock her closet, take forth paper, fold it, write upon't, read it, afterwards seal it, and again return to bed; yet all this while in a most fast sleep.

DOCTOR: A great perturbation in nature, to receive at once the benefit of sleep, and do the effects of watching! In this slumb'ry agitation, besides her walking and other actual performances, what, at any time, have you heard her say?

GENTLEW.: That, sir, which I will not report after her.

DOCTOR: You may to me: and 'tis most meet you should.

GENTLEW.: Neither to you nor any one; having no witness to confirm my speech.

Enter LADY MACBETH, *with a taper*

Lo you, here she comes! This is her very guise; and, upon my life, fast asleep. Observe her; stand close.

DOCTOR: How came she by that light?

GENTLEW.: Why, it stood by her. She has light by her continually; 'tis her command.

DOCTOR: You see, her eyes are open.

GENTLEW.: Ay, but their sense is shut.

DOCTOR: What is it she does now? Look, how she rubs her hands.

GENTLEW.: It is an accustom'd action with her, to seem thus washing her hands. I have known her continue in this a quarter of an hour.

LADY M.: Yet here's a spot.

DOCTOR: Hark! she speaks. I will set down what comes from her, to satisfy my remembrance the more strongly.

LADY M.: Out, damnèd spot! out, I say!—One: two: why, then 'tis time to do't. —Hell is murky!—Fie, my lord, fie! a soldier, and afeard? What need we fear who knows it, when none can call our power to account?—Yet who would have thought the old man to have had so much blood in him?

DOCTOR: Do you mark that?

LADY M.: The thane of Fife had a wife; where is she now?—What, will these hands ne'er be clean?—No more o' that, my lord, no more o' that; you mar all with this starting.

DOCTOR: Go to, go to; you have known what you should not.

GENTLEW.: She has spoke what she should not, I am sure of that; Heaven knows what she has known.

LADY M.: Here's the smell of the blood still; all the perfumes of Arabia will not sweeten this little hand. Oh, oh, oh!

DOCTOR: What a sigh is there! The heart is sorely charg'd.

GENTLEW.: I would not have such a heart in my bosom for the dignity of the whole body.

DOCTOR: Well, well, well,—

GENTLEW.: Pray God it be, sir.

DOCTOR: This disease is beyond my practice; yet I have known those which have walk'd in their sleep who have died holily in their beds.

LADY M.: Wash your hands, put on your nightgown; look not so pale.—I tell you yet again, Banquo's buried; he cannot come out on's grave.

DOCTOR: Even so?

LADY M.: To bed, to bed! there's knocking at the gate. Come, come, come, come, give me your hand. What's done cannot be undone. To bed, to bed, to bed! *(Exit)*

DOCTOR: Will she go now to bed?

GENTLEW.: Directly.

DOCTOR: Foul whisp'rings are abroad; unnatural deeds
Do breed unnatural troubles: infected minds
To their deaf pillows will discharge their secrets.
More needs she the divine than the physician.
God, God forgive us all! Look after her;
Remove from her the means of all annoyance,
And still keep eyes upon her. So, good-night!
My mind she has mated and amaz'd my sight.
I think, but dare not speak.

GENTLEW.: Good-night, good doctor.

(Exeunt)[19]

SHAKESPEARE

LISTEN TO A PROSE NARRATIVE

One of the most fascinating story-tellers on the podium was Charles Laughton. This dynamic personality read into words—usually skimmed over by many—perceptive meanings and expressed them through a co-ordinated "body-vocal" impact—a *toute d'une piece* performance. He held his audience literally spellbound, when, after placing a huge Bible on the lectern, he proceeded to breathe into the black marks of the "Good Book" the vigor and imagination of a creator. At times, one would even doubt the vitalized words were really printed within the vast volume—until some research satisfied an idea that *something* other than words had been added: the *something*, of course, was Charles Laughton. His was not the

[19] The Caedmon recording, SHS-M-231 D, of *Macbeth* is quite different in its interpretation, particularly that of Lady Macbeth, Macbeth and the Doctor. You will note more hysteria; you will hear the upward inflection on Lady Macbeth's "We fail;" you will hear heavy breathing in the sleep-walking scene. Listen to Anthony Quayle as Macbeth and Gwen Ffrangcon Davies as Lady Macbeth.

ordinary pulpit "reading" of non-existent characters who uttered lifeless words. Instead, he brought to life characterizations of those who met obstacles, uttered fiery and passionate words, grappled with and directed the conflict of peoples. His recording of *Reading from the Bible*[20] gives you a presentation that is memorable but not as vivid as his total interpretation on the podium. You will hear vocal quality having much of the same irresistible power as that of Dylan Thomas in the recording of his narrative *A Child's Christmas in Wales*,[21] especially in its rhythmical cadences and controlled ease.

One of your first tasks in preparing an interpretative presentation is to consider what kind of vocal quality will best indicate the meaning as expressed through the narrator or characters. At first your vocal potential in resonation will seem limited, but eventually you will enjoy developing and amplifying your tones and combining other vocal factors to establish dramatic characterizations and episodes. If possible listen to Edward O'Brien's recording of Crane's *The Red Badge of Courage*, Caedmon TC 1040. The quick shifting of O'Brien's vocal quality for identification of characters in this dramatic narrative is excellent.

For an initial project, select a poem in which the narrator has a distinctive vocal quality, as in the two poems listed below. In "The Creation," you have the added problem of finding the most impressive tonal quality for the character of God. The tone of this poem calls for naive simplicity and wonderment. The feeling of the awesome power of creation, rather than an exaggerated dramatic intensity, must be shown in the full resonance of the voice. God's statements "That's good!" and "I'm lonely still" and "I'll make me a man" are not the dramatic tones or cries of the superman. Give some thought to the solemnity of God's acts, but observe that the narrator appears to believe God's control is immediate and easeful.

The Creation
(*A Negro Sermon*)

And God stepped out on space,
And He looked around and said,
"*I'm lonely—*
I'll make me a world."

And as far as the eye of God could see
Darkness covered everything,
Blacker than a hundred midnights
Down in a cypress swamp.

[20] *Reading from the Bible*, recorded by Charles Laughton, Decca DL 9031.
[21] *A Child's Christmas in Wales* by Dylan Thomas, recorded by Dylan Thomas, Caedmon TC 1002.

Then God smiled,
And the light broke,
And the darkness rolled up on one side,
And the light stood shining on the other,
And God said, *"That's good!"*

Then God reached out and took the light in His hands,
And God rolled the light around in His hands
Until He made the sun;
And He set that sun a-blazing in the heavens.
And the light that was left from making the sun
God gathered it up in a shining ball
And flung it against the darkness,
Spangling the night with the moon and stars.
Then down between
The darkness and the light
He hurled the world;
And God said, *"That's good!"*

Then God Himself stepped down—
And the sun was on His right hand,
And the moon was on His left;
The stars were clustered about His head,
And the earth was under His feet.
And God walked, and where He trod
His footsteps hollowed the valleys out
And bulged the mountains up.

Then He stopped and looked and saw
That the earth was hot and barren.
So God stepped over to the edge of the world
And He spat out the seven seas;
He batted His eyes, and the lightnings flashed;
He clapped His hands and the thunders rolled;
And the waters above the earth came down,
The cooling waters came down.

Then the green grass sprouted,
And the little red flowers blossomed,
The pine tree pointed his finger to the sky,
And the oak spread out his arms,
The lakes cuddled down in the hollows of the ground,
And the rivers ran down to the seas;
And God smiled again,
And the rainbow appeared,
And curled itself around His shoulder.

Then God raised His arm and He waved His hand
Over the sea and over the land,

And He said, *"Bring forth! Bring forth!"*
And quicker than God could drop His hand,
Fishes and fowls
And beasts and birds
Swam the rivers and the seas,
Roamed the forests and the woods,
And split the air with their wings.
And God said, *"That's good!"*

Then God walked around,
And God looked around
On all that He had made.
He looked at His sun,
And He looked at His moon,
And He looked at His little stars;
He looked on His world
With all its living things,
And God said, *"I'm lonely still."*

Then God sat down
On the side of a hill where He could think;
By a deep, wide river He sat down;
With His head in His hands,
God thought and thought,
Till He thought, *"I'll make me a man!"*

Up from the bed of the river
God scooped the clay;
And by the bank of the river
He kneeled Him down;
And there the great God Almighty
Who lit the sun and fixed it in the sky,
Who flung the stars to the most far corner of the night,
Who rounded the earth in the middle of His hand;
This Great God,
Like a mammy bending over her baby,
Kneeled down in the dust
Toiling over a lump of clay
Till He shaped it in His own image;

Then into it He blew the breath of life,
And man became a living soul.
Amen. Amen.

JAMES WELDON JOHNSON[22]

Like many of Pound's poems and translations, "The River-Merchant's Wife: A Letter" leaves much untold in its narrative. Siobhan McKenna's vocal quality would give the restrained emotional appeal to the lines; perhaps yours will too.

The River Merchant's Wife: A Letter

While my hair was still cut straight across my forehead
I played about the front gate, pulling flowers.
You came by on bamboo stilts, playing horse,
You walked about my seat, playing with blue plums.
And we went on living in the village of Chokan:
Two small people, without dislike or suspicion.

At fourteen I married My Lord you.
I never laughed, being bashful.
Lowering my head, I looked at the wall.
Called to, a thousand times, I never looked back.

At fifteen I stopped scowling,
I desired my dust to be mingled with yours
Forever and forever and forever.
Why should I climb the look out?

At sixteen you departed,
You went into far Ku-to-yen, by the river of swirling eddies,
And you have been gone five months.
The monkeys make sorrowful noise overhead.

You dragged your feet when you went out.
By the gate now, the moss is grown, the different mosses,
Too deep to clear them away!
The leaves fall early this autumn, in wind.
The paired butterflies are already yellow with August
Over the grass in the West garden;
They hurt me. I grow older.
If you are coming down through the narrows of the river Kiang,
Please let me know beforehand,
And I will come out to meet you
       As far as Cho-fu-Sa.[23]

BY RIHAKU

TRANSLATED BY EZRA POUND FROM *Li Po*

Another helpful project at this stage of your learning skills should involve a dialogue with two but not more than three characters, who show differentiating vocal qualities. For instance, how would you vary the vocal quality of each person in the following scene from *Suppressed Desires?* To appreciate the involvement triggered at the unhappy breakfast episode, you should read this short play. Perhaps you can even now guess what "Step-Hen!, Step-Hen!" eventually means to Henrietta as she pursues her psychological study of dreams.

This typical husband-wife breakfast altercation offers excellent contrasts in voices and mood, aided by the disgruntled look of Steve, the psychoanalytic expression of Henrietta and the early-bird sweetness of sister Mabel. Vocal characterizations should bring laughter; keep the tone light and the movement fast.

from *Suppressed Desires*

*There is a breakfast table set for three, but only two seated at it—*HENRIETTA *and* STEPHEN BREWSTER. *As the curtains withdraw* STEVE *pushes back his coffee cup and sits dejected.*

HENRIETTA: It isn't the coffee, Steve dear. There's nothing the matter with the coffee. There's something the matter with you.

STEVE *(doggedly)*: There may be something the matter with my stomach.

HENRIETTA *(scornfully)*: Your stomach! The trouble is not with your stomach but in your subconscious mind.

STEVE: Subconscious piffle!

HENRIETTA: Steve, you never used to be so disagreeable. You certainly have got some sort of complex. You're all inhibited. You're no longer open to new ideas. You won't listen to a word about psychoanalysis.

STEVE: A word! I've listened to volumes!

HENRIETTA: You've ceased to be creative in architecture—your work isn't going well. You're not sleeping well—

STEVE: How can I sleep, Henrietta, when you're always waking me up in the night to find out what I have been dreaming?

HENRIETTA: But dreams are so important, Steve. If you'd tell yours to Dr. Russell he'd find out exactly what's wrong with you.

STEVE: There's nothing wrong with me.

HENRIETTA: You don't talk as well as you used to.

STEVE: Talk? I can't say a thing without you looking at me in that dark fashion you have when you're on the trail of a complex.

HENRIETTA: This very irritability indicates that you are suffering from some suppressed desire.

STEVE: I'm suffering from a suppressed desire for a little peace.

HENRIETTA: Dr. Russell is doing simply wonderful things with nervous cases. Won't you go to him, Steve?

STEVE (*slamming down his newspaper*): No, Henrietta, I won't!

HENRIETTA: But, Stephen—!

STEVE: Tst! I hear Mabel coming. Let's not be at each other's throats the first day of her visit.

MABEL: Good morning.

HENRIETTA: Oh, here you are, little sister.

STEVE: Good morning, Mabel.

HENRIETTA: It's so good to have you here. I was going to let you sleep, thinking you'd be tired after the long trip. Sit down. There'll be fresh toast in a minute and will you have—

MABEL: Oh, I ought to have told you, Henrietta. Don't get anything for me. I'm not eating breakfast.

HENRIETTA: Not eating breakfast? (*She sits down, then leans toward Mabel and scrutinizes her.*)

STEVE (*half to himself*): The psychoanalytical look!

HENRIETTA: Mabel, why aren't you eating breakfast?

MABEL (*a little startled*): Why, no particular reason. I just don't care much for breakfast, and they say it keeps down—that is, it's a good thing to do without it.

HENRIETTA: Don't you sleep well? Did you sleep well last night?

MABEL: Oh yes, I sleep all right. Yes, I did have the funniest dream!

STEVE: S—h! S—t!

HENRIETTA: What did you dream, Mabel?

STEVE: Look-a-here, Mabel, I feel it's my duty to put you on. Don't tell Henrietta your dreams. If you do she'll find out that you have an underground desire to kill your father and marry your mother—

HENRIETTA: Don't be absurd, Stephen Brewster. (*sweetly to Mabel*) What was your dream, dear?

MABEL: Well, I dreamed I was a hen.

HENRIETTA: A hen?

MABEL: Yes; and I was pushing along through a crowd as fast as I could, but being a hen, I couldn't walk very fast—it was like having a tight skirt, you know; and there was some sort of creature in a blue cap—you know how mixed up dreams are—and it kept shouting after me and saying, "Step, Hen! Step, Hen!" until I got all excited and just couldn't move at all.

HENRIETTA (*resting chin in palm and peering*): You say you became much excited?

MABEL (*laughing*): Oh, yes; I was in a terrible state.

HENRIETTA (*murmurs*): This is significant.

STEVE: She dreams she's a hen. She is told to step lively. She becomes violently agitated. What can it mean?

HENRIETTA: Mabel, do you know anything about psychoanalysis?

MABEL: Oh—not much. No—I— (*brightening*) It's something about the war, isn't it?

STEVE: Not that kind of war.

MABEL: I thought it might be the name of a new explosive.

STEVE: It is.

MABEL: You see, Henrietta, I—we do not live in touch with intellectual things, as you do. Bob being a dentist—somehow—our friends—
STEVE: Oh, to be a dentist![24]

GEORGE CRAM COOK AND SUSAN GLASPELL

[24] © 1951 by Walter H. Baker Company. Reprinted with permission of BAKER'S PLAYS, Boston, Mass. 02110.

10

Vocal Intensity

PRESSURE OF VOCAL ATTACK

THE TERM "INTENSITY"

The term *intensity* has been used often throughout discussions of the author's tone and mood, his emotional expression; and also as indicating a concentrated source of strength in episodic progression, in which all assembled parts point up and heighten the desired effect. Imagery intensifies by the vividness of its word connotations; word choice and arrangement intensify mood, atmosphere, rhythm; certain word associations through their symbolism intensify, deepen and expand the author's meaning. In this sense, intensity implies the strengthening of, and adding to, the flow of energy and the deepening of the impression through selectivity of literary devices.

CONTROL OF VOCAL INTENSITY

In speaking of *vocal* intensity, the same associative pattern is followed: some concentrated force or stress important for the literary meaning necessitates a change of pressure against the vocal folds to give added strength, energy and depth to the production of the vocal tones. This attribute is called vocal intensity, vocal force and loudness. One term is as good as another in this study if you understand that the amount of air pressure involving vocal cord tension and tonal amplification makes possible the degree of vocal intensity—the magnitude or loudness of the auditory sensation.

Loudness usually refers to extensity of tone rather than to intensity. Because of the connotation of loudness, you are likely to think that you must shout or use a tremendously big voice in your interpretation. If, however, you understand loudness in terms of desired audibility, of strengthening and amplifying the voice so you can be heard, then you are thinking correctly. Varying degrees of intensity, force, loudness or stress are necessary to create sensitive impressions. The continual use of the sharp, intense voice, the too weak or too forceful voice, the too loud or too soft voice should be eliminated from your interpretative attempts.

The control of vocal intensity lies mainly in the way the breath stream is expelled against the approximated or adducted vocal folds. You will have to control the attack of the breath stream made on the folds, depending on whether you want your vocal intensity to be abrupt, soft, hard, staccato or smooth. Involuntary breathing presents few problems in ordinary smooth-flowing speech, but in animated speaking or interpreting, the rhythm of breathing is dependent upon rhythm of ideas or grouping of thoughts. If your interpretation is to appear controlled, breathing must be subordinated to the grouping of phrases and sentences of the literary selection and to the emphasis necessary to intensify and sustain the meaning.

A weak vocal attack usually means that muscular support being expended for vocal production is insufficient. Sometimes this lack of intensity is due to ignorance of knowing *how* to strengthen tones; most of the time it is caused by the physical and psychological make-up of the individual—he "just cannot live or speak in any other way." Certainly speech will have little animation if the body is not primed to the joy of energetic living. A voice that *never* attacks vigorously indicates the person is likely to be unresponsive in a lively communicative manner. Those who do not bother to employ more than the minimum energy in speaking usually have colorless, weak voices. On the other hand, some one who attacks vigorously most of the time, who likes to boom out his voice above every other voice and who insists on being emphatic over every verbal transaction or activity, becomes tiresome and boring.

The aim of the interpreter should be, then, to present animated, lively, purposeful speech sustained through the control of the respiratory musculature. The audience likes your voice to sound as if you are sincerely alert to the enjoyment you offer. Your body, especially the face, will do much to show this interest; so must your voice demonstrate varying intensity and responsiveness to the situation.

CONTINUED LOUDNESS

In this discussion, loudness means vocal "carrying" power: a voice that reaches a great crowd without amplification; makes itself heard over the noise of an indoor swimming pool or the practice on an athletic field; produces the biggest yell at an exciting game. Unfortunately, this continued vocal intensity often causes undue strain and tension on the action of the vocal folds and their attendant muscles as well as throat muscles; whereas correctly projected voices show no resultant strain. Even the interpreter, in an effort to make his voice carry in a large room, sometimes tenses laryngeal and throat musculature; the voice, consequently, may become harsh, high-pitched, nasal. If this tension is long continued or becomes a habit, the tones may become husky or hoarse, or vocalization may be impossible.

During World War II, when young student officers were being pushed through their military training at a tremendous rate, many were unable to vocalize above a whisper after thirty minutes of issuing commands in a "loud" voice. At the end of the day, they could not even emit a whisper. Their vocal and breathing mechanisms were intact, but the way in which they were tensing their vocal mechanisms was quite wrong. They were trying to secure "carrying power" by shouting, thereby expelling all their breath on the initial words of "readying"; and consequently, issuing the final command on residual air. Strain in the delicate muscles that control the vocal folds was reduced only after the men had been taught to secure force and energy from the pressure of abdominal muscles; then to control and release abnormal tension from the throat and shoulder muscles. To sustain the outgoing breath stream properly was most important so that the final issuance of the command would have the necessary intensity.

VARIETY IN INTENSITY

POETRY

Many emotional effects can be created by the manner in which vocal sounds are projected—whether spoken forcibly, eased into with gentleness and smoothness or given certainty, vigor and animation. Sometimes the brisk, staccato attack is necessary as heard in Sarett's interpretation of his poem, "The Squaw Dance,"[1] one stanza of which is reprinted here. Sarett, who lived at various times among northern Indian tribes, was made an honorary member of the Chippewa Tribe and named *Pay-Sheeg-Ah-Deek*, meaning "Lone Caribou." Since he was allowed to participate in the tribal activities, he learned their dancing rhythms and speaking habits. In his recording, you hear the sharp "beat, beat, beat . . ." as he uses a strong vocal stress to communicate intensity of speech reflected by the rhythm of the dance. You hear also the exultant staccato calls of "Hi! Hi!" This sharp attack is initiated by a sudden hard pressure below the vocal folds, thus producing tones that are powerful and sudden.

One week before his death, Sarett wrote, apropos of vocal restraint and intensity as shown in his recording, the following letter:[2]

I am so glad that you liked my record. It has had a wonderful sale. I feel that readers of my poems should know how the author of them *meant* them

[1] *Lew Sarett: Reading from His Collected Poems.* Columbia, XTV-15494, 15495.
[2] From a letter to the authors dated July 28, 1954.

to be read, or again, how the author *himself* reacts to them, for good or for ill. That should be helpful. For example, in the recording—and always on the platform—I read "Four Little Foxes" and "Wind in the Pine" with great and deep feeling inwardly but always with great *restraint;* I never express outwardly one half of what I feel. I do this because that is the way I am made. But also it happens to be the most effective way to read these moving poems; they have a head of steam when they are read with restraint. So also with the Indian poems—readers should learn much from the recording. I doubt that anybody ever saw fully the beauty of the Indian sleep-story, "Wéeng," until he got the melodic pattern established in the recording. . . . As you say, "Requiem," is succinct. It says a lot in a few words—and they cut deep. Another favorite of mine is "Deep Wet Moss." It is a smooth and deep little poem.

from *The Squaw Dance*

Beat, beat, beat, beat, beat upon the tom-tom,
Beat, beat, beat, beat, beat upon the drum.
Hóy-eeeeeee-yáh! Hóy-eeeeeee-yáh!
Shuffle to the left, shuffle to the left,
Shuffle, shuffle, shuffle to the left, to the left.
Fat squaws, lean squaws, gliding in a row,
Grunting, wheezing, laughing as they go;
Bouncing up with a scuffle and a twirl,
Flouncing petticoat and hair in a whirl.
Rheumatic hags of gristle and brawn,
Rolling in like a ponderous billow;
Fair squaws lithe as the leaping fawn,
Swaying with the wind and bending with the willow;
Bouncing buttock and shriveled shank,
Scuffling to the drumbeat, rank on rank;
Stolid eye and laughing lip,
Buxom bosom and jiggling hip,
Weaving in and weaving out,
Hí! Hí! Hí! with a laugh and a shout,
To the beat, beat, beat, beat, beat upon the tom-tom,
Beat, beat, beat, beat, beat upon the drum;
To the drum-beat, drum-beat, drum-beat, drum-beat, drum-beat, drum-
    beat, drum-beat—
Hóy-eeeeeee-yáh! Hóy-eeeeeee-yáh!
Hí! Hí! Hí! Hí! Hóy-eeeeeeeeeeeeeee-yáh![3]

                                                      LEW SARETT

Byron, who was usually quite intense in his poetry, also wrote melodious lyrics with a smoothness and gentleness of tone: "So We'll Go No

[3] From COVENANT WITH EARTH by Lew Sarett. Gainesville: University of Florida Press, 1956. Reprinted by permission of Mrs. Lew Sarett.

More A Roving" (page 226) and "She Walks in Beauty" are two lyrical classics.

She Walks in Beauty

She walks in beauty, like the night
  Of cloudless climes and starry skies;
And all that's best of dark and bright
  Meet in her aspect and her eyes:
Thus mellow'd to that tender light
  Which heaven to gaudy day denies.

One shade the more, one ray the less,
  Had half impaired the nameless grace
Which waves in every raven tress,
  Or softly lightens o'er her face;
Where thoughts serenely sweet express
  How pure, how dear their dwelling-place.

And on that cheek, and o'er that brow,
  So soft, so calm, yet eloquent,
The smiles that win, the tints that glow,
  But tell of days in goodness spent,
A mind at peace with all below,
  A heart whose love is innocent!

GEORGE GORDON, *Lord Byron*

How would you vary the intensity of these poems?

Lament

Listen, children;
Your father is dead.
From his old coats
I'll make you jackets;
I'll make you trousers
From his old pants.
There'll be in his pockets
Things he used to put there,
Keys and pennies
Covered with tobacco;
Dan shall have the pennies
To save in his bank;
Anne shall have the keys
To make a pretty noise with.

Life must go on,
And the dead be forgotten;
Life must go on
Though good men die;
Anne, eat your breakfast;
Dan, take your medicine;
Life must go on;
I forget just why.[4]

EDNA ST. VINCENT MILLAY

Prospice

Fear death?—to feel the fog in my throat,
   The mist in my face,
When the snows begin, and the blasts denote
   I am nearing the place,
The power of the night, the press of the storm,
   The post of the foe;
Where he stands, the Arch Fear in a visible form,
   Yet the strong man must go:
For the journey is done and the summit attained,
   And the barriers fall,
Though a battle's to fight ere the guerdon be gained,
   The reward of it all.
I was ever a fighter, so—one fight more,
   The best and the last!
I would hate that death bandaged my eyes and forbore,
   And bade me creep past.
No! let me taste the whole of it, fare like my peers
   The heroes of old,
Bear the brunt, in a minute pay glad life's arrears
   Of pain, darkness and cold.
For sudden the worst turns the best to the brave,
   The black minute's at end,
And the elements' rage, the fiend-voices that rave,
   Shall dwindle, shall blend,
Shall change, shall become first a peace, out of pain,
   Then a light, then thy breast,
O thou soul of my soul! I shall clasp thee again
   And with God be the rest![5]

ROBERT BROWNING

[4] From COLLECTED POEMS, Harper & Row. Copyright 1913, 1921, 1923, 1940, 1948, 1951 by Edna St. Vincent Millay and Norma Millay Ellis. Reprinted by permission of Norma Millay Ellis.

[5] *Masterpieces of Literature: Great Themes in Poetry.* Browning recorded by Basil Rathbone. Columbia, E 11-10, sponsored by the National Council of Teachers of English.

Killers

I am singing to you
Soft as a man with a dead child speaks;
Hard as a man in handcuffs,
Held where he cannot move:

Under the sun
Are sixteen million men,
Chosen for shining teeth,
Sharp eyes, hard legs,
And a running of young warm blood in their wrists.

And a red juice runs on a green grass;
And a red juice soaks the dark soil.
And the sixteen million are killing . . . and killing and killing.

I never forget them day or night:
They beat on my head for memory of them;
They pound on my heart and I cry back to them;
To their homes and women, dreams and games.

I wake in the night and smell the trenches,
And hear the low stir of sleepers in lines—
Sixteen million sleepers and pickets in the dark:
Some of them long sleepers for always,

Some of them tumbling to sleep to-morrow for always,
Fixed in the drag of the world's heartbreak,
Eating and drinking, toiling . . . on a long job of killing,
Sixteen million men.[6]

CARL SANDBURG

In his interpretations, Sandburg creates poetic intensity and a unique rhythm.[7]

PROSE

Vocal intensity varies greatly in prose narratives because of the different types of characters and episodes, as well as shifts in tone and movement. The choice of vocal approach at the beginning of a story is

[6] From CHICAGO POEMS by Carl Sandburg. Copyright 1916 by Holt, Rinehart and Winston, Inc. Copyright 1944 by Carl Sandburg. Reprinted by permission of Holt, Rinehart and Winston, Inc.
[7] *Carl Sandburg: Reading His Poems.* Caedmon, 1150.

especially important in securing the author's intention for environment, tone, atmosphere and mood. If the opening paragraphs merely explain or introduce characters, your vocal stress should be moderate, not too soft and not too strong, but certainly communicative. Many interpreters have a tendency to hurry over the beginning of a story without the proper intensity and emphasis; consequently, the heart of the action and significance of some character may not be readied for the final outcome.

The four contrasting opening scenes below, along with the beginning of Aiken's story "Impulse" (page 233), require some thought as to the proper degree of intensity and correct emphasis to anticipate the author's central meaning. Four scenes are from short stories: Aiken's "Impulse"; Faulkner's "Spotted Horses" and "A Rose for Emily"; and Joyce's "Counterparts"; one is from the novel *A Tree Grows in Brooklyn* by Smith. Even though the excerpts are short, they give clues to the intensity of the vocal approach. If you have read the complete stories, your difficulties will be few; if you are unacquainted with the narratives, guess as to your procedure and then read the narrative for accurate clues. Look for the following:

1. Are the titles suggestive of characterization or action?
2. What is author's point of view?
3. Who is the narrator? Objective or subjective approach?
4. What impression has been established as an introductory interest?
5. Does the scene progress far enough for the interpreter to guess whether characterization, dramatic action, exposition or description will be dominant in the telling of the story?
6. Has the author used any contrasts?
7. Does the scene appear to be static, without progression?
8. Has imagery given any clues as to the kind of story the author has planned? How about character clues?
9. How do Faulkner's two scenes differ?
10. How would you employ vocal intensity and quality in each scene?
11. Which scene would you *guess* might offer the best interpretative material? Why?

from *Spotted Horses*

OPENING SCENE 1

A little while before sundown the men lounging about the gallery of the store saw, coming up the road from the south, a covered wagon drawn by mules and followed by a considerable string of obviously alive objects which in the levelling sun resembled vari-sized and -colored tatters torn at random from large billboards—circus posters, say—attached to the rear of the wagon and inherent with its own separate and collective motion, like the tail of a kite.

"What in the hell is that?" one said.

"It's a circus," Quick said. They began to rise, watching the wagon. Now they could see that the animals behind the wagon were horses. Two men rode in the wagon.

"Hell fire," the first man—his name was Freeman—said. "It's Flem Snopes." They were all standing when the wagon came up and stopped and Snopes got down and approached the steps. He might have departed only this morning. He wore the same cloth cap, the minute bow against the white shirt, the same gray trousers. He mounted the steps.

"Howdy, Flem," Quick said. The other looked briefly at all of them and none of them, mounting the steps. "Starting you a circus?"

"Gentlemen," he said. He crossed the gallery; they made way for him. Then they descended the steps and approached the wagon, at the tail of which the horses stood in a restive clump, larger than rabbits and gaudy as parrots and shackled to one another and to the wagon itself with sections of barbed wire. Calico-coated, small-bodied, with delicate legs and pink faces in which their mismatched eyes rolled wild and subdued, they huddled, gaudy, motionless, and alert, wild as deer, deadly as rattlesnakes, quiet as doves. The men stood at a respectful distance, looking at them. At that moment Jody Varner came through the group, shouldering himself to the front of it.

"Watch yourself, doc," a voice said from the rear. But it was already too late. The nearest animal rose on its hind legs with lightning rapidity and struck twice with its forefeet at Varner's face, faster than a boxer, the movement of its surge against the wire which held it travelling backward among the rest of the band in a wave of thuds and lunges. "Hup, you broom-tailed, hay-burning sidewinders," the same voice said. This was the second man who had arrived in the wagon. He was a stranger. He wore a heavy, densely black moustache, a wide pale hat. When he thrust himself through and turned to herd them back from the horses they saw, thrust into the hip pockets of his tight jeans pants, the butt of a heavy pearl-handled pistol and a florid carton such as small cakes come in. "Keep away from them, boys," he said. "They've got kind of skittish, they ain't been rode in so long."[8]

WILLIAM FAULKNER

from *A Rose for Emily*

OPENING SCENE 2

When Miss Emily Grierson died, our whole town went to her funeral: the men through a sort of respectful affection for a fallen monument, the women mostly out of curiosity to see the inside of her house, which no one save an old man-servant—a combined gardener and cook—had seen in at least ten years.

It was a big, squarish frame house that had once been white, decorated with cupolas and spires and scrolled balconies in the heavily lightsome style of the seventies, set on what had once been our most select street. But garages and cotton gins had encroached and obliterated even the august names of that neighborhood; only Miss Emily's house was left, lifting its stubborn and co-quettish decay above the cotton wagons and the gasoline pumps—an eyesore among eyesores. And now Miss Emily had gone to join the representatives of those august names where they lay in the cedar-bemused cemetery among the ranked and anonymous graves of Union and Confederate soldiers who fell at the battle of Jefferson.[9]

William Faulkner

from *Counterparts*

OPENING SCENE 3

The bell rang furiously and, when Miss Parker went to the tube, a furious voice called out in a piercing North of Ireland accent: "Send Farrington here!"

Miss Parker returned to her machine, saying to a man who was writing at a desk: "Mr. Alleyne wants you upstairs."

The young man muttered *"Blast* him!" under his breath and pushed back his chair to stand up. When he stood up he was tall and of great bulk. He had a hanging face, dark wine-colored, with fair eyebrows and mustache: his eyes bulged forward slightly and the whites of them were very dirty. He lifted up the counter and passing by the clients, went out of the office with a heavy step.

He went heavily upstairs until he came to the second landing, where a door bore a brass plate with the inscription: Mr. Alleyne. Here he halted, puf-fing with labor and vexation, and knocked. The shrill voice cried: "Come in!"

The man entered Mr. Alleyne's room. Simultaneously Mr. Alleyne, a little man wearing gold-rimmed glasses on a clean-shaven face, shot his head up over a pile of documents. The head itself was so pink and hairless it seemed like a large egg reposing on the papers. Mr. Alleyne did not lose a moment: "Far-rington? What is the meaning of this: Why have I always to complain to you? May I ask why you haven't made a copy of that contract between Bodley and Kirwan? I told you it must be ready by four o'clock."

"But Mr. Shelley said, sir—"

"*Mr. Shelley said, sir.* Kindly attend to what I say and not to what *Mr. Shelley says, sir.*"[10]

James Joyce

[9] From "A Rose for Emily," copyright 1930 and renewed 1957 by William Faulkner. Reprinted from COLLECTED STORIES OF WILLIAM FAULKNER, by permission of Random House, Inc.
[10] From DUBLINERS by James Joyce. Originally published by B. W. Heubsch, Inc. in 1916. Reprinted by permission of The Viking Press, Inc.

from *A Tree Grows in Brooklyn*

OPENING SCENE 4

SERENE was a word you could put to Brooklyn, New York. Especially in the summer of 1912. Somber, as a word, was better. But it did not apply to Williamsburg, Brooklyn. Prairie was lovely and Shenandoah had a beautiful sound, but you couldn't fit those words into Brooklyn. Serene was the only word for it; especially on a Saturday afternoon in summer.

Late in the afternoon the sun slanted down into the mossy yard belonging to Francie Nolan's house, and warmed the worn wooden fence. Looking at the shafted sun, Francie had that same feeling that came when she recalled the poem they recited in school.

> *This is the forest primeval. The murmuring*
> *pines and the hemlocks,*
> *Bearded with moss, and in garments green,*
> *indistinct in the twilight,*
> *Stand like Druids of eld.*

The one tree in Francie's yard was neither a pine nor a hemlock. It had pointed leaves which grew along green switches which radiated from the bough and made a tree which looked like a lot of opened green umbrellas. Some people called it the Tree of Heaven. No matter where its seed fell, it made a tree which struggled to reach the sky. It grew in boarded-up lots and out of neglected rubbish heaps and it was the only tree that grew out of cement. It grew lushly, but only in the tenements districts.[11]

BETTY SMITH

Characterization through dialogue in prose selections is extremely significant to the author's central meaning. The progression of a story can go astray if the interpreter has not been able to characterize through proper stress. Although elements of pitch and intonation are probably most important, vocal quality and intensity must harmonize with the temperament of the character; otherwise, the characterizations will be one-dimensional.

The following selection shows obvious differences in vocal intensity that point up the distinctive personality of the two characters, God and Noah. "De Lawd" walks calmly through *The Green Pastures*, a folk drama, with the full confidence of a great, all-powerful man who can offer a cigar to a worthy follower of "De Lawd's"; so he speaks with a deep, resonant bass voice and a serene, "heavenly" manner of power. Noah is one of "De

[11] From A TREE GROWS IN BROOKLYN by Betty Smith. Copyright 1943, 1947 by Betty Smith. Reprinted by permission of Harper & Row, Publishers.

Lawd's" workers getting a directive. He is talkative, persistent and a good organizer with definite tastes. The element of timing enters into these two characterizations also—one is deliberate and slow; the other is more than ready to fill in the gaps with ideas, especially concerning the forty days and nights with only one keg for medicinal purposes.

from *The Green Pastures*

PART I, SCENE 8

The scene is the dining room of NOAH's *cabin.* NOAH's *wife is preparing dinner, as* NOAH *appears with a stranger.*

NOAH: Company, darlin'. (NOAH's WIFE *takes* NOAH's *and* GOD's *hats.*) Dis gemman's a preacher, too. He's jest passin' through de country.

GOD: Good mo'nin', sister.

NOAH's WIFE: Good mo'nin'. You jest ketch me when I'm gettin' dinner ready. You gonter stay with us?

GOD: If I ain't intrudin'. Brother Noah suggested—

NOAH's WIFE: You set right down yere. I got a chicken in de pot an' it'll be ready in 'bout five minutes. I'll go out de back and call Shem, Ham 'n' Japheth. (*to* GOD) Dey's our sons. Dey live right acrost de way but always have Sunday dinner wid us. You mens make yo'selves comf'table.

GOD: Thank you, thank you kindly.

NOAH: You run along, we all right. (GOD *and* NOAH *seat themselves.* NOAH's *wife exits.*)

GOD: You got a fine wife, Brother Noah.

NOAH: She pretty good woman.

GOD: Yes, suh, an' you got a nice little home. Have a ten-cent seegar? (GOD *offers him one.*)

NOAH: Thank you, much obliged. (*Both men lean back restfully in their chairs.*)

GOD: Jest what seems to be de main trouble 'mong mankind, Noah?

NOAH: Well, it seems to me de main trouble is dat de whol' distric' is wide open. Now you know dat makes fo' loose livin'. Men folks spen's all dere time fightin', loafin' an' gamblin', an' makin' bad likker.

GOD: What about de women?

NOAH: De women is worse dan de men. If dey ain't makin' love powder dey out beg, borrow an' stealin' money for policy tickets. Doggone, I come in de church Sunday fo' las' 'bout an hour befo' de meetin' was to start, and dere was a woman stealin' de altar cloth. She was goin' to hock it. Dey ain't got no moral sense. Now you take dat case las' month, over in East Putney. Case of dat young Willy Roback.

GOD: What about him?

NOAH: Dere is a boy sebenteen years old. Doggone, if he didn't elope with his aunt. Now, you know, dat kin' of goin' on is bad fo' a neighborhood.

GOD: Terrible, terrible.

NOAH: Yes, suh. Dis use' to be a nice, decent community. I been doin' my best

to preach de Word, but seems like every time I preach de place jest goes
a little mo' to de dogs. De good Lawd only knows what's gonter happen.

GOD: Dat is de truth. *(There is a pause. Each puffs his cigar. Suddenly* NOAH
grasps his knee, as if it were paining him, and twists his foot.)

NOAH: Huh!

GOD: What's de matter?

NOAH: I jest got a twitch. My buck-aguer I guess. Every now and then I gets
a twitch in de knee. Might be a sign of rain.

GOD: That's just what it is. Noah, what's de mos' rain you ever had 'round dese
parts?

NOAH: Well, de water come down fo' six days las' April an' de ribber got so
swole it bust down de levee up 'bove Freeport. Raise cain all de way down
to de delta.

GOD: What would you say was it to rain for forty days and nights?

NOAH: I'd say dat was a *complete* rain!

GOD: Noah, you don't know who I is, do you?

NOAH *(puzzled)*: Yo' face looks easy, but I don' think I recall de name. (GOD
*rises slowly, and as he reaches his full height, there is a crash of lightning,
a moment's darkness, and a roll of thunder. It grows light again.* NOAH *is
on his knees in front of* GOD.) I should have known you. I should have
seen de glory.

GOD: Dat's all right, Noah. You didn' know who I was.

NOAH: I'm jes' ol' preacher Noah, Lawd, an' I'm yo' servant. I ain' very much,
but I'se all I got.

GOD: Sit down, Noah. Don' let me hear you shamin' you'se'f, caize you' a good
man. *(Timidly* NOAH *waits until* GOD *is seated, and then sits, himself.)* I
jest wanted to fin' out if you was good, Noah. Dat's why I'm walkin' de
earth in de shape of a natchel man. I wish dey was mo' people like you.
But, far as I kin see, you and yo' family is jest de only respectable people
in de worl'.

NOAH: Dey jes all poor sinners, Lawd.

GOD: I know. I am your Lawd. I am a god of wrath and vengeance an' dat's
why I'm gonter destroy dis' worl'.

NOAH *(almost in a whisper; drawing back)*: Jest as you say, Lawd.

GOD: I ain't gonter destroy you, Noah. You and yo family, yo' sheep an' cattle,
an' all de udder things dat ain't human I'm gonter preserve. But de rest is
gotta go. *(Takes a pencil and a sheet of paper from his pocket)* Look yere,
Noah. (NOAH *comes over and looks over his shoulder.)* I want you to build
me a boat. I want you to call it de "Ark," and I want it to look like dis.
(He is drawing on the paper. Continues to write as he speaks) I want you
to take two of every kind of animal and bird dat's in de country. I want
you to take seeds an' sprouts an' everythin' like dat an' put them on dat
Ark, because dere is gonter be all dat rain. Dey's gonter to be a deluge,
Noah, an dey's goin' to be a flood. De levees is gonter bust an' everythin'
dat's fastened down is comin' loose, but it ain't gonter float long, caize I'm
gonter make a storm dat'll sink everythin' from a hencoop to a barn. Dey
ain't a ship on de sea at'll be able to fight dat tempest. Dey all got to go.
Everythin'. Everythin' in dis pretty worl' I made, except one thing, Noah.

You an' yo' family an' de things I said are goin' to ride dat storm in de Ark. Yere's de way it's to be. (*He hands* NOAH *the paper.* NOAH *takes it and reads.*)

NOAH (*pause; looks at paper again*): Yes, suh, dis seems to be complete. Now 'bout the animals, Lawd, you say you want everythin'?

GOD: Two of everythin'.

NOAH: Dat would include jayraffes an' hippopotamusses?

GOD: Everythin' dat is.

NOAH: Dey was a circus in town las' week. I guess I kin fin' dem. Co'se I kin git all de rabbits an' possums an' wil' turkeys easy. I'll sen' de boys out. Hum, I'm jest wonderin'—

GOD: 'Bout what?

NOAH: 'Bout snakes. Think you'd like snakes, too?

GOD: Certainly. I want snakes.

NOAH: Oh, I kin git snakes, lots of 'em. Co'se, some of 'em's a little dangerous. Maybe I better take a kag of likker, too?

GOD: You kin take a kag of likker.

NOAH (*musingly*): Yes, suh, dey's a awful lot of differ'nt kin's of snakes, come to think about it. Dey's water moccasins, cotton-moufs, rattlers—mus' be a hund'ed kin's of other snakes down in de swamps. Maybe I better take two kags of likker.

GOD (*mildly*): I think de one kag's enough.

NOAH: No. I better take two kags. Besides I kin put one on each side of de boat, an' balance de ship wid dem as well as havin' dem fo' medicinal use.

GOD: You kin put one kag in de middle of de ship.

NOAH (*buoyantly*): Jest as easy to take two kags, Lawd.

GOD: I think one kag's enough.

NOAH: Yes, Lawd, but you see forty days—an' forty nights— (*There's a distant roll of thunder.*)

GOD (*firmly*): One kag, Noah.

NOAH: Yes, Lawd, one kag.[12]

MARC CONNELLY

CLIMAX

The word *climax* derived from the Greek word meaning *ladder,* usually pertains to a "building up"; it can also indicate a high point arrived at unexpectedly. It may be created in several ways: by artistic selectivity of episodes; by choice of words and sentence arrangements; by intensity and speed of movement; by domination of one character; and by some unexpected turn or twist of words or events. The interpreter builds toward the climax auditorially—by the voice. He follows the movement of the selection, modulating his vocal intensity—either quietly or forcefully—and tim-

[12] From THE GREEN PASTURES by Marc Connelly. Copyright 1929, 1930, © 1957, 1958 by Marc Connelly. Reprinted by permission of Holt, Rinehart and Winston, Inc. Part I, scene 8, p. 63.

ing his vocal expression—either increasing the tempo or breaking it by pauses in crucial places.

Vocal intensity usually varies within a poem; for instance, if the narrative element is dominant, different kinds of stress in characterization and incidents are necessary. This element of attack, along with vocal quality and timing, not only presents differentiation in tone and mood but assists in progression of ideas, quick turns of phrases and sentences to the highest point of interest and action as in the dramatic monologue.

DRAMATIC MONOLOGUES

Two of Browning's dramatic monologues, "My Last Duchess" and "Soliloquy of the Spanish Cloister," show varying intensity and different types of climax. Eliot's "Journey of the Magi," using an entirely different tone, is included for further contrast with Browning's poems.

My Last Duchess

SCENE: FERRARA

That's my last Duchess painted on the wall,
Looking as if she were alive. I call
That piece a wonder, now: Frà Pandolf's hands
Worked busily a day, and there she stands.
Will 't please you sit and look at her? I said
"Frà Pandolf" by design, for never read
Strangers like you that pictured countenance,
The depth and passion of its earnest glance,
But to myself they turned (since none puts by
The curtain I have drawn for you, but I)
And seemed as they would ask me, if they durst,
How such a glance came there; so, not the first
Are you to turn and ask thus. Sir, 'twas not
Her husband's presence only, called that spot
Of joy into the Duchess' cheek: perhaps
Frà Pandolf chanced to say, "Her mantle laps
Over my Lady's wrist too much," or "Paint
Must never hope to reproduce the faint
Half-flush that dies along her throat:" such stuff
Was courtesy, she thought, and cause enough
For calling up that spot of joy. She had
A heart—how shall I say?—too soon made glad,
Too easily impressed: she liked whate'er
She looked on, and her looks went everywhere.
Sir, 'twas all one! My favor at her breast,
The dropping of the daylight in the West,

The bough of cherries some officious fool
Broke in the orchard for her, the white mule
She rode with round the terrace—all and each
Would draw from her alike the approving speech,
Or blush, at least. She thanked men,—good! but thanked
Somehow—I know not how—as if she ranked
My gift of a nine-hundred-years-old name
With anybody's gift. Who'd stoop to blame
This sort of trifling? Even had you skill
In speech—(which I have not)—to make your will
Quite clear to such an one, and say, "Just this
Or that in you disgusts me; here you miss,
Or there exceed the mark"—and if she let
Herself be lessoned so, nor plainly set
Her wits to yours, forsooth, and made excuse,
—E'en then would be some stooping; and I choose
Never to stoop. Oh, sir, she smiled, no doubt,
Whene'er I passed her; but who passed without
Much the same smile? This grew; I gave commands;
Then all smiles stopped together. There she stands
As if alive. Will 't please you rise? We'll meet
The company below, then. I repeat,
The Count your master's known munificence
Is ample warrant that no just pretence
Of mine for dowry will be disallowed;
Though his fair daughter's self, as I avowed
At starting, is my object. Nay, we'll go
Together down, sir. Notice Neptune though,
Taming a seahorse, thought a rarity,
Which Claus of Innsbruck cast in bronze for me!

ROBERT BROWNING

Soliloquy of the Spanish Cloister

Gr-r-r—there go, my heart's abhorrence!
　　Water your damned flower-pots, do!
If hate killed men, Brother Lawrence,
　　God's blood, would not mine kill you!
What? your myrtle-bush wants trimming?
　　Oh, that rose has prior claims—
Needs its leaden vase filled brimming?
　　Hell dry you up with its flames!

At the meal we sit together;
　　Salve tibi! I must hear
Wise talk of the kind of weather,

Sort of season, time of year:
Not a plenteous cork-crop: scarcely
Dare we hope oak-galls, I doubt:
What's the Latin name for "parsley"?
Whats the Greek name for Swine's Snout?

Whew! We'll have our platter burnished,
Laid with care on our own shelf!
With a fire-new spoon we're furnished,
And a goblet for ourself,
Rinsed like something sacrificial
Ere 'tis fit to touch our chaps—
Marked with L. for our initial!
(He-he! here his lily snaps!)

Saint, forsooth! While brown Dolores
Squats outside the Convent bank
With Sanchicha, telling stories,
Steeping tresses in the tank,
Blue-black, lustrous, thick like horse-hairs,
—Can't I see his dead eye glow,
Bright as 'twere a Barbary corsair's?
(That is, if he'd let it show!)

When he finishes refection,
Knife and fork he never lays
Cross-wise, to my recollection,
As do I, in Jesu's praise.
I, the Trinity illustrate,
Drinking watered orange-pulp—
In three sips the Arian frustrate;*
While he drains his at one gulp!

Oh, those melons! If he's able
We're to have a feast; so nice!
One goes to the Abbot's table,
All of us get each a slice.
How go on your flowers? None double?
Not one fruit-sort can you spy?
Strange!—And I, too, at such trouble,
Keep them close-nipped on the sly!

There's a great text in Galatians,
Once you trip on it, entails
Twenty-nine distinct damnations,
One sure, if another fails;

* *Arian frustrate:* Christ, created by God, is inferior to Him in dignity.

If I trip him just a-dying,
    Sure of heaven as sure can be,
Spin him round and send him flying
    Off to hell, a Manichee?

Or, my scrofulous French novel
    On gray paper with blunt type!
Simply glance at it, you grovel
    Hand and foot in Belial's gripe:
If I double down its pages
    At the woeful sixteenth print,
When he gathers his greengages,
    Ope a sieve and slip it in't?

Or, there's Satan—one might venture
    Pledge one's soul to him, yet leave
Such a flaw in the indenture
    As he'd miss, till, past retrieve,
Blasted lay that rose-acacia
    We're so proud of! *Hy Zy, Hine.* . . .*
'St, there's Vespers! *Plena gratiâ*
    Ave, Virgo!† Gr-r-r—you swine!

ROBERT BROWNING

Journey of the Magi

'A cold coming we had of it,
Just the worst time of the year
For a journey, and such a long journey:
The ways deep and the weather sharp,
The very dead of winter.'
And the camels galled, sore-footed, refractory,
Lying down in the melting snow,
There were times we regretted
The summer palaces on slopes, the terraces,
And the silken girls bringing sherbet.
Then the camel men cursing and grumbling
And running away, and wanting their liquor and women,
And the night-fires going out, and the lack of shelters,
And the cities hostile and the towns unfriendly
And the villages dirty and charging high prices:
A hard time we had of it.
At the end we preferred to travel all night,

---

* *Hy, Zy, Hine:* a curse on the Friar
† *Plena gratiâ, Ave, Virgo:* full of grace, Hail Virgin

Sleeping in snatches,
With the voices singing in our ears, saying
That this was all folly.

Then at dawn we came down to a temperate valley,
Wet, below the snow line, smelling of vegetation;
With a running stream and a water-mill beating the darkness,
And three trees on a low sky,
And an old white horse galloped away in the meadow.
Then we came to a tavern with vine-leaves over the lintel,
Six hands at an open door dicing for pieces of silver,
And feet kicking the empty wine-skins.
But there was no information, and so we continued
And arrived at evening, not a moment too soon
Finding the place; it was (you may say) satisfactory.

All this was a long time ago, I remember,
And I would do it again, but set down
This set down
This: were we led all that way for
Birth or Death? here was a Birth, certainly,
We had evidence and no doubt. I had seen birth and death,
But had thought they were different; this Birth was
Hard and bitter agony for us, like Death, our death.
We returned to our places, these Kingdoms,
But no longer at ease here, in the old dispensation,
With an alien people clutching their gods.
I should be glad of another death.[13]

T. S. ELIOT

These three monologues, so different in the characterizations, reveal the creative techniques of poets. Since you may not be so well-informed concerning Eliot's "Journey of the Magi," immediate attention should be given to several directional points that focus on and support the meaning.

The narrator is recognized as one of the Magi who traveled to the birthplace of Christ. The source of the first five lines in quotes, according to critics, comes from a Christmas Day sermon in 1622 by Bishop Lancelot Andrews, one of the translators of the Authorized Version of the Bible. At first, the shock of understatement and reversal of the traditional revelation of a new "star" in the heavens is almost unbelievable. You expect some kind of spiritual uplift or hallowed atmosphere. The poet, however, gives no colorful imagery to lift the spirits, neither does he mention the gifts of the Magi. Instead the narrator's tone is one of sorrowful regret as he item-

[13] From COLLECTED POEMS 1909-1962 by T. S. Eliot, copyright, 1936, by Harcourt, Brace & World, Inc.; copyright, © 1963, 1964, by T. S. Eliot. Reprinted by permission of the publishers.

izes many comforts left behind and discomforts endured: just the worst time of year . . . the dead of winter . . . for such a long journey . . . men missing the summer palaces on the slopes . . . the silken girls . . . the nightfires going out . . . lack of shelters . . . unfriendly towns . . . dirty villages . . . high prices . . . traveling all night . . . and more; ending with the conclusion that the "journey was folly." To make the tone more monotonous and grim, the poet has joined all these discomforts with "and" . . . "and" . . . "and." Finally when they arrived, "it was (you may say) satisfactory." Could any phrase be more bleak for an experience that has illuminated literature for centuries?

In the second stanza, Eliot indirectly suggests symbols that tie the present episode to incidents in the life of Christ. If you do not recognize them, look in the Bible: the white horse (try *Revelations*); the three trees etched on the low sky (the story of the crucifixion); the pieces of silver (the thirty pieces of silver in the betrayal).

If by this time you have caught the matter-of-fact, desultory tone, you will not be surprised at the bitter paradoxical conclusion of the third stanza—"I would do it again, but set down/ This set down/ This: were we led all that way for/ Birth or Death?" (note the way the poet gets emphasis); this he concludes was "Hard and bitter agony" for them, because of the death of their kingdoms, their death. Then the fulcrum readies you for the last sentence, "I should be glad of another death," thus providing the shift in thought.

You should proceed further in your analysis of the preceding monologue by comparing it with the two Browning poems. Some of your questions about the Eliot poem have been answered, but you have more to observe. This outline should help you:

Narrator:
   1. Who is he? In what age range would you place him?
   2. To whom is he speaking?
   3. Is the auditor named? Is he important?
   4. Is the narrator revealed through his actions? through his speech?
   5. What psychological traits are evidenced? Cite phrases and lines.
Situation:
   1. What kind of environment is revealed? How?
   2. What events have preceded this situation?
   3. Is this particular dramatic moment well-prepared for?
Theme:
   1. What is the theme? the central meaning?
   2. Point out various incidents or thoughts which support the meaning.
Tone:
   1. How does the poet set the tone?
   2. Is it well-controlled?

Atmosphere and Mood:
1. Are mood or atmosphere noticeably important? If so, how obtained?
2. Which poem is most dramatic in either of these elements?

Form:
1. Study the idea of each stanza; if not arranged in stanzaic form, where do the ideas shift or change?
2. Do the ideas follow a logical progression?
3. Do the ideas become more intense? If so, where and how?
4. Study the phraseology, the length of the lines, the smoothness of the sentences, the breaks, the pauses.
5. Do these elements influence the speech of the narrator? Cite instances.

Movement:
1. Is there a noticeable progression in ideas, action or characterization?
2. How does the rhythm of the lines assist in the motion of the poem?
3. Contrast the three poems as to ease of movement and to tension.
4. Is there a climax? a denouement?
5. Is the general movement rapid, slow or varied?

Imagery:
1. How is imagery employed—metaphorically? symbolically?
2. Which poem offers the most vivid sensory reactions?

Speech Characteristics:
1. Does each narrator have a distinctive speech rhythm? Does it characterize him?
2. How would you analyze his speech rhythm? Does it fit in with his particular environment? his emotional reactions?
3. What vocal quality and intensity would best fit his characteristic speech?

Empathy:
1. Which poem gives you the best opportunity to project into the character?
2. What is the nature of that empathy? For instance, do you empathize more in the understanding of the Duke's reactions than you do with the story of the fate of the last Duchess? Has the story of the "Journey of the Magi" made you feel the agony of the journey so that your ideas of the Star of Bethlehem have been punctured? With whom or with what are you identifying?

You might like to compare these dramatic monologues with Tennyson's "Ulysses," Arnold's "Dover Beach," Eliot's "The Love Song of J. Alfred Prufrock" or "Rhapsody on a Windy Night." One of them should provide excellent interpretative material for characterization.

Since many students are doubtful about the fate of the Duke's Duchess, an anecdote of interest should be repeated here. When Browning was once asked whether the Duke had the Duchess put to death, the poet did not answer immediately; after a pause, he said, "Yes, the commands were that she be put to death." Then, after another pause, Browning added with his typical rebound, as if he had just thought of the idea, "Of course, it is possible he might have had her shut up in a convent." So you may choose the action most characteristic of the Italian Duke.

SONNETS

One poet whose vocal intensity can always be heard in his sonnets is Hopkins, probably because he believes in "inscape" of speech melody; that is, pattern of sound as shown in poetry. Whether you can say that to know Hopkins is to understand his poetry, or to know Hopkins's poetry is to understand the poet, is questionable because his personality and basic theories merge so completely in his poems. You are acquainted with his sonnet "Windhover," (page 166) and "Pied Beauty" (page 50) so you know what to expect in the meaning of "God's Grandeur." It is a sonnet of protest against man's materialistic indifference to the natural beauty of God's world, a beauty which lives on forever through the generations. The innermost thought is based on the need of man to understand the individualistic beauty of nature that reflects the image and glory of God —this is the basic approach in his "inscape" theory. The intensity in this poem differs from "Pied Beauty," which is delightful in tone, yet grounded in reverence. As Frankenberg points out in his ingenious manner, the rhythm of the first line of "Pied Beauty" with its reminiscent colloquial Irish expression "Glory be to God" in comparison with its more exalted praise of God, is typical of the lighter tone of the dappled and pied. The poem ends, however, with the more serious utterance of "Praise him."[14] In "God's Grandeur," the intensity of the tone cannot be doubted. Compare your interpretation of these three poems with that of Cusack.[15]

God's Grandeur

The world is charged with the grandeur of God.
　It will flame out, like shining from shook foil;
　It gathers to a greatness, like the ooze of oil
Crushed. Why do men then now not reck his rod?
Generations have trod, have trod, have trod;
　And all is seared with trade; bleared, smeared with toil;
　And wears man's smudge and shares man's smell: the soil
Is bare now, nor can foot feel, being shod.

[14] Lloyd Frankenberg, *Invitation to Poetry* (New York: Doubleday & Company, Inc., 1956), p. 249.
[15] *Poetry of Gerard Manley Hopkins.* Recorded by Cyril Cusack. Caedmon, 1111.

And for all this, nature is never spent;
  There lives the dearest freshness deep down things;
And though the last lights off the black West went
  Oh, morning, at the brown brink eastward, springs—
Because the Holy Ghost over the bent
  World broods with warm breast and with ah! bright wings.[16]

GERARD MANLEY HOPKINS

The first line of the first quatrain sets the tone of exaltation, "The world is charged with the grandeur of God." Note the force of the words and enlarged images evoked by *world, charged, grandeur, God;* and how they seem to boom out in sonorous tones. Moreover, the continuation of the metaphor, based on vivid imagery and sound devices, calls for strong vocal intensity to convey deep seriousness, quite different from the charm of "Pied Beauty." The first line has its source in the poet's explanation of the "inscape" theory: "All things therefore are charged with love, are charged with God, and if we know how to touch them, give off sparks and take fire, yield drops and flow, ring and tell of Him."[17]

In the second quatrain, the weight of the compelling first line creates a hard impact with its repetitious phrase, "have trod," covering the time in which generations have made the soil bare with gains other than the glory of God, as man became "seared with trade," and "bleared, smeared with toil." The sextet lifts and returns you to the hope and glorification of God's natural beauty, in which there lives the "dearest freshness deep down things." *How* does this image mean? Remember Hopkins is likely to pile up adjectives and nouns and omit prepositions and conjunctions that are unimportant to him. As you come to the last line, the upsurge of a climactic emotion gives the deep feeling of warmth, security and brightness of wings to carry you onward: "broods with warm breast and ah! bright wings." Note the emphasis contrived by the fulcrum. As you were taken through the sonnet of Hopkins, now try your imaginative skill in comparing his poem with Millay's "God's World." The titles are similar but the tone, intensity, mood, structure and the climax are different; and so a different meaning is developed.

God's World

O world, I cannot hold thee close enough!
  Thy winds, thy wide grey skies!
  Thy mists, that roll and rise!

[16] From *Poems of Gerard Manley Hopkins,* Third Edition, edited by W. H. Gardner. Copyright 1948 by Oxford University Press, Inc. Reprinted by permission.
[17] From Gerard Manley Hopkins, *Journals and Papers* (New York: Oxford University Press, 1953), p. 332.

Thy woods, this autumn day, that ache and sag
And all but cry with colour! That gaunt crag
To crush! To lift the lean of that black bluff!
World, World, I cannot get thee close enough!

Long have I known a glory in it all,
　　But never knew I this:
　　Here such a passion is
As stretcheth me apart—Lord, I do fear
Thou'st made the world too beautiful this year;
　　My soul is all but out of me,—let fall
No burning leaf; prithee, let no bird call.[18]

EDNA ST. VINCENT MILLAY

As each of these sonnets expresses with deep feeling the glory and grandeur of God's world, so another sonnet by Keats proclaims with youthful passion his great revelation upon reading Chapman's translation of Homer. At twenty-two years of age, Keats was transported into new realms of literary discovery by an incident that motivated the creation of his famous sonnet, "On First Looking into Chapman's Homer." The title may lessen your curiosity, if you are not interested in Homer and do not know of Chapman. Moreover, it carries none of Keats's exuberance.

The story of how the sonnet was written is repeated in every book of literature, probably because of the amazing dexterity shown by a young poet after a few hours of composition. Keats and his friend Clark had spent most of one night speaking "out loud and bold" from the translation of Homer by Chapman, an Elizabethan. Then Keats, arriving home early in the morning and enraptured with the moving recreation of the translation, wrote the sonnet before retiring and sent it to Clark the next morning. So from the experience of two young men speaking with gusto and evidently with appreciation, the heritage of the poem has become yours.

The often-quoted line, "Till I heard Chapman speak out loud and bold," carries the exciting motivation and tone which Keats experienced. This intensity, which increases from line to line, must be created by the interpreter, as well as the exuberance of discovery.

On First Looking Into Chapman's Homer

Much have I travelled in the realms of gold,
　　And many goodly states and kingdoms seen;
　　Round many western islands have I been
Which bards in fealty to Apollo hold.

Oft of one wide expanse had I been told ·
  That deep-browned Homer ruled as his demesne;
  Yet never did I breathe its pure serene
Till I heard Chapman speak out loud and bold.
Then felt I like some watcher of the skies
  When a new planet swims into his ken;
Or like stout Cortez when with eagle eyes
  He stared at the Pacific—and all his men
Looked at each other with a wild surmise—
  Silent, upon a peak in Darien.

JOHN KEATS

The fervor of a young man's enthusiasm, sparkle and awe is inherent in the sonnet. Perhaps the full youthful vigor is not so obvious in the first lines weighted down by words reminiscent of Homer: "realms of gold," "goodly states," "kingdom," "bards of fealty," "Apollo," "demesne," "ken." The meaning gradually emerges from metaphors like traveling in realms of gold to those more typical of his experience and era. He feels like the "watcher of the skies" as he sights a "new planet"; and he identifies with Cortez (in reality, Balboa) as he stared with wonder and awe at the Pacific, "silent on a peak in Darien." These metaphors support the sudden and tremendous emotion felt by Keats as he experiences the discovery of an unknown and unexpected literary adventure.

Not too often is an inspiring interpretation heard with the vibrant tone building to a crescendo. If you decide to interpret the sonnet, sense the dramatic upsurge to the close of the poem. The need for appropriate pauses to create suspense, excitement and wonder is most important. Richardson's interpretation may interest you. Compare the recordings of Keats's poems as listed below.[19]

Another sonnet of interesting vocal intensity is Donne's "Death, Be Not Proud."

Death, Be Not Proud

Death, be not proud, though some have called thee
Mighty and dreadful, for thou art not so;
For those whom thou think'st thou dost overthrow
Die not, poor Death; nor yet canst thou kill me.
From rest and sleep, which but thy pictures be,
Much pleasure; then from thee much more must flow;
And soonest our best men with thee do go—
Rest of their bones, and souls' delivery!
Thou'rt slave to fate, chance, kings, and desperate men,

[19] *Poet's Gold,* V. 2, see p. 261; and *The Poetry of Keats.* Recorded by Sir Ralph Richardson. Caedmon 1087.

And dost with poison, war, and sickness dwell;
And poppy or charms can make us sleep as well
And better than thy stroke. Why swell'st thou then?
One short sleep past, we wake eternally,
And Death shall be no more: Death, thou shalt die.

JOHN DONNE

As in all of Donne's poetry, the poet's personal emotion is expressed: in this one, the meaning is made more intense by paradox. Can you select ideas and phrases that present the uncertainty of paradoxical meaning? Are you aware of the rhythmical pattern coinciding with the poet's reactions; and of the decisive finality in the last four lines, reaching a conclusive climax by means of four words of equal metrical value—two spondee feet?

Compare the thought of Donne's sonnet with Shelley's "Ozymandias." Remember: from the face of the wrecked statue of long, long ago with its frown, wrinkled lip and sneer of cold command, the character of one who was once proud and powerful still survives through the hands of the sculptor. Look for symbolic significance and irony, namely: that immortality exists in art and in nature as shown in boundless and bare sands that continue to stretch forever in endless distances—as opposed to the decay of human life, and with it, the loss of man's power, glory and pride.

No group of sonnets would be complete without Wordsworth's "Lines Composed Upon Westminster Bridge." The tone of the poem is immediate and personal. The incident which motivated the sonnet is related by Dorothy Wordsworth in her *Journals*.[20] She and her brother William were crossing Westminster Bridge on the Dover Coach one clear morning: "It was a beautiful morning. The city, St. Paul's, with the river and a multitude of little boats, made a most beautiful sight as we crossed Westminster Bridge. The houses were not overhung by their cloud of smoke, and they were spread out endlessly, yet the sun shone so brightly, with such a fierce light, that there was something like the purity of one of nature's own grand spectacles." Wordsworth, choosing the medium of the sonnet, wrote the verse, as he records, on the "roof of a coach, on my way to France." He captured all that his sister saw and felt, and added to her visual enchantment the tone of quietness, calmness, silence, presented by the scene.

Lines Composed upon Westminster Bridge

Earth has not anything to show more fair:
Dull would be he of soul who could pass by
A sight so touching in its majesty:
This City now doth, like a garment, wear

[20] Dorothy Wordsworth, *Journals of Dorothy Wordsworth*, E. de Selincourt, ed. (New York: St. Martin's Press, 1941), Vol. 1, pp. 172-173.

The beauty of the morning; silent, bare,
Ships, towers, domes, theatres, and temples lie
Open unto the fields, and to the sky;
All bright and glittering in the smokeless air.
Never did sun more beautifully steep
In his first splendor, valley, rock, or hill;
Ne'er saw I, never felt, a calm so deep!
The river glideth of his own sweet will:
Dear God! the very houses seem asleep;
And all that mighty heart is lying still!

WILLIAM WORDSWORTH

Wordsworth is overwhelmed by an unsuspected beauty and majesty in the deep calm of a morning steeped in the first splendor of the rising sun, bright and glittering; by the quietness of the river gliding at its will; and by the overtones of serenity in the great city, usually smoke-filled and bustling, now a city whose mighty heart is lying still. In contrast to the peace of an early morning in a city asleep, Frost, in his masterful poetic manner, achieves the tone and atmosphere of the haunting loneliness and isolation with which night can surround man in his sonnet, "Acquainted With The Night."

Acquainted with the Night

I have been one acquainted with the night.
I have walked out in rain—and back in rain.
I have outwalked the furthest city light.

I have looked down the saddest city lane.
I have passed by the watchman on his beat
And dropped my eyes, unwilling to explain.

I have stood still and stopped the sound of feet
When far away an interrupted cry
Came over houses from another street,

But not to call me back or say good-bye;
And further still at an unearthly height,
One luminary clock against the sky

Proclaimed the time was neither wrong nor right.
I have been one acquainted with the night.[21]

ROBERT FROST

[21] From COMPLETE POEMS OF ROBERT FROST. Copyright 1916, 1921, 1923, 1928, 1930, 1939 by Holt, Rinehart and Winston, Inc. Copyright 1936, 1942, 1944, 1951, © 1956, 1958 by Robert Frost. Copyright © 1964 by Lesley Frost Ballantine. Reprinted by permission of Holt, Rinehart and Winston, Inc.

No tremendous outburst of emotion is shown here. Where, however, could anyone find a deeper sense of the desolation of man's aloneness, separation, withdrawal from the world of men? Through carefully selected images, Frost has made the night more lonely, more silent, more aloof. The mystery of night immediately suggests a symbolic significance centered around the darkness. The narrator walks alone in the dark and rain —even to the city's farthest light—beyond which an impenetrable darkness is imagined; he passes the saddest city lane; with his eyes down, he wanders by the watchman, always a symbol of aloneness; he hears no sound except his footfall and an "interrupted cry . . . from another street," frightening because of the stillness and eeriness of the night's blackness. Finally, looking up high to an "unearthly height" he sees the lighted face of the clock, proclaiming that time is neither right nor wrong, nor can it be changed. This image again isolates man, evoking the thought that time passes on, unchanging and indifferent to man's suffering, and that man must find his own way of salvation in the darkness surrounding him. The mood created is not one of man's helplessness nor of his need for assistance; rather, man's independence in meeting the experiences of the "dark" is suggested. The tone of the narrator is one of calm detachment quite different from the peaceful calm of Wordsworth's sonnet. Neither is there an implied symbol indicated in the latter poem.

These sonnets have been chosen not only for their variety in form but also, as Eliot writes, "for the skill and power with which the poet makes the pattern comply with what he has to say."[22] For instance, is Frost's structure employing the tercet rima pattern forced or is it an asset to the tone, atmosphere and meaning? The following analysis of these lyrics may help your interpretation:

1. Does the poet's approach set the tone of emotional impact or is it too formal for the intended thought?
2. Does the sentence structure give the impression of having been worked over too precisely or does it heighten meaning through rhythmical cadences?
3. Do the lines give the illusion of a natural and gradual crescendo to the fulcrum or are they directed too suddenly and deliberately into a climax?
4. Is the break between the octet and sestet one that is meaningful?
5. Has the poet considered the impact of images and symbols to establish vivid meaning or is he too concerned with form?
6. How will the vocal intensity of the interpreter vary in each sonnet to emphasize nuances of thought?

[22] T. S. Eliot, *On Poetry and Poets* (New York: Farrar, Straus & Giroux, 1957), p. 37.

7. Which poem will create empathic responses if impressively interpreted?
8. Which sonnet will a student audience enjoy most? appreciate most? understand the least?

PROSE

Prose that shows contrast and conflict of forces, characters or ideas usually builds to a climax. Even in descriptive and expository essays a crescendo of ideas will be evident. The high point of suspense in the essay, however, will never reach the peak of interest found in a story, novel or play. In these latter forms the conflict is shown through a succession of mounting incidents that include characters in action: that activity may demonstrate what the characters are thinking and why they react as they do, as in Woolfe's "The New Dress" (page 117); or may show persons under the control of the environment, as in Mansfield's story, "The Daughters of the Late Colonel" (page 518).

You, as an interpreter, must decide on the direction the author has taken to create suspense in fiction and drama. Very seldom will you select, as has been done in this book, scenes that are at the climactic point of interest. Your audience is usually introduced to one or two scenes that lead up to the final powerful action. The high point of any literature cannot be appreciated unless the conflicting forces are shown in opposition and then related to the progressive movement directed to the author's central idea. To repeat, you must know the literature as a whole if you are to interpret only a part of it.

At the end of Hemingway's novel *For Whom the Bell Tolls*, the last moments of Jordan's life are tense with pain and expectation but precisioned by heroic courage. This final scene has been called one of "grace under pressure" because of the author's unique presentation. If you do not recall the scenes depicting the forward movement to this dramatic scene, refresh your memory by rereading some preceding episodes. The environment of the final action is reminiscent of the opening setting in which Jordan, a bomber of bridges, lies on the ground amid pine trees to survey his target point. In the first episode, the reader's anticipation of the danger in the bombing of the bridge is cleverly initiated by the author; in the final scene, the tone of anxiety is intensified many times by Jordan's excruciating pain from his smashed leg and the grim knowledge that he intends to stay alive to kill. Jordan, having sent away those who had helped him, including Maria, awaits his death alone in the forest of pine with unbelievable stoicism—waiting for the bell to toll for him. He wonders if he can endure the pain long enough to kill the officer in command as he comes through the hills and into the opening, at which Jordan's gun is pointed.

from *For Whom the Bell Tolls*

"I can't wait any longer now," he said. "If I wait any longer I'll pass out. I know because I've felt it starting three times now and I've held it. I held it all right. But I don't know about any more . . . It would be all right to do it now. Really, I'm telling you now that it would be all right."

And if you wait and hold them up even a little while or just get the officer that may make all the difference. One thing well done can make—

"All right," he said. And he lay very quietly and tried to hold on to himself that he felt slipping away from himself as you feel snow starting to slip sometimes on a mountain slope, and he said, now quietly, "Then let me last until they come."

Robert Jordan's luck held very good because he saw, just then, the cavalry ride out of the timber and cross the road. He watched them coming riding up the slope. He saw the trooper who stopped by the gray horse and shouted to the officer who rode over to him. He watched them both looking down at the gray horse. They recognized him of course. He and his rider had been missing since the early morning of the day before.

Robert Jordan saw them there on the slope, close to him now, and below he saw the road and the bridge and the long lines of vehicles below it. He was completely integrated now and he took a good long look at everything. Then he looked up at the sky. There were big white clouds in it. He touched the palm of his hand against the pine needles where he lay and he touched the bark of the pine trunk that he lay behind.

Then he rested as easily as he could with his two elbows in the pine needles and the muzzle of the submachine gun resting against the trunk of the pine tree.

As the officer came trotting now on the trail of the horses of the band he would pass twenty yards below where Robert Jordan lay. At that distance there would be no problem. The officer was Lieutenant Berrendo. He had come up from La Granja when they had been ordered up after the first report of the attack on the lower post. They had ridden hard and had then had to swing back, because the bridges had been blown, to cross the gorge high above and come around through the timber. Their horses were wet and blown and they had to be urged into the trot.

Lieutenant Berrendo, watching the trail, came riding up, his thin face serious and grave. His submachine gun lay across the saddle in the crook of his left arm. Robert Jordan lay behind the tree, holding onto himself very carefully and delicately to keep his hands steady. He was waiting until the officer reached the sunlit place where the first trees of the pine forest joined the green slope of the meadow. He could feel his heart beating against the pine needle floor of the forest.[23]

ERNEST HEMINGWAY

[23] Excerpt from the work of Ernest Hemingway is used by permission of Charles Scribner's Sons: FOR WHOM THE BELL TOLLS (Copyright 1940 Ernest Hemingway).

In the following excerpt, Francie is the little girl who grows up in Brooklyn in Betty Smith's novel *A Tree Grows in Brooklyn*. This is a memorable incident in her childhood, an experience that reveals Francie's character even at the age of ten years. This same perseverance, this shrewd dealing at the bargain-counter and the intuitive understanding of the man behind the sales, this knowledge of how people really *mean*, this unbelievable acceptance of those who belong to her world and shape her way of living and this wish for beauty—even the greenness and scent of the Christmas tree—all these are captured in this brief episode and are part of her desire to belong, as she "grows up" in Brooklyn.

The seller of trees is a foil for Francie. Be sure you discover his appropriate vocal quality and intensity; and also catch the rhythm of his speech—and the feeling in his heart.

from *A Tree Grows in Brooklyn*

The spruce trees began coming into the neighborhood the week before Christmas. Their branches were corded to hold back the glory of their spreading and probably to make shipping easier. Vendors rented space on the curb before a store and stretched a rope from pole to pole and leaned the trees against it. All day they walked up and down this one-sided avenue of aromatic leaning trees, blowing on stiff ungloved fingers and looking with bleak hope at those people who paused. A few ordered a tree set aside for the day; others stopped to price, inspect and conjecture. But most came just to touch the boughs and surreptitiously pinch a fingerful of spruce needles together to release the fragrance. And the air was cold and still, and full of the pine smell and the smell of tangerines which appeared in the stores only at Christmas time and the mean street was truly wonderful for a little while.

There was a cruel custom in the neighborhood. It was about the trees still unsold when midnight of Christmas Eve approached. There was a saying that if you waited until then, you wouldn't have to buy a tree; that "they'd chuck 'em at you." This was literally true.

At midnight on the Eve of our dear Saviour's birth, the kids gathered where there were unsold trees. The man threw each tree in turn, starting with the biggest. Kids volunteered to stand up against the throwing. If a boy didn't fall down under the impact, the tree was his. If he fell, he forfeited his chance at winning a tree. Only the roughest boys and some of the young men elected to be hit by the big trees. The others waited shrewdly until a tree came up that they could stand against. The little kids waited for the tiny, foot-high trees and shrieked in delight when they won one.

On the Christmas Eve when Francie was ten and Neely nine, mama consented to let them go down and have their first try for a tree. Francie had picked out her tree earlier in the day. She had stood near it all afternoon and evening praying that no one would buy it. To her joy, it was still there at midnight. It was the biggest tree in the neighborhood and its price was so high that no one could afford to buy it. It was ten feet high. Its branches were bound with new white rope and it came to a sure point at the top.

The man took this tree out first. Before Francie could speak up, a neighborhood bully, a boy of eighteen known as Punky Perkins, stepped forward and ordered the man to chuck the tree at him. The man hated the way Punky was so confident. He looked around and asked:

"Anybody else wanna take a chanct on it?"

Francie stepped forward. "Me, Mister."

A spurt of derisive laughter came from the tree man. The kids snickered. A few adults who had gathered to watch the fun, guffawed.

"Aw g'wan. You're too little," the tree man objected.

"Me and my brother—we're not too little together."

She pulled Neeley forward. The man looked at them—a thin girl of ten with starveling hollows in her cheeks but with the chin still baby-round. He looked at the little boy with his fair hair and round blue-eyes—Neeley Nolan, all innocence and trust.

"Two ain't fair," yelped Punky.

"Shut your lousy trap," advised the man who held all power in that hour. "These here kids is got nerve. Stand back, the rest of youse. These kids is goin' to have a show at this tree."

The others made a wavering lane. Francie and Neeley stood at one end of it and the big man with the big tree at the other. It was a human funnel with Francie and her brother making the small end of it. The man flexed his great arms to throw the great tree. He noticed how tiny the children looked at the end of the short lane. For the split part of a moment, the tree thrower went through a kind of Gethsemane.

"Oh, Jesus Christ," his soul agonized, "why don't I just give 'em the tree, say Merry Christmas and let 'em go? What's the tree to me? I can't sell it no more this year and it won't keep till next year." The kids watched him solemnly as he stood there in his moment of thought. "But then," he rationalized, "if I did that, all the others would expect to get 'em handed to 'em. And next year, nobody a-tall would buy a tree off of me. They'd all wait to get 'em handed to 'em on a silver plate. I ain't a big enough man to give this tree away for nothin'. No, I ain't big enough. I ain't big enough to do a thing like that. I gotta think of myself and my own kids." He finally came to his conclusion. "Oh, what the hell! Them two kids is gotta live in this world. They *got* to get used to it. They got to learn to give and to take punishment. And by Jesus, it ain't give but *take, take, take* all the time in this God-damned world." As he threw the tree with all his strength, his heart wailed out, "It's a God-damned, rotten, lousy world!"

Francie saw the tree leave his hands. There was a split bit of being when time and space had no meaning. The whole world stood still as something dark and monstrous came through the air. The tree came towards her blotting out all memory of her ever having lived. There was nothing—nothing but pungent darkness and something that grew and grew as it rushed at her. She staggered as the tree hit them. Neeley went to his knees but she pulled him up fiercely before he could go down. There was a mighty swishing sound as the tree settled. Everything was dark, green and prickly. Then she felt a sharp pain at the side of her head where the trunk of the tree had hit her. She felt Neeley trembling.

When some of the older boys pulled the tree away, they found Francie and her brother standing upright, hand in hand. Blood was coming from scratches on Neeley's face. He looked more like a baby than ever with his bewildered blue eyes and the fairness of his skin made more noticeable because of the clear red blood. But they were smiling. Had they not won the biggest tree in the neighborhood? Some of the boys hollered "Hooray!" A few adults clapped. The tree man eulogized them by screaming.

"And now get the hell out of here with your tree, you lousy bastards."

Francie had heard swearing since she had heard words. Obscenity and profanity had no meaning as such among those people. They were emotional expressions of inarticulate people with small vocabularies; they made a kind of dialect. The phrases could mean many things according to the expression and tone used in saying them. So now, when Francie heard themselves called lousy bastards, she smiled tremulously at the kind man. She knew that he was really saying, "Goodbye—God bless you."

It wasn't easy dragging that tree home. They had to pull it inch by inch. They were handicapped by a boy, who ran alongside yelping, "Free ride! All aboard!" who'd jump on and make them drag him along. But he got sick of the game eventually and went away.

In a way, it was good that it took them so long to get the tree home. It made their triumph more drawn out. Francie glowed when she heard a lady say, "I never saw such a big tree!" A man called after them, "You kids musta robbed a bank to buy such a big tree." The cop on their corner stopped them, examined the tree, and solemnly offered to buy it for ten cents—fifteen cents if they'd delivered it to his home. Francie nearly burst with pride although she knew he was joking. She said she wouldn't sell it for a dollar, even. He shook his head and said she was foolish not to grab the offer. He went up to a quarter but Francie kept smiling and shaking her head, "no."

It was like acting in a Christmas play where the setting was a street corner and the time, a frosty Christmas Eve and the characters, a kind cop, her brother and herself. Francie knew all the dialogue. The cop gave his lines right and Francie picked up her cues happily and the stage directions were the smiles between the spoken lines.

They had to call up to papa to help them get the tree up the narrow stairs. Papa came running down. To Francie's relief, he ran down straight and not sideways which proved that he was still sober.

Papa's amazement at the size of the tree was flattering. He pretended to believe that it wasn't theirs. Francie had a lot of fun convincing him although she knew all the while that the whole thing was make-believe. Papa pulled in front and Francie and Neeley pushed in back and they began forcing the big tree up the three narrow flights of stairs. Johnny was so excited that he started singing, not caring that it was rather late at night. He sang, "Holy Night." The narrow walls took up his clear sweet voice, held it for a breath and gave it back with doubled sweetness. Doors creaked open and families gathered on the landings, pleased and amazed at the something unexpected being added to that moment of their lives.

. . . They set the tree up in the front room after spreading a sheet to protect the carpet of pink roses from falling pine needles. The tree stood in a big tin bucket with broken bricks to hold it upright. When the rope was cut away, the branches spread out to fill the whole room. They draped over the piano and it was so that some of the chairs stood among the branches. There was no money to buy tree decorations or lights. But the great tree standing there was enough. The room was cold. It was a poor year, that one—too poor for them to buy the extra coal for the front room stove. The room smelled cold and clean and aromatic. Every day, during the week the tree stood there, Francie put on her sweater and zitful cap and went in and sat under the tree. She sat there and enjoyed the smell and the dark greenness of it.

Oh, the mystery of a great tree, a prisoner in a tin wash bucket in a tenement front room![24]

BETTY SMITH

In contrast to Francie's story of sharp and courageous bargaining for an evergeen tree is the story told by Dylan Thomas of his visit as a child to his grandpa's house. Francie no doubt could have coped with "grandpa," even though the stubborn old gentleman belongs to the tradition and atmosphere of Welsh legends. No one, however, but Thomas could have written this tale of a small boy, in the dead of night, peering through the candlelight at his "grandpa," wearing a white flannel nightshirt and a red waistcoat with walnut-sized brass buttons, and shouting "Gee-up" to his horses who were taking him over a rough road in the traveling bed. Nor could anyone but this Welsh author have touched the heart with "grandpa's" desire to find a "comfy spot" for burial—a place where "you can twitch your legs without putting them in the sea."

Compare images and incidents typically Welsh in character and action with those of Francie's experience in the Brooklyn environment. The rhythmic movement and character contrasts vary in each. Inasmuch as the Welsh story is a unit, these elements build toward and enhance the fantasy and mystical tone of the final scene where "grandpa" stands firmly on the bridge, clutching his bag to his side, and staring at the flowing river and sky. Would the fantasy have been affected if the author had permitted "grandpa" to go home? Listen to Thomas's recording of this narrative,[25] and also of "A Child's Christmas in Wales" for an excellent story-telling technique.

[24] From A TREE GROWS IN BROOKLYN by Betty Smith. Copyright 1943, 1947 by Betty Smith. Reprinted by permission of Harper & Row, Publishers.
[25] *Stories of Dylan Thomas*, V.5. Recorded by Dylan Thomas. Caedmon, TC 1132.

A Visit to Grandpa's

In the middle of the night I woke from a dream full of whips and lariats as long as serpents, and runaway coaches on mountain passes, and wide, windy gallops over cactus field, and I heard the old man in the next room crying, "Gee-up!" and "Whoa!" and trotting his tongue on the roof of his mouth.

It was the first time I had stayed in grandpa's house. The floorboards had squeaked like mice as I climbed into bed, and the mice between the walls had creaked like wood as though another visitor was walking on them. It was a mild summer night, but curtains had flapped and branches beaten against the window. I had pulled the sheets over my head, and soon was roaring and riding in a book.

"Whoa there, my beauties!" cried grandpa. His voice sounded very young and loud, and his tongue had powerful hooves, and he made his bedroom into a great meadow. I thought I would see if he was ill, or had set his bed-clothes on fire, for my mother had said that he lit his pipe under the blankets, and had warned me to run to his help if I smelt smoke in the night. I went on tiptoe through the darkness to his bedroom door, brushing against the furniture and upsetting a candlestick with a thump. When I saw there was a light in the room I felt frightened, and as I opened the door I heard grandpa shout, "Gee-up!" as loudly as a bull with a megaphone.

He was sitting straight up in bed and rocking from side to side as though the bed were on a rough road; the knotted edges of the counterpane were his reins; his invisible horses stood in a shadow beyond the bedside candle. Over a white flannel nightshirt he was wearing a red waistcoat with walnut-sized brass buttons. The over-filled bowl of his pipe smouldered among his whiskers like a little, burning hayrick on a stick. At the sight of me, his hands dropped from the reins and lay blue and quiet, the bed stopped still on a level road, he muffled his tongue into silence, and the horses drew softly up.

"Is there anything the matter, grandpa?" I asked, though the clothes were not on fire. His face in the candlelight looked like a ragged quilt pinned upright on the black air and patched all over with goat-beards.

He stared at me mildly. Then he blew down his pipe, scattering the sparks and making a high, wet dog-whistle of the stem, and shouted: "Ask no questions."

After a pause, he said slyly: "Do you ever have nightmares, boy?"

I said: "No."

"Oh, yes, you do," he said.

I said I was woken by a voice that was shouting to horses.

"What did I tell you?" he said. "You eat too much. Who ever heard of horses in a bedroom?"

He fumbled under his pillow, brought out a small tinkling bag, and carefully untied its strings. He put a sovereign in my hand, and said "Buy a cake." I thanked him and wished him good night.

As I closed my bedroom door, I heard his voice crying loudly and gaily, "Gee-up!, gee-up!" and the rocking of the travelling bed.

In the morning I woke from a dream of fiery horses on a plain that was littered with furniture, and of large, cloudy men who rode six horses at a time and whipped them with burning bed-clothes. Grandpa was at breakfast, dressed in deep black. After breakfast he said, "There was a terrible loud wind last night," and sat in his arm-chair by the hearth to make clay balls for the fire. Later in the morning he took me for a walk, through Johnstown village and into the fields on the Llanstephan road.

A man with a whippet said, "There's a nice morning, Mr. Thomas," and when he had gone, leanly as his dog, into the short-treed green wood he should not have entered because of the notices, grandpa said: "There, do you hear what he called you? Mister!"

We passed by small cottages, and all the men who leant on the gates congratulated grandpa on the fine morning. We passed through the wood full of pigeons, and their wings broke the branches as they rushed to the tops of the trees. Among the soft, contented voices and the loud, timid flying, grandpa said, like a man calling across a field: "If you heard those old birds in the night, you'd wake me up and say there were horses in the trees."

We walked back slowly, for he was tired, and the lean man stalked out of the forbidden wood with a rabbit held as gently over his arm as a girl's arm in a warm sleeve.

On the last day but one of my visit I was taken to Llanstephan in a governess cart pulled by a short, weak pony. Grandpa might have been driving a bison, so tightly he held the reins, so ferociously cracked the long whip, so blasphemously shouted warning to boys who played in the road, so stoutly stood with his gaitered legs apart and cursed the demon strength and wilfulness of his tottering pony.

"Look out, boy!" he cried when we came to each corner, and pulled and tugged and jerked and sweated and waved his whip like a rubber sword. And when the pony had crept miserably round each corner, grandpa turned to me with a sighing smile: "We weathered that one, boy."

When we came to Llanstephan village at the top of the hill, he left the cart by the "Edwinsford Arms" and patted the pony's muzzle and gave it sugar, saying: "You're a weak little pony, Jim, to pull big men like us."

He had strong beer and I had lemonade, and he paid Mrs. Edwinsford with a sovereign out of the tinkling bag; she inquired after his health, and he said that Llangadock was better for the tubes. We went to look at the church-yard and the sea, and sat in the wood called the Sticks, and stood on the concert platform in the middle of the wood where visitors sang on midsummer nights and, year by year, the innocent of the village was elected mayor. Grandpa paused at the churchyard and pointed over the iron gate at the angelic headstones and the poor wooden crosses. "There's no sense in lying there," he said.

We journeyed back furiously: Jim was a bison again.

I woke late on my last morning, out of dreams where the Llanstephan sea carried bright sailing-boats as long as liners; and heavenly choirs in the Sticks, dressed in bards' robes and brass-buttoned waistcoats, sang in a strange Welsh to the departing sailors. Grandpa was not at breakfast; he rose early. I walked in the fields with a new sling, and shot at the Towy gulls and the rooks in the parsonage trees. A warm wind blew from the summer points of the weather;

a morning mist climbed from the ground and floated among the trees and hid the noisy birds; in the mist and the wind my pebbles flew lightly up like hailstones in a world on its head. The morning passed without a bird falling.

I broke my sling and returned for the midday meal through the parson's orchard. Once, grandpa told me, the parson had bought three ducks at Carmarthen Fair and made a pond for them in the centre of the garden; but they waddled to the gutter under the crumbling doorsteps of the house, and swam and quacked there. When I reached the end of the orchard path, I looked through a hole in the hedge and saw that the parson had made a tunnel through the rockery that was between the gutter and the pond and had set up a notice in plain writing: "This way to the pond."

The ducks were still swimming under the steps.

Grandpa was not in the cottage. I went into the garden, but grandpa was not staring at the fruit-trees. I called across to a man who leant on a spade in the field beyond the garden hedge: "Have you seen my grandpa this morning?"

He did not stop digging, and answered over his shoulder: "I seen him in his fancy waistcoat."

Griff, the barber, lived in the next cottage. I called to him through the open door: "Mr. Griff, have you seen my grandpa?"

The barber came out in his shirtsleeves.

I said: "He's wearing his best waistcoat." I did not know if it was important, but grandpa wore his waistcoat only in the night.

"Has grandpa been to Llanstephan?" asked Mr. Griff anxiously.

"We went there yesterday in a little trap," I said.

He hurried indoors and I heard him talking in Welsh, and he came out again with his white coat on, and he carried a striped and coloured walking-stick. He strode down the village street and I ran by his side.

When we stopped at the tailor's shop, he cried out, "Dan!" and Dan Tailor stepped from his window where he sat like an Indian priest but wearing a derby hat. "Dai Thomas has got his waistcoat on," said Mr. Griff, "and he's been to Llanstephan."

As Dan Tailor searched for his overcoat, Mr. Griff was striding on. "Will Evans," he called outside the carpenter's shop, "Dai Thomas has been to Llanstephan, and he's got his waistcoat on."

"I'll tell Morgan now," said the carpenter's wife out of the hammering, sawing darkness of the shop.

We called at the butcher's shop and Mr. Price's house, and Mr. Griff repeated his message like a town crier.

We gathered together in Johnstown square. Dan Tailor had his bicycle, Mr. Price his pony-trap. Mr. Griff, the butcher, Morgan Carpenter, and I climbed into the shaking trap, and we trotted off towards Carmarthen town. The tailor led the way, ringing his bell as though there were a fire or a robbery, and an old woman by the gate of a cottage at the end of the street ran inside like a pelted hen. Another woman waved a bright handkerchief.

"Where are we going?" I asked.

Grandpa's neighbours were as solemn as old men with black hats and jackets on the outskirts of a fair. Mr. Griff shook his head and mourned: "I didn't expect this again from Dai Thomas."

"Not after the last time," said Mr. Price sadly.

We trotted on, we crept up Constitution Hill, we rattled down into Lammas Street, and the tailor still rang his bell and a dog ran, squealing, in front of his wheels. As we clip-clopped over the cobbles that led down to the Towy bridge, I remembered grandpa's nightly noisy journeys that rocked the bed and shook the walls, and I saw his gay waistcoat in a vision and his patchwork head tufted and smiling in the candlelight. The tailor before us turned round on his saddle, his bicycle wobbled and skidded. "I see Dai Thomas!" he cried.

The trap rattled on to the bridge, and I saw grandpa there; the buttons of his waistcoat shone in the sun, he wore his tight, black Sunday trousers and a tall, dusty hat I had seen in a cupboard in the attic, and he carried an ancient bag. He bowed to us. "Good morning, Mr. Price," he said, "and Mr. Griff and Mr. Morgan and Mr. Evans." To me, he said, "Good morning, boy."

Mr. Griff pointed his coloured stick at him.

"And what do you think you are doing on Carmarthen bridge in the middle of the afternoon," he said sternly, "with your best waistcoat and your old hat?"

Grandpa did not answer, but inclined his face to the river wind, so that his beard was set dancing and wagging as though he talked, and watched the coracle men move, like turtles, on the shore.

Mr. Griff raised his stunted barber's pole. "And where do you think you are going," he said, "with your old black bag?"

Grandpa said: "I am going to Llangadock to be buried." And he watched the coracle shells slip into the water lightly, and the gulls complain over the fish-filled water as bitterly as Mr. Price complained:

"But you aren't dead yet, Dai Thomas."

For a moment grandpa reflected, then: "There's no sense in lying dead in Llanstephan," he said. "The ground is comfy in Llangadock; you can twitch your legs without putting them in the sea."

His neighbours moved close to him. They said: "You aren't dead, Mr. Thomas."

"How can you be buried, then?"

"Nobody's going to bury you in Llanstephan."

"Come on home, Mr. Thomas."

"There's strong beer for tea."

"And cake."

But grandpa stood firmly on the bridge, and clutched his bag to his side, and stared at the flowing river and the sky, like a prophet who has no doubt.[26]

DYLAN THOMAS

The power of dramatic writing found in Conrad's *Heart of Darkness* is well-known to you. You recall how Marlowe began his jungle search for Mr. Kurtz, who was known to have succumbed to the savagery of the jungle natives. Two of the harrowing scenes—as Marlowe and his men travel the reach that was "narrow, straight, with high sides like a railway cutting" by means of a broken down steamer—provide excellent interpretative material. The atmosphere of the first episode pushes in on you from all sides until you are stifled, rigid, almost frozen in fear.

from *The Heart of Darkness*

EPISODE 1

The dusk came gliding into it long before the sun had set. The current ran smooth and swift, but a dumb immobility sat on the banks. The living trees, lashed together by the creepers and every living bush of the undergrowth, might have been changed into stone, even to the slenderest twig, to the lightest leaf. It was not sleep—it seemed unnatural, like a state of trance. Not the faintest sound of any kind could be heard. You looked on amazed, and began to suspect yourself of being deaf—then the night came suddenly, and struck you blind as well. About three in the morning some large fish leaped, and the loud splash made me jump as though a gun had been fired. When the sun rose there was a white fog, very warm and clammy, and more blinding than the night. It did not shift or drive; it was just there, standing all round you like something solid. At eight or nine, perhaps, it lifted as a shutter lifts. We had a glimpse of the towering multitude of trees, of the immense matted jungle, with the blazing little ball of the sun hanging over it—all perfectly still—and then the white shutter came down again, smoothly, as if sliding in greased grooves. I ordered the chain, which we had begun to heave in, to be paid out again. Before it stopped running with a muffled rattle, a cry, a very loud cry, as of infinite desolation, soared slowly in the opaque air. It ceased. A complaining clamour, modulated in savage discords, filled our ears. The sheer unexpectedness of it made my hair stir under my cap. I don't know how it struck the others; to me it seemed as though the mist itself had screamed, so suddenly, and apparently from all sides at once, did this tumultuous and mournful uproar arise. It culminated in a hurried outbreak of almost intolerably excessive shrieking, which stopped short, leaving us stiffened in a variety of silly attitudes, and obstinately listening to the nearly as appalling and excessive silence. "Good God! What is the meaning-----" stammered at my elbow one of the pilgrims. . . . Two others remained open-mouthed a whole minute, then dashed into the little cabin, to rush out incontinently and stand darting scared glances, with Winchesters at "ready" in their hands. What we could see was just the steamer we were on, her outlines blurred as though she had been on the point of dissolving, and a misty strip of water, perhaps two feet broad, around her—and that was all. The rest of the world was nowhere, as far as our eyes and ears were concerned. Just nowhere. Gone, disappeared; swept off without leaving a whisper or a shadow behind.[27]

As Marlowe, the narrator, took the trail into the jungle after being warned of danger involving Kurtz and the savages, he felt the deadly

[27] From YOUTH AND TWO OTHER STORIES by Joseph Conrad, "Heart of Darkness." Reprinted by permission of J. M. Dent & Sons Ltd., Publishers and the Trustees of the Joseph Conrad Estate, pp. 101-102.

terror of the impenetrable darkness; he was aware of shadowy figures
lurking around him; he was startled by "abrupt bursts of yells" coming
through the night; he was terrified by the "weird incantations" and the
"monotonous beating of a big drum" and the muffled sounds of many men
against the "flat wall of woods"; he sensed the incredible fear and danger
of a "sudden onslaught and massacre." Yet he must track down that gray
shadow of the jungle that was Kurtz, the "unseen presence of victorious
corruption."

Marlowe finally found a broad trail over which he strode rapidly with
clenched fists and "imbecile thoughts" of falling on Kurtz and overwhelming him. He remembers how he confused the beat of the drum with the
beating of his heart and was glad it was keeping such a steady beat. He
was intensely aware of dark motion around him, of "black things that
stood very still." He began to imagine that he would never get back to
the steamer and would have to spend the rest of his life living alone and
unarmed among the dark jungle forces. Then seeing some kind of motion
ahead of him, he quickly swung around in a wide semicircle to circumvent
Kurtz and to outwit the dark forms.

EPISODE 2

I came upon him, and, if he had not heard me coming, I would have fallen
over him, too, but he got up in time. He rose, unsteady, long, pale, indistinct,
like a vapour exhaled by the earth, and swayed slightly, misty and silent before
me; while at my back the fires loomed between the trees, and the murmur of
many voices issued from the forest. I had cut him off cleverly; but when actually confronting him I seemed to come to my senses, I saw the danger in its
right proportion. It was by no means over yet. Suppose he began to shout?
Though he could hardly stand, there was still plenty of vigour in his voice. "Go
away—hide yourself," he said, in that profound tone. It was very awful. I
glanced back. We were within thirty yards from the nearest fire. A black figure
stood up, strode on long black legs, waving long black arms, across the glow. It
had horns—antelope horns, I think—on its head. Some sorcerer, some witch-man,
no doubt: it looked fiend-like enough. "Do you know what you are doing?" I
whispered. "Perfectly," he answered, raising his voice for that single word: it
sounded to me far off and yet loud, like a hail through a speaking-trumpet. If
he makes a row we are lost, I thought to myself. This clearly was not a case
for fisticuffs, even apart from the very natural aversion I had to beat that Shadow—this wandering and tormented thing. "You will be lost," I said—"utterly
lost." One gets sometimes such a flash of inspiration, you know. I did say the
right thing, though indeed he could not have been more irretrievably lost than
he was at this very moment, when the foundations of our intimacy were being
laid—to endure—to endure—even to the end—even beyond.

"I had immense plans," he muttered irresolutely. "Yes," said I; "but if you
try to shout I'll smash your head with------" There was not a stick or a stone
near. "I will throttle you for good," I corrected myself. "I was on the threshold
of great things," he pleaded, in a voice of longing, with a wistfulness of tone

that made my blood run cold. "And now for this stupid scoundrel-----" "Your success in Europe is assured in any case," I affirmed, steadily. I did not want to have the throttling of him, you understand—and indeed it would have been very little use for any practical purpose. I tried to break the spell—the heavy, mute spell of the wilderness—that seemed to draw him to its pitiless breast by the awakening of forgotten and brutal instincts, by the memory of gratified and monstrous passions. This alone, I was convinced, had driven him out to the edge of the forest, to the bush, towards the gleam of fires, the throb of drums, the drone of weird incantations; this alone had beguiled his unlawful soul beyond the bounds of permitted aspirations. And, don't you see, the terror of the position was not in being knocked on the head—though I had a very lively sense of that danger, too—but in this, that I had to deal with a being to whom I could not appeal in the name of anything high or low.[28]

Kurtz was carried to the steamer, while from the woods came "quivering, bronze bodies" shouting from the slope something that was rapid and breathless in utterance. The group was led by a savage, superb woman with "helmeted head," magnificent in fringed draperies with the glint of yellow metal. Her tawny face wore a tragic look and her eyes were wild in their appeal. Kurtz listened to the chorus of voices with wistfulness and hate merging in his face and with "fiery and longing eyes," as the steamer started on its way.

During the journey back to civilization, Marlowe remembers the eloquence of Kurtz's voice as he explained his accumulation of ivory and how his voice "rang deep to the very last" in superb and lofty expression. Marlowe found a man intensely concentrated on himself; an intelligence that was clear but a soul that knew "no restraint, no faith, no fear"; a man who was struggling "blindly."

EPISODE 3

His was an impenetrable darkness. I looked at him as you peer down at a man who is lying at the bottom of a precipice where the sun never shines. But I had not much time to give him, because I was helping the engine-driver to take to pieces the leaky cylinders, to straighten a bent connecting-rod, and in other such matters. I lived in an infernal mess of rust, filings, nuts, bolts, spanners, hammers, ratchet-drills—things I abominate, because I don't get on with them. I tended the little forge we fortunately had aboard; I toiled wearily in a wretched scrap-heap—unless I had the shakes too bad to stand.

One evening coming in with a candle I was startled to hear him say a little tremulously, "I am lying here in the dark waiting for death." The light was within a foot of his eyes. I forced myself to murmur, "Oh, nonsense!" and stood over him as if transfixed.

Anything approaching the change that came over his features I have never seen before, and hope never to see again. Oh, I wasn't touched. I was fascinated. It was as though a veil had been rent. I saw on that ivory face the ex-

[28] *Ibid.*, pp. 142-144.

pression of sombre pride, of ruthless power, of craven terror—of an intense and hopeless despair. Did he live his life again in every detail of desire, temptation, and surrender during that supreme moment of complete knowledge? He cried in a whisper at some image, at some vision—he cried out twice, a cry that was no more than a breath—

"The horror! The horror!"

I blew the candle out and left the cabin. The pilgrims were dining in the mess-room, and I took my place opposite the manager, who lifted his eyes to give me a questioning glance, which I successfully ignored. He leaned back, serene, with that peculiar smile of his sealing the unexpressed depths of his meanness. A continuous shower of small flies streamed upon the lamp, upon the cloth, upon our hands and faces. Suddenly the manager's boy put his insolent black head in the doorway, and said in a tone of scathing contempt—

"Mistah Kurtz—he dead."[29]

JOSEPH CONRAD

Earlier the narrator's point of view in Crane's narratives, *The Open Boat* and *The Red Badge of Courage*, was discussed. As you proceed with the following episodes of the former story, compare the vividness of the experiences of each, remembering the creative source of one was motivated by the author's real experience with three men in a small open boat and the source of the other was purely imaginative. If each narrative is read in its entirety, the tonal impact of dramatic and ironic images and incidents building to a crescendo in both stories will bring overwhelming empathic responses.

In the following episodes from *The Open Boat*, the mood is taut, tense and fearful in one scene; is relaxed in the next moment; moves to high tension; then to hope; and finally, dwindles to despair. In these short sketches of drama you empathize with the voyagers tossed about by huge waves with "snarling crests"—each one a hill from which the men momentarily survey "a broad tumultuous expanse, shining and wind-riven," with the play of the sea, "wild with lights of emerald and white and amber." You are bounced about in the boat, "a wee thing wallowing, miraculously top-up, at the mercy of five oceans" whose "great spreads of water, like white flames," "swarming over" the cargo of four men: men whose faces in the "wan light must have been gray" and whose "eyes must have glinted in strange ways as they gazed steadily astern."

Thus Crane takes you through the back-breaking struggle of the men to keep the craft afloat,[30] through hunger, weariness and cold and their anxious scanning of the thin black line of land—a line "thinner than paper." As the wind dies down, the cook and correspondent take up the oars again. "And the oiler rowed, and then the correspondent rowed. Then the

[29] *Ibid.*, pp. 149-150.

[30] Crane's biographers report the author's physical condition was greatly impaired after this hazardous sea incident, which may have been the precipitating cause of his early death.

oiler rowed. It was a weary business." You pull with the tired oarsmen numbed by back pains; you feel the tension of trying to seek some hope; you are aching and cramped as they sink exhausted in the bed of cold sea water swashing back and forth in the bottom of the dinghy. Then as they approach closer to the thin black line, "it becomes a line of black and a line of white trees and sand"; the captain sees a house on shore. You find momentary release from your fear. The eyes of the men are strained toward the shore, as they utter their exclamations:

from *The Open Boat*

EPISODE 1

"Look! There's a man on the shore!"

"Where?"

"There! See 'im? See 'im?"

"Yes, sure! He's walking along."

"Now he's stopped. Look! He's facing us!"

"He's waving at us!"

"So he is! By thunder!"

"Ah, now we're all right! Now we're all right! There'll be a boat out here for us in half an hour."

"He's going on. He's running. He's going up that house there."

The remote beach seemed lower than the sea, and it required a searching glance to discern the little black figure. The captain saw a floating stick and they rowed to it. A bath-towel was by some weird chance in the boat, and, tying this on the stick, the captain waved it. The oarsman did not dare turn his head, so he was obliged to ask questions.

"What's he doing now?"

"He's standing still again. He's looking, I think. . . . There he goes again. Toward the house. . . . Now he's stopped again."

"'Is he waving at us?"

"No, not now! He was, though."

"Look! There comes another man!"

"He's running."

"Look at him go, would you."

"Why, he's on a bicycle. Now he's met the other man. They're both waving at us. Look!"

"There comes something up the beach."

"What the devil is that thing?"

"Why, it looks like a boat."

'Why, certainly, it's a boat."

"No; it's on wheels."

"Yes, so it is. Well, that must be the life-boat. They drag them along the shore on a wagon."

"That's the life-boat, sure."

"No, by ------, it's—it's an omnibus."

"I tell you it's a life-boat."

"It is not! It's an omnibus. I can see it plain. See? One of these big hotel omnibuses."

"By thunder, you're right. It's an omnibus, sure as fate. What do you suppose they are doing with an omnibus? Maybe they are going around collecting the life-crew, hey?"

"That's it, likely. Look! There's a fellow waving a little black flag. He's standing on the steps of the omnibus. There come those other two fellows. Now they're all talking together. Look at the fellow with the flag. Maybe he ain't waving it."

"That ain't a flag, is it? That's his coat. Why, certainly, that's his coat."

"So it is. It's his coat. He's taken it off and is waving it around his head. But would you look at him swing it!"

"Oh, say, there isn't any life-saving station there. That's just a winter resort hotel omnibus that has brought over some of the boarders to see us drown."

"What's that idiot with the coat mean? What's he signaling, anyhow?"

"It looks as if he were trying to tell us to go north. There must be a life-saving station up there."

"No; he thinks we're fishing. Just giving us a merry hand. See? Ah, there, Willie!"

"Well, I wish I could make something out of those signals. What do you suppose he means?"

"He doesn't mean anything. He's just playing."

"Well, if he'd just signal us to try the surf again, or to go to sea and wait, or go north, or go south, or go to hell, there would be some reason in it. But look at him! He just stands there and keeps his coat revolving like a wheel."

"There come more people."

"Now there's quite a mob. Look! Isn't that a boat?"

"Where? Oh, I see where you mean. No, that's no boat."

"That fellow is still waving his coat. . . ."

"Wonder how long he can keep that up. He's been revolving his coat ever since he caught sight of us. . . . Why don't he do something?"

"Oh, it's all right now."

"They'll have a boat out here for us in less than no time, now that they've seen us."

A faint yellow tone came into the sky over the low land. The shadows on the sea slowly deepened. The wind bore coldness with it, and the men began to shiver.

"Holy smoke!" . . . "If we keep on monkeying out here! If we've got to flounder out here all night!"

"Oh, we'll never have to stay here all night! Don't you worry. They've seen us now, and it won't be long before they'll come chasing out after us."

The shore grew dusky. The man waving a coat blended gradually into this gloom, and it swallowed in the same manner the omnibus and the group of people. The spray, when it dashed uproariously over the side, made the voyagers shrink and swear like men who were being branded. . . ."

In the meantime, the oiler rowed, and then the correspondent rowed, and then the oiler rowed. Grey-faced and bowed forward, they mechanically, turn by turn, plied the leaden oars. The form of the lighthouse had vanished from the southern horizon, but finally a pale star appeared, just lifting from the sea. The streaked saffron in the west passed before the all-merging darkness, and the sea to the east was black. The land had vanished, and was expressed only by the low and drear thunder of the surf.

"If I am going to be drowned—if I am going to be drowned—if I am going to be drowned, why, in the name of the seven mad gods who rule the sea, was I allowed to come thus far and contemplate sanu and trees? Was I brought here merely to have my nose dragged away as I was about to nibble the sacred cheese of life?"

A night on the sea in an open boat is a long, long night; the icy waves showered over the men huddled in the water in the bottom of the boat— asleep. . . . Finally, as the night deepened the correspondent at the oars was suddenly conscious of an invader.

EPISODE 2

There was a long, loud swishing astern of the boat, and a gleaming trail of phosphorescence, like blue flame, was furrowed on the black waters. It might have been a monstrous knife.

Then there came a stillness, while the correspondent breathed with the open mouth and looked at the sea.

Suddenly there was another swish and another long flash of bluish light, and this time it was alongside the boat, and might almost have been reached with an oar. The correspondent saw an enormous fin speed like a shadow through the water, hurling the crystalline spray and leaving the long glowing trail. . . .

Finally, the thing which had followed the boat and waited had evidently grown bored at the delay. There was no longer to be heard the splash of the cutwater, and there was no longer the flame of the long trail. . . . The wind came stronger, and sometimes a wave suddenly raged out like a mountain-cat, and there was to be seen the sheen and sparkle of a broken crest. . . .

When the correspondent awoke in the morning, the "sea and the sky were each of the gray hue of the dawning." On the distant shore, he could see many little black cottages and a tall white windmill, but no man or dog, nothing alive appeared on the beach. A conference was held: the boat was to be turned toward the beach—it could not withstand the lashing much longer.

EPISODE 3

There were no hurried words, no pallor, no plain agitation. The men simply looked at the shore. "Now, remember to get well clear of the boat when you jump," said the captain.

Seaward the crest of a roller suddenly fell with a thunderous crash, and the long, white comber came roaring down upon the boat.

"Steady now," said the captain. The men were silent. They turned their eyes from the shore to the comber and waited. The boat slid up the incline, leaped at the furious top, bounced over it, and swung down the long back of the wave. Some water had been shipped and the cook bailed it out.

But the next crest crashed also. The tumbling, boiling flood of white water caught the boat and whirled it almost perpendicular. Water swarmed in from all sides. . . . The little boat, drunken with the weight of water, reeled and snuggled deeper into the sea. . . .

The third wave moved forward, huge, furious, implacable. It fairly swallowed the dinghy, and almost simultaneously the men tumbled into the sea. A piece of life-belt had lain in the bottom of the boat, and as the correspondent went overboard he held this to his chest with his left hand.

The January water was icy. . . . The water was cold.

When he came to the surface he was conscious of little but the noisy water. Afterward he saw his companions in the sea. The oiler was ahead in the race. He was swimming strongly and rapidly. Off to the correspondent's left, the cook's great white and corked back bulged out of water, and in the rear the captain was hanging with his one good hand to the keel of the overturned dinghy . . . he paddled leisurely. . . .

But finally he arrived at a place in the sea where travel was beset with difficulty. He did not pause swimming to inquire what manner of current had caught him, but there his progress ceased. . . .

The correspondent remained in the grip of this strange new enemy—a current. The shore, with its white slope of sand and its green bluff, topped with little silent cottages, was spread like a picture before him. . . .

He thought: "I am going to drown? Can it be possible? Can it be possible? Can it be possible?" Perhaps an individual must consider his own death to be the final phenomenon of nature.

But later a wave perhaps whirled him out of this small, deadly current, for he found suddenly that he could again make progress toward the shore. Later still, he was aware that the captain, clinging with one hand to the keel of the dinghy, had his face turned away from the shore and toward him, and was calling his name. "Come to the boat! Come to the boat!"

In his struggle to reach the captain and the boat, he reflected that when one gets properly wearied drowning must really be a comfortable arrangement—a cessation of hostilities accompanied by a large degree of relief. . . .

Presently he saw a man running along the shore. He was undressing with most remarkable speed. Coat, trousers, shirt, everything flew magically off him.

"Come to the boat!" called the captain.

"All right, Captain." As the correspondent paddled, he saw the captain let himself down to the bottom and leave the boat. Then the correspondent performed his one little marvel of the voyage. A large wave caught him and flung him with ease and supreme speed completely over the boat and far beyond it. It struck him even then as an event in gymnastics, and a true miracle of the sea. An overturned boat in the surf is not a plaything to a swimming man.

The correspondent arrived in water that reached only to his waist, but his condition did not enable him to stand for more than a moment. Each wave knocked him into a heap, and the undertow pulled at him.

Then he saw the man who had been running and undressing, and undressing and running, come bounding into the water. He dragged ashore the cook, and then waded toward the captain, but the captain waved him away, and sent him to the correspondent. He was naked—naked as a tree in winter; but a halo was about his head, and he shone like a saint. He gave a strong pull, and a long drag, and a bully heave at the correspondent's hand. The correspondent, schooled in the minor formulae, said: "Thanks, old man." But suddenly the man cried, "What's that?" He pointed a swift finger. The correspondent said, "Go."

In the shallows, face downward, lay the oiler. His forehead touched sand that was periodically, between each wave, clear of the sea.

The correspondent did not know all that transpired afterward. When he achieved safe ground he fell, striking the sand with each particular part of his body. It was as if he dropped from a roof, but the thud was grateful to him.

It seemed that instantly the beach was populated with men with blankets, clothes, and flasks, and women with coffee-pots and all the remedies sacred to their minds. The welcome of the land to the men from the sea was warm and generous; but a still and dripping shape was carried slowly up the beach, and the land's welcome for it could only be the different and sinister hospitality of the grave.

When it came night, the white waves paced to and fro in the moonlight, and the wind brought the sound of the great sea's voice to the men on shore, and they felt that they could then be interpreters.[31]

STEPHEN CRANE

Crane secures many of his tense crescendos by means of short repetitive phrases and sentences. This is particularly evident in the narrating of the back-breaking task of plying the oars, in the description of the continual bombardment of the waves on the small craft, in ironic phrases like "If I'm going to be drowned" or in the lines—"Maybe they think we're out here in sport. Maybe they think we're fishing. Maybe they think we're damned fools."

The undercurrent of the struggle between nature and man cannot be fully understood nor can the impact of the last line be appreciated unless the entire story is read. You need to follow through on thoughts like "If I'm going to be drowned" with "If this old ninny-woman Fate, cannot do better than this, she should be deprived of the management of men's fortunes. She is an old hen who knows not her intention." Later when the men decide to leave the boat, the correspondent looked at the tall wind-tower and thought, "This tower was a giant, standing with its back to the plight of ants. It represented in a degree the serenity of nature amid the struggles of the individual—nature in the wind, and nature in the vision of

[31] Stephen Crane, *The Open Boat and Other Tales of Adventure* (New York: Doubleday & Company, 1898), pp. 29-36, 41-48, 55-63.

men. She did not seem cruel to him then, nor beneficent, nor treacherous, nor wise. But she was indifferent, flatly indifferent." Finally, when he was safe on land, the correspondent was able to interpret the voice of the sea.

Although you have not yet completed the technique of identifying characters through their full speech pattern, check these excerpts for speech that personalizes each man: his responses, his choice of words, his attitude toward danger. Picture each man in his position of authority, culture, profession; then as each one reacts psychologically to others and events. One may speak rapidly, one deliberately, one impatiently, one obediently, one emotionally. Certainly the Captain has a deep resonant voice, characterized by kindliness and understanding and with lessened vitality because of his injury. The actual names of the men were Captain Murphy, Montgomery (cook), Billie Higgins (oiler). Captain Murphy was quoted in the papers of 1897 as saying that Crane was the "spunkiest fellow out," a "thoroughbred" and a "brave man with plenty of grit." If you can give them distinctive characters, then you can omit introductory phrases or tags as "the oiler said," "the captain replied." An interpreter depends on his voice to carry the impression of the person's attitude and character; and on the direction of the eyes and stance of the body for further identification.

CLIMAX THROUGH IRONY

POETRY

The tone of irony is sometimes used most effectively for the climax of understatement, achieved through the sudden turn of the phrase, the skillful use of syntactical order of words or phrases, the pause to secure the quick shift of ideas or turn of events. Instead of the typical crescendo for a climax, the poet can suggest an evenness of tone in a restrained understatement of ideas or common-place relating of events. Consequently, the turn in ideas, events or character activity is not anticipated. When the break occurs in the thought continuum, the change is sudden, unexpected and surprising in its climax. Sometimes, an ironic tone may pervade most of the lines, so the poem may lose power in the climax. In a lyric or dramatic poem, the building of conflict and the contrast of ideas, events or images usually results from the poet's clever use of syntactical order of words, phrases and sentences that must be shown by vocal stress and intensity.

The interpretation of a climaxing sentence, such as the one with which Robinson so adroitly ends this next poem, takes intonational precision. The tone is casual; the stunning shock is due to what is left unsaid; the poem is dramatic, even though the words are stated with quiet forthrightness and simplicity; the contrasts are quietly implied. If this simplicity can be sustained, the climax will be unusually effective. A force-ful attack will not give the audience the intended shock since it will betray the fact that something of great moment is going to happen. Obviously, Robinson was striving for climax through ironic understate-ment: the words "one calm summer night" set the tone of quietness; the short phrase "went home" adds to the everyday event. A pause after "went home" and then quietly, "and put a bullet through his head" conveys the ironic tone. Instead of a forceful climax, you are caught off guard by a climax of understatement, powerful in its quiet intensity and its contrast with what is anticipated.

Richard Cory

Whenever Richard Cory went down town,
We people on the pavement looked at him:
He was a gentleman from sole to crown,
Clean-favored, and imperially slim.

And he was always quietly arrayed,
And he was always human when he talked;
But still he fluttered pulses when he said,
"Good-morning," and he glittered when he walked.

And he was rich—yes, richer than a king,
And admirably schooled in every grace:
In fine, we thought that he was everything
To make us wish that we were in his place.

So on we worked, and waited for the light,
And went without the meat, and cursed the bread;
And Richard Cory, one calm summer night,
Went home and put a bullet through his head.[32]

EDWIN ARLINGTON ROBINSON

Hardy gives a superlative finish to the following well-known poem. He uses the question-answer technique to create suspense for the climax and then prepares the reader carefully for the expected fidelity of a dog for its master. If this poem is interpreted for listeners who are not ac-quainted with it, their faces usually anticipate their pleasure in the dog's faithfulness; to some, consequently, the last stanza comes as a surprise; but to all, it is a rueful and ironic climax.

[32] Edwin Arlington Robinson, *The Children of the Night* (New York: Charles Scribner's Sons, 1897), p. 82.

"Ah, Are You Digging on My Grave?"

"Ah, are you digging on my grave
   My beloved one?—planting rue?"
—"No: yesterday he went to wed
One of the brightest wealth has bred,
'It cannot hurt her now,' he said,
   'That I should not be true.' "

"Then who is digging on my grave?
   My dearest, dearest kin?"
—"Ah, no: they sit and think, 'What use!
What good will planting flowers produce?
No tendance of her mound can loose
   Her spirit from Death's gin.' "

"But some one digs upon my grave?
   My enemy?—prodding sly?"
—"Nay: when she heard you had passed the Gate
That shuts on all flesh soon or late,
She thought you no more worth her hate,
   And cares not where you lie."

"Then, who is digging on my grave?
   Say—since I have not guessed!"
—"O, it is I, my mistress dear,
Your little dog, who still lives near,
And much I hope my movements here
   Have not disturbed your rest?"

"Ah, yes! *You* dig upon my grave . . .
   Why flashed it not on me
That one true heart was left behind!
What feeling do we ever find
To equal among human kind
   A dog's fidelity?"

"Mistress, I dug upon your grave
   To bury a bone, in case
I should be hungry near this spot
When passing on my daily trot.
I am sorry, but I quite forgot
   It was your resting-place."[33]

THOMAS HARDY

[33] Reprinted with permission of the Macmillan Company from COLLECTED POEMS OF THOMAS HARDY. Copyright 1925 by The Macmillan Company.

Dickinson's poems are not so easy to interpret as the simplicity of word choice and line arrangement might indicate at first glance. Here is another poem of understatement. The outward tone of tense quietness, interrupted by a buzzing fly, covers a meaning that leaves you stunned. The succinct phrasing carries the weight and depth of a death scene—and "then there interposed a fly," perhaps an inconsequential fly—but no, it is a buzzing fly—into the stillness of the room. What contrasts are used effectively in these lines? What is the tone—tragic, ironic, wondering, or what? This climax calls for a quiet but rigid vocal intensity. Do you agree with Julie Harris's interpretation?[34]

I Heard a Fly Buzz When I Died

I heard a fly buzz when I died;
　　The stillness round my form
Was like the stillness in the air
　　Between the heaves of storm.

The eyes beside had wrung them dry,
　　And breaths were gathering sure
For that last onset, when the king
　　Be witnessed in his power.

I willed my keepsakes, signed away
　　What portion of me I
Could make assignable,—and then
　　There interposed a fly,

With blue, uncertain, stumbling buzz,
　　Between the light and me;
And then the windows failed, and then
　　I could not see to see.[35]

EMILY DICKINSON

Contrast the Dickinson poem with Sarett's "Requiem for a Modern Croesus," in form, tone, imagery, intensity, climax. Is the metaphoric language effective? What is the significance of the word "pennies"? In Sarett's recording of this poem,[36] he observes that it is the length of a telegram but contains the story of an entire lifetime. The vigor of his voice in these explanatory remarks is heard again in the interpretation of the poem but

[34] *Poems and Letters of Emily Dickinson.* Recorded by Julie Harris, Caedmon, 1119.
[35] Emily Dickinson, *The Complete Poems of Emily Dickinson* (Boston: Little, Brown and Company, 1960).
[36] *Lew Sarett: Reading from His Collected Poems.* Columbia, XTV–15494, 15495.

the difference in tone and intensity given to the poetic lines is quite noticeable.

Requiem for a Modern Croesus

To him the moon was a silver dollar, spun
Into the sky by some mysterious hand; the sun
Was a gleaming golden coin—
His to purloin;
The freshly minted stars were dimes of delight
Flung out upon the counter of the night.

In yonder room he lies,
With pennies on his eyes.[37]

LEW SARETT

In "Dirge," Kenneth Fearing hits you *biff! bam! wham!* and leaves you bewildered with his slugging ironic intensity. What was your first impression of these quick, decisive attacks depicting life's progression in a city that cares little as it takes more and more? What characterizes the narrator?

Now reread to observe the metaphorical language instead of the slang vernacular of a city. As you proceed, line by line, note whether all the images describe negatively. Are there some that connote a positive life with an undercurrent of real living, some that seem to fight the outward false city pressures? At whom is Fearing's onslaught of vociferous words hurled?

Dirge

1-2-3 was the number he played but today the number came
3-2-1;
bought his Carbide at 30 but it went to 29; had the
favorite at Bowie but the track was slow—

O, executive type, would you like to drive a floating power,
knee action, silk-upholstered six? Wed a Hollywood star?
Shoot the course in 58? Draw to the ace, king, jack?
O, fellow with a will who won't take no, watch out for three
cigarettes on the same, single match; O democratic voter
born in August under Mars, beware of liquidated rails—

[37] From *Covenant with Earth*, by Lew Sarett. Gainesville: University of Florida Press, 1956. Reprinted by permission of Mrs. Lew Sarett.

Dénouement to dénouement, he took a personal pride in the
    certain, certain way he lived his own, private life,
    but nevertheless, they shut off his gas; nevertheless,
    the bank foreclosed; nevertheless, the landlord called;
    nevertheless, the radio broke,

And twelve o'clock arrived just once too often,
    just the same he wore one gray tweed suit, bought one
        straw hat, drank one straight Scotch, walked one short
        step, took one long look, drew one deep breath,
    just one too many,

And wow he died as wow he lived,
    going whop to the office and blooie home to sleep and
        biff got married and bam had children and oof got fired,
    zowie did he live and zowie did he die,

With who the hell are you at the corner of his casket,
    and where the hell we going on the right hand silver
    knob, and who the hell cares walking second from the
    end with an American Beauty wreath from why the hell
    not.

Very much missed by the circulation staff of the New York
    Evening Post; deeply, deeply mourned by the B.M.T.,*

Wham, Mr. Roosevelt; pow, Sears Roebuck; awk, big dipper;
    bop, summer rain;
    bong, Mr., bong, Mr., bong, Mr., bong.[38]

                                        KENNETH FEARING

Stevens writes his poem, "The Emperor of Ice-Cream," in a less flamboyant, derisive mood, but nevertheless with an ironic tone that may connote mocking humor or a tongue-in-cheek poke at death.

The Emperor of Ice-Cream

Call the roller of big cigars,
The muscular one, and bid him whip
In kitchen cups concupiscent curds.
Let the wenches dawdle in such dress
As they are used to wear, and let the boys

---

* The Bowie Race Track is in Maryland; the B.M.T. refers to the Brooklyn-Manhattan Transit line of the New York City subway.

[38] Kenneth Fearing, "Dirge," *New and Selected Poems* (Bloomington, Ind.: Indiana University Press, 1956). Reprinted by permission.

Bring flowers in last month's newspapers.
Let be be finale of seem.
The only emperor is the emperor of ice-cream.

Take from the dresser of deal,
Lacking the three glass knobs, that sheet
On which she embroidered fantails once
And spread it so as to cover her face.
If her horny feet protrude, they come
To show how cold she is, and dumb.
Let the lamp affix its beam.
The only emperor is the emperor of ice-cream.[39]

WALLACE STEVENS

To some analysts, the problem in this poem is "the imaginative ambiguity inherent" in the images; to others, as suggested by Wells,[40] the
poet, in his amusing, lusty and ironic role may have been "merely taking
the undertaker for a ride." In his scandalous manner, he mocks the "vac-
uous decorum of modern funeral customs by imagining obsequies in an
ultraproletarian style." The critic continues: "In brazen confidence he
addresses death in the most demotic terms possible, as lord of that most
perishable of foods, ice cream."

Blackmur,[41] on the other hand, would call the poem "Directions for a
Funeral with Two Epitaphs"—the couplets at the end of each stanza. The
ambiguity arising from two unrelated and unusual images—one of a corpse
with protruding horny feet and the other of a muscular one "whipping
desirable desserts in the kitchen"—is united by the epitaphs. The first one
—"Let be be finale of seem"—means "Take whatever seems to be, as really
being"; the second one—"Let the lamp affix its beam"—states that "this
woman is dead" and "these things," as ambiguous as they may be, "are as
they are." Friar and Brinnin[42] also comment on the first couplet as meaning "Let that which is, put an end to that which seems." Blackmur has
probably epitomized the poet's idea—although he received no affirmation
from Stevens—when he concludes that the "only power worth heeding is
the power of the moment, of what is passing, of the flux." In other words,
the only emperor is the emperor of ice-cream—or "the king is dead; long
live the king."

[39] Copyright 1923; renewed 1951 by Wallace Stevens. Reprinted from THE
COLLECTED POEMS OF WALLACE STEVENS by permission of Alfred A.
Knopf, Inc.

[40] Henry W. Wells, *Introduction to Wallace Stevens* (Bloomington, Ind.: Indiana
University Press, 1964), p. 75.

[41] Richard P. Blackmur, *Language as Gesture* (New York: Harcourt, Brace &
World, Inc., 1952), pp. 228-229.

[42] Friar Kimon and John Malcolm Brinnin, *Modern Poetry* (New York: Appleton-
Century-Crofts, 1951), p. 87.

Your vocal tone may connote meaning by being lightly amusing or derisive or full of lustful delight; nevertheless, you cannot ignore the ironic touch. Your phrasing and pausing for emphasis and reinforcement must support your meaning. How does this poem compare in intensity with "Dirge"?

Compare the themes of these two poems dealing with the same subject—the end of the world: Frost's "Fire and Ice" and MacLeish's "The End of the World."

Fire and Ice

Some say the world will end in fire,
Some say in ice.
From what I've tasted of desire
I hold with those who favor fire.
But if it had to perish twice,
I think I know enough of hate
To say that for destruction ice
Is also great
And would suffice.[43]

ROBERT FROST

The End of the World

Quite unexpectedly, as Vasserot
The armless ambidextrian was lighting
A match between his great and second toe,
And Ralph the lion was engaged in biting
The neck of Madame Sossman while the drum
Pointed, and Teeny was about to cough
In waltz-time swinging Jocko by the thumb—
Quite unexpectedly the top blew off:

And there, there overhead, there, there hung over
Those thousands of white faces, those dazed eyes,
There in the starless dark the poise, the hover,
There with vast wings across the cancelled skies,
There in the sudden blackness the black pall
Of nothing, nothing, nothing—nothing at all.[44]

ARCHIBALD MACLEISH

[43] Frost, see p. 309.
[44] "The End of the World" from THE COLLECTED POEMS OF ARCHIBALD MACLEISH. Copyright 1952 by Archibald MacLeish. Reprinted by permission of the publisher, HOUGHTON MIFFLIN COMPANY.

In Frost's poem, you recognize irony of understatement; in the Mac-Leish sonnet, irony of situation. How would you compare the point of view of each poet? Which poem gives the greater ironic impact? Does Frost's terse, cool appraisal strike you as merciless—even icy in its understatement? Do you have the feeling that a sharp thin-bladed knife is cutting through man's fear of ultimate disaster—much as a surgeon's scalpel makes a sharp, clean incision? Observe how the two contrasting words— *fire* and *ice*—suggest the metaphorical undercurrent of the contrasting emotions—*desire* and *hate*—thus adding intensity to the thought. Note also how the repetition of the rhyme sounds of *a* and *i* tighten rather than soothe or relax one, as would the sounds *oo* or *ah*. "Desire," "ice," "fire," "twice," "suffice" support a brittle, curt appraisal and abrupt tone of aloofness and objectivity.

Instead of understatement, MacLeish builds his situation around a metaphor: the circus is the world, a world of performers grotesque and outlandish in their abilities. Then suddenly, dramatically, while everyone is demonstrating his agility, the "top" blows off. In the sestet, the contrasts in images—the thousands of white faces, the dazed eyes in the sudden blackness, the repetitions of "groping" words are empathically powerful, so powerful that you may wonder how you can ever reach the climax of the last line.

PROSE

Vocal intensity, when employed in the interpretation of prose literature with an ironic tone, takes a different timing as in *The Open Boat* and *The Heart of Darkness*. In poetry, the irony is usually more evident at the turn of the last sentence than throughout the poem. In prose, the ironic intensity is sustained for a longer time—perhaps through pages. The voice cannot be too heavy or too light in its attack; usually it should have a two-edged approach—a gloss, a veneer of saying something in mock-seriousness covering a contrasting undercurrent of reality. Of course, facial and eye expressions as well as vocal tones will play a part in letting the audience realize the secret of saying one thing and meaning another. This procedure is difficult and subtle in performance and certainly not easy to explain on paper. If you strive too intently to convey the underlying meaning to the audience, the thought will not be released, and the audience will not know whether or not to laugh. You have heard this meaning with an "edge" expressed and have enjoyed the turns and twists of phrases and have been helped by the lift of the eyebrow, the narrowing of the eyes, the slight smile on the lips or the quick change in vocal intensity.

Because most university students know the writer Dwight MacDonald, several paragraphs from his essay "Homogenized Culture" will provide an interesting piece for interpretation of ironic tone. Consider the word *homogenized*. Is the word double-edged for the meaning implied? Are the images as vivid as those you have found in poetry or the essays printed earlier in this text? Which contrasts give you the most effective impression of irony? Is there a climax? Is it ironic?

from *Homogenized Culture*

Like nineteenth-century capitalism, Mass Culture is a dynamic, revolutionary force, breaking down the old barriers of class, tradition, taste, and dissolving all cultural distinctions. It mixes and scrambles everything together, producing what might be called homogenized culture, after another American achievement, the homogenization process that distributes the globules of cream evenly throughout the milk instead of allowing them to float separately on top. It thus destroys all values, since value judgments imply discrimination. Mass Culture is very, very democratic: it absolutely refuses to discriminate against, or between, anything or anybody. All is grist to its mill, and all comes out finely ground indeed.

Consider *Life*, a typical homogenized mass-circulation magazine. It appears on the mahogany library tables of the rich, the glass end-table of the middle-class and the oilcloth-covered kitchen tables of the poor. Its contents are as thoroughly homogenized as its circulation. The same issue will contain a serious exposition of atomic theory alongside a disquisition on Rita Hayworth's love life; photos of starving Korean children picking garbage from the ruins of Pusan and of sleek models wearing adhesive brassieres; an editorial hailing Bertrand Russell on his eightieth birthday ("A GREAT MIND IS STILL ANNOYING AND ADORNING OUR AGE") across from a full-page photo of a housewife arguing with an umpire at a baseball game ("MOM GETS THUMB"); a cover announcing in the same size type "A NEW FOREIGN POLICY, BY JOHN FOSTER DULLES" and "KERIMA: HER MARATHON KISS IS A MOVIE SENSATION"; nine color pages of Renoirs plus a memoir by his son, followed by a full-page picture of a roller-skating horse. The advertisements, of course, provide even more scope for the editor's homogenizing talents, as when a full-page photo of a ragged Bolivian peon grinningly drunk on coca leaves (which Mr. Luce's conscientious reporters tell us he chews to narcotize his chronic hunger pains) appears opposite an ad of a pretty smiling well-dressed American mother with her two pretty, smiling, well-dressed children (a boy and a girl, of course—children are always homogenized in American ads) looking raptly at a clown on a TV set ("RCA VICTOR BRINGS YOU A NEW KIND OF TELEVISION—SUPER SETS WITH 'PICTURE POWER' "). The peon would doubtless find the juxtaposition piquant if he could afford a copy of *Life* which, fortunately for the Good Neighbor Policy, he cannot.[45]

Dwight MacDonald

[45] From *Diogenes*, No. 3, Summer 1953, The International Council for Philosophy and Humanistic Studies, Unesco, Paris. Reprinted by permission of the publisher.

11

Vocal Tempo

As a student of interpretation, you will benefit from a pleasant, *resonant* voice that can be adapted to the character and meaning of the literature. The necessity for appropriate vocal intensity has also been stressed in order to obtain vitality of meaning: a weak vocal attack on vigorously written lines makes them colorless and heavy vocal intensity given to a gentle, melodious selection makes meaning ludicrous.

GENERAL TEMPO

You are now ready to go one step further in developing an effective speech pattern for interpretative purposes by studying the tempo of your vocal utterance: the general timing and rate of movement as shown through inherent short and long quantities of sounds, phraseology and pauses. These devices of movement convey not only rhythmical cadences but intensify meaning by adding tone, mood and atmosphere.

TIMING FOR PATTERN OF MEANING

Since your timing is usually controlled by the style of the literature, the author's pattern of writing should be carefully considered. The significance of an interpretative meaning may be missed by wrong phrasing, pausing and general timing. You would find it difficult, for instance, to interpret a love scene with a fast tempo unless it happens to be a scene from a comedy or farce where speed is required for laughter or some reversal of action; and certainly sorrow is seldom expressed by a quick, staccato rate. When you speak rapidly, others think you are hurried, tense or excited; when you speak slowly, you give the impression of being deliberate, calm or perhaps indifferent. One attention-getting device of announcers of football and basketball games is a rapid tempo, partly because of the speed of the playing, partly because they try to create empathically the excitement of the sport. Watch a room full of people listening to any action sport: notice how they lean forward and attend to the staccato and forceful voice recounting the activity of the players with occasional bursts of enthusiasm and mounting crescendos. Then listen to the same announcer control his speech tempo after the game. Such control is essential for those who wish to interpret literature, but is extended more subtly into nuances of meaning. No one expects you to race from start to finish or stumble over words or hurry through sentence after sentence; neither are you expected to amble along in a consistent and contented manner. Interpretation that includes no change of pace within the phrase, sentence or whole pattern will always be ineffective unless monotony of tempo is called for by the author's atmosphere or mood.

Lucky was the playwright of the early and mid-twentieth century if his comedy was in the artistic hands of the popular acting couple known as "The Lunts." Everyone who has enjoyed a performance of this engaging couple will agree with John Mason Brown, drama critic, that they have a sense of timing that is phenomenal, a characteristic that *makes* a comedy, no matter how skillfully lines have been written. Few can write as delightfully as Brown does after seeing "The Lunts" in the New York production of *O' Mistress Mine:*

A cat could not have more fun with catnip than they do with the lines they speak. They do not hammer them, and roll on them. They know how to hold a sentence back, and then send it scurrying suddenly to its conclusion. They never miss the meaningful or explosive word, and never overstress it. They are shrewd judges of what to underscore and what to throw away. They realize that the very act of seeming to throw a phrase or a word away is in itself a form of emphasis. They are no less adroit in altering the pace of their single sentences. What is more, their watches are always synchronized.[1]

SOUND QUANTITIES

The duration within the word, called *quantity,* is one of the most subtle devices the author employs to establish his desired tempo. Every speech sound, vowel and consonant, possesses quantity. The plosives—*k, g, p, b, t, d*—tend to be short and staccato; the nasal continuants—*m, n, ng*—are long and continuous, if you choose to make them so; the fricatives and sibilants—*th, f, v, s, sh*—may vary but usually are not continuous or prolonged; the vowels—*oo* as in *who, ou* as in *out, a* as in *all, a* as in *father, o* as in *go, oi* as in *oil*—are inherently long; *o* as in *got, a* as in *at, e* as in *met, i* as in *fit, u* as in *hut* are by nature short and quick.

In effective interpretation, the problem of deciding whether or not to yield to the inherent quantities of the sounds is always present. Most important is the necessity of recognizing how the poet has developed tempo, rhythmical pattern or certain moods by the device of word quantities. This

[1] From SATURDAY REVIEW. "Reunion in New York" by John Mason Brown. February 16, 1946. Reprinted by permission of Saturday Review and the author, p. 34.

matter should not be so stressed that the interpretation becomes exaggerated in tonal quality; rather the sound should come through subtly so that the audience hears it but is not conscious of the "timing device." In the use of imagery, the writer chooses words for the sound as well as connotative values.

For instance, in the excerpt from Gilbert's *Iolanthe*, the short phrases give the impression of speed and tension even though many pauses are effective. Most of the phrases seem to fall on top of one another in their speed, creating greater confusion. To add to this impression, the words were evidently selected for their abruptness and quickness in sound production, with emphasis on hard consonantal sounds rather than prolonged vowels as in *moon, brood, home, father, all.* Listen to some of the alliterative and plosive sounds employed: *blanketing, tickles, like mixed pickles, sharp is the pricking, tumble and toss, pick them in a tangle, regular wreck, crick in your neck, needles and pins, flesh is a-creep, fluff in your lungs, ditto, ditto.* Infectious laughter can greet the interpreter who pauses imperceptively in the seemingly fast tempo that takes one through this night of discomfort.

from *Iolanthe*

When you're lying awake with a dismal headache, and repose is tabooed by
    anxiety,
I conceive you may use any language you choose to indulge in without impro-
    priety,
For your brain is on fire—the bedclothes conspire of usual slumber to plunder
    you:
First your counterpane goes and uncovers your toes, and your sheet slips
    demurely from under you;
Then the blanketing tickles—you feel like mixed pickles, so terribly sharp is the
    prickling;
And you're hot and you're cross, and you tumble and toss till there's nothing
    'twixt you and the ticking;
Then your bedclothes all creep to the floor in a heap, and you pick 'em all up
    in a tangle;
Next your pillow resigns and politely declines to remain at its usual angle.
Well, you get some repose in the form of a doze, with hot eyeballs and head
    ever-aching;
But your slumbering teems with such horrible dreams that you'd very much
    better be waking.
You're a regular wreck, with a crick in your neck,
And no wonder you snore, for your head's on the floor,
And you've needles and pins from your soles to your shins,
And your flesh is a-creep, for your left leg's asleep,
And some fluff in your lungs, and a feverish tongue,

And a thirst that's intense, and a general sense
That you haven't been sleeping in clover.
But the darkness has passed, and it's daylight at last,
And the night has been long—ditto, ditto, my song—
And thank goodness, they're both of them over!

W. S. GILBERT

PHRASING FOR MEANING

Usually the author patterns his phrases to show emphasis or contrast
in meaning. You must decide how he intends to have his words mean
through his arrangement of words and phrases. Give appropriate emphasis
and contrast to the following excerpts:

1. Never in the field of human conflict was so much owed by so many to so few.
2. What I like in a good author is not what he says but what he whispers.
3. He who has little silver in his pouch must have more silk on his tongue.
4. "Praise the Lord, and pass the ammunition," he shouted; but I prayed,
   "Praise the Lord, the ammunition has passed me."
5. The heart of the fool is in his mouth but the mouth of a wise man is in his
   heart.
6. There is no indispensable man.
7. Life is a foreign language: all men mispronounce it.
8. He who knows and knows he knows,
       He is wise. Follow him.
   He who knows and knows not he knows,
       He is asleep. Wake him.
   He who knows not and knows not he knows not,
       He is a fool. Shun him.
   He who knows not and knows he knows not,
       He is a child. Teach him.
9.   . . . That we would do
   We should do when we would: for this "would" changes,
   And hath abatements and delays as many
   As there are tongues, are hands, are accidents,
   And then this "should" is like a spendthrift sigh,
   That hurts by easing.

Too often the interpreter phrases, not according to meaning, but according to his involuntary breathing pattern. If he is in the habit of using
short, quick breaths, then he may tend to break up the line into broken
phrases; or if he is the long-winded person, he may keep on and on without any attention given to the phrase pause that clarifies meaning. His interpretation will sound more like jargon, and eventually he will be gasping
for breath or speaking on residual air. Learn to subordinate natural
breathing habits to the rhythmical pattern and meaning.

PAUSE FOR MEANING

Actors, like "The Lunts," know that a pause in the right place with the right timing and stress is one of the marks of their professional status. Lack of pause is the surest stamp of the amateur—unless laughter is sought by a certain type of comedy character. You should realize that a silence can often be more effective than a jumble of words. Even the most ordinary meaning gains in importance by revealing breaks in the flow of sound. The subtleties of expression possible in sentient use of pause are beyond calculation. Watch and listen to the professionals who know the values of timing in order to get laughs or achieve dramatic suspense. They know, for instance, that by intelligent pausing—not too long and not too short—they can "squeeze a laugh" or emphasize a dramatic or ironic or pointed meaning. They also know that merely to pause is not enough, since anticipation and a "follow-through" sustained by facial expression and bodily poise are necessary. Listen to Bob Hope for an example of excellent timing, even to the fraction of a second. Watch him sustain the pause for a laugh. At times the laughter might not come were it not for the added help from his eye expression and bodily control. He knows when the response seems not to be readily forthcoming and may remark about how funny the joke failed to be—and so everyone laughs because the joke is on him. If you observe him often, you will anticipate the moment he will break the silence. This is not so easy to accomplish as it appears. Perhaps you have had the experience of laughing heartily at a story. Somehow when you tried to repeat it, no one even smiled or responded, except by another kind of pause—the pause of bewilderment.

The same principle of pausing holds true in the interpretation of poetry. Inasmuch as the lines are more concentrated in form, mistakes cannot be made in gauging what word or phrase needs the pause to point up meaning with added strength. The caesura is the imperceptible pause that is permissive in the metrical pattern of the poet's line; usually it comes after a cadenced phrase in the medial position of the line. If, however, you are looking only for the caesura and decide no other pauses are allowable for emphasis, reinforcement or suspense, then your potential for interpretation of great literature needs more awareness. You may discover after listening to yourself that your pattern is sing-song, a mechanical interpretation that lacks variety and vitality of expression, even to the point of chanting poetic lines with an even tempo and with a sustained pitch level. Although Yeats believed the voice in poetry must show spontaneity and "speech so natural and dramatic" that the hearer would feel the emotions of the poet, he is not always impressive in creating discriminating meaning with his Welsh singing quality.

PAUSE FOR REINFORCEMENT

Meaning can be reinforced by correctly placed pauses. When an author has written a particularly impressive piece of literature, the mere retelling is not enough. Remember that people grasp ideas more slowly through the ear than through the eye, so the importance of the thought should be highlighted by the reinforcing pause. The listener is then given a moment to grasp and to react. If you pause before the effective word or phrase, you tend to direct the listener's attention and curiosity. A pause after a phrase adds emphasis, even to the point where your listeners may find themselves repeating quietly what has been said. So if the thought is to be made vivid and emphatic, pause for reinforcement.

The following short poems are so written as to indicate obvious places for pauses. The exuberance of the phrases in the first poem leads naturally to a pause for reinforcement after "add" (7th line); thus bringing delight and satisfaction with the repetition of the phrase "Jenny kiss'd me." By the way, "Jenny" is reported to have been Mrs. Thomas Carlyle.

Jenny Kiss'd Me

Jenny kiss'd me when we met,
    Jumping from the chair she sat in;
Time, you thief, who love to get
    Sweets into your list, put that in!
Say I'm weary, say I'm sad,
    Say that health and wealth have missed me,
Say I'm growing old, but add,
    Jenny kiss'd me.

Leigh Hunt

Brown has so worded this lyric that you cannot ignore the pauses to express the whimsical tone.

I Bended Unto Me

I bended unto me a bough of May,
That I might see and smell:
It bore it in a sort of way,
It bore it very well.
But when I let it backward sway,
Then it were hard to tell
With what a toss, with what a swing,

The dainty thing
Resumed its proper level,
And sent me to the devil.
I know it did—you doubt it?
I turned, and saw them whispering about it.[2]

THOMAS EDWARD BROWN

The pauses in "Cupid Swallowed" are half-beats—as if you were catching your breath in excitement. The line "in a cup/ Of my wine, I plunged and sank him" swings into definite action with *plunged* and *sank;* the question of the next line quickens in tempo, then stops for the pause before the gleeful answer "I drank him!"

Cupid Swallowed

T'other day, as I was twining
Roses for a crown to dine in,
What, of all things, midst the heap,
Should I light on, fast asleep,
But the little desperate elf—
The tiny traitor—Love himself!
By the wings I pinched him up
Like a bee, and in a cup
Of my wine, I plunged and sank him,
And what d'ye think I did?—I drank him!
Faith, I thought him dead. Not he!
There he lives with ten-fold glee;
And now this moment, with his wings,
I feel him tickling my heart-strings.

LEIGH HUNT

You will enjoy making Dickinson's pauses meaningful—she helps you!

I'm Nobody

I'm Nobody! Who are you?
Are you—Nobody—too?
Then there's a pair of us!
Don't tell! they'd banish us—you know!

How dreary—to be—Somebody!
How public—like a Frog—

[2] Thomas E. Brown, *Collected Poems* (New York: The Macmillan Company, 1908).

To tell your name—the livelong June—
To an admiring Bog!³

EMILY DICKINSON

Tennyson has packed the philosophy of the Christian world into these six lines. In your interpretation, give the audience time to grasp the meaning. Even though pauses for reinforcement are found in the poem, the rhythm remains melodious and smooth. The longest pause—it should not drag—is after the phrase "all in all."

Flower in the Crannied Wall

Flower in the crannied wall,
I pluck you out of the crannies,
I hold you here, root and all, in my hand,
Little flower—but *if* I could understand
What you are, root and all, and all in all,
I should know what God and man is.

ALFRED TENNYSON

The right timing in the following verse can bring a laugh on the last line if you recognize the half-beat or syncopated pause after "Mamma" (accent is on last syllable) before you quickly and lightly add, "And that's my earliest recollection."

A Terrible Infant

I recollect a nurse called Ann,
   Who carried me about the grass,
And one fine day a fine young man
   Came up, and kissed the pretty lass:
She did not make the least objection!
   Thinks I, "*Aha!*
When I can talk, I'll tell Mamma."
—And that's my earliest recollection.

FREDERICK LOCKER-LAMPSON

In prose, the same principle of pausing holds true. No finer example of reinforcement exists than one by the master of the King's English, Sir Winston Churchill. His lines have the rhythm and cadenced tone of

³ Emily Dickinson, *The Complete Poems of Emily Dickinson* (Boston: Little, Brown and Company, 1960).

poetry. Study this famous excerpt carefully, noting the melodious cadences of the phrases, the reinforcement of the central idea through pauses and the poetic vigor rather than prosaic dullness. Read aloud to feel the movement toward the climax. Also listen to Churchill's phrasing and rhythm as well as his vocal quality and emphasis in his recording.[4]

from *Blood, Sweat and Tears*

I have myself full confidence that if all do their duty, if nothing is neglected, and if the best arrangements are made, as they are being made, we shall prove ourselves once again able to defend our island home, ride out the storms of war, and outlive the menace of tyranny, if necessary, for years, if necessary, alone.

At any rate, that is what we are going to do. That is the resolve of His Majesty's Government—every man of them. That is the will of Parliament and the nation. The British Empire and the French Republic, linked together in their cause and their need, will defend to the death their native soils, aiding each other like good comrades to the utmost of their strength. Even though large tracts of Europe and many old and famous States have fallen or may fall into the grip of the Gestapo and all the odious apparatus of Nazi rule, we shall not flag or fail. We shall go on to the end; we shall fight in France; we shall fight on the seas and oceans; we shall fight with growing confidence and growing strength in the air; we shall defend our Island, whatever the cost may be; we shall fight on the beaches; we shall fight on the landing grounds; we shall fight in the fields and in the streets; we shall fight in the hills. We shall never surrender, and even if, which I do not for a moment believe, this Island or a large part of it were subjugated and starving, then our Empire beyond the seas, armed and guarded by the British Fleet, will carry on the struggle, until, in God's good time, the New World, with all its power and might, steps forth to the rescue and the liberation of the old.[5]

WINSTON CHURCHILL

PAUSE FOR SUSPENSE

An audience likes nothing better than the unexpected turn of the phrase to give impelling meaning. The pause in anticipation of what is to come gives added penetration in an interpretation. The logic of the author's meaning in prose or the rhythm of the poem will not permit you to interpret the meaning in *your* particular way; instead you can find a clue to the direction of intended emphasis and contrast leading to the high point of interest. By pausing to create suspense, and at the same time to

[4] *Famous Wartime Speeches.* Recorded by Sir Winston Churchill. Cap., TBO—2192.
[5] From BLOOD, SWEAT AND TEARS by Sir Winston Churchill. Copyright, 1941 by Winston Churchill. Reprinted by permission of G. P. Putnam's Sons.

reinforce, you can bring the listener to expectancy, thus adding tremendously to the effectiveness of the author's pattern of meaning.

The famous opening scene of *Hamlet* creates suspense immediately and plunges the reader into the heart of the plot, as the watching guards sense the forboding of unusual events on this dark night. Notice the shifts in dramatic movement, the quick staccato opening, the desire of these watchers to be on their way. With Horatio's entrance, the tempo slows until the Ghost appears again. Then the tempo quickens in frightening suspense until his exit. The atmosphere of fear and hushed expectancy, increased by the time of night, can only be shown by muted voices that utilize suspense pauses. Are you conscious also of the rhythmical pattern leading to the climax of this opening scene; and of the contrasts in vocal quality that support the forward movement?[6]

from *Hamlet*

ACT I, SCENE 1

Elsinore. A platform before the castle. FRANCISCO *at his post. Enter to him* BERNARDO.

BER.: Who's there?

FRAN: Nay, answer me: stand, and unfold yourself.

BER.: Long live the king!

FRAN.: Bernardo?

BER.: He.

FRAN.: You come most carefully upon your hour.

BER.: 'Tis now struck twelve; get thee to bed, Francisco.

FRAN.: For this relief much thanks: 'tis bitter cold,
    And I am sick at heart.

BER.: Have you had quiet guard?

FRAN.:   Not a mouse stirring.

BER.: Well, good night.
    If you do meet Horatio and Marcellus,
    The rivals of my watch, bid them make haste.

FRAN.: I think I hear them. Stand, ho! Who's there?

Enter HORATIO *and* MARCELLUS

HOR.: Friends to this ground.

MAR.:   And liegeman to the Dane.

FRAN.: Give you good night.

MAR.:   O, farewell, honest soldier:
    Who hath relieved you?

FRAN.:   Bernardo has my place.

[6] This scene is interesting to interpret if different students assume the various roles, each person demonstrating a different vocal quality, appropriate intensity and tempo in order to build dramatic movement.

Give you good night.   (*Exit*)

MAR.:   Holla! Bernardo!
BER.:   Say,
       What, is Horatio there?
HOR.:   A piece of him.
BER.: Welcome, Horatio: welcome, good Marcellus.
MAR.: What, has this thing appear'd again tonight?
BER.: I have seen nothing.
MAR.: Horatio says 'tis but our fantasy, . . .
HOR.: Tush, tush, 'twill not appear. . . .

                          Enter GHOST

MAR.: Peace, break thee off; look, where it comes again!
BER.: In the same figure, like the king that's dead.
MAR.: Thou art a scholar; speak to it, Horatio.
BER.: Looks it not like the king? mark it, Horatio.
HOR.: Most like: it harrows me with fear and wonder.
BER.: It would be spoke to.
MAR.:   Question it, Horatio.
HOR.: What art thou that usurp'st this time of night
       . . . By heaven I charge thee, speak!
MAR.: It is offended.
BER.:   See, it stalks away!
HOR.: Stay! speak, speak! I charge thee, speak! (*Exit* GHOST)

Later Hamlet is told of the Ghost's appearance. Again the suspense
occurs by fast-moving lines, interspersed with suspense pauses and repetitive phrases.

HAM.: Indeed, indeed, sirs, but this troubles me.
       Hold you watch to-night?
MAR.: ⎱
BER.: ⎰   We do, my lord.
HAM.: Arm'd, say you?
MAR.: ⎱ Arm'd, my lord.
BER.: ⎰
HAM.: From top to toe?
BER.: ⎱
MAR.: ⎰   My lord, from head to foot,
HAM.: Then saw you not his face?
HOR.: O, yes, my lord; he wore his beaver up.
HAM.: What, look'd he frowningly?
HOR.: A countenance more in sorrow than in anger.
HAM.: Pale or red?
HOR.: Nay, very pale.
HAM.:   And fix'd his eyes upon you?
HOR.: Most constantly.
HAM.:   I would I had been there.

HOR.: It would have much amazed you.

HAM.: Very like, very like. Stay'd it long?

MAR.:
BER.: } Longer, longer.

HOR.: Not when I saw't.

HAM.:   His beard was grizzled,—no?

HOR.: It was, as I have seen it in his life,
    A sable silver'd.

HAM.: I will watch to-night;
    Perchance 'twill walk again.

SHAKESPEARE

E. E. Cummings sometimes gives clues to the interpretation of his poetic meaning by means of typographical arrangement, thus suggesting pauses for reinforcement and suspense. In his poem "in Just-" from his collection *Chansons Innocentes,* he puts some words together and spaces others in such a manner that the interpreter can ignore neither the rhythmical effect nor the atmosphere and tone. His recording of his poems reveals his vocal versatility in emphasizing meaning.[7]

The combined words—"balloonman," "eddieandbill," "puddle-wonderful," "bettyandisbel," "hop-scotch," "jump-rope"— belong to the enchantment of children's play; the spacing of words as in "whistles   far and   wee,"   is part of the child's imaginative fun; the steps downward on "and the goat-footed" and the timing of the last words "far and   wee" recall the melody and range of the child's voice at play, dying away—just as the balloonman's whistle—when they turn the corner.

"in Just—"

in Just
spring   when the world is mud-
luscious the little
lame balloonman

whistles   far   and wee

and eddieandbill come
running from marbles and
piracies and it's
spring

when the world is puddle-wonderful

the queer
old balloonman whistles

[7] *E. E. Cummings: Reading His Poems.* Caedmon, TC 1017.

far   and   wee
and bettyandisbel come dancing

from hop-scotch and jump-rope and

it's
spring
and
            the

                    goat-footed

balloonMan   whistles
far
and
wee[8]

E. E. CUMMINGS

As you can observe, Cummings is unique in establishing a tone of voice that leaves little doubt concerning the mood of his poetry—often ironic, sometimes biting and mocking in its sarcasm, sometimes romantic and sensuous. In the above poem, he has with his usual linguistic approach given images that tingle children with the joy of spring. Although he has extended his meaning symbolically, the poem has tone mainly because he has captured the sensations of the wonderful inner happiness of children. The "balloonman" may suggest a symbol to you, if you look a second time at the descriptive "goat-footed." Mrs. Elizabeth Qualey, Cummings's sister, writes of their exciting experiences as children every spring, which no doubt gave the poet the idea for the poem: "The first and most exciting sign that spring had really come was the balloon man. First you heard his whistle in the distance, then he would come walking down the street, carrying a basket full of balloons of all colors tugging at their strings."[9]

By this time, you realize that your vocal quality and light vocal attack must fit the atmosphere of the joy and mystery of spring to the child. If you follow the poet's suggestions, the pauses for reinforcement and suspense will carry his meaning. Above all, feel the joyous rhythm of spring.

The following lyrics of Humbert Wolfe are ingenious in their simplicity of form and language. Do not be deceived, however, into thinking they are easy to interpret. Some ingenuity on your part will be needed to decide where and how long to pause in order to capture the rhythm and gentle irony of some of the lines. Do you find the metaphorical meaning interesting? How do the poems differ in tone?

[8] Copyright, 1923, 1951 by E. E. Cummings. Reprinted from his volume POEMS 1923-1954 by permission of Harcourt, Brace & World, Inc.
[9] Charles Norman, *E. E. Cummings: The Magic Maker* (New York: Duell, Sloan and Pearce, 1964), p. 21.

Thrushes

The City Financier
walks in the gardens,
stiffly, because of
his pride and his burdens.

The daisies, looking
up, observe
only a self-
respecting curve.

The thrushes only
see a flat
table-land
of shiny hat.

He looks importantly
about him,
while all the spring
goes on without him.[10]

HUMBERT WOLFE

The Gray Squirrel

Like a small gray
coffee-pot,
sits the squirrel.
He is not

all he should be,
kills by the dozens
trees, and eats
his red-brown cousins.

The keeper, on the
other hand
, who shot him, is
a Christian, and

loves his enemies,
which shows
the squirrel was not
one of those.[11]

HUMBERT WOLFE

[10] From KENSINGTON GARDENS, Copyright 1927, by Humbert Wolfe. Reprinted by permission of Miss Ann Wolfe.
[11] *Ibid.*

The Lilac

Who thought of the lilac?
"I," dew said,
"I made up the lilac
out of my head."

"She made up the lilac!
Pooh!" thrilled a linnet,
and each dew-note had a
lilac in it.[12]

HUMBERT WOLFE

Queen Victoria

Queen Victoria's
statue is
the work of her
daughter Beatrice.

The shape's all wrong,
and the crown don't fit,
but—bless her old heart!
she was proud of it.[13]

HUMBERT WOLFE

Things Lovelier

You cannot dream
Things lovelier
Than the first love
I had of her.

Nor air is any
By magic shaken
As her first breath in
The first kiss taken.

And who, in dreaming,
Understands

[12] *Ibid.*
[13] *Ibid.*

Her hands stretched like
A blind man's hands?

Open, trembling,
    Wise they were—
You cannot dream
    Things lovelier.[14]

HUMBERT WOLFE

PATTERNS OF RHYTHM

ORGANIC RHYTHM

Rhythm is sometimes conceded to be the ultimate difference between poetry and prose. To believe that some types of literature—as free verse or prose—do not have rhythmic cadences is to believe that man has no organic rhythm. Yet you know you do have an innate pattern of breathing, walking, living, feeling and reacting—even eating. Rhythm cannot be isolated from you or the writer, for it is an integral part of man and helps him to live more comfortably. Man's functioning habits are geared to his neuromuscular system, which in turn establishes the pattern peculiar to his body matrix. You may not be conscious of your breathing or bodily rhythm; if, however, you aspirate a small foreign object, you will soon realize the havoc that can be caused to your breathing and your heartbeat, resulting in a-rhythmical activity of bodily movements as you gasp for oxygen. Hopefully you may live—if your bodily patterns are restored! These same unacknowledged rhythms are revealed in the cadenced pattern of your daily speech, unless you deliberately seek to modify them. So, too, the writer follows the pattern typical of his physiological and psychological structure as shown in the tonicity of his muscles. All great literature is built on the author's basic rhythmic reactions, whether he is writing prose or poetry, unless he chooses to delegate the telling of his story or poem to a narrator who has his own characteristic speech pattern.

RHYTHMICAL DEVICES

Rhythm in poetry, as discussed earlier, is built on a pattern involving a framework of meter, alliteration, rhyme, word and phrase arrangements according to the poet's melody. In prose, rhythm involves timing of ideas and episodes—their ebb and flow—in a larger movement as well as attention to repetitive and varying sound cadences of sentences. The difference lies mainly in the concentration of the pattern: poetry is structured in a capsule form powered for immediate impact; prose *appears* to be a

[14] *Ibid.*

more leisurely kind of reading in which the total rhythmical reactions are not absorbed so quickly. Much of the prose arrangement is lost to the casual reader, because prose has not been read aloud in the past. You can now, however, tune in to the rhythmical charm of prose by listening to recordings of Thomas, Proust, McKenna, Laughton, Perelman and the British interpreters (see pages 423, 424). Rhythm in literature must be heard to be appreciated empathically, as music is heard, as the rhythm of the dance must be sensed and heard.

Instead of the observable literary devices found in the melody of poetry, the pattern of prose will be more irregular, more diffuse and cover a larger plan than the concentrated pattern of poetry. It is not always obvious how the prose writer secures his effect. You should be able to recognize a movement of the whole, a rhythm acknowledged through the progression of sentence arrangements, ideas, events, characters, through the use of contrast and balance and through patterns of speech rhythm.

RHYTHM & METER IN POETRY

Many persons think of meter and rhythm as interchangeable elements in poetry, but the distinguishing mark lies in the fact that meter, fashioned according to mechanical rules, is not a means of communicating meaning. Rhythm, on the other hand, has much to do with conveying thought through its melody, its sensory responses. Interpretation is given its most personal touch through rhythm because it contains an element not found in meter: the emotional factor or empathic, surging movement, initiated by the spirit, swing, mood, recurrent cadences of the selection—never noticeable in scanning verse aloud.

Who can define what rhythm is, except to say that it is the *blending* of recurrent stressed and unstressed syllables into a flowing, continuous pattern or melody. To put it another way, rhythm is a varying pattern of sound and pause but with enough regularity and repetition in the variations that the ear catches the cadences, usually bringing an empathic pleasure to the listener. Meter can be said to exist on the printed page, for it can be marked off by rule with mechanical precision; it can be paced like the beat of a drum or the click-clack of train wheels. Meter is the basic structure for rhythm, for the intricate patterns of cadence and melody, for the varying excursions within the metrical pattern. Rhythm is impossible to pin-point because, although it is inherent in the selection, it must strike a sympathetic response in and be identified with the interpreter's feeling. You have watched ballet troupes—the basic pattern of the dance is interpreted by various groups on the stage into different rhythms; finally, these patterns are blended, as melodies are in a symphonic or-chestration, into one intricate rhythmical pattern. Dance orchestras also provide a background pattern interpreted by dancing couples according to the rhythms popular at the time or according to the dancers' inherent rhythm. Similarly, the interpreter may find more than one rhythmical pattern in a poem. If your sense of rhythm is latent, then you may have difficulty finding it in any poem. To repeat: no perceptive interpretation is possible in scanning meter, for all interpreters do it alike; and what all do alike is not interpretation.

The difference lies between the mechanical rendition of an exercise and the spirited or moving production of a finished interpretation. Rhythm conforms to no rule of its own; it is always a matter of the interpreter's ingenuity, versatility and rhythmic development in employing a happy combination of all the principles that make up lively speech. "You are a poet if you interpret a poem well." The poetry is in the interpreter—and the hearer—or else there is none. Meter is like a church hymn sung by the congregation; rhythm is like the rendition of an artist giving expression to his inmost soul. Meter has no surprises; rhythm never reveals its secrets. It is one surprise after another and each one of them is a pleasure. It catches the listeners off guard and makes them glad. It titillates attention and interest by the everlasting uncertainty of what is going to happen next.

The interpreter needs no *detailed* study of prosody to interpret a poem effectively. In fact, some students could probably interpret "This is the forest primeval" with truer rhythmic sense if they had not been urged at various times to scan it. Over-emphasis on scansion distorts speech rhythm and is likely to lead to a monotonous, droning interpretation of poetry—even to sing-song. Experience in training the ear may overcome this mechanical rendition. Consequently, the instructor's exhortation to utilize the units of regular scansion within the structured free verse is puzzling and needs explanation. A certain value may exist in being conscious of the poet's metrical pattern. When that awareness becomes paramount so that the interpreter thinks in terms of iambs and dactyls, then interpretation has suffered its worst blow: stress is distorted, timing becomes mechanical, pitch is nil, quality becomes inflexible and meaning is diminished. When an interpreter says, "I was miserable listening to him mutilate Shakespeare's iambic pentameter," he has lost, if he ever had it, the joy of Shakespeare's melody and rhythm. Anyone who reads blank verse for the sake of blank verse instead of the meaning does not have a realization of the poet's aim. Certainly no poet would say, "See how well I write blank verse," but rather "Note how well I can gain rhythmical effects by using a framework of blank verse." No poet ever wrote blank verse for the sake of blank verse.

Meter is not an end in itself but a means to an end. It should be considered a sort of convenience, a guidepost, a framework which shows the general arrangement of the poem, and from which various rhythmical patterns emerge. As an interpreter of poetry, you are anxious to convey a rhythmical impression which is not a matter of scansion but of muscles and glands. You live rhythmically, you move rhythmically and you should be able to interpret rhythmically. Your task is to discover and improve the variability of your vocal expression so that you can adapt cadences to meaning for the pleasure of the audience.

RHYTHMICAL INTERPLAY OF VOICES

Since the best way to experience rhythm is to hear and sense it through empathic response, listen to recordings of professional performances employing a montage of voices. Shaw's "Don Juan in Hell," performed by the "First Drama Quartet," was the initial production demonstrating this rhythmic interplay of voices. Today you may hear this kind of vocal portrayal on any university campus under the present name of "Readers Theatre."

READERS THEATRE

Inasmuch as you are interested in tempo and movement of literature through vocal and bodily expression, this is an opportune time to discuss briefly the initial efforts of the venture called "Readers Theatre." This kind of performance places emphasis on a collage, sometimes called a montage of voices, rather than on a one-man show, as John Gielgud's The *Ages of Man*.[15] The "readers" initially were professional actors who arranged themselves on a stage devoid of atmosphere or props except for chairs or high stools, lecterns and scripts. Shaw's *Don Juan In Hell*,[16] Benét's *John Brown's Body*[17] and Thomas's *Under Milk Wood*[18] were outstanding *first* performances.

Today the format may include a long poem or a series of poems from one poet; a story or series of incidents from various stories or plays of an author. The professional trend has been to feature a writer as in *The World of Carl Sandburg*[19] (the poet's poems, songs and narrative of Lincoln); *Brecht on Brecht*[20] ("a glimpse into the heart and workshop of the poet and playwright"); *Dear Liar*[21] (correspondence between those two

---

[15] *The Ages of Man,* featuring Sir John Gielgud. Columbia LP, OL 590.
[16] *Don Juan in Hell,* see p. 363.
[17] *John Brown's Body,* see p. 365.
[18] *Under Milk Wood,* see p. 363.
[19] *The World of Carl Sandburg,* with Leif Erickson and Bette Davis.
[20] *Brecht on Brecht,* a Crawford production with Dane Clark, Anne Jackson, Lotte Lenya, Viveca Lindfors and George Voskovec. Columbia LP, 02S-203.
[21] *Dear Liar,* featuring Katherine Cornell and Brian Aherne.

scintillating artists, Mrs. Patrick Campbell and George Bernard Shaw); *Pictures in the Hallway*[22] (the charm and wit of Sean O'Casey); *Spoon River Anthology*[23] (a collection of Edgar Lee Masters's vignettes); *An Evening's Frost*[24] (excerpts from Frost's prose and poetry). University groups have learned how to delve into the complete works of a writer, showing near professional as well as grotesque performances. It is rewarding to know, however, that interpreters are becoming "author-conscious," "personality-interested" and that many wise and temperate directors are working for the success of this vocal project.

Readers Theatre is obviously inadequately named; even New York critics have difficulty in naming the theatrical attempt that is not theatre and the reading attempt that is more than reading. Certainly the name "Actors Theatre" found in the New York papers is redundant. The change from "The Spoon River Anthology" to "The Spoon River Revue" in one of the midwest papers is due partly to the "ineffectual occasional music" about the "essence of love" occurring during the intermission. An interlude of this sort is likely to mean that the director is on the defensive in his attempt to entertain so he "provides" beyond the vignettes from Masters.

Readers Theatre may be considered a hybrid of interpretation and acting—a vocal close-up shot of characters. Because of the inbreeding of these two highly sensitive arts, many variations may and do occur. Some results grow into weeds, which later may be difficult to eliminate; a few performances have appeared to go beyond interpretation into impersonation, even to the outer edge of ineffective acting; and a few cannot be named at all. Certainly the end-result is neither impersonation nor, unfortunately, acting. If the art of this group interpretative technique can be kept under professional control, an enviable future for those interested is envisioned: the professional interpreter might discover a more lucrative vocation, if discriminating taste becomes the byword.

READERS THEATRE: TOTAL EFFECT

The total effect should not be merely vocal demonstrations of each person "reading" a part; rather it should be considered a total movement by means of spoken words, a kaleidoscopic tempo that flows into a rhythmic whole through voice *and* facial expression *and* bodily tension *and* attitude. The interpreter *suggests* at a high level of performance through bodily tensions that give awareness of an attitude. To try to

[22] *Pictures in the Hallway*, a Paul Shyre production with Mildred Dunnock, Martyn Green and Paul Shyre.

[23] *Spoon River Anthology*, a Joseph Cates production with original Broadway cast: Betty Garrett, Robert Elston, Joyce Van Patten, Charles Aidman, Naomi Hirshhorn and Hal Lynch. Columbia LP, S2-2410.

[24] *An Evening's Frost*, a Donald Hall production, directed by Marcella Cisney and Robert Schnitzer, with Jacqueline Brookes and Will Geer.

obliterate the body in the interpretation and *then* permit many extraneous bodily mannerisms in the handling of oneself as an interpreter is one of the great errors of the typical collegiate Readers Theatre. In this technique, communication does not end with one person "reading" the script and another one taking up the lines where the last voice stopped; rather the meaning must be carried from one interpreter to another, much in the manner of picking up cues on the stage. Beyond that, the interpreter should not venture in extensity of overt movement. Consequently, any intervening action that has nothing to do with meaning should be obliterated as much as possible; at least, attention should not be focused in the wrong direction. The body attitude must be kept in focus with the voice: no sagging at the waistline, no dislocated hip while waiting the next turn at the script, no aimless handling of the script, no moving of the head from side to side to see if the audience approves or how the rest of the cast is reacting. The picture of the "whole" must be kept intact—the word "theatre" implies this; unfortunately, the word "reading" does not. An impression of impressions should be received by the audience—an output of the "whole." Apropos of this thought, Henry Hewes, critic for *Saturday Review*,[25] writes perceptively about the "Spoon River" performance:

What is missing, however, is the cumulative, imaginary creation of a town, in the mind's eye of the poet, or an insistent, passionate attitude toward life driven home by one character. Instead, the evening becomes a series of amusing and touching minor vignettes interspersed with folk songs that are unimportant interludes. They succeed in breaking up something that is already much too segmented.

If, moreover, an attempt is made to be ultra-artistic in an effort to outdo the next-door university group, then the director may be stepping "out-of-bounds"—too close to the acting area yet producing neither near-professional acting nor even poor acting and certainly not "reading." Neither would interpreters accept the performance, for it carries no *illusion* of an artistic endeavor. Some hybrids, however, show these unusual formations in the vagaries of growth. Then, too, many university theater groups look askance at the efforts as "merely reading rehearsals such as precede our acting rehearsals"; others arouse some skepticism when they remark that Readers Theatre is a "bonanza" in "whipping up" an assembly program or in "rushing" a one-act play to the hungry Rotarians.

The director and the students must decide whether or not they wish to be on the periphery of acting—providing a hasty unloading of unwanted passengers for the stage—or interested in the play of voices. The director must also decide whether or not he will work for *suggestion*, as lighting a face at an appropriate time, grouping his characters to show opposition

[25] *Saturday Review*, October 19, 1963.

or toning down costumes. He must not carry these additional features farther than suggestion or he will not create an artistic performance. You can learn from the professionals, however, who usually stop short of acting, costuming, elaborate and fantastic lighting and grotesque make-up.

One of the first techniques an actor learns is how to approach a chair, sit on it, grace it while sitting and how to leave it with economy of effort. The problem is greatly accentuated in Readers Theatre when high stools are affected because of their theatrical high stance—or as observed, their advanced leg level. The management of the lower extremities as they encircle the high stools is sometimes quite a show—and can easily divert attention—if no lectern is in front of them or if the director has his cast leaving the stools to move forward stage front with every speech. Added to these eccentricities, sinister black-robed creatures may take turns walking from their high stools to the apron of the stage, their faces representing death masks, their eyes staring straight ahead in an unseeing, unfeeling "great stone-face" look; then having supposedly "read" from the script held rigidly in clenched hands, they slump on their seats after their small contribution and carelessly wind their legs around the spindles of the tall stool and gropingly look for their next bit in the manuscript.

If the person in charge will remember this is a hearing project, grounded in the rise and fall of tempo, in the flow of voices—and teach the student to LISTEN—then perhaps the tempo will move coordinately; and not with the spasmodic movement that says "All right, your turn, go ahead while I find my next cue." Furthermore, let the one who takes care of stage directions know that his expository interpretation is extremely important in keeping listeners informed and interpreters on a unified level of performance: his voice must be alive with information rather than dead with inertia and must work into the idea of a cohesive whole rather than of parts.

O'Connor's love of the cadences of voice is the goal participating students should seek in listening to voices. O'Connor reports he is not interested in the color of a girl's eyes or the dress she is wearing, but he gets a feeling about the person through hearing her voice—the cadences, words and phrases she uses. Neither can he finish a story unless he knows how everyone in it speaks—then he sees and knows the individual.[26]

Before this discussion is concluded, you should be reminded that the manipulation of a script should be subordinated to the total interpretative impression. You must consider it your most important property: handle it with reverence but focus only background attention on it. Concentration on the script to the extent that it secures more attention than the meaning is not acceptable. You must learn to glance at it as if it contained meaning and treat it as the masterpiece of the author—or else do

[26] *Paris Interview Series*, p. 169.

not have it in your hand. Remember it is not dead material. As a show-piece, it is a nonentity; as a piece of artistic writing, it holds great power. You may recall earlier remarks about Laughton's handling of the Bible: his turning of the thin pages of the huge Book, as if he revered the contents, helped to make the experiences memorable to the audience.

Today Readers Theatre is presented under many guises. At this point, the direction in which it will proceed and the signposts to be observed in university environs will depend on the discriminating control of the Interpretation Interest Group in the Speech Association of America. In a few years perhaps, performances can reach the artistic level of the music heard from a chamber string quartet or quintet, the charm of which is created through the sound of recurrent melodies. One musician plays his melody and another starts his—and so on—until all blend together in a harmonious musical sound. The pleasure comes from *hearing* the contrapuntal movement of the various tunes rather than *watching* the musicians. The same importance of strengthening *vocal* precision for emotional meanings to secure the tempo and rhythmical flow of voices should be realized in Readers Theatre. Jacques Barzun's discussion of the vocal melodies heard in the recording of *Don Juan In Hell* echoes this pleasure.

READERS THEATRE: EARLY PERFORMANCES

Initially, the performances on Broadway, beginning in 1951 with *Don Juan in Hell,* were unstylized, without properties and with emphasis on vocal patterns. In the recording of this excerpt from Shaw's *Man and Superman,* the tonal discrimination is intriguing. Listen for the melodic pattern of voices: the vocal quality of each character impresses the listener with its flexibility, resonance and tonality; the intensity emphasizes meaning and atmosphere; the rhythm moves to tremendous climaxes; the changes in pitch reveal meaning which originally few but Shaw had sensed.

More than that, as Barzun suggests, one becomes aware of a counter-point of vocal melodies skillfully arranged: sometimes with one melody overlapping another; sometimes with a vocal pattern rising in crescendo to be picked up by another vocal theme that mounts to a climax, only to be softened by another melody. You may not *hear* this counterpoint of vocal melodies at first, but you will be enchanted by the play of vocal quality once you become familiar with the lines and can submerge the fascination of Shaw's verbal dexterity. Barzun, in the *Notes* that accompany the recording, writes aptly of this contrapuntal arrangement:

What Shaw does is to compose with words and ideas a quartet in one great movement, or perhaps a fugue for four voices. It would be going beyond the facts to say that the piece was consciously written in musical form, but is undoubtedly oratorical (which is why it holds an audience so easily), and musical forms are patterned on the basic oratorical scheme of introduction, exposition, development, and recapitulation. The result is that in listening to Shaw's verbal sonata you do not, as in reading, mind the returns and repeats, you welcome them. And even though some have been cut from the present performance, the shape of the vocal rendering gives pleasure—the pleasure of an almost bodily satisfaction—quite apart from the satisfaction of wit, eloquence, and living philosophy.[27]

As you listen further, you can identify each character by his speech rhythm, vocal quality and intensity. Listen to Doña Anna's voice interpreted by Agnes Moorehead, first as a woman of 77 years and then as a young girl of 27 years. As an old woman, her vocal quality and intonations belong to a person who is assured, confident of authority, worldly, sophisticated, demanding; and the throaty, slightly husky laugh adds to the impression of a woman who has lived fully and luxuriously. As soon as Doña Anna decides that she will be 27 years old while in Hell, her vocal quality becomes lighter and softer and not so resonant.

The voices of the three men—the Devil, the Commander and Don Juan—reveal through their nuances of inflection, attack, rhythm and quality, clear-cut characterizations. The Devil's voice belongs to a person who is detached, aloof, commanding, ironical, impatient—and certainly to one who is not moved by the philosophy of others. The Commander's voice reveals a man of the world, a dilettante—suave, mellow, casual, not easily provoked because he enjoys security and prestige. Don Juan's voice portrays a most interesting contrast to the other masculine voices inasmuch as he is the pivot about which the others move. His vibrant, intense quality indicates a highly emotional, impetuous and decisive personality. His last long speech, beginning with the line, "On the contrary, here I have everything appointed me," builds to a breathtaking climax, showing a voice under the finest control. If you are genuinely alert to the sound of vocal characteristics, you will be intrigued with *Don Juan in Hell*,[28] not for one hour's listening but for many hours—and furthermore, for the first time you may discover Shaw's dexterity and skill in arrangement of words.

Two performances of professional significance were presented and recorded in 1953: Dylan Thomas's *Under Milk Wood*[29] with a subtitle,

---

[27] Copyright, 1953, by Jacques Barzun. Reprinted by permission of the author. The excerpt recorded in this album is from the full-length play, *Man and Superman* by George Bernard Shaw. The complete play is contained in George Bernard Shaw, *Nine Plays* (New York, Dodd, Mead & Company, Inc., 1935).

[28] *Don Juan in Hell*, an excerpt from Bernard Shaw's *Man and Superman*, recorded by the First Drama Quartet, with Charles Laughton, as director, Charles Boyer, Agnes Moorehead and Cedric Hardwicke. Columbia, OSL-166.

[29] *Under Milk Wood*, featuring Dylan Thomas with the original Broadway cast, including Dion Allen, Allen F. Collins, Roy Poole, Sada Thompson, Nancy Wickwire. Caedmon, TC 2005.

"A Play for Voices"—a natural for Readers Theatre; and Benét's American epic, *John Brown's Body*. Because Thomas was involved as author, director and member of the cast, biographers have written about his personal part in the production: his anxiety as to the outcome, his last minute polishing attempts and his joy at the jubilant audience reaction. The following comment by Brinnin records a life-like picture of what happened on May 15, 1953, the night of the first performance of this "zany comedy and its final mellow embrace of a whole village of the living and the dead." Thomas opened his performance in this atmosphere as described by Brinnin: "The stage was dim until a soft breath of light showed Dylan's face" as he began:

> To begin at the beginning: It is Spring, moonless night in the small town, starless and bible-black, the cobblestreets silent and the hunched, courters'-and-rabbits' wood limping invisible down to the sloeback, slow, black, crowblack, fishingboat-bobbing sea. The houses are blind as moles (though moles see fine tonight in the snouting, velvet dingles) or blind as Captain Cat there in the muffled middle by the pump and the town clock, the shops in mourning, the Welfare Hall in widows' weeds. And all the people of the lulled and dumbfound town are sleeping now. . . .
>
> Only you can hear the houses sleeping in the streets in the slow deep salt and silent black bandaged night. Only you can see, in the blinded bedrooms, the combs and petticoats over the chairs, the jugs and basins, the glasses of teeth, Thou Shalt Not on the wall, and the yellowing dickybird-watching pictures of the dead. Only you can hear and see, behind the eyes of the sleepers, the movements and countries and mazes and colours and dismays and rainbows and tunes and wishes and flight and fall and despairs and big seas of their dreams.[30]

DYLAN THOMAS, *Under Milk Wood*

Brinnin continues with his description of audience reaction:

One by one, the faces of the other actors came into view as the morning light of Milk Wood broadened and Dylan's voice, removed and godlike in tone, yet pathetically human in the details upon which it dwelt, made a story, a mosaic and an *aubade* of the beginning movements of a village day. Expectant, hushed, and not at all prepared to laugh, the audience seemed as deep in concentration as the actors on the stage until, finally, unable not to recognize the obvious bawdy meaning of some of the play's early lines, two or three people laughed outright. But still there was a general uneasiness, an incomprehension, as if these outbursts had been mistaken laughter. Then, as soon as it became evident that this story of a village was as funny as it was loving and solemn, a chain of laughter began and continued until the last line. When the lights slowly faded and the night had swallowed up the last face and muffled the last voice in the village, there was an unexpected silence both on stage and off. The thousand spectators sat as if stunned, as if the slightest handclap might violate a spell. But within a few moments the lights went up and applause crescendoed and bravos were shouted by half the standing audience while the cast came back for curtain call after curtain call until, at the fifteenth of these, squat and boyish in his happily flustered modesty, Dylan stepped out alone.[31]

JOHN MALCOLM BRINNIN, *Dylan Thomas in America*

The performance of *John Brown's Body*[32] by the First Drama Quartet of professional actors, directed by Charles Laughton, preceded *Under Milk Wood* by three months. The Quartet was supported by the singing of ballads and spirituals created by Walter Schumann and sung by the well-known Hall Johnson Choir. Here is your opportunity to hear the varied rhythm and spirit of ballads. As Brooks Atkinson wrote in the *New York Times,* February 16, 1953, "The severe beauty of choral singing is an integral part of this imaginative planned performance."

The theme of this epic is one of the perplexing contemporary issues—the problem of race equality but of one hundred years ago. The conflicting characters and war episodes of the North and South are excellently dramatized through characterizations of the leaders—Lincoln, Lee, Jackson, John Brown; through fictional individuals—Clay Wingate, Cudjo, Lucy Weatherby, Mary Lou, Sally Dupré, symbols of Southern life; through Jack Ellyat and Bailey of the Northern soldiers; and through Melora of the "hide-out" group. The poet portrays John Brown as the symbol of the motivating spirit of civil rights, recalling his execution continually by the weird and hollow echo of his song from the eerie atmosphere of the grave: "There Is a Song in My Bones."

These recordings permit you to *hear* how the voice carries meaning. A Reader's Theatre performance should be one that sharpens your ears to hear whereas a play is a production for which you polish your lens to see and also hope to hear. Listen now to excerpts from *John Brown's Body.*[33]

[31] From DYLAN THOMAS IN AMERICA by John Malcolm Brinnin. Copyright 1955, by John Malcolm Brinnin. Reprinted by permission of Atlantic—Little, Brown and Company, pp. 209-210.

[32] *John Brown's Body* by Stephen Vincent Benét. Recorded by Tyrone Power, Judith Anderson, Raymond Massey, Richard White, directed by Charles Laughton; and supported by the Hall Johnson Choir. Columbia, 5 SL-181. The recorded version of this long poem varies slightly in its format from the printed poem but can be easily followed.

[33] Compare the Columbia recording with the CBS Television Adaptation. Recorded by Richard Boone, narrator, Douglas Campbell, Peter Donat, Lester Rawlins, Nancy Wickwire with supporting cast, Burt Brinckerhoff, John Colicos, Sean Garrison, Maxwell Glanville, Jeremiah Morris. Distributed by the Anti-Defamation League of B'nai B'rith, New York, N.Y.

There Is a Song in My Bones

John Brown's body lies a-mouldering in the grave.
He will not come again with foolish pikes
And a pack of desperate boys to shadow the sun.
He has gone back North. The slaves have forgotten his eyes.
John Brown's body lies a-mouldering in the grave.
John Brown's body lies a-mouldering in the grave.
Already the corpse is changed, under the stone,
The strong flesh rotten, the bones dropping away.
Cotton will grow next year, in spite of the skull.
Slaves will be slaves next year, in spite of the bones.
Nothing is changed, John Brown, nothing is changed.

"There is a song in my bones. There is a song
In my white bones."

I hear no song. I hear
Only the blunt seeds growing secretly
In the dark entrails of the preparate earth,
The rustle of the cricket under the leaf,
The creaking of the cold wheel of the stars.

"Bind my white bones together—hollow them
To skeleton pipes of music. When the wind
Blows from the budded Spring, the song will blow."

I hear no song. I only hear the roar
Of the Spring freshets, and the gushing voice
Of mountain-brooks that overflow their banks,
Swollen with melting ice and crumbled earth.

"That is my song.
It is made of water and wind. It marches on."

No, John Brown's body lies a-mouldering,
A-mouldering.

"My bones have been washed clean
And God blows through them with a hollow sound,
And God has shut his wildfire in my dead heart."

I hear it now,
Faint, faint as the first droning flies of March,
Faint as the multitudinous, tiny sigh
Of grasses underneath a windy scythe.

"It will grow stronger."

It has grown stronger. It is marching on.
It is a throbbing pulse, a pouring surf,
It is the rainy gong of the Spring sky
Echoing,
John Brown's body,
John Brown's body.
But still it is not fierce. I find it still
More sorrowful than fierce.

"You have not heard it yet. You have not heard
The ghosts that walk in it, the shaking sound."

Strong medicine,
Bitter medicine of the dead,
I drink you now. I hear the unloosed thing,
The anger of the ripe wheat—the ripened earth
Sullenly quaking like a beaten drum
From Kansas to Vermont. I hear the stamp
Of the ghost-feet. I hear the ascending sea.

  "Glory, Glory, Hallelujah,
  Glory, Glory, Hallelujah,
  Glory, Glory, Hallelujah!"

What is this agony of the marching dust?
What are these years ground into hatchet blades?

"Ask the tide why it rises with the moon,
My bones and I have risen like that tide
And an immortal anguish plucks us up
And will not hide us till our song is done."

The phantom drum diminishes—the year
Rolls back. It is only winter still, not spring,
The snow still flings its white on the new grave,
Nothing is changed, John Brown, nothing is changed
John . . . Brown . . .[34]

    STEPHEN VINCENT BENÉT

Benét has established certain rhythms for his characters depending on their environmental and cultural background. Wingate Hall, the symbol of Southern gentility and happy living, has for its mistress, Mary Lou, and for its young master, her son Clay. The Wingate rhythm, as Benét

[34] FROM: SELECTED WORKS OF STEPHEN VINCENT BENÉT. Published by Holt, Rinehart & Winston. Copyright 1927, 1928 by Stephen Vincent Benét. Copyright renewed © 1955, by Rosemary Carr Benét. Reprinted by permission of Brandt & Brandt.

remarks in his "Foreword," reflects the lightness and swiftness of dancing and riding, with the dash and courtesy of the pre-war South.

Here is Clay Wingate—

> Riding back through the Georgia Fall
> To the white-pillared porch of Wingate Hall.
> Fall of the possum, fall of the 'coon,
> And the lop-eared hound-dog baying the moon. . . .
>
> A smokiness so vague in the air
> You feel it rather than see it there— . . .
>
> A pine-cone fire and a banjo-tune,
> And a julep mixed with a silver spoon. . . .
>
> Wingate checked on his horse's rein
> With a hand as light as a butterfly
> And drank content in body and brain
> As he gazed for a moment at the sky.
> This was his Georgia, this his share
> Of pine and river and sleepy air.

Benét reveals the characteristic southern touch of gentility as he portrays Mary Lou, matriarch of the proud Georgian family of Wingate Hall—

> She knew her Bible—and how to flirt
> With a swansdown fan and a brocade skirt.
> For she trusted in God but she liked formalities
> And the world and Heaven were both realities. . . .
>
> Gentility must keep to gentility—

so reasoned Mary Lou, a woman of many passions; for she could hate—

> The terrible hate of women's ire,
> The smoky, the long-consuming fire.

Cudjo and Aunt Bess, as chief caretakers of the mansion and its inmates, provide a jovial background with their particular tunes. You hear the banjos "planking" whenever Cudjo speaks—in fact you hear the rhythm of his shuffling feet. Listen as he watches Sally Dupré, daughter of the former French dancing master—

> Cudjo watched her as she went by,
> "She's got a light foot," thought Cudjo, "Hi!
> A light, swif' foot and a talkin' eye!

> But you'll need more'n dat, Miss Sally Dupré
> Before you proposals with young Marse Clay—"

or as he prepares for the gay festivities—

> There's goin' to be mixin's and mighty doin's,
> Chicken-fixin's and barbecuin's,
> Old Marse Billy's a-comin' home!
> He's slewn a brigade with a ha'nts's jaw-bone,
> He's slewn an army with one long sabre,
> He's scared old Linkum 'most to death,
> Now he's comin' home to rest from he labor,
> Play on he fiddle and catch he breath!

and who could forget how fat Aunt Bess in her ice-wool shawl—

> Spends the hoarded knowledge her heart is rich in
> On oceans of trifle and floating island.

If you are still having difficulty sensing various rhythms, try this "laughing" tempo—

> The negro laughter, the blue-black rose,
> The laughter that doesn't end with the lips
> But shakes the belly and curls the toes
> And prickles the ends of the fingertips.

In the Southern picture also is Sally Dupré, who could look "like a saint in plaster"—

> But when the fiddles began to play
> And her feet beat fast but her heart beat faster
> An alien grace inhabited them
> And she looked like her father, the dancing master.
> The scapegoat elegant, "French Dupré, . . .

Sally, in love with Clay Wingate, has not always been accepted by the Southern women even though her father married an "Appleton." Here is another example of the rhythm of Southern gentility—

> And slander is sinful and gossip wrong,
> And country memories are long,
> The Appleton clan is a worthy clan
> But we remember the dancing-man.
> The girl is pretty, the girl seems wise,
> The girl was born with her father's eyes. . . .

We wouldn't hurt her to save our souls.
But after all—and nevertheless—
For one has to think—and one must confess—
And one must admit—but one never knows—
So it has gone, and so it goes, . . .

Till, little by little and stitch by stitch
The girl is put in her proper niche— . . .

For some good reason, Lucy Weatherby, *The Dixie Angel,* is not included in the format of the recording, even though she serves as a foil for Sally Dupré. The following scenes contrast portraits of these two Southern women: check on the choice of words and the speech pattern of each woman. Lucy is in love with her own charms and beauty and rationalizes about her love for her country and the "dear brave boys." Sally reacts with restraint to a panoramic scene of Clay and Lucy with the Black Horse Troop. The pauses are extremely important in conveying Sally's reactions, especially her stunned feeling as expressed in the last four lines containing a preponderance of monosyllabic words. How has the poet made the speech rhythm of each woman differ according to her temperament?

The Dixie Angel

Lucy Weatherby, cuddled up in her bed,
Drifted along toward sleep with a smile on her mouth,
"I was pretty tonight," she thought, "I was pretty tonight.
Blue's my color—blue that matches my eyes.
I always ought to wear blue. I'm sorry for girls
Who can't wear that sort of blue. Her name is Sally
But she's too dark to wear the colors I can,
I'd like to give her my blue dress and see her wear it,
She'd look too gawky, poor thing.
                                        He danced with her
For a while at first but I hadn't danced with him then,
He danced with me after that. He's rather a dear.
I wonder how long he'll be here. I think I like him.
I think I'm going to be pretty while I am here. . . .

Poor Curly—I ought to answer his mother's letter
But it's hard answering letters."
                                        She cried a little,
Thinking of Curly. The tears were fluent and warm,
They did not sting in her eyes. . . .
                                        She dried the tears

And thought to herself with a pleasant little awe,
"You really are mighty brave, dear. You really are.
Nobody would think your beau was killed in Manassas."
—She could hardly remember Curly any more—
She tried to make Curly's face come out of the darkness
But it was too hard—the other faces kept coming—. . . .

Boys who were privates, boys who were majors and captains,
Nice old Generals who patted your shoulder,
Darling convalescents who called you an angel—
A whole great lucky-bag of nice, thrilling boys,
Fighting for you—and the South and the Cause, of course.
You were a flame for the Cause. You sang songs about it.
You sent white feathers to boys who didn't enlist
And bunches of flowers to boys who were suitably wounded.
You wouldn't dream of making peace with the North
While a single boy was left to fight for the Cause
And they called you the Dixie Angel. . . .[35]

STEPHEN VINCENT BENÉT

The Black Horse Troop Returns to War

Sally Dupré, from the high porch of her house
Stared at the road.
                    They would be here soon enough.
She had waved a flag the last time they went away.
This time she would wave her hand or her handkerchief.
That was what women did. The column passed by
And the women waved, and it came back and they waved,
And, in between, if you loved, you lived by a dull
Clock of long minutes that passed like sunbonneted women
Each with the same dry face and the same set hands. . . .

They were coming now.
She remembered the first time.
They were different now. They rode with a different rein.
They rode all together. They knew where they were going.
They were famous now, but she wondered about the fame.
And yet, as she wondered, she felt the tears in her blood
Because they could ride so easily.
                                He was there.
She fed her heart to the hawk and watched him ride. . . .

Then she thought. "No, no, I can't bear it. It cannot be borne."
And knowing this, bore it.
                        He saw her. He turned his horse.

[35] Benét, see p. 367.

"If he comes here, I can't keep it back. I can't keep it back,
I can't stand it, don't let him come." He was coming now.
He rides well, she thought, while her hands made each other cold.
I will have to remember how. And his face is sharper.
The mustache quite changes his face. The face that I saw
While he was away was clean-shaven and darker-eyed.
I must change that, now. I will have to remember that.
It is very important.
                         He swung from Black Whistle's back.
His spurs made a noise on the porch. She twisted her hands.
"If I shut my eyes, I can make him kiss me. I will not."

They were saying good-by, now. She heard polite voices saying it.
Then the voices ended. "No, no, it is not to be borne,
It is the last twist of the vise."
                              Her will snapped then.
When she looked at him, she knew that the knives were edgeless.
In an instant life would begin, life would be forever.

His eyes wavered. There was a thin noise in her ears,
A noise from the road.
                         The instant fell and lay dead
Between them like something broken.

She turned to see what had killed it.

Lucy Weatherby, reining a bright bay mare,
Played with the braided lash of a riding-whip . . .
And the whole troop clustered about her.
                                   Her habit was black
But she had a knot of bright ribbons pinned at her breast,
Red and blue—the Confederate colors.
                              They had cheered her,
They had cheered her, riding along with her colored ribbons.
It was that which had killed the instant.
                                   Sally looked
At the face with the new mustache she had to remember.
"Good-bye," she said. The face bent over her hand
And kissed it acceptably.
                         Then the face had gone.
He was back with the others now. She watched for a minute.
Lucy was unpinning her knot of ribbons.
She saw a dozen hands go up for the knot
And Lucy laugh her sweet laugh and shake her bright head,
Glance once at Huger Shepley and once at Clay,
And then toss the colored knot to the guidon-bearer
Who grinned and tied the ribbons around the staff
While some of them cheered again.
                              Then the horses moved.

They went by Lucy. Lucy was waving her hand.
She had tears in her eyes and was saying brave words to the soldiers.
Sally watched a back and a horse go out of sight.
She was tired, then.
When the troop had quite disappeared
Lucy rode up to the house.
                    The two women kissed
And talked for a while about riding-habits and war.
"I just naturally love every boy in the Black Horse Troop,
Don't you, Sally darling? They're all so nice and polite,
Quite like our Virginia boys, and the Major's a dear,
And that nice little one with the guidon is perfectly sweet.
You ought to have heard what he said when I gave him the knot.
Though, of course, I can tell why you didn't come down to the road,
War's terrible, isn't it? All those nice boys going off—
I feel just the way you do darling—we just have to show them
Whenever we can that we know they are fighting for us,
Fighting for God and the South and the cause of the right— . . .
We've all got to do what we can in this horrible war."
Sally agreed that we had, and drank from a cup.
She thought. "Lucy Weatherby. Yes. I must look for a doll.
I must make a doll with your face, an image of wax.
I must call that doll by your name."[36]

STEPHEN VINCENT BENÉT

In addition to the foregoing examples of rhythms emphasizing situations and characters, here is the melodious ballad of the young girl, Melora, who tended the wounded Jack Ellyat as he strayed into the "hiders" area. Listen to the ballad Melora sings.

Melora's Song

Love came by from the riversmoke,
    When the leaves were fresh on the tree,
But I cut my heart on the blackjack oak
    Before they fell on me.

The leaves are green in the early Spring,
    They are brown as linsey now,
I did not ask for a wedding-ring
    From the wind in the bending bough.

Fall lightly, lightly, leaves of the wild,
    Fall lightly on my care,
I am not the first to go with child
    Because of the blowing air.

[36] *Ibid.*

I am not the first nor yet the last
    To watch a goosefeather sky,
And wonder what will come of the blast
    And the name to call it by.

Snow down, snow down, you whitefeather bird,
    Snow down, you winter storm,
Where the good girls sleep with a gospel word
    To keep their honor warm.

The good girls sleep in their modesty,
    The bad girls sleep in their shame,
But I must sleep in the hollow tree
    Till my child can have a name.

I will not ask for the wheel and thread
    To spin the labor plain,
Or the scissors hidden under the bed
    To cut the bearing-pain.

I will not ask for the prayer in church
    Or the preacher saying the prayer,
But I will ask the shivering birch
    To hold its arms in the air.

Cold and cold and cold again,
    Cold in the blackjack limb
The winds of the sky for his sponsor-men
    And a bird to christen him.

Now listen to me, you Tennessee corn,
    And listen to my word,
This is the first child ever born
    That was christened by a bird.

He's going to act like a hound let loose
    When he comes from the blackjack tree,
And he's going to walk in proud shoes
    All over Tennessee.

I'll feed him milk out of my own breast
    And call him Whistling Jack.
And his dad'll bring him a partridge nest,
    As soon as his dad comes back.[37]

                        STEPHEN VINCENT BENÉT

[37] *Ibid.*

Hear the hushed atmosphere of the Song of the Hiders.

> This is the hidden place that hiders know.
> This is where hiders go,
> Step softly, the snow that falls here is different snow,
> The rain has a different sting.
> Step softly, step like a cloud, step softly as the least
> Whisper of air against the beating wing,
> And let your eyes be sealed
> With two blue muscadines
> Stolen from secret vines,
> Or you will never find in the lost field
> The table spread, the signs of the hidden feast.[38]
>
> STEPHEN VINCENT BENÉT

As explained by Benét, the rhythm of the war scenes is purposely "rough." The episodes are also particularly effective because of the vivid characterizations of the leaders, North and South. You hear Massey portraying Lincoln with his home-spun philosophy from the prairie land of Illinois. You are moved by the remarkable images of Jackson, Lee and Sherman, especially the latter's march to the sea, introduced by the stirring ballad, "Jubili, Jubilo."

In the following episode of the war, you will discover a rhythm different in its cadences from those of the Wingate Hall environs. Jack Ellyat attempts an escape, prodded by his war pal, Bailey. Note how the lines build to a dramatic crescendo through the broken rhythm and then die away as Ellyat collapses.

Escape

> It was night now. The column still marched. But Bailey and Ellyat
> Had dropped to the rear of the column, planning escape.
> There were few guards and the guards were as tired as they.
> Two men could fall in a ditch by the side of the road
> And get away, perhaps, if they picked a good time.
> They talked it over in stupid whispers of weariness.
> The next bend—no, the guard was coming along.
> The next bend after—no, there was a light for a moment
> From a brief star, then clouded—the top of the hill—
> The bottom of the hill—and they still were marching.
> Rain began to fall, a drizzle at first, then faster.
> Ellyat's eyes were thick. He walked in a dream,
> A heavy dream, cut from leaden foil with blunt shears.

[38] *Ibid.*

Then Bailey touched him—he felt the tired bones of his skull
Click with a sudden spark—his feet stopped walking—
He held his breath for an instant,
And then wearily slumped in the ditch with enormous noise,
Hunching his shoulders against a phantom bayonet.

But when he could raise his head, the column had gone.
He felt fantastic. They couldn't escape like this.
You had to escape like a drawing in *Harper's Weekly*
With stiff little men on horses like sickle-pears
Firing round frozen cream-puffs into your back.
But they had escaped.
                  Life came back to him in a huge
Wave of burnt stars. He wanted to sing and yell.
He crackled out of the ditch and stood beside Bailey.
Had he ever hated Bailey? It could not have been.
He loved Bailey better than anything else in the world.

They moved slyly toward the woods, they were foxes escaped.
Wise foxes sliding away to a hidden earth
To a sandy floor, to the warm fawn-flanks of sweet sleep. . . .
And then an awful molasses-taffy voice
Behind them yelled "Halt!" and "Halt!" and—sudden explosion
Of desultory popcorn in iron poppers—
Wild running at random—a crash among broken boughs—
A fighting second—Bailey's voice, half-strangled but clear,
"Run like hell, Jack, they'll never catch you!"
                   He ran like hell.

Time passed like the rain. Time passed and was one with the rain.[39]

                        STEPHEN VINCENT BENÉT

Probably the climax of all rhythm scenes is the ballroom episode at Wingate Hall, in which superficial gayety and inner tension are sustained as Sally and Clay fight inwardly rather than verbally. This episode is an experience in irony. The background incantation of "This is the last" haunts the scene, starting as an echoing whisper and mounting in terrifying accents; penetrating Mary Lou's innermost thoughts; dinning the ear of Clay Wingate with its insistence; and finally, blending as an undercurrent into the rhythm of the music.

Listen to the differences in vocal quality and intensity of the two dancers, Sally and Clay, who utter "small talk" as they follow the gay, dancing melody, but inwardly think intensely of their mutual relationship through the inner "stream of consciousness." The final crescendo stem-

[39] *Ibid.*

ming from the strife between Sally and Clay and the symbolic tumbling down of Wingate Hall is superb; the climax is tense, quickening, disastrous with the ironic overtones of the gay lilt of music. The last lines of the ballroom scene are reprinted below in full for your pleasure as you listen to the recording:

Sally Dupré and Wingate Talk with the Music

That's good music. It beats in your head.

(It beats in the head, it beats in the head,
It ties the heart with a scarlet thread,
This is the last,
This is the last,
Hurry, hurry, this is the last.
We dance on a floor of polished sleet,
But the little cracks are beginning to meet,
Under the play of our dancing feet.
I do not care. I am Wingate still.
The corn unground by the watermill.
And I am yours while the fiddles spill,
But my will has a knife to cut your will,
My birds will never come to your hill.

You are my foe and my only friend,
You are the steel I cannot bend,
You are the water at the world's end.

But Wingate Hall must tumble down,
Tumble down, tumble down,
A dream dissolving, a ruined thing,
Before we can melt from the shattered crown
Gold enough for a wedding-ring.
And Wingate Hall must lie in the dust,
And the wood rot and the iron rust
And the vines grow over the broken bust,
Before we meet without hate or pride,
Before we talk as lover and bride,
Before the daggers of our offence
Have the color of innocence,
And nothing is said and all is said,
And we go looking for secret bread,
And lie together in the same bed.)

Yes, it's good music, hear it lift.

(It is too mellow, it is too swift,
I am dancing alone in my naked shift,
I am dancing alone in the snowdrift.
You are my lover and you my life,
My peace and my unending strife
And the edge of the knife against my knife.
I will not make you a porcelain wife.

We are linked together for good and all,
For the still pool and the waterfall,
But you are married to Wingate Hall.
And Wingate Hall must tumble down,
Tumble down, tumble down,
Wingate Hall must tumble down,
An idol broken apart,
Before I sew on a wedding gown
And stitch my name in your heart.) [40]

STEPHEN VINCENT BENÉT

RHYTHM IN DRAMATIC POETRY

Since every enduring poem usually has dramatic power and intensity, a classification of dramatic poetry may seem superfluous. Some poets, however, dramatize the theme by means of narrative and descriptive elements supported by varying rhythms, imagery, atmosphere and mood. Keats's "The Eve of St. Agnes" has been accorded the muted richness of Renaissance tapestry depicting the romantic atmosphere of that period. In contrast, Vachel Lindsay's dramatic poem "The Congo," sometimes called a fantasy, is reminiscent in its various moods of spirituals, primitive rituals and racial superstitions expressed with the superb innate rhythms of the negro race and set in a Congo background of vivid color and vigorous vitality. Instead of muted tapestried elegance in a restrained but melodious rhythm, you are presented with impressionistic splashes of "red as wine," "diamond dust," "gold-leaf crust," "gold and ivory and elephant bone," "ebony palace," "suits of flame," highlighted by syncopated rhythmic beats as well as melodious cadences.

Although the poet gives vocal cues in the margin concerning *his* interpretation, his recording[41] shows that he must have reached an exciting high peak of chanting this poem in his troubadour travels. His marginal notes, however, indicate a wide variation in inflectional tones, pauses, vocal tempo, intensity and quality for rhythmic changes.

[40] *Ibid.*
[41] *Vachel Lindsay: Reading His Poetry.* Caedmon, TC 1041.

The Congo

A Study of the Negro Race

I. THEIR BASIC SAVAGERY

Fat black bucks in a wine-barrel room,
Barrel-house kings, with feet unstable,   *A deep rolling*
Sagged and reeled and pounded on the table,   *bass.*
Pounded on the table,
Beat an empty barrel with the handle of a broom,
Hard as they were able,
Boom, boom, BOOM,
With a silk umbrella and the handle of a broom,
Boomlay, boomlay, boomlay, BOOM.
THEN I had religion, THEN I had a vision.
I could not turn from their revel in derision.
THEN I SAW THE CONGO, CREEPING THROUGH THE   *More deliberate.*
 BLACK,   *Solemnly chanted.*
CUTTING THROUGH THE JUNGLE WITH A GOLDEN
 TRACK.
Then along that riverbank
A thousand miles
Tattooed cannibals danced in files;
Then I heard the boom of the blood-lust song
And a thigh-bone beating on a tin-pan gong.
And "Blood!" screamed the whistles and the fifes of   *A rapidly piling*
 the warriors,   *climax of speed*
"Blood!" screamed the skull-faced, lean witch-doctors; *and racket.*
"Whirl ye the deadly voo-doo rattle,
Harry the uplands,
Steal all the cattle,
Rattle-rattle, rattle-rattle,
Bing!
Boomlay, boomlay, boomlay, BOOM!"   *With a philosophic*
A roaring, epic, rag-time tune   *pause.*
From the mouth of the Congo
To the Mountains of the Moon.
Death is an Elephant,
Torch-eyed and horrible,
Foam-flanked and terrible.
BOOM, steal the pygmies,   *Shrilly and with*
BOOM, kill the Arabs,   *a heavily accented*
BOOM, kill the white men,   *metre.*
Hoo, HOO, HOO.
Listen to the yell of Leopold's ghost   *Like the wind in*
Burning in Hell for his hand-maimed host.   *the chimney.*

Hear how the demons chuckle and yell
Cutting his hands off, down in Hell.
Listen to the creepy proclamation,
Blown through the lairs of the forest-nation,
Blown past the white-ants' hill of clay,   *All the O sounds*
Blown past the marsh where the butterflies play:—   *very golden.*
"Be careful what you do,   *Heavy accents*
Or Mumbo-Jumbo, God of the Congo,   *very heavy.*
And all of the other   *Light accents*
Gods of the Congo,   *very light. Last*
Mumbo-Jumbo will hoo-doo you,   *line whispered.*
Mumbo-Jumbo will hoo-doo you,
Mumbo-Jumbo will hoo-doo you,

II. THEIR IRREPRESSIBLE HIGH SPIRITS

Wild crap-shooters with a whoop and a call   *Rather shrill and*
Danced the juba in their gambling-hall   *high.*
And laughed fit to kill, and shook the town,
And guyed the policemen and laughed them down
With a boomlay, boomlay, boomlay, BOOM. . . .
THEN I SAW THE CONGO, CREEPING THROUGH THE
     BLACK,
CUTTING THROUGH THE JUNGLE WITH A GOLDEN   *Read exactly as*
     TRACK.   *in first section.*
A negro fairyland swung into view,   *Lay emphasis on*
A minstrel river   *the delicate ideas.*
Where dreams come true.   *Keep as light-*
The ebony palace soared on high   *footed as*
Through the blossoming trees to the evening sky.   *possible.*
The inlaid porches and casements shone
With gold and ivory and elephant-bone.
And the black crowd laughed till their sides were sore
At the baboon butler in the agate door,
And the well-known tunes of the parrot band
That trilled on the bushes of that magic land.

A troupe of skull-faced witch-men came   *With pomposity.*
Through the agate doorway in suits of flame,
Yea, long-tailed coats with a gold-leaf crust
And hats that were covered with diamond-dust.
And the crowd in the court gave a whoop and a call
And danced the juba from wall to wall.
But the witch-men suddenly stilled the throng.   *With a great*
With a stern cold glare, and a stern old song: *deliberation and*
"Mumbo-Jumbo will hoo-doo you." . . .   *ghostliness.*

Just then from the doorway, as fat as shotes
Came the cake-walk princes in their long red coats,
Canes with a brilliant lacquer shine,
And tall silk hats that were red as wine.
And they pranced with their butterfly partners there,
Coal-black maidens with pearls in their hair,
Knee-skirts trimmed with the jessamine sweet,
And bells on their ankles and little black feet.
And the couples railed at the chant and the frown
Of the witch-men lean, and laughed them down.
(Oh, rare was the revel, and well worth while
That made those glowering witch-men smile.)

With overwhelming assurance, good cheer, and pomp.
With growing speed and sharply marked dance rhythm.

The cake-walk royalty then began
To walk for a cake that was tall as a man
To the tune of "Boomlay, boomlay, Boom,"
While the witch-men laughed, with a sinister air,
And sang with the scalawags prancing there:
"Walk with care, walk with care,
Or Mumbo-Jumbo, God of the Congo,
And all of the other
Gods of the Congo,
Mumbo-Jumbo will hoo-doo you,
Beware, beware, walk with care,
Boomlay, boomlay, boomlay, boom.
Boomlay, boomlay, boomlay, boom,
Boomlay, boomlay, boomlay, boom,
Boomlay, boomlay, boomlay,
Boom."
Oh, rare was the revel, and well worth while
That made those glowering witch-men smile.

With a touch of negro dialect and as rapidly as possible toward the end.

Slow philosophic calm.

III. THE HOPE OF THEIR RELIGION

A good old negro in the slums of the town
Preached at a sister for her velvet gown,
Howled at a brother for his low-down ways,
His prowling, guzzling, sneak-thief days.
Beat on the Bible till he wore it out,
Starting the jubilee revival shout.
And some had visions, as they stood on chairs,
And sang of Jacob, and the golden stairs.
And they all repented, a thousand strong,
From their stupor and savagery and sin and wrong
And slammed their hymn books till they shook the
room
With "Glory, glory, glory,"

Heavy bass.
With a literal imitation of camp-meeting racket, and trance.

And "Boom, boom, Boom."
THEN I SAW THE CONGO, CREEPING THROUGH THE   *Exactly as in the first*
    BLACK,   *section.*
CUTTING THROUGH THE JUNGLE WITH A GOLDEN
    TRACK.
And the gray sky opened like a new-rent veil
And showed the Apostles with their coats of mail.
In bright white steel they were seated round,
And their fire-eyes watched where the Congo wound.
And the twelve Apostles, from their thrones on high,
Thrilled all the forest with their heavenly cry:—   *Sung to the tune of*
"Mumbo-Jumbo will die in the jungle;   *"Hark, ten thousand*
Never again will he hoo-doo you.   *harps and voices."*
Never again will he hoo-doo you."

Then along that river, a thousand miles   *With growing delibera-*
The vine-snared trees fell down in files.   *tion and joy.*
Pioneer angels cleared the way
For a Congo paradise, for babes at play,
For sacred capitals, for temples clean.
Gone were the skull-faced witch-men lean.
There, where the wild ghost-gods had wailed   *In a rather high key—*
A million boats of the angels sailed   *as delicately as*
With oars of silver, and prows of blue   *possible.*
And silken pennants that the sun shone through.
'Twas a land transfigured, 'twas a new creation.
Oh, a singing wind swept the negro nation
And on through the backwoods clearing flew:—
"Mumbo-Jumbo is dead in the jungle.
Never again will he hoo-doo you.
Never again will he hoo-doo you."

Redeemed were the forests, the beasts and the men,
And only the vulture dared again
By the far, lone mountains of the moon
To cry, in the silence, the Congo tune:—   *Dying off into a*
"Mumbo-Jumbo will hoo-doo you,   *penetrating, terrified*
Mumbo-Jumbo will hoo-doo you.   *whisper.*
Mumbo . . . Jumbo . . . will . . . hoo-doo . . . you."[42]

VACHEL LINDSAY

You may test your versatility in making changes in vocal quality, intensity and tempo according to sound values in "The Congo." One essential attitude must be accepted: the poem can be successfully interpreted

[42] Reprinted with permission of The Macmillan Co. from THE CONGO AND
OTHER POEMS by Vachel Lindsay. Copyright 1914 by The Macmillan Co., renewed 1942 by Elizabeth C. Lindsay.

only with an alert, spirited bodily activity that shifts in tension with every change in mood, intensity and rhythm. The body must play a definite part in *suggesting* rhythm. This poem illustrates the principle that rhythm is within you; it is your muscular feeling *into*—your empathic response to the black marks—that produces the rhythmic sensation. You can interpret with many rhythms and melodies: the rhythm can be chanted effectively but is likely to become monotonous; it can be based on the beat of the tom-tom in the background—or on modern rhythms. The interesting total rhythmic pattern, however, shows a combination of various cadences that should not be bound by one type of beat. Even those who do not enjoy the poem as an artistic fantasy, nevertheless admit Lindsay's unusual ability to fit specific images into the movement.

A few hints may help you to extend yourself into a lively interpretation:

1. You should be able to hear the tom-tom rhythm in the background of the lines, "Then I saw the Congo, creeping through the black."
2. The tom-tom should beat with a more syncopated rhythm beginning "Then along that riverbank."
3. The voodoo accents build up in the lines beginning, "Be careful what you do."
4. The Charleston or even the modern dance rhythms are obvious in the lines beginning, "Wild crap-shooters with a whoop and a call."
5. The waltz tempo swings into rhythm with the lines beginning "A negro fairyland swung into view."
6. The "soft-shoe" in slow motion rhythm fits in nicely with the lines that follow "A group of skull-faced witch-men came."
7. The cake-walk bodily posture (the strut) and tempo take over on the lines beginning "Just then from the doorway as fat as shotes."
8. Again you sense the slow motion soft-shoe rhythm, finally swinging into a definite beat of the voodoo tempo beginning, "While the witch-men laughed, with a sinister air" and ends with "Boom!" You have a deep, resonant, intense tone here or rise to a climax of high intensity.
9. Instead of these tempo changes, the whole poem can follow modern impressionistic rhythms. This has been done effectively by students of interpretative art as an exercise in rhythm. Certainly empathy can be experienced from the unusual arrangement and pacing of words in this poem. This kind of rhythmic performance, however, is not a substitute for a distinctive interpretation; it will give you, however, some appreciation of how words can be put together in rhythmic cadences.

Besides these suggestions, many ways are available for you to acknowledge word quantities and apply vocal quality and intensity: in "Boomlay, boomlay, boomlay, Boom"; in "Rattle-rattle, rattle-rattle, Bing!"—try rising gradually to a high prolonged tone suggestive of the sound of the last word, "Bing!" Then note the deep vocal intensity in "Boom," compared to the high, quick tone of "steal the pygmies." The poet continues the same pattern until "Hoo, Hoo, Hoo," using either prolonged or shortened vowels, as well as various kinds of vocal quality and intensity. Other word quantities differ greatly: contrast "And a thigh-bone beating on a tin-pan gong" (stressing the *n* sound and harsh vowels) with the long drawn out tones of "burning in Hell for his hand-maimed host/ Hear how the demons chuckle and yell," and with "Mumbo-Jumbo will hoo-doo you." Then interpret the quick short quantities in "Wild crap-shooters with a whoop and a call/ Danced the juba in their gambling hall," followed by colorful passage of the cake-walk beginning, "Yea, long-tailed coats with a gold-leaf crust." Certainly no one could miss the staccato sounds suggestive of the dancing of "Coal black maidens with pearls in their hair/ Knee skirts trimmed with the jessamine sweet/ And bells on their ankles and little black feet." The images appeal to the kinesthetic sense. Visual imagery is also prevalent—both in color and contrast. You must have been conscious of the reds and golds; you must have caught the impression of the ebony palace soaring on high through the blossoming trees—with the richness of inlaid porches, casements of gold, ivory and elephant bone and the agate door—silhouetted against the evening sky.

The meaning of the poem becomes more evident after the imagery, sound values and line rhythms are sensed. To merely look at "The Congo" and decide it is a medley of sound patterns is not to do justice to the poet's meaning. First of all, if you consider the symbol of the Congo River, then you understand the progression of the three parts, climaxed in Part III with a "Congo paradise." Although Part III deviates from the first two parts in its tone and rhythm, it carries the religious undercurrent and fervor of the Negro group so that "only the vulture dared again/ By the far, lone mountains of the moon,/ (note vowel quantities) To cry in the silence, the Congo tune." An attempt has been made to help you "get the feel" of obvious rhythmical cadences of some poetic lines in the hope you can more deeply appreciate the fact that rhythm does not exist alone nor can it be isolated from literature. It is governed to a certain extent by the central meaning; by the tone, mood and atmosphere, all of which support that meaning; by syntax arrangements in which the poet's tendency to stress words gently or intensely is observable; by meter arrangement, sometimes faintly recognized as in free verse; and other times noticeably present, as in the beat of the tom-tom that can be heard and felt in Parts I and II; by imagery as expressed through word and sound patterns; by pauses for phrasing, reinforcement and suspense; and by literary devices as alliteration, rhyme, consonance, assonance. Most of all, it is determined by the poet's own rhythm, the way he feels his meaning innately, physically. In turn, your expression of it depends on your empathy to the pattern.

Thomas's "Fern Hill" is a poem with that luxurious inner longing one likes to revel in because of its strong empathic pleasure. For this reason, it has garnered many approving judgments in critical books: "luminous with all the weathers of childhood," "miraculous beauty," "the greatest threnody," "his finest composition." In an effort to be truly critical, some write of the motifs and the levels of meaning found in its lines; but surpassing everything that the poem contains are the cadences, the melody of the lines.[43] It is reprinted here for that purpose: read the lines aloud, put them through a mellowing process, bask in the goldenness and joy and gracious liberty of his memories. You will long remember the cadences of phrases like "as I was young and easy," "as the grass was green," "time let me play and be golden," "all the sun long," "it was air and playing," "all the moon long I heard," "green and golden I was huntsman," "happy as the heart was long," "golden in the heydays," "my wishes raced through the house-high hay."

Fern Hill

Now as I was young and easy under the apple boughs
About the lilting house and happy as the grass was green,
    The night above the dingle starry,
      Time let me hail and climb
    Golden in the heydays of his eyes,
And honoured among wagons I was prince of the apple towns
And once below a time I lordly had the trees and leaves
      Trail with daisies and barley
    Down the rivers of the windfall light.

And as I was green and carefree, famous among the barns
About the happy yard and singing as the farm was home,
    In the sun that is young once only,
      Time let me play and be
    Golden in the mercy of his means,
And green and golden I was huntsman and herdsman, the calves
Sang to my horn, the foxes on the hills barked clear and cold,
      And the sabbath rang slowly
    In the pebbles of the holy streams.

All the sun long it was running, it was lovely, the hay—
Fields high as the house, the tunes from the chimneys, it was air

[43] *"A Child's Christmas in Wales" and Five Poems.* Recorded by Dylan Thomas. Caedmon, TC-1002. This recording contains "Fern Hill."

And playing, lovely and watery
        And fire green as grass.
And nightly under the simple stars
As I rode to sleep the owls were bearing the farm away,
All the moon long I heard, blessed among stables, the night-jars
        Flying with the ricks, and the horses
                Flashing into the dark.

And then to awake, and the farm, like a wanderer white
With the dew, come back, the cook on his shoulder: it was all
        Shining, it was Adam and maiden,
                The sky gathered again
        And the sun grew round that very day.
So it must have been after the birth of the simple light
In the first, spinning place, the spellbound horses walking warm
        Out of the whinnying green stable
                On to the fields of praise.

And honoured among foxes and pheasants by the gay house
Under the new made clouds and happy as the heart was long,
        In the sun born over and over,
                I ran my heedless ways,
        My wishes raced through the house-high hay
And nothing I cared, at my sky blue trades, that time allows
In all his tuneful turning so few and such morning songs
        Before the children green and golden
                Follow him out of grace,

Nothing I cared, in the lamb white days, that time would take me
Up to the swallow thronged loft by the shadow of my hand,
        In the moon that is always rising,
                Nor that riding to sleep
        I should hear him fly with the high fields
And wake to the farm forever fled from the childless land.
Oh as I was young and easy in the mercy of his means,
        Time held me green and dying
        Though I sang in my chains like the sea.[44]

DYLAN THOMAS

   You are able to follow the personal development of Thomas, interwoven with the images: the carefree, ecstatic joy of the "very young-in-
heart Thomas" running heedless ways, never realizing that time allows
only a few morning songs "Before the children green and golden/Follow
him out of grace," and not caring that time would take him "Up to the

swallow thronged loft by the shadow of my hand/In the moon that is always rising/ . . . And wake to the farm forever fled from the childless land." This last stanza subtly brings his happiness and memories, with an undercurrent of regret, into focus on a minor note.

Eliot's "The Hollow Men" has been placed next because of its contrast to "Fern Hill":

The Hollow Men
Mistah Kurtz—he dead.

A penny for the Old Guy

I

We are the hollow men
We are the stuffed men
Leaning together
Headpiece filled with straw. Alas!
Our dried voices, when
We whisper together
Are quiet and meaningless
As wind in dry grass
Or rats' feet over broken glass
In our dry cellar

Shape without form, shade without colour,
Paralysed force, gesture without motion;

Those who have crossed
With direct eyes, to death's other Kingdom*
Remember us—if at all—not as lost
Violent souls, but only
As the hollow men
The stuffed men.

II

Eyes I dare not meet in dreams
In death's dream kingdom†
These do not appear:
There, the eyes are
Sunlight on a broken column
There, is a tree swinging
And voices are
In the wind's singing

* *death's other Kingdom:* over the river Acheron to Hell.
† *death's dream kingdom:* the kingdom of the hollow men, meaningless, empty.

More distant and more solemn
Than a fading star.

   Let me be no nearer
In death's dream kingdom
Let me also wear
Such deliberate disguises
Rat's coat, crowskin, crossed staves
In a field
Behaving as the wind behaves
No nearer—

   Not that final meeting
In the twilight kingdom.

III

This is the dead land
This is cactus land
Here the stone images
Are raised, here they receive
The supplication of a dead man's hand
Under the twinkle of a fading star.

   Is it like this
In death's other kingdom
Waking alone
At the hour when we are
Trembling with tenderness
Lips that would kiss
Form prayers to broken stone.

IV

The eyes are not here
There are no eyes here
In this valley of dying stars
In this hollow valley
This broken jaw of our lost kingdoms

In this last of meeting places
We grope together
And avoid speech
Gathered on this beach of the tumid river

Sightless, unless
The eyes reappear
As the perpetual star
Multifoliate rose

Of death's twilight kingdom
The hope only
Of empty men.

v

Here we go round the prickly pear
Prickly pear prickly pear
Here we go round the prickly pear
At five o'clock in the morning.

Between the idea
And the reality
Between the motion
And the act
Falls the shadow
                    For Thine is the Kingdom

Between the conception
And the creation
Between the emotion
And the response
Falls the Shadow
                    Life is very long

Between the desire
And the spasm
Between the potency
And the existence
Between the essence
And the descent
Falls the Shadow
                    For Thine is the Kingdom

For Thine is
Life is
For Thine is the

This is the way the world ends
This is the way the world ends
This is the way the world ends
Not with a bang but a whimper.[45]

T. S. Eliot

First, compare the connotations of the two titles. Then note the narrator's voice is a collective "we," which should give a certain personal approach to the dramatic poem: in this instance, however, no contact is conveyed. Instead of Thomas's surging feeling of sunlight and warmth, "all shining," the atmosphere surrounding the narrator is a dry, arid, inescapable one in a kingdom among effigies lacking meaning and vision (note the fading and dying stars as compared to the direct eyes of vision).

By what means has the poet expressed this impressively deadening tone? Eliot has first managed to secure hollowness by means of short, broken phrases that are not melodiously cadenced and die away before they are experienced. The rhythm has no lilt, life or uplift in any of the desultory moods, even in the line "Here we go round the prickly pear." He has further created empathic images by his unusual word selection: connotations and sound values that make the throat choke with rigidity, the mouth dry, the head empty of any reality, the eyes sightless and the body inert, paralyzed, groping, acted upon by the spiritual deterioration extending to the static point of nothingness. In addition to this penetration, the poet has contrived to intensify mood by almost every literary device: alliteration, consonance, assonance, repetition, rhyme—all sound values.

In searching for the meaning, decide first how the epigraphs are related to the central idea. Are Guy Fawkes and "Mistah Kurtz" alike? Is the "Old Guy," for whom children sell effigies for pennies, representative of the hollow men? How does "Mistah Kurtz," a lost, violent man, fit into the characterization of the hollow men? From what source is the conflict derived? Turn your attention to the symbols: the dying star, the Shadow, the multifoliate rose, the tumid river.

Where is the irony in Part V? This dramatic monologue offers an opportunity for variety in vocal intensity, quality and tempo. If you secure the mood, the pitch changes will follow the tone of your voice.

These next scenes from the poetic play, *Cyrano de Bergerac*, demonstrate effectively how the speech rhythm of two characters, in their responses to one another, can present a total melodious pattern, even though the phrases are sometimes broken by well-timed pauses. If you picture Cyrano as the spirited swordsman who enjoys a fight under any pretext (particularly when motivated by a remark about his enormous nose), you can then imagine how his bodily tension and attitudes fit into the silences with quick turns and actions to supplement the rhythm of his speech. He acts and speaks with great animation and spirit. (Note recording of Sir Ralph Richardson as Cyrano.[46]) Le Bret is the foil to feed Cyrano cues for his poetical expression, thus providing opportunities for increase of dramatic tension through Cyrano's *tour de force.*

[46] *Cyrano de Bergerac.* Recorded by Sir Ralph Richardson, Anna Massey, Peter Wyngard and supporting cast. Caedmon, S-306.

This first scene introduces you to Cyrano as the lover. Unfortunately, Roxane's affections favor a handsome young lover who has neither the skill, dash nor ingenuity of Cyrano—nor can he write poetry for her. Read the play to appreciate the dramatist's psychological as well as dramatic portrayal of the hero.

The second scene reveals Cyrano as a man of contradictory moods and actions: a dreamer, a proud swordsman who chooses to stand alone among his enemies, a poet whose love is unrequited. You will recognize the extrovert, covering up his heartbreak and hurts by bravado and pride.

from *Cyrano de Bergerac*

ACT I, SCENE 2

CYRANO: My old friend—look at me,
And tell me how much hope remains for me
With this protuberance! Oh I have no more
Illusions! Now and then—bah! I may grow
Tender, walking alone in the blue cool
Of evening, through some garden fresh with flowers
After the benediction of the rain;
My poor big devil of a nose inhales
April . . . and so I follow with my eyes
Where some boy, with a girl upon his arm,
Passes a patch of silver . . . and I feel
Somehow, I wish I had a woman too,
Walking with little steps under the moon,
And holding my arm so, and smiling. Then
I dream—and I forget. . . .
       And then I see
The shadow of my profile on the wall!

LE BRET: My friend! . . .

CYRANO: My friend, I have my bitter days,
Knowing myself so ugly, so alone.
Sometimes—

LE BRET: You weep?

CYRANO (*quickly*): Oh, not that ever! No,
That would be too grotesque—the tears trickling down
All the way along this nose of mine?
I will not so profane the dignity
Of sorrow. Never any tears for me!
Why there is nothing more sublime than tears,
Nothing!—Shall I make them ridiculous
In my poor person?

LE BRET: Love's no more than chance!

CYRANO (*shakes his head*): No. I love Cleopatra; do I appear

Caesar? I adore Beatrice; have I
The look of Dante?
LE BRET: But your wit—your courage—
Why, that poor child who offered you just now
Your dinner! She—you saw with your own eyes,
Her eyes did not avoid you.
CYRANO (*thoughtfully*): That is true . . .
LE BRET: Well then! Roxane herself, watching your duel,
Paler than—
CYRANO: Pale?—
LE BRET: Her lips parted, her hand
Thus, at her breast—I saw it! Speak to her!
Speak, man!
CYRANO: Through my nose? She might laugh at me;
That is the one thing in this world I fear![47]

EDMOND ROSTAND

ACT II, SCENE 1

CYRANO: . . . To sing, to laugh, to dream,
To walk in my own way and be alone,
Free, with an eye to see things as they are,
A voice that means manhood—to cock my hat
Where I choose— At a word, a *Yes*, a *No*,
To fight—or write. To travel any road
Under the sun, under the stars, nor doubt
If fame or fortune lie beyond the bourne—
Never to make a line I have not heard
In my own heart; yet, with all modesty
To say: "My soul, be satisfied with flowers,
With fruit, with weeds even; but gather them
In the one garden you may call your own."
So, when I win some triumph, by some chance,
Render no share to Caesar—in a word,
I am too proud to be a parasite,
And if my nature wants the germ that grows
Towering to heaven like the mountain pine,
Or like the oak, sheltering multitudes—
I stand, not high it may be—but alone!
LE BRET: Alone, yes!—But why stand against the world?
What devil has possessed you now, to go
Everywhere making yourself enemies?
CYRANO: Watching you other people making friends
Everywhere—as a dog makes friends! I mark
The manner of these canine courtesies

And think: "My friends are of a cleaner breed;
    Here comes—thank God!—another enemy!"
LE BRET: But this is madness!
CYRANO: Method, let us say.
    It is my pleasure to displease. I love
    Hatred. Imagine how it feels to face
    The volley of a thousand angry eyes—
    The bile of envy and the froth of fear
    Spattering little drops about me— You—
    Good nature all around you, soft and warm—
    You are like those Italians, in great cowls
    Comfortable and loose— Your chin sinks down
    Into the folds, your shoulders droop. But I—
    The Spanish ruff I wear around my throat
    Is like a ring of enemies; hard, proud,
    Each point another pride, another thorn—
    So that I hold myself erect perforce.
    Wearing the hatred of the common herd
    Haughtily, the harsh collar of Old Spain,
    At once a fetter and—a halo![48]

EDMOND ROSTAND

Frost always attains the dramatic in his poetic lines, often through understatement of climax or unusual arrangement of words to give rhythm and vocal tone or through overtones of philosophical meaning. In his two well-known dramatic sketches showing conflicting forces at play between husband and wife—"The Death of the Hired Man" and "Home Burial"— he has set his stage much as a playwright would. In the former dialogue, which is not reprinted but which you have read, he puts his characters on the back porch of a farm home; he adds special lighting with a moon shining down on Mary and a little silver cloud high overhead, as she waits for Warren's return from Silas. Frost tunes the voices to the quiet of the moonlight night; he relies on the conflict and characteristic rhythm of voices rather than overt action. He keeps you in suspense about the main character, Silas, whom you never meet but who is none-the-less developed into a distinct character as portrayed by the gentle persuasion of Mary and the efficient, brusque, masculine attitude of Warren. The quietness of the climax is prepared for by the setting, by Mary's temperate philosophy and plea to Warren to be kind to Silas. The climax is brought about by Warren's return—too soon it seemed to Mary; then sitting beside her and clasping her hand—and waiting—Warren finally utters the one word, "Dead."[49]

Now contrast this approach with that of "Home Burial."

[48] *Ibid.*
[49] *Robert Frost: Reading His Poetry*. Caedmon, 1060.

Home Burial

He saw her from the bottom of the stairs
Before she saw him. She was starting down,
Looking back over her shoulder at some fear.
She took a doubtful step and then undid it
To raise herself and look again. He spoke
Advancing toward her: "What is it you see
From up there always—for I want to know."
She turned and sank upon her skirts at that,
And her face changed from terrified to dull.
He said to gain time: "What is it you see,"
Mounting until she cowered under him.
"I will find out now—you must tell me, dear."
She, in her place, refused him any help
With the least stiffening of her neck and silence.
She let him look, sure that he wouldn't see,
Blind creature; and a while he didn't see.
But at last he murmured, "Oh," and again, "Oh."

"What is it—what?" she said.

                              "Just that I see."

"You don't," she challenged. "Tell me what it is."

"The wonder is I didn't see at once.
I never noticed it from here before.
I must be wonted to it—that's the reason.
The little graveyard where my people are!
So small the window frames the whole of it.
Not so much larger than a bedroom, is it?
There are three stones of slate and one of marble,
Broad-shouldered little slabs there in the sunlight
On the sidehill. We haven't to mind *those*.
But I understand: it is not the stones,
But the child's mound—"

                              "Don't, don't, don't, don't," she cried.

She withdrew shrinking from beneath his arm
That rested on the bannister, and slid downstairs;
And turned on him with such a daunting look,
He said twice over before he knew himself:
"Can't a man speak of his own child he's lost?"

"Not you! Oh, where's my hat? Oh, I don't need it!
I must get out of here. I must get air.

I don't know rightly whether any man can."

"Amy! Don't go to someone else this time.
Listen to me. I won't come down the stairs."
He sat and fixed his chin between his fists.
"There's something I should like to ask you, dear."

"You don't know how to ask it."

     "Help me, then."

Her fingers moved the latch for all reply.
"My words are nearly always an offense.
I don't know how to speak of anything
So as to please you. But I might be taught,
I should suppose. I can't say I see how.
A man must partly give up being a man
With women-folk. We could have some arrangement
By which I'd bind myself to keep hands off
Anything special you're a-mind to name.
Though I don't like such things 'twixt those that love.
Two that don't love can't live together without them.
But two that do can't live together with them."
She moved the latch a little. "Don't—don't go.
Don't carry it to someone else this time.
Tell me about it if it's something human.
Let me into your grief. I'm not so much
Unlike other folks as your standing there
Apart would make me out. Give me my chance.
I do think, though, you overdo it a little.
What was it brought you up to think it the thing
To take your mother-loss of a first child
So inconsolably—in the face of love.
You'd think his memory might be satisfied——"

"There you go sneering now!"

     "I'm not, I'm not!
You make me angry. I'll come down to you.
God, what a woman! And it's come to this,
A man can't speak of his own child that's dead."

"You can't because you don't know how to speak.
If you had any feelings, you that dug
With your own hand—how could you?—his little grave;

I saw you from that very window there,
Making the gravel leap and leap in air,
Leap up, like that, like that, and land so lightly
And roll back down the mound beside the hole.

I thought, Who is that man? I didn't know you.
And I crept down the stairs and up the stairs
To look again, and still your spade kept lifting.
Then you came in. I heard your rumbling voice
Out in the kitchen, and I don't know why,
But I went near to see with my own eyes.
You could sit there with the stains on your shoes
Of the fresh earth from your own baby's grave
And talk about your everyday concerns.
You had stood the spade up against the wall
Outside there in the entry, for I saw it."

"I shall laugh the worst laugh I ever laughed.
I'm cursed. God, if I don't believe I'm cursed."

"I can repeat the very words you were saying.
'Three foggy mornings and one rainy day
Will rot the best birch fence a man can build.'
Think of it, talk like that at such a time!
What had how long it takes a birch to rot
To do with what was in the darkened parlor.
You couldn't care! The nearest friends can go
With anyone to death, comes so far short
They might as well not try to go at all.
No, from the time when one is sick to death,
One is alone, and he dies more alone.
Friends make pretense of following to the grave,
But before one is in it, their minds are turned
And making the best of their way back to life
And living people, and things they understand.
But the world's evil. I won't have grief so
If I can change it. Oh, I won't, I won't!"

"There, you have said it all and you feel better.
You won't go now. You're crying. Close the door.
The heart's gone out of it: why keep it up.
Amy! There's someone coming down the road!"

"You—oh, you think the talk is all. I must go—
Somewhere out of this house. How can I make you____"

"If—you—do!" She was opening the door wider.
"Where do you mean to go? First tell me that.
I'll follow and bring you back by force, I *will!*____"[50]

ROBERT FROST

[50] From COMPLETE POEMS OF ROBERT FROST. Copyright 1916, 1921, 1923, 1928, 1930, 1939 by Holt, Rinehart and Winston, Inc. Copyright 1936, 1942, 1944, 1951, © 1956, 1958, by Robert Frost. Copyright © 1964 by Lesley Frost Ballantine. Reprinted by permission of Holt, Rinehart and Winston, Inc.

In "Home Burial," Frost again presents a husband and wife, whose conflict, as shown in the intensely disturbed and sometimes hysterical voices, arises from the sight of the mound of their dead child, whose grave the husband has just completed, and which can be seen from the window by the stairs. Frost sets this scene on that stairway, utilizing the dramatic changes of movement as the two characters take their separate places on the stairway to look through the window framing the small graveyard where the mound can be seen. This physical movement indicated in very brief, indirect stage directions adds significantly to the building of the tone of the conflicting voices. First the husband sees Amy from the bottom of the stairs as she starts down; he continues to mount, until she sinks on the stair. Then he happens to look out the window and "sees"—for the first time. The next movement shows his wife shrinking from beneath his arm that rests on the bannister and sliding down the stairs. Now he is above her; he sits on the stairs and fixes his chin between his fists. She has moved to the door; her fingers move the latch slightly; then she begins to cry; her fingers on the latch are opening the door wider—wider—and she is gone, as her husband's voice rises to the last word, "I'll follow and bring you back by force. I *will!—*"

The poet also cues you into the emotional reactions of his characters. Note these phrases: "She took a doubtful step"; "her face changed from terrified to dull"; "she cowered under him"; "the least stiffening of her neck and silence." Only a dramatist could arrange the movements and reactions of this scene so cleverly within such a short time to point up the crescendo of voices, permitting the emotional gap between husband and wife to become wider as the door opens wider—and Amy is gone. This significant movement, this great tension and conflict, as well as the wife's hysteria, are in direct contrast to the general tempo of "The Death of the Hired Man."

In each dialogue, however, Frost plunges you into the climax of a series of events in which you have not participated. In "Home Burial," you become aware of the previous incidents which have keyed this particular action to a high emotional pitch. You learn shortly what the husband has done and what he has said to make his wife hysterical. Then you begin to wonder about their lack of sensitivity and understanding for one another. Is there another undercurrent which has precipitated this emotional outburst on the part of Amy? Is the husband, covering his grief with the physical effort of digging the grave and talking about the birch rot to show outward control? Then his plea—"Don't go to some one else this time"—intimates that these two married people had not reached a unified happiness even before the death of their child. Grief can easily upset one's emotional balance, but the cry of the mother seems to go deeper than this incident. Think over the responses of each character to find, if you can, the emotional timbre of each. With which one do you empathize?

In the interpretation of this scene, you must watch the tempo controlling the interlocking of the speech responses, the interplay of interruptions that moves the scene rhythmically and also reveals in the timing two different temperaments. In the speech rhythm of each one, Frost gives tonal reality and quality to his characters and so, to the incident. It talks —it moves rapidly—by means of "speech" characterization. The tonal inflections are emphasized by repetitions and pauses, thus giving the "heard" voice of the characters. Think over the pitch changes as well as intensity, quality and rhythm, that will be most effective in the following phrases: "But at last he murmured, 'Oh,' and again 'Oh.'" (Try variations of pitch on the *Oh* and watch the pauses.); "What is it—what!" "Don't, don't, don't, don't," she cried. (What of the crescendo here?); "Don't— don't go." "I'm not, I'm not." "I shall laugh the worst laugh I ever laughed. I'm cursed. God, if I don't believe I'm cursed."; "You *couldn't* care."; "If— you—do!"; "I *will*—" (What do the italics and dash do for the meaning?).

Certainly these two dramatic dialogues fulfill Frost's belief that poems must be different in approach, thought and character. Since climax has been discussed recently, center your interest on how one incident drops to a climax of understatement and the other builds to near-hysteria, with no denouement or completion of future action.

BALLADS

Now turn your attention to the special narrative poem, the ballad, usually expressed through understatement. The following group suggests varying rhythms. Try to make each poem distinctive inasmuch as no two are alike. You will recognize the early folk ballad, the later ballad with its lighter tone and joyous refrain, the parody, the famous barrack-room ballad and the most notable nineteenth-century literary ballad.

The first poem, "The Twa Corbies" (ravens), belongs to the folk group. The suggested irony is worth your attention: the murder of the knight provides food for the ravens and permits the maid to go to her lover.

The Twa Corbies

As I was walking all alane,
I heard two corbies making a mane;*
The tane unto the t'other say,
"Where sall we gang and dine today?"

"In behint yon auld fail dyke,†
I wot there lies a new-slain knight;

* *mane:* moan.
† *dyke:* old turf wall.

And naebody kens that he lies there,
But his hawk, his hound, and lady fair.

"His hound is to the hunting gane,
His hawk to fetch the wild-fowl hame,
His lady's ta'en another mate,
So we may mak our dinner sweet.

"Ye'll sit on his white hause-bane,°
And I'll pick out his bonny blue een;
Wi ae lock o' his dowden hair
We'll theek our nest when it grows bare.

"Mony a one for him makes mane,
But nane sall ken where he is gane:
O'er his white banes when they are bare,
The wind sall blaw for evermair."

Bartlett Jere Whiting adds an interesting note to this well-known folk ballad of a lady's hard-heartedness toward her lover. He writes that Samuel Pepys enjoyed the ballad, but "some of the pleasure may have come from its singer, the actress Mrs. Knepp, to whom Pepys was devotedly attached.[51] So sing it!

Bonny Barbara Allan

It was in and about the Martinmas time,
    When the green leaves were a falling,
That Sir John Græme, in the West Country,
    Fell in love with Barbara Allan.

He sent his man down through the town,
    To the place where she was dwelling:
"O haste and come to my master dear,
    Gin ye be Barbara Allan."

O hooly, hooly rose she up,
    To the place where he was lying,
And when she drew the curtain by,
    "Young man, I think you're dying."

"O it's I'm sick, and very, very sick,
    And 't is a' for Barbara Allan:"

° *hause-bane:* neck-bone.

[51] Bartlett Jere Whiting, ed., *Traditional British Ballads* (New York: Appleton-Century-Crofts, 1955), p. 39.

"O the better for me ye's never be,
    Tho your heart's blood were a spilling.

"O dinna ye mind, young man," said she,
    "When ye was in the tavern a drinking,
That ye made the healths gae round and round,
    And slighted Barbara Allan?"

He turnd his face unto the wall,
    And death was with him dealing:
"Adieu, adieu, my dear friends all,
    And be kind to Barbara Allan."

And slowly, slowly raised she up,
    And slowly, slowly left him,
And sighing said, she could not stay,
    Since death of life had reft him.

She had not gane a mile but twa,
    When she heard the dead-bell ringing,
And every jow that the dead-bell geid,
    It cry'd, "Woe to Barbara Allan!"

"O mother, mother, make my bed!
    O make it saft and narrow!
Since my love died for me to-day,
    I'll die for him to-morrow."

"Get Up and Bar the Door" offers a change in subject matter. Note the appeal of the domestic incident and the brevity with which it is treated in this version. What phrase in the last stanza brings about the humorous climax?

Get Up and Bar the Door

It fell about the Martinmas time,
    And a gay time it was then,
When our goodwife got puddings to make,
    And she's boild them in the pan.

The wind sae cauld blew south and north,
    And blew into the floor;
Quoth our goodman to our goodwife,
    "Gae out and bar the door."

"My hand is in my hussyfskap,
   Goodman, as ye may see;
An it should nae be barrd this hundred year,
   It's no be barrd for me."

They made a paction tween them twa,
   They made it firm and sure,
That the first word whaeer shoud speak,
   Shoud rise and bar the door.

Then by there came two gentlemen,
   At twelve o'clock at night,
And they could neither see house nor hall,
   Nor coal nor candle-light.

"Now whether is this a rich man's house,
   Or whether is it a poor?"
But neer a word wad ane o them speak,
   For barring of the door.

And first they ate the white puddings,
   And then they ate the black;
Tho muckle thought the goodwife to hersel,
   Yet neer a word she spake.

Then said the one unto the other,
   "Here, man, tak ye my knife;
Do ye tak aff the auld man's beard.
   Ann I'll kiss the goodwife."

"But there's nae water in the house,
   And what shall we do than?"
"What ails ye at the pudding-broo,
   That boils into the pan?"

O up then started our goodman,
   An angry man was he:
"Will ye kiss my wife before my een,
   And scad me wi pudding-bree?"

Then up and started our goodwife,
   Gied three skips on the floor:
"Goodman, you've spoken the foremost word,
   Get up and bar the door!"

On the light side, this old English ballad may catch your fancy:

Robin-a-thrush

Old Robin-a-thrush he married a wife
With a hoppitty moppitty mow now.
She proved to be the plague of his life.
With a hig jig jiggitty, ruffetty petticoat,
Robin-a-thrush cries mow now.

She never gets up till twelve o'clock
With a hoppitty moppitty mow now.
Puts on her gown and above it her smock.
With a hig jig jiggitty, ruffetty petticoat,
Robin-a-thrush cries mow now.

Her butter she made in an old man's boot
With a hoppitty moppitty mow now.
And to churn it well she put in her foot.
With a hig jig jiggitty, ruffetty petticoat,
Robin-a-thrush cries mow now.

Her cheese when made was put on the shelf
With a hoppitty moppitty mow now.
And it never was turned till it turned itself.
With a hig jig jiggitty ruffetty petticoat,
Robin-a-thrush cries mow now.

This song it was made for gentlemen
With a hoppitty moppitty mow now.
If you want any more you must sing it again.
With a hig jig jiggitty ruffetty petticoat,
Robin-a-thrush cries mow now.

Many have sung:

Johnny at the Fair

Oh dear, what can the matter be!
Dear, dear, what can the matter be!
Oh, dear, what can the matter be
Johnny's so long at the fair!

He promised to bring me a faring to please me,
And then for a kiss, oh he said he would tease me.
He promised to buy me a bunch of blue ribbons
To tie up my bonnie brown hair.

> *Oh dear, what can the matter be!*
> *Dear, dear, what can the matter be!*
> *Oh, dear, what can the matter be*
> *Johnny's so long at the fair!*

He promised to buy me a basket of posies,
  A garland of lilies, a garland of roses,
A little straw hat to set off the blue ribbons
  That tie up my bonnie brown hair.

> *Oh dear, what can the matter be!*
> *Dear, dear, what can the matter be!*
> *Oh, dear, what can the matter be*
> *Johnny's so long as the fair!*

In Dame Edith Evans's recording of Carroll's ballad-parody, "Father William,"[52] you hear an excellent demonstration of how not to dawdle in the interpretation of the poem. Her spirited timing provides the light, humorous touch that would not be noticeable in a slowly-paced rhythm. The question-and-answer technique is reminiscent of the folk ballad.

Father William

"You are old, Father William," the young man said,
  "And your hair has become very white;
And yet you incessantly stand on your head—
  Do you think, at your age, it is right?"

"In my youth," Father William replied to his son,
  "I feared it might injure the brain;
But, now that I'm perfectly sure I have none,
  Why, I do it again and again."

"You are old," said the youth, "as I mentioned before,
  And have grown most uncommonly fat;
Yet you turned a back-somersault in at the door—
  Pray, what is the reason of that?"

"In my youth," said the sage, as he shook his gray locks,
  "I kept all my limbs very supple

---

[52] *The Voice of Poetry*, sponsored by the National Council of Teachers of English, and recorded by Dame Edith Evans. Columbia MM, 375. In this recording, you will note the fine quality of Evans's voice, well-sustained tones, but which sometimes die out at the end of a phrase. There is excellent contrast, however, between her rollicking cadences of the lullaby, "Sweet and Low," compared to the clipped abruptness of "Father William." Her interpretation of Blake's "The Tiger" will also interest you.

By the use of this ointment—one shilling the box—
   Allow me to sell you a couple?"

"You are old," said the youth, "and your jaws are too weak
   For anything tougher than suet;
Yet you finished the goose, with the bones and the beak—
   Pray, how did you manage to do it?"

"In my youth," said the father, "I took to the law,
   And argued each case with my wife;
And the muscular strength which it gave to my jaw
   Has lasted the rest of my life."

"You are old," said the youth, "one would hardly suppose
   That your eye was as steady as ever;
Yet you balanced an eel on the end of your nose—
   What made you so awfully clever?"

"I have answered three questions, and that is enough,"
   Said his father. "Don't give yourself airs!
Do you think I can listen all day to such stuff?
   Be off, or I'll kick you down-stairs!"

                            LEWIS CARROLL

You may be interested to know that Carroll supposedly wrote "Father William" as a parody on Heywood's poem:

Jack and His Father

"Jack," quoth his father, "how shall I ease take?
If I stand, my legs ache; and if I kneel
My knees ache; if I go, then my feet ache;
If I lie, my back aches; if I sit, I feel
My hips ache; and lean I never so weel,
My elbows ache." "Sir," quoth Jack, "pain to exile,
Since all these ease not, best ye hang awhile."

                            JOHN HEYWOOD

An interpretation of Kipling's "Gunga Din" must have the cockney vowels and intonational stress to characterize the rhythm. "Din" is pronounced "Deen," rhyming with *spleen, been, green.* If you recall the pronduction of *My Fair Lady,* the memory of the cockney speech rhythm and the songs, "With a Little Bit of Luck" and "Get Me to the Church on Time," may help you to swing into the rhythm of the narrator, even though the mood is different. Intensity and rhythmical stress at the end of each stanza must be watched, particularly the noticeable change in the last lines. The story is alive with vitality so empathic response should not be difficult.

Gunga Din

You may talk o' gin an' beer
When you're quartered safe out 'ere,
An, you're sent to penny-fights an' Aldershot it;
But when it comes to slaughter
You will do your work on water,
An' you'll lick the bloomin' boots of 'im that's got it.
Now in Injia's sunny clime,
Where I used to spend my time
A-servin' of 'Er Majesty the Queen,
Of all them black-faced crew
The finest man I knew
Was our regimental *bhisti,*° Gunga Din.

    It was "Din! Din! Din!
    You limping lump o' brick-dust, Gunga Din!
    Hi! *slippy hitherao!*†
    Water, get it! *Panee lao!*‡
    You squidgy-nosed old idol, Gunga Din!"

The uniform 'e wore
Was nothin' much before,
An' rather less than 'arf o' that be'ind,
For a twisty piece o' rag
An' a goatskin water-bag
Was all the field-equipment 'e could find.
When the sweatin' troop-train lay
In a sidin' through the day,
Where the 'eat would make your bloomin' eyebrows crawl,
We shouted "*Harry By!*"§
Till our throats were bricky-dry,
Then we wopped 'im 'cause 'e couldn't serve us all.

    It was "Din! Din! Din!
    You 'eathen, where the mischief 'ave you been?
    You put some *juldee*‖ in it,

° *bhisti:* water-carrier.
† *slippy hitherao:* make it on the double over here.
‡ *panee lao:* bring water quickly.
§ "*Harry by!*": "Hey, you!"
‖ *juldee:* speed.

Or I'll *marrow** you this minute,
If you don't fill up my helmet, Gunga Din!"

'E would dot an' carry one
Till the longest day was done,
An' 'e didn't seem to know the use o' fear.
If we charged or broke or cut,
You could bet your bloomin' nut,
'E'd be waitin' fifty paces right flank rear.
With 'is *mussick*† on 'is back,
'E would skip with our attack,
An' watch us till the bugles made "Retire."
An' for all 'is dirty 'ide,
'E was white, clear white, inside
When 'e went to tend the wounded under fire!

It was "Din! Din! Din!
With the bullets kickin' dust-spots on the green.
When the cartridges ran out,
You could 'ear the front-files shout:
"Hi! ammunition-mules an' Gunga Din!"

I sha'n't forgit the night
When I dropped be'ind the fight,
With a bullet where my belt-plate should 'a' been.
I was chokin' mad with thirst,
An' the man that spied me first
Was our good old grinnin', gruntin' Gunga Din.
'E lifted up my 'ead,
An' 'e plugged me where I bled,
An' 'e guv me 'arf-a-pint o' water—green;
It was crawlin' an' it stunk,
But of all the drinks I've drunk,
I'm gratefulest to one from Gunga Din.

It was "Din! Din! Din!
'Ere's a beggar with a bullet through 'is spleen;
'E's chawin' up the ground
An' 'e's kickin' all around:
For Gawd's sake, git the water, Gunga Din!"

'E carried me away
To where a *dooli*‡ lay,
An' a bullet come an' drilled the beggar clean.
'E put me safe inside,

* *marrow:* strike.
† *mussick:* large container for water made of hide.
‡ *dooli:* a litter, usually with canvas cover and wheels.

An' just before 'e died:
"I 'ope you liked your drink," sez Gunga Din.
So I'll meet 'im later on
In the place where 'e is gone—
Where it's always double drill and no canteen;
'E'll be squattin' on the coals
Givin' drink to pore damned souls,
An' I'll get a swig in Hell from Gunga Din!

Din! Din! Din!
You Lazarushian-leather* Gunga Din!
Tho' I've belted you an' flayed you,
By the livin' Gawd that made you,
You're a better man than I am, Gunga Din![53]

RUDYARD KIPLING

Dip into the pages of *The Hobbit*[54] for ballads with various rhythms. Note how the character and quantity value of the words and phrasing establish the movement of the song: the deep-throated sweet singing of the dwarves with the accompaniment of their fiddles, flutes, clarinets, drum, viols and gold harp in "Far Over the Misty Mountains Cold" as well as their juggling "Chip the Glasses and Crack the Plates"; the goblins singing and shaking their prisoners, as they keep time with the "flap of their flat feet" in "Clap! Snap! the Black Crack!"; Bilbo's attempt to infuriate the spiders with his "Old Fat Spider Spinning in the Tree"; the barrel ballad, "Down the Swift Dark Stream You Go"; and the elves greeting Bilbo on his return, "Come! Tra-la-la-lally!" Try to feel the rhythmical melody so that you too can sing as the elves, goblins and dwarves.

The literary ballad of Keats, "La Belle Dame Sans Merci," has been placed in this collection of narrative poems. Compare your interpretation of this ballad with Richardson's in his recording of *The Poetry of Keats.*[55]

La Belle Dame Sans Merci

BALLAD

"O what can ail thee, knight-at-arms,
Alone and palely loitering!

* *Lazarushian-leather:* a combination of two allusions: *Lazarus,* the water-carrier who was taken to "Abraham's bosom" by the angels (Luke 16:19) and *Russian leather,* hides tanned to make them especially supple and durable.

[53] "Gunga Din" from DEPARTMENTAL DITTIES AND BALLADS AND BARRACK-ROOM BALLADS by Rudyard Kipling. Published in the United States by Doubleday & Company, Inc.

[54] J. R. R. Tolkien, *The Hobbit* (Boston: Houghton Mifflin Company, 1965).

[55] *The Poetry of Keats.* Recorded by Sir Ralph Richardson, Caedmon TC-1087.

The sedge has wither'd from the lake,
    And no birds sing.

"O what can ail thee, knight-at-arms!
    So haggard and so woe-begone?
The squirrel's granary is full,
    And the harvest's done.

"I see a lily on thy brow
    With anguish moist and fever dew,
And on thy cheeks a fading rose
    Fast withereth too."

"I met a lady in the meads,
    Full beautiful—a faery's child,
Her hair was long, her foot was light,
    And her eyes were wild.

"I made a garland for her head,
    And bracelets too, and fragrant zone;
She look'd at me as she did love,
    And made sweet moan.

"I set her on my pacing steed,
    And nothing else saw all day long.
For sidelong would she bend, and sing
    A faery's song.

"She found me roots of relish sweet,
    And honey wild, and manna dew,
And sure in language strange she said—
    'I love thee true.'

"She took me to her elfin grot,
    And there she wept, and sigh'd full sore,
And there I shut her wild wild eyes
    With kisses four.

"And there she lullèd me asleep,
    And there I dream'd—ah! woe betide!—
The latest dream I ever dream'd
    On the cold hill's side.

"I saw pale kings, and princes too,
    Pale warriors, death-pale were they all;
They cried—'La Belle Dame sans Merci
    Hath thee in thrall!'

"I saw their starv'd lips in the gloam,
  With horrid warning gapèd wide;
And I awoke, and found me here
  On the cold hill's side.

"And this is why I sojourn here,
  Alone and palely loitering,
Though the sedge is wither'd from the lake,
  And no birds sing."

JOHN KEATS

Keats provides the ethereal atmosphere of fantasy by dream images that suggest the faery-like, romantic world of unreality; the world of *La Belle Dame*, who sang a faery's song; the world where the narrator "saw pale kings and princes too,/Pale warriors, death pale were they all." So the climax is reached in deathly pale images; and the denouement is planned most effectively by the repetition of the first stanza with its "unfinished" desolate line, "And no birds sing."

Do you think "La Belle Dame" is the symbol of woman's treachery or unfaithfulness—as many do? How does Keats employ the folk-ballad technique: point of view; narrative element as it involves the factor of time; expansion of theme; dramatic tone and dialogue; atmosphere and mood; metaphorical language; refrain.

LYRICS

In this group of lyrics, integrate rhythm with meaning, tone, mood and atmosphere. In other words, decide on the tone or attitude of the narrator and adapt lightness or heaviness of attack accordingly, as well as determining the best vocal quality for the general effectiveness. Then decide whether or not your interpretation fits the rhythm. If you change one vocal element, probably you will have to adjust the others for the desired total impression.

Watch the vowel quantities, rhyme schemes, pauses necessary for phrasing, reinforcement, suspense; also the poet's caesuras and fulcrums. An audience always empathizes with lyrical rhythm if the body and voice of the interpreter seem to be in tune with the poem.

In his recording,[56] Sarett tells the delightful story of this Indian lullaby. The poet's control of rhythm, sensitive softness of attack, sustained pauses, should motivate you to be aware of lyrical possibilities. Remember that a lullaby never becomes more intense in attack but dies away with the slumber of the child.

[56] *Lew Sarett: Reading from His Collected Poems.* Columbia, XTV-15494, 15495.

Wéeng

(AN INDIAN SLUMBER-SONG)

Hush! my baby, or soon you will hear
The Sleepy-eye, Wéeng-oosh, hovering near;
Out of the timber he will come,
A little round man as small as your thumb.
Swinging his torch of a red fire-fly,
Out of the shadows old Sleepy-eye,
With sound of a ghost, on the wind will creep
To see if a little boy lies alseep;
Over your cheeks old Wéeng will go,
With feet as soft as the falling snow—
Tip-toe . . . . tip-toe.

Hush! my little one, close your lids tight,
Before old Sleepy-eye comes to-night;
Hi-yáh! if he finds you are still awake,
He draws from his quiver a thistledown stake;
With an acorn for club he pounds on its butt,
Till Sleepy-eye hammers the open eye shut;
Then from his bundle he pulls out another,
Hops over your nose and closes the other;
Up and down with his club he will rap
On the open lid till he closes the gap—
Tap-tap . . . . tap-tap.

If Wéeng-oosh comes at the end of this day,
And finds you asleep he will hurry away . . .
Do you hear him cry on the winds that blow?—
And walk on the earth as soft as a doe?—
To-and-fro . . . . to-and-fro. . .
Hi-yáh! he has crept away from my lap!
For he found my little boy taking a nap.
Oh, weep no more and whisper low,
I hear the feet of Sleepy-eye go—
Tip-toe . . . . tip-toe.[57]

LEW SARETT

Siegfried Sassoon, a war poet, is known for his bitter, ironic tones. This lyric, however, sings its way into your heart with its unrestrained joy of *every one* singing the song of great freedom. The poem creates em-

[57] From COVENANT WITH EARTH, by Lew Sarett. Gainesville: University of Florida Press, 1956. Reprinted by permission of Mrs. Lew Sarett.

pathy as the melody suddenly soars like the flight of recently imprisoned birds, "winging wildly across the white/Orchard and dark green fields; on; on; . . ."

Every One Sang

Every one suddenly burst out singing;
And I was filled with such delight
As prisoned birds must find in freedom
Winging wildly across the white
Orchard and dark green fields; on; on; and out of sight.

Every one's voice was suddenly lifted,
And beauty came like the setting sun.
My heart was shaken with tears; and horror
Drifted away. . . O but every one
Was a bird; and the song was wordless; the singing will never be done.[58]

SIEGFRIED SASSOON

Someone has written somewhere that an appropriate subtitle to this flying bit of rhythm would be "The Short Happy Life of the Little Man Who Was Carried Away by a Kite." Be sure to keep him in the air "far beyond far," and do not drop him on the last line.

'o by the by'

o by the by
has anybody seen
little you-i
who stood on a green
hill and threw
his wish at blue

with a swoop and a dart
out flew his wish
(it dived like a fish
but it climbed like a dream)
throbbing like a heart
singing like a flame

[58] From COLLECTED POEMS OF SIEGFRIED SASSOON. Copyright 1920 by E. P. Dutton & Co., 1948 by Siegfried Sassoon. Reprinted by permission of The Viking Press, Inc.

blue took it my
far beyond far
and high beyond high
bluer took it your
but bluest took it our
away beyond where

what a wonderful thing
is the end of a string
(murmurs little you-i
as the hill becomes nil)
and will somebody tell
me why people let go[59]

E. E. CUMMINGS

This Sandburg lyric is not typical of the poet's great spirit extolling American democracy nor of his free verse rhythm. For those who have difficulty sensing the rhythm of his verse, here is a poem with an intriguing and satisfying pulse. Watch the timing of the pauses; do not hurry if you wish to express the melody.

The Great Hunt

I cannot tell you now;
    When the wind's drive and whirl
    Blow me along no longer,
    And the wind's a whisper at last—
Maybe I'll tell you then—
                    some other time.

    When the rose's flash to the sunset
    Reels to the wrack and the twist,
    And the rose is a red bygone,
    When the face I love is going
    And the gate to the end shall clang,
    And it's no use to beckon or say, "So long"—
Maybe I'll tell you then—
                    some other time.

I never knew any more beautiful than you:
    I have hunted you under my thoughts,
    I have broken down under the wind

And into the roses looking for you.
I shall never find any

greater than you.[60]

CARL SANDBURG

If you listen intently as you read Auden's poem aloud several times, the melody of the lines expressing the various rhythms of the sea movements will enter "the channels of the ear" so that you may catch the "swaying sound of the sea." Auden uses his rhyme schemes subtly by means of near-rhymes as in "ledges" and "lodges," and "chalk," "pluck," "knock"; end and internal rhymes, especially words ending in "er,"—"stranger," "discover," "wander," "harbour," "mirror," "summer," "water," "saunter." Interpret the rhythm of these lines based on sound values, "When the chalk wall falls to the foam and its tall ledges/Oppose the pluck/And knock of the tide,/And the shingle scrambles after the sucking surf." In other words, visualize and sense what the water is doing—rhythmically.

Look, Stranger, on This Island Now

Look, stranger, on this island now
The leaping light for your delight discovers
Stand stable here
And silent be,
That through the channels of the ear
May wander like a river
The swaying sound of the sea.

Here at the small field's ending pause
When the chalk wall falls to the foam and its tall ledges
Oppose the pluck
And knock of the tide,
And the shingle scrambles after the sucking surf,
And the gull lodges
A moment on its sheer side.

Far off like floating seeds the ships
Diverge on urgent voluntary errands,
And the full view
Indeed may enter
And move in memory as now these clouds do,

[60] From CHICAGO POEMS by Carl Sandburg. Copyright 1916 by Holt, Rinehart and Winston, Inc. Copyright 1944 by Carl Sandburg. Reprinted by permission of Holt, Rinehart and Winston, Inc.

That pass the harbour mirror
And all the summer through the water saunter.[61]

W. H. AUDEN

John Crowe Ransom will always startle you because he appears to be so immune to any sentiment. You can expect "objectivity plus" in the expression of his meaning; strangely enough, however, you discover rhythmic cadences in his cool appraisals. Note how the last line of the first three stanzas of "Blue Girls" leaves you suspended in doubt; and how the last line of the fourth stanza clinches his unhappy exhortation of the future.

Ciardi,[62] with his typical insight, points out how Ransom sometimes selects words for their root meanings rather than for the meaning involving present habitual usage: for instance, "publish" in this poem has the root meaning "to make public" rather than to "issue" a book, journal or newspaper; "establish," in the same way, means "to make stable." So too he suggests that "practice" and "perfection," which you might check in the dictionary, express added meaning through their root meanings. Do you find irony in the word "blue"?

Blue Girls

Twirling your blue skirts, traveling the sward
Under the towers of your seminary,
Go listen to your teachers old and contrary
Without believing a word.

Tie the white fillets then about your lustrous hair
And think no more of what will come to pass
Than bluebirds that go walking on the grass
And chattering on the air.

Practice your beauty, blue girls, before it fail;
And I will cry with my loud lips and publish
Beauty which all our power shall never establish,
It is so frail.

For I could tell you a story which is true:
I know a lady with a terrible tongue,
Blear eyes fallen from blue,

[61] Copyright 1937 and renewed 1964 by W. H. Auden. Reprinted from THE COLLECTED POETRY OF W. H. AUDEN, by permission of Random House, Inc.
[62] John Ciardi, *How Does a Poem Mean* (Boston: Houghton Mifflin Company, 1959), p. 803.

> All her perfections tarnished—and yet it is not long
> Since she was lovelier than any of you.[63]

JOHN CROWE RANSOM

If you enjoy Marianne Moore's poetry, then you expect a distinctive, near-scientific and objective approach in her poems; also unusual relationships in contrasts and similarities among objects and ideas; strange word groupings and vivid color combinations—almost reminiscent of Hopkins; images that have precision without any lush softness conveyed. If you expect these characteristics, as well as irregularity of lines, you will not be disappointed. Certainly you will not fall into a deep relaxing pose because of a cadenced rhythm that lulls you into peaceful inertia and meditation. Instead you will find yourself going back over phrases, wondering if in some way you have missed a phrase or two as you try to ease into the next relationship of quite dissimilar objects.

Her structural pattern is irregular but the startling metaphorical expressions overshadow the unusual "Moore" forms, which appear to be a technique to emphasize "sense" stress and accent. The phrases in themselves have a distinctive rhythm but they are often interspersed with bits of philosophy that do not permit a flow of cadences. The mind to her is "an enchanting thing like the glaze on a katydid-wing" (here is a rhythmic phrase). The octopus is "deceptively reserved and flat" with "dots of cyclamen-red and maroon on its clearly defined pseudo-podia" (you are startled), "creeping slowly as with meditated stealth" (you are kinesthetically aware of danger)—and more than that he kills his prey with the "concentric crushing rigour of the python" (you writhe in empathy). How do you react to "picking periwinkles from the cracks" (crackles delicately with plosive sounds)? And of the snail, who but Moore could find the relationship—"if 'compression is the first grace of style,'/you have it" (phrase from Demetrius *On Style*); or of the crape myrtle, "the stiff-leafed tree's blue-/pink dregs-of-wine pyramids/of mathematical/circularity" (colorful, circular rhythm). Her images are formed into sharply etched similes and metaphors, restrained in sensuous appeal but unique in intellectual approach—much like the scientist who knows anatomical structure, which was part of Moore's early training.

Try the rhythm of "Peter":

Peter

Strong and slippery, built for the midnight grass-party
confronted by four cats,

[63] Copyright 1927 by Alfred A. Knopf, Inc. Renewed 1955 by John Crowe Ransom. Reprinted from SELECTED POEMS, Revised Edition, by John Crowe Ransom, by permission of Alfred A. Knopf, Inc.

he sleeps his time away—the detached first claw on the
      foreleg, which corresponds
to the thumb, retracted to its tip; the small tuft of
      fronds
   or katydid-legs above each eye, still numbering the
        units in each group;
     the shadbones regularly set about the mouth, to
        droop or rise

in unison like the porcupine's quills—motionless. He
        lets himself be flat-
tened out by gravity, as it were a piece of seaweed
        tamed and weakened by
exposure to the sun; compelled when extended, to lie
     stationary. Sleep is the result of his delusion
        that one must do as
     well as one can for himself; sleep—epitome of
        what is to

him as to the average person, the end of life. Demonstrate
        to him how
the lady caught the dangerous southern snake, placing a
        forked stick on either
side of its innocuous neck; one need not try to stir
     him up; his prune-shaped head and alligator eyes are
        not a party to the
        joke. Lifted and handled, he may be dangled like an
        eel or set

up on the forearm like a mouse; his eyes bisected by pupils
        of a pin's
width, are flickeringly exhibited, then covered up. May
        be? I should say
might have been; when he has been got the better of in a
     dream—as in a fight with nature or with cats—we all
        know it. Profound sleep is
     not with him a fixed illusion. Springing about with
        froglike ac-

curacy, emitting jerky cries when taken in the hand, he is
        himself
again; to sit caged by the rungs of a domestic chair would
        be unprofit-
able—human. What is the good of hypocrisy? It
     is permissible to choose one's employment, to abandon
        the wire nail, the
     roly-poly, when it shows signs of being no longer a
        pleas-

ure, to score the adjacent magazine with a double line of
      strokes. He can
talk, but insolently says nothing. What of it? When one
      is frank, one's very
presence is a compliment. It is clear that he can see
      the virtue of naturalness, that he is one of those who
         do not regard
      the published fact as a surrender. As for the disposi-
         tion

invariably to affront, an animal with claws wants to have to
      use
them; that eel-like extension of trunk into tail is not an
      accident. To
leap, to lengthen out, divide the air—to purloin, to pur-
      sue.
    To tell the hen: fly over the fence, go in the wrong
        way in your perturba-
      tion—this is life; to do less would be nothing but
        dishonesty.[64]

MARIANNE MOORE

In contrast to Moore's poem, Theodore Roethke's "Big Wind" moves as the big wind-waves with a terrific velocity until the quiet of the last two lines is reached. The poet shows in much of his poetry a compulsive spirit characteristic of intensive moods and action, like the memory of the torrential onslaught on the Michigan greenhouse of his childhood. This background serves symbolically in many of his later poems as the origin and ending of the life-span.

Big Wind

Where were the greenhouses going,
Lunging into the lashing
Wind driving water
So far down the river
All the faucets stopped?—
So we drained the manure-machine
For the steam plant,
Pumping the stale mixture
Into the rusty boilers,
Watching the pressure gauge

Waver over to red,
As the seams hissed
And the live steam
Drove to the far
End of the rose-house,
Where the worst wind was,
Creaking the cypress window-frames,
Cracking so much thin glass
We stayed all night,
Stuffing the holes with burlap;
But she rode it out,
That old rose-house,
She hove into the teeth of it,
The core and pith of that ugly storm,
Ploughing with her stiff prow,
Bucking into the wind-waves
That broke over the whole of her,
Flailing her sides with spray,
Flinging long strings of wet across the roof-top,
Finally veering, wearing themselves out, merely
Whistling thinly under the wind-vents;
She sailed into the calm morning,
Carrying her full cargo of roses.[65]

THEODORE ROETHKE

The literary devices employed in the selection and arrangement of words and phrases in the Roethke poem provide the force and movement which give urgency and intensity to the rhythmical pattern. Listen to the poet's sensitive but powerful interpretation.[66]

To summarize: the many elements merged into the creation of poetic rhythm permit a more elusive pattern of movement than meter which can be diagramed or scanned. Knowledge of the classical metrical patterns will not produce an interpreter—it may only help one to understand poetic structure and to speak the literary language—and so appear knowledgeable.

RHYTHMICAL PATTERNS IN PROSE

The rhythm of prose does not have the "felt" concentration of movement found in a poem. The essay, story, novel, drama, as artistic produc-

[65] "Big Wind" by Theodore Roethke. Copyright 1947 by the United Chapters of Phi Beta Kappa. From the book, THE LOST SON AND OTHER POEMS by Theodore Roethke. Reprinted by permission of Doubleday & Company, Inc.

[66] *Words for the Wind and Other Poems.* Recorded by Theodore Roethke. Folk, 9736.

tions and experiences, will have a pattern conceived on an expanded playing board, the manner depending on how the writer wishes to use his controls. The essayist, in his animated personal writing, has a kind of over-all pattern growing out of his reactions to his subject. He takes the plunge without much ado in order to catch the attention of the reader. The novelist selects episodes to build progressively through increasing but varying repetition to portray his characters in action. If he wishes to hold the attention of his readers, every item will be projected by means of a patterned movement and tempo, and will, as James has written, "try to catch the rhythm of life." The short story author strikes quickly and so selects more perceptively, depending to a great extent on his approach through characterization, events or simple narration. Drama, if successful, shows a rhythm that accentuates, interrupts, dips slightly now and then and finally quickens in tempo as it reaches the climax. Certainly both prose and poetic drama show the writer's attention to words, his highlighting to give innuendos, meaning and rhythm—in much the same fashion as observed in the poetic form of the dramatic monologue, but extended over many episodes and many pages.

THE SYMBOL

In addition to the general rhythmic pattern of the whole, some novelists use the expanded symbol that supports the meaning by its *varied* repetition and thereby gives rhythmic unity. E. K. Brown, in *The Rhythm of the Novel*,[67] believes this type of symbolism takes the place of the poets' literary devices for rhythmic effects. The writer of fiction, like the poet, wishes to communicate a glimpsed emotion through a symbol in an area that extends beyond the characters and their environment. He does not wish, according to Brown, to fasten the symbol down in an explicit manner; he instead hopes to have it weave through his story implicitly, so that it will be felt by those responsive to the author's central meaning. If this symbol can be an "expanding" rather than a "fixed" symbol, then it will be successful in holding together the rhythmic sequence—probably much as the motifs in music. If, as Brown reports, the symbol is fixed, then you discover repetition of pattern without variation. This is the equivalent probably of a verse pattern thoroughly dependent on the jingle rhyme scheme in which melody is lacking and a pattern of beats is prominent. As an example of the fixed symbol, Brown cites Wilder's Pulitzer award story, *The Bridge of San Luis Rey*. You will recall that three unrelated groups, including five individuals, have the same illumination that the kind of love each has had in the past for a certain individual has been selfish love. These five involved persons have decided on a change in the

[67] E. K. Brown, *Rhythm of the Novel* (Toronto: University of Toronto Press, 1950), pp. 42-43.

quality and approach of their past behavior. Coincidentally, they start on their respective journeys on the same day to seek reappraisal of their love by a reunion with the involved persons. As they start over the bridge leading to their particular paths, the bridge collapses, carrying all five individuals to their death. Brown is correct in saying that each pattern is repetitive; the differences, however, in characterizations, motivations and approach keep the reader curious and engrossed. Wilder reveals his symbolic meaning when he ends the story by having the Abbess Maria remark, "There is a land of the living and the dead and the bridge is love." This is only one example of many expanded symbols to be found in the novel—a device which must be recognized if you decide to interpret certain scenes from a novel.

CHARACTERIZATION

The speech rhythm of characters, in contrast, conflict and balance with one another, is the author's most vivid way of identifying the internal thought and activity of each person; and of building the illusion of reality for the over-all movement of his narrative. In Faulkner's novel, *The Sound and The Fury,* the pattern achieved by the author through the speech of his characters pulls his story together into a rhythmic unit. Faulkner's selection of the speech phrases for Caddy, Dilsey, and even Benjy, makes the reader pause to wonder how he conceived such realistic patterns of speech. Each is colloquial—as Huck Finn's is—and seemingly natural to the environment and to character reaction, especially in the silences; each is rooted deeply in how the person thinks, feels and acts in his environment. The same element is remembered in the four characters of *The Glass Menagerie* by Williams: characterization is gained not so much by the actions as through speech patterns. No one can forget the fluttering, persistent, self-engrossed voice of the dominating mother, as she reiterates the "blown-up" memories of her past; nor can one forget Tom's voice at the other extreme, impatient, at times belligerent, unaccepting—but creating a powerful emotional impact through its poetic rhythm in the last scene; and in between these two is the lost, bewildered voice of Laura. The fourth character from the outside world of reality offers normal speech rhythm and attitude in contrast to the other persons, each of whom is looking within his own shell for escape.

Although you are acquainted with Dickens's *A Christmas Carol,* you may not realize how beautifully spaced and high-lighted the scenes are to show contrast and conflict of the voices. The author gives each character his own particular speech, again for the sake of conflict: Scrooge has his; his nephew has his; Tiny Tim has his own way of being an echo. Finally, they are blended together into a unifying mosaic by bringing the conflicting character of Scrooge into the Christmas spirit with his vocal change to good cheer. The counterplay of characters and episodes shows a rhythmical progression to the final bursting point of hearty Christmas fellowship. This balance and contrast of scenes is indeed part of Dickens's unity of impression, beautifully and rhythmically executed.

Through their verbal idiocyncrasies, characters can bring laughter. A well-known example is Mrs. Malaprop, so named by Sheridan in *The Rivals* because of her grotesque misuse of words. Her "malapropism" stems from her love of the sound of polysyllabic words that fit into the rhythm, if not the meaning, of her speech. Her tirades reveal her vain, superficial character in contrast to the speech of the other characters.

In the following episode, Lydia, the niece of Mrs. Malaprop, has just left the room after refusing to marry Mrs. Malaprop's marriage choice for her—Sir Anthony's son, Captain Absolute. Unknown to either of the elders, young Absolute, masquerading as "Beverly" to Lydia, is planning to elope with the young lady. Although the play hinges on this thin thread of deceit, Sheridan has given it a hilarious tone because of Mrs. Malaprop's word idiocyncrasies. Lydia has been ordered to her room because of her rebellious spirit concerning her choice of a husband, leaving Mrs. Malaprop with Sir Anthony. On the stage, this scene is always punctured with many laughs, so that Lydia's aunt has to sustain her air of authority during the laughter. Of course, she will not seem humorous to you unless you know the meaning of the words she misuses.

from *The Rivals*

MRS MAL.: There's a little intricate hussy for you!

SIR ANTH.: It is not to be wonder'd at, Ma'am—all this is a natural consequence of teaching girls to read.—Had I a thousand daughters, by heaven! I'd as soon have them taught the black art as the alphabet!

MRS MAL.: Nay, nay, Sir Anthony, you are an absolute misanthrope.

SIR ANTH.: In my way hither, Mrs Malaprop, I observed your niece's maid coming forth from a circulating library!—She had a book in each hand— they were half bound volumes, with marble covers!—From that moment I guess'd how full of duty I should see her mistress!

MRS MAL.: Those are vile places, indeed!

SIR ANTH.: Madam, a circulating library in a town is as an ever green tree of diabolical knowledge!—It blossoms through the year!—And depend on it, Mrs Malaprop, that they who are so fond of handling the leaves, will long for the fruit at last.

MRS MAL.: Fie, fie, Sir Anthony, you surely speak laconically.

SIR ANTH.: Why, Mrs Malaprop, in moderation, now, what would you have a woman know?

MRS MAL.: Observe me, Sir Anthony.—I would by no means wish a daughter of mine to be a progeny of learning; I don't think so much learning becomes a young woman; for instance—I would never let her meddle with Greek, or Hebrew, or Algebra, or Simony, of Fluxions, or Paradoxes, or such inflammatory branches of learning—neither would it be necessary for her to handle any of your mathematical, astronomical, diabolical instruments:—But, Sir Anthony, I would send her, at nine years old, to a boarding-school, in order to learn a little ingenuity and artifice.—Then, Sir, she should have a supercilious knowledge in accounts;— as she grew up, I would have her instructed in geometry, that she might know something of the contagious countries;—but above all, Sir Anthony, she should be mistress of orthodoxy, that she might not misspell, and mispronounce words so shamefully as girls usually do; and likewise that she might reprehend the true meaning of what she is saying—This, Sir Anthony, is what I would have a woman know;—and I don't think there is a superstitious article in it.

SIR ANTH.: Well, well, Mrs Malaprop, I will dispute the point no further with you. —But, Mrs Malaprop, to the more important point in debate,—you say, you have no objection to my proposal.

MRS MAL.: None, I assure you.—I am under no positive engagement with Mr Acres, and as Lydia is so obstinate against him, perhaps your son may have better success.

SIR ANTH.: Well, madam, I will write for the boy directly.—He knows not a syllable of this yet, though I have for some time had the proposal in my head. He is at present with his regiment.

MRS MAL.: We have never seen your son, Sir Anthony; but I hope no objection on his side—

SIR ANTH.: Objection!—let him object if he dare!—No, no, Mrs Malaprop, Jack knows that the least demur puts me in a phrenzy directly.—My process was always very simple—in their younger days, 'twas "Jack, do this;"—if he demurr'd—I knock'd him down—and if he grumbled at that—I always sent him out of the room.

MRS MAL.: Aye, and the properest way, o'my conscience!—nothing is so conciliating to young people as severity.—Well, Sir Anthony, I shall give Mr Acres his discharge, and prepare Lydia to receive your son's invocations; —and I hope you will represent *her* to the Captain as an object not altogether illegible.

SIR ANTH.: Madam, I will handle the subject prudently.—Well, I must leave you—and let me beg you, Mrs Malaprop, to enforce this matter roundly to the girl;—take my advice—keep a tight hand—if she rejects this proposal—clap her under lock and key: and if you were just to let the servants forget to bring her dinner for three or four days, you can't conceive how she'd come about! (*Exit* SIR ANTH.)[68]

RICHARD SHERIDAN

[68] *The Rivals* by Richard Sheridan. Recorded by Dame Edith Evans, Pamela Brown, Michael MacLiammoir and supporting cast. Dame Edith Evans, as Mrs. Malaprop, times her speech pattern with the finesse of a professional comedian, thereby preparing for laughs on the malapropisms and also creating a distinctive character. Caedmon, TC 2020 S.

Another example of humor—this time brought about through rhythmical contrast of real and fantasy episodes, as well as verbal patterns—is contained in the characterization in Thurber's story, "The Secret Life of Walter Mitty." Inasmuch as the contrasts in Mitty's voice depend greatly on pitch changes, as well as other vocal attributes, the story has been reprinted in chapter 12. Read it over now to observe the way in which Thurber has secured part of his humor through his rhythmical vocal and episodal techniques.

STYLISTIC PATTERNS

As mentioned earlier, the arrangement of phrases and sentences in prose usually shows a rhythmical pattern—more diffusable, irregular and not so observable as in poetry. It will also offer pleasurable sensations due to motor responses but the awareness is not so distinct as in poetry. According to psychologists, every rhythm, *if felt*, consists of actual bodily movements due to the emotional reaction through associations and suggestions. This is the principle of empathy.

Your task is to let the lines speak for themselves so that the author's movement is recognized, instead of imposing your own melody. If your rhythm of thought and writing is different from the writer's or if you are a passively rhythmic person, you may experience some difficulty. You can learn, however, to sense varying cadences, even as you do in dancing. Remember the author thought his pattern would establish tone, mood or atmosphere to intensify meaning. Since these elements contribute to patterns of melody, then not only the timing is important, but also vocal pitch, intensity and quality in the establishment of a distinguishing style. The movement may be abrupt, terse, decisive; it may have the smoothness of some poetry; it may be rapid and tense; it may be characterized by highly condensed and repetitive sentences. The best way to identify the particular stylistic pattern is to practice aloud, easing into phrases and letting them carry your voice, instead of trying to make them fit your particular vocal pattern. The way of an author with word combinations, imagery, stressing and unstressing to get the full sweep of emotional meaning must be heard—so start listening. As Stevenson has written— "One sound suggests, echoes, demands and harmonizes with another, and the art of using these concordances is the final art of literature."

Recordings of prose are available to offer excellent ear training: the British recorders of many English prose writers[69]; the varying vocal patterns of McKenna and Marshall in "The Soliloquies of Molly and Leopold Bloom[70]"; the versatile and resonant voice of Cusack as he presents

[69] *The Cambridge Treasury of English Prose: Austen to Brontë*, V. 4 and *Dickens to Butler*, V. 5. Caedmon, TC 1058.

[70] *Ulysses*: "The Soliloquies of Molly and Leopold Bloom" by James Joyce, recorded by Siobhan McKenna and E. G. Marshall. Caedmon, TC 1063.

Stephen Dedalus in action and in prayer as well as in contemplative moments from *A Portrait of the Artist as a Young Man*[71]; the change in vocal rhythm of Sir Ralph Richardson in "Swann in Love[72]"; the timing through vocal adaptations to fit mood and meaning of McKenna and Cusack as they interpret from *Finnegan's Wake*[73]—so that suddenly the meaning is revealed. These latter recordings are evidence of the sensitive potential of voice in carrying meaning through the inner stream of consciousness. In contrast, Perelman[74] employs his own particular pausing and rhythm to give pleasure. The most dramatic cadences of speech rhythm can be heard in unrehearsed narratives of historical events in the album *I Can Hear It Now*[75] (3 vols.: 1919-1949). For instance, the broadcast of Hubert Morrison describing the four-hour crossing and initial landing of the German dirigible, *Hindenburg*, at Lakehurst, New Jersey in 1937, is suddenly climaxed by his horrified and gasping recounting of the burning of the dirigible with its human cargo of first patrons caught in the fiery blast. Your sensitivity to rhythmical patterns will be heightened as you listen to these and other recordings—if, as psychologists report, you are aggressively rhythmical in responding empathically.

Try your voice on the following cadenced patterns of style: can you *feel* the difference in the rhythm of Capote's story, "A Christmas Memory," and Cary's opening to his novel, *The Horse's Mouth*?

from *A Christmas Memory*

Imagine a morning in late November. A coming of winter morning more than twenty years ago. Consider the kitchen of a spreading old house in a country town. A great black stove is its main feature; but there is also a big round table and a fireplace with two rocking chairs placed in front of it. Just today the fireplace commenced its seasonal roar.

A woman with shorn white hair is standing at the kitchen window. She is wearing tennis shoes and a shapeless gray sweater over a summery calico dress. She is small and sprightly, like a bantam hen; but, due to a long youthful illness, her shoulders are pitifully hunched. Her face is remarkable—not unlike Lincoln's, craggy like that, and tinted by sun and wind; but it is delicate too, finely boned, and her eyes are sherry-colored and timid. "Oh my," she exclaims, her breath smoking the windowpane, "it's fruitcake weather!"

[71] *A Portrait of the Artist as a Young Man* by James Joyce, recorded by Cyril Cusack. Caedmon, TC 1110.

[72] *Remembrance of Things Past:* "Swann in Love" by Marcel Proust, recorded by Sir Ralph Richardson. Caedmon, TC 2017.

[73] *Finnegan's Wake* by James Joyce, recorded by Siobhan McKenna and Cyril Cusack. Caedmon, TC 1086.

[74] S. J. Perelman Record. Sp. Arts, 705.

[75] *I Can Hear It Now* (3 vols.: 1919-1949) narrated by Edward Murrow. Hindenburg incident recorded by Hubert Morrison, V. 1. Columbia, 5 ML, 4095.

The person to whom she is speaking is myself. I am seven; she is sixty-something. We are cousins, very distant ones, and we have lived together —well, as long as I can remember. Other people inhabit the house, relatives; and though they have power over us, and frequently make us cry, we are not, on the whole, too much aware of them. We are each other's best friend. She calls me Buddy, in memory of a boy who was formerly her best friend. The other Buddy died in the 1880's, when she was still a child. She is still a child.

"I knew it before I got out of bed," she says, turning away from the window with a purposeful excitement in her eyes. "The courthouse bell sounded so cold and clear. And there were no birds singing; they've gone to warmer country, yes indeed. Oh, Buddy, stop stuffing biscuit and fetch our buggy. Help me find my hat. We've thirty cakes to bake."

It's always the same: a morning arrives in November, and my friend, as though officially inaugurating the Christmas time of year that exhilarates her imagination and fuels the blaze of her heart, announces: "It's fruitcake weather! Fetch our buggy. Help me find my hat."

The hat is found, a straw cartwheel corsaged with velvet roses out-of-doors has faded: it once belonged to a more fashionable relative. Together, we guide our buggy, a dilapidated baby carriage, out to the garden and into a grove of pecan trees. The buggy is mine, that is, it was bought for me when I was born. It is made of wicker, rather unraveled, and the wheels wobble like a drunkard's legs. But it is a faithful object; springtimes, we take it to the woods and fill it with flowers, herbs, wild fern for our porch pots; in the summer, we pile it with picnic paraphernalia and sugar-cane fishing poles and roll it down to the edge of a creek; it has its winter uses, too: as a truck for hauling firewood from the yard to the kitchen, as a warm bed for Queenie, our tough little orange and white rat terrier, who has survived distemper and two rattlesnake bites. Queenie is trotting beside it now.

Three hours later we are back in the kitchen hulling a heaping buggy-load of windfall pecans. Our backs hurt from gathering them: how hard they were to find (the main crop having been shaken off the trees and sold by the orchard's owners, who are not us) among the concealing leaves, the frosted deceiving grass. Caarackle! A cheery crunch, scraps of miniature thunder sound as the shells collapse and the golden mound of sweet oily ivory meat mounts in the milk-glass bowl. Queenie begs to taste, and now and again my friend sneaks her a mite, though insisting we deprive ourselves. "We musn't, Buddy. If we start, we won't stop. And there's scarcely enough as there is. For thirty cakes." The kitchen is growing dark. Dusk turns the window into a mirror: our reflections mingle with the rising moon as we work by the fireside in the firelight. At last, when the moon is quite high, we toss the final hull into the fire and with joined sighs, watch it catch flame. The buggy is empty, the bowl is brimful.[76]

Truman Capote

---

[76] From "A Christmas Memory," © Copyright 1956 by Truman Capote. Reprinted from BREAKFAST AT TIFFANY'S, by Truman Capote, by permission of Random House, Inc.

from *The Horse's Mouth*

I was walking by the Thames. Half-past morning on an autumn day. Sun in a mist. Like an orange in a fried fish shop. All bright below. Low tide, dusty water and a crooked bar of straw, chicken boxes, dirt and oil from mud to mud. Like a viper swimming in skim milk. The old serpent, symbol of nature and love.

> Five windows light the caverned man; through one he breathes the air;
> Through one hears music of the spheres; through one can look
> And see small portions of the eternal world.

Such as Thames mud turned into a bank of nine carat gold rough from the fire. They say a chap just out of prison runs into the nearest cover; into some dark little room, like a rabbit put up by a stoat. The sky feels too big for him. But I like it. I swam in it. I couldn't take my eyes off the clouds, the water, the mud. And I must have been hopping up and down Greenbank Hard for half an hour grinning like a gargoyle, until the wind began to get up my trousers and down my back, and to bring me to myself, as they say. Meaning my liver and lights. . . .

I had two and six left from my prison money. I reckoned that five pounds would set me up with bed, board, and working capital. That left four pounds seventeen and six to be won. From friends. But when I went over my friends, I seemed to owe them more than that; more than they could afford.

The sun had crackled into flames at the top; the mist was getting thin in places, you could see crooked lines of gray, like old cracks under spring ice. Tide on the turn. Snake broken up. Emeralds and sapphires. Water like varnish with bits of gold leaf floating thick and heavy. Gold is the metal of the intellect.[77]

JOYCE CARY

At first glance, the sentences of each excerpt appear to be of the same length, but on closer observation, you note that Cary's are mostly phrases shot through with vivid imagery. The cadences are different because of the word arrangement and the narrator's tone. Cary's short and brusque sentences or thoughts carry a unique mood and tone of suppressed exhilaration of remembered as well as of present experience—at an adult level.

The stylistic pattern of Capote's delightful reminiscence from the remembered point of view of a seven-year-old child is also impressionistic but mellow in recall. Incidents are presented so effectively with naive charm that the reader becomes completely immersed in the episodes and

[77] From THE HORSE'S MOUTH by Joyce Cary. Copyright 1944 by Joyce Cary. Reprinted by permission of Harper & Row, Publishers.

characters, including Queenie. Try your skill in contrasting tone, mood and rhythm of the excerpts.

The images create immediate but different responses: in the Cary passage, the sensation of intense participation with the freedom of the environment; the quick excitement and absorption of old landmarks, even bathing in the muddy Thames; and the joy of recapturing the vivid colors, intensified for the artist who has just been released from prison. In the Capote nostalgic memory, the delicious joy of a child's "long ago" participation in the festive event of baking cakes is sensed: the mood is accomplished in muted tones, yet is familiar to everyone as a childhood experience. You are more likely to identify with the child than with the artist who is exulting in immediate experiences, unfamiliar to you.

According to Trilling, style has little to do with grammar or pronunciation; rather it is concerned mainly with the ease and freedom in employing language; the rhythm of word groups and intonations of the speaking voice. Since he cites Mark Twain as the great master of prose rhythm, try to ease into Huck Finn's colloquial rhythm in this opening passage of his story. In the foreword of his volume, Mark Twain remarks "In this book a number of dialects have been used, to wit: The Missouri negro dialect, the ordinary 'Pike County' dialect, and four modified varieties of this last." He adds that the distinction has not been haphazard work; rather it has been accomplished through personal familiarity with these speech forms. So Huck is speaking his own particular dialect, the intonational rhythm heard throughout this classic.

Observe how these passages from Capote, Cary and Mark Twain reveal the personality of the narrator.

from *The Adventures of Huckleberry Finn*

You don't know about me without you have read a book by the name of *The Adventures of Tom Sawyer;* but that ain't no matter. That book was made by Mr. Mark Twain, and he told the truth, mainly. There was things which he stretched, but mainly he told the truth. That is nothing. I never seen anybody but lied one time or another, without it was Aunt Polly, or the widow, or maybe Mary. Aunt Polly—Tom's Aunt Polly, she is—and Mary, and the Widow Douglas is all told about in that book, which is mostly a true book, with some stretchers, as I said before.

Now the way that the book winds up is this: Tom and me found the money that the robbers hid in the cave, and it made us rich. We got six thousand dollars apiece—all gold. It was an awful sight of money when it was piled up. Well, Judge Thatcher he took it and put it out at interest, and it fetched us a dollar a day apiece all the year round—more than a body could tell what to do with. The Widow Douglas she took me for her son, and allowed she would sivilize me; but it was rough living in the house all the time, considering how dismal regular and decent the widow was in all her ways; and so when I couldn't stand it no longer I lit out. I got into my old rags and my sugar hogshead again, and was free and satisfied. But Tom Sawyer he hunted me up and said he was going to start a band of robbers, and I might join if I would go back to the widow and be respectable. So I went back.

The widow she cried over me, and called me a poor lost lamb, and she called me a lot of other names, too, but she never meant no harm by it. She put me in them new clothes again, and I couldn't do nothing but sweat and sweat, and feel all cramped up. Well, then, the old thing commenced again. The widow rung a bell for supper, and you had to come to time. When you got to the table you couldn't go right to eating, but you had to wait for the widow to tuck down her head and grumble a little over the victuals, though there warn't really anything the matter with them—that is, nothing only everything was cooked by itself. In a barrel of odds and ends it is different; things get mixed up, and the juice kind of swaps around, and the things go better.

After supper she got out her book and learned me about Moses and the Bulrushes, and I was in a sweat to find out all about him; but by and by she let it out that Moses had been dead a considerable long time; so then I didn't care no more about him, because I don't take no stock in dead people.[78]

MARK TWAIN

This next narrative needs no explanatory remarks since everyone remembers the story of Scrooge. Dickens, like Mark Twain, carries the atmosphere and mood through his rhythmic pattern. The narrator is the omniscient one who sees all. Do you feel the lack of the personality of the narrator who takes part in the activities?

Look in on this animated moving picture with Scrooge as he watches one of the scenes of his younger days. The festivities of Christmas eve are under way as old Fezziwig "adjusted his capacious waistcoat, laughed all over himself, from his shoes to his organ of benevolence and called out, in a comfortable, oily, rich, fat, jovial voice: 'Yo ho, my boys. No more work to-night, Christmas eve. . . . Let's have the shutters up before a man can say Jack Robinson.'" You may remember how those fellows, Dick and Ebenezer "went at it."

from *A Christmas Carol*

Clear away! There was nothing they wouldn't have cleared away, or couldn't have cleared away, with old Fezziwig looking on. It was done in a minute. Every movable was packed off, as if it were dismissed from public life forevermore; the floor was swept and watered, the lamps were trimmed, fuel was heaped upon the fire; and the warehouse was as snug, and warm, and dry, and bright a ballroom as you would desire to see upon a winter's night.

[78] Mark Twain (Samuel Clemens), *The Adventures of Huckleberry Finn*, Author's National Edition, Vol. XIII (New York: Harper & Brothers, 1899), pp. 1-2.

In came a fiddler with a music-book, and went up to the lofty desk, and made an orchestra of it, and tuned like fifty stomach-aches. In came Mrs. Fezziwig, one vast, substantial smile. In came the three Miss Fezziwigs, beaming and lovable. In came the six young followers whose hearts they broke. In came all the young men and women employed in the business. In came the housemaid, with her cousin, the baker. In came the cook, with her brother's particular friend, the milkman. . . . In they all came, one after another; some shyly, some boldly, some gracefully, some awkwardly, some pushing, some pulling; in they all came, anyhow and everyhow. Away they all went, twenty couples at once; hands half round and back again the other way; down the middle and up again; round and round in various stages of affectionate grouping; old top couple always turning up in the wrong place; new top couple starting off again, as soon as they got there; all top couples at last, and not a bottom one to help them! . . .

But if they had been twice as many—ah, four times—old Fezziwig would have been a match for them, and so would Mrs. Fezziwig. As to *her*, she was worthy to be his partner in every sense of the term. . . . A positive light appeared to issue from Fezziwig's calves. They shone in every part of the dance like moons. You couldn't have predicted, at any given time, what would become of them next. And when old Fezziwig and Mrs. Fezziwig had gone through the dance: advance and retire, both hands to your partner, bow and curtsey, corkscrew, thread-the-needle, and back again to your place, Fezziwig "cut"—cut so deftly, that he appeared to wink with his legs, and came upon his feet again without a stagger.

Charles Dickens

You will also discover individual rhythms peculiar to various essayists that should increase your appreciation for stylistic rhythm. Perhaps the passage most famous for its poetic pattern is from Walter Pater's essay on "Leonardo Da Vinci." The essayist is writing of the "Mona Lisa" portrait. Pater, in the early portion of the essay, remarks of the great painter, "Out of the secret places of unique temperament he brought strange blossoms and fruits hitherto unknown; and for him, the novel impression conveyed, the exquisite effect woven, counted as an end in itself—a perfect end." Before the essayist describes the penetrating expressiveness of "Mona Lisa" he questions, "What was the relationship of a living Florentine to this creature of his thought? By what strange affinities had the dream and the person grown up thus apart, and yet so closely together? . . . That there is much of mere portraiture in the picture is attested by the legend that by artificial means, the presence of mimes and flute-players, that subtle expression was protracted on her face. . . ." Here is your opportunity to feel *poetic* rhythm in prose:

The presence that rose thus so strangely beside the waters, is expressive of what in the ways of a thousand years men had come to desire. Hers is the head upon which all "the ends of the world are come" and the eyelids are a little

weary. It is a beauty wrought out from within upon the flesh, the deposit, little
cell by cell, of strange thoughts and fantastic reveries and exquisite passions.
Set it for a moment beside one of those white Greek goddesses or beautiful
women of antiquity, and how would they be troubled by this beauty, into
which the soul with all its maladies has passed! All the thoughts and experience of the world have etched and moulded there, in that which they have of
power to refine and make expressive the outward form, the animalism of
Greece, the lust of Rome, the mysticism of the middle age with its spiritual ambition and imaginative loves, the return of the Pagan world, the signs of the
Borgias. She is older than the rocks among which she sits; like the vampire, she
has been dead many times, and learned the secrets of the grave; and has been a
diver in deep seas, and keeps their fallen days about her; and trafficked for
strange webs with Eastern merchants; and, as Leda, was the mother of Helen
of Troy, and, as Saint Anne, the mother of Mary; and all this has been to her
but as the sound of lyres and flutes, and lives only in the delicacy with which
it has moulded the changing lineaments, and tinged the eyelids and the hands.
The fancy of a perpetual life, sweeping together ten thousand experiences, is
an old one; and modern philosophy has conceived the idea of humanity as
wrought upon by, and summing up in itself, all modes of thought and life. Certainly Lady Lisa might stand as the embodiment of the old fancy, the symbol
of the modern idea.[79]

WALTER PATER

You have just read rhythmic prose that is poetic—without meter!

[79] From Walter Pater, "Leonardo Da Vinci," *The Renaissance* (New York: The
Macmillan Company, 1873, 1888, 1901, 1910), pp. 124-126.

12
Vocal Pitch

WHAT IS VOCAL PITCH?

VOCAL PITCH: MEANING INDICATOR

All vocal factors studied thus far—vocal quality, intensity and tempo—will assist in the creation of the writer's meaning, tone, mood and atmosphere. The vocal element, however, that is the most sensitive indicator of your reactions, feelings, ideas and attitudes toward meaning is *vocal pitch*. By various manifestations of pitch—inflections, steps and key —you can achieve not only the logical import of literature but also the more subtle, connotative and emotional meanings. Proper control of pitch changes along with syllabic stress are the main requirements for the development of speech melody or an intonational pattern—even for the enhancement of your conversational speech.

VOCAL PITCH: FREQUENCY OF VOCAL FOLD VIBRATIONS

Simply, pitch is the highness and lowness of your voice as the sound waves impinge upon the ear. More technically, pitch is the auditory sensation produced by the rate at which the vocal folds vibrate. This rate, or frequency, is determined mainly by the length, thickness or mass, and tension of the vocal folds. As in all vibrating mechanisms, the greater the number of vibrations per second, the higher the pitch. In vocal pitch, those persons whose vocal folds are longer and show greater mass than average, normally will have low-pitched voices because fewer vibrations per second occur; those whose folds are short and show less mass will usually have high-pitched voices because more vibrations per second occur. This general statement may be affected by other factors not within the realm of your study of interpretation.

Children usually have high-pitched voices until they reach the age of puberty. If the high pitch remains during adulthood, it may be due to the failure of development of the laryngeal mechanism or to the inability of the person to adjust to the growth of the larynx. Sometimes, in this period, the adolescent will pass through a period of huskiness, showing poor approximation of the vocal folds or glottal edges. In men, particularly, the vocal pitch should become lower as the individual approaches maturity. Certainly any male who still has a high-pitched voice at the age of eighteen or over should find the reason for it and seek the necessary therapy.

OPTIMUM PITCH

The range of pitch level or key at which the voice operates with the greatest ease is called the optimum pitch. Under normal tension, it is the range at which the least effort is necessitated for the action of your vibrating mechanism—the vocal folds. As your fundamental tone is increased in intensity, the optimum range will become higher. When you phonate "ah," without imitation of another voice, you will vocalize within your optimum range. For women, the optimum pitch is usually slightly higher than 256 double vibrations per second (middle C); and for men, it is near 150 double vibrations per second or about one octave lower than for women.

Some people, however, through poor habits or bodily tensions, employ a much higher pitch range than is pleasing to the listener; others speak at a pitch level that is too low, so that vocal quality often becomes breathy or guttural or indistinct. You must not forget that the tension of the vocal folds is determined by the action of the intrinsic and extrinsic muscles of the larynx, which in turn are affected to a great extent by general bodily tension. Anyone—man or woman—who lives in a state of hypertension or becomes suddenly frightened, will usually have a voice that is higher than that person's optimum or normal pitch range. If no organic dysfunction is causing the high-pitched voice, the range can often be lowered by merely finding the optimum pitch or by easing general bodily tension.

FLEXIBILITY OF PITCH

SPEECH MELODY: INTONATIONAL PATTERN

The discussions on literary meanings have emphasized how the author's stylistic pattern sets the tone of the selection. So too, the melody of a person's speech expresses his attitude through vocal tone. Melody is the overall delicate combination of pitch changes with syllabic stress. It should be flexible so as to indicate your feelings, your general health and happiness. It usually is an index of what is taking place within the speaker or conversationalist. The individual with personality and temperament shows his love of life through his inflectional and stress patterns. The plaintive person has a depressing melody or intonational pattern, due to monotony of either too many upward or downward slides and a minimum of stressed syllables. The lively, happy-go-lucky individual has a breezy melody showing a variety of speech changes with stress accents that are very contagious. Speech that lacks melody is uninteresting and unconvincing.

Many people do not hear their own speech melody; some are offended when they are told their voices are monotonous and lacking in verve and sensitiveness. Every would-be interpreter should be tested for pitch discrimination: the *Seashore Measures of Musical Talent* are effective in ascertaining aptitude in this respect. The person who is not sensitive to pitch variations in his own voice cannot profitably criticize his or another's interpretation. For the interpreter, the refinement of refinements, both in understanding literature and in expressing its meaning, lies in his ability to show pitch flexibility for discriminating meaning.

MEANING THROUGH SLIDE, STEP, KEY

You are aware of the subtle meanings expressed through skillful use of pitch changes and can learn about people's attitudes—perhaps unconsciously—through their vocal flexibility. Monotony of voice may also stem from too much of the same vocal intensity and a repetitive tempo pattern or from too much flexibility. This latter fault is not too common; a person, however, may give the impression of "talking down to an audience" due to excessive inflections.

Pitch flexibility may be effected in three ways: by *slide*, by *step* and by *key*. The changes produced by the appropriate use of these three vocal devices will indicate the proportion of sense and feeling in the literary material. Slides, the upward and downward movements of the voice *within* the word or syllable, must be present in discriminating meaning. Steps, the upward and downward movements of the voice *between* words and syllables, are necessary for increased emphasis and contrast and play an equally interesting part in feeling. Key, the *level* or particular range of tone, indicates the intensity of the mood, atmosphere and tonal quality of the selection.

THE SLIDE

The variations of slides in vocal pitch are many, but the three classifications usually spoken of are the *upward* (/), the *downward* (\), and the *wave* (∧∨ ∧∧ ∧). The upward slide, if used with discretion, gives a very interesting lilt and melody to the voice; it must be employed, however, not exclusively, but in nice admixture with the downward slide. The upward slide, if overdone, suggests an indecisive note—one of hesitation, of inconclusiveness. The speech of most people, however, shows a preponderance of upward rather than downward slides. If the downward slide is practiced consistently, the meaning is likely to become too dogmatic, certain, sure, pedantic. The discriminating downward slide gives a sense of assurance; it clinches the thought and offers a feeling of satisfaction. The wave, a combination of the upward and downward slides, can excite subtle and delicate meanings and add much to an interesting melody and rhythm. The gossip employs it—overtime; the sarcastic person gets most of his effects from the use of the wave; the actor always uses a combination of slides to provoke a new meaning for the audience. Slang phrases are interesting because of slides and steps that suggest a double meaning.

In a way, pitch slides or inflections carry the essence of meaning in effective interpretation. You may have difficulty detecting your own speech pattern, but you can always listen to others and observe what their voices are showing through the vocal glides. Sometimes you can even hear inflections in the quickest syllables that are held for any length of time. One way to note this phenomenon is to listen to a recording, especially as it slows down.

In any group of words, you can discover a score of meanings. Take the sentence *I will go,* and try combinations of inflections and stress to express different reactions. First you can mean, "I am leaving" (downward slides on all words); or "I am determined to go whether you like it or not" (long upward slide *or* downward slide on *will*); or "You expect me to go? (long upward slide on *I* and short upward slides on *will* and *go*). You can suggest many more subtleties. In the interpretative situation, the inflectional tone must fit into the total concept of the meaning.

As you become more conscious of the possibilities offered by different inflectional patterns, you will increase your sensitivity and ability to express them. The writer indicates his idea as well as he can by phrasing and selection of words, syntactical order for emphasis and sometimes, by punctuation—if other literary devices block the way to understanding.

When Lady Macbeth and Macbeth are debating the advisability of killing Duncan, the following dialogue takes place:

> MACBETH: If we should fail?
> LADY M: We fail. But, screw your courage to the sticking place,
>   And we'll not fail.

Another Shakespearean editor has printed this text:

> MACBETH: If we should fail?
> LADY M: We fail! But screw your courage to the sticking place,
>   And we'll not fail.

Here are two clearly defined meanings. How is the difference indicated? Is it the punctuation? That seems reasonable. You must remember, however, that punctuation does not make meaning; it only records and suggests it. The real meaning is in the writer or the interpreter. You can see it is not in the words for the words in the above dialogue are precisely the same, yet they may have two different meanings—maybe more. In the first passage, *fail* in Lady Macbeth's speech has a definite downward inflection, indicating a decision has been made; in the second passage, the emphasis is placed on *we*, that takes on the tone of incredulity and paves the way for the upward slide on *fail*. Other inflections may be possible if they fit in with Lady Macbeth's indomitable spirit.

Sarett's "Four Little Foxes" is an interesting study demonstrating how, by certain words and cadences, a poet can express the intonations he would expect you to interpret for an audience. He has also marked the pacing to cue you to the rhythmical phrases: note the punctuation mark at the end of every third line; and the short phrase of the fourth line with its gentleness of approach accomplished by the pause before the words and by the echo of the two words from the first line. The poet, however, has placed a period after each fourth line which unfortunately indicates to many a downward, decisive slide, whereas the voice should have the persuasive note of the upward slide.[1] The note of sympathy and pleading and the repetition of the words *gently, softly, lightly*, should persuade the interpreter than an upward inflection is necessary:

Four Little Foxes

Speak gently, Spring, and make no sudden sound;
For in my windy valley, yesterday I found
New-born foxes squirming on the ground—
       Speak gently.

Walk softly, March, forbear the bitter blow;
Her feet within a trap, her blood upon the snow,
The four little foxes saw their mother go—
       Walk softly.

Go lightly, Spring, oh, give them no alarm;
When I covered them with boughs to shelter them from harm,
The thin blue foxes suckled at my arm—
       Go lightly.

Step softly, March, with your rampant hurricane;
Nuzzling one another, and whimpering with pain,
The new little foxes are shivering in the rain—
       Step softly.[2]

LEW SARETT

[1] *Lew Sarett: Reading from His Collected Poems.* Columbia, XTV—15494, 15495.
[2] From COVENANT WITH EARTH, by Lew Sarett. Gainesville: University of Florida Press, 1956. Reprinted by permission of Mrs. Lew Sarett.

SONG-NOTES

The slide or inflection can be emphasized best by knowing its oppo-site—the "song-note"—held at an intonational level, with little or no movement up and down. In singing, the slide is the exception rather than the rule. In musical comedies and vaudeville acts you occasionally detect an actor merely reciting instead of singing the words of a song. What is the difference? The talking singer inflects slightly; the singer keeps his words at the pitch level of the note.

Court criers, circus ballyhooers and auctioneers (especially in to-bacco selling) use song-notes. Men speaking in large auditoriums or in the open air without public address systems incline to song-notes. The reason for this is worth marking: a slide involves greater exertion than a tone held at one level; and, furthermore, one can be heard more easily. The louder the sound of the voice, the more difficult it is to run up and down the scale in meaningful spech. Fortunately, the amplification system is helping to rid the platform of the song-note speaker, although he is sometimes still heard on the air. When this happens, the effect is rather ludicrous because the one speaking or interpreting and the listeners *know* this kind of indirectness is not necessary over so intimate a means of communication as the microphone. The interpreter must learn to talk in tune and in pitch with the times.

By omitting or reducing the gliding motion of the voice, you impair your conversational ease in any situation; you sound indirect, stilted, monotonous, meaningless. You lack the effect of the "first time over," a term used by actors to characterize the impression of easy, direct inter-pretation. When instructors of speech ask their students in interpretation to be more "natural," they really mean "use slides more intelligently." They may also mean that you probably ought to make some changes in your personal habits and attitudes because the flexibility of your intona-tional pattern may reflect, unfortunately, your liabilities. The changing of habits may have to start from within. Mechanical awareness is perfunc-tory compared to the real work of improving your attitude and physical well-being. Whenever possible, however, listen to your own inflectional efforts with a critical ear via the tape-recorder.

No character in literature is more adept in accomplishing his evil plot through insinuation than Iago is in Shakespeare's play *Othello*. The following passage portrays Iago's shrewdness and craftiness. Iago is at-tempting to make the unsuspecting Othello suspicious of Desdemona. Consequently, the slides employed by the two characters will be entirely different. Every line of Iago's speeches must have a double meaning by means of insinuating inflections. Notice the one word "Indeed!" in line 11. Try various slides before you decide which one will carry Iago's meaning most expertly. Do the same thing with the phrases, "Honest, my lord?" and "Think, my lord!" Watch Othello's lines for imitation and for reversal of slides on the same words. Bear in mind that the last words, "Thou dost mean something," are uttered by an angry and impatient Othello.

IAGO: My noble lord,—
OTHELLO: What dost thou say, Iago?
IAGO: Did Michael Cassio, when you woo'd my lady,
    Know of your love?
OTH.: He did, from first to last. Why dost thou ask?
IAGO: But for a satisfaction of my thought;
    No further harm.
OTH.:   Why of thy thought, Iago?
IAGO: I did not think he had been acquainted with her.
OTH.: O, yes; and went between us very oft.
IAGO: Indeed!
OTH.: Indeed! ay, indeed. Discern'st thou aught in that?
    Is he not honest?
IAGO: Honest, my lord?
OTH.:   Honest! ay, honest.
IAGO: My lord, for aught I know.
OTH.: What dost thou think?
IAGO: Think, my lord!
OTH.:   Think, my lord!
    By heaven, he echoes me,
    As if there were some monster in his thought
    Too hideous to be shown.—Thou dost mean something.

> SHAKESPEARE, *Othello,*
> Act III, Scene 3

Study slide possibilities in the next selection. Remember Cyrano is a poet, philosopher, wit. Remember too that any offense to his enormous nose means death from his sword. The Vicomte de Valvert has just witnessed the death of the Meddler because of his reference to Cyrano's nose. He is attempting just before this episode to put the swordsman in his place by telling him his nose is too large. Cyrano's reply gives suggestions for inflectional tones with great variation. See if you can match your vocal pitch changes to his descriptive words.

from *Cyrano de Bergerac*

ACT I

CYRANO: Ah, no, young sir!
    You are too simple. Why, you might have said—
    Oh, a great many things! Mon dieu, why waste
    Your opportunity? For example, thus:—

Aggressive: I, sir, if that nose were mine,
I'd have it amputated—on the spot!
Friendly: How do you drink with such a nose?
You ought to have a cup made specially.
Descriptive: 'Tis a rock—a crag—a cape—
A cape? say rather, a peninsula!
Inquisitive: What is that receptacle—
A razor-case or a portfolio?
Kindly: Ah, do you love the little birds
So much that when they come and sing to you,
You give them this to perch on? *Insolent:*
Sir, when you smoke, the neighbors must suppose
Your chimney is on fire. *Cautious:* Take care—
A weight like that might make you topheavy.
Thoughtful: Somebody fetch my parasol—
Those delicate colors fade so in the sun!
Pedantic: Does not Aristophanes
Mention a mythologic monster called
Hippocampelephantocamelos?
Surely we have here the original!
Familiar: Well, old torchlight! Hang your hat
Over that chandelier—it hurts my eyes.
Eloquent: When it blows, the typhoon howls,
And the clouds darken. *Dramatic:* When it bleeds—
The Red Sea! *Enterprising:* What a sign
For some perfumer! *Lyric:* Hark—the horn
Of Roland calls to summon Charlemagne!
Simple: When do they unveil the monument?
Respectful: Sir, I recognize in you
A man of parts, a man of prominence—
Rustic: Hey? What? Call that a nose? Na, na—
I be no fool like what you think I be—
That there's a blue cucumber! *Military:*
Point against cavalry! *Practical:* Why not
A lottery with this for the grand prize?
Or—parodying Faustus in the play—
"Was this the nose that launched a thousand ships
And burned the topless towers of Ilium?
These, my dear sir, are things you might have said
Had you some tinge of letters, or of wit
To color your discourse. But wit,—not so,
You never had an atom—and of letters,
You need but three to write you down—an Ass.
Moreover,—if you had the invention, here
Before these folk to make a jest of me—
Be sure you would not then articulate
The twentieth part of half a syllable
Of the beginning! For I say these things

> Lightly enough myself, about myself,
> But I allow none else to utter them.[3]

EDMOND ROSTAND

THE STEP

The slide or inflection is the movement up and down *within* the word or syllable; the step is the change of pitch level *between* words and syllables. Steps emphasize and contrast meaning. Monopitch, characterized by narrow steps or none at all, is tiresome and without vitality. Many times it has its place, however, in moments that involve moods of intense hatred, sullenness, sorrow, scheming. Sometimes it is employed as an indication of low intelligence. On the other hand, some go to the opposite extreme and cultivate enormously wide steps: for instance, the storyteller of the children's hour or the neighborly gossip or the long-lost friend who ejaculates over her happiness in seeing you again. Neither one of these extremes is convincing in good conversation, but the interpreter must be able to discriminate and to study them as "character types." In lively, rhythmic speech, the voice often takes wide steps repeatedly from the highest to the lowest notes and then, quite as often, employs steps that are barely perceptible. When a certain measure of abandon and spontaneity is to be expressed, pitch changes both in slides and in steps are wide, almost to the limit of the voice's range. A typical example of how the meaning can be changed by the use of wide or narrow steps is shown in the following diagram. The dotted line may be considered the normal level of the voice. The space indicated between each syllable is the step; some intervals are narrow, others are quite wide, depending on the meaning:

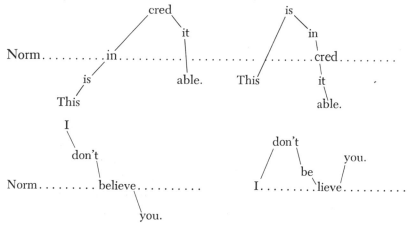

[3] From CYRANO DE BERGERAC by Edmond Rostand, Brian Hooker Translation. Copyright 1923 by Holt, Rinehart and Winston, Inc. Copyright 1951 by Doris C. Hooker. Reprinted by permission of Holt, Rinehart and Winston, Inc. Act I, p. 40.

A wide range of pitch is one of the sure ways of expressing meaningful, tense and highly emotional scenes. When you are speaking wholeheartedly, without restraint and fear of consequences, you tend to use wide steps. This is usually true in extreme anger, happiness, jealousy or fear. When you are beset with doubts, fears, indifference or are torn between two opinions or feelings, you are more likely to use narrow steps or a more level pitch. For instance, in extreme fear, the voice may sound the whole gamut; whereas with a fear that is the result of a clash of opinions or feelings, the voice tends to hold a more level tone. If you cry out in terror, "They are killing me!" you may use the whole range of your voice. On the other hand, when Lady Macbeth finds that Macbeth has blundered in the plans for concealing the murder of Duncan, she is frightened and yet she wishes to correct the fatal mistake; so she says with a level voice, the very evenness of which shows the conflict within her, "Why did you bring those daggers from the room!"

In the same way, sentiments of serenity, love, adoration, solemnity are likely to employ narrow steps, due to the factor of restraint. One does not bark at the beauty of the moon or orate his devotion to his beloved—if he means what he says. Thus Romeo, full of "rapture and a wild desire," yet fearful of being caught in the Capulet garden, cries out *softly:*

> Soft, what light through yonder window breaks?
> It is the east, and Juliet is the sun!

If you will reread the scene between Horatio and the guards (page 349), you will sense, by the way Shakespeare has written the short staccato lines beginning "Peace, break thee off!," the repression of fear at the sight of the ghost of their former king in the dead of the night. Shakespeare has written into the sentence structure the intonational pattern of the scene; the tones are almost on one level, free from wide steps and inflections. On the other hand, you remember the Cudjo lines in Benét's *John Brown's Body* have an infinite range of slides and wide steps.

THE KEY

Key, the general level or range of vocal pitch along the musical scale, is an indicator of mood; a device used by the interpreter to express emotional levels. Your own particular key level will not be acceptable in all interpretations, especially characterizations. In general, but not necessarily, a light, moderately high key may be used for moods of serenity, gaiety, calmness. Browning's lyric from "Pippa Passes" takes an optimistic tone as the young girl sings her song:

> The year's at the spring
> And Day's at the morn;

Morning's at seven;
The hill-side's dew-pearl'd;
The lark's on the wing;
The snail's on the thorn:
God's in his heaven—
All's right with the world!

ROBERT BROWNING,
Pippa Passes

The highest key, a shrill shriek, is reserved for extreme rage or terror—when someone has lost control of himself; one can also employ a low key depending on the situation and the voice of the character. When Emilia discovers that Othello has killed Desdemona, his innocent wife, she cries out, first probably in a medium key, then in a high level, and finally, with a shriek of fear and horror:

EMILIA: Thou hast not half that power to do me harm
As I have to be hurt. O gull! O dolt!
As ignorant as dirt! thou hast done a deed—
I care not for thy sword; I'll make thee known,
Though I lost twenty lives.—Help! help! ho! help!
The moor hath kill'd my mistress! Murder! murder!

SHAKESPEARE, *Othello,*
Act V, Scene 2

A medium key usually represents sincerity, quiet happiness; and is generally a good key for exposition, description, for the main character unless he is playing an eccentric. In other words, it is often a good starting key level from which one can reach higher or lower keys for meaning, contrast in scenes, characters, climax, mood or atmosphere. The following selections offer great variety in pitch flexibility.

SELECTIONS

This moderate range with appropriate pauses is effective in these philosophical lines by Moore—but keep your vitality through inflections and intensity.

What Are Years?

What is our innocence,
what is our guilt? All are
naked, none is safe. And whence
is courage: the unanswered question,

the resolute doubt,—
dumbly calling, deafly listening—that
in misfortune, even death,
    encourages others
    and in its defeat, stirs

  the soul to be strong? He
sees deep and is glad, who
    accedes to mortality
and in his imprisonment rises
upon himself as
the sea in a chasm, struggling to be
free and unable to be,
    in its surrendering
    finds its continuing.

  So he who strongly feels,
behaves. The very bird,
    grown taller as he sings, steels
his form straight up. Though he is captive,
his mighty singing
says, satisfaction is a lowly
thing, how pure a thing is joy.
    This is mortality,
    this is eternity.[4]

MARIANNE MOORE

Sarett has indicated very clearly how the meaning should be interpreted in his poem "The Sheepherder." The casual but varied pitch changes of the narrator are quite different from the monotony of the words of the sheepherder, as evidenced by the description of his actions and speech: "fiercely intent," "furtive of manner," "blazing of eye," as he counts his sheep, "one sheep, two sheep, three sheep." The cues are thus given for the speech rhythm and for narrow steps and few inflections: in other words, the speech will be monotonous in rhythm and in pitch. These differences in the speech patterns of the narrator and sheepherder also support variation in tone and mood.

The Sheepherder

Loping along on the day's patrol,
I came on a herder in Madison's Hole;
Furtive of manner, blazing of eye,

[4] Reprinted with permission of The Macmillan Co. from COLLECTED POEMS by Marianne Moore. Copyright 1941 by Marianne Moore.

He never looked up when I rode by;
But counting his fingers, fiercely intent,
Around and around his herd he went:

> *One sheep, two sheep, three sheep, four . . .*
> *Twenty and thirty . . . forty more;*
> *Strayed—nine ewes; killed—ten rams;*
> *Seven and seventy lost little lambs.*

He was the only soul I could see
On the lonely range for company—
Save one lean wolf and a prairie-dog,
And a myriad of ants at the foot of a log;
So I sat the herder down on a clod—
But his eyes went counting the ants in the sod:

> *One sheep, two sheep, three sheep, four . . .*
> *Fifty and sixty . . . seventy more;*
> *There's not in this flock a good bell-wether!*
> *Then how can a herder hold it together!*

Seeking to cheer him in his plight,
I flung my blankets down for the night;
But he wouldn't talk as we sat by the fire—
Corralling sheep was his sole desire;
With fingers that pointed near and far,
Mumbling, he herded star by star:

> *One sheep, two sheep, three—as before!*
> *Eighty and ninety . . . a thousand more!*
> *My lost little lambs—one thousand seven!*
> *Are wandering over the hills of Heaven.*[5]

Lew Sarett

The famous witch scene from *Macbeth* is difficult to interpret—unless three or more interpreters work together—because of the bodily rhythm integrated with the poetic rhythm. You will be paid dividends, however, through the practice of wide and changing vocal slides, steps and key. The playwright's artistry in securing a continuous, blended rhythm through the chant of the weird sisters is extraordinary in its eerie melody. Be careful to show the marked contrast in the voices of Macbeth and Banquo. Remember the hour is late and the news of the witches is a foreboding of events to come.

[5] From COVENANT WITH EARTH, by Lew Sarett. Gainesville: University of Florida Press, 1956. Reprinted by permission of Mrs. Lew Sarett.

from *Macbeth*

ACT I, SCENE 3

This scene takes place late at night on a heath near Forres. It is stormy and thunder is heard.

FIRST WITCH: Where hast thou been, sister?

SECOND WITCH: Killing swine.

THIRD WITCH: Sister, where thou?

1. WITCH: A sailor's wife had chestnuts in her lap,
    And munch'd, and munch'd, and munch'd. "Give me," quoth I.
    "Aroint thee, witch!" the rump-fed ronyon cries.
    Her husband's to Aleppo gone, master o' the Tiger;
    But in a sieve I'll thither sail,
    And, like a rat without a tail,
    I'll do, I'll do, and I'll do.

2. WITCH: I'll give thee a wind.

1. WITCH: Thou'rt kind.

3. WITCH: And I another.

1. WITCH: I myself have all the other,
    And the very ports they blow,
    All the quarters that they know
    I' the shipman's card.
    I'll drain him dry as hay.
    Sleep shall neither night nor day
    Hang upon his pent-house lid;
    He shall live a man forbid.
    Weary se'nnights nine times nine
    Shall he dwindle, peak, and pine:
    Though his bark cannot be lost,
    Yet it shall be tempest-tost.
    Look what I have.

2. WITCH: Show me, show me.

1. WITCH: Here I have a pilot's thumb,
    Wreck'd as homeward he did come. (*Drums within*)

3. WITCH: A drum, a drum!
    Macbeth doth come.

ALL: The weird sisters, hand in hand,
    Posters of the sea and land,
    Thus do go about, about;
    Thrice to thine, and thrice to mine.
    And thrice again, to make up nine.
    Peace! the charm's wound up.

Enter MACBETH *and* BANQUO

MACBETH: So foul and fair a day I have not seen.

BANQUO: How far is't call'd to Forres? What are these
　　　So wither'd and so wild in their attire,
　　　That look not like the inhabitants o' the earth,
　　　And yet are on't? Live you? or are you aught
　　　That man may question? You seem to understand me,
　　　By each at once her choppy finger laying
　　　Upon her skinny lips. You should be women,
　　　And yet your beards forbid me to interpret
　　　That you are so.
MACBETH: Speak, if you can. What are you?
1. WITCH: All hail, Macbeth! hail to thee, thane of Glamis!
2. WITCH: All hail, Macbeth! hail to thee, thane of Cawdor!
3. WITCH: All hail, Macbeth, that shalt be King hereafter!
BANQUO: Good sir, why do you start, and seem to fear
　　　Things that do sound fair? (*To the witches*) I' the name of truth,
　　　Are ye fantastical, or that indeed
　　　Which outwardly ye show? My noble partner
　　　You greet with present grace and great prediction
　　　Of noble having and of royal hope,
　　　That he seems rapt withal; to me you speak not.
　　　If you can look into the seeds of time,
　　　And say which grain will grow and which will not,
　　　Speak then to me, who neither beg nor fear
　　　Your favours nor your hate.
1. WITCH: Hail!
2. WITCH: Hail!
3. WITCH: Hail!
1. WITCH: Lesser than Macbeth, and greater.
2. WITCH: Not so happy, yet much happier.
3. WITCH: Thou shalt get kings, though thou be none;
　　　So all hail, Macbeth and Banquo!
1. WITCH: Banquo and Macbeth, all hail!
MACBETH: Stay, you imperfect speakers, tell me more.
　　　By Sinel's death I know I am thane of Glamis;
　　　But how of Cawdor? The thane of Cawdor lives,
　　　A prosperous gentleman; and to be king
　　　Stands not within the prospect of belief
　　　No more than to be Cawdor. Say from whence
　　　You owe this strange intelligence, or why
　　　Upon this blasted heath you stop our way
　　　With such prophetic greeting. Speak, I charge you.
　　　　　　　　WITCHES *vanish*

　　　　　　　　　　　　　　　SHAKESPEARE

In this brief dialogue between Alice and Humpty Dumpty, Carroll's italicized words indicate that particular emphasis should be given to certain inflectional tones. Find various slides, steps and differences in key range to get the contrast of the condescending and presumptuous voice of Humpty Dumpty with Alice's unsophisticated intonational pattern, especially her tone of wonderment.

Alice, in her journey through Wonderland, comes upon an egg and expects any moment that it will be transformed into a tree:

from *Humpty Dumpty*

However, the egg only got larger and larger, and more and more human: when she had come within a few yards of it, she saw that it had eyes and a nose and mouth; and when she had come close to it, she saw clearly that it was HUMPTY DUMPTY himself. "It can't be anybody else!" she said to herself. "I'm as certain of it, as if his name were written all over his face."

It might have been written a hundred times, easily, on that enormous face. Humpty Dumpty was sitting with his legs crossed, like a Turk, on the top of a high wall—such a narrow one that Alice quite wondered how he could keep his balance—and, as his eyes were steadily fixed in the opposite direction, and he didn't take the least notice of her, she thought he must be a stuffed figure after all.

"And how exactly like an egg he is!" she said aloud, standing with her hands ready to catch him, for she was every moment expecting him to fall.

"It's *very* provoking," Humpty Dumpty said after a long silence, looking away from Alice as he spoke, "to be called an egg—*very!*"

"I said you *looked* like an egg, Sir," Alice gently explained. "And some eggs are very pretty, you know," she added, hoping to turn her remark into a sort of compliment.

"Some people," said Humpty Dumpty, looking away from her as usual, "have no more sense than a baby!" . . . "But tell me your name and your business."

"My *name* is Alice, but—"

"It's a stupid name enough!" Humpty Dumpty interrupted impatiently. "What does it mean?"

"*Must* a name mean something?" Alice asked doubtfully.

"Of course it must," Humpty Dumpty said with a short laugh: "*my* name means the shape I am—and a good handsome shape it is, too. With a name like yours, you might be any shape, almost."

"Why do you sit out here all alone?" said Alice, not wishing to begin an argument.

"Why, because there's nobody with me!" cried Humpty Dumpty. "Did you think I didn't know the answer to *that?* Ask another."

"Don't you think you'd be safer down on the ground?" Alice went on, not with any idea of making another riddle, but simply in her good-natured anxiety for the queer creature. "That wall is so *very* narrow!"

"What tremendously easy riddles you ask!" Humpty Dumpty growled out. "Of course I don't think so! Why, if ever I *did* fall off—which there's no chance of—but *if* I did—" Here he pursed up his lips and looked so solemn and grand that Alice could hardly help laughing. "*If I did* fall," he went on, "*the King has promised me*—ah, you may turn pale, if you like! You didn't think I was going to say that, did you? *The King has promised me—with his very own mouth—to—to—*"

"To send all his horses and all his men," Alice interrupted, rather unwisely.

"Now I declare that's too bad!" Humpty Dumpty cried, breaking into a sudden passion. "You've been listening at doors—and behind trees—and down chimneys—or you couldn't have known it!"

"I haven't indeed!" Alice said very gently. "It's in a book."

"Ah, well! They may write such things in a *book*," Humpty Dumpty said in a calmer tone. "That's what you call a History of England, that is. Now, take a good look at me! I'm one that has spoken to a King, *I* am: mayhap you'll never see such another: and to show you I'm not proud, you may shake hands with me!" And he grinned almost from ear to ear, as he leant forwards (and as nearly as possible fell off the wall in doing so) and offered Alice his hand. She watched him a little anxiously as she took it. "If he smiled much more, the ends of his mouth might meet behind," she thought: "and then I don't know *what* would happen to his head! I'm afraid it would come off!"

"Yes, all his horses and all his men," Humpty Dumpty went on. "They'd pick me up again in a minute, *they* would! However, this conversation is going on a little too fast: let's go back to the last remark but one."

"I'm afraid I can't quite remember it," Alice said very politely.

"In that case we start fresh," said Humpty Dumpty, "and it's my turn to choose a subject"— . . . "So here's a question for you. How old did you say you were?"

Alice made a short calculation, and said "Seven years and six months."

"Wrong!" Humpty Dumpty exclaimed triumphantly. "You never said a word like it!"

"I thought you meant 'How old *are* you?' " Alice explained.

"If I'd meant that, I'd have said it." . . .

"When *I* use a word," Humpty Dumpty said in rather a scornful tone, "it means just what I choose it to mean—neither more nor less."

"The question is," said Alice, "whether you *can* make words mean so many different things."

"The question is," said Humpty Dumpty, "which is to be master—that's all."

Alice was too much puzzled to say anything, so after a minute Humpty Dumpty began again. "They've a temper, some of them—particularly verbs: they're the proudest—adjectives you can do anything with, but not verbs—however, *I* can manage the whole lot of them! Impenetrability! That's what *I* say!"

"Would you tell me, please," said Alice, "what *that* means?"

"Now you talk like a reasonable child," said Humpty Dumpty, looking very much pleased. "I meant by 'impenetrability' that we've had enough of that subject, and it would be just as well if you'd mention what you mean to do next, as I suppose you don't mean to stop here all the rest of your life."

"That's a great deal to make one word mean," Alice said in a thoughtful tone.

"When I make a word do a lot of work like that," said Humpty Dumpty, "I always pay it extra."

"Oh!" said Alice. She was too much puzzled to make any other remark.

"Ah, you should see 'em come round me of a Saturday night," Humpty Dumpty went on, wagging his head gravely from side to side: "for to get their wages, you know."[6]

Lewis Carroll, *Through the Looking Glass*

Mark Twain, in *The Innocents Abroad*,[7] comes in contact with bustling guides as they march sightseers through "miles of pictures and sculptures" and "frescoes enough to fresco the heavens"—all done by "Michael Angelo." He and his American party, getting exasperated with the parrot-like talk of the guides, decide never to go into ecstasies over anything, to keep "impassible faces and stupid indifference in the presence of the sublimest wonders" and to keep their serenity at all times. The doctor in their group is chosen to ask the questions because he can "keep his countenance and look more like an inspired idiot and throw more imbecility into the tone of his voice than any other man alive." Here is an excerpt concerning their antics with a French guide in Genoa.

from *The Innocents Abroad*

The guides in Genoa are delighted to secure an American party, because Americans so much wonder, and deal so much in sentiment and emotion before any relic of Columbus. Our guide there fidgeted about as if he had swallowed a spring mattress. He was full of animation—full of impatience. He said:

"Come wis me, genteelmen!—come! I show you ze letter-writing by Christopher Colombo!—write it himself!—write it wis his own hand!—come!"

He took us to the municipal palace. After much impressive fumbling of keys and opening of locks, the stained and aged document was spread before us. The guide's eyes sparkled. He danced about us and tapped the parchment with his finger:

"What I tell you, genteelmen! Is it not so? See! handwriting Christopher Colombo!—write it himself!"

We looked indifferent—unconcerned. The doctor examined the document very deliberately, during a painful pause. Then he said, without any show of interest:

"Ah—Ferguson—what—what did you say was the name of the party who wrote this?"

"Christopher Colombo! ze great Christopher Colombo!"

[6] Martin Gardner notes in his "Introduction and Notes," *The Annotated Alice* (New York: Clarkson N. Potter, Inc., 1960), p. 268, that Humpty Dumpty is Carroll's philologist and philosopher, "skilled primarily in linguistic matters"; that the author was "fully aware of the profundity of Humpty Dumpty's whimsical discourse on semantics." Gardner points out that Carroll gave him the point of view of "nominalism," namely that universal terms are nothing but verbal utterances, a view now "held by almost all contemporary logical empiricists."

[7] Mark Twain (Samuel Clemens), *The Innocents Abroad* (New York: The American Publishing Company, 1870), V. I, Ch. 27, pp. 303-307.

Another deliberate examination.

"Ah—did he write it himself, or—or how?"

"He write it himself!—Christopher Colombo! he's own handwriting, write by himself!"

Then the doctor laid the document down and said:

"Why, I have seen boys in America only fourteen years old that could write better than that."

"But zis is ze great Christo—"

"I don't care who it is! It's the worst writing I ever saw. Now you mustn't think you can impose on us because we are strangers. We are not fools, by a good deal. If you have got any specimens of penmanship of real merit, trot them out!—and if you haven't, drive on!"

We drove on. The guide was considerably shaken up, but he made one more venture. He had something which he thought would overcome us. . . .

"Ah, genteelmen, you come wis me! I show you beautiful, oh, magnificent bust Christopher Colombo!—splendid, grand, magnificent!"

He brought us before the beautiful bust—for it *was* beautiful—and sprang back and struck an attitude:

"Ah, look, genteelmen!—beautiful, grand,—bust Christopher Colombo!—beautiful bust, beautiful pedestal!"

The doctor put up his eyeglass—procured for such occasions:

"Ah—what did you say this gentleman's name was?"

"Christopher Colombo!—ze great Christopher Colombo!"

" 'Christopher Colombo—ze great Christopher Colombo.' Well, what did *he* do?"

"Discover America!—discover America, oh, ze devil!"

"Discover America. No—that statement will hardly wash. We are just from America ourselves. We heard nothing about it. Christopher Colombo—pleasant name—is—is he dead?"

"Oh, *corpo di Baccho!*—three hundred year!"

"What did he die of?"

"I do not know!—I cannot tell."

"Smallpox, think?"

"I do not know, genteelmen!—I do not know *what* he die of!"

"Measles, likely?"

"Maybe—maybe—I do *not* know—I think he die of somethings."

"Parents living?"

"Im-posseeble!"

"Ah—which is the bust and which is the pedestal?"

"Santa Maria!—*zis* ze bust!—*zis* ze pedestal!"

"Ah, I see, I see—happy combination—very happy combination, indeed. Is —is this the first time this gentleman was ever on a bust?"

That joke was lost on the foreigner—guides cannot master the subtleties of the American joke.

. . . Yesterday we spent three or four hours in the Vatican again, that wonderful world of curiosities. We came very near expressing interest, some-times—even admiration—it was very hard to keep from it. We succeeded though. Nobody else did, in the Vatican museums. The guide was bewildered—non-plussed. . . . He had reserved what he considered to be his greatest wonder till the last—a royal Egyptian mummy, the best-preserved in the world, perhaps. He took us there. He felt so sure, this time, that some of his old enthusiasm came back to him:

"See, genteelmen!—Mummy! Mummy!"

The eyeglass came up as calmly, as deliberately as ever.

"Ah,—Ferguson—what did I understand you to say the gentleman's name was?"

"Name?—he got no name!—Mummy!—'Gyptian mummy!"

"Yes, yes. Born here?"

"No! *'Gyptian* mummy!"

"Ah, just so. Frenchman, I presume?"

"No!—*not* Frenchman, not Roman!—born in Egypta!"

"Born in Egypta. Never heard of Egypta before. Foreign locality, likely. Mummy—mummy. How calm he is—how self-possessed. Is, ah—is he dead?"

"Oh, *sacré bleu,* been dead three thousan' year!" The doctor turned on him savagely:

"Here, now, what do you mean by such conduct as this! Playing us for Chinamen because we are strangers and trying to learn! Trying to impose your vile second-hand carcasses on *us!*—thunder and lightning, I've a notion to—to— if you've got a nice *fresh* corpse, fetch him out!—or, by George, we'll brain you!"

We make it exceedingly interesting for this Frenchman. However, he has paid us back, partly, without knowing it. He came to the hotel this morning to ask if we were up, and he endeavored as well as he could to describe us, so that the landlord would know which persons he meant. He finished with the casual remark that we were lunatics.

Mark Twain

The mastery of the imitation of any person's speech depends on the sensitivity of the ear to intonational stress, vocal inflections and speech rhythm. Mark Twain, who usually wrote stories in many dialects peculiar to the Mississippi River environment in Missouri, has caught in this sketch the French dialectal rhythm produced by inflectional and stress patterns that in turn influence vocal intensity. The humor of the situation lies in the differences of temperaments shown through the speech and general bodily tonicity: as in the contrast between the highly excitable guide and the flat, noncommittal attitude of the disconcerting and seemingly stupid American doctor.

With an entirely different approach from that of Mark Twain, Thurber provokes laughter in *The Secret Life of Walter Mitty* through vocal changes of his main character in contrasting episodes. The author thrusts his apparently weak and unwilling victim of a nagging wife into unexpected and highly imaginative scenes of courageous undertakings staffed by Walter Mitty in various roles. Thus he presents a complete reversal of personality through speech rhythm, attitude and bodily activity.

Inasmuch as you will have been exposed to three of Thurber's stories, you should at this point know the great humorist personally and should listen to him speak of his technique in securing humor. When he was asked by an interviewer if dealing with humor slowed down his literary production, Thurber remarked:

With humor you have to look out for traps. You're likely to be very gleeful with what you've first put down, and you think it's fine, very funny. One reason you go over and over it is to make the piece sound less as if you were having a lot of fun with it yourself. You try to play it down. In fact, if there's such a thing as a *New Yorker* style, that would be it—playing it down. . . .

Someone once wrote a definition of the difference between English and American humor. I wish I could remember his name. I thought his definition very good. He said that the English treat the commonplace as if it were remarkable and the Americans treat the remarkable as if it were commonplace. I believe that's true of humorous writing. . . . In "The Secret Life of Walter Mitty" I tried to treat the remarkable as commonplace.

The author explains why he wrote *The Thurber Album,* which includes "The Secret Life of Walter Mitty":

The Thurber Album was written at a time when in America there was a feeling of fear and suspicion. It's quite different from *My Life and Hard Times,* which was written earlier and is a funnier and better book. The *Album* was kind of an escape—going back to the Middle West of the last century and the beginning of this, when there wasn't any fear and hysteria. I wanted to write the story of some solid American characters, more or less as an example of how Americans started out and what they should go back to—to sanity and soundness and away from this jumpiness. It's hard to write humor in the mental weather we've had, and that's likely to take you into reminiscence. Your heart isn't in it to write anything funny. In the years 1950 to 1953 I did very few things, nor did they appear in *The New Yorker.*[8]

As you get acquainted with Mr. Mitty, study the contrasts in speech rhythm and episode timing. Think too about the name *Mitty*—does it belong to a strong, daring, resourceful, masterful man of action and courage?

The Secret Life of Walter Mitty

"We're going through!" The Commander's voice was like thin ice breaking. He wore his full-dress uniform, with the heavily braided white cap pulled down rakishly over one cold gray eye. "We can't make it, sir. It's spoiling for a hurricane, if you ask me." "I'm not asking you, Lieutenant Berg," said the Commander. "Throw on the power lights! Rev her up to 8,500! We're going through!" The pounding of the cylinders increased: ta-pocketa-pocketa-pocketa-*pocketa-pocketa.* The Commander stared at the ice forming on the pilot window. He walked over and twisted a row of complicated dials. "Switch on No. 8

[8] *Paris Interview Series,* pp. 88, 97.

auxiliary!" he shouted. "Switch on No. 8 auxiliary!" repeated Lieutenant Berg. "Full strength in No. 3 turret!" shouted the Commander. "Full strength in No. 3 turret!" The crew, bending to their various tasks in the huge, hurtling eight-engined Navy hydroplane, looked at each other and grinned. "The Old Man'll get us through," they said to one another. "The Old Man ain't afraid of Hell!" . . .

"Not so fast! You're driving too fast!" said Mrs. Mitty. "What are you driving so fast for?"

"Hmm?" said Walter Mitty. He looked at his wife, in the seat beside him, with shocked astonishment. She seemed grossly unfamiliar, like a strange woman who had yelled at him in a crowd. "You were up to fifty-five," she said. "You know I don't like to go more than forty. You were up to fifty-five." Walter Mitty drove on toward Waterbury in silence, the roaring of the SN202 through the worst storm in twenty years of Navy flying fading in the remote, intimate airways of his mind. "You're tensed up again," said Mrs. Mitty. "It's one of your days. I wish you'd let Dr. Renshaw look you over."

Walter Mitty stopped the car in front of the building where his wife went to have her hair done. "Remember to get those overshoes while I'm having my hair done," she said. "I don't need overshoes," said Mitty. She put her mirror back into her bag. "We've been all through that," she said, getting out of the car. "You're not a young man any longer." He raced the engine a little. "Why don't you wear your gloves? Have you lost your gloves?" Walter Mitty reached in a pocket and brought out the gloves. He put them on, but after she had turned and gone into the building and he had driven on to a red light, he took them off again. "Pick it up, brother!" snapped a cop as the light changed, and Mitty hastily pulled on his gloves and lurched ahead. He drove around the streets aimlessly for a time, and then he drove past the hospital on his way to the parking lot.

. . . "It's the millionaire banker, Wellington McMillan," said the pretty nurse. "Yes?" said Walter Mitty, removing his gloves slowly. "Who has the case?" "Dr. Renshaw and Dr. Benbow, but there are two specialists here, Dr. Remington from New York and Mr. Pritchard-Mitford from London. He flew over." A door opened down a long, cool corridor and Dr. Renshaw came out. He looked distraught and haggard. "Hello, Mitty," he said. "We're having the devil's own time with McMillan, the millionaire banker and close personal friend of Roosevelt. Obstreosis of the ductal tract. Tertiary. Wish you'd take a look at him." "Glad to," said Mitty.

In the operating room there were whispered introductions: "Dr. Remington, Dr. Mitty. Mr. Pritchard-Mitford, Dr. Mitty." "I've read your book on streptothricosis," said Pritchard-Mitford, shaking hands. "A brilliant performance, sir." "Thank you," said Walter Mitty. "Didn't know you were in the States, Mitty," grumbled Remington. "Coals to Newcastle, bringing Mitford and me up here for a tertiary." "You are very kind," said Mitty. A huge, complicated machine, connected to the operating table, with many tubes and wires, began at this moment to go pocketa-pocketa-pocketa. "The new anesthetizer is giving way!" shouted an interne. "There is no one in the East who knows how to fix it!" "Quiet, man!" said Mitty, in a low, cool voice. He sprang to the machine, which was now going pocketa-pocketa-queep-pocketa-queep. He began fingering delicately a row of glistening dials. "Give me a fountain pen!" he snapped. Someone handed him a fountain pen. He pulled a faulty piston out of the machine and inserted the pen in its place. "That will hold for ten minutes," he said. "Get on with the operation." A nurse hurried over and whispered to Renshaw, and Mitty saw the man turn pale. "Coreopsis has set in," said Renshaw nervously. "If you would take over, Mitty?" Mitty looked at him and at the craven figure of Benbow, who drank, and at the grave, uncertain faces of the two great specialists. "If you wish," he said. They slipped a white gown on him; he adjusted a mask and drew on thin gloves; nurses handed him shining. . . .

"Back it up, Mac! Look out for that Buick!" Walter Mitty jammed on the brakes. "Wrong lane, Mac," said the parking-lot attendant, looking at Mitty closely. "Gee. Yeh," muttered Mitty. He began cautiously to back out of the lane marked "Exit Only." "Leave her sit there," said the attendant. "I'll put her away." Mitty got out of the car. "Hey, better leave the key." "Oh," said Mitty, handing the man the ignition key. The attendant vaulted into the car, backed it up with insolent skill, and put it where it belonged.

They're so damn cocky, thought Walter Mitty, walking along Main Street; they think they know everything. Once he had tried to take his chains off, outside New Milford, and he had got them wound around the axles. A man had had to come out in a wrecking car and unwind them, a young, grinning garageman. Since then Mrs. Mitty always made him drive to a garage to have the chains taken off. The next time, he thought, I'll wear my right arm in a sling; they won't grin at me then. I'll have my right arm in a sling and they'll see I couldn't possibly take the chains off myself. He kicked at the slush on the sidewalk. "Overshoes," he said to himself, and he began looking for a shoe store.

When he came out into the street again, with the overshoes in a box under his arm, Walter Mitty began to wonder what the other thing was his wife had told him to get. She had told him twice, before they set out from their house for Waterbury. In a way he hated these weekly trips to town—he was always getting something wrong. Kleenex, he thought, Squibb's, razor blades? No. Toothpaste, toothbrush, bicarbonate, carborundum, initiative and referendum? He gave it up. But she would remember it. "Where's the what's-its-name?" She would ask. "Don't tell me you forgot the what's-it-name." A newsboy went by shouting something about the Waterbury trial.

. . . "Perhaps this will refresh your memory." The District Attorney suddenly thrust a heavy automatic at the quiet figure on the witness stand. "Have you ever seen this before?" Walter Mitty took the gun and examined it expertly. "This is my Webley-Vickers 50.80," he said calmly. An excited buzz ran around the courtroom. The judge rapped for order. "You are a crack shot with any sort of firearms, I believe?" said the District Attorney, insinuatingly. "Objection!" shouted Mitty's attorney. "We have shown that the defendant could not have fired the shot. We have shown that he wore his right arm in a sling on the night of the fourteenth of July." Walter Mitty raised his hand briefly and the bickering attorneys were stilled. "With any known make of gun," he said evenly, "I could have killed Gregory Mitzhurst at three hundred feet *with my left hand.*" Pandemonium broke loose in the courtroom. A woman's scream rose above the bedlam and suddenly a lovely, dark-haired girl was in Walter Mitty's arms. The District Attorney struck at her savagely. Without rising from his chair, Mitty let the man have it on the point of the chin. "You miserable cur!" . . .

"Puppy biscuit," said Walter Mitty. He stopped walking and the buildings of Waterbury rose up out of the misty courtroom and surrounded him again. A woman who was passing laughed. "He said 'Puppy biscuit,'" she said to her companion. "That man said 'Puppy biscuit' to himself." Walter Mitty hurried on. He went into an A. & P., not the first one he came to but a smaller one farther up the street. "I want some biscuit for small, young dogs," he said to the clerk. "Any special brand, sir?" The greatest pistol shot in the world thought a moment. "It says 'Puppies Bark for It' on the box," said Walter Mitty.

His wife would be through at the hairdresser's in fifteen minutes, Mitty saw in looking at his watch, unless they had trouble drying it; sometimes they had trouble drying it. She didn't like to get to the hotel first; she would want him to be there waiting for her as usual. He found a big leather chair in the lobby, facing a window, and he put the overshoes and the puppy biscuit on the floor beside it. He picked up an old copy of *Liberty* and sank down into the chair. "Can Germany Conquer the World Through the Air?" Walter Mitty looked at the pictures of bombing planes and of ruined streets.

. . . "The cannonading has got the wind up in young Raleigh, sir," said the sergeant. Captain Mitty looked up at him through tousled hair. "Get him to bed," he said wearily. "With the others. I'll fly alone." "But you can't, sir," said the sergeant anxiously. "It takes two men to handle that bomber and the Archies are pounding hell out of the air. Von Richtman's circus is between here and Saulier." "Somebody's got to get that ammunition dump," said Mitty. "I'm going over. Spot of brandy?" He poured a drink for the sergeant and one for himself. War thundered and whined around the dugout and battered at the door. There was a rending of wood and splinters flew through the room. "A bit of a near thing," said Captain Mitty carelessly. "The box barrage is closing in," said the sergeant. "We only live once, Sergeant," said Mitty, with his faint, fleeting smile. "Or do we?" He poured another brandy and tossed it off. "I never see a man could hold his brandy like you, sir," said the sergeant. "Begging your pardon, sir." Captain Mitty stood up and strapped on his huge Webley-Vickers automatic. "It's forty kilometers through hell, sir," said the sergeant. Mitty finished one last brandy. "After all," he said softly, "what isn't?" The pounding of the cannon increased; there was the rat-tat-tatting of machine guns, and from somewhere came the menacing pocketa-pocketa-pocketa of the new flame-throwers. Walter Mitty walked to the door of the dugout humming "Auprès de Ma Blonde." He turned and waved to the sergeant. "Cheerio!" he said. . . .

Something struck his shoulder. "I've been looking all over this hotel for you," said Mrs. Mitty. "Why do you have to hide in this old chair? How did you expect me to find you?" "Things close in," said Walter Mitty vaguely. "What?" Mrs. Mitty said. "Did you get the what's-its-name? The puppy biscuit? What's in that box?" "Overshoes," said Mitty. "Couldn't you have put them on in the store?" "I was thinking," said Walter Mitty. "Does it ever occur to you that I am sometimes thinking?" She looked at him. "I'm going to take your temperature when I get you home," she said.

They went out through the revolving doors that made a faintly derisive whistling sound when you pushed them. It was two blocks to the parking lot. At the drugstore on the corner she said, "Wait here for me. I forgot something.

I won't be a minute." She was more than a minute. Walter Mitty lighted a cigarette. It began to rain, rain with sleet in it. He stood up against the wall of the
drugstore, smoking. . . . He put his shoulders back and his heels together. "To
hell with the handkerchief," said Walter Mitty scornfully. He took one last drag
on his cigarette and snapped it away. Then, with that faint, fleeting smile playing about his lips, he faced the firing squad; erect and motionless, proud and
disdainful, Walter Mitty the Undefeated, inscrutable to the last.[9]

JAMES THURBER

Thurber has made it easy for you to identify with Mitty's release
from the bombardment of a demanding, feminine voice; you are ready
and anxious to rise to great imaginative heights to enjoy his spurts of
operational skill and bravery. You not only understand but appreciate the
hero's need to escape. You anticipate the next associative hint which will
put him in a situation as the top member of the echelon group. Thurber's
technique of suggesting through his narrator certain associations that start
Mitty into his dreams of greatness and bring him back to his duties of
buying overshoes and puppy biscuit are ridiculously funny: the plunge
into the dare-devil "Operation-Speed" with Commander Mitty at the helm
—"The Old Man who ain't afraid of Hell"—and thence to the back-seat
driving of an efficient wife of small affairs, urging him to curb his speed
and to take care of mundane matters of shopping; driving past a hospital
sends Dr. Mitty to "emergency" in the operating room; the newsboy shouting "something about a trial" finds the hero as a defendant in a murder
case, demonstrating his ability to swing his mighty left at the District
Attorney; "you miserable cur" recalls the purchase of puppy biscuit (not
dog food); magazine pictures of "bombing planes and ruined streets" hurl
Captain Mitty into heavy battle with the careless remark, "We live only
once, Sergeant"; when something strikes him on the shoulder, he is verbally and physically pulled out of his chair by his wife with a shower of
questions; and the final effort—to stand against the wall of a drugstore to
avoid the rain—brings on the firing squad—and no doubt, his wife. Walter
Mitty—the Undefeated!

You can now understand how the infectious humor is created through
the sudden changes in episodes and the contrast of the "superior" heroic
speech rhythm—characterized by clichés of professional phrases and short,
taut, tense, decisive tones in moments of great crises—with the non-com-
mittal mutterings and troubled thoughts of forgotten instructions ordered
by the voice of Mitty's superior home officer, his unimaginative and per-
severing wife. Through these reversals, especially the escape episodes,
Thurber presents a sympathetic as well as humorous portrayal; consequently, the empathic response is strong.

[9] *The Secret Life of Walter Mitty* by James Thurber. Copyright © 1939, James
Thurber. Originally published in *The New Yorker*. Reprinted with permission of Mrs.
James Thurber.

In the previous chapter, the effect of intensity on the ironic tone in literature was discussed. Probably the innuendoes through discriminating pitch changes to express a *double entendre* pattern are more important than the vocal attack. Everyone does it in daily conversation and usually thinks inwardly, "I got by with that all right." You, the listener, may think, "Now did he really mean what he said?" Some indulge in this double talk continually and soon acquire an insincerity.

You observed ironic humor in MacDonald's sketch. Another humor—a gentle, self-imposed irony—is found in Perelman's "Young As You Feel." This selection shows how a prose writer can stir up laugh-provoking images and thoughts through ironic contrasts; and combine the personal tone of braggadocio—"young as you feel"—with a blithe rationalization of how he keeps young and dapper while his friends grow so obviously old. No one but Perelman could write such a delightfully funny sentence as this: "Simultaneously, a factory whistle deep in my thyroid gave a long, piercing blast to signalize the close of business, and before I could claw open my collar to equalize the pressure, I was a forty-six-year-old alumnus entirely surrounded by floor." What in these kinesthetic images makes you laugh? Ego, of course, tinged with irony! Your fancy is also tickled by the clever assortment of inappropriate words to describe the fall of the ego. The contrast of what the narrator thinks he is as a beau brummel and what he really is as he leans toward the older age line is pointed up several times with tongue-in-cheek nonchalance.

Can you laugh with this character who blows himself up into an inflated balloon of carbon dioxide only to find that it collapses when a pinpoint fractures it; and who decides with a final slightly ironic tone that after all, "I love young people, but they're so darn *shallow*"? Watch the timing and inflections of the last sentence and do not attack too strongly with your voice for the author is only secretly laughing at himself—and enjoying the ironic touch.

Young As You Feel

The stroke that really sent my traducers slithering into their holes, though, and forever extracted their venom, was dealt them the night of my twenty-fifth college reunion. Between ourselves, I had been reluctant to attend, suspecting that the sight of a jaunty figure and hair as black as the raven's wing would shame my doddering classmates, but I weakly gave in when they persuaded me to appear, if only for contrast. Notwithstanding, I thought as I entered the ballroom where our silver jubilee dance was in progress that I had blundered into some ghostly quadrille. These decrepit, shrunken gaffers waltzing stately about, with their wigs askew and dentures flapping—could they be the youths I had rollicked with in the Jazz Age? My worst misgivings were justified; one after the other, seamed faces nodded welcome and called out greetings in voices that croaked like Aristophanes' *Frogs.* Just as I was deciding to steal away to some milieu on my own age level, say a Fifty-second Street jam session, an elderly fogy clapped me boisterously on the back.

"Didn't recognize you, Skinny," he quavered. "You're as flabby as those old quilts we used when we roomed together." I shook hands distantly and remarked that, unlike his, my teeth were still first edition.

"They look it," he chuckled, presenting the young lady with him and vanishing into the bar. For some reason I could not fathom, unless that she noticed my fleeting resemblance to Vernon Castle the creature began pressing me to dance with her. I declined gracefully, explaining that I gave only charity exhibitions now, but she deliberately chose to misunderstand.

"I know—it's the arteries," she said. "Wait a minute, Pops—I'll find you a chair." My blood boiled up at the injustice of the slur; an instant later, we were circling the floor dizzily, pirouetting and dipping like swallows, our bodies moving as two to the savage beat of the music. The other dancers, electrified by skill they could not hope to rival, gave ground and applauded us on; the orchestra quickened its rhythm to match our flying feet. Around and round we went, shifting from the Cubanola glide into the toddle, from the bunny-hug to the maxixe and the balconade. The saxaphones were sobbing. "La Veeda, Maid of Spain," and I was whirling my breathless partner through the intricacies of the camel walk when I noticed to my consternation that she had developed two heads and that steam was issuing from both. Simultaneously, a factory whistle deep in my thyroid gave a long, piercing blast to signalize the close of business, and before I could claw open my collar to equalize the pressure, I was a forty-six-year-old alumnus entirely surrounded by floor.

Well, men, say what you will, there's nothing like a few weeks on the horizontal to tone up the system. You catch up on your reading and you get plenty of exercise, too, slamming down the phone when your friends call up to commiserate. Just for the record, I feel right as rain, fine as silk, and sound as a nut, and the moment the doc gives me the nod, I figure to get down to the seashore for a nice rest. Some place without too many young flibbertigibbets cavorting about and raising Cain till all hours. I love young people, but they're so darn *shallow.* You never know what they're thinking—and maybe it's just as well.[10]

S. J. PERELMAN

13

Total Expression of the Impression

Throughout this book your vocal and bodily controls have been emphasized. Your personality as a performer has been mentioned only casually because the student interpreter gradually develops his own individualistic approach as his interest in literary problems increases. Now a few pages are in order on *how* you can present yourself as an individual and *how* you can meet the audience situation.

THE INTERPRETER

In your final attempt to secure and express meaningful impressions through vocal and bodily integration, your willingness to create an *esprit de corps* in an interpretative situation is the culminating asset in creating *total* enjoyment. If you choose to be the interpreter of a story, event, incident or characterization found in poetry, prose or drama, then you must be the pivotal figure around which attention and interest will center. You must mean to others by being organically alive, alert in an immediate manner, not merely systematically, mechanically or functionally alive; not even just intelligently alive, because in some instances that attitude might imply a dull passivity to your listeners.

YOU—THE INDIVIDUAL

You mean first as an individual: a person with a certain temperament, attitude, approach, vocal flexibility—plus particular reactions that make you personable. You cannot be just anybody interpreting anybody's literature in anybody's manner. You *mean* as a distinctive individual vitalizing your impressions so that the urgency of communication with others is felt in a special memorable way. With ease of manner and economy of effort, an inner intensity of belief in self, literature and audience response should be present. As an interpreter, Sandburg has this distinctiveness for he *means* in his own particular rhythmical manner; Thomas shows a sustained buoyancy and sensitivity that is typically Thomas and thus lifts his poems and stories to an impressive level. His is a personal approach; so is Frost's; so is Laughton's; so is McKenna's; so is Helen Hayes's.

This extra-perceptive quality that intensifies meaning for others must seem to evolve and become vivid through your own inner potential instead of being pushed on an audience in a mechanical way. To speak of inner responses may seem inappropriate to some who write vaguely about the mind; but not to famous present-day neurologists who are continually tapping and stimulating nerve endings to stir up response.[1] You should be aware that today the mind is considered a nebulous circuit of nerve fibers relaying, through their wandering chains, chemical or electrical "touch-offs" to reacting muscles, thus arousing associations closely related to the presented stimulus. Some individuals have a greater intuitive and instinctive appreciation (nerve stimulations) of the impression to be created; some may not recognize relationships (synaptic reactions) nor be so well-adjusted in controlling the output machinery (relay circuits in the brain).

DISCRIMINATING LITERARY TASTE

Discriminating taste in the selection of literature will definitely characterize you as a perceptive individual. Explanatory discussions will never benefit you in the way that actual experience does. You have to learn the effect on an audience of placing your standards too high or too low. At times you need a multidirectional program for a mixed audience; other times, you may wish to limit your interpretations to a certain intellectual level; sometimes your goal may be to present a light and entertaining program. Generally an audience enjoys literature for the connotative associations that stir up empathic responses; they are more likely to enjoy the impression if they can say to themselves, "Yes, I know—I remember."

If you decide to demonstrate the philosophy of the poet through his poetry, then you must prepare your audience, footnote as you proceed, amplify and extend the exposition of the poetry. For instance, Donne's general acceptance as a metaphysical poet will not guarantee an interpretation that will reinforce this reputation, unless you help the audience to follow and thus to appreciate. Look again at Millay's "The Ballad of the Harp-Weaver." You may be confused, as some are, with the mystical meanings of the images—"wind with a wolf's head," "harp with a woman's head"—and the relationship of the Madonna and Magi themes. Certainly these images add to the mysticism of the theme. The final interpretative effect of the ballad, however, lies in the tone you give the narrative because of images, smoothness of the lines with their clear-cut, simple di-

[1] *Speech and Brain Mechanisms* by Wilder Penfield and Lamar Roberts is a volume you can understand and appreciate. Published by Princeton University Press, 1959.

rectness and yet mystical wonder. Robert Lowell, after his experiences during a summer of lectures in the East, remarks that the best poems are not always the ones that capture the interest of the audience or the ones that should be read aloud, for inspiration is no substitute for humor, shock, narrative and a hypnotic voice, the four musts for an oral interpretation."[2]

Woolbert, one of the greatest teachers of and promoters for speech in the early twentieth century, once wrote on the fly-leaf of an 1865 edition of Elizabethan lyrics these notes:

1. What is poetry? A visible form? No—something heard.
2. When is poetry good? When it talks.
3. The lyric must talk.
4. What of Elizabethan lyrics? Some talked; some showed off.

This was the end of the lecture outline, but typical of Woolbert's communicative approach in teaching interpretation. You, as an interpreter, must know how to make literature "talk"; you must also realize some literary writing is written to remain on the printed page. You have come in contact with certain excerpts in this book that would interest only a particular type of audience and would not "talk" to a heterogeneous group. Keep your literary taste on a high level; always think, however, in terms of talking value rather than a philosophy that cannot be interpreted easily —and so cannot be understood, even by a sophisticated group. The most important questions in your thoughts should be: "Can I meet the spirit of the occasion with this literature?" "Can I break down the barriers of conscious attentiveness and awareness of the listeners to create empathy with this literary approach?" Woolbert, the pragmatist, would have agreed with Ciardi: "Questions of art are questions of execution."[3]

This chapter has been planned to give you further experience in various types of literature, theme, approach, stylistic and rhythmical patterns, characterizations. Many other poems, prose narratives and dramatic scenes in the earlier pages could be profitably examined again, since you are now working toward a total interpretation by means of all discussed techniques.

POETRY, PROSE & DRAMA

The minor differences in interpreting poems, prose narratives and dramas revolve, to a large degree, around the concentration employed in getting them started. In poetry, you expect to be plunged immediately into an environment, conflict, idea or characterization. You cannot cut or

[2] Robert Lowell, "On Robert Lowell's 'Skunk Hour,'" *The Contemporary Poet as Artist and Critic,* Anthony Ostroff, ed. (Boston: Little, Brown and Company, 1964), p. 108.
[3] From DIALOGUE WITH AN AUDIENCE by John Ciardi. Copyright © 1958 by John Ciardi. Published by J. B. Lippincott Company.

substitute words, phrases or lines without destroying the poet's imagery and rhythmical pattern. You must learn to pinpoint his meaning in a finely directed attempt.

The narrative may begin with an exposition, a background environment, dialogue, inner thoughts of a character, description of a character or scene or at the climax of the story. No matter what kind of beginning the author chooses, a narrative thread eventually unites the various story-telling elements: what happens, why it happens, how it happens, where it happens and to whom it happens. If parts are eliminated because of the time limit in presentation, explanations are in order so the audience can get the total meaning.

These statements are true also of a scene or two extracted from a play. The audience must be kept informed in such a way as not to destroy the manner in which the story is unfolded. Some explanation is needed to set the specific background, revealed on the stage through decor suggesting time, place and atmosphere. The scenes should be picked carefully to show progression of events or development and conflict of characters—whichever the playwright is emphasizing. The story, of course, is told through the speech and activity of the actors. Consequently, effective interpretation from dramas depends greatly on audience preparation for the scenes and characters selected, as well as upon your bodily attitude, facial expression and voice.

POETRY

GENERAL ASSESSMENT

Since you know something about the development of a speech pattern, as well as the investigation of meaning, now examine these poems for total expression—working *toute d'une piece*. A few comments have been inserted to intrigue and motivate you but not necessarily to have you agree. *All* vocal factors should be integrated with bodily attitude to present the impression. The important principle is two-fold: understanding *why* and *how* the author has given a certain meaning; and *how* to re-create it through communicative ability. This point has been emphasized throughout these several hundred pages as the philosophy underlying the art of interpretative speech.

LITERARY ANALYSIS

The following poems are mainly lyrics. You will have to decide whether the expository, narrative, descriptive, emotional or dramatic elements predominate in each one and interpret accordingly. Your poetic classification should be justified by your interpretative impression and expression. After this prosaic directive, you may find an effective antidote in Kazantzakis's poetic principle that "Life is what inspiration is to a poem": if you are to comprehend a poem, something other than words— that "only obstruct the flow of inspiration"—is needed. The poet writes: "We must plunge into its heart, we must live in its inspiration, we must enter into a rhythmical harmony with the poet himself, for only then may the words lose their rigidity and inflexibility or may the current rush on its way once more and the poem seethe in us with its true essence, and which a grammatical analysis can never discover."[4]

POEMS FOR STUDY

Sandburg's tone in his poem "Cool Tombs" is one of philosophical wonder, so be careful of a dominant, aggressive attitude.

Cool Tombs

When Abraham Lincoln was shoveled into the tombs, he forgot the
copperheads and the assassin . . . in the dust, in the cool tombs.

And Ulysses Grant lost all thought of con men and Wall Street, cash
and collateral turned ashes . . . in the dust, in the cool tombs.

Pocahontas' body, lovely as a poplar, sweet as a red haw in November, or a pawpaw in May, did she wonder? does she remember?
. . . in the dust, in the cool tombs?

Take any streetful of people buying clothes and groceries, cheering a
hero or throwing confetti and blowing tin horns . . . tell me if
the lovers are losers . . . tell me if any get more than the lovers
. . . in the dust . . . in the cool tombs.[5]

CARL SANDBURG

Too many downward slides will not give the listener's imagination a chance to wander into the paths of the poet's thoughts. Keep the query, the doubt, in your voice through your inflections. Decide whether or not

[4] From Nikos Kazantzakis, "Introduction," *The Odyssey, A Modern Sequel,* trans. by Kimon Friar. Copyright © 1958 by Simon and Schuster, Inc. Reprinted by permission of the publishers, p. xvii.

[5] From CORNHUSKERS by Carl Sandburg. Copyright 1918 by Holt, Rinehart and Winston, Inc. Copyright 1946 by Carl Sandburg. Reprinted by permission of Holt, Rinehart and Winston, Inc.

you should change the key as you merge into the refrain of "in the dust, in the cool tombs," which requires special timing through pauses. You will notice that the tone is in a minor key so intensity is moderate.

Careful consideration must be given to the contrast in moods in "Naming of the Parts." Read it over, observing Henry Reed's technique in changing from one mood to another.

Naming of Parts

To-day we have naming of parts. Yesterday,
We had daily cleaning. And to-morrow morning,
We shall have what to do after firing. But to-day,
To-day we have naming of parts. Japonica
Glistens like coral in all of the neighbouring gardens,
     And to-day we have naming of parts.

This is the lower sling swivel. And this
Is the upper sling swivel, whose use you will see,
When you are given your slings. And this is the piling
    swivel,
Which in your case you have not got. The branches
Hold in the gardens, their silent, eloquent gestures,
     Which in our case we have not got.

This is the safety-catch, which is always released
With an easy flick of the thumb. And please do not let me
See anyone using his finger. You can do it quite easy
If you have any strength in your thumb. The blossoms
Are fragile and motionless, never letting anyone see
     Any of them using their finger.

And this you can see is the bolt. The purpose of this
Is to open the breech, as you see. We can slide it
Rapidly backwards and forwards: we call this
Easing the spring. And rapidly backwards and forwards
The early bees are assaulting and fumbling the flowers:
     They call it easing the Spring.

They call it easing the Spring: it is perfectly easy
If you have any strength in your thumb: like the bolt,
And the breech, and the cocking-piece, and the point of
    balance,
Which in our case we have not got; and the almond-
    blossom

Silent in all of the gardens and the bees going backwards
and forwards,
For to-day we have naming of parts.[6]

HENRY REED

A quick transference from mechanical matters to enjoyment of spring
is necessitated by the narrator's sudden shift in thought, time and environment. The outward matter-of-fact tone of the moment is in control and
command, not too successfully covering up the inner emotional remembrance of spring.

The vocal inflections used to explain facts are sometimes more obvious in their flexibility than those recalling images of sensory appeal. The
key range will change back and forth as you go from the instructional tone
to the memory tone; but the steps will be narrowed in the spring episodes
as well as the vocal slides.

Vocal intensity will be softened in recalling spring compared to the
stress employed to make the parts named clearly understood. So too, will
the sound quantities be given more attention in the colorful images in
contrast to the abrupt attack on naming the parts. Your vocal flexibility
will naturally show the different rhythms in the author's word choice and
phrasing.

Some find an ironic tinge to phrases like "easing the spring" and "you
have not got" and "point of balance"; others find merely the pun on words
and phrases—of which you may find more in this poem. Whatever meaning
you accept, your upward and wave-like inflections will have to show the
two-edged meaning with appropriate pauses—but pauses that are not too
long because of the blending of the two rhythmical patterns.

Your delight in Cummings's "atmospheric" lyric will motivate you to
try interesting vocal variety.

hist whist

hist   whist
little ghostthings
tip-toe
twinkle-toe

little twitchy
witches and tingling
goblins
hob-a-nob   hob-a-nob

[6] From A MAP OF VERONA AND OTHER POEMS, copyright, 1947, by
Henry Reed. Reprinted by permission of Harcourt, Brace & World, Inc.

little hoppy happy
toad in tweeds
tweeds
little itchy mousies

with scuttling
eyes   rustle and run   and
hidehidehide
whisk

whisk   look out for the old woman
with the wart on her nose
what she'll do to yer
nobody knows

for she knows the devil   ooch
the devil   ouch
the devil
ach   the great

green
dancing
devil
devil

devil
devil
        wheeEEE[7]

          E. E. CUMMINGS

You could interpret this "twitchy, tingling, scuttling" poem in many ways. The title offers clues to the tone and atmosphere. Wide as well as narrow steps with eerie vocal quality and intensity should be your endeavor. Pauses—sustained by bodily posture—will clinch an interesting climax.

The personal touch in "Toby" gives a distinctive appeal that is difficult to resist.

Toby Goes to Market

We shipped the calf to the market—
Toby, the brindle-bull,

With his face of perpetual wonder,
  And his tail like stuck-out wool.

Toby, who wallowed in mischief:
  Who squirmed through the pasture-rails,
Trampled my garden of melons,
  Battered my milking-pails.

Toby, who cried in the downpour,
  Too frugal of brindle brain
To dash from the storm into shelter,
  Or rump himself to the rain.

We tried to corral him for market;
  He blatted, his fear intense,
Straddled his legs on a railing,
  And hung himself on the fence.

We cornered him and roped him,
  He flung out his legs and sprawled;
We dragged him into the cow-pen,
  And there bewildered he bawled.

I drove him into the runway
  That leads to the cattle-cars;
He rattled his heels on the pickets
  And battered his head on the bars.

Pierre jammed him in with the cattle,
  Beside his bellowing cow;
She lowed to her suckling gently
  And licked the blood from his brow.

And Toby trembled beside her,
  Fear in his big brown eyes,
As he heard the thunder and tumult
  Of clamoring cattle rise.

A lurch of the snorting engine
  Flung him beneath the feet
Of steers that trampled him earthward;
  And Toby began to bleat.

He was on his way to the market,
  Toby, the neighborhood pet,
Who had licked the salt from my fingers
  And slavered my hands with wet.

> He was off on the big adventure;
> He was reluctant to go
> On a jaunt that had no returning—
> Oh, Toby, how did you know![8]

Lew Sarett

If you listen with a discriminating ear to Sarett's recording of "Toby,"[9] you will hear the poet's subtle use of slides to show personal sympathy for the calf and thus to awaken a similar response in his listeners. Since the emotional meaning is gained through descriptive narrative, be careful of being too dramatic. Pauses will intensify Toby's predicament.

Marvell's poem, "To His Coy Mistress," is usually discussed with great interest within interpretative groups because of the meaning that students, with their various backgrounds, read into the lines. You will do well to remember that Marvell wrote in the seventeenth century at a time when poetry was structured around conceits, wit and ingenuity of phrase; and the tone was never heavily serious.

To His Coy Mistress

> Had we but world enough, and time,
> This coyness, lady, were no crime.
> We would sit down, and think which way
> To walk, and pass our long love's day.
> Thou by the Indian Ganges' side
> Shouldst rubies find: I by the tide
> Of Humber would complain. I would
> Love you ten years before the Flood,
> And you should, if you please, refuse
> Till the conversion of the Jews.
> My vegetable love should grow
> Vaster than empires and more slow:
> An hundred years should go to praise
> Thine eyes, and on thy forehead gaze;
> Two hundred to adore each breast,
> But thirty thousand to the rest;
> An age at least to every part,
> And the last age should show your heart.
> For, lady, you deserve this state,
> Nor would I love at lower rate.

But at my back I always hear
Time's wingèd chariot hurrying near,
And yonder all before us lie
Deserts of vast eternity.
Thy beauty shall no more be found,
Nor, in thy marble vault, shall sound
My echoing song; then worms shall try
That long-preserved virginity,
And your quaint honor turn to dust,
And into ashes all my lust.
The grave's a fine and private place,
But none, I think, do there embrace.

Now, therefore, while the youthful hue
Sits on thy skin like morning dew,
And while thy willing soul transpires
At every pore with instant fires,
Now let us sport us while we may,
And now, like amorous birds of prey,
Rather at once our time devour,
Than languish in his slow-chapped power.
Let us roll all our strength and all
Our sweetness up into one ball,
And tear our pleasures with rough strife
Thorough the iron gates of life;
Thus, though we cannot make our sun
Stand still, yet we will make him run.

ANDREW MARVELL

Disagreement about the tone of intensity will always provide argument. This is partly due to the failure of realizing that the three sections of the poem build progressively through three ideas, each one of which is expressed with an increasingly meaningful attitude; and partly due to the lack of awareness of the narrator's change of tone in accordance with the idea expressed. Follow through on the particular tone of each section, realizing that the sentient thought of each part calls for discriminating inflections and stress patterns.

Decide also on the temper and age of the narrator. Is he facetious, sophisticated, suave or is he sincere and seriously persuasive; or does he employ a mixture of these attitudes? What factor in the development of the meaning does he use with different intensity for its persuasive power? *Time!* If you cannot observe that *time* is urgent for the narrator, count the number of years he spends in praising and adoring his mistress in the first section. Then look again at those two famous lines at the beginning of the second part, "But at my back I always hear / Time's wingèd chariot hurrying near." Notice also the fine irony in "The grave's a fine and private place,/ But none, I think, do there embrace." Is he merely sportive? Check again on *time* in the last section, especially the last two lines.

Vocal pitch changes, lightness and heaviness of attack and various shifts in quality are all-important in characterizing the narrator's attitudes.

Remember the typical Hardy poem will probably pull the last ironic drop out of the unusual and make it appear real. A skeleton serves as the narrator of "Channel Firing."

Channel Firing

That night your great guns unawares,
Shook all our coffins as we lay,
And broke the chancel window squares,
We thought it was the Judgment-day

And sat upright. While drearisome
Arose the howl of wakened hounds:
The mouse let fall the altar-crumb,
The worms drew back into the mounds,

The glebe cow drooled. Till God called, "No;
It's gunnery practice out at sea
Just as before you went below;
The world is as it used to be:

"All nations striving strong to make
Red war yet redder. Mad as hatters
They do no more for Christés sake
Than you who are helpless in such matters.

"That this is not the judgment-hour
For some of them's a blessed thing,
For if it were they'd have to scour
Hell's floor for so much threatening, . . .

"Ha, ha. It will be warmer when
I blow the trumpet (if indeed
I ever do; for you are men,
And rest eternal sorely need)."

So down we lay again. "I wonder,
Will the world ever saner be,"
Said one, "than when He sent us under
In our indifferent century!"

And many a skeleton shook his head.
"Instead of preaching forty year,"
My neighbour Parson Thirdly said,
"I wish I had stuck to pipes and beer."

Again the guns disturbed the hour,
Roaring their readiness to avenge,
As far inland as Stourton Tower,
And Camelot, and starlit Stonehenge.[10]

THOMAS HARDY

The poet is unbelievably casual in approaching his theme, and yet startling and haunting in tone as he creates the ghastly picture of skeletons sitting upright and wondering whether the booming of great guns at sea is their call to Judgment Day; of the howling of awakened hounds; of the frightened mouse dropping an altar crumb (a fragment of the consecrated host?); of worms retreating from waves of sound; of a parson's drooling cow. God then appears, not in a burst of glory or compassion, but in petulant annoyance to say "No," to state the facts and to add that the living do as little for the sake of Christ as the dead, who are no longer able to do anything. If those responsible for the noisy commotion were now called to final judgment, they would be condemned to scour the floor of Hell. Then, with ironic laughter, he thinks how unmistakable *his* trumpet call will be—if indeed he finally does decide to arouse the human dead, who need all the rest they can get. The disappointed dead settle back, wondering sadly whether men will ever become more reasonable as century follows century. And a parson regrets devoting a lifetime to preaching salvation rather than to unthinking pleasures. The guns' continued roar does not let the dead rest; it even rolls inland over monuments, each progressively remote in time: a fourteenth-century church tower, the cite of the vanished capital of King Arthur, a prehistoric circle of large stones. Note that the last stanza is thus a coda: the guns renew their roar (first two lines), which spreads out and dies away (last two lines).

At first, the stanzas may fool you, until their grim horror burrows deeply into your conscience and you begin dreaming about them. Hardy has indeed touched the gamut of emotions in developing his theme of unchanging evil in an indifferent humanity. Experiment with various pitch intonations to carry the caustic undercurrent. How does the melody of the last stanza change from the preceding lines to create the final tone and mood of receding silence?

The setting of the next poem is an art gallery. The narrator is observing how the "Old Masters" portray suffering and tragedy of the moment as the rest of the world goes its way, selfish and indifferent—even callous—about another's "martyrdom" to life.

The incident of Brueghel's *The Fall of Icarus* is set in a framework of concentrated intensity, every stroke of the poet's pen revealing the totality of the impression. Even if you do not know this master canvas, you can visualize the passive tragedy of the scene; if you do know it, you will want to see it again after this poetical account.

Musée Des Beaux Arts

About suffering they were never wrong,
The Old Masters: how well they understood
Its human position; how it takes place
While someone else is eating or opening a window or just walking
    dully along;
How, when the aged are reverently, passionately waiting
For the miraculous birth, there always must be
Children who did not specially want it to happen, skating
On a pond at the edge of the wood:
They never forgot
That even the dreadful martyrdom must run its course
Anyhow in a corner, some untidy spot
Where the dogs go on with their doggy life and the torturer's horse
Scratches its innocent behind on a tree.

In Breughel's *Icarus*, for instance: how everything turns away
Quite leisurely from the disaster; the ploughman may
Have heard the splash, the forsaken cry,
But for him it was not an important failure; the sun shone
As it had to on the white legs disappearing into the green
Water; and the expensive delicate ship that must have seen
Something amazing, a boy falling out of the sky,
Had somewhere to get to and sailed calmly on.[11]

W. H. AUDEN

Although this lyric has dramatic power, the intensity is restrained by the meditative manner in which the story, philosophy and descriptive elements are narrated. Vocal intonations and pacing of lines should give an impression of the stark indifference of people to tragedy, at a time when assistance is needed. Vocal intensity, quiet but deep, should be focused on building to the climax of understatement.

Friar and Brinnin have this helpful footnote in their volume *Modern Poetry*, which reads,

[11] Copyright 1940 by W. H. Auden. Reprinted from THE COLLECTED POETRY OF W. H. AUDEN, by permission of Random House, Inc.

"Musée des Beaux Arts": The Museum of Fine Arts in Brussels where is hung *The Fall of Icarus* by Pieter Brueghel. See reproduction in color opposite p. 222 in Thomas Craven's *A Treasury of Modern Art*, and Mr. Craven's comment: "It is the greatest conception of indifference in painting—an indifference which seems to flood the landscape, reducing the whole notion of classified mythology to a couple of lower extremities."[12]

Ransom's "Bells for John Whiteside's Daughter" is one of the most thought-provoking lyrics in modern poetry and one of the most difficult to interpret.

Bells for John Whiteside's Daughter

There was such speed in her little body,
And such lightness in her footfall,
It is no wonder that her brown study
Astonishes us all.

Her wars were bruited in our high window.
We looked among orchard trees and beyond,
Where she took arms against her shadow,
Or harried unto the pond

The lazy geese, like a snow cloud
Dripping their snow on the green grass,
Tricking and stopping, sleepy and proud,
Who cried in goose, Alas,

For the tireless heart within the little
Lady with rod that made them rise
From their noon apple-dreams, and scuttle
Goose-fashion under the skies!

But now go the bells, and we are ready;
In one house we are sternly stopped
To say we are vexed at her brown study,
Lying so primly propped.[13]

                                            JOHN CROWE RANSOM

The title of the poem is intriguing because of its irony: "bells" you discover are funeral bells, not the happy tinkling bells of a child's play

    [12] Kimon Friar and John Malcolm, eds., *Modern Poetry* (New York: Appleton-Century-Crofts, 1951), p. 444.

and they ring for the unnamed daughter of John Whiteside, a well-known and probably respected member of his community. Which words are emphasized in the title? Meanings can be extended—try a few.

The poem shocks you with its understatement and ironic restraint. On the surface, the emotional impression is not one of grief but astonishment and disbelief. The words "astonishes," "brown study," "vexed," "primly propped" halt you because of their contrast with the child's wonderland, where there danced one with "speed in her little body" and "lightness in her footfall"; one who played as all children play, warred in and out among the orchard trees and beyond with her own shadow (perhaps with no one else for a playmate); shooed the lazy geese in the pond from their "noon apple-dreams" so that they cried "Alas" at the little tireless "lady with rod," a scepter no doubt of her reign in the orchard. Now her "brown study" astonishes all, and in one house they are sternly stopped to say they are vexed at her brown study, "lying so primly propped."

Critics, especially Brooks and Warren,[14] fathom deeply into the "savage irony" created by putting two well-known clichés side by side: "Won't that child ever be still, she is driving me distracted" and "She was so active—who would have guessed that she would die so quickly." This attitude turns the attention from the child to the parents. In other words, the child, whom *they* wished would be quiet and still, is indeed now forever still in her "brown study." Some think of the child as the "image of war"— she appears as a warrior. (And who but adults teach children to war on every object they see?) Even so, the connotation of the word "war" should not be carried beyond the confines of childhood and into adult experiences of "war."

Explore your impressions of the poem. Whenever understatement occurs, you are given leeway to gather meaning according to your own experiences. If you have known only naughty, noisy children who make war in their play, to the exasperation and frustration of the parents, then you may read naughtiness in the child's fanciful experiences. If, on the other hand, you see an orchard of trees, a pond with lazy white geese aroused from their noon apple-dreams, a home with a high window—perhaps a picture window looking out toward this child's paradise—*then* the wonder and astonishment of the brown study takes on another meaning. The "brown study" to the parents may be a more believable and acceptable event than death of the active sprite. The poem leaves one strangely moved because of the poet's ironic understatement intensified by the sudden surprise of "astonished" and "vexed."

Changes in vocal quality, pitch and intensity are mandatory as the mood changes, but restraint is also important. The phrasing, as in the "goose" phrases, is difficult but rhythmical. Pauses to reinforce imagery

---

[14] Cleanth Brooks and Robert Penn Warren, *Understanding Poetry*, 3rd ed. (New York: Holt, Rinehart and Winston, Inc., 1960), p. 237.

and create suspense must be controlled. Finally, inflections must express a two-edged meaning and create the shock of the last lines.

Ransom's poem recalls Dickinson's "After Great Pain a Formal Feeling Comes." Although they are not similar in approach or form, the latter aids in the understanding of the emotion contained in Ransom's poem.

After Great Pain a Formal Feeling Comes

After great pain a formal feeling comes—
The nerves sit ceremonious like tombs;
The stiff Heart questions—was it He who bore?
And yesterday—or centuries before?

The feet mechanical go round
A wooden way
Of ground or air or Ought,
Regardless grown,
A quartz contentment like a stone.

This is the hour of lead
Remembered if outlived
As freezing persons recollect
The snow—
First chill, then stupor, then
The letting go.[15]

EMILY DICKINSON

Do not overlook the emotional impact of the images: "stiff Heart," "nerves sit ceremonious like tombs," "feet mechanical go round," "wooden way," "quartz contentment like a stone," "hour of lead," "freezing persons," "chill," "stupor." Be sensitive to the emotional progression of images that create bodily reactions after the death or loss of a loved one: the immobility; then the wooden, mechanical moving round; finally, the freezing, chill and stupor before the "letting go."

The significance of allusions, as they direct attention to emotional and philosophical reinforcement of meaning, is dramatically demonstrated in Frost's Poem "Out, Out—." The title is from Macbeth's soliloquy on the brevity and hopelessness of life—lines seldom matched in concentration of emotional impact. Macbeth, having run the gamut of murderous deeds for his own gain, contemplates his past as he ruefully admits, "I

15 Emily Dickinson, *The Complete Poems of Emily Dickinson* (Boston: Little, Brown and Company, 1960).

have supp'd full of horrors." Then word of Lady Macbeth's death is brought to him. In despair, Macbeth mutters in heavy, anguished and bitter tones—

> She should have died hereafter;
> There would have been a time for such a word.
> To-morrow, and to-morrow, and to-morrow,
> Creeps in this petty pace from day to day
> To the last syllable of recorded time,
> And all our yesterdays have lighted fools
> The way to dusty death. Out, out, brief candle!
> Life's but a walking shadow, a poor player
> That struts and frets his hour upon the stage
> And then is heard no more: it is a tale
> Told by an idiot, full of sound and fury,
> Signifying nothing.
>
> SHAKESPEARE, Macbeth
Act V, Scene 5

Observe the low key level and narrow pitch changes for the mood, beginning "To-morrow, and to-morrow, and to-morrow/ Creeps in this petty pace from day to day"; and how the metaphorical image fits into the picture of inescapable despair and doom. The mood reflects the total effect of man's struggle "from day to day," as he paces his way through the futility of living like a walking shadow, a poor player who struts and frets and then is heard no more on his way to "dusty death."

Now read Frost's poem, "Out, Out—."

"Out, Out—"

> The buzz-saw snarled and rattled in the yard
> And made dust and dropped stove-length sticks of wood,
> Sweet-scented stuff when the breeze drew across it.
> And from there those that lifted eyes could count
> Five mountain ranges one behind the other
> Under the sunset far into Vermont.
> And the saw snarled and rattled, snarled and rattled,
> As it ran light, or had to bear a load.
> And nothing happened: day was all but done.
> Call it a day, I wish they might have said
> To please the boy by giving him the half hour
> That a boy counts so much when saved from work.
> His sister stood beside them in her apron
> To tell them "Supper." At the word, the saw,
> As if to prove saws knew what supper meant,

Leaped out at the boy's hand, or seemed to leap—
He must have given the hand. However it was,
Neither refused the meeting. But the hand!
The boy's first outcry was a rueful laugh,
As he swung toward them holding up the hand
Half in appeal, but half as if to keep
The life from spilling. Then the boy saw all—
Since he was old enough to know, big boy
Doing a man's work, though a child at heart—
He saw all spoiled. "Don't let them cut my hand off—
The doctor, when he comes. Don't let him, sister!"
So. But the hand was gone already.
The doctor put him in the dark of ether.
He lay and puffed his lips out with his breath.
And then—the watcher at his pulse took fright.
No one believed. They listened at his heart.
Little—less—nothing!—and that ended it.
No more to build on there. And they, since they
Were not the one dead, turned to their affairs.[16]

ROBERT FROST

You are aware of how skillfully the poet has stated his title, for the dash takes the place of the words "brief candle" and gives an unfinished touch even as the young life was cut off so suddenly. Again Frost restrains his tone and casually drops the reader gasping with the last line.

Remember to interpret with the knowledge of Frost's sensitive understatement rather than with an exaggeration through many wide steps and slides. A narrow range of key with inflections that indicate varying tension will assist in a dramatic portrayal. The broken rhythm, conveyed by the incomplete phrases, is basic for the emotional meaning, made stark by long, reinforcing and suspenseful pauses.

Compare the empathic response of these selections. Which gives you the greater emotional reaction?

These two poems by Dickinson and Lawrence have the same subject —the snake. Their treatment, however, produces quite different themes.

A Narrow Fellow in the Grass

A narrow fellow in the grass
Occasionally rides;

You may have met him,—did you not?
His notice sudden is.

The grass divides as with a comb,
A spotted shaft is seen;
And then it closes at your feet
And opens further on.

He likes a boggy acre,
A floor too cool for corn.
Yet when a child, and barefoot,
I more than once, at morn,

Have passed, I thought, a whip-lash
Unbraiding in the sun,—
When, stooping to secure it,
It wrinkled, and was gone.

Several of nature's people
I know, and they know me;
I feel for them a transport
Of cordiality;

But never met this fellow,
Attended or alone,
Without a tighter breathing,
And zero at the bone.[17]

EMILY DICKINSON

Snake

A snake came to my water-trough
On a hot, hot day, and I in pyjamas for the heat,
To drink there.

In the deep, strange-scented shade of the great dark carob-tree
I came down the steps with my pitcher
And must wait, must stand and wait, for there he was at the trough
    before me.

He reached down from a fissure in the earth-wall in the gloom
And trailed his yellow-brown slackness soft-bellied down, over the
    edge of the stone trough
And rested his throat upon the stone bottom,
And where the water had dripped from the tap, in a small clearness,

[17] Dickinson, *op. cit.*

He sipped with his straight mouth,
Softly drank through his straight gums, into his slack long body,
Silently.

Someone was before me at my water-trough,
And I, like a second comer, waiting.

He lifted his head from his drinking, as cattle do,
And looked at me vaguely, as drinking cattle do,
And flickered his two-forked tongue from his lips, and mused a
    moment,
And stooped and drank a little more,
Being earth-brown, earth-golden from the burning burning bowels of
    the earth
On the day of Sicilian July, with Etna smoking.

The voice of my education said to me
He must be killed,
For in Sicily the black, black snakes are innocent, the gold are
    venomous.

And voices in me said, If you were a man
You would take a stick and break him now, and finish him off.

But must I confess how I liked him,
How glad I was he had come like a guest in quiet, to drink at my
    water-trough
And depart peaceful, pacified, and thankless,
Into the burning bowels of this earth?

Was it cowardice, that I dared not kill him?
Was it perversity, that I longed to talk to him?
Was it humility, to feel so honoured?
I felt so honoured.

And yet those voices:
If you were not afraid, you would kill him!

And truly I was afraid, I was most afraid,
But even so, honoured still more
That he should seek my hospitality
From out the dark door of the secret earth.

He drank enough
And lifted his head, dreamily, as one who has drunken,
And flickered his tongue like a forked night on the air, so black,
Seeming to lick his lips,

And looked around like a god, unseeing, into the air,
And slowly turned his head,
And slowly, very slowly, as if thrice adream,
Proceeded to draw his slow length curving round
And climb again the broken bank of my wall-face.

And as he put his head into that dreadful hole,
And as he slowly drew up, snake-easing his shoulders, and entered
farther,
A sort of horror, a sort of protest against his withdrawing into that
horrid black hole,
Deliberately going into the blackness, and slowly drawing himself
after,
Overcame me now his back was turned.

I looked round, I put down my pitcher,
I picked up a clumsy log
And threw it at the water-trough with a clatter.

I think it did not hit him,
But suddenly that part of him that was left behind convulsed in
undignified haste,
Writhed like lightning, and was gone
Into the black hole, the earth-lipped fissure in the wall-front,
At which, in the intense still noon, I stared with fascination.

And immediately I regretted it.
I thought how paltry, how vulgar, what a mean act!
I despised myself and the voices of my accursed human education.

And I thought of the albatross,
And I wished he would come back, my snake.

For he seemed to me again like a king,
Like a king in exile, uncrowned in the underworld,
Now due to be crowned again.

And so, I missed my chance with one of the lords
Of life.
And I have something to expiate;
A pettiness.[18]

Taormina

D. H. Lawrence

[18] From THE COMPLETE POEMS OF D. H. LAWRENCE, ed. Vivian de Sola Pinto and F. Warren Roberts. Copyright 1923, 1950 by Frieda Lawrence. Reprinted by permission of The Viking Press, Inc.

As you study these two poems, analyze these points:

1. Do the narrators differ in point of view, tone and attitude?
2. Are these attitudes contrasted in the titles? in meaning? in poetic form? in the conflict? in imagery? in mood? in atmosphere?
3. Which poem startles more intensely and makes one cringe by its empathic impact?
4. Does either poem treat the snake as a symbol of evil?
5. How would the narrators differ in vocal presentation?
6. Compare the resolving of the conflict in each one. One critic writes the denouement of Lawrence's "Snake" is within the character. What does this mean?

Yeats and Eliot will offer a challenge in your study of these two poetic masterpieces. If you have difficulty understanding them, turn to some of the references cited below.[19] Here is your chance to compare two variably structured poems on the same subject but with a different extension of the theme: each narrator is a senior citizen acknowledging the problem of meeting old age but each speaks with his own personal attitude and tone, perspective, desire and commitment toward a new kind of living; and each finds a denouement. After an initial analysis, you can travel alone with Prufrock through the foggy streets and on his troubled way to find the remnants of his youth. Your way with Yeats, however, takes another kind of route with comfortable traveling because he is "sailing," not to find sensual pleasure in his old age but rather to find Byzantium, symbolic of the world of eternal artistic life.

The Love Song
of J. Alfred Prufrock

S'io credesse che mia risposta fosse
A persona che mai tornasse al mondo,
Questa fiamma staria senza piu scosse.
Ma perciocche giammai di questo fondo
Non torno vivo alcun, s'i'odo il vero,
Senza tema d'infamia ti rispondo.

Let us go then, you and I,
When the evening is spread out against the sky

[19] Paul Engle and Warren Carrier, *Reading Modern Poetry* (Chicago: Scott, Foresman and Company, 1955). George Williamson, *A Reader's Guide to Eliot* (New York: The Noonday Press, 1953). Cleanth Brooks and Robert Penn Warren, *Understanding Poetry* (New York: Holt, Rinehart and Winston, Inc., 1960). Kimon Friar and John Malcolm Brinnin, *Modern Poetry* (New York: Appleton-Century-Crofts, 1951). Elder Olson, *Sailing to Byzantium* (Kansas City: University of Kansas City *Review,* VIII). James Miller and Bernice Slote, *The Dimensions of Poetry* (New York: Dodd, Mead and Company, 1962).

Like a patient etherized upon a table;
Let us go, through certain half-deserted streets,
The muttering retreats
Of restless nights in one-night cheap hotels
And sawdust restaurants with oyster-shells:
Streets that follow like a tedious argument
Of insidious intent
To lead you to an overwhelming question . . .
Oh, do no ask, "What is it?"
Let us go and make our visit.

In the room the women come and go
Talking of Michelangelo.

The yellow fog that rubs its back upon the window-panes,
The yellow smoke that rubs its muzzle on the window-panes
Licked its tongue into the corners of the evening,
Lingered upon the pools that stand in drains,
Let fall upon its back the soot that falls from chimneys,
Slipped by the terrace, made a sudden leap,
And seeing that it was a soft October night,
Curled once about the house, and fell asleep.

And indeed there will be time
For the yellow smoke that slides along the street,
Rubbing its back upon the window-panes;
There will be time, there will be time
To prepare a face to meet the faces that you meet;
There will be time to murder and create,
And time for all the works and days of hands
That lift and drop a question on your plate;
Time for you and time for me,
And time yet for a hundred indecisions,
And for a hundred visions and revisions,
Before the taking of a toast and tea.

In the room the women come and go
Talking of Michelangelo.

And indeed there will be time
To wonder, "Do I dare?" and, "Do I dare?"
Time to turn back and descend the stair,
With a bald spot in the middle of my hair—
[They will say: "How his hair is growing thin!"]
My morning coat, my collar mounting firmly to the chin,
My necktie rich and modest, but asserted by a simple pin—
[They will say: "But how his arms and legs are thin!"]
Do I dare

Disturb the universe?
In a minute there is time
For decisions and revisions which a minute will reverse.

    For I have known them all already, known them all:—
Have known the evenings, mornings, afternoons,
I have measured out my life with coffee spoons;
I know the voices dying with a dying fall
Beneath the music from a farther room.
      So how should I presume?

    And I have known the eyes already, known them all—
The eyes that fix you in a formulated phrase,
And when I am formulated, sprawling on a pin,
When I am pinned and wriggling on the wall,
Then how should I begin
To spit out all the butt-ends of my days and ways?
      And how should I presume?

    And I have known the arms already, known them all—
Arms that are braceleted and white and bare
[But in the lamplight, downed with light brown hair!]
Is it perfume from a dress
That makes me so digress?
Arms that lie along a table, or wrap about a shawl.
      And should I then presume?
      And how should I begin?

               . . . . .

Shall I say, I have gone at dusk through narrow streets
And watched the smoke that rises from the pipes
Of lonely men in shirt-sleeves, leaning out of windows? . . .

    I should have been a pair of ragged claws
Scuttling across the floors of silent seas.

               . . . . .

And the afternoon, the evening, sleeps so peacefully!
Smoothed by long fingers,
Asleep . . . tired . . . or it malingers,
Stretched on the floor, here beside you and me.
Should I, after tea and cakes and ices,
Have the strength to force the moment to its crisis?
But though I have wept and fasted, wept and prayed,
Though I have seen my head [grown slightly bald] brought in upon
      a platter,
I am no prophet—and here's no great matter;
I have seen the moment of my greatness flicker,

And I have seen the eternal Footman hold my coat, and snicker,
And in short, I was afraid.

And would it have been worth it, after all,
After the cups, the marmalade, the tea,
Among the porcelain, among some talk of you and me,
Would it have been worth while,
To have bitten off the matter with a smile,
To have squeezed the universe into a ball
To roll it toward some overwhelming question,
To say: "I am Lazarus, come from the dead,
Come back to tell you all, I shall tell you all"—
If one, settling a pillow by her head,
    Should say: "That is not what I meant at all.
    That is not it, at all."

And would it have been worth it, after all,
Would it have been worth while,
After the sunsets and the dooryards and the sprinkled streets,
After the novels, after the teacups, after the skirts that trail along the
    floor—
And this, and so much more?—
It is impossible to say just what I mean!
But as if a magic lantern threw the nerves in patterns on a screen:
Would it have been worth while
If one, settling a pillow or throwing off a shawl,
And turning toward the window, should say:
    "That is not it at all,
    That is not what I meant, at all."

           . . . . .

No! I am not Prince Hamlet, nor was meant to be;
Am an attendant lord, one that will do
To swell a progress, start a scene or two,
Advise the prince; no doubt, an easy tool,
Deferential, glad to be of use,
Politic, cautious, and meticulous;
Full of high sentence, but a bit obtuse;
At times, indeed, almost ridiculous—
Almost, at times, the Fool.

    I grow old . . . I grow old . . .
I shall wear the bottoms of my trousers rolled.

    Shall I part my hair behind? Do I dare to eat a peach?
I shall wear white flannel trousers, and walk upon the beach.
I have heard the mermaids singing, each to each.

I do not think that they will sing to me.

I have seen them riding seaward on the waves
Combing the white hair of the waves blown back
When the wind blows the water white and black.

We have lingered in the chambers of the sea
By sea-girls wreathed with seaweed red and brown
Till human voices wake us, and we drown.[20]

T. S. ELIOT

Sailing to Byzantium

I

That is no country for old men. The young
In one another's arms, birds in the trees,
—Those dying generations—at their song,
The salmon-falls, the mackerel-crowded seas,
Fish, flesh, or fowl, commend all summer long
Whatever is begotten, born, and dies.
Caught in that sensual music all neglect
Monuments of unageing intellect.

II

An aged man is but a paltry thing,
A tattered coat upon a stick, unless
Soul clap its hands and sing, and louder sing
For every tatter in its mortal dress,
Nor is there singing school but studying
Monuments of its own magnificence;
And therefore I have sailed the seas and come
To the holy city of Byzantium.

III

O sages standing in God's holy fire
As in the gold mosaic of a wall,
Come from the holy fire, perne in a gyre,
And be the singing-masters of my soul.
Consume my heart away; sick with desire
And fastened to a dying animal
It knows not what it is; and gather me
Into the artifice of eternity.

[20]From COLLECTED POEMS 1909-1962 by T. S. Eliot, copyright, 1936, by Harcourt, Brace & World, Inc.; copyright, © 1963, 1964, by T. S. Eliot. Reprinted by permission of the publishers.

IV

Once out of nature I shall never take
My bodily form from any natural thing,
But such a form as Grecian goldsmiths make
Of hammered gold and gold enamelling
To keep a drowsy Emperor awake;
Or set upon a golden bough to sing
To lords and ladies of Byzantium
Of what is past, or passing, or to come.[21]

WILLIAM BUTLER YEATS

First look at the titles. "The Love Song of J. Alfred Prufrock" makes you pause to chuckle good-naturedly over Eliot's subterfuge, then brings poignancy as you realize the lyrics belong to a song with a repetitive refrain, "I grow old," and end on a minor note with "we drown." The "love song" Prufrock would like to sing is never sung, except wishfully and inwardly, and then perhaps with overtones of the ineffectual "off-key" melody of old age. How do you feel about the name of the narrator? The "J. Alfred" sounds a bit pretentious; and "Alfred"—well, Alfred may connote many things to many people. "Prufrock" is reminiscent of the portmanteau words discussed in Carroll's "Jabberwocky." What words are merged together in this name?

According to his title, Yeats, at sixty years, is contemplating a sailing venture that will help him escape from a world of physical deterioration to Byzantium, the eternal city. His "Byzantium" is not in reality Constantinople, but a symbol representing a world of imagination, spirit, eternal and golden art; a world of no decay, deterioration or fleeting sensory experiences; a place of permanence and artistic immortality, abstract and man-made—an "artifice of eternity."[22] At first glance, Yeats's connotations may appear simpler than Eliot's. If you really want to know Yeats's "Byzantium," a civilization which flourished in his Phase 15, during the phase of the full moon, and his theories about the centrifugal gyrations of the world, read his essays and "The Vision." Some critics question whether you should know Yeats's concepts before you read his poetry[23] or try to find the meaning in his poetic lines, and then discover, for instance, what a phrase like "perne in a gyre" could possibly mean. To help you through this particular moment, the word "perne" is an Irish word meaning spool or bobbin, on which thread is wound. Here, according to analysts, the

[21] Reprinted with permission of The Macmillan Co. from COLLECTED POEMS by William Butler Yeats. Copyright 1928 by The Macmillan Co., renewed 1956 by Bertha Georgie Yeats.

[22] Does this thought remind you of Keats's "Ode on a Grecian Urn" and of Ciardi's discussion of Stevens's "Anecdote of a Jar"?

[23] W. B. Yeats, *Essays; Discoveries* (New York: The Macmillan Co., 1929). W. B. Yeats, *Mythologies* (New York: The Macmillan Co., 1959).

word is used as a verb, meaning to "spiral down." "Gyre" belongs in his concept of whirling, centrifugal energy, discussed earlier with his poem, "The Second Coming." These words "perne" and "gyre" are basic to his belief of the rotations of generations: "each age unwinds the thread another age has wound."

Before you proceed to study these poems, look at this translation of Eliot's epigraph and resolve its relationship to the meaning. These lines are from Dante's *Inferno*, Canto XXVII. When one of the flames in Hell—that of the spirit of a Count—was asked why he was being punished, his answer was introduced by this remark:

"If I thought my answer were to one who ever could return to the world, this flame would shake no more; but since no one did ever return alive from this depth, if what I hear be true, without fear of infamy I shall answer you."

Now observe the approach of the distinctive characters who act as narrators. One acknowledges that youth enjoys transient sensual joys but rationalizes that youth cannot, however, enter into the permanence of the world of the spirit; so hopefully, he, Yeats, can "sail to Byzantium" for his escape from deterioration. The other narrator thinks inwardly—or interiorly—about his personal deficiencies as he walks through the streets of yellow fog on an evening that is "etherized," hears the women talking of Michelangelo and wonders if anyone will notice "how his hair is growing thin," "his arms and legs are growing thin" and how he is at times "almost ridiculous—/Almost, at times, the Fool."

The attitudes are different. Yeats is the narrator facing his conflict brought on by old age in a straightforward manner and is quite aware that he is voicing his predicament and his desire for a more satisfying life. Prufrock is thinking aloud but timidly communing with himself: "Let us go, you and I." Remembering the epigraph, you know he is not talking to an audience. Many have speculated about this line: some believe the "I" is the reader; others that "I" is Prufrock's ego. You will identify the technique of the "stream of consciousness" employed by the poet. Prufrock is cogitating about his conflict, always finding delay in "time"—"there will be time" . . . "time for you and time for me." That tone of inner revelation pervades the poem rather than the outspoken story of how he feels; he will continue to wear his mask even though he knows it is ineffectual.

Prufrock's song is one of discordant psychological overtones. He is webbed in by his environment, caught in the yellow fog of his own baffling fear of old age as it affects his sartorial appearance and indirectly his "love song." After the first two lines in which an invitation is extended for a casual evening walk, you are plunged into an etherized street, one-night cheap hotels, sawdust restaurants and a fog that gets thicker as the narrator moves on his way trying to solve his particular idiosyncrasies of old age. It is a smothering, toxic atmosphere, choking you at every step, making you reel for want of oxygen. In this way you enter into the first verse of Prufrock's song.

Eliot's beginning is very different from Yeats's abrupt, pointed and spontaneous line, "That is no country for old men." This is the basis for his thesis, and in a logically formed structure, the poet proceeds to discuss, by means of contrast, his conflict between transient and permanent pleasures—according to his concepts—and arrives at a denouement. The conclusions differ because of the disposition of the narrators: Yeats resolves his difficulty, one of principle rather than the tormenting rationalization of a psychological situation; Prufrock permits his problem to die away inadequately without positive resolution, as he listens to the singing of the mermaids who probably will not sing to him, and alas, no "human voices wake us"—so "we (you and I) drown."

This is your start for a complete analysis of *meaning*. For your interpretation, study how allusions, metaphorical language and sound devices —alliteration, consonance, assonance, repetition and rhyme—aid in creating atmosphere in this interior monologue. In order to capture tone, mood and atmosphere, be careful of an exaggerated interpretation of certain phrases, such as "indecisions, visions and revisions" or of one too dramatic as in the line "When I am pinned and wriggling on the wall." Note also how Prufrock's speech rhythm follows his inner stream of consciousness. Consequently, his lines shift and break with his transitions in thought, as in "But I digress," "Do I dare," "And how should I presume," "And how should I begin." This broken rhythmic pattern, emphasized by the poet's punctuation and phrasing, indicates Prufrock's struggle to think his way through the maze of his "love song." You can employ almost every vocal principle in the expression of the Prufrock monologue. Yeats's poem, on the other hand, calls for a more formal approach inasmuch as the narrator's ideas are not as personal or familiar to an audience, nor couched in the intimate conversational tone and dramatic phrasing of Eliot. Furthermore, Yeats is "outward bound" and knows where he wants to go.

In Arnold's "Dover Beach," (page 100), another narrator contemplates *religious* deterioration of man in a world without faith. This setting is beautiful: calm sea, full tide, moon lies fair, tranquil bay with glimmering lights. The imagery, however, begins to take on depth symbolically: the grating roar of pebbles brings "the eternal note of sadness" into the turbid "ebb and flow" cadences. So, too, "The Sea of Faith/ Was once, too, at the full," but now the poet can hear only its "long, withdrawing roar" (the retreating tide is symbolic of the loss of faith among men). Even though he and his love are on a darkling plain "Swept with confused alarms of struggle and flight,/ Where ignorant armies clash at night," they must be steadfast and true to one another. In this well-known dramatic monologue, you create another character with a particular attitude and mood through inflectional innuendoes.

As you work on your analysis, clarify your impressions by jotting down personality clues of each narrator, his conflict as it involves the central meaning, climax and denouement. Then characterize by selecting the most revealing vocal quality and intensity and also the various pitch changes, especially inflections that show discriminating traits. The speech rhythm of each narrator will be affected by your tonal impression. Finally, put the central meaning into a total expression of that character. Do you have dominant traits of the person? If not, did you forget that bodily attitude is an important part of the total expression?

You may be helped by listening to "Sailing to Byzantium"[24] and "The Love Song of J. Alfred Prufrock"[25] as recorded by Cusack and Eliot.

PROSE

GENERAL ASSESSMENT

For the interpreter, the interesting features of the short story and novel are the individuality, the unique approach and follow-through to the "illuminating moment," much discussed in critical analyses. Each narrative must be studied within its own framework, observing the author's characteristic style of writing. The interpreter's first act is to see from all sides the "moment" of the story; or as James writes, "The power to guess the unseen from the seen, to trace the implication of things, to judge the whole piece by the pattern, the condition of feeling life in general so completely that you are well on your way to knowing any particular corner of it—this cluster of gifts may also be said to constitute experience. . . . If experience consists of impression, it may be said that impressions *are* experience. . . . Therefore, I add, 'Try to be one of the people on whom nothing is lost.' "[26]

You must assess not only the literature but your close involvement in the story. Before you interpret any narrative, be sure that the impression you wish to evoke is implicit in the progression of events and in your conception of the theme. Frost's remark, "No tears in the writer, no tears in the reader," and "No surprise for the writer, no surprise for the reader,"[27] can be paraphrased by saying "No tears in the interpreter, no tears in the listeners; no surprise for the interpreter, no surprise for the listeners."

[24] *Poetry of Yeats*, recorded by Cyril Cusack. Caedmon, TC 1081.
[25] *T. S. Eliot: Reading Poems and Choruses*. Caedmon, TC 1045.
[26] Henry James, *The Art of Fiction* in answer to Besant.
[27] Robert Frost, "The Figure a Poem Makes," *Complete Poems of Robert Frost* (New York: Holt, Rinehart and Winston, Inc., 1964), p. vi.

LITERARY ANALYSIS

In narratives, both of the essay or dramatic type, you should check on the following:

1. *Point of View*
   a. Who is the narrator?
   b. What part does he have in the action?
   c. Can he observe all characters with objectivity so that he obtains a complete perspective?
   d. What is the limiting factor of the particular point of view?
2. *Plot Exposition*
   a. State in a short paragraph what happens.
3. *Theme*
   a. What is the theme?
   b. Does the author succeed in combining literary elements to intensify the theme?
   c. Is the theme reached mainly through characterization, events, conflict of ideas or symbolic intent?
4. *Setting or Environment*
   a. How would you characterize the setting, the environment?
   b. Does it set the tone, atmosphere or mood?
   c. Is it important as a background to the characters or action?
   d. Does it emphasize the psychological or physical action?
5. *Time*
   a. How has time been established?
   b. Is it important to the movement of the story?
   c. Does it affect seriously the motives, thoughts, actions of any of the characters?
   d. Is the present influenced by the past to the extent that the past takes over as a constant control of events?
   e. Is the flash-back technique used?
6. *Design and Form*
   a. Does the author utilize expository, descriptive, narrative, character or dramatic elements in opening his story?
   b. Does he make one element dominant as the narrative continues?
   c. Is the movement of the whole static, tense, rapid, casual, introspective or climactic?
   d. How does the progression of events relate to the meaning, climax, denouement?
   e. Is a specific tone established?
7. *Conflict*
   a. What is the main conflict? How is it influenced by minor conflicts?

b. What motives are involved in the conflict—emotional, analytical, philosophical, psychological?

c. How is conflict presented—through suspense, inner revelation, contrast, paradox, coincidence, characterization, episodes, dialogue, exposition?

8. *Characters*

a. How are characters revealed?

b. Which character is the pivot about which others converge?

c. Which character furthers the action?

d. How does the main character respond to pressures of environment, friends, enemies, family, community?

e. Do characters give the illusion of reality? Are they exaggerations, caricatures?

f. Do any of the main characters change? If so, in what way—physically, psychologically, morally?

g. Which characters give the greatest empathic responses?

h. Characterize each person with details offered by the author.

9. *Style*

a. Is the author direct or indirect?

b. What is the inter-relationship of symbolic meaning, imagery, rhythmical pattern, literary devices to the theme, design, tone, atmosphere and mood? Be specific.

CHARACTERIZATION THROUGH DIALOGUE

Your analysis of character impressions must not be overlooked as you gain ideas from your literary analysis. You may recall how Mansfield told of reading her story, "Miss Brill," aloud, over and over, so that every detail would fit her main character at each particular moment on that particular day. The author wanted to hear the sound values that would personalize Miss Brill, even though she did not participate in conversation. In the same way, your adeptness in responding empathically to the spirit of character interplay and reactions in narratives, and also in drama, is a necessity.

The fully charged momentum of any piece of literature cannot be secured mechanically. If the selection promotes no response in you, do not try to interpret it. Without your own feel for the movement and, particularly, the trend of the dialogue, the conflict and revelation of characters in contrasting situations and emotional portrayals, your interpretation is likely to be static, monotonous and without vitality. Dialogue, for instance, is not a "one-and," "two-and," "three-and" separation of individual responses; it *is* a "one-plus-two-plus-three-plus" continuing and integrating flow of speech rhythm. One response dovetails into another either by acquiescing, over-riding, hesitating, stumbling, refuting, bombarding or declining in a manner which could connote surprise, fear, bitterness, irony, joy, anger, understanding, hatred. The opportunities are many!

SPEECH PATTERN & BODILY ATTITUDE

Vocal patterns must be established for each character. No two people have the same speech rhythm, except in some interpretative attempts when the scene is crowded with too many people. Avoid this hazard. Adapt the speech rhythm to the personality of the character. Characterizations can be differentiated mainly by pitch intonations and key level, as well as by quality, intensity, rhythm. Vocal changes must be instantaneous in the quick interplay of speeches and should be watched as each character picks up cues. The key range will help to show contrasts in masculine and feminine characters. If you are a man, do not use an unreal falsetto or unpleasant nasal voice for a feminine character (unless she is unpleasant). Rather, soften the intensity and give her less pharyngeal resonance and a slightly higher key range than the male. If you are of the feminine gender, you will be wise not to select a scene or story with two or three males of muscle and brawn. Pitch changes occur, as you know by this time, with shifts in vocal intensity, quality and tempo, to create the emotional timbre of the scene. The ability, too, to start the speech response of one person in a different key level and rhythm from that of the previous character must be cultivated. The beginning of each response should show motivation either by some change in voice, eye movement or bodily tension, but not a plunging difference. Learn how to blend the speeches into a unit of vocal interaction with meaningful bodily attitude.

Corresponding with these vocal patterns are the bodily tensions and postures that differentiate characters. Be careful of excessive movement; learn how to grow into the character's attitude. Watch people around you to get ideas. Be careful also of an over-indulgence in certain pattern types, as the portrayal of age by the shaking body supported by an invisible cane and a quivering, scratchy voice; or the young girl who continually flicks the ashes from her cigarette. These are not subtle points in character portrayal.

The center of facial attraction is the eye expression, but not necessarily the wide-open "baby-stare." The eyes through their many minute movements can often show how a character's thoughts are forming, how he is responding inwardly, how he understands another's thoughts, how he is not going to be able to withstand the emotional outbreak. The eyes will also give direction cues of one character speaking to another or of one being introduced to another.

PROSE NARRATIVES FOR STUDY

Jean Kerr's essay type of literature with emphasis on delightfully funny anecdotes follows. The dialogue excerpts, with which the author keeps the humor alive, will recall experiences for most audiences, not only among women but also men.

from *How To Talk To A Man*

Of course, I have no statistics, and nobody ever tells me anything. But I suspect one reason marriages break up is that some wives, after spending a full hour in rich, deeply shared silence with the beloved, are apt to remark, "In heaven's name, *say* something, will you?"

The problem stems quite naturally from the fact that women speak because they wish to speak, whereas a man speaks only when driven to speech by something outside himself—like, for instance, he can't find any clean socks, or he has just read in a headline that Herbert Hoover foresees no depression in 1960. A wife who really feels cheerful and chatty early in the morning (a circumstance that can be explained only by a faulty metabolism) can always inveigle her husband into conversation by using a little imagination and by learning to snap up cues. She might say, "Speaking of clean socks reminds me, did you read John Hutchens' review of *The Mackerel Plaza?*" Now he's on the spot. He has to say something, even if it is only to comment on the total absence of any connection between his socks and *The Mackerel Plaza*.

I have a rather engaging little trick, for stirring my own husband into statement. I just quote a few lines from the balcony scene of *Romeo and Juliet*.

"He speaks," I say in mock lyrical tones, "but he says nothing. What of that? His eye discourses. I will answer *it*." Thus prodded, he is apt to say things he will have to retract later, but there are risks to everything.

Actually, if you had wanted a husband who would be a stimulating conversationalist, you should have married a mechanic or even a gardener—certainly not an author or a professional man, or, last of all, a lecturer. When we got married, my husband was a lecturer and professor of drama and I used to imagine the stimulating, intellectual conversation we were going to have at breakfast. Like this:

ME: That play last night was interesting, didn't you think?

HIM: Very. Of course, the author is still heavily in debt to Chekhov—the despairing protagonist, the shackling environment, the complete stasis in the third act and, of course, the total absence of climax.

ME: Yes, he has an almost kinetic sense of atmosphere, but he never licked the story line.

HIM: Licked it? He should have joined it.

    (Appreciative chuckles all around.)

This, however, is a transcript of the actual conversation:

HIM: (Despairingly) I'll bet this is diet bread.

ME: What's the matter with diet bread?

HIM: (After a pause) Everything. Why don't we eat things other people eat?

ME: Such as—

HIM: (Passionately) Those flat sticky things with jam inside them. Or muffins. Why don't we ever have muffins?

ME: (Evenly) Very well, dear, we'll have muffins.

HIM: (Suspiciously) Oh, I know you. You'll get diet muffins.

We really should have our own radio show.

It's interesting to observe the phenomenon that will cause a husband who hasn't opened his yap in weeks suddenly to find the gift of speech. Just order a new coat that differs in any way at all from the last five coats you have owned and watch Big Chief Still Waters blossom into Alistaire Cooke, a veritable fount of articulation. "Yes, I know it's the new style, but we haven't got a space ship yet. Oh, I see, all the fullness in the back is *supposed* to make you look as if you're standing in a head wind! Well, never mind. It'll be economical, anyway —in the summer you can take it to the beach and use it as a cabana." Etc.

There is a cure for this. Just take him with you when you go to Bonwit Teller's. Once you deposit him on that chaste Empire sofa in Misses' Suits, his whole attitude will change—not to mention his pulse, temperature, and rate of breathing. Precisely what causes men to go into shock in Bonwit's I can't imagine. My husband keeps looking from right to left in a state of ashen panic, as though he feared at any moment one of those elegant salesladies was going to snatch him and set his hair. But at any rate he brings a more judicious attitude to the subject of high style. "Yeah, yeah," he mutters at my first appearance from the depths of the dressing room, "it looks great, let's get out of here."

HOW TO TALK TO A MAN IN A FASHIONABLE RESTAURANT

I once read an interview with the Duchess of Windsor in which she said that she and the Duke hated to eat in public restaurants because they had to converse so animatedly and affect such feverish interest in each other—lest rumors start that they were estranged—that she never could enjoy a bite of her dinner. It ought to be (but somehow it isn't) helpful to tell yourself that you're not the Duchess of Windsor and that nobody is even the tiniest bit interested in whether you and your husband have spoken since 1943. The point is that in a restaurant (like Sardi's, for instance) where you are surrounded by the tinkling laughter of beautiful models engaged in vivacious conversation with movie actors, you do feel somehow that you can't just sit there, specters at the feast, looking like two people who have just learned that their 1958 income-tax return was being investigated. Of course, there are lots of things on your mind that you could say ("Well, you saw that Chris got D in Health Habits again," or, "The man came about the drier and he says we need a whole new unit"), but this doesn't seem to be the time or the place.

A couple I know have solved the problem beautifully. She just tells him the story of The Three Bears, a narrative which is admirable for the purpose because of its many rising inflections. And he helps her out by occasionally inter-jecting a remark like "By George, you mean she ate every last bite of the baby bear's porridge?" Do try it some time. Anybody overhearing you will conclude that you are discussing a new television spectacular—either that, or you're both a little bit dotty. If you should be concerned about this aspect of the matter, or if you should happen to intercept a stunned glance from the waiter, you can always drop in a covering remark like "Red Buttons—*there's* your Baby Bear!"

HOW TO TALK TO A MAN WHEN HE'S TAKING A SHOWER

Here you have a captive audience and an ideal opportunity to tell a hus-band a number of things that you don't want him to hear. (Later on you can say, "Of course I told you, you just don't listen!") There is no limit to the amount of unwelcome information you can get off your chest at one clip in these circumstances: "The man from Macy's was here and I took thirty dollars out of your wallet," and "Betty called, she and George are going to drop in," and "The children are going to be in a Humpty-Dumpty play tonight—Col is playing Humpty and John is one of the king's men and we both have to go."

HOW TO TALK TO A MAN AFTER YOU'VE TOLD HIM IF HE DOESN'T STOP FIDDLING WITH THAT OLD TOASTER HE IS GOING TO BLOW A FUSE, AND HE DOES

There is no way. Just light a candle and count ten or your blessings, which-ever is greater.[28]

JEAN KERR, *The Snake Has All The Lines*

These passages from Kerr will provide entertainment if insinuating inflections with the imperceptible pause and certain knowing eye expres-sions are employed. The interpretative attempt should not be exaggerated but gleefully, diabolically and lightly managed to get the laughter. The author is skillful in building and timing her conversational episodes; and she is quite adept at the quick turn of the phrase. Show your enjoyment for the light tone and touch of the author.

In this excerpt from the delightful stylist, John Mason Brown, the humor comes not so much from the actual episode as it does from the narrator's reactions to Belle's "inner butterflies" and physical activities.

We Have with Us Tonight

To some chairmen, perhaps quite naturally since talking is their business, lecturers do not seem like human beings, filled with human fears and standing in need of last-minute concentration. The war of nerves is supposed to hold no

[28] From "How To Talk To A Man" copyright © 1958 by Jean Kerr. From the book, THE SNAKE HAS ALL THE LINES by Jean Kerr. Reprinted by permission of Doubleday & Company, Inc., pp. 49-52, 55-56, 59.

terrors for them. They are talking machines; sound tracks with bodies; the kind of offspring a Victrola might have if wedded to a windmill. Such an attitude, even though it puts you in the robot class, is flattering when, because of it, you suddenly find yourself miscast as a knight-errant.

In the automobile on the way to the auditorium you can tell when you will have to hoist your faded plume and rub the dust off your broken armor.

"Now, Belle, it's going to be all right," says the husband of the lady who is to present you and who has suddenly begun to keen in the front seat like a chorus of unhappy fisherwomen in an Irish play. "I know you will be fine. Won't Belle be fine, Mr. Brown?" Forgetting what you were trying to remember about your own speech, you bow to the inevitable. "Of course, she will. Don't worry. It's easy."

"But I can't! I won't go on." There is a pause. Then a sudden rally. "You see, I'm dreadfully scared, Mr. Brown, because this is the first time I have had to do this kind of thing. I wish I'd never gotten into it! I know it's silly, but I'm petrified. Henry, I'm *petrified!* I'm sure I'll disgrace you. I'll have to read it, even though I promised Grace this afternoon that I wouldn't. I tell you I'm PETRIFIED! I was scared at luncheon—but NOW! Oh, Henry! Henry, did you bring the aromatics?"

By this time the auditorium has been reached, and you have begun to feel as nervous about Belle as Belle does and as Henry does. Henry has disappeared, mopping his brow. "Good luck, girlie," he has said in parting. "Chin up! You couldn't be worse than Evelyn was." With that, Henry has gone to take his place out front. Belle has meanwhile been drawn to the mirror above the dressing table like an astronomer to the Milky Way. The drone of the audience through the curtains and the open door might appeal to an apiarist, but it unnerves Belle.

"My tummy! My tummy!" she sighs, with an expression usually reserved for the English Channel. "It's full of butterflies!"

Your one hope is that moths won't emerge.

"Now calm yourself, Mrs. Tremens," you say, patting her on the back as if she were a baby about to bring up a bubble, and trusting her husband will understand if he returns. "It'll soon be over. All things come to an end."

"No! No! No! It won't," she insists, opening her evening bag to spread a neatly written manuscript before her on the dressing table. "I knew it! I knew it! I can't remember a word of it, and I had it all by heart."

"May I help you?" you ask, putting your own notes in your suitcase and locking it. Suddenly an intern's calm descends upon you.

"Oh, I know it's silly, but would you?" Belle passes her manuscript to you in a hand quaking with palsy.

"Now, then, let's try it."

" 'Ladies and gentlemen,' " begins Belle, clearing her throat like a motorboat having a hard time getting started, and at last speaking in an astral voice, " 'Ladies and gentlemen—!' There! I told you. I haven't the vaguest idea what comes next."

" 'Ladies and gentlemen,' " you repeat, " 'the—' "

"No! No! Don't tell me," she insists. " 'The—the—' Now let's see. How could it go on from there?"

" 'Ladies and gentlemen,' " you say firmly, reading her script to her, " 'the Broadway theatre is a long way from here, but we are hoping it will be nearer to us to-night. It gives me great pleasure to introduce—' "

By now it is ten minutes after the announced starting time.

"Don't you think we really ought to get going?" you ask. "Why don't you just read it? No one will know."

"Never! Never!" says Belle. "I promised Grace I wouldn't. And anyway she said she'd kill me if I did."

Someone knocks timidly on the door. It is Henry. "Dear," says he, puffing from the dash up the aisle of the auditorium, the plunge down the stairs by the box office, the long run through the basement corridor, and the climb up the truncated steps leading to the stage, "Grace thinks you ought to begin. They're getting restless."

So out you go, forgetting Henry as he sits down to mop his face, and following Belle onto the stage to those chairs. For what seems an eternity, Belle remains seated, doing her best to resemble Queen Mary at the Durbar. You try to whisper a few nothings to her, to indicate how much at home you both are. But, in addition to palsy, Belle now seems to have developed a sudden and acute attack of deafness. After five repulses, which have entirely shaken your confidence and made the audience wonder what you could possibly have done to insult Mrs. Tremens in the wings, Belle at last rises. Swaying somewhat unsteadily, she advances to the lectern to grab hold of it as if it were a mast and she a sailor imperiled in a Conrad typhoon. Clutched in her hand you can see the manuscript of her introduction. In a moment or two she spreads this out before her and reaches in her handbag with magnificent defiance for her tortoise-shell glasses.

A new peace—a calm decidedly outward—has descended upon her. Only to the speaker is Belle's fear now evident. He, after all, can see what the audience cannot. Though Belle's voice is firm when she starts off with "Ladies and gentlemen," and her hands are propped so that they cannot shake, Belle's back contrives to tremble beneath her tight satin skirt like Jello in the wind.

"Ladies and gentlemen," she begins, bowing right and left at the sheet of paper before her as if the whole audience were sitting on it. Thereafter she never lifts her eyes from her written speech until, with a very pained look, she has expressed the pleasure it has given her to introduce you. Whereupon, turning her head to the side of the stage where you aren't, she points to an empty chair, realizes her error, looks around in tragic confusion, smiles when she has at last spotted you, and rushes back to her seat to reread the manuscript, fearful lest she may have omitted part of it. Just as you step forward, murmuring, "You were fine; Henry will be very proud of you," Henry comes walking down the aisle to retake his place, still mopping his head, and having missed the big moment, when comparisons with Evelyn were in order.[29]

JOHN MASON BROWN

Interpret with the narrator's easy, assured manner. Brown's tone is light, inwardly gleeful in retrospect at woman's frailty in speaking before

[29] From *Accustomed As I Am,* by John Mason Brown. W. W. Norton & Co., 1942. Reprinted with permission of the author, pp. 30-34.

an audience, almost wicked in his "tongue-in-cheek" attitude. He is not obviously flippant, however, but covers all with a mock-seriousness. This tone is necessary for a revealing interpretation. If you want laughter from your audience, work for inflections that are not too broad or exaggerated and also for reinforcing pauses enlightened by eye and facial expression.

Flush, the cocker spaniel, who changed his habitat from the country home at Three Mile Cross to the luxurious room of Elizabeth Barrett of Wimpole Street, learns how to conduct himself among London dangers and in Regent's Park. The young male aristocrat, through his sensitive smell and intelligent observations of reactions of those observing him, becomes aware of his environment and his proper place as a dog of high fashion. In the following passage he takes stock of his good points through a most understanding narrator, whose point of view should interest you.

from *Flush*

For the first time he heard his nails click upon the hard paving-stones of London. For the first time the whole battery of a London street on a hot summer's day assaulted his nostrils. He smelt the swooning smells that lie in the gutters; the bitter smells that corrode iron railings; the fuming, heady smells that rise from basements. . . . And also as he trotted up Wimpole Street behind Miss Barrett's chair he was dazed by the passage of human bodies. Petticoats swished at his head; trousers brushed his flanks; sometimes a wheel whizzed an inch from his nose; the wind of destruction roared in his ears and fanned the feathers of his paws as a van passed. Then he plunged in terror. Mercifully the chain tugged at his collar; Miss Barrett held him tight, or he would have rushed to destruction.

At last, with every nerve throbbing and every sense singing, he reached Regent's Park. And then when he saw once more, after years of absence it seemed, grass, flowers and trees, the old hunting cry of the fields hallooed in his ears and he dashed forward to run as he had run in the fields at home. But now a heavy weight jerked at his throat; he was thrown back on his haunches. Were there not trees and grass? he asked. Were these not the signals of freedom? Had he not always leapt forward directly Miss Mitford started on her walk? Why was he a prisoner here? He paused. Here, he observed, the flowers were massed far more thickly than at home; they stood, plant by plant, rigidly in narrow plots. The plots were intersected by hard black paths. Men in shiny top-hats marched ominously up and down the paths. At the sight of them he shuddered closer to the chair. He gladly accepted the protection of the chain. Thus before many of these walks were over a new conception had entered his brain. Setting one thing beside another, he had arrived at a conclusion. Where there are flower-beds there are asphalt paths; where there are flower-beds and asphalt paths and men in shiny top-hats, dogs must be led on chains. Without being able to decipher a word of the placard at the Gate, he had learnt his lesson—in Regent's Park dogs must be led on chains.

And to this nucleus of knowledge, born from the strange experiences of the summer of 1842, soon adhered another: dogs are not equal, but different. At Three Mile Cross Flush had mixed impartially with taproom dogs and the Squire's greyhounds; he had known no difference between the tinker's dog and himself. Indeed it is probable that the mother of his child, though by courtesy called Spaniel, was nothing but a mongrel, eared in one way, tailed in another. But the dogs of London, Flush soon discovered, are strictly divided into different classes. Some are chained dogs, some run wild. Some take their airings in carriages and drink from purple jars; others are unkempt and uncollared and pick up a living in the gutter. Dogs, therefore, Flush began to suspect, differ; some are high, others low; and his suspicions were confirmed by snatches of talk held in passing with the dogs of Wimpole Street. "See that scallywag? A mere mongrel! . . . By gad, that's a fine Spaniel. One of the best in Britain! . . . Pity his ears aren't a shade more curly. . . . There's a topknot for you!" . . .

Flush knew before the summer had passed that there is no equality among dogs; there are high dogs and low dogs. Which then was he? No sooner had Flush got home than he examined himself carefully in the looking-glass. Heaven be praised, he was a dog of birth and breeding! His head was smooth; his eyes were prominent but not gozzled; his feet were feathered; he was the equal of the best-bred cocker in Wimpole Street. He noted with approval the purple jar from which he drank—such are the privileges of rank; he bent his head quietly to have the chain fixed to his collar—such are its penalties. When about this time Miss Barrett observed him staring in the glass, she was mistaken. He was a philosopher, she thought, meditating the difference between appearance and reality. On the contrary, he was an aristocrat considering his points.[30]

VIRGINIA WOOLF

Your pitch changes will reveal your appreciative attitude of Flush's gradual awareness of his importance as a "high" dog. Notice the appeal of the "dog" imagery; and the manner in which Virginia Woolf puts you into the patter of the four paws. How does the author connote Flush's lively personality and appearance?

Thurber was once a student at Ohio State University so you should be able to identify with his educational experiences and enjoy the scholastic efforts of the campus "great."

from *University Days*

I passed all the other courses that I took at my University, but I could never pass botany. This was because all botany students had to spend several hours a week in a laboratory looking through a microscope at plant cells, and I

[30] From FLUSH by Virginia Woolf, copyright 1933, by Harcourt, Brace & World, Inc.; copyright, 1961, by Leonard Woolf. Reprinted by permission of the publishers, pp. 37-40.

could never see through a microscope. I never once saw a cell through a microscope. This used to enrage my instructor. He would wander around the laboratory pleased with the progress all the students were making in drawing the involved and, so I am told, interesting structure of flower cells, until he came to me. I would just be standing there. "I can't see anything," I would say. He would begin patiently enough, explaining how anybody can see through a microscope, but he would always end up in a fury, claiming that I could *too* see through a microscope but just pretended that I couldn't. "It takes away from the beauty of the flowers anyway," I used to tell him. "We are not concerned with beauty in this course," he would say. "We are concerned solely with what I may call the *mechanics* of flars." "Well," I'd say, "I can't see anything." "Try it just once again," he'd say, and I would put my eye to the microscope and see nothing at all, except now and then a nebulous milky substance —a phenomenon of maladjustment. You were supposed to see a vivid, restless clockwork of sharply defined plant cells. "I see what looks like a lot of milk," I would tell him. This, he claimed, was the result of my not having adjusted the microscope properly, so he would readjust it for me, or rather, for himself. And I would look again and see milk.

I finally took a deferred pass, as they called it, and waited a year and tried again. (You had to pass one of the biological sciences or you couldn't graduate.) The professor had come back from vacation as brown as a berry, bright-eyed, and eager to explain cell-structure again to his classes. "Well," he said to me, cheerily, when we met in the first laboratory hour of the semester, "we're going to see cells this time, aren't we?" "Yes, sir," I said. Students to right of me and to left of me and in front of me were seeing cells; what's more, they were quietly drawing pictures of them in their notebooks. Of course, I didn't see anything.

"We'll try it," the professor said to me, grimly, "with every adjustment of the microscope known to man. As God is my witness, I'll arrange this glass so that you see cells through it or I'll give up teaching. In twenty-two years of botany, I—" he cut off abruptly for he was beginning to quiver all over, like Lionel Barrymore, and he genuinely wished to hold onto his temper; his scenes with me had taken a great deal out of him.

So we tried with every adjustment of the microscope known to man. With only one of them did I see anything but blackness or the familiar lacteal opacity, and that time I saw, to my pleasure and amazement, a variegated constellation of flecks, specks, and dots. These I hastily drew. The instructor, noting my activity, came back from an adjoining desk, a smile on his lips and his eyebrows high in hope. He looked at my cell drawing. "What's that?" he demanded, with a hint of a squeal in his voice. "That's what I saw," I said. "You didn't, you didn't, you *didn't!*" he screamed, losing control of his temper instantly, and he bent over and squinted into the microscope. His head snapped up. "That's your eye!" he shouted. "You've fixed the lens so that it reflects! You've drawn your eye!"

Another course that I didn't like, but somehow managed to pass, was economics. I went to that class straight from the botany class, which didn't help me any in understanding either subject. I used to get them mixed up. But not as mixed up as another student in my economics class who came there direct

from a physics laboratory. He was a tackle on the football team, named Bolenciecwcz. At that time Ohio State University had one of the best football teams
in the country, and Bolenciecwcz was one of its outstanding stars. In order to be
eligible to play it was necessary for him to keep up in his studies, a very difficult matter, for while he was not dumber than an ox he was not any
smarter. Most of his professors were lenient and helped him along. None gave
him more hints, in answering questions, or asked him simpler ones than the
economics professor, a thin, timid man named Bassum. One day when we were
on the subject of transportation and distribution, it came Bolenciecwcz's turn
to answer a question. "Name one means of transportation," the professor said
to him. No light came into the big tackle's eyes. "Just any means of transportation," said the professor. Bolenciecwcz sat staring at him. "That is," pursued the
the professor, "any medium, agency, or method of going from one place to
another." Bolenciecwcz had the look of a man who is being led into a trap. "You
may choose among steam, horse-drawn, or electrically propelled vehicles," said
the instructor. "I might suggest the one which we commonly take in making
long journeys across land." There was a profound silence in which everybody
stirred uneasily, including Bolenciecwcz and Mr. Bassum. Mr. Bassum abruptly
broke this silence in an amazing manner. "Choo—choo—choo," he said, in a low
voice, and turned instantly scarlet. He glanced appealingly around the room.
All of us, of course, shared Mr. Bassum's desire that Bolenciecwcz should stay
abreast of the class in economics, for the Illinois game, one of the hardest and
most important of the season, was only a week off. "Toot, toot, too-toooooot!"
some student with a deep voice moaned, and we all looked encouragingly at Bolenciecwcz. Somebody else gave a fine imitation of a locomotive letting off
steam. Mr. Bassum himself rounded off the little show. "Ding, dong, ding,
dong," he said, hopefully. Bolenciecwcz was staring at the floor now, trying to
think, his great brow furrowed, his huge hands rubbing together, his face red.

"How did you come to college this year, Mr. Bolenciecwcz?" asked the
professor. "*Chuf*fa, chuffa, *chuf*fa chuffa."

"M'father sent me," said the football player.

"What on?" asked Bassum.

"I git an 'lowance," said the tackle, in a low, husky voice, obviously embarrassed.

"No, no," said Bassum. "Name a means of transportation. What did you
ride here on?"

"Train," said Bolenciecwcz.[31]

JAMES THURBER

Thurber's professor, characterized as a dedicated instructor, may not
be typical at your university but he has been observed on certain campus
environments. Give him some wide steps as he gets more and more irritated with Thurber's inability to see cells. After all, he was probably hired
to *teach* and not to investigate his student's visual difficulty—and anyway
he believed in the powerful potential of microscopes.

In the latter part of this selection, your audience may come close to hysteria if you can make this particular professor and the classmates offer the right vocal assistance to Bolenciecwcz by means of contrast.

Henry Miller needs no introduction to his entertaining type of literature. This farcical dialogue with its ironic overtones needs more than the black marks on the page to help others enjoy it completely. As you read, what character types do you recognize?

from *Soirée in Hollywood*

The hostess was running about like a wet hen. Trying to rustle up enough hands for a game of bridge. A desperate soul, surrounded by the booty of a thousand battles. "I understand you're a writer," she said, as she tried to carom from my corner of the room to the bar. "Won't you have something to drink— a highball or something? Dear me, I don't know what's come over everybody this evening. I do hate to hear these political discussions. That young man is positively rude. Of course I don't approve of insulting the President of the United States in public but just the same he might have used a little more tact. After all, Mr. So-and-so is an elderly man. He's entitled to some respect, don't you think? Oh, there's So-and-so!" and she dashed off to greet a cinema star who had just dropped in.

The old geezer who was still tottering about handed me a highball. I tried to tell him that I didn't want any but he insisted that I take it anyway. He wanted to have a word with me, he said, winking at me as though he had something very confidential to impart.

"My name is Harrison," he said. "H-a-r-r-i-s-o-n," spelling it out as if it were a difficult name to remember.

"Now what is your name, may I ask?"

"My name is Miller—M-i-l-l-e-r," I answered, spelling it out in Morse for him.

"Miller! Why, that's a very easy name to remember. We had a druggist on our block by that name. Or course. *Miller*. Yes, a very common name.

"So it is," I said.

"And what are you doing out here, Mr. Miller? You're a stranger, I take it?"

"Yes," I said, "I'm just a visitor."

"You're in business, are you?"

"No, hardly. I'm just visiting California."

"I see. Well, where do you come from—the Middle West?"

"No, from New York."

"From New York City? Or from up State?"

"From the city."

"And have you been here very long?"

"No, just a few hours."

"A few hours? My, my . . . well, that's interesting. Very interesting. And will you be staying long, Mr. Miller?"

"I don't know. It depends."

"I see. Depends on how you like it here, is that it?"

"Yes, exactly."

"Well, it's a grand part of the world, I can tell you that. No place like California, I always say. Of course, I'm not a native. But I've been out here almost thirty years now. Wonderful climate. And wonderful people, too."

"I suppose so," I said, just to string him along. I was curious to see how long the idiot would keep up his infernal nonsense.

"You're not in business, you say?"

"No, I'm not."

"On a vacation, is that it?"

"No, not precisely. I'm an ornithologist, you see."

"A what? Well, that's interesting."

"*Very*," I said, with great solemnity.

"Then you may be staying with us for a while, is that it?"

"That's hard to say. I may stay a week and I may stay a year. It all depends. Depends on what specimens I find."

"I see. Interesting work, no doubt."

"*Very!*"

"Have you ever been to California before, Mr. Miller?"

"Yes, twenty-five years ago."

"Well, well, is that so? *Twenty-five years ago!* And now you're back again."

"Yes, back again."

"Were you doing the same thing when you were here before?"

"You mean ornithology?"

"Yes, that's it."

"No, I was digging ditches then."

"Digging ditches? You mean you were—*digging ditches?*"

"Yes, that's it, Mr. Harrison. It was either dig ditches or starve to death."

"Well, I'm glad you don't have to dig ditches any more. It's not much fun —*digging ditches*, is it?"

"No, especially if the ground is hard. Or if your back is weak. Or vice versa. Or let's say your mother has just been put in the mad house and the alarm goes off too soon."

"I beg your pardon! *What did you say?*"

"If things are not just right, I said. You know what I mean—bunions, lumbago, scrofula. It's different now, of course. I have my birds and other pets. Mornings I used to watch the sun rise. Then I would saddle the jackasses—I had two and the other fellow had three. . . ."

"This was in California, Mr. Miller?"

"Yes, twenty-five years ago. I had just done a stretch in San Quentin. . . ."

"*San Quentin?*"

"Yes, attempted suicide. I was really gaga but that didn't make any difference to them. You see, when my father set the house afire one of the horses kicked me in the temple. I used to get fainting fits and then after a time I got homicidal spells and finally I became suicidal. Of course I didn't know that the revolver was loaded. I took a pot shot at my sister, just for fun, and luckily I missed her. I tried to explain it to the judge but he wouldn't listen to me. I never carry a revolver anymore. If I have to defend myself I use a jack-knife. The best thing, of course, is to use your knee. . . ."

"Excuse me, Mr. Miller, I have to speak to Mrs. So-and-so a moment. Very interesting what you say. *Very interesting indeed.* We must talk some more. Excuse me just a moment. . . ."

I slipped out of the house unnoticed and started to walk towards the foot of the hill. The highballs, the red and white wines, the champagne, the cognac were gurgling inside me like a sewer. I had no idea where I was, whose house I had been in or whom I had been introduced to.[32]

Henry Miller

Those small "knowing" facial expressions must punctuate the vocal inflections in order to highlight the nonsense offered in such a blithe spirit. The narrator's friend, who feeds back so much mental vacancy, will be enjoyed if you can give him the delayed response reaction with some bewilderment as he gradually tries to understand—or to listen. The contrast in voices can be easily worked out to create a ridiculous scene.

Some critics speak of Mansfield's "Miss Brill" as a revealing characterization rather than a narrative. Miss Brill, however, *is* the action, revealing a tremendous amount of conflicting activity.

Miss Brill

Although it was so brilliantly fine—the blue sky powdered with gold and great spots of light like white wine splashed over the Jardins Publiques—Miss Brill was glad that she had decided on her fur. The air was motionless, but when you opened your mouth there was just a faint chill, like a chill from a glass of iced water before you sip, and now and again a leaf came drifting—from nowhere, from the sky. Miss Brill put up her hand and touched her fur. Dear little thing! It was nice to feel it again. She had taken it out of its box that afternoon, shaken out the moth-powder, given it a good brush, and rubbed the life back into the dim little eyes. "What has been happening to me?" said the sad little eyes. Oh, how sweet it was to see them snap at her again from the red eiderdown! . . . But the nose, which was of some black composition, wasn't at all firm. It must have had a knock, somehow. Never mind—a little dab of black sealing-wax when the time came—when it was absolutely necessary. . . . Little rogue! Yes, she really felt like that about it. Little rogue biting its tail just by her left ear. She could have taken it off and laid it on her lap and stroked it. She felt a tingling in her hands and arms, but that came from walk-

[32] From THE AIR-CONDITIONED NIGHTMARE by Henry Miller. Copyright 1945 by New Directions. Reprinted by permission of the publishers, New Directions, New York.

ing, she supposed. And when she breathed, something light and sad—no, not sad, exactly—something gentle seemed to move in her bosom.

There were a number of people out this afternoon, far more than last Sunday. And the band sounded louder and gayer. That was because the Season had begun. For although the band played all the year round on Sundays, out of season it was never the same. It was like some one playing with only the family to listen; it didn't care how it played if there weren't any strangers present. Wasn't the conductor wearing a new coat, too? She was sure it was new. He scraped with his foot and flapped his arms like a rooster about to crow, and the bandsmen sitting in the green rotunda blew out their cheeks and glared at the music. Now there came a little "flutey" bit—very pretty!—a little chain of bright drops. She was sure it would be repeated. It was; she lifted her head and smiled.

Only two people shared her "special" seat: a fine old man in a velvet coat, his hands clasped over a huge carved walking-stick, and a big old woman, sitting upright, with a roll of knitting on her embroidered apron. They did not speak. This was disappointing, for Miss Brill always looked forward to the conversation. She had become really quite expert, she thought, at listening as though she didn't listen, at sitting in other people's lives just for a minute while they talked round her.

She glanced, sideways, at the old couple. Perhaps they would go soon. Last Sunday, too, hadn't been as interesting as usual. An Englishman and his wife, he wearing a dreadful Panama hat and she button boots. And she'd gone on the whole time about how she ought to wear spectacles; she knew she needed them; but that it was no good getting any; they'd be sure to break and they'd never keep on. And he'd been so patient. He'd suggested everything—gold rims, the kind that curved round your ears, little pads inside the bridge. No, nothing would please her. "They'll always be sliding down my nose!" Miss Brill had wanted to shake her.

The old people sat on the bench, still as statues. Never mind, there was always the crowd to watch. To and fro, in front of the flower-beds and the band rotunda, the couples and groups paraded, stopped to talk, to greet, to buy a handful of flowers from the old beggar who had his tray fixed to the railings. Little children ran among them, swooping and laughing; little boys with big white silk bows under their chins, little girls, little French dolls, dressed up in velvet and lace. And sometimes a tiny staggerer came suddenly rocking into the open from under the trees, stopped, stared, as suddenly sat down "flop," until its small high-stepping mother, like a young hen, rushed scolding to its rescue. Other people sat on the benches and green chairs, but they were nearly always the same, Sunday after Sunday, and—Miss Brill had often noticed—there was something funny about nearly all of them. They were odd, silent, nearly all old, and from the way they stared they looked as though they'd just come from dark little rooms or even—even cupboards!

Behind the rotunda the slender trees with yellow leaves down drooping, and through them just a line of sea, and beyond the blue sky with gold-veined clouds.

Tum-tum-tum tiddle-um! tiddle-um! tum tiddley-um tum ta! blew the band.

Two young girls in red came by and two young soldiers in blue met them, and they laughed and paired and went off arm-in-arm. Two peasant women with funny straw hats passed, gravely, leading beautiful smoke-coloured donkeys. A cold, pale nun hurried by. A beautiful woman came along and dropped her bunch of violets, and a little boy ran after to hand them to her, and she took them and threw them away as if they'd been poisoned. Dear me! Miss Brill didn't know whether to admire that or not! And now an ermine toque and a gentleman in grey met just in front of her. He was tall, stiff, dignified, and she was wearing the ermine toque she'd bought when her hair was yellow. Now everything, her hair, her face, even her eyes, was the same colour as the shabby ermine, and her hand, in its cleaned glove, lifted to dab her lips, was a tiny yellowish paw. Oh, she was so pleased to see him—delighted! She rather thought they were going to meet that afternoon. She described where she'd been—everywhere, here, there, along by the sea. The day was so charming— didn't he agree? And wouldn't he, perhaps? . . . But he shook his head, lighted a cigarette, slowly breathed a great deep puff into her face, and, even while she was still talking and laughing, flicked the match away and walked on. The ermine toque was alone; she smiled more brightly than ever. But even the band seemed to know what she was feeling and played more softly, played tenderly, and the drum beat, "The Brute! The Brute!" over and over. What would she do? What was going to happen now? But as Miss Brill wondered, the ermine toque turned, raised her hand as though she'd seen some one else, much nicer, just over there, and pattered away. And the band changed again and played more quickly, more gaily than ever, and the old couple on Miss Brill's seat got up and marched away, and such a funny old man with long whiskers hobbled along in time to the music and was nearly knocked over by four girls walking abreast.

Oh, how fascinating it was! How she enjoyed it! How she loved sitting here, watching it all! It was like a play. It was exactly like a play. Who could believe the sky at the back wasn't painted? But it wasn't till a little brown dog trotted on solemn and then slowly trotted off, like a little "theatre" dog, a little dog that had been drugged, that Miss Brill discovered what it was that made it so exciting. They were all on the stage. They weren't only the audience, not only looking on; they were acting. Even she had a part and came every Sunday. No doubt somebody would have noticed if she hadn't been there; she was part of the performance after all. How strange she'd never thought of it like that before! And yet it explained why she made such a point of starting from home at just the same time each week—so as not to be late for the performance—and it also explained why she had quite a queer, shy feeling at telling her English pupils how she spent her Sunday afternoons. No wonder! Miss Brill nearly laughed out loud. She was on the stage. She thought of the old invalid gentleman to whom she read the newspaper four afternoons a week while he slept in the garden. She had got quite used to the frail head on the cotton pillow, the hollowed eyes, the open mouth and the high pinched nose. If he'd been dead she mightn't have noticed for weeks; she wouldn't have minded. But suddenly he knew he was having the paper read to him by an actress! "An actress!" The old head lifted; two points of light quivered in the old eyes. "An actress—are ye?" And Miss Brill smoothed the newspaper as though it were the manuscript of her part and said gently: "Yes, I have been an actress for a long time."

The band had been having a rest. Now they started again. And what they played was warm, sunny, yet there was just a faint chill—a something, what was it?—not sadness—no, not sadness—a something that made you want to sing. The tune lifted, lifted, the light shone; and it seemed to Miss Brill that in another moment all of them, all the whole company, would begin singing. The young ones, the laughing ones who were moving together, they would begin, and the men's voices, very resolute and brave, would join them. And then she too, she too, and the others on the benches—they would come in with a kind of accompaniment—something low, that scarcely rose or fell, something so beautiful—moving. . . . And Miss Brill's eyes filled with tears and she looked smiling at all the other members of the company. Yes, we understand, we understand, she thought—though what they understood she didn't know.

Just at that moment a boy and a girl came and sat down where the old couple had been. They were beautifully dressed; they were in love. The hero and heroine, of course, just arrived from his father's yacht. And still soundlessly singing, still with that trembling smile, Miss Brill prepared to listen.

"No, not now," said the girl. "Not here, I can't."

"But why? Because of that stupid old thing at the end there?" asked the boy. "Why does she come here at all—who wants her? Why doesn't she keep her silly old mug at home?"

"It's her fu-fur which is so funny," giggled the girl. "It's exactly like a fried whiting."

"Ah, be off with you!" said the boy in an angry whisper. Then: "Tell me, ma petite chérie—"

"No, not here," said the girl. "Not *yet*."

On her way home she usually bought a slice of honey-cake at the baker's. It was her Sunday treat. Sometimes there was an almond in her slice, sometimes not. It made a great difference. If there was an almond it was like carrying home a tiny present—a surprise—something that might very well not have been there. She hurried on the almond Sundays and struck the match for the kettle in quite a dashing way.

But to-day she passed the baker's by, climbed the stairs, went into the little dark room—her room like a cupboard—and sat down on the red eiderdown. She sat there for a long time. The box that the fur came out of was on the bed. She unclasped the necklet quickly; quickly, without looking, laid it inside. But when she put the lid on she thought she heard something crying.[33]

KATHERINE MANSFIELD

As you study the eccentricities of Miss Brill, you become involved in an intimate, poignant empathic response to her small joys; you know every detail that characterizes her so completely in her introspective environment: details of thought, movement, dress, participation, imagination, appreciation, awareness, listening, sensitivity—all of which find expression in her limited, but to her, complete activity of living.

Miss Brill has been etched with sensitivity and restraint; first, against a red eiderdown quilt (Mansfield's touches of color are always interesting) with an old fur-piece cuddled in her arms; later as a still, quiet figure at a band-concert. She is a small, lonely (but not in her thinking) soul living within the confines of a cupboard room and her own thoughts. You become a part of her activity as she fondles the one possession that *belongs* to her and gives her comfort, even as a child clings to his favorite blanket. You are with her as she enjoys the happiness of an outdoor concert; you project yourself into the action of the Jardin Publiques. You watch as she gets her small ounce of joy imagining she is a gay participant, and as she plays her silent—but to her, important—part as an actress on that stage every Sunday; you follow her after the performance as she buys a small bit of pastry with a chance almond to make it a treat; you hurry home with her on "almond Sundays" to strike the match for the "kettle in quite a dashing way." You wish someone would talk to her, would notice her— and ironically someone does see her—and the fur piece. Mansfield says nothing of her devastating isolation "but today she passed the baker's by, climbed the stairs, went into the little dark room . . ." What a bleak and joyless ending to a "brilliantly fine" afternoon with the "blue sky powdered with gold!" The author has kept the inner happiness of Miss Brill intact with never a suggestion of her wish for greater happiness nor even a whisper that she might be lonely. Consequently, the last line must be in the same temper of restraint so that it will not become sentimental or maudlin. It can be done!

Forster is acknowledged not only as the most influential fiction writer of the 1930's but also as an essayist and speaker. Many of his stories are built into a structure of fantasy. This is true of "The Other Side of the Hedge," an allegory that is a near-relative to the symbolic tale inasmuch as it carries an abstract meaning relating to its obvious physical meaning. It may be thought of as an extended metaphor, in which one thing or idea is related or portrayed in the likeness or similarity to another. No difficulty will be experienced in securing the allegorical meaning but the story may have to be read several times in order to realize how completely and smoothly the author has carried through on the allegorical meaning.

The Other Side of the Hedge

My pedometer told me that I was twenty-five; and, though it is a shocking thing to stop walking, I was so tired that I sat down on a milestone to rest. People outstripped me, jeering as they did so, but I was too apathetic to feel resentful, and even when Miss Eliza Dimbleby, the great educationist, swept past, exhorting me to persevere, I only smiled and raised my hat.

At first I thought I was going to be like my brother, whom I had had to leave by the roadside a year or two round the corner. He had wasted his breath on singing, and his strength on helping others. But I had travelled more wisely, and now it was only the monotony of the highway that oppressed me —dust under foot and brown crackling hedges on either side, ever since I could remember.

And I had already dropped several things—indeed, the road behind was strewn with the things we all had dropped; and the white dust was settling down on them, so that already they looked no better than stones. My muscles were so weary that I could not even bear the weight of those things I still carried. I slid off the milestone into the road, and lay there prostrate, with my face to the great parched hedge, praying that I might give up.

A little puff of air revived me. It seemed to come from the hedge; and, when I opened my eyes, there was a glint of light through the tangle of boughs and dead leaves. The hedge could not be as thick as usual. In my weak, morbid state, I longed to force my way in, and see what was on the other side. No one was in sight, or I should not have dared to try. For we of the road do not admit in conversation that there is another side at all.

I yielded to the temptation, saying to myself that I would come back in a minute. The thorns scratched my face, and I had to use my arms as a shield, depending upon my feet alone to push me forward. Halfway through I would have gone back, for in the passage all the things I was carrying were scraped off me, and my clothes were torn. But I was so wedged that return was impossible, and I had to wriggle blindly forward, expecting every moment that my strength would fail me, and that I should perish in the undergrowth.

Suddenly cold water closed round my head, and I seemed sinking down for ever. I had fallen out of the hedge into a deep pool. I rose to the surface at last, crying for help, and I heard someone on the opposite bank laugh and say: "Another!" And then I was twitched out and laid panting on the dry ground.

Even when the water was out of my eyes, I was still dazed, for I had never been in so large a space, nor seen such grass and sunshine. The blue sky was no longer a strip, and beneath it the earth had risen grandly into hills— clean, bare buttresses, with beech trees in their folds, and meadows and clear pools at their feet. But the hills were not high, and there was in the landscape a sense of human occupation—so that one might have called it a park, or garden, if the words did not imply a certain triviality and constraint.

As soon as I got my breath, I turned to my rescuer and said:

"Where does this place lead to?"

"Nowhere, thank the Lord!" said he, and laughed. He was a man of fifty or sixty—just the kind of age we mistrust on the road—but there was no anxiety in his manner, and his voice was that of a boy of eighteen.

"But it must lead somewhere!" I cried, too much surprised at his answer to thank him for saving my life.

"He wants to know where it leads!" he shouted to some men on the hill side, and they laughed back, and waved their caps.

I noticed then that the pool into which I had fallen was really a moat which bent round to the left and to the right, and that the hedge followed it continually. The hedge was green on this side—its roots showed through the clear water, and fish swam about in them—and it was wreathed over with dog-roses and Traveller's Joy. But it was a barrier, and in a moment I lost all pleasure in the grass, the sky, the trees, the happy men and women, and realized that the place was but a prison, for all its beauty and extent.

We moved away from the boundary, and then followed a path almost parallel to it, across the meadows. I found it difficult walking, for I was always trying to out-distance my companion, and there was no advantage in doing this if the place led nowhere. I had never kept step with anyone since I left my brother.

I amused him by stopping suddenly and saying disconsolately, "This is perfectly terrible. One cannot advance: one cannot progress. Now we of the road——"

"Yes. I know."

"I was going to say, we advance continually."

"I know."

"We are always learning, expanding, developing. Why, even in my short life I have seen a great deal of advance—the Transvaal War, the Fiscal Question, Christian Science, Radium. Here for example—"

I took out my pedometer, but it still marked twenty-five, not a degree more.

"Oh, it's stopped! I meant to show you. It should have registered all the time I was walking with you. But it makes me only twenty-five."

"Many things don't work in here," he said. "One day a man brought in a Lee-Metford, and that wouldn't work."

"The laws of science are universal in their application. It must be the water in the moat that has injured the machinery. In normal conditions everything works. Science and the spirit of emulation—those are the forces that have made us what we are."

I had to break off and acknowledge the pleasant greetings of people whom we passed. Some of them were singing, some talking, some engaged in gardening, hay-making, or other rudimentary industries. They all seemed happy; and I might have been happy too, if I could have forgotten that the place led nowhere.

I was startled by a young man who came sprinting across our path, took a little fence in fine style, and went tearing over a ploughed field till he plunged into a lake, across which he began to swim. Here was true energy, and I exclaimed: "A cross-country race! Where are the others?"

"There are no others," my companion replied; and, later on, when we passed some long grass from which came the voice of a girl singing exquisitely to herself, he said again: "There are no others." I was bewildered at the waste in production, and murmured to myself, "What does it all mean?"

He said: "It means nothing but itself"—and he repeated the words slowly, as if I were a child.

"I understand," I said quietly, "but I do not agree. Every achievement is worthless unless it is a link in the chain of development. And I must not trespass on your kindness any longer. I must get back somehow to the road, and have my pedometer mended."

"First, you must see the gates," he replied, "for we have gates, though we never use them."

I yielded politely, and before long we reached the moat again, at a point where it was spanned by a bridge. Over the bridge was a big gate, as white as ivory, which was fitted into a gap in the boundary hedge. The gate opened outwards, and I exclaimed in amazement, for from it ran a road—just such a road as I had left—dusty under foot, with brown crackling hedges on either side as far as the eye could reach.

"That's my road!" I cried.

He shut the gate and said: "But not your part of the road. It is through this gate that humanity went out countless ages ago, when it was first seized with the desire to walk."

I denied this, observing that the part of the road I myself had left was not more than two miles off. But with the obstinacy of his years he repeated: "It is the same road. This is the beginning, and though it seems to run straight away from us, it doubles so often, that it is never far from our boundary and sometimes touches it." He stooped down by the moat, and traced on its moist margin an absurd figure like a maze. As we walked back through the meadows, I tried to convince him of his mistake.

"The road sometimes doubles, to be sure, but that is part of our discipline. Who can doubt that its general tendency is onward? To what goal we know not—it may be to some mountain where we shall touch the sky, it may be over precipices into the sea. But that it goes forward—who can doubt that? It is the thought of that that makes us strive to excel, each in his own way, and gives us an impetus which is lacking with you. Now that man who passed us—it's true that he ran well, and jumped well, and swam well; but we have men who can run better, and men who can jump better, and who can swim better. Specialization has produced results which would surprise you. Similarly, that girl——"

Here I interrupted myself to exclaim: "Good gracious me! I could have sworn it was Miss Eliza Dimbleby over there, with her feet in the fountain!"

He believed that it was.

"Impossible! I left her on the road, and she is due to lecture this evening at Tunbridge Wells. Why, her train leaves Cannot Street in—of course my watch has stopped like everything else. She is the last person to be here."

"People always are astonished at meeting each other. All kinds come through the hedge, and come at all times—when they are drawing ahead in the race, when they are lagging behind, when they are left for dead. I often stand near the boundary listening to the sounds of the road—you know what they are —and wonder if anyone will turn aside. It is my great happiness to help someone out of the moat, as I helped you. For our country fills up slowly, though it was meant for all mankind."

"Mankind have other aims," I said gently, for I thought him well-meaning; "and I must join them." I bade him good evening, for the sun was declining, and I wished to be on the road by nightfall. To my alarm, he caught hold of me, crying: "You are not to go yet!" I tried to shake him off, for we had no interests in common, and his civility was becoming irksome to me. But for all my struggles the tiresome old man would not let go; and, as wrestling is not my specialty, I was obliged to follow him.

It was true that I could have never found alone the place where I came in, and I hoped that, when I had seen the other sights about which he was worrying, he would take me back to it. But I was determined not to sleep in the country, for I mistrusted it, and the people too, for all their friendliness. Hungry though I was, I would not join them in their evening meals of milk and fruit, and, when they gave me flowers, I flung them away as soon as I could do so unobserved. Already they were lying down for the night like cattle—some out on the bare hillside, others in groups under the beeches. In the light of an orange sunset I hurried on with my unwelcome guide, dead tired, faint for want of food, but murmuring indomitably: "Give me life, with its struggles and victories, with its failures and hatreds, with its deep moral meaning and its unknown goal!"

At last we came to a place where the encircling moat was spanned by another bridge, and where another gate interrupted the line of the boundary hedge. It was different from the first gate; for it was half transparent like horn, and opened inwards. But through it, in the waning light, I saw again just such a road as I had left—monotonous, dusty, with brown crackling hedges on either side, as far as the eye could reach.

I was strangely disquieted at the sight, which seemed to deprive me of all self-control. A man was passing us, returning for the night to the hills, with a scythe over his shoulder and a can of some liquid in his hand. I forgot the destiny of our race. I forgot the road that lay before my eyes, and I sprang at him, wrenched the can out of his hand, and began to drink.

It was nothing stronger than beer, but in my exhausted state it overcame me in a moment. As in a dream, I saw the old man shut the gate, and heard him say: "This is where your road ends, and through this gate humanity—all that is left of it—will come in to us."

Though my senses were sinking into oblivion, they seemed to expand ere they reached it. They perceived the magic song of nightingales, and the odour of invisible hay, and stars piercing the fading sky. The man whose beer I had stolen lowered me down gently to sleep off its effects, and, as he did so, I saw that he was my brother.[34]

E. M. FORSTER

The central meaning of this allegory emerges to voice Forster's disbelief in science and the machine that produce a mechanized world in which men (in this instance, a young man of twenty-five years) struggle to seek reputation and personal gain. To support his theme, the author has followed his theory of the difference between pattern and rhythm in a narrative.[35] Pattern "springs mainly from the plot" revealed here in the contrasting actions of characters caught in "flash" incidents. Rhythm, a "heard" rhythm, which relates movements similar to the echo of a recurring phrase in a symphony, unites the "movements as a whole." It is not present all the time like the pattern but comes and goes as a recalled

---

[34] Copyright 1947 by Alfred A. Knopf, Inc. Reprinted from THE COLLECTED TALES OF E. M. FORSTER, by permission of Alfred A. Knopf, Inc.

[35] Edward Morgan Forster, "Pattern and Rhythm," *Aspects of the Novel* (New York: Harcourt, Brace & World, Inc., 1929, 1937), pp. 213-242.

memory, which by its "lovely waxing and waning" fills the reader with "surprise and freshness and hope." The rhythmic counterbalancing of the two sides of the hedge contrast symbolically the sound and bustle of the dusty road with the freedom and relaxation of the open country. One side of the hedge with its brown crackling brush facing the open road symbolizes the hectic, competitive values of hurried reality and society's demand for progress; the "other side of the hedge" symbolizes the permanent values of vision and imagination in which pressures, necessities and mechanization do not impinge on easeful and thoughtful living. The "flash" incidents forming the background of the "other side" present a "heard rhythm" which strengthens movement and recall as the climax is reached.

Forster culminates the pattern of his allegory by two gates: the ivory gate opening outwardly—the gate through which "humanity went out countless ages ago"; and the gate of horn opening inwardly to the "other side of the hedge." According to critics, the author was probably alluding to the incident in Homer's *Odyssey* in which Penelope discusses the portent of dreams with Odysseus and remarks: "Two gates there are for dreams, one made of horn and one of ivory. The dreams which pass through the carved ivory delude and bring us tales that turn to naught; those that pass through polished horn accomplish real things, whenever seen."

Vocal attention to imagery that describes characteristics and movements of the two sides of the hedge will intensify meaning. Inflections should reflect the incredulity of the narrator, his wonderment and inability to grasp or accept the new direction of his life road in contrast to the guide who is relaxed, casual and understanding.

Consider also the intent of the last sentence, "I saw that he was my brother." Can the meaning of blood-relationship be extended to the brotherhood of man? How will your voice carry this latter thought? Most of all, timing is extremely important: make good use of appropriate pauses with corresponding facial expression to gain reinforcement and suspense.

"Bombardment" is an interpreter's paradise because the stylistic arrangement offers opportunity to contrast images, tone, timing and intensity, as well as pitch changes.

from *Bombardment*

Slowly, without force, the rain drops into the city. It stops a moment on the carved head of Saint John, then slides on again, slipping and trickling over his stone cloak. It splashes from the lead conduit of a gargoyle, and falls from it in turmoil on the stones in the Cathedral square. Where are the people, and why does the fretted steeple sweep about in the sky? Boom! The sound swings against the rain. Boom, again! After it, only water rushing in the gutters, and the turmoil from the spout of the gargoyle. Silence. Ripples and mutters. Boom!

The room is damp, but warm. Little flashes swarm about from the fire-light. The lustres of the chandeliers are bright, and clusters of rubies leap in the bohemian glasses on the *étagère*. Her hands are restless, but the white masses of her hair are quite still. Boom! Will it never cease to torture, this iteration! Boom! The vibration shatters a glass on the *étagère*. It lies there, formless and glowing, with all its crimson gleams shot out of pattern, spilled, flowing red, blood-red. A thin bell-note pricks through the silence. A door creaks. The old lady speaks: "Victor, clear away that broken glass." "Alas! Madam, the bohemian glass!" "Yes, Victor, one hundred years ago my father brought it—" Boom! The room shakes, the servitor quakes. Another goblet shivers and breaks. Boom!

It rustles at the window-pane, the smooth, streaming rain, and he is shut within its clash and murmur. Inside is his candle, his table, his ink, his pen, and his dreams. He is thinking, and the walls are pierced with beams of sunshine, slipping through young green. A fountain tosses itself up at the blue sky, and through the spattered water in the basin he can see copper carp, lazily floating among cold leaves. A wind-harp in a cedar-tree grieves and whispers, and words blow in his brain, bubbled, iridescent, shooting up like flowers of fire, higher and higher. Boom! The flame-flowers snap on their slender stems. The fountain rears up into long broken spears of dishevelled water and flattens into the earth. Boom! And there is only the room, the table, the candle, and the sliding rain. Again, Boom!—Boom!—Boom! He stuffs his fingers into his ears. He sees corpses, and cries out in fright. Boom! It is night, and they are shelling the city! Boom! Boom.!"[36]

AMY LOWELL

The short dramatic sentences in "Bombardment" must be voiced with discriminating pitch intonations, sometimes on a level monotone key and other times showing wide steps and a great range of key. They also support the rhythm which builds to a crescendo in each episode. You can experiment with the variations offered to produce the contrasting moods of the characters.

Do not expend all your vocal power at the beginning of each vignette, however, even though the situation is tense. You can keep your tone taut throughout but be sure to create anticipation for the next air onslaught. Gradually increase your intensity, remembering that pauses are extremely important in providing the necessary shifts from slight tension to fright to extreme terror.

[36] "Bombardment" by Amy Lowell from THE COMPLETE POETICAL WORKS OF AMY LOWELL. Copyright 1955 by Houghton Mifflin Company. Reprinted by permission of the publisher, Houghton Mifflin Company.

To create a story on the subject of "courage," Fitzgerald has placed two brothers of differing personalities in a series of dramatic war episodes.

Courage

When they were youngsters of ten and twelve, the Sprague boys used to walk home alone after Sunday evening services. Peter was the elder, a stocky, unimaginative child, dark-skinned and awkward. Davy had nice features. He was fair like his mother's people.

As they neared the foot of Pride's Hill, Peter would take his brother's hand. Davy was afraid. That was on account of the old Baptist cemetery. The stones gleamed, and there were noises in the underbrush that fringed the road. As they topped the rise, the younger boy would draw away a little, and start chattering again.

Even in those days Peter had understood. Davy was different; things bothered him more.

When the war came, it was inevitable that the Sprague boys should be among the first from Baintree to go.

Davy enlisted in Boston, on his way home from his freshman year at Tufts. Two weeks later, when he left to report for duty, Peter went with him.

It was September. The transport was rocking to the first long swells of the outer harbor. The brothers stood by the rail, watching their convoy nose out ahead. Somewhere in the distance behind them the fog was blurring out the ragged Hoboken water front. . . .

Beneath their feet the great shafts plunged and recoiled—pushing them steadily, relentlessly, toward the unknown.

It was December. The third battalion had halted along the road beyond Ménil-la-Tour. At eight that night the division would take over a sector from the French. The men had done twelve muddy miles since noon, and they were profanely tired.

The rain had ceased falling and the sky was drawing away, cold and hard. A heavy rumbling came and went among the hills up ahead. A gray-blue camion lumbered by. Its bearded chauffeur dexterously caught a cigarette and grinned his thanks. The poplars dripped. Out of the clumps of O. D., blue shreds of smoke eddied.

Sergeant Sprague, working down the line, reached his brother's squad. Davy was sitting on his unslung pack, a little withdrawn from the others.

"How are the feet, Davy?"

"They're sore, Pete. Got any water?"

"Plenty." He reached for his canteen.

As he took the canteen back, he paused, his fingers on its cover. Out of the distance had come a purring noise—high up. A soft purr with a recurring throb in it. The men grew silent. The noise came louder and louder. Far up in the sky, somewhat off to the right, a tiny black insect was sailing slowly toward them.

"He's looking for the road," remarked Pete. Slipping the canteen back in his belt Pete snapped-to the felt covers. The word was passed along to cut out the cigarettes and lie flat.

The Boche plane was droning almost directly overhead. The men lay still. The plane swooped down toward the road. A bomb struck in the field behind them; the explosion beat on them—the Boche had passed over.

A voice came from the next squad, "Missed us, you——!" A tense suppressed laugh. The Boche came circling back again. The drone of his engine grew louder and louder. It would be close this time. Davy's hand came into Pete's line of vision. It was very still—the hand. Then slowly, spasmodically it twitched. It twitched as a shot rabbit twitches—convulsively. He was aware suddenly of a fear that had been with him from the beginning. Davy couldn't stand it. He was different. He wished to God the war would end—soon.

A flash, and the crash came. On the other side of the road—a bit of iron rang on a helmet.

The plane didn't return. It hummed off toward Ménil-la-Tour. The men sat up and followed it with jeering comments. Davy clambered to his feet, laughing unsteadily.

Sprague grew leisurely awake. There was a patch of sunlight on the dugout floor. That meant afternoon. Pete had a vague memory of noise, heavy muffled sounds. He had slept since daylight. It was quiet outside. It had been a quiet two weeks. By this time to-morrow they would be back in reserve. The first battalion would be in to relieve them by dawn. He heard someone passing outside; the creak of heavy boots on the duckboards. Fritz had been lying low. It was a bad sign, that. Well—they'd be out to-morrow. He'd speak to the captain then about Davy. It was nothing to be ashamed of. Davy was sick. His nerves were screwed tight—to the breaking point. They could see for themselves.

He sat up and reached for his shoes, but the image of his brother's white face, the tense look of his eyes, persisted. Only one more day. The bags at the head of the stairs pushed in. It was Sergeant Ferber.

"Sleep through the row?" he grunted, pushing back his helmet.

"I heard something."

"They threw some Berthas over—knocked in a piece of the support trench."

Ferber stood watching Pete winding on his spirals.

"Your brother's out of luck."

Sprague straightened up and waited—tense.

"He sneaked off post five when the fuss started. They picked him up cryin' like a kid."

It had come.

Sprague drew a quick sharp breath and bent again over his leggings, his back to Ferber. He tucked in the tape ends and turned.

"The kid's all in—he's sick."

Ferber spat his disgust. "He will be when they get through with him," he remarked judicially.

Sprague's eyes flamed. Then, without speaking, he went past Ferber to the stairs.

The sky was blue overhead. The guns were quiet, oppressively quiet. There was a soft thud above him. A little sand scattered down. Davy—Davy!

The lantern at Captain Doane's elbow flared and smoked. The shadow on the wall behind him bulked grotesquely. He gave no sign. Sprague spoke with an effort, a sense of futility dragging down his words. When he had done, the officer raised his eyes. He looked past Sprague.

"The court can consider his physical condition. That's not up to me," he said wearily.

Sprague's voice was steady. "Will you recommend clemency, sir?"

"I can't, Sprague. When your brother crawled off his post, he endangered the whole battalion. I can't let any feeling for you—"

There was more; something about justice and Pete's own record. The words blurred together. It didn't matter. Davy would be put under guard in the morning when they started out. They wouldn't shoot him—it would be Leavenworth. The *Concord Times* would have it. Jim Wetherby would bring the paper out to his mother.

The phone stuttered. As Doane reached for the set, Sprague saluted stiffly and turned away.

He was passing out of the orderlies' room when someone grabbed his elbow. "Are you deaf, Sarge? The old man wants you back."

The captain was waiting, drumming nervously on the table. "Price is on number nine. He thinks they've sneaked in and set up a machine gun off to his left."

As Pete listened, his brother's face grew indistinct. The ground sloped off to the left of number nine.

"They could get the support trench from that position, sir."

The captain jerked forward, scowling. "If they've got that support trench covered, they've got wind we're going to be relieved. They're going to strafe us when we start out! You know the men. Send someone out to look it over. If the Boches are there, we'll hold up the movement and shell them out in the morning."

A sense of relief—of escape—flashed on him. It would be a way out. Doane was waiting—giving him his chance.

A way out—for him. He stood silent.

The captain stirred impatiently. "Well? Tell the man who goes, we'll make him if he gets back. That's all, Sergeant."

Sprague wormed his way out through the narrow connecting ditch to number nine post. A fine rain was beginning to fall. The night was black and warm. Price pointed out through the dark. Crouching together, they waited till a flare of light shot up.

"Off to your left," whispered Price, "there's a shell hole. You can't see nothing, but there's a couple of Heinies in there with a machine gun or I'll—"

"All right, Price. I'll send someone out to look it over. Don't open up if you hear us. I'll go part way myself."

Price cursed fervently under his breath. His whisper followed Sprague. "There's a ticket west waiting for the bird that goes."

Sprague knew it.

Davy lay crouched, his face to the wall. At the touch of his brother's hand he shivered and turned to stare up at him hopelessly. He tried to smile. His lips twitched.

Pete's face was granite. "Davy, get your shoes on. The C. O. wants you." . . .

In the trench outside, Pete gripped his shoulder. "You've got to get out and get out quick. They're going to line you up in the morning."

"My God, Pete! They wouldn't do that!"

"They've got to on account of the others." He put his arms around the boy and held him close. Then gently he broke the grasp of his fingers. "You're going over to the Boches, Davy. They will ship you back to a prison camp. After this thing is over, people won't remember."

He was glad of the darkness.

"I can't, Pete." There was nothing left but fear.

"It's your only chance. Sure you can. Come."

The boy shrank back.

"It's that or the firing squad, Davy."

A moment later they were on their faces crawling beneath the wire. Out by number nine post. He could hear Davy breathing—quick forced gasps. Groping, he reached and found his hand. They crept on. Out past the vague hump that was number nine post. Five—ten yards beyond. A flare went up, and before the light failed he had aligned the suspected crater.

Drawing close, he whispered, "I've got to go back now, Dave. Keep straight on till you strike a shell hole, twenty-five yards out. Crawl in there till it starts to get light and then go over."

He drew swiftly back before Dave could hesitate, lest he refuse to go on. He could still get him back. He dug his fingers into the earth. The silence pushed down on him—it was too late now. The seconds hung back.

A roar shattered the night. The waiting Boche had swung his gun on the black smudge that had crept too near. A sharp staccato of shots. The silence settled down again. Sprague crept back under the wire. His lips were bleeding.

Captain Doane looked up anxiously. "Well, Sprague?"

"There's a machine gun there, sir. Thirty yards off post nine." There was a note of exhaustion in his voice. "He opened up and got our man."

Doane fumbled for his pipe. Their eyes met. "Who went, Sergeant?"

Pete lifted a suffering face. "Private Sprague, sir," he said proudly. Then his voice went flat.

"Your lantern's smoking, sir. I'll send Webber in."

He stopped in the orderlies' room, and then went back to his brother's dugout—to gather up Davy's things. They would send them back to his mother.[37]

BRASSIL FITZGERALD

The conflict in "Courage" can be heightened if you show, through your speech pattern, the contrasting and revealing characteristics of the two brothers in a demanding environment. Careful pacing of events and dialogue on your part, as well as the varying speech rhythms and pitch

[37] From THE ATLANTIC MONTHLY. "Courage" by Brassil Fitzgerald, November 1925. Reprinted with permission of the author and publishers.

intonations of the brothers, will strengthen the mood, add to the intensity of the final situation, and so build to a bitter climax and denouement.

"The week after was one of the busiest weeks of their lives." So writes Mansfield in a typical plunge into the heart of her story "The Daughters of the Late Colonel." Through a series of episodes, Josephine and Constantia, or "Jug" and "Con," huddle together within their narrow world dominated by their father, the late Colonel, who though dead, still controls their way of living with his baleful eye and the thump of his stick. These flash incidents could easily be dramatized into a series of scenes within a play structure because of the objectivity in approach and because of Mansfield's sharply etched detail work in dialogue and movement that betray the inner thoughts of the sisters. This technique, you will recall from "Miss Brill," is characteristic of the author's literary style.

Only episodes 1, 2, 3, 5, and 6 out of 12 have been reprinted, with the hope that these scenes will provide motivation to read the story in its entirety. These five scenes portray Jug and Con reflecting the tone and shadow of their past life, limited to their relationships with their father, a nurse and a maid. The scene with the minister (Episode 4), who suggests to their horror a "little communion" in the parlor, has been omitted in this sequence.

The crushing tragedy involves two sisters who cannot separate themselves from the life of the past because they cannot efface the memory or *presence* of the Colonel. Their concepts and daily habits are so deeply embedded in the past that "time" becomes the important part of the story's theme—escape from time "that is no more" into the reality of the present. You continually hope that each scene may show a brave start into a real adventure. Although there may be a glimmer at times, it is only a brief light that cannot be rekindled and so dies quickly with tragic hopelessness.

from *The Daughters of the Late Colonel*

1

The week after was one of the busiest weeks of their lives. Even when they went to bed it was only their bodies that lay down and rested; their minds went on, thinking things out, talking things over, wondering, deciding, trying to remember where . . .

Constantia lay like a statue, her hands by her sides, her feet just overlapping each other, the sheet up to her chin. She stared at the ceiling.

"Do you think father would mind if we gave his top-hat to the porter?"

"The porter?" snapped Josephine. "Why ever the porter? What a very extraordinary idea!"

"Because," said Constantia slowly, "he must often have to go to funerals.

And I noticed at—at the cemetery that he only had a bowler." She paused. "I thought then how very much he'd appreciate a top-hat. We ought to give him a present, too. He was always very nice to father."

"But," cried Josephine, flouncing on her pillow and staring across the dark at Constantia, "father's head!" And suddenly, for one awful moment, she nearly giggled. Not, of course, that she felt in the least like giggling. It must have been habit. Years ago, when they had stayed awake at night talking, their beds had simply heaved. And now the porter's head, disappearing, popped out, like a candle, under father's hat. . . . The giggle mounted, mounted; she clenched her hands; she fought it down; she frowned fiercely at the dark and said "Remember" terribly sternly.

"We can decide to-morrow," she sighed.

Constantia had noticed nothing; she sighed.

"Do you think we ought to have our dressing-gowns dyed as well?"

"Black?" almost shrieked Josephine.

"Well, what else?" said Constantia. "I was thinking—it doesn't seem quite sincere, in a way, to wear black out of doors and when we're fully dressed, and then when we're at home—"

"But nobody sees us," said Josephine. She gave the bedclothes such a twitch that both her feet became uncovered, and she had to creep up the pillows to get them well under again.

"Kate does," said Constantia. "And the postman very well might."

Josephine thought of her dark-red slippers, which matched her dressing-gown, and of Constantia's favourite indefinite green ones which went with hers. Black! Two black dressing-gowns and two pairs of black woolly slippers, creeping off to the bathroom like black cats.

"I don't think it's absolutely necessary," said she.

Silence. Then Constantia said, "We shall have to post the papers with the notice in them to-morrow to catch the Ceylon mail. . . . How many letters have we had up till now?"

"Twenty-three."

Josephine had replied to them all, and twenty-three times when she came to "We miss our dear father so much" she had broken down and had to use her handkerchief, and on some of them even to soak up a very light-blue tear with an edge of blotting-paper. Strange! She couldn't have put it on—but twenty-three times. Even now, though, when she said over to herself sadly, "We miss our dear father *so* much" she could have cried if she'd wanted to.

"Have you got enough stamps?" came from Constantia.

"Oh, how can I tell?" said Josephine crossly. "What's the good of asking me that now?"

"I was just wondering," said Constantia mildly.

Silence again. There came a little rustle, a scurry, a hop.

"A mouse," said Constantia.

"It can't be a mouse because there aren't any crumbs," said Josephine.

"But it doesn't know there aren't," said Constantia.

A spasm of pity squeezed her heart. Poor little thing! She wished she'd left a tiny piece of biscuit on the dressing table. It was awful to think of it not finding anything. What would it do?

"I can't think how they manage to live at all," she said slowly.

"Who?" demanded Josephine.

And Constantia said more loudly than she meant to, "Mice."

Josephine was furious. "Oh, what nonsense, Con!" she said. "What have mice got to do with it? You're asleep."

"I don't think I am," said Constantia. She shut her eyes to make sure. She was.

Josephine arched her spine, pulled up her knees, folded her arms so that her fists came under her ears, and pressed her cheek hard against the pillow.

2

Another thing which complicated matters was they had Nurse Andrews staying on with them that week. It was their own fault; they had asked her. It was Josephine's idea. On the morning—well, on the last morning, when the doctor had gone, Josephine had said to Constantia, "Don't you think it would be rather nice if we asked Nurse Andrews to stay on for a week as our guest?"

"Very nice," said Constantia.

"I thought," went on Josephine quickly, "I should just say this afternoon, after I've paid her, 'My sister and I would be very pleased, after all you've done for us, Nurse Andrews, if you would stay on for a week as our guest.' I'd have to put that in about being our guest in case—"

"Oh, but she could hardly expect to be paid!" cried Constantia.

"One never knows," said Josephine sagely.

Nurse Andrews had, of course, jumped at the idea. But it was a bother. It meant they had to have regular sit-down meals at the proper times, whereas if they'd been alone they could just have asked Kate if she wouldn't have minded bringing them a tray wherever they were. And meal-times now that the strain was over were rather a trial.

Nurse Andrews was simply fearful about butter. Really they couldn't help feeling that about butter, at least, she took advantage of their kindness. And she had that maddening habit of asking for just an inch more bread to finish what she had on her plate, and then, at the last mouthful, absent-mindedly—of course it wasn't absent-mindedly—taking another helping. Josephine got very red when this happened, and she fastened her small, bead-like eyes on the tablecloth as if she saw a minute strange insect creeping through the web of it. But Constantia's long, pale face lengthened and set, and she gazed away—away—far over the desert, to where that line of camels unwound like a thread of wool. . . .

"When I was with Lady Tukes," said Nurse Andrews, she had such a dainty little contrayvance for the buttah. It was a silvah Cupid balanced on the —on the bordah of a glass dish, holding a tayny fork. And when you wanted some buttah you simply pressed his foot and he bent down and speared you a piece. It was quite a gayme."

Josephine could hardly bear that. But "I think those things are very extravagant" was all she said.

"But whey?" asked Nurse Andrews, beaming through her eye-glasses. "No one, surely, would take more buttah than one wanted—would one?"

"Ring, Con," cried Josephine. She couldn't trust herself to reply.

And proud young Kate, the enchanted princess, came in to see what the old tabbies wanted now. She snatched away their plates of mock something or other and slapped down a white, terrified blancmange.

"Jam, please, Kate," said Josephine kindly.

Kate knelt and burst open the sideboard, lifted the lid of the jam-pot, saw it was empty, put it on the table, and stalked off.

"I'm afraid," said Nurse Andrews a moment later, "there isn't any."

"Oh, what a bother!" said Josephine. She bit her lip. "What had we better do?"

Constantia looked dubious. "We can't disturb Kate again," she said softly.

Nurse Andrews waited, smiling at them both. Her eyes wandered, spying at everything behind her eye-glasses. Constantia in despair went back to her camels. Josephine frowned heavily—concentrated. If it hadn't been for this idiotic woman she and Con would, of course, have eaten their blancmange without. Suddenly the idea came.

"I know," she said. "Marmalade. There's some marmalade in the sideboard. Get it, Con."

"I hope," laughed Nurse Andrews, and her laugh was like a spoon tinkling against a medicine-glass—"I hope it's not very bittah marmalayde."

3

But, after all, it was not long now, and then she'd be gone for good. And there was no getting over the fact that she had been very kind to father. She had nursed him day and night at the end. Indeed, both Constantia and Josephine felt privately she had rather overdone the not leaving him at the very last. For when they had gone in to say good-bye Nurse Andrews had sat beside his bed the whole time, holding his wrist and pretending to look at her watch. It couldn't have been necessary. It was so tactless, too. Supposing father had wanted to say something—something private to them. Not that he had. Oh, far from it! He lay there, purple, a dark, angry purple in the face, and never even looked at them when they came in. Then, as they were standing there, wondering what to do, he had suddenly opened one eye. Oh, what a difference it would have made, what a difference to their memory of him, how much easier to tell people about it, if he had only opened both! But no—one eye only. It glared at them a moment and then . . . went out.

5

Well, at any rate, all that part of it was over, though neither of them could possibly believe that father was never coming back. Josephine had had a moment of absolute terror at the cemetery, while the coffin was lowered, to think that she and Constantia had done this thing without asking his permission. What would father say when he found out? For he was bound to find out sooner or later. He always did. "Buried. You two girls had me *buried!*" She heard his stick thumping. Oh, what would they say? What possible excuse could they make? It sounded such an appallingly heartless thing to do. Such a wicked advantage to take of a person because he happened to be helpless at the moment. The other people seemed to treat it all as a matter of course. They were strangers; they couldn't be expected to understand that father was the very last person for such a thing to happen to. No, the entire blame for it all would fall on her and Constantia. And the expense, she thought, stepping into the tight-buttoned cab. When she had to show him the bills. What would he say then?

She heard him absolutely roaring, "And do you expect me to pay for this gimcrack excursion of yours?"

"Oh," groaned poor Josephine aloud, "we shouldn't have done it, Con!"

And Constantia, pale as a lemon in all that blackness, said in a frightened whisper, "Done what, Jug?"

"Let them bu-bury father like that," said Josephine, breaking down and crying into her new, queer-smelling mourning handkerchief.

"But what else could we have done?" asked Constantia wonderingly. "We couldn't have kept him, Jug—we couldn't have kept him unburied. At any rate, not in a flat that size."

Josephine blew her nose; the cab was dreadfully stuffy.

"I don't know," she said forlornly. "It is all so dreadful. I feel we ought to have tried to, just for a time at least. To make perfectly sure. One thing's certain"—and her tears sprang out again—"father will never forgive us for this—never!"

6

Father would never forgive them. That was what they felt more than ever when, two mornings later, they went into his room to go through his things. They had discussed it quite calmly. It was even down on Josephine's list of things to be done. *Go through father's things and settle about them.* But that was a very different matter from saying after breakfast:

"Well, are you ready, Con?"

"Yes, Jug—when you are."

"Then I think we'd better get it over."

It was dark in the hall. It had been a rule for years never to disturb father in the morning, whatever happened. And now they were going to open the door without knocking even. . . . Constantia's eyes were enormous at the idea; Josephine felt weak in the knees.

"You—you go first," she gasped, pushing Constantia.

But Constantia said, as she always had said on those occasions, "No, Jug, that's not fair. You're eldest."

Josephine was just going to say—what at other times she wouldn't have owned to for the world—what she kept for her very last weapon, "But you're tallest," when they noticed that the kitchen door was open, and there stood Kate. . . .

"Very stiff," said Josephine, grasping the door-handle and doing her best to turn it. As if anything ever deceived Kate!

It couldn't be helped. That girl was. . . . Then the door was shut behind them, but—but they weren't in father's room at all. They might have suddenly walked through the wall by mistake into a different flat altogether. Was the door just behind them? They were too frightened to look. Josephine knew that if it was it was holding itself tight shut; Constantia felt that, like the doors in dreams, it hadn't any handle at all. It was the coldness which made it so awful. Or the whiteness—which? Everything was covered. The blinds were down, a cloth hung over the mirror, a sheet hid the bed; a huge fan of white paper filled the fireplace. Constantia timidly put out her hand; she almost expected a snowflake to fall. Josephine felt a queer tingling in her nose, as if her nose was freezing. Then a cab klop-klopped over the cobbles below, and the quiet seemed to shake into little pieces.

"I had better pull up a blind," said Josephine bravely.

"Yes, it might be a good idea," whispered Constantia.

They only gave the blind a touch, but it flew up and the cord flew after, rolling round the blindstick, and the little tassel tapped as if trying to get free. That was too much for Constantia.

"Don't you think—don't you think we might put it off for another day?" she whispered.

"Why?" snapped Josephine, feeling as usual, much better now that she knew for certain that Constantia was terrified. "It's got to be done. But I do wish you wouldn't whisper, Con."

"I didn't know I was whispering," whispered Constantia.

"And why do you keep on staring at the bed?" said Josephine, raising her voice almost defiantly. "There's nothing *on* the bed."

"Oh, Jug, don't say so!" said poor Connie. "At any rate, not so loudly."

Josephine felt herself that she had gone too far. She took a wide swerve over to the chest of drawers, put out her hand, but quickly drew it back again.

"Connie!" she gasped, and she wheeled round and leaned with her back against the chest of drawers.

"Oh, Jug—what?"

Josephine could only glare. She had the most extraordinary feeling that she had just escaped something simply awful. But how could she explain to Constantia that father was in the chest of drawers? He was in the top drawer with his handkerchiefs and neckties, or.in the next with his shirts and pyjamas, or in the lowest of all with his suits. He was watching there, hidden away—just behind the door-handle—ready to spring.

She pulled a funny old-fashioned face at Constantia, just as she used to in the old days when she was going to cry.

"I can't open," she nearly wailed.

"No, don't, Jug," whispered Constantia earnestly. "It's much better not to. Don't let's open anything. At any rate, not for a long time."

"But—but it seems so weak," said Josephine, breaking down.

"But why not be weak for once, Jug?" argued Constantia, whispering quite fiercely. "If it is weak." And her pale stare flew from the locked writing-table—so safe—to the huge glittering wardrobe, and she began to breathe in a queer, panting way. "Why shouldn't we be weak for once in our lives, Jug? It's quite excusable. Let's be weak—be weak, Jug. It's much nicer to be weak than to be strong."

And then she did one of those amazingly bold things that she'd done about twice before in their lives; she marched over to the wardrobe, turned the key, and took it out of the lock. Took it out of the lock and held it up to Josephine, showing Josephine by her extraordinary smile that she knew what she'd done, she'd risked deliberately father being in there among his overcoats.

If the huge wardrobe had lurched forward, had crashed down on Constantia, Josephine wouldn't have been surprised. On the contrary, she would have thought it the only suitable thing to happen. But nothing happened. Only the room seemed quieter than ever, and bigger flakes of cold air fell on Josephine's shoulders and knees. She began to shiver.

"Come, Jug," said Constantia, still with that awful callous smile, and Josephine followed just as she had that last time, when Constantia had pushed Benny into the round pond.[38]

KATHERINE MANSFIELD

Instead of broad sweeping discussions, Mansfield, as usual, selects detailed action interwoven with scraps of dialogue to portray dramatically the inner reaction and thoughts of her characters. She interposes no comment nor does she characterize the sisters as indecisive. You merely become conscious of ineffectual, hesitant words that seem to die away into "thin air," for no culmination occurs in any of the episodes. You also begin to understand the futility of the sisters' escape and are likely to mutter after each incident, "Too late, too late!"

The influences of the past—like "life in a tunnel"—have thoroughly impregnated their living habits. They have freedom but are incapable of exercising any movement of escape. Furthermore, the Colonel is not dead; his presence is very much alive—his stick still thumps, his one menacing eye still glistens and glares, he objects to being buried, roaring, "And do you expect me to pay for this gimcrack excursion of yours?" These flashing incidents vividly suggest the complete hypnotic power of Father. The entrance into the Colonel's room is hesitating, terrifying, until Kate, who knows the answers to everything, appears—then the quick shutting of the door and the sisters are inside; but certainly not inside their father's room for everything is white, nor is he lying on the bed! Of course, he may be hiding in the chest of drawers or in the wardrobe, ready to spring out; so with an extremely brave and bold movement, Con *locks* the wardrobe door.

Each episode reiterates, as shown by the reactions and intense remarks of these two personalities, that they are caught in the pattern of the past. As the curtain drops on each revealing scene, the sisters continue to flounder in a maze of yesterday's directives and to search feebly for an escape into the present. No matter what tiny outlet they seek, they are pushed back because of their inability to realize the possibility of living without the dominance of their father. Even Kate and the nurse, who might have helped, are grim reminders of the fortress built around them. They intensify the shadows of scorn, harsh ingratitude and indifference pervading the darkened home.

This is the irony of the story: the situation has freed the sisters of the bondage to the Colonel, but their characters cannot perceive the way into a different life and no one is near to help them. In the last episode Mansfield dramatizes their hopelessness through the symbolism of the sun's rays. For a few moments, the pale red sunlight falls upon the Indian carpet, is gone and then comes again; it deepens and shines almost golden on the relics of the past that imprison the daughters of the Colonel. The sun touches Jud gently, drawing her to the window. She struggles inwardly to understand her need. Con too muses silently on the infrequent but joyous freedom of earlier days when she escaped to the seaside to watch the restless waters and to sing her happiness of the moment in the moonlight—only to go back to the rigidity of the "tunnel life" with father. "Perhaps now . . ." and they instinctively turn to each other, start to phrase their longing but the unfinished sentences fade away and are lost in the moment of indecision. A big cloud blots out the sun as each one admits vaguely she forgot what she was going to say.

Mansfield writes about Jug and Con:

There was a moment when I first had "the idea" when I saw the two sisters as *amusing:* but the moment I looked deeper, . . . I bowed down to the beauty hidden in their lives. . . . All was meant, of course, to lead up to that last paragraph, when my two flowerless ones turned with that timid gesture, to the sun. "Perhaps *now* . . ." And after that, it seemed to me, they died as surely as Father was dead.[39]

In an interpretation of these episodes, the dialogue, the restrained movements of the sisters, the mannerisms of their speech, the incomplete thoughts, the fearful atmosphere of an unrealistic world must be studied carefully. The inconclusiveness of their phrases should characterize two bewildered women with their dominating and frightening prop always with them, even though they buried that gentleman in an abnormal fear of his wrath at such dastardly conduct. This ineffectiveness of dealing with reality—even in the insignificant daily chores of providing necessities like butter and jam—must permeate the atmosphere. Much can be suggested through vocal intensity, quality and inflections to contrast the sisters: which is the more emotional; which appears to be in command; which serves as a shadow for the other; which is closer to freedom; what vocal change is needed for an expression of their inner thoughts?

One's first confession must be an event that requires some outward control of inner tension, even if the sins are few. So if you are a small boy of possibly seven years, not schooled too well in the conduct within a confessional, with murder in your heart for your grandmother who gives pennies to your sister but not to you, you might be "half-stupefied with

[39] Katherine Mansfield, *Letters of Katherine Mansfield* (New York: Alfred A. Knopf, Inc., 1929), Letter: June 23, 1921, p. 389, v. 2.

terror" as you are led not too kindly to the church. How would you know in the "pitch darkness" of the confessional which wall to kneel before or that a small shelf was for folded hands in prayer instead of knees bent in confession?

from *First Confession*

All the trouble began when my grandfather died and my grandmother— my father's mother—came to live with us. Relations in the one house are a strain at the best of times, but, to make matters worse, my grandmother was a real old countrywoman and quite unsuited to the life in town. She had a fat, wrinkled old face, and, to Mother's great indignation, went round the house in bare feet—the boots had her crippled, she said. For dinner she had a jug of porter and a pot of potatoes with—sometimes—a bit of salt fish, and she poured out the potatoes on the table and ate them slowly, with great relish, using her fingers by way of a fork. . . .

When Mother was at work and my grandmother made the dinner I wouldn't touch it. Nora once tried to make me, but I hid under the table from her and took the bread-knife with me for protection. Nora let on to be very indignant . . . and came after me. I lashed out at her with the bread-knife, and after that she left me alone. I stayed there till Mother came in from work and made my dinner, but when Father came in later Nora said in a shocked voice: "Oh, Dadda, do you know what Jackie did at dinnertime?" Then, of course, it all came out; Father gave me a flaking; Mother interfered, and for days after that he didn't speak to me and Mother barely spoke to Nora. And all because of that old woman! God knows, I was heart-scalded.

Then, to crown my misfortunes, I had to make my first confession and communion. . . . I was scared to death of confession. The day the whole class went I let on to have a toothache, hoping my absence wouldn't be noticed; but at three o'clock, just as I was feeling safe, along comes a chap with a message from Mrs. Ryan that I was to go to confession myself on Saturday and be at the chapel for communion with the rest. To make it worse, Mother couldn't come with me and sent Nora instead.

Now, that girl had ways of tormenting me that Mother never knew of. She held my hand as we went down the hill, smiling sadly and saying how sorry she was for me, as if she were bringing me to the hospital for an operation.

"Oh, God help us!" she moaned. "Isn't it a terrible pity you weren't a good boy? Oh, Jackie, my heart bleeds for you! How will you ever think of all your sins? Don't forget you have to tell him about the time you kicked Gran on the shin."

"Lemme go!" I said, trying to drag myself free of her. "I don't want to go to confession at all."

"But sure, you'll have to go to confession, Jackie," she replied in the same regretful tone. "Sure, if you didn't, the parish priest would be up to the house, looking for you. 'Tisn't, God knows, that I'm not sorry for you. Do you remember the time you tried to kill me with the bread-knife under the table? And the language you used to me? I don't know what he'll do with you at all, Jackie. He might have to send you up to the bishop."

I remember thinking bitterly that she didn't know the half of what I had to tell—if I told it. I knew I couldn't tell it, and understood perfectly why the fellow in Mrs. Ryan's story made a bad confession. . . . I remember that steep hill down to the church, and the sunlit hillsides beyond the valley of the river, which I saw in the gaps between the houses like Adam's last glimpse of Paradise.

Then, when she had manoeuvred me down the long flight of steps to the chapel yard, Nora suddenly changed her tone. She became the raging malicious devil she really was.

"There you are!" she said with a yelp of triumph, hurling me through the church door. "And I hope he'll give you the penitential psalms, you dirty little caffler."

I knew then I was lost, given up to eternal justice. The door with the coloured-glass panels swung shut behind me, the sunlight went out and gave place to deep shadow, and the wind whistled outside so that the silence seemed to crackle like ice under my feet. Nora sat in front of me by the confession box. There were a couple of old women ahead of her, and then a miserable-looking poor devil came and wedged me in at the other side, so that I couldn't escape even if I had the courage. He joined his hands and rolled his eyes in the direction of the roof, muttering aspirations in an anguished tone, and I wondered had he a grandmother too. . . .

Nora's turn came, and I heard the sound of something slamming, and then her voice as if butter wouldn't melt in her mouth, and then another slam, and out she came. God, the hypocrisy of women! Her eyes were lowered, her head was bowed, and her hands were joined very low on her stomach, and she walked up the aisle to the side altar looking like a saint. You never saw such an exhibition of devotion; and I remembered the devilish malice with which she had tormented me all the way from our door, and wondered were all religious people like that, really. It was my turn now. With the fear of damnation in my soul I went in, and the confessional door closed of itself behind me.

It was pitch-dark and I couldn't see priest or anything else. Then I really began to be frightened. In the darkness it was a matter between God and me, and He had all the odds. He knew what my intentions were before I even started; I had no chance. All I had ever been told about confession got mixed up in my mind, and I knelt to one wall and said: "Bless me, father, for I have sinned; this is my first confession." I waited for a few minutes, but nothing happened, so I tried it on the other wall. Nothing happened there either. He had me spotted all right.

It must have been then that I noticed the shelf at about one height with my head. It was really a place for grown-up people to rest their elbows, but in my distracted state I thought it was probably the place you were supposed to kneel. Of course, it was on the high side and not very deep, but I was always good at climbing and managed to get up all right. Staying up was the trouble. There was room only for my knees, and nothing you could get a grip on but a sort of wooden moulding a bit above it. I held on to the moulding and repeated the words a little louder, and this time something happened all right. A slide was slammed back; a little light entered the box, and a man's voice said: "Who's there?"

" 'Tis me, father," I said for fear he mightn't see me and go away again. I couldn't see him at all. The place the voice came from was under the moulding, about level with my knees, so I took a good grip of the moulding and swung myself down till I saw the astonished face of a young priest looking up at me. He had to put his head on one side to see me, and I had to put mine on one side to see him, so we were more or less talking to one another upside-down. It struck me as a queer way of hearing confessions, but I didn't feel it my place to criticize.

"Bless me, father, for I have sinned; this is my first confession," I rattled off all in one breath, and swung myself down the least shade more to make it easier for him.

"What are you doing up there?" he shouted in an angry voice, and the strain the politeness was putting on my hold of the moulding, and the shock of being addressed in such an uncivil tone, were too much for me. I lost my grip, tumbled, and hit the door an unmerciful wallop before I found myself flat on my back in the middle of the aisle. The people who had been waiting stood up with their mouths open. The priest opened the door of the middle box and came out, pushing his biretta back from his forehead; he looked something terrible. Then Nora came scampering down the aisle.

"Oh, you dirty little caffler!" she said. "I might have known you'd do it. I might have known you'd disgrace me. I can't leave you out of my sight for one minute."

Before I could even get to my feet to defend myself she bent down and gave me a clip across the ear. This reminded me that I was so stunned I had even forgotten to cry, so that people might think I wasn't hurt at all, when in fact I was probably maimed for life. I gave a roar out of me.

"What's all this about?" the priest hissed, getting angrier than ever and pushing Nora off me. "How dare you hit the child like that, you little vixen?"

"But I can't do my penance with him, father," Nora cried, cocking an outraged eye up at him.

"Well, go and do it, or I'll give you some more to do," he said, giving me a hand up. "Was it coming to confession you were, my poor man?" he asked me.

" 'Twas, father," said I with a sob.

"Oh," he said respectfully, "a big hefty fellow like you must have terrible sins. Is this your first?"

" 'Tis, father," said I.

"Worse and worse," he said gloomily. "The crimes of a life-time. I don't know will I get rid of you at all to-day. You'd better wait now till I'm finished with these old ones. You can see by the looks of them they haven't much to tell."

"I will, father," I said with something approaching joy.

The relief of it was really enormous. Nora stuck out her tongue at me from behind his back, but I couldn't even be bothered retorting. I knew from the very moment that man opened his mouth that he was intelligent above the ordinary. When I had time to think, I saw how right I was. It only stood to reason that a fellow confessing after seven years would have more to tell than people that went every week. The crimes of a lifetime, exactly as he said. It was only what he expected, and the rest was the cackle of old women and girls with their talk of hell, the bishop, and the penitential psalms. That was all they knew. I started to make my examination of conscience, and barring the one bad business of my grandmother it didn't seem so bad.

The next time, the priest steered me into the confession box himself and left the shutter back the way I could see him get in and sit down at the further side of the grille from me.

"Well, now," he said, "what do they call you?"

"Jackie, father," said I.

"And what's a-trouble to you, Jackie?"

"Father," I said, feeling I might as well get it over while I had him in a good humour, "I had it all arranged to kill my grandmother."

He seemed a bit shaken by that, all right, because he said nothing for quite a while.

"My goodness," he said at last, "that'd be a shocking thing to do. What put that into your head?"

"Father," I said, feeling very sorry for myself, "she's an awful woman."

"Is she?" he asked. "What way is she awful?"

"She takes porter, father," I said, knowing well from the way Mother talked of it that this was a mortal sin, and hoping it would make the priest take a more favourable view of my case.

"Oh, my!" he said, and I could see he was impressed.

"And snuff, father," said I.

"That's a bad case, sure enough, Jackie," he said.

"And she goes round in her bare feet, father," I went on in a rush of self-pity, "and she knows I don't like her, and she gives pennies to Nora and none to me, and my da sides with her and flakes me, and one night I was so heart-scalded I made up my mind I'd have to kill her."

"And what would you do with the body?" he asked with great interest.

"I was thinking I could chop that up and carry it away in a barrow I have," I said.

"Begor, Jackie," he said, "do you know you're a terrible child?"

"I know, father," I said, for I was just thinking the same thing myself. "I tried to kill Nora too with a bread-knife under the table, only I missed her."

"Is that the little girl that was beating you just now?" he asked.

" 'Tis, father."

"Someone will go for her with a bread-knife one day, and he won't miss her," he said rather cryptically. "You must have great courage. Between ourselves, there's a lot of people I'd like to do the same to but I'd never have the nerve. Hanging is an awful death."

"Is it, father?" I asked with the deepest interest—I was always very keen on hanging. "Did you ever see a fellow hanged?"

"Dozens of them," he said solemnly. "And they all died roaring."

"Jay!" I said.

"Oh, a horrible death!" he said with great satisfaction. "Lots of the fellows I saw killed their grandmothers too, but they all said 'twas never worth it."

He had me there for a full ten minutes talking, and then walked out the chapel yard with me. I was genuinely sorry to part with him, because he was the most entertaining character I'd ever met in the religious line. Outside, after the shadow of the church, the sunlight was like the roaring of waves on a beach; it dazzled me; and when the frozen silence melted and I heard the screech of the trams on the road my heart soared. I knew now I wouldn't die in the night and come back, leaving marks on my mother's furniture. It would be a great worry to her, and the poor soul had enough.

Nora was sitting on the railing, waiting for me, and she put on a very sour puss when she saw the priest with me. She was mad jealous because a priest had never come out of the church with her.

"Well," she asked coldly, after he left me, "what did he give you?"

"Three Hail Marys," I said.

"Three Hail Marys," she repeated incredulously. "You mustn't have told him anything."

"I told him everything," I said confidently.

"About Gran and all?"

"About Gran and all."

(All she wanted was to be able to go home and say I'd made a bad confession.)

"Did you tell him you went for me with the bread-knife?" she asked with a frown.

"I did to be sure."

"And he only gave you three Hail Marys?"

"That's all."

She slowly got down from the railing with a baffled air. Clearly this was beyond her. As we mounted the steps back to the main road she looked at me suspiciously.

"What are you sucking?" she asked.

"Bullseyes."

"Was it the priest gave them to you?"

" 'Twas."

"Lord God," she wailed bitterly, "some people have all the luck! 'Tis no advantage to anybody trying to be good. I might just as well be a sinner like you."[40]

FRANK O'CONNOR

You must have enjoyed this Irish story. If your laughter is not hearty, you may have missed the "inner working," not only of Jackie but of the child psychologist in the priest's robe. What is unsaid makes the story— so interpret as completely as you can. Let your audience know what is implied by means of facial expressions, vocal inflections and pauses. Each of these male characters is skillfully epitomized in the dialogue; Nora, on the other hand, is obvious in her "vixen" ways. What an excellent story in which to show your total versatility as a priest talking "man to man" to

Jackie! If you have difficulty in getting a bit of the Irish lilt into your speech rhythm, listen again to McKenna in her recordings of Irish poems.

DRAMA

GENERAL ASSESSMENT

Literary analysis of drama for interpretative purposes is not too different from that of the narrative. You will have to read the complete play as you did the short story and the novel; you will study the plot, theme, progression of scenes, movement, time, place, design, conflict—and *characters*. The point of view is not an essential part of your analysis, since most plays are written objectively. If the playwright has written a drama impregnated with his moral philosophy, however, you will be interested in how he approaches his theme. Other factors, as action, atmosphere and environment, are taken care of by stage directions and setting. The structure of the play is definitely outlined, so you may check very easily on the progression of events and whether the movement proceeds with mounting tension and relates to the theme.

The general tone may be expressed mainly by the kind of play the author has written. As an interpreter, you must know the heavy, serious touch of the *tragedy* and its necessary character delineation and development; the gay, humorous touch of *light comedy* that portrays characters—seemingly normal but caught in typical and often difficult situations of everyday living and usually quick and alert in their speech responses and actions; the exaggeration of *farce*, broad in its concept of rather improbable characters caught in almost impossible situations, events, activity, that causes hilarity because of unusual combinations of people and situations; the light conversation of *high comedy* with its sophisticated and often intellectual attitudes, gay innuendoes and repartee; and the glow and charm of the *romantic comedy* with its intrigue and love episodes.

CHARACTERIZATION IN PLAYS

The two literary elements usually found in narratives—exposition and description—will not be found in the drama except as stage directions. Your presentation of scenes will be centered entirely on the revealing of characters through their speech patterns and bodily attitudes. For this reason, it is better not to select scenes dominated by action; for instance, comedy scenes where people come and go continually. Those moments that show contrasts in characterization, conflict, development or move the theme forward to its climax are important for interpretative interest.

Since you will have no interrelating expository passages from the playwright, watch your cue-pick-up so that reaction, movement and crescendo are shown, not too obviously but with discerning vocal and bodily expression. Again you are warned not to talk at the same key level for all the characters, especially when you cue into a response. The speech pattern of the whole scene must be studied for its high and low points and its rhythmical flow of speech. The body, too, as with distinguished actors on the stage, will show distinctive muscular tensions for each character so that the mood and movement of a scene will be intensified.

In group projects, important breaks or pauses between speeches must be sustained by bodily attitude and facial expression. A character must never seem to move in and out of a scene. Watch distinguished actors who know the value of holding the body meaningfully still to reveal their part in the total emotional movement.

No advice about the cutting of literature is being offered here because this operation is a hazardous one and may destroy the author's style. Consult your instructor on this matter because each piece of literature has its own life and form and should not be slashed by an amateur.

The following dramatic scenes are varied in setting, emotional tone, conflict, characters, rhythmical speech, climax and language. An attempt has been made to indicate certain high points in each literary selection.

DRAMATIC SCENES FOR STUDY

This episode from *Mary, Mary* by Jean Kerr is very much alive with the conversation of two attractive persons, Mary and Dirk. Mary, unhappily divorced from Bob McKellaway, publisher, has come to Bob's apartment at the request of their lawyer to settle some items of deduction for Bob's income tax report. Here Mary meets a young author and actor, Dirk Winston, whose manuscript Bob is checking for publication. Mary and Dirk have just returned from dinner and are waiting for Bob and his bride-to-be, Tiffany, who are expected shortly.

After some casual talk about writers and actors, a "small silence" occurs; then Dirk begins a more personal conversation.

from *Mary, Mary*

ACT II

DIRK: Your eyes are so blue—and so liquid. I feel they might spill right down your cheeks.

MARY *(quick with the answer):* That's because I need glasses and won't wear them.

DIRK *(curious and interested):* Why do you do that?

MARY: Do what?

DIRK: You jump when you get a compliment.

MARY (*too quickly*): No I don't.

DIRK: You're actually embarrassed.

MARY (*a shade too defensively*): Why should I be embarrassed?

DIRK: I don't know. But you are. You come bustling in to change the subject, like a nervous hostess who's discovered that two of the guests are quarreling. (*Imitating the hostess*) "Now, come along, Harry—there's somebody very nice I want you to meet."

MARY: All right. Pay me pretty compliments and I won't change the subject.

DIRK: And you won't make jokes?

Mary is stunned by the echo of Bob's previous remark.

MARY: What? What?

DIRK: Shouldn't I have said that?

MARY: No, that's all right. It's been said before. Just recently, in fact. I suppose I should take a course and find out what a girl should answer when a gentleman says, "Tell me, pretty maiden, are there any more at home like you?" Though it would hardly pay. It doesn't come up that often.

DIRK: I thought little girls learned things like that when they were three years old.

MARY: Oh, but I'm a very retarded case. It's only just this year I learned how to put my hair up in rollers.

DIRK: What did you do before that?

MARY: I wore it pinned back in a bun. And when it had to be cut, I cut it, or I went somewhere and *they* cut it. Lately I've been going to Elizabeth Arden, and I want you to know that it's a whole new way of life.

DIRK: So I'm told.

MARY: At Arden's they don't just cut your hair—never. They *shape* it. And they honestly think a good shaping is as important as a cure for cancer. The hairdresser really blanched when he saw my bun. I could hear him thinking, "Thank God she came to me—another month and it might have been too late."

DIRK: Well, I think your hair looks lovely. Now say thank you.

MARY: Thank you.

DIRK: See how easy it is?

MARY (*self-conscious*): I—Oh—Tell me about your book.

DIRK: What can I tell you? It weighs three quarters of a pound. It takes eighty-four cents in stamps to mail it.

MARY: Don't talk like that. You musn't lose faith in it just because Bob didn't like it. Bob's a good publisher but he makes mistakes. Did you have any help with this book?

DIRK: You mean, did I *tell* it to somebody? No.

MARY: I'm glad. All these "as told to" books have such a spooky flavor about them. First the personality is all drained off. Then, to compensate, something else is pumped in—sex or religion or Scott Fitzgerald. I fully expect that any day now we're going to have The Confessions of Saint Augustine —as told to Gerold Frank.

DIRK: Mary—

MARY: What?

DIRK: You just said Bob makes mistakes. But how did he ever let you slip through his fingers?

MARY: Just lucky, I guess.

DIRK: I think I am beginning to see the clue to this little puzzle.

MARY: What puzzle?

DIRK: You.

MARY: I'd love to think I was a puzzle. A woman of mystery. Smiling and enigmatic on the surface—but underneath, a tigress. *(Change of mood, straightforward)* I hate to admit it, but what you see is all there is. Underneath this plain, girlish exterior, there's a very plain girl.

DIRK: Ah, but what happened to make you *decide* it was such a plain exterior? It was the divorce, wasn't it? It was Bob.

MARY: Bob? I decided *that* when I was thirteen years old. We can't blame Bob for everything.

DIRK: At thirteen, all by yourself, you decided that?

MARY: Oh, there were people around, but I can't say they gave me any argument. Do you ever look at little girls?

DIRK: How little?

MARY *(rather intensely, as she remembers and thinks about it)*: You take two little girls. One of them is pink and round, with curly hair and yards of eyelashes. The other one is pale and bony, with thin, wispy hair and two little ears poking through—like the handles on a sugar bowl. Okay, which one of these little girls is going to have to wear braces on her teeth?

DIRK: The wispy one.

MARY *(as though awarding him a prize)*: You've got it. That was me. Braces on my teeth, Band-Aids on my knees, freckles on my nose. All elbows and shoulder blades. For two years running I got picked to play the consumptive orphan in *Michael O'Halloran.*

DIRK: That was talent.

MARY: That was typecasting.

DIRK: All adolescents go through something. I had the worst case of acne in the history of the world. For three years I was a technicolor marvel. You wouldn't remember when Fleischmann's Yeast was the big thing. I used to eat Fleischmann's Yeast and drink water until I couldn't move without gurgling. I imagine I was actually fermenting.

MARY: I never ate yeast, but once I sent away secretly for Stillman's freckle cream. I guess I used too much, because I just peeled and peeled. I had to pretend it was a sunburn.

DIRK: I used to pretend I hated everybody. Especially girls, because I was too self-conscious to talk to them.

MARY: You made a spectacular recovery.

DIRK: I may even have overdone it. But why didn't you—

MARY: Make a recovery? Well, it was sort of different with me. When I was a kid, I mean really a kid, I never worried about the way I looked, because I thought—I *knew*—I'd grow up to be beautiful just like my sister Clara.

DIRK: Was she so beautiful?

MARY: Clara? She had bright red hair and brown eyes and she always had a faintly startled look, as if she'd just come out of a dark theatre into the sunlight. People who met her would be so busy staring they'd forget to finish their sentences.

DIRK: I can see that would have been something of a cross for you.

MARY: No, I thought it was insurance. Clara was six years older than I was, and I thought "I'll grow up to look just like that." One day I was measuring myself—I was about fourteen—and I realized I hadn't grown at all, not an inch, in a whole year. And then it came to me. I wasn't going to grow any more. I was *up*. And I didn't look anything at all like Clara.

DIRK: And you weren't satisfied to look like Mary?

MARY: I certainly was not. I went rushing to my father, and I asked him when I was going to look like Clara. Poor man. He didn't know what to say.

DIRK: What did he say?

MARY: He said "Darling, we wouldn't want two Claras. You're the bright one." That did it. I could have faced being plain, but to be plain *and* bright! In the high school I went to, that was a beatable combination.

DIRK: So you decided to get on the debating team.

MARY: How did you know?

DIRK: Girls who feel they are not going to be invited to dances always get on the debating team.

MARY: And I worked on the school newspaper. And I imagined all the time I was really Catherine Earnshaw.

DIRK: Catherine who?

MARY: The girl in *Wuthering Heights*. Cathy.

DIRK: Oh, Merle Oberon.

MARY: That's right. I used to dream that somewhere there was a strange, dark man whose heart was quietly breaking for me. On rainy nights I'd open the window and imagine I could hear him calling—"Oh, my wild, sweet Cathy!" The colds I got! And of course the only dark man I ever saw was a middle-aged dentist who used to adjust the braces on my teeth.

DIRK: And you're still cross about it.

MARY: Is that how I sound? I don't feel that way. I feel wistful. I think of that sappy little girl and I wonder what happened to her.

DIRK: Nothing happened. She hasn't changed at all.

MARY: You mean I haven't changed at all? That's a hell of a thing to say.

DIRK: Oh, I'm certain you've changed in appearance. That's clear enough. But you yourself haven't changed. Somewhere inside you, you're *still* wearing braces on your teeth.

MARY: Oh, come, come. I came to the big city. I learned to tip waiters. I read *The New Yorker*. I got married.

DIRK: And nothing took. Do you know what's strange?

MARY: What?

DIRK: Here you are—so lovely. And nobody falls in love with you.

MARY: Oh, is that so? And where did you get that idea?

DIRK: From you.

MARY: You're crazy. I never said—listen, lots of people—well, Bob was certainly in love with me—

DIRK: You really thought so?

MARY: Of course! Why else would he marry me? There was no dowry, or anything.

DIRK: I don't know. Why did he?

MARY *(seriously unsettled beneath her insistent assurance):* Because he felt that —because we both—listen, what is this? I haven't answered so many idiotic questions since I tried to open a charge account at Saks! There must be a genteel, ladylike way of telling you that it's none of your damn business!

DIRK: I knew I'd get a rise out of you when I said that about Bob.

MARY: Then why did you say it?

DIRK: Of course Bob was in love with you. But you don't believe it. You never believed it.

MARY: What did he tell you?

DIRK: Nothing. You're the evidence. Women who believe they're attractive have a certain air about them. You don't. Your reflexes are off.

MARY *(now furious):* I will match my reflexes with your manners any old day! And now, unless you have some other little speech all rehearsed, I suggest you go upstairs or downstairs or wherever it is you call home![41]

JEAN KERR

The dialogue between Mary and Dirk is buoyant in its quick "give and take," thus characterizing each person. Dirk serves as the cue man— very much like a skillful psychologist—to reveal Mary's temperament as it has been conditioned by her early background and her present difficulties. Build for high spots and watch quick changes in emotional reactions —using varying vocal patterns to keep the scene moving.

Nowhere in literature will you find a more dynamic picture of Browning than in *The Barretts of Wimpole Street*. The following scene dramatizes the first meeting of Browning and Elizabeth Barrett, an invalid confined to her room for many months in the Barrett home on Wimpole Street.

from *The Barretts of Wimpole Street*

ACT II

HENRIETTA: Mr. Robert Browning.

> ROBERT BROWNING *enters. He is a dark, handsome man in the middle thirties, faultlessly, perhaps even a trifle foppishly dressed. Over his shoulder he wears a cape fastened with a chain at the throat. He carries his high hat, lemon-coloured gloves, and clouded cane.* BROWNING'S *manner is sincere and ardent; his speech rapid, voluble, and emphasized by free gestures.* HENRIETTA *goes out.*

[41] From MARY, MARY by Jean Kerr. Copyright © 1960, 1961, 1963 by Jean Kerr. Reprinted by permission of Doubleday & Company, Inc. Act 2, pp. 73-85.

BROWNING (*pausing for a moment a few steps beyond the threshold*): Miss Barrett?

ELIZABETH (*stretching out her hand*): How-do-you-do, Mr. Browning?

BROWNING (*quickly lays aside his hat, and gloves, and crossing to the sofa, takes her hand in both of his*): Dear Miss Barrett—at last! (*Raises her hand to his lips*) At last!

ELIZABETH (*still all nerves, and rather overcome by the ardour and unconventionality of his manner*): I—I've had to put off the pleasure of meeting you much longer than I wished. . . .

BROWNING (*still holding her hand*): Would you ever have received me if I hadn't been so tiresomely insistent?

ELIZABETH: As you know from my letters, I've not been at all well during the winter, and I—(*Realizing that her hand is still in his, she gently withdraws it*) But won't you take off your cape?

BROWNING: Thank you.

ELIZABETH: I—I hope you don't find the room very close, Mr. Browning?

BROWNING: No, no. . . .

ELIZABETH: My doctor obliges me to live in what I am afraid must be to you a—a hot-house temperature. . . .

BROWNING (*who has thrown a quick glance round the room*): Wonderful! You may think, Miss Barrett, that this is the first time I've been here. You're quite wrong, you know!

ELIZABETH: But—

BROWNING: Quite wrong. I have seen this room more times than I can remember. It's as familiar to me as my own little study at home! Before I came in, I knew just how your books were arranged, just how that tendril of ivy slanted over the window panes—and those busts of Homer and Chaucer are quite old friends, and have looked down on me often before!

ELIZABETH (*smilingly protesting*): No, really—!

BROWNING: But I could never make out who the other fellows were on the top of the wardrobe, and—

ELIZABETH (*laughing, and now quite at her ease*): Oh, come, Mr. Browning! I know that dear Mr. Kenyon is never tired of talking about his friends; but I can't believe that he described my poor little room to you in detail!

BROWNING (*seating himself beside her*): I dragged all the details I possibly could out of him—and my imagination supplied the rest. Directly after I had read your brave and lovely verses I was greedy for anything and everything I could get about you.

ELIZABETH (*smilingly*): You frighten me, Mr. Browning!

BROWNING: Why?

ELIZABETH: Well, you know how Mr. Kenyon's enthusiasms run away with his tongue? He and I are the dearest of friends. What he told you about poor me I quite blush to imagine!

BROWNING: You mean, Miss Barrett, about you—you *yourself*?

ELIZABETH: I feel it would be hopeless for me to try to live up to his description.

BROWNING: He never told me anything about you—personally—which had the slightest interest for me.

ELIZABETH (*puzzled*): Oh?

BROWNING: Everything he could give me about your surroundings and the circumstances of your life I snatched at with avidity. But all he said about *you* was quite beside the point, because I knew it already—and better than Mr. Kenyon, old friend of yours though he is!

ELIZABETH: But—Oh, Mr. Browning, do my poor writings give me so hopelessly away?

BROWNING: Hopelessly—utterly—entirely—to *me!* . . . I can't speak for the rest of the world.

ELIZABETH (*smilingly*): You frighten me again!

BROWNING: No?

ELIZABETH: But you do! For I'm afraid it would be quite useless my ever trying to play-act with you!

BROWNING: Quite useless!

ELIZABETH: I shall always have to be—just myself?

BROWNING: Always.

ELIZABETH: Oh . . . (*quickly*) And you too, Mr. Browning?

BROWNING: Always—just myself! (*He stretches out his hand; she takes it with a smile. Then, with a sudden laugh*) But really, you know, Miss Barrett, I sha'n't be able to take much credit for that! Being myself comes to me as easily as breathing. It's play-acting I can't manage—and the hot water I've got into in consequence . . . If life's to run smoothly we should all be mummers. Well, I can't mum!

ELIZABETH: Yes, I can believe that now I know you. But isn't it extraordinary? When you are *writing* you never do anything else but—play-act.

BROWNING: I know—

ELIZABETH: You have never been yourself in any one of your poems. It's always somebody else speaking through you.

BROWNING: Yes. And shall I tell you why? I am a very modest man. (*Quickly, after a slight pause*) I am really!

ELIZABETH (*with suppressed amusement*): I didn't question it, Mr. Browning.

BROWNING: So modest, I fully realize that if I wrote about myself—my hopes and fears, hates and loves, and the rest of it—my poems would be intolerably dull.

ELIZABETH (*laughing, vivaciously*): Well—since we are pledged to nothing but the truth, I won't contradict you—until I know you better!

BROWNING (*with a laugh*): Bravo!

ELIZABETH (*ardently*): Oh, but these poems, with their glad and great-hearted acceptance of life—you can't imagine what they mean to me! Here am I shut in by four walls, the view of Wimpole Street my only glimpse of the world. And they troop into the room and round my sofa, these wonderful people of yours out of every age and country, and all so tingling with life! life! life! No, you'll never begin to realize how much I owe you!

BROWNING (*with emotion*): You—you really mean that?

ELIZABETH: Why, why Mr. Browning—

BROWNING: But of course you do, or you wouldn't say it! And you'll believe me when I tell you that what you have said makes up to me a thousand times over for all the cold-shouldering I've had from the public?

ELIZABETH *(fiercely):* Oh, it infuriates me! Why can we never know an eagle for an eagle until it has spread its wings and flown away from us for good? Sometimes—I detest the British public!

BROWNING *(lightly):* Oh, no, no! Dear old British public! At least it gives us generously the jolly pastime of abusing it! And mind you, Miss Barrett, I've an uneasy feeling that my style is largely to blame for my unpopularity.

ELIZABETH *(a little too eagerly):* Oh, surely not!

BROWNING: Didn't we agree never to play-act with each other?

ELIZABETH *(with a laugh): Touché!* Well, perhaps, there *are* passages in your work a little invol—I mean a little too—too profound for the general reader.

BROWNING: Oh, no! It's not what I say, but how I say it.

ELIZABETH: Oh, but—

BROWNING: And yet to me it's all simple and easy as the rule of three! And to you?

ELIZABETH: Well . . . not *quite* always. Sometimes there *are* passages. . . . *(She picks up a book.)* I have marked one or two in your "Sordello" which rather puzzle me. Here, for instance . . . *(She opens the book and hands it to him.)*

BROWNING *(taking the book):* Oh, "Sordello!" Somebody once called it "a horror of great darkness!" I've done my best to forget it. However—*(He reads the passage to himself, smiling. The smile fades; he passes his hand over his brow and reads it again. She watches him, covertly smiling. He mutters.)* Extraordinary. . . . But—but a passage torn from its context. . . .

He rises and goes to the window, as though to get more light on the subject, and reads the passage a third time. ELIZABETH *has some difficulty in suppressing her amusement. He turns to her with an expression of humorous chagrin.*

ELIZABETH: Well?

BROWNING: Well, Miss Barrett—when that passage was written only God and Robert Browning understood it. Now only God understands it.[42]

RUDOLF BESIER

In the foregoing scene, the speech rhythm characterizes each individual in an unusually brilliant manner: Browning—a dashing, brisk, vital extrovert; Elizabeth—hesitant, nervous at the situation, reticent but alert, a woman of culture who cannot hide her surprise at the impetuous, vigorous Robert Browning.[43] Here are innuendoes which your vocal inflections must master—as in the laugh hidden in the last lines. Timing, as controlled through pauses, is important throughout the scene; the vocal attack and quality of the two voices must be differentiated.

[42] Copyright 1930, 1958 by Rudolf Besier. From THE BARRETTS OF WIMPOLE STREET by Rudolf Besier, by permission of Little, Brown and Co. Act 2, pp. 59-66.

[43] *Sonnets from the Portuguese / The Barretts of Wimpole Street,* recorded by Katherine Cornell and Anthony Quayle. Caedmon TC 1071.

Woolf, in her fascinating portrayal of Flush (page 128), describes the exciting reactions of this first meeting of the two "great lovers" in literature through the jealous eyes of the cocker spaniel. Flush observed with consternation the "dreadful boldness which marked every movement of the 'Hooded Man'." He heard the stranger finally run down the stairs and "smartly" bang the door behind him. As for Miss Barrett, she appeared to glow while Flush lay ignored; in fact, she seemed not to remember him. The climax of the day, however, arrived at dinner, for "that night she ate her chicken to the bone," with nary a scrap thrown to Flush.

Although you may know the William Saroyan play, *Hello Out There*, probably you have never attempted to formulate your impression of the theme. You may remember the presence of two young people groping for the happiness of living and also the tragedy of a young man's death because of a husband who is trying to save his own name. If you intend to interpret the reprinted scene, however, you will have to study the connotative power centered in the three words of the title, repeated under different circumstances and gaining in momentum and poignancy to the end. Certainly they are not the shouts of an extrovert who wants to be heard all the time. That interpretation would be monotonous and not characteristic of the superb artistry of Saroyan. As you read this first half of the short drama, think of the intent of the title and observe how the words are woven into the narrative. The reactions in an interpretative group will bring out many meanings to help the movement of the play.

from *Hello Out There*

> *There is a fellow in a small-town prison cell, tapping slowly on the floor with a spoon. After tapping half a minute, as if he were trying to telegraph words, he gets up and begins walking around the cell. At last he stops, stands at the center of the cell, and doesn't move for a long time. He feels his head, as if it were wounded. Then he looks around. Then he calls out dramatically, kidding the world.*

YOUNG MAN: Hello—out there! *(Pause)* Hello—out there! Hello—out there! *(Long pause)* Nobody out there. *(Still more dramatically, but more comically, too)* Hello—out there! Hello—out there!

A GIRL'S VOICE *is heard, very sweet and soft.*

THE VOICE: Hello.
YOUNG MAN: Hello—out there.
THE VOICE: Hello.
YOUNG MAN: Is that you, Katey?
THE VOICE: No—this here is Emily.
YOUNG MAN: Who? *(Swiftly)* Hello out there.

THE VOICE: Emily.

YOUNG MAN: Emily who? I don't know anybody named Emily. Are you that girl I met at Sam's in Salinas about three years ago?

THE VOICE: No—I'm the girl who cooks here. I'm the cook. I've never been in Salinas. I don't even know where it is.

YOUNG MAN: Hello out there. You say you cook here?

THE VOICE: Yes.

YOUNG MAN: Well, why don't you study up and learn to cook? How come I don't get no jello or anything good?

THE VOICE: I just cook what they tell me to. *(Pause)* You lonesome?

YOUNG MAN: Lonesome as a coyote. Hear me hollering? Hello out there!

THE VOICE: Who you hollering to?

YOUNG MAN: Well—nobody, I guess. I been trying to think of somebody to write a letter to, but I can't think of anybody.

THE VOICE: What about Katey?

YOUNG MAN: I don't know anybody named Katey.

THE VOICE: Then why did you say Is that you, Katey?

YOUNG MAN: Katey's a good name. I always did like a name like Katey. I never *knew* anybody named Katey, though.

THE VOICE: *I* did.

YOUNG MAN: Yeah? What was she like? Tall girl, or little one?

THE VOICE: Kind of medium.

YOUNG MAN: Hello out there. What sort of a looking girl are *you?*

THE VOICE: Oh, I don't know.

YOUNG MAN: Didn't anybody ever tell you? Didn't anybody ever talk to you that way?

THE VOICE: What way?

YOUNG MAN: You know. Didn't they?

THE VOICE: No, they didn't.

YOUNG MAN: Ah, the fools—they should have. I can tell from your voice you're O.K.

THE VOICE: Maybe I am and maybe I ain't.

YOUNG MAN: I never missed yet.

THE VOICE: Yeah, I know. That's why you're in jail.

YOUNG MAN: The whole thing was a mistake.

THE VOICE: They claim it was rape.

YOUNG MAN: No—it wasn't.

THE VOICE: That's what they claim it was.

YOUNG MAN: They're a lot of fools.

THE VOICE: Well, you sure are in trouble. Are you scared?

YOUNG MAN: Scared to death. *(Suddenly)* Hello out there!

THE VOICE: What do you keep saying that for all the time?

YOUNG MAN: I'm lonesome. I'm as lonesome as a coyote. *(A long one)* Hello—out there!

THE GIRL *appears, over to one side. She is a plain girl in plain clothes.*

THE GIRL: I'm kind of lonesome, too.

YOUNG MAN *(turning and looking at her):* Hey— No fooling? Are you?

THE GIRL: Yeah— I'm almost as lonesome as a coyote myself.

YOUNG MAN: Who *you* lonesome for?

THE GIRL: I don't know.

YOUNG MAN: It's the same with me. The minute they put you in a place like this you remember all the girls you ever knew, and all the girls you didn't get to know, and it sure gets lonesome.

THE GIRL: I bet it does.

YOUNG MAN: Ah, it's awful. *(Pause)* You're a pretty kid, you know that?

THE GIRL: You're just talking.

YOUNG MAN: No, I'm not just talking—you *are* pretty. Any fool could see that. You're just about the prettiest kid in the whole world.

THE GIRL: I'm not—and you know it.

YOUNG MAN: No—you are. I never saw anyone prettier in all my born days, in all my travels. I knew Texas would bring me luck.

THE GIRL: Luck? You're in jail, aren't you? You've got a whole gang of people all worked up, haven't you?

YOUNG MAN: Ah, that's nothing. I'll get out of this.

THE GIRL: Maybe.

YOUNG MAN: No, I'll be all right—*now.*

THE GIRL: What do you mean—now?

YOUNG MAN: I mean after seeing you. I got something now. You know for a while there I didn't care one way or another. Tired. *(Pause)* Tired of trying for the best all the time and never getting it. *(Suddenly)* Hello out there!

THE GIRL: Who you calling now?

YOUNG MAN: You.

THE GIRL: Why, I'm right here.

YOUNG MAN: I know. *(Calling)* Hello out there!

THE GIRL: Hello.

YOUNG MAN: Ah, you're sweet. *(Pause)* I'm going to marry *you.* I'm going away with *you.* I'm going to take you to San Francisco or some place like that. I *am,* now. I'm going to win myself some real money, too. I'm going to study 'em real careful and pick myself some winners, and we're going to have a lot of money.

THE GIRL: Yeah?

YOUNG MAN: Yeah. Tell me your name and all that stuff.

THE GIRL: Emily.

YOUNG MAN: I know that. What's the rest of it? Where were you born? Come on, tell me the whole thing.

THE GIRL: Emily Smith.

YOUNG MAN: Honest to God?

THE GIRL: Honest. That's my name—Emily Smith.

YOUNG MAN: Ah, you're the sweetest girl in the whole world.

THE GIRL: Why?

YOUNG MAN: I don't know why, but you are, that's all. Where were you born?

THE GIRL: Matador, Texas.

YOUNG MAN: Where's that?

THE GIRL: Right here.

YOUNG MAN: Is this Matador, Texas?

THE GIRL: Yeah, it's Matador. They brought you here from Wheeling.

YOUNG MAN: Is that where I was—Wheeling?

THE GIRL: Didn't you even know what town you were in?

YOUNG MAN: All towns are alike. You don't go up and ask somebody what town you're in. It doesn't make any difference. How far away is Wheeling?

THE GIRL: Sixteen or seventeen miles. Didn't you know they moved you?

YOUNG MAN: How could I know, when I was out—cold? Somebody hit me over the head with a lead pipe or something. What'd they hit me for?

THE GIRL: Rape—that's what they *said*.

YOUNG MAN: Ah, that's a lie. *(Amazed, almost to himself)* She wanted me to give her money.

THE GIRL: Money?

YOUNG MAN: Yeah, if I'd have known she was a woman like that—well, by God, I'd have gone on down the street and stretched out in a park somewhere and gone to sleep.

THE GIRL: Is that what she wanted—money?

YOUNG MAN: Yeah. A fellow like me hopping freights all over the country, trying to break his bad luck, going from one poor little town to another, trying to get in on something good somewhere, and she asks for money. I thought she was lonesome. She *said* she was.

THE GIRL: Maybe she was.

YOUNG MAN: She was *something*.

THE GIRL: I guess I'd never see you, if it didn't happen, though.

YOUNG MAN: Oh, I don't know—maybe I'd just mosey along this way and see you in this town somewhere. I'd recognize you, too.

THE GIRL: Recognize me?

YOUNG MAN: Sure, I'd recognize you the minute I laid eyes on you.

THE GIRL: Well, who would I be?

YOUNG MAN: Mine, that's who.

THE GIRL: Honest?

YOUNG MAN: Honest to God.

THE GIRL: You just say that because you're in jail.

YOUNG MAN: No, I mean it. You just pack up and wait for me. We'll high-roll the hell out of here to Frisco.

THE GIRL: You're just lonesome.

YOUNG MAN: I been lonesome all my life—there's no cure for that—but you and me—we can have a lot of fun hanging around together. You'll bring me luck, I know it.

THE GIRL: What are you looking for luck for all the time?

YOUNG MAN: I'm a gambler. I don't work. I've *got* to have luck, or I'm a bum. I haven't had any decent luck in years. Two whole years now—one place to another. Bad luck all the time. That's why I got in trouble back there in Wheeling, too. That was no accident. That was my bad luck following me around. So here I am, with my head half busted. I guess it was her old man that did it.

THE GIRL: You mean her father?

YOUNG MAN: No, her husband. If I had an old lady like that, I'd throw her out.

THE GIRL: Do you think you'll have better luck, if I go with you?

YOUNG MAN: It's a cinch. I'm a good handicapper. All I need is somebody like you with me. It's no good always walking around in the streets for anything that might be there at the time. You got to have somebody staying with you all the time—through winters when it's cold, and springtime when it's pretty, and summertime when it's nice and hot and you can go swimming—through *all* the times—rain and snow and all the different kinds of weather a man's got to go through before he dies. You got to have somebody who's right. Somebody who knows you, from away back. You got to have somebody who even knows you're wrong but likes you just the same. I know I'm wrong, but I just don't want anything the hard way, working like a dog, or the *easy* way, working like a dog—working's the hard way and the easy way both. All I got to do is beat the price, always —and then I don't feel lousy and don't hate anybody. If you go along with me, I'll be the finest guy anybody ever saw. I won't be wrong any more. You know when you get enough of that money, you *can't* be wrong any more—you're right because the money says so. I'll have a lot of money and you'll be just about the prettiest, most wonderful kid in the whole world. I'll be proud walking around Frisco with you on my arm and people turning around to look at us.

THE GIRL: Do you think they will?

YOUNG MAN: Sure they will. When I get back in some decent clothes, and you're on my arm—well, Katey, they'll turn around and look, and they'll see something, too.

THE GIRL: Katey?

YOUNG MAN: Yeah—that's your name from now on. You're the first girl I ever called Katey. I've been saving it for you. O.K.?

THE GIRL: O.K.

YOUNG MAN: How long have I been here?

THE GIRL: Since last night. You didn't wake up until late this morning, though.

YOUNG MAN: What time is it now? About nine?

THE GIRL: About ten.

YOUNG MAN: Have you got the key to this lousy cell?

THE GIRL: No. They don't let me fool with any keys.

YOUNG MAN: Well, can you get it?

THE GIRL: No.

YOUNG MAN: Can you *try?*

THE GIRL: They wouldn't let me near any keys. I cook for this jail, when they've got somebody in it. I clean up and things like that.

YOUNG MAN: Well, I want to get out of here. Don't you know the guy that runs this joint?

THE GIRL: I know him, but he wouldn't let you out. They were talking of taking you to another jail in another town.

YOUNG MAN: Yeah? Why?

THE GIRL: Because they're afraid.

YOUNG MAN: What are they afraid of?

THE GIRL: They're afraid these people from Wheeling will come over in the middle of the night and break in.

YOUNG MAN: Yeah? What do they want to do that for?

THE GIRL: Don't *you* know what they want to do it for?

YOUNG MAN: Yeah, I know all right.

THE GIRL: Are you scared?

YOUNG MAN: Sure I'm scared. Nothing scares a man more than ignorance. You can argue with people who ain't fools, but you can't argue with fools— they just go to work and do what they're set on doing. Get me out of here.

THE GIRL: How?

YOUNG MAN: Well, go get the guy with the key, and let me talk to him.

THE GIRL: He's gone home. Everybody's gone home.

YOUNG MAN: You mean I'm in this little jail all alone?

THE GIRL: Well—yeah—except me.

YOUNG MAN: Well, what's the big idea—doesn't anybody stay here all the time?

THE GIRL: No, they go home every night. I clean up and then I go, too. I hung around tonight.

YOUNG MAN: What made you do that?

THE GIRL: I wanted to talk to you.

YOUNG MAN: Honest? What did you want to talk about?

THE GIRL: Oh, I don't know. I took care of you last night. You were talking in your sleep. You liked me, too. I didn't think you'd like me when you woke up, though.

YOUNG MAN: Yeah? Why not?

THE GIRL: I don't know.

YOUNG MAN: Yeah? Well, you're wonderful, see?

THE GIRL: Nobody ever talked to me that way. All the fellows in town—*(Pause)*.

YOUNG MAN: What about 'em? Come on—tell me.

THE GIRL: They laugh at me.

YOUNG MAN: Laugh at *you?* They're fools. What do they know about anything? You go get your things and come back here. I'll take you with me to Frisco. How old are you?

THE GIRL: Oh, I'm of age.

YOUNG MAN: How old are you?—Don't lie to me! Sixteen?

THE GIRL: I'm seventeen.

YOUNG MAN: Well, bring your father and mother. We'll get married before we go.

THE GIRL: They wouldn't let me go.

YOUNG MAN: Why not?

THE GIRL: I don't know, but they wouldn't. I know they wouldn't.

YOUNG MAN: You go tell your father not to be a fool, see? What is he, a farmer?

THE GIRL: No—nothing. He gets a little relief from the government because he's supposed to be hurt or something—his side hurts, he says. I don't know what it is.

YOUNG MAN: Ah, he's a liar. Well, I'm taking you with me, see?

THE GIRL: He takes the money I earn, too.

YOUNG MAN: He's got no right to do that.

THE GIRL: I know it, but he does it.

YOUNG MAN *(almost to himself):* This world stinks. You shouldn't have been born in this town, anyway, and you shouldn't have had a man like that for a father, either.

THE GIRL: Sometimes I feel sorry for him.

YOUNG MAN: Never mind feeling sorry for him. (*Pointing a finger*) I'm going to talk to your father some day. I've got a few things to tell that guy.

THE GIRL: I know you have.

YOUNG MAN (*suddenly*): Hello—out there! See if you can get that fellow with the keys to come down and let me out.

THE GIRL: Oh, I couldn't.

YOUNG MAN: Why not?

THE GIRL: I'm nobody here—they give me fifty cents every day I work.

YOUNG MAN: How much?

THE GIRL: Fifty cents.

YOUNG MAN (*to the world*): You see? They ought to pay money to *look* at you. To breathe the *air* you breathe. I don't know. Sometimes I figure it never is going to make sense. Hello—out there! I'm scared. You try to get me out of here. I'm scared them fools are going to come here from Wheeling and go crazy, thinking they're heroes. Get me out of here, Katey.

THE GIRL: I don't know what to do. Maybe I could break the door down.

YOUNG MAN: No, you couldn't do that. Is there a hammer out there or anything?

THE GIRL: Only a broom. Maybe they've locked the broom up, too.

YOUNG MAN: Go see if you can find anything.

THE GIRL: All right. (*She goes.*)

YOUNG MAN: Hello—out there! Hello—out there! (*Pause*) Hello—out there! Hello —out there! (*Pause*) Putting me in jail. (*With contempt*) Rape! Rape! *They* rape everything good that was ever born. His side hurts. They laugh at her. Fifty cents a day. Little punk people. Hurting the only good thing that ever came their way. (*Suddenly*) Hello—out there!

THE GIRL (*returning*): There isn't a thing out there. They've locked everything up for the night.

YOUNG MAN: Any cigarettes?

THE GIRL: Everything's locked up—all the drawers of the desk, all the closet doors—everything.

YOUNG MAN: I ought to have a cigarette.

THE GIRL: I could get you a package maybe, somewhere. I guess the drug store's open. It's about a mile.

YOUNG MAN: A mile? I don't want to be alone that long.

THE GIRL: I could run all the way, and all the way back.

YOUNG MAN: You're the sweetest girl that ever lived.

THE GIRL: What kind do you want?

YOUNG MAN: Oh, any kind—Chesterfields or Camels or Lucky Strikes—any kind at all.

THE GIRL: I'll go get a package. (*She turns to go.*)

YOUNG MAN: What about the money?

THE GIRL: I've got some money. I've got a quarter I been saving. I'll run all the way. (*She is about to go.*)

YOUNG MAN: Come here.

THE GIRL: (*going to him*) What?

YOUNG MAN: Give me your hand. (*He takes her hand and looks at it, smiling. He lifts it and kisses it.*) I'm scared to death.

THE GIRL: I am, too.

YOUNG MAN: I'm not lying—I don't care what happens to me, but I'm scared nobody will ever come out here to this God-forsaken broken-down town and find you. I'm scared you'll get used to it and not mind. I'm scared you'll never get to Frisco and have 'em all turning around to look at you. Listen—go get me a gun, because if they come, I'll kill 'em! They don't understand. Get me a gun!

THE GIRL: I could get my father's gun. I know where he hides it.

YOUNG MAN: Go get it. Never mind the cigarettes. Run all the way. *(Pause, smiling but seriously)* Hello, Katey.

THE GIRL: Hello. What's *your* name?

YOUNG MAN: Photo-Finish is what they *call* me. My races are always photo-finish races. You don't know what that means, but it means they're very close. So close the only way they can tell which horse wins is to look at a photograph after the race is over. Well, every race I bet turns out to be a photo-finish race, and my horse never wins. It's my bad luck, all the time. That's why they call me Photo-Finish. Say it before you go.

THE GIRL: Photo-Finish.

YOUNG MAN: Come here. (THE GIRL *moves close and he kisses her.*) Now, hurry. Run all the way.

THE GIRL: I'll run. (THE GIRL *turns and runs. The* YOUNG MAN *stands at the center of the cell a long time.* THE GIRL *comes running back in. Almost crying)* I'm afraid. I'm afraid I won't see you again. If I come back and you're not here, I—

YOUNG MAN: Hello—out there!

THE GIRL: It's so lonely in this town. Nothing here but the lonesome wind all the time, lifting the dirt and blowing out to the prairie. I'll stay *here*. I won't *let* them take you away.

YOUNG MAN: Listen, Katey. Do what I tell you. Go get that gun and come back. Maybe they won't come tonight. Maybe they won't come at all. I'll hide the gun and when they let me out you can take it back and put it where you found it. And then we'll go away. But if they come, I'll kill 'em! Now, hurry—

THE GIRL: All right. *(Pause)* I want to tell you something.

YOUNG MAN: O.K.

THE GIRL *(very softly)*: If you're not here when I come back, well, I'll have the gun and I'll know what to do with it.

YOUNG MAN: You know how to handle a gun?

THE GIRL: I know how.

YOUNG MAN: Don't be a fool. *(Takes off his shoe, brings out some currency)* Don't be a fool, see? Here's some money. Eighty dollars. Take it and go to Frisco. Look around and find somebody. Find somebody alive and halfway human, see? Promise me—if I'm not here when you come back, just throw the gun away and get the hell to Frisco. Look around and find somebody.

THE GIRL: I don't *want* to find anybody.

YOUNG MAN *(swiftly, desperately)*: Listen, if I'm not here when you come back, how do you know I haven't gotten away? Now, do what I tell you. I'll meet you in Frisco. I've got a couple of dollars in my other shoe. I'll see you in San Francisco.

THE GIRL *(with wonder)*: San Francisco?

YOUNG MAN: That's right—San Francisco. That's where you and me belong.

THE GIRL: I've always wanted to go to *some* place like San Francisco—but how could I go alone?

YOUNG MAN: Well, you're not alone any more, see?

THE GIRL: Tell me a little what it's like.

YOUNG MAN (*very swiftly, almost impatiently at first, but gradually slower and with remembrance, smiling, and* THE GIRL *moving closer to him as he speaks*): Well, it's on the Pacific to begin with—ocean water all around. Cool fog and seagulls. Ships from all over the world. It's got seven hills. The little streets go up and down, around and all over. Every night the fog-horns bawl. But they won't be bawling for you and me.

THE GIRL: What else?

YOUNG MAN: That's about all, I guess.

THE GIRL: Are people different in San Francisco?

YOUNG MAN: People are the same everywhere. They're different only when they love somebody. That's the only thing that makes 'em different. More people in Frisco love somebody, that's all.

THE GIRL: Nobody anywhere loves anybody as much as I love you.

YOUNG MAN (*shouting, as if to the world*): You see? Hearing you say that, a man could die and still be ahead of the game. Now, hurry. And don't forget, if I'm not here when you come back, get the hell to San Francisco where you'll have a chance. Do you hear me?

THE GIRL *stands a moment looking at him, then backs away, turns and runs. The* YOUNG MAN *stares after her, troubled and smiling. Then he turns away from the image of* THE GIRL. *After a while he sits down and buries his head in his hands.*[44]

WILLIAM SAROYAN

The playwright, eliminating the precipitating action, starts with the beginning of the culminating movement of the play. The opening scene seems almost a static situation: a young man is in jail, apparently with no other person to serve as a contact with the outside world. Consequently, Saroyan starts action by having the hero attempt communication with someone—anyone—"out there." This unique beginning plunges the reader immediately into the theme so succinctly indicated in the title: the young man's universal need to communicate with another person; the uniting thread with the young girl who needs companionship also; later, ironically, the communication with the "other" people—out there—who become responsible for his death; and the culminating echo of the three words by the sobbing girl as she whispers her desperate need, "Hello—out there! Hello—out—there!"

This necessity to communicate, to have someone understand, centers around the meeting of two young souls: the young man with the exuberance and "know-how" of youth, who says, "I have been lonesome all my

[44] From "Hello Out There" in RAZZLE-DAZZLE, copyright, 1942, by William Saroyan. Reprinted by permission of Harcourt, Brace and World, Inc., pp. 357-380.

life—there's no cure for that"; and the young girl, hired as a cook at fifty cents a day and having little contact with people except those of Matador, Texas. (Inasmuch as you are now word-conscious, what irony do you find in the name Matador—after reading the entire play?) The youthful extrovert, who never works, is impulsive and optimistic about his talents. To the young girl, skeptical at first, he becomes convincing. He is a dreamer in a world that owes him a living; and he is a philosopher of sorts, always seeking greener grounds and less loneliness and some good luck—all of which bring a responsive understanding in the reader. Who has not hoped for a better chance and only a little luck! This feeling is universal; and is heightened here because the young man is in jail with no friends, except the hope of the girl's friendship.

So when that young voice answers his greeting "out there," he responds in a typical masculine protective manner—more than is usual. Then he finds someone else needs understanding and help. His rationalization about his own failure and his rosy future has the ring of youth—and to the girl, the ring of truth and hope. She listens, falls into his expressed pattern as of a man who knows the world—at least, San Francisco; he understands and will take her out of Matador. As for him, he transfers his gratefulness for an understanding voice into love; for he will make the gesture of taking her away, of showing her charm to passers-by, of finding the money which has so far eluded him, as well as good fortune. She is his answer to good luck! The dreams of youth? Why not? Nothing new here, you might say. Sentimental, you decide! True, if interpreted merely as the dreams of young people. Saroyan, however, has written dialogue that dovetails effectively into a universal pattern of everyone's need for understanding and communication with one's fellow-men: even the youth is fearful of his own lack of perceptive knowledge concerning his captors, thus creating a foreboding of the outcome.

The play in all its tangents centers around the lack or meagerness of understanding, the havoc and tragedy of not communicating adequately. So "Hello Out There" becomes an unconscious inner call for help in a world that cares little. And who at some time has not felt this same inadequacy and wished for an answering voice?

The dialogue does not have the sparkling fluency of two sophisticated persons—therein lies its charm. It does have an underlying emotional urgency. The speech pattern of each character offers a scene of contrast and speculation: the kind of articulate speech which two young people, not too wise, not too skillful, not too certain about themselves, use in groping for an inner feeling to give them assurance.

Before you decide how the voice should reflect emotional value, try to feel the loneliness of a cell in a strange locale; the probable hazardous outcome of a predicament (which the young man foresees and you sense); the wishfulness and urgency for communication with someone; the hope aroused in the youth due to the girl's need for protection; and the assurance, the feeling that she will bring him the good luck which has too long passed him by. After thinking over this situation, pull in the reins of control lest you permit the lines to run away with too much sentiment. Restraint will emphasize the intent of the play.

Due to the nuances of the two voices, this portion of the play is more difficult to interpret than the later dramatic action of death for the youth and desolation for the girl. The characters are established in this scene—as is the theme. Contrast in the range of key and intensity of the two voices will add to the dramatic effectiveness. Inasmuch as the three words, "Hello —out there" deepen in meaning as the conversation proceeds, consider carefully the changes in vocal quality, tempo, inflections, key and attack.

You have been in contact with Williams's motivation for his play *The Glass Menagerie* (page 56); you have observed Tom Wingfield serve as narrator in introducing this memory play (page 122); and have heard him after his unwilling return to the dreary stultifying atmosphere of his former home. Before you study the following scene, reread Tom's descriptive prelude to this scene.

from *The Glass Menagerie*

AMANDA *(calling)*: Tom?

TOM: Yes, Mother.

AMANDA: We can't say grace until you come to the table!

TOM: Coming, Mother: *(He bows slightly and withdraws, reappearing a few moments later in his place at the table.)*

AMANDA *(to her son)*: Honey, don't *push* with your *fingers*. If you have to push with something, the thing to push with is a crust of bread. And chew— chew! Animals have sections in their stomachs which enable them to digest food without mastication, but human beings are supposed to chew their food before they swallow it down. Eat food leisurely, son, and really enjoy it. A well-cooked meal has lots of delicate flavors that have to be held in the mouth for appreciation. So chew your food and give your salivary glands a chance to function!

Tom deliberately lays his imaginary fork down and pushes his chair back from the table.

TOM: I haven't enjoyed one bite of this dinner because of your constant directions on how to eat it. It's you that makes me rush through meals with your hawk-like attention to every bite I take. Sickening—spoils my appetite —all this discussion of—animals' secretion—salivary glands—mastication!

AMANDA *(lightly)*: Temperament like a Metropolitan star! *(He rises and crosses down stage.)* You're not excused from the table.

TOM: I'm getting a cigarette.

AMANDA: You smoke too much.

LAURA *rises.*

LAURA: I'll bring in the blanc mange.

AMANDA *(rising):* No, sister, no, sister—you be the lady this time and I'll be the darky.

LAURA: No, I'm already up.

AMANDA: Resume your seat, little sister—I want you to stay fresh and pretty —for gentlemen callers!

LAURA: I'm not expecting gentlemen callers.

AMANDA *(crossing out to kitchenette. Airily):* Sometimes they come when they are least expected! Why I remember one Sunday afternoon in Blue Mountain— *(Enters kitchenette)*

TOM: I know what's coming!

LAURA: Yes. But let her tell it.

TOM: Again?

LAURA: She loves to tell it.

AMANDA *returns with bowl of dessert.*

AMANDA: One Sunday afternoon in Blue Mountain—your mother received— *seventeen!*—gentlemen callers! Why, sometimes there weren't chairs enough to accommodate them all. We had to send over to bring in folding chairs from the parish house.

TOM *(remaining at the portieres):* How did you entertain those gentlemen callers?

AMANDA: I understood the art of conversation!

TOM: I bet you could talk.

AMANDA: Girls in those days *knew* how to talk, I can tell you.

TOM: Yes?

AMANDA: They knew how to entertain their gentlemen callers. It wasn't enough for a girl to be possessed of a pretty face and a graceful figure—although I wasn't slighted in either respect. She also needed to have a nimble wit and a tongue to meet all occasions.

TOM: What did you talk about?

AMANDA: Things of importance going on in the world! Never anything common or vulgar. . . . My callers were gentlemen—all! Among my callers were some of the most prominent young planters of the Mississippi Delta—planters and sons of planters! *(Her eyes lift, her face glows, her voice becomes rich and elegiac.)*

There was young Champ Laughlin who later became vice-president of the Delta Planters Bank.

Hadley Stevenson who was drowned in Moon Lake and left his widow one hundred and fifty thousand in Government bonds.

There were the Cutrere brothers, Wesley and Bates. Bates was one of my bright particular beaux! He got in a quarrel with that wild Wainwright boy. They shot it out on the floor of Moon Lake Casino. Bates was shot through the stomach. Died in the ambulance on his way to Memphis. His widow was also well-provided for, came into eight or ten thousand acres, that's all. She married him on the rebound—never loved her—carried my picture on him the night he died!

And there was that boy that every girl in the Delta had set her cap for! That beautiful, brilliant young Fitzhugh boy from Greene County!

TOM: What did he leave his widow?

AMANDA: He never married! Gracious, you talk as though all of my old admirers had turned up their toes to the daisies!

TOM: Isn't this the first you've mentioned that still survives?

AMANDA: That Fitzhugh boy went North and made a fortune—came to be known as the Wolf of Wall Street! He had the Midas touch, whatever he touched turned to gold!

And I could have been Mrs. Duncan J. Fitzhugh, mind you! But—I picked your *father!*

LAURA *(rising)*: Mother, let me clear the table.

AMANDA: No, dear, you go in front and study your typewriter chart. Or practice your shorthand a little. Stay fresh and pretty—It's almost time for our gentlemen callers to start arriving. *(She flounces girlishly toward the kitchenette.)* How many do you suppose we're going to entertain this afternoon?

TOM *throws down the paper and jumps up with a groan.*

LAURA: I don't believe we're going to receive any callers, Mother.

AMANDA *(reappearing, airily)*: What? No one—not one? You must be joking! *(LAURA nervously echoes her laugh. She slips in a fugitive manner through the half-open portieres and draws them gently behind her. A shaft of very clear light is thrown on her face against the faded tapestry of the curtains.)* Not one gentleman caller? It can't be true! There must have been a flood, there must have been a tornado!

LAURA: It isn't a flood, it's not a tornado, Mother. I'm just not popular like you were in Blue Mountain. . . . *(TOM utters another groan. LAURA glances at him with a faint, apologetic smile, her voice catching a little.)* Mother's afraid I'm going to be an old maid.[45]

TENNESSEE WILLIAMS

In this opening episode, the playwright immediately personalizes the three main characters; the scene, however, is definitely Amanda's. She is described as a "little woman of great but confused vitality clinging frantically to another time and place." This is the first impression she gives through the predominately ineffectual tone of her chatter. Her world is not that of an alley apartment with the fire escape as its only entrance and exit, but the memory existence of Southern grace, popularity and gentility.

[45] From THE GLASS MENAGERIE, by Tennessee Williams. Copyright 1945 by Tennessee Williams and Edwina D. Williams. Reprinted by permission of Random House, Inc.

Williams adds, in his description of her, that there is "much to admire, to love and to pity" because of these tendencies in her "slight person."[46]

Amanda's daughter, Laura, probably more crippled with inner thoughts than physically, is the mild, seemingly conforming daughter who lives her life within the boundaries of her collection of small fragile glass animals. She has no desire to escape from her customary isolation. The flicker of interest observed in the scene with her former school-mate apparently dies after his exit.

Tom seeks another kind of life not so stifling and binding, not so encumbered with past memories, not so numbing with Laura's contentment within her own world of glass objects. Then too, the picture of his father, smiling "ineluctably" is an ever-present reminder of how one person left and never came back. So Tom leaves with Amanda's words taunting him, "Then go to the moon—you selfish dreamer!" Later he returns briefly—the memory of Laura's inescapable life haunting him—to whisper, "Blow out your candles, Laura—and so good-bye. . . ." The symbolism throughout the play should interest you—even the blowing out of the candles.

The interpretation of the difficult character of Amanda is a challenge for a young person. If you read the play—and you should—you discover she is not the typical nagging housewife and mother. She lives in the expectations of her past experiences being repeated for Laura and in the "memory-happiness" that blots out her present surroundings. This is her escape—into memory of the past. Tom, being a man, takes flight; Laura has no escape—and seeks none!

A series of dramatic episodes revolving around the escape of Matt Denant from the prison grounds forms the structure of Galsworthy's *Escape*. The playwright presents a kaleidoscopic impression of the philosophy of the play by thrusting Matt into seemingly inescapable situations after his arrest. In the prelude Matt defends a girl whom a plain-clothes man is arresting for vagrancy. During a violent struggle between the two men, Matt knocks the officer down. Unfortunately the man is killed as his head hits a rail and Matt is imprisoned for five years for manslaughter.

After the "escape" episode—reprinted here—Matt is alert in eluding his hunters but continually withdraws from probable safety in order that his helpers may not be embarrassed. Even with the help of kindly people, physical escape is made impossible because of Matt's sporting attitude in not wishing to involve other persons. When he finally gives himself up to the law to avoid difficulty for a sympathetic parson, he reveals in his last line Galsworthy's central meaning: "It's one's decent self one can't es-

---

[46] Listen to the album of *The Glass Menagerie*. Recorded by Montgomery Clift, Julie Harris, Jessica Tandy and David Wayne with supporting cast. Caedmon, TRS—M-301.

cape." Interwoven with this idea is the motivating force which plunged an innocent Matt into the catastrophic situation of imprisonment—"Original Sin." At the end of the prelude—when Matt realizes that the officer is dead—a policeman asks him what the row was about. Matt, bowed down in despair with his head in his hands says, "Oh! God knows! Original Sin!" When these last two words were heard on the professional stage, the actor's inflections portrayed a young man non-plussed by the horrible reality of an accidental situation that engulfed him.

In the following scene, two voices with tense, muffled undertones come out of the foggy and quiet atmosphere where two blurred crouching figures are huddled over a row of potatoes. Galsworthy has very cleverly placed emphasis on the voices—as he does throughout the play for the dramatic progression of the episodes.

from *Escape*

PART I, EPISODE I

More than a year has passed since MATT DENANT *has been thrown in prison for killing a policeman in defense of a girl. The following scene is on the prison farm, Dartmoor, in a heavy fog. The stone wall of the field runs along the back and a stone wall joins it on the left.* MATT DENANT *and a* FELLOW CONVICT *are picking up the potatoes they have dug up earlier. They are but dimly seen in the fog, flinging the potatoes right and left into two baskets between them. They are speaking in low voices.*

MATT: The poor blighter was dead, and I got five years for manslaughter.
FELLOW CONVICT: Cripes! A cop! You were lucky not to swing, mate.
MATT: The girl stood by me like a brick. If she hadn't come forward—
F. C.: Lucky there, too. Most of 'em wouldn't. They're too mortal scared. 'Ow much you got left to do?
MATT: Three years, if I behave like a plaster saint.

He stops and straightens himself.

F. C.: I got four. I say, you're a torf, yn't you?
MATT: Toff! (*With a laugh*) Item, one Oxford accent; item, one objection to being spoken to like a dog.
F. C.: Hush! (*Jerking his thumb toward the wall*) Fog don't prevent 'em hearin', blight 'em!
MATT: It's come up mighty sudden. Think it's going to last?
F. C.: After a wet spell—this time o' year, when the wind's gone—yus. They'll be roundin' us up in a minute, you'll see—and 'ome to Blighty. Makes 'em nervous—fog. That's when you get the escapes.
MATT: No one's ever got away from here, they say.
F. C.: There've been a good few tries, though.
MATT: Gosh! I'd like to have one.

F. C.: Don't you do it, mate. You want clothes, you want money, you want a car, to give you a dawg's chance. And then they'd get you. This moor's the 'ell of a place. I say, you must 'ave hit that cop a fair knock!

MATT: Just an ordinary knock-out on the jaw. It wasn't that. He landed the back of his head on the Row rail. Poor devil! He wasn't married, luckily.

F. C.: Luckily? Well, you never know about *that*. But get 'im off your chest, mate—'e wouldn't sit on mine—no more than an 'Un did in the War. That's a good fair potato.

The figure of a Warder is dimly seen coming along from the Right under the wall. He stops.

WARDER: No talking there! When you've finished that row, pick back the next and then stand by to fall in. *(No answer from the convicts)* Hear me? Answer, can't you?

F. C.: Right, Sir! *(The Warder's figure is seen moving back.)* Nice man, ain't he? Wot'd I tell you? Early 'ome to tea.

MATT *(very low)*: Like a dog! Three more years—like a dog!

F. C.: 'E's all right, reely. It's the fog. Fog makes 'em nervous; an' when a man's nervous I've always noticed 'e speaks like that.

MATT: Yes: well, *I* can't get used to it.

F. C.: Too particular, you torfs—get too much corn when you're two-year-olds.

MATT *(sharp and low)*: *You* know the moor—where's Two Bridges?

F. C.: There—a mile.

MATT: And Tavistock?

F. C. *(pointing right back)*: Seven. Guv'nor—don't do it. There ain't a chance in a million. You'll only get pneumonium in this stinkin' wet, and they'll have you into the bargain, sure as eggs—bread and water, cells, and the rest of it.

MATT: I got out of Germany.

F. C.: Out of Germany? Cripes! That was none so dusty!

MATT: They've got no dogs here now, have they?

F. C.: Don't fancy they 'ave. But, Guv'nor, the whole countryside round 'ere's agynst you. They don't like convicts. Funny yn't it?

They have reached the end of the row, and stop, stooping, with their heads close together.

MATT: Draw me a plan with this stick.

F. C.: Blimy! *(Marking the earth)* 'Ere's the main road, and 'ere's the cross road to Tavistock. 'Ere's the Inn at Two Bridges, and 'ere's Post Bridge. 'Ere's Bee Tor Cross, ten to twelve mile. Chagford up there, Moreton 'ampstead 'ere.

MATT: What's across the main road from Two Bridges?

F. C.: Moor. A long bit o' wood about 'ere; then 'Ambleton then you drops into fields to Widecombe; then up, and more moor to Heytor and Bovey. There's rail at Bovey or Lustleigh, and much good that'll do you with everybody as eager to see you as if you was the Prince of Wyles! Out this way you got Fox Tor Mire—ruddy bad bog, that!

A moment's silence while MATT *studies the chart in the soil.*

WARDER'S VOICE: Hurry up with that last row—you two men!

The fog grows thicker.

MATT (*smearing out the chart with his foot*): It's real thick now. Gosh! I'll have a shot!

They move back, beginning the last row.

F. C. (*jerking his thumb left*): There's another blighter thirty yards out on the wall there. 'E'll shoot.

MATT: I know. I'm going over that wall in the corner, and then along under his nose on the near side. Ten to one he'll be looking out on the off side in this fog. If that chap there doesn't spot me, I'll get by.

F. C.: You're mad, Guv'nor. They'll shoot at sight. And if they don' see you—in ten minutes I'll have finished this row, an' they're bound to know you're gone. You 'aven't the chance of a cock-louse.

MATT: All right, friend, don't worry! A bullet'd be a nice change for me. If I don't get one—I'll give 'em a run for their money.

F. C.: Well, if you must go, mate— Strike the main road and run that way. In this fog they'll 'ave to take us back before they dare start after you. You'll find a scrap of a wood a bit beyond the river on the left side. Get into it and cover yourself with leaves till it's dead dark. Then you'll still be close to the road and you can myke shift in a stack or something till the morning. If you go wandering about the moor all night in this fog, you won't get nowhere, and you'll be done in stiff before dawn.

MATT: Thanks. Sooner the better, now— Never stop to look at a fence. Next time the steam's full on. (*Puts some potatoes in his pocket*) . . . Can you eat these raw? I ate turnips in Germany.

F. C.: Never tried, Guv'nor. Tyke this. (*He holds out a slice of bread.*)

MATT: Thanks awfully. You're a good chap.

F. C.: Wish you luck. Wish I was comin' too, but I 'aven't got the pluck, an' that's a fact.

MATT: Now! Turn your head the other way and keep it there. Remember me to Blighty. So long!

He moves three steps away from his fellow convict, pauses a few seconds, then suddenly, stooping low, runs to the wall, and is over it like a cat. In the minute of silence that follows, one can see the CONVICT *listening.*

F. C. (*counting the seconds to himself, up to twenty, in an excited murmur*): Gawd! 'E's past that blighter! (*Listens again*) Gawd! 'E's orf! (*With realization of his fellow's escape comes an itch to attempt it himself*) Shall I 'ave a shoot meself? Shall I? Gawd! I must!

He has just turned to sneak off, when the WARDER'S *voice is heard off, Right.*

WARDER: You, man, there! Where's your mate?

F. C.: 'Ad a call, sir. (*He stands still.*)

WARDER: What d'you mean?

F. C.: Went over that wall, Sir.

WARDER: He's not there. Now then! Where is he?

F. C.: No use arstin' me. *I* don't know where he is.

WARDER: Come with me. *(He marches sharply along the wall back. Halting)* Convict! Out there! Answer! Warder! You, Williams! Anyone passed you? Lost a man here!

VOICE OF SECOND WARDER: No one's passed.

FIRST WARDER: Sharp, then! There's a man gone!

SECOND WARDER *appears at the top of the wall.*

SECOND WARDER: He must ha' got past *you,* then.

FIRST WARDER: Curse this fog! Fire a shot for warning. No, don't, or we'll have others running for it. Muster sharp and get off home and report—that's the only thing. Here, you! Keep your mouth shut. You know all about it, I bet.

F. C.: Not me, Sir. 'E just said 'e 'ad a call to 'ave tea with the Duchess; an' I went on pickin' up, knowin' you was in an 'urry.

FIRST WARDER: Mind your lip! Come on, Williams. March, you![47]

JOHN GALSWORTHY

The speech pattern of the Fellow Convict reveals the cockney rhythm of a seasoned convict. Matt voices his own personality pedigree: "item, one Oxford accent; item, one objection to being talked to like a dog." The contrast should prove an exciting one for you, especially with the third voice of the Warder adding further tension. The inflectional patterns are distinctive for the three men; so are vocal intensity and quality. Do not let any phrase slip by without listening a second time for the best slides and key to convey the mood and meaning. Give the ending of the scene the dramatic lift Galsworthy intended with the release of ironic humor from the Fellow Convict.

Ludwig Lewisohn subtitles his play *Adam,* "A Dramatic History in a Prologue, Seven Scenes and an Epilogue." His protagonist, a British multi-millionaire, is never seen or heard. His characterization is presented through a series of episodes involving him in his relationships with socialites; business associates; his young American wife who is seeking a divorce; a German actress whom Adam has loved and her present admirer; a Poet; three Jews who are hoping for a financial contribution; and his mother and father. The last scene, the seventh, is reprinted here. As in most episodic structures of this type, little, if any, continuity is expected between each episode. This is true also of Mansfield's story, "The Daughters of the Late Colonel."

You learn cautiously through the dramatic scenes that Adam is a Jew. This is whispered at first, then admitted by the actress and finally dis-

[47] Reprinted with the permission of Charles Scribner's Sons from "Escape" by John Galsworthy. Copyright 1926 Charles Scribner's Sons; renewal copyright 1954 by Ada Galsworthy.

cussed by the three Jews. You learn also from the latter that Adam changed his name to Elhar, "pure Hebrew": *El*—God and *har*—the mountain "burned with fire unto the heart of heaven." They realize its "indefinable, slightly exotic elegance," which Gentiles do not recognize as Jewish. The first Jew feels that Adam fled not only from Germany but from his own self, "that original Jewish self" which had been wounded in some way. The reader is kept in suspense about the wound, the deep hurt, until the scene between his father and mother occurs. Meanwhile, his wife has admitted that she found an "emptiness" about him, a hate for people and a heart with no warmth and a figure that was ghostly. According to the socialites, Adam was a "devilish elegant chap," "notoriously seen with a foreign actress at Deauville and Cannes." The German actress saw him as a "wounded and divided soul, full of generosity and sadness; a man who with his millions could not buy "earth, home, speech, inner oneness, inner security"; and from the Poet came the closest approach to the playwright's theme: Adam was "almost the wandering Jew; almost the symbol of the legend and the curse."

The story then begins to center around Adam's background. Piece by piece the idea of his flight from his inner self takes form: namely that his Jewish self had to be crushed, the self that was so easily hurt; that he had to have power for defense so he accumulated wealth and became a British citizen; that his wounded spirit finally sought the nearest shelter, only to discover its dangers. In the scene between his father and mother, the distressed mother reveals she has never known why her son had left his home so suddenly nor where he had gone. Finally, Adam's father tells the story to his wife. An Anti-Semite professor, eloquent, yet subtle in teaching the "Jewish danger," began his duties in Adam's school. Gradually the Jewish boys were avoided and then ostracized. One day, under some pretext, the professor asked all Jewish boys to stand up. Adam remained seated. At dismissal time, he was chased, pounded, beaten and left exhausted, with his clothes in shreds. Two days later he disappeared from his home.

Since this play may not be known to many, this resumé has been recounted so that the empathic impact of this last scene between the Minnesota pilot and the British valet can be appreciated.

from *Adam*

THE SEVENTH SCENE

Out of a dim sky projects the private aeroplane of Mr. Adam Elhar. Definitely visible are his American PILOT *in his place and behind him Mr. Elhar's British* VALET. *The metallic whir of the motors accompanies the scene.*

THE PILOT: Lousy weather.

THE VALET: Oh rotten!

THE PILOT: I told the boss.

THE VALET: Didn't do much good.

THE PILOT: Na-a! Gee!

THE VALET: Mr. Elhar's been very restless recently.

THE PILOT: Restless? Nuts! Say, is he always that way?

THE VALET: Not exactly.

THE PILOT: You ought to know. You been with him long enough.

THE VALET: He has these fits—

THE PILOT: Fits is right. D'you ever see a cat have 'em. Christ!

THE VALET: It's been getting worse. During the war and a few years after he worked sixteen and seventeen hours a day. He seemed quite happy. Then he stopped—

THE PILOT: Made his pile, I guess.

THE VALET: Oh yes, Mr. Elhar is very wealthy. But since then he's been growing more and more restless. I thought he would settle down when he married. But that didn't last long.

THE PILOT: No. So I saw by the papers.

THE VALET: Hope you don't mind: but you mustn't believe everything in the American papers.

THE PILOT: Sure not. That's all right. 'Cause when you get to know the boss you see he's a kind of a good guy.

THE VALET: He's been very good to me.

THE PILOT: I believe you. You know: I felt kindo sorry for him yesterday. I guess you didn't hear?

THE VALET: No. I was packing or out on errands.

THE PILOT: Well, say: First he wanted to fly to Berlin. Luncheon at Cologne. All right. I been that way often. Next he calls me in. No. We're hoppin' off to Paris. *All* right. Same to me, you know. Then he calls me in again and shows me maps. He wants to go to a little God-forsaken town in Germany. Right on the Polish line. Can I do it? Sure, I say. Why not? First to Berlin—No, he says. He don't want to go by Berlin. Then he says he don't think he'll go. He was pale and had whiskey and soda on the table.

THE VALET: Just before luncheon?

THE PILOT: Yeh. That's right.

THE VALET: I noticed it because he almost never touches liquor.

THE PILOT: That's right too. Well, after luncheon, *if* you please, he'd changed his mind again. We'll wait a day and fly to Königsberg. From there he'd take a car. By that time I felt kindo razzle-dazzled. I said: You're sure now, Mr. Elhar? My former boss woulda bawled me out!

THE VALET: Not Mr. Elhar.

THE PILOT: No. He grinned kindo sickly. He says: I don't blame you, Larsen, he says. I oughta know my own mind at my time o' life. He's so dam' human.

THE VALET: He is that.

THE PILOT: So I got me some extra maps an' I doped out the route. I didn't hardly see how you could avoid Berlin. By that time it was afternoon an' he called me in again. He looked like all hell.

THE VALET: I begged him to go to bed and rest up or call a doctor.

THE PILOT: I don't blame you. Anyhow he said: Sorry, Larsen, to have changed my mind again. Just to Paris, as usual. Then we'll see. So that was the last I saw of him till this morning. He didn't look any too good when we started.

THE VALET: No. He didn't. And he acted queer enough last night. I wouldn't tell you this if I didn't think you respected and liked Mr. Elhar.

THE PILOT: Sure I do. He's a good guy.

THE VALET: Well, last night, just as I was going to turn off the lights he called me back. Timkins, he said, I'd like to ask you an intimate question. I said: Certainly, sir; anything you like, sir.

THE PILOT: What'd he ask you?

THE VALET: He said: Are you happy, Timkins?

THE PILOT: Gee—!

THE VALET: I said: Why, after a manner of speaking, sir, I am. So he says: tell me more. Why, I said, you know I'm a widower, sir. And you know that my boy and girl are growing up. You've helped me with their education right along. So he said: Yes, yes, go on! Well, I said, it took me years to get over the loss of my wife. I loved her, sir, I said. But the children have been a great compensation, if I may say so. They're both going to rise above their father's station in the world, I said, thanks to you. Not that I'm not satisfied and self-respecting, as you know, sir. And the children are devoted to me, I said. So he said: yes, and how about the future? Why, I said, I take a real satisfaction working for you, sir, and I'm buying a little place in the country—a very nice little place—for my old age where the children and maybe *their* children can come and visit me summers, and I'll have a garden. I always did like gardens. But you'll excuse me, sir, I said, for talking so much. Only it's your own fault, sir. And what do you think he said?

THE PILOT: I got a hunch.

THE VALET: He said: Timkins, he said, I envy you from the bottom of my heart. . . .

THE PILOT: Elhar is a gentleman. What's eatin' him?

THE VALET: I sometimes think it's because he don't practise his religion.

THE PILOT: Aw, come off.

THE VALET: He's an Israelite, you know.

THE PILOT: Well, supposin'! America's full o' Jews. All kinds. I've worked for one or two. Not bad people. But you couldn't call 'em religious.

THE VALET: Oh, it's just an idea of mine. I'm Church of England myself. I don't know as I believe very much. But my people have been Church of England for maybe hundreds of years an' so—

THE PILOT: Yeh, I know what you mean. I'm from Minnesota myself. When I'm home I don't seem to mind Ma draggin' me to the Norwegian Lutheran Church. People are funny that way.

THE VALET: Funny, as you say. But natural.

THE PILOT: Natu— . . . Say, that's a lousy wind we're runnin' into.

THE VALET: Rotten.

THE PILOT: Dark there.

THE VALET: Nasty.
THE PILOT: Try to get up over—
THE VALET: Better.
THE PILOT: What's that knockin'?
THE VALET: Do you hear it, too?
THE PILOT: Do I? Don't like it. Slammin'. Gee! Go'n look. Quick!

THE VALET *disappears. The motors whir more metallically and loudly.*

THE VALET (*reappears. He trembles. His face is livid. His jaw shakes*): Larsen!
THE PILOT: Well?
THE VALET: It's the door! Unlocked!
THE PILOT: Christ! No! And Mr. Elhar?
THE VALET: Gone!
THE PILOT: Aw, don't tell me a thing—
THE VALET: I looked. I looked. He opened the door. He jumped out. He's gone. In the channel—(*He hides his face in his hands.*)
THE PILOT: Jesus Christ!

THE VALET *sobs convulsively into his hands.*

THE PILOT: Jesus Christ!
THE VALET *sobs and shakes.*

CURTAIN.[48]

LUDWIG LEWISOHN

The rhythmical intonations of two dialects should show contrast not only in British and American speech patterns but also in the personalities of the men; the vocal quality and tempo will also be sharply different. Pauses for suspense and reinforcement are frequent so that the moods of the men will be heightened. The quiet intensity at the climactic point can be powerful if executed properly; above all, meaningful intonations must be sought for the ejaculation, "Jesus Christ" so that it will convey the amazement and awe of a prayerful utterance.

Miller has previously recounted how certain structural images from his own experiences served as a background for "Death of a Salesman" (page 55). Now reread one of the great dramatic plays of the American theater and study the progression of events through the manifestation of Willy's inner thoughts as they lead to the powerful climax.

In his "Introduction," the playwright states that "any dramatic form is an artifice, a way of transforming a subjective feeling into something that can be comprehended through public symbols." He also has the underlying concept that "nothing in this life comes next"; rather everything

[48] From Ludwig Lewisohn, *Adam* (New York: Harper & Row, Inc., 1929). Permission is granted by Mrs. Ludwig Lewisohn, literary executrix. Seventh scene, pp. 85-91.

exists within individuals *at the same time;* a person *is his past,* for the present is the only past to which he is capable of reacting. This belief explains the form of the play about Willy Loman, whose past is his present. Miller admits he began the drama with the idea that Willy was to kill himself; he was not sure how he would do it. He decided that if he could make Willy remember enough, he would destroy himself; consequently, he structured the scenes in such a way that Willy's memories would taunt him "like a mass of tangled roots without end or beginning." Within five minutes of the opening of the play, Willy is portrayed, according to the playwright, as one tormented by the conflict with Biff, his son.

Willy and Linda are the parents of Biff and Happy—names that connote pleasant family living in earlier days. Now, Willy, the unsuccessful salesman in his tired years, hopes in vain for the same love, admiration and acceptance from his sons as when they were young. Furthermore, he tries to keep up the pretense of success; he cannot face the reality of failure; and avoids this fear of known defeat by escape into dreams of a pleasant yesterday. Miller writes that he did not intend to employ the flashback technique; rather he wished to show Willy in retrospect. To the playwright, the drama is a "sort of confession."

Linda, a devoted wife, protects Willy even to the point of suggesting that Biff leave home because of Willy's unrest whenever Biff returns from his unsuccessful jobs.

Biff, the ne'er-do-well shadow of Willy, who has so far lived a similar "phony" existence, finally decides to face his lack of moral stamina in business, leave his home and try for a new experience in real living. Although Miller reports that he did not want a mounting tension—rather a "single chord of suspense" presented at the beginning "within which all strains and melodies would be already contained"—the reader or observer of the play will feel the tension mount toward the last scene.

Preceding the following scene, Linda, fearful of Willy's health, has urged Biff to leave his home. Biff, who has failed earlier in the day to secure a job, goes into the garden "in the blue of the night," and forces his unwilling father to bring his seeds, flashlight and hoe into the house. Before entering, he explains to Willy that he is leaving and will not be back. Inside, Biff tries to shake his father's hand in a good-bye gesture; Willy refuses and rebelliously resents Biff's startling declaration of his illusion of success through stealing. Nor can he endure Biff's accusation of himself (Willy) as a "phony." Later, when Biff breaks down at the conclusion of this verbal battle, Willy glows with the realization that Biff still loves him.

After the rest of the family has gone upstairs, Willy make a decisively tragic but redeeming move for one who has been unable to face defeat. Linda and her sons hear the car, with Willy at the wheel, roar off to destruction. Miller explains this action: Willy has been given a "powerful" piece of knowledge, namely, that he is loved by his son, Biff; and has been embraced by him and forgiven. His "fatherhood" has been achieved; he can only prove his existence with dignity by offering "power"—the price of his insurance policy—for his posterity.[49]

This summary includes only a portion of the tragic undercurrents inherent in the drama. Read the complete play to experience the interplay of characters. The following scene takes place after Biff and Willy come in from the garden.

from *Death of a Salesman*

BIFF *repeats his decision before* LINDA *and* HAPPY:

BIFF: Dad, you're never going to see what I am, so what's the use of arguing? If I strike oil I'll send you a check. Meantime forget I'm alive.

WILLY (*to* LINDA): Spite, see?

BIFF: Shake hands, Dad.

WILLY: Not my hand.

BIFF: I was hoping not to go this way.

WILLY: Well, this is the way you're going. Good-by.

BIFF *looks at him a moment, then turns sharply and goes to the stairs.*

WILLY (*stops him with*): May you rot in hell if you leave this house!

BIFF (*turning*): Exactly what is it that you want from me?

WILLY: I want you to know, on the train, in the mountains, in the valleys, wherever you go, that you cut down your life for spite!

BIFF: No, no.

WILLY: Spite, spite, is the word of your undoing! And when you're down and out, remember what did it. When you're rotting somewhere beside the railroad tracks, remember, and don't you dare blame it on me!

BIFF: I'm not blaming it on you!

WILLY: I won't take the rap for this, you hear?

HAPPY *comes down the stairs and stands on the bottom step, watching.*

BIFF: That's just what I'm telling you!

WILLY (*sinking into a chair at the table, with full accusation*): You're trying to put a knife in me—don't think I don't know what you're doing!

BIFF: All right, phony! Then let's lay it on the line. (*He whips the rubber tube out of his pocket and puts it on the table.*)

HAPPY: You crazy—

LINDA: Biff! (*She moves to grab the hose, but* BIFF *holds it down with his hand.*)

BIFF: Leave it there! Don't move it!

WILLY (*not looking at it*): What is that?

[49] Arthur Miller, "Introduction," *Collected Plays* (New York: The Viking Press, 1954).

BIFF: You know goddam well what that is.

WILLY (*caged, wanting to escape*): I never saw that.

BIFF: You saw it. The mice didn't bring it into the cellar! What is this supposed to do, make a hero out of you? This supposed to make me sorry for you?

WILLY: Never heard of it.

BIFF: There'll be no pity for you, you hear it? No pity!

WILLY (*to* LINDA): You hear the spite!

BIFF: No, you're going to hear the truth—what you are and what I am!

LINDA: Stop it!

WILLY: Spite!

HAPPY (*coming down toward* BIFF): You cut it now!

BIFF (*to* HAPPY): The man don't know who we are! The man is gonna know! (*To* WILLY) We never told the truth for ten minutes in this house!

HAPPY: We always told the truth!

BIFF (*turning on him*): You big blow, are you the assistant buyer? You're one of the two assistants to the assistant, aren't you?

HAPPY: Well, I'm practically—

BIFF: You're practically full of it! We all are! And I'm through with it. (*To* WILLY) Now hear this, Willy, this is me.

WILLY: I know you!

BIFF: You know why I had no address for three months? I stole a suit in Kansas City and I was in jail. (*To* LINDA, *who is sobbing*) Stop crying. I'm through with it. (LINDA *turns away from them, her hands covering her face.*)

WILLY: I suppose that's my fault!

BIFF: I stole myself out of every good job since high school!

WILLY: And whose fault is that?

BIFF: And I never got anywhere because you blew me so full of hot air I could never stand taking orders from anybody! That's whose fault it is!

WILLY: I hear that!

LINDA: Don't, Biff!

BIFF: It's goddam time you hear that! I had to be boss big shot in two weeks, and I'm through with it!

WILLY: Then hang yourself! For spite, hang yourself!

BIFF: No! Nobody's hanging himself, Willy! I ran down eleven flights with a pen in my hand today. And suddenly I stopped, you hear me? And in the middle of that office building, do you hear this? I stopped in the middle of that building and I saw—the sky. I saw the things that I love in this world. The work and the food and time to sit and smoke. And I looked at the pen and said to myself, what the hell am I grabbing this for? Why am I trying to become what I don't want to be? What am I doing in an office, making a contemptuous, begging fool of myself, when all I want is out there, waiting for me the minute I say I know who I am! Why can't I say that, Willy? (*He tries to make* WILLY *face him, but* WILLY *pulls away and moves to the left.*)

WILLY (*with hatred, threateningly*): The door of your life is wide open!

BIFF: Pop! I'm a dime a dozen, and so are you!

WILLY (*turning on him now in an uncontrolled outburst*): I am not a dime a dozen! I am Willy Loman, and you are Biff Loman!

BIFF *starts for* WILLY, *but is blocked by* HAPPY. *In his fury,* BIFF *seems on the verge of attacking his father.*

BIFF: I am not a leader of men, Willy, and neither are you. You were never anything but a hard-working drummer who landed in the ash can like all the rest of them! I'm one dollar an hour, Willy! I tried seven states and couldn't raise it. A buck an hour! Do you gather my meaning? I'm not bringing home any prizes any more, and you're going to stop waiting for me to bring them home!

WILLY (*directly to* BIFF): You vengeful, spiteful mut!

BIFF *breaks from* HAPPY. WILLY, *in fright, starts up the stairs.* BIFF *grabs him.*

BIFF (*at the peak of his fury*): Pop, I'm nothing! I'm nothing, Pop. Can't you understand that? There's no spite in it any more. I'm just what I am, that's all.

BIFF's *fury has spent itself, and he breaks down, sobbing, holding on to* WILLY, *who dumbly fumbles for* BIFF's *face.*

WILLY (*astonished*): What're you doing? What're you doing? (*To* LINDA) Why is he crying?

BIFF (*crying, broken*): Will you let me go? Will you take that phony dream and burn it before something happens? (*Struggling to contain himself, he pulls away and moves to the stairs.*) I'll go in the morning. Put him—put him to bed. (*Exhausted,* BIFF *moves to the stairs.*)

WILLY (*after a long pause, astonished, elevated*): Isn't that remarkable? Biff— he likes me!

LINDA: He loves you, Willy!

HAPPY (*deeply moved*): Always did, Pop.

WILLY: Oh, Biff! (*Staring wildly*) He cried! Cried to me! (*He is choking with his love, and now cries out his promise.*) That boy—that boy is going to be magnificent!

[Linda and Happy follow Biff upstairs, but Willy remains below, thinking about Biff's love for him, and imagining the magnificence of Biff with twenty thousand dollars in his pocket! Linda has called several times asking Willy to come upstairs but Willy is lost in his dream thoughts. Finally she calls again:]

LINDA (*calling*): Willy, you coming up?

WILLY (*uttering a gasp of fear, whirling about as if to quiet her*): Sh! (*He turns around as if to find his way; sounds, faces, voices, seem to be swarming in upon him and he flicks at them, crying*) Sh! Sh! (*Suddenly music, faint and high, stops him. It rises in intensity, almost to an unbearable scream. He goes up and down on his toes, and rushes off around the house.*) Shhh!

LINDA: Willy?

There is no answer. LINDA *waits.* BIFF *gets up off his bed. He is still in his clothes.* HAPPY *sits up.* BIFF *stands listening.*

LINDA (*with real fear*): Willy, answer me! Willy!

There is the sound of a car starting and moving away at full speed.

LINDA: No!
BIFF (*rushing down the stairs*): Pop!

As the car speeds off, the music crashes down in a frenzy of sound, which becomes the soft pulsation of a single cello string.[50]

ARTHUR MILLER

The lines speak because of Miller's dynamic and moving way with words. The scene advances quickly, the conflict and tension among the characters increase and build to an unexpected, sudden departure of Willy in the death car. You can try to keep up with the playwright's dramatic power by presenting the deeply involved persons through ever-changing vocal patterns. You may not have a top interpretative performance in characterization and movement as in the professional recording,[51] but you will have learned how skillfully Miller has created one of the classics of the theater.

THE PRIVILEGE OF SHOWING "HOW"

Perhaps you can now realize how the techniques in this book revolve around the word *How:* how the student reaches meaning, how he expresses that meaning and how all elements can be integrated by a spirited interpreter in a total expression. Woolbert wrote years ago—

I for one am still a small boy in the face of interesting phenomena; I always want to know why? and how? I have the elemental desire to take things apart to see what makes them tick. And once I have found out . . . I impulsively attempt to state the guiding principle so that others can know *how.* Teaching I conceive to be a process of *showing how.*

The intention of these pages has not been to make you a polished interpreter. The goal was rather to have you aim toward sincerity in developing your awareness of literary meanings; and to find enjoyment in your ability to communicate those memorable impressions as an interpreter of spirit and creative potential. Faulkner has said, "Always dream and shoot higher than you know you can do. Don't try to be better than your contemporaries. . . . Try to be better than yourself."[52]

[50] From DEATH OF A SALESMAN by Arthur Miller. Copyright © 1949 by Arthur Miller. Reprinted by permission of The Viking Press, Inc.
[51] *Death of a Salesman.* Recorded by Lee J. Cobb, Mildred Dunnock and members of the original Broadway cast. Caedmon, 310-S.
[52] From WRITERS AT WORK: PARIS INTERVIEW SERIES, ed. Malcolm Cowley. Copyright 1963 by The Paris Review, Inc. By permission of The Viking Press.

Hopefully, some of the Woolbertian spirit for interpretative speech will be remembered by you, for this great teacher and psychologist had unswerving faith in the energy and ability of students. Let him speak for himself as a teacher of speech:

We must help make well-rounded men of our students; far beyond other teachers, we have a great opportunity. If any member of the profession gets more fun out of it than I do, I envy him sincerely. . . . I sympathize feelingly with my colleagues who find their charges empty of head and dead of heart. I count it as a personal privilege to be in a profession that offers unusual opportunities to fill one and vitalize the other.[53]

Woolbert operated as a great teacher of students through lively communication; perhaps that spirit of communicative energy will be reflected in your interpretative speech performances!

[53] Charles Henry Woolbert, "A Problem in Pragmatism," *Quarterly Journal of Speech*, II (1916), pp. 272-274.

INDEX OF NAMES

Italic page numbers indicate the pages on which the selection is reprinted.

INDEX OF SELECTIONS

Italic page numbers indicate the pages on which the selection is reprinted.